Second Edition

Psychotherapy
Through
Imagery

Joseph E. Shorr, Ph.D.

1983
Thieme-Stratton Inc.   *Georg Thieme Verlag*
New York   *Stuttgart · New York*

Publisher: Thieme-Stratton Inc.
381 Park Avenue South
New York, New York 10016

This monograph is a revised and updated edition of Dr. Shorr's two previous publications *Psycho-Imagination Therapy* and *Psychotherapy Through Imagery*.

Printed in the United States of America.
Cover design by M. Losaw.

Psychotherapy Through Imagery
Joseph E. Shorr, Ph.D.

TSI ISBN 0–86577–083–2
GTV ISBN 3–13–606302–3

Last digit is print number 5 4 3 2 1

Contents

Section I

Psycho-Imagination Therapy: The Integration of Phenomenology and Imagination

Section II

Psychotherapy Through Imagery

Foreword to the Second Edition

In the past two decades we have witnessed an exciting upsurge of research and clinical applications of man's basic capacity for forming images or related mental representations of external experience or internal memories and emotions. Joseph E. Shorr is a pioneer in the development of the human's potential for using imagination as a basis for a diagnostic and psychotherapeutic intervention method. He was one of the first clinicians in America to expand the use of imagery beyond its limited employment in the early psychodynamic treatment approaches and to recognize its enormous power for evoking emotion and providing a sense of cognitive clarity for clients trapped in unexpressed or unidentifiable conflicts.

There are now a variety of approaches for the use of imagery in psychotherapy. Some rely on continuous imagery "trips" – following a stream, climbing a mountain, exploring a cave – that initiate a sequence of continuing fantasies through a therapeutic hour. Dr. Shorr, who works more within a neo-Freudian psychodynamic orientation, follows Sullivan in emphasizing the interactive communication between client and therapist. Thus, the image is used to help the client clarify his or her own self awareness and then, further, to communicate clearly with the therapist.

Few people I know are as ingenious and imaginative as Dr. Shorr in generating situations that can evoke from patients powerful and meaningful imagery. It is amazing how quickly clients become engaged and respond with elaborate, seemingly unplanned images to requests such as seeing themselves in a mirror, looking down a deep hole, seeing their parents in various unexpected settings, or completing a phrase like, "Never refer to me as _____." I have seen a remarkable response to such suggestions from presumably sophisticated professionals participating in some of his workshops.

It seems likely that most of us walk through life constantly producing little verbal glosses or visual imagery associations to the thousands of people we pass on the street or see on movie or TV screens. Our night dreams in their strangeness pick up some of these daytime metaphors but in modern times only clever writers like Donald Barthelme or John Irving can represent these preconscious, seemingly bizarre waking images that characterize the stream of thought. Dr. Shorr, recognizing this distinctive human pattern of fleeting and, then, with practice, crystallized metaphor, has developed in his vast armamentarium of suggested situations a remarkable key to unlocking the rich variety of moving pictures we carry around with us as representatives of interpersonal relationships.

Jerome L. Singer, Ph.D.
Director of Clinical Training
Yale University, New Haven
Connecticut

Preface to the Second Edition

In the last five years the fund of knowledge about imagery with patients and the general population in workshops and classes has grown four-fold. Since that time developments in the use of imagery as a method of revealing subjective meaning from introspective reporting of imagery production have opened various avenues of exploration. Those that were not previously reported are self-image imagery, special imagery (unique indicators of personality organization), unconscious imagery, parental imagery, resistance and imagery, the Shorr Imagery Test and its Supplementary form, the Group Shorr Imagery Test, the Shorr Parental Imagery Test, general imagery, and the therapist's own imagery.

In the first decade I was able to explore in depth such constructs as Dual Imagery, Body Imagery, Sexual Imagery, Task Imagery, Cathartic Imagery, and the use of imagery in group therapy. The active introduction of directed imagery, plus selected use of spontaneous imagery woven into the fabric of the dialogical process, gave rapid meaning and facilitated the uncovering of difficult material. Utilizing Task Imagery as well as Cathartic Imagery helped patients to define themselves more in line with their true identity.

An important development (1978) was the organizing of the imagery productions into useful therapeutic categories for appropriate clinical use. In this manner the nearly three thousand imaginary situations, finish-the-sentences, most-and-least questions, plus the self-and-other questions can not only be categorized but are available as a reservoir of clinically experienced material to be appropriately used.

In writing a preface, I would be remiss if I did not mention my emphasis on waking imagery. For example, when I have asked people *not* to imagine something, a funny thing happens. As a personal example, allow me to ask you *not* to imagine a red giraffe. No doubt, despite yourself, you are "seeing" a red giraffe. It is effortless, instantaneous, and ubiquitous. In fact, the apparent ease of this constant flow of images in our heads makes us take our own images for granted.

My own view is that this stream of images needs to be tuned in as if they were radio waves. Whether a person pays attention to his own flow of images, or is asked to report the spontaneous images that occur to him, or to respond to directed imaginary situations, he is getting in touch with the ongoing flow of images. In a sense, the more one is able to allow the flow of images, the richer one can experience his inner life.

My preference is for the term "waking imagery." Human beings during waking hours are involved in waking imagery (in sleep they are involved in dream activity). My preference then allows me to include daydreaming, fantasies, reveries, etc., as forms of waking imagery. One could not daydream without the flow of waking imagery, yet one can be involved in waking imagery without daydreaming. The same can be said for fantasizing as well as other forms of waking imagery.

If we establish waking imagery as an effortless, instantaneous, and ubiquitous flow in our minds, we must also see that most persons take it for granted – unless, of course, we are daydreaming, or we have hallucinated visually, or we are having an unbidden image.

Furthermore, if we are involved in memory images which I call reminiscent imagery, we are tapping the flow of images in our minds. When we are worrying or anticipating the future we must use our imagination and imagery.

Child psychologists studying the phenomenon of imaginary companions long have realized the role of waking imagery as the vehicle for such behavior and thought. Certainly children's play, so fascinating to observe, could not be possible unless the child could manipulate his or her waking images into the playful pattern.

Television shows us so much, it leaves little for our imagination. Not so for radio, which allows us to create in our minds the action and images related to the story we are listening to.

Even such concepts as reincarnation, whether one believes in it or not, depend on waking imagery for its creation. What about nostalgia, or even one's idea of paradise – could this be possible without the resource of waking imagery?

In empathy or sympathy, we need to imagine the other person's feelings, action or plight.

Recently enormous interest has centered on the feelings of terror that have come from Dracula, Jaws, and the Body Snatchers – a fascination for such events that also allows us to experience in imagination inexplicable feelings of dread and fear. The old Harold Lloyd pictures where he is perilously dangling from tall buildings bears this point out well.

Imagery may well be the powerful ingredient that unites perception, motivation, emotion, subjective meaning and realistic abstract thought.

Waking imagery's relevance to psychotherapy is perceived when one asks a patient to imagine an imaginary situation. In so doing all persons, when they report their imagery flow, are revealing how they are viewing their world. Essentially each person, as he reveals his images, tells how he sees himself and how he sees others, as well as how others see him.

Since imagery may bypass the censorship of the individual, imagery has a projective quality that leads to subjective meaning. In therapy this principle can then be used for heightening the awareness of a conflict as well as for the resolution of a conflict.

Using the projective qualities of imagery, the Shorr Imagery Test (SIT), developed in 1974 from the most useful imaginary situations and finish-the-sentence tests, is now used in several hundred clinics and hospitals. A group form was developed in 1977 by C. Smith, T. Kard, L. Squire and M. Vale. In 1978 a Supplementary Shorr Imagery Test was developed from the most useful imaginary situations and finish-the-sentence tests coming out of the work since 1974. Originally the idea was to develop an alternate form of the SIT, but it was subsequently discovered that certain items on the original SIT were not possible to duplicate in another form. Consequently, the Supplementary test was developed both as a means of testing the limits of the first or by itself as a faster instrument, since it contains one half as many items.

Under construction at present is the Shorr Parental Imagery Test. This test, using parental imagery, can be given to children from their point of view and then nearly identical items given to the parents from their point of view. The phenomenological in-viewing can be an invaluable aid in diagnosis and therapy. Results of this work will be reported at a later date.

Also underway at this time is the Shorr Couples Imagery Test, one of the most significant outgrowths of the parent-child imagery test. Nearly all of the items that the parents respond to in their imagination are then used in relation to each of the parents.

For example, the father, husband, or male member of the couple is asked to imagine staring at his wife's (or female member of the couple's) naked back, and then to report what he sees, does and feels. The wife, or female, is then asked to stare at the naked back of the husband, or male, and report what she sees, feels and does. Preliminary use of the Shorr Couples Imagery Test shows it taps some of the unconscious interactional factors between men and women. Since this test can be scored for conflict between couples quantitatively, it can potentially be a valuable research tool. Qualitative interpretation of the material adds dimensions heretofore not seen in projective tests with couples.

In 1979 in Los Angeles the Institute for Psycho-Imagination Therapy was the organizing force behind the first annual conference of the American Association for the Study of Mental Imagery.

I would like to thank the members of my staff—Jack Connella, Pennee Robin, and Gail Sobel—who were instrumental in developing with me the new imagery tests, and are so helpful in the many facets of the Institute.

Thanks are due to all the patients, workshop participants in Sweden, France and England, and all those in the 10- and 20-week training classes here in Los Angeles.

I wish also to thank my wife, Ruth, for the continued support that made this book possible.

I would also like to thank Jane Stewart for her help in preparing the manuscript and her invaluable suggestions.

Joseph Shorr, Ph.D.

Los Angeles
1983

Preface To The First Edition

It seems ordinary to say one owes it all to one's patients. Not with me. For without their imagery productions, difficulties, tendencies, unique styles and feelings, the explorations would be severely limited. The infinite range and variety of visual imagery in psychotherapeutic experience are oftentimes dazzling. Added to this are some spectacular individual variations, ubiquitously unfolding and providing fresh challenges to meanings. The imagery can have the quality of mystery that each newborn child possesses. What will it look like? What will it grow into? What will it be?

As a result, most of the formulations about imagery come from reported and observable experiences, including my own imagery.

How a person changes in psychotherapy is a fascinating process. But, fascinating as it may be, it is also multifaceted, complex, sometimes inexplicable, sometimes dramatic. In this book I emphasize the use of imagery in the process of psychotherapy, but I do not believe imagery in and of itself is all of what makes people change in the course of therapy. To my way of thinking it is one of the most important dimensions that can be utilized in therapy, but we have only opened the doors. There is more to learn and do. A few years ago I never imagined what new dimensions imagery had in store for me. I cannot exactly imagine what lies ahead. When I close my eyes I see a beautiful field of flowers with the purple mountains in the distance. What does it mean? Time will tell.

In human experience when men spoke of the "five senses," vision was considered the noblest. Today the special status or significance of vision has lost none of its importance. Most of us can experience much more of the world visually than through any other sense modality. We can perceive visually events and objects distant and near and otherwise not available to our senses. Visual memory, moreover, seems to be especially vivid and permanent; we are more likely to forget or mistake someone's voice than his face, and it is easier to summon up a visual image than a tactile or olfactory one.

I refer to "imagery" essentially as visual imagery. On occassion, I might ask a person to imagine listening to some other person speaking to him; or how he or she might feel touching others or solid substances or how certain imagined substances might taste. The auditory, olfactory and tactile images are not omitted, but the visual predominates.

Imagery seems to play a part in nearly all of the proliferating new psychotherapeutic techniques. When solid theoretical constructs as the source of these techniques are not incorporated, we are on shaky ground. Spectacular use of imagery is no substitute for experience in the solid use of imagery. That is why I have tried to connect theoretical bases for the specific uses of imagery. Otherwise, transfer of skill is technique-centered and can leave the therapist bereft of genuine resource and theory.

Apart from therapy, human curiosity and imagination appears mired in contemporary man beset by an alienated, sometimes meaningless, sometimes absurd world. To free one's imagination and to stir curiosity is for me a desired goal in an age of reduction.

I have been asked many times how I became interested in imagery and the concept of Psycho-Imagination Therapy. It came from many directions. I cannot name them all. The two more important influences are as follows. Foremost was the book *The Self and Others* in 1962 and the *Divided Self* shortly thereafter in 1963. These helped me formulate and concretize what I had already learned from Rollo May. (Surprisingly few psychotherapists I met were specifically aware of Laing's work until 1967, with his *Politics of Experience.*) Second, about the same time I came across the works of Desoille, Ven Den Berg (Caslant) and a little later Hanscarl Leuner and Roberto Assajioli and their studies in imagery. It seemed that the phenomenology of Laing and May et al. needed to be integrated with the developing work in imagery through a natural bridge – psychotherapeutic imagery productions. Out of this (plus other influences) emerged Psycho-Imagination Therapy, which then assimilated its own experiences and directions.

The "other influences" upon my work refer to those investigators who are not directly involved in psychotherapy but who nevertheless have helped expand the importance of the role of imagination and imagery in human living. Imagination and fantasy is now recognized as an indispensable resource in human life. Full accessibility to their own private imagery are the hallmarks of creative persons (Dellas and Gaier, 1970). It is known that vivid imagery does not obfuscate the accurate viewing of the real world (Sheehan, 1966). Contrary to previous thought, Jerome L. Singer has shown that the better able one is to make images, the better one is capable of fun, able to live more imaginatively, to discriminate between fantasy and reality better, and to be less disconcerted by unexpected thoughts and images (Singer, 1966).

It has been my observation that the intensive use of imagery in psychotherapy heightens therapist motivation and involvement because of the interesting and dramatic nature of the material that is elicited. The probability is great that the vividness and intensity of the patient's imagery productions serves as a catalyst to his or her own therapeutic motivations.

Some of the developments in the book came from a class I gave in "Identity and Imagination" at UCLA. Other material was developed from the many workshops given in Wurzburg, Tokyo, Hawaii, Montreal and in Los Angeles. As consultant to the California School of Professional Psychology, I helped participate in research projects involving imagery.

I wish to acknowledge those persons who read portions of the manuscript and who offered encouragement, criticism and suggestions. They are Dr. Jerome L. Singer of Yale; Dr. David L. Shapiro of the Center for Forensic Psychiatry, Ann Arbor, Michigan; Dr. Lili Wolf, N.Y.U. School of Social Work; Dr. Peter Wolson, President of Los Angeles Society of Clinical Psychologists; Dr. Hans Rosenwald of the Albert Schweitzer Colleges; Raymond J. Vespe of Palo Alto; and Jess Millman, Milton Shapiro, Dr. Ernest L. Rossi, Dr. Karl Pottharst and Dr. David Bilovsky of Los Angeles.

Introduction to the Second Edition

It is a pleasure to participate even in this small way in Dr. Shorr's grand enterprise, which is nothing less than the development of an entire new armamentarium of psycho-diagnostic and treatment methods based on the examination of patients' mental imagery.

The approach described here uses patients' mental imagery as the plastic, affect-laden medium for revealing and working through the psychological complexities that created each patient's problems. Each step characteristically begins with an instruction by the therapist, such as setting up an imaginary situation or asking the patient to complete a sentence stem aimed at the source of difficulty. There are special procedures designed to reveal various kinds of intrapsychic and interpersonal conflicts, at revealing aspects of the self-concept or of fundamental drives, fears, and wishes. The resulting imagery may provide the focus for discussion aimed at insight or it may provide the mental arena for exploring and resolving difficulties. The spontaneous nature of mental imagery seemingly incorporates both resistances and the contents defended against, thereby partially bypassing the resistances. The pictorial, visual quality of most imagery provides a range and variety of information that is hardly possible with linear verbal discourse.

This venture follows two previous lines of development. The first is that of the directed waking dream therapies of Desoille, Virel and Fretigny in France and of Leuner in Germany, as well as other approaches that make heavy use of imagery, such as Assagioli's psychosynthesis. The second tradition is that of projective assessment techniques, which have refused to die under the heavy double-barreled onslaught of academic criticism and of rejection by behaviorally oriented clinicians (as recently as 1976, the Rorschach and Thematic Apperception Test were still the tests most frequently recommended by clinical psychologists for study by graduate students). Nevertheless, Shorr's psycho-imagination therapy is significantly different from the therapies of his predecessors in the directed waking dream movement and his assessment techniques provide some form of information not ordinarily or systematically available with previous projective techniques.

Psycho-imagination therapy differs from the therapies of Desoille and Leuner in that it provides the therapist with a wide range of specific imaginal techniques that are intended to be used whenever the clinician senses that they will be productive. They are not intended to be used in any particular sequence. They can be combined flexibly to serve as the core of the therapy or they can be used adjunctively in a wide variety of therapeutic contexts. In either instance, they are intended as tools to "open the patient up" to imaginal and affective experiences that are either missing from the patient's normal conscious flow or are systematically unattended when they occur. Thus, even therapists who believe that other approaches, such as behavioral, cognitive, or verbal-associative approaches are in general more efficient, may turn to psycho-imagination therapy techniques as techniques of choice when therapy has stalled. For this reason, the techniques described in this book may be absorbed more readily than other imaginal techniques into the repertoire of the average therapist.

Psycho-imagination therapy contrasts with its main imaginal competitors in accepting a rather eclectic theoretical framework. This handbook plainly reflects the influences of Freud, Sullivan, Horney, Jung, Desoille, Leuner, Rogers, symbolic interactionism, various existential therapists, and the empirical tradition of general psychology. It brings these elements into relationship with one another within a single orientation and set of techniques. It does not attempt an explicit unification of them into a monolithic theoretical system, and it therefore remains open to absorbing new ideas as they emerge and are compatible with the varying theoretical orientations of most practicing clinicians.

Joseph E. Shorr is among the most fertile contemporary creators of psychotherapeutic techniques. His approach to his clinical practice has been one of pushing back the boundaries, experimenting clinically, attempting particular techniques to optimize their impact, and carefully observing the effects. His clinical experience tells him – and the cases he reports strongly suggest – that he has brought together a powerful clinical method.

This method clearly warrants the next step, which is to examine its procedures, processes, and outcomes quantitatively. Like virtually every major psychological treatment approach, psycho-imagination therapy was developed in the consulting room rather than in the laboratory, was applied before receiving controlled, quantitative scrutiny. Its ultimate success in gaining widespread adoption will depend in substantial part on its validation as an efficient treatment method. Few observers are as intensely aware of this need for controlled, quantitative study as Shorr himself. At least with respect to his assessment methods, he and his colleagues have already begun to perform these studies.

I recall my sense of bemusement upon first looking through the first edition of the manual for the Shorr Imagery Test (SIT), which reported some initial norms and reliabilities. Here was a table of contents that was a model for test manuals under American Psychological Association guidelines, but the text consisted in substantial part of promissory notes. The manual was as much as anything a blueprint for future research, a prospectus inviting the user of the test to take hold and contribute. Gradually, the undone research is getting underway. Norms are growing in scope. Some validity studies have been reported or are in progress.

Among the studies that appear now to be most urgent are therapy outcome validation studies, assessment validation studies, and studies of the processes and parameters of treatment. One might envision the following kinds of investigations:

Outcome studies: The principal criticism that Psycho—Imagination therapy will have to meet is that levied against the older dynamic therapies: that it takes longer to achieve results with its imaginal methods than with more direct verbal or behavioral methods and that it offers no additional benefits – that, as Lindzey and Tejessey concluded about TAT scores, the results of imagery techniques may provide little more than the clinician could have obtained from the patient by simply asking.

There is no *a priori* reason to accept this criticism, and clinical experience militates against it. In fact, one of the supposed advantages of imaginal techniques is precisely that they cut through resistances and confusion more quickly than their competitors. But this must now be demonstrated. The demonstration will require evidence that information that the patient can translate into desirable behavior change emerges more readily with the introduction of psycho-imagination techniques than with cognitive or behavioral approaches that lack psycho-imagination components.

It is also possible that the use of imaginal techniques enables therapy to have a more encompassing and hence more enduring effect on the patient, because the open-ended nature of imaginal response may work to prevent premature closure on the part of both patient and therapist regarding the nature and scope of the clinical problem. This possibility, and perhaps other added benefits of psycho-imagination therapy, also call for careful outcome investigations.

Assessment validation: Traditional psychodiagnostic methods are typically used in institutional settings as screening procedures. They have often been criticized for providing little information that the therapist can employ in the particulars of designing treatment plans or arriving at decisions about what to do at the many puzzling junctures that occur in therapy. Many practitioners, perhaps particularly in individual practice, use no formal assessment devices or employ behavioral assessment procedures highly targeted to specific presenting complaints.

The Shorr Imagery Test (SIT) falls somewhere in between these extremes. It may eventually be developed into a general screening method, but it is designed to provide particular information about the patients' problems and imaginal processes. Its superiority for these purposes remains to be demonstrated.

Research must answer a number of pressing questions: Which kinds of treatment decisions are easier to formulate with the responses to the SIT than without it? Is therapy preceded by the SIT shorter (because more effective) than without it or with the use of alternative assessment procedures? Does the SIT enhance the therapist's ability to predict the nature of the patient's subsequent insights, affects, resistances and behaviors?

Process studies: any treatment method gains with understanding how it works. In the instance of Psycho—Imagination therapy, it is important to understand the nature of the imaginal processes that it harnesses and the variables that determine them – patients' response repertoires, current concerns, internally generated cues, therapist-generated cues and instructions, patients' physiological states, species-specific response tendencies, and so on. The more we know about these fundamentals the better psycho-imagination therapists will be able to optimize their methods and to suit them to particular existing conditions and constraints.

The questions for research posed above have not to my knowledge been answered in a controlled, quantitative manner for any of the imaginal therapies and only to a variable and highly limited extent for the other psychological therapies. An approach with the promise of the one described in this book deserves urgent attention of this kind.

Clinicians and researchers will find Psychotherapy Through Imagery an important and most interesting avenue into the world of imagery and its psychotherapeutic uses.

Eric Klinger

University of Minnesota
Morris, Minnesota

Psycho-Imagination Therapy
The Integration of
Phenomenology and Imagination

CHAPTER I

The Self and Others

"Thus every relationship at least implies a definition of self by other and other by self."

R. D. Laing

"You danced. You danced to each other's tune. You both wrote a musical play and cast each other in the leading roles. A farce – a tragedy – take your pick."

The Novel, *The Edge*
Shirley Mezvinsky

In order to take the bold leap into the new dimension of existential phenomenological thinking in relation to present-day techniques of psychotherapy, it might be well to by-pass much of the intellectualization that has blighted a great deal of the literature in this field.

As Raymond Vespe commented, "It further appeared to me that as existentialists we seem so averse to conceptualizing our knowledge and formalizing our procedures that after some thirty years the existential in psychotherapy is in need of some kind of laxative! How fertile will existential psychotherapy be and how relevant will it become if its meaning cannot be grasped or communicated? . . . we are interested in firmly grounding existential psychotherapy in a phenomenological attitude and methodology." (Vespe, 1969, p. 85.)

It seems to me to be valid, then, to try to communicate some of the ways in which I have approached not only an understanding of my patients' inner worlds but have also tried, via the methods of using imaginary situations and existential questioning, to reveal their principal areas of conflict.

Many years ago I realized that the therapeutic session must be a truly alive one in the sense that the phenomenologists stress, namely, that to know fully *what* we are doing, to feel it, to experience it all through our being, is more important than to know *why*. If we fully know the *what*, the *why* will come along by itself. For, as Hora stated, "Complete understanding of one's mode of being tends to bring about a shift in world view, that is, a changed attitude toward life. Change occurs the moment man can see the totality of his situation." (Hora, 1962, p. 37.)

Also I have been greatly indebted to the English existentialist, Dr. R. D. Laing, for so brilliantly pointing the way to further research in the area of the relationship of the self-to-others. Quite clearly, man has always been intrigued, engrossed,

3

sometimes obsessed, in his efforts to define or analyze his own human reality or identity. The "I" that Lizai searched for in 866 A.D.; the "essence" that Sartre elucidates; and Rollo May's idea of "centeredness," all spark like varied points of light from the myriad-hued crystal of the concept of *self*.

Philosophers, poets, mystics, and more recently, psychologists and psycho-analysts, have tried to come to terms with this enigma from different points of view, but each must lead inevitably to the fact that the existant one must analyze is oneself. As May (1958, p. 56) states, "The world of this particular patient must be grasped from the inside, be known and seen so far as possible from the angle of the one who exists in it."

But the complex architecture of the self, as realized by the consciousness of the self, is not an *isolated* one, as many persons tend to feel. It is inevitably interrelated, even interpenetrated, by the other selves. As Dr. Laing so concisely states: "It is clear that a person's 'own' identity can never be completely abstracted from his identity-for-others. His identity-for-himself depends to some extent on the identity others ascribe to him, but also on the identities he attributes to the others and hence on the identity or identities he attributes to the other(s) as attributing to him." (Laing, 1962, p. 75.) But this is not always apparent to either the individual or the other person, let alone an observer of the relationship.

People, from their initial encounters, are constantly defining their inter-penetrating relationships, guided by largely unconscious "rules." But these rules tend to be stable or balanced. Jackson (1957) drew attention to this phenomenon and introduced the term "family homeostasis." However, this very well may apply to any two people, and to paraphrase, may be called "dyadic homeostasis."

Dr. Otto Allen Will, Jr. shows this point quite clearly in relation to the very early life of the child and mother. "After birth, the vital needs of the infant — for food, fluid, motor integrity, restricted temperature range, bodily contact and other forms of sensory stimulation — must be met through activities with another person, who, to a considerable extent, learns with the infant to recognize and respond adequately to its needs. In this activity, needs of the mother are also revealed, developed, and met. A reciprocal relationship is formed, in which requirements of both partners are expressed, satisfied or frustrated, identified, and increasingly conceptualized in interpersonal terms." (Will, 1964, p. 4.)

Laing takes it on from there: "One is in the first instance the person that other people say one is. As one grows older one either *endorses,* or tries to *discard* the ways in which the others have defined one. One can decide to be what it has been said one is. One may try not to be what, nevertheless, one has practically inevitably come to assume one is, in one's heart of hearts. Or one may try to tear out from oneself this 'alien' identity that one has been endowed with or condemned to, and create by one's own actions an identity for oneself, which one tries to force others to confirm." (Laing, 1962, p. 84.)

It is the ability of each individual to either endorse his given identity or to *successfully change it,* that will determine his mental and emotional development and stability.

The Stake in the Relationship

It is important to understand that between one person and another there is always a stake in keeping the definition of the relationship intact. For, it is my contention that between any two people, each has a stake in the other in order that the individual's identity be preserved. In a mental hospital, one may see a woman huddled in a corner who has yielded almost all of her identity to the world in order to preserve just enough identity to survive. Her stake is to preserve whatever little sense of self she can.

The individual who feels anxious when he drives up to a gas station may be anxious because he has a stake in preserving his identity even to the gas station attendant. He has to protect himself against what he feels might be a negative judgment on the part of the gas station attendant (the other) about himself (the self). Or, he may have a stake in not being taken advantage of and, to protect his identity, he may act tough or curt.

Of course, the concept of "stake" is close to what we call *resistance* in psychotherapy. Every patient has a stake in resisting or using whatever rationalizations, explanations, or uninvolvements he may deem necessary to protect his ego against the therapist's attempt to make him cope with his world. The greater the loss of identity the patient has, the greater the stake in sustaining and maintaining his own security operations.

Wheelis states this quite clearly when he writes, "The extended awareness is also an effect of the loss of identity for the reason that, being unsure of who one is and where one stands, it behooves one to be more alert and perceptive." (Wheelis, 1958, p. 21.)

The novelist, Saul Bellow, in *Herzog* (1964, p. 169) shows how much stake we have in feeling miserable even when things are obviously going well: *"To tell the truth, I never had it so good . . . but I lacked the strength of character to bear such joy.* That was hardly a joke. When a man's breast feels like a cage from which all the dark birds have flown – he is free, he is light. And he longs to have his vultures back again. He wants his customary struggles, his nameless, empty works, his anger, his afflictions and his sins."

Sometimes we have to yield a part of ourselves through inhibitions, repression, regression, denial, reaction formation, or detachment, in order to maintain our identity. Or, we may have to conquer, dominate, engulf, destroy, or shape other people's lives for them to preserve our own identity. There are countless strategies people will employ to try to manage their ontological insecurity, which may range from unconsciously perpetrating their parents' reaction upon others, to the self-illusory maneuver of *pretending* to be such and such a person instead of actually being it.

Sartre captures this ploy beautifully: "Let us consider this waiter in the café. His movement is quick and forward, a little too precise, a little too rapid . . . He bends forward a little too eagerly; his voice, his eyes express an interest a little too solicitous for the order of the customer . . . All his behaviour seems to us a game. . . But what is he playing? We need not watch long before we can explain it: he is playing at *being* a waiter in a café." (Laing, 1962, p. 27.)

In fact the ways are so numerous and sometimes so ingenious and subtle that it indeed presents one of the most formidable barriers to understanding which confronts both the patient and the therapist.

Rollo May uses the word "centeredness" in place of identity, but the following clearly indicates the same formulation: *"I assume that this person, like all beings, is centered in himself, and an attack on this centeredness is an attack on his existence.* He is here in my office because this centeredness has broken down or is precariously threatened. Neurosis, then, is seen not as a deviation from my particular theories of what a person ought to be, but precisely as the method the individual uses to preserve his own centeredness, his own existence. His symptoms are his way of shrinking the range of his world in order that his centeredness may be protected from threat; a way of blocking off aspects of his environment that he may be adequate to the remainder." (May, 1964, p. 28.)

Phenomenological In-Viewing

It is very difficult to get "inside" a man as he enters a room full of strangers. How does he view himself? How will the others view him? How does he think they will think of his view of them? How does he think they will think of his view of their view of him? As you see, it gets complicated!

In group therapy I have sometimes asked one patient, Jim, how he thought Mary thought of Bill in the same group. Also, what did Bill think that Jim was going to say about Mary? This phenomenological in-viewing is admittedly complicated, but also extremely revealing, as the insight often seems to be more correct and to have more depth than the more usual "depth interpretation" in orthodox psychoanalysis.

For example, when Jim was asked to say what he thought Mary was thinking about Bill, Jim said, "Mary thinks that Bill sees her as an attractive woman with whom he would like to be sexually intimate."

But Bill thought Jim would say, "That I *pretend* interest in Mary because I really feel anxious around her. As a matter of fact, I feel she is a castrator."

Mary agreed with Jim's insight about her, but both were taken aback by Bill's statement about his actual world. Mary in this case had a self-definition in relation to others that she was attractive to all men. And Bill had a self-definition that he was not going to be accepted by women and furthermore they would engulf him.

So, without this intervention of in-viewing the definition of their relationships might have continued unchanged. However, the stake in sustaining the definition was not able to withstand this attack of openness in a group therapy session.

Fantasy

I believe that any person who has accepted an "alien identity" received from significant others has a marked tendency towards denial. To give a child an "alien identity" a parent must deny the child many aspects of his existence. For example, one might ask a patient what I call an existential question such as, "What did your (mother, father, or whoever) deny in you?" One person might answer, "My existence, they never knew that I was alive." Yet another might say, "My sexuality – they never wanted to acknowledge that sex existed." Invariably it is the thing that was denied to him that the individual will feel guilty about having for himself for the rest of his life.

If a person cannot come to terms with his "alien identity" he will be left with only one possibility – fantasy. In his fantasy things can happen to him "safely" and still allow the significant others to define the relationship. In reality imbued with this "alien identity" he plays the roles set up by his relationships, but only in fantasy can he feel he is a "real" person.

The Need to Make a Difference to Someone

Therapeutic experience has convinced me that in addition to all the needs, or hierarchy of needs, that Murray or Maslow have suggested, to which I agree wholeheartedly, our alienated society has forced man into re-emphasizing two other main needs of an existential nature.

Foremost is the need to make a difference to someone. There is nothing that leads to frustration and despair more quickly than the feeling that you are indeed not making a difference to anybody.

How often have we heard of the desperately lonely person committing one act, no matter how "crazy" it may seem, so that at least, "I made a difference to someone." Suicide notes very often suggest the same phenomenon. "If I kill myself who would really care anyway?" Many potential suicides are deterred by the fact that possibly the person does make a difference to a child, a husband, wife, or even a cause. Or, perhaps, as Nietzsche once remarked, just the thought of suicide has saved many lives!

Man's great fear seems to be that he will not make a difference to anyone – that he will be alone. Any observer of American life can verify the large numbers of people who, though seemingly otherwise "successful," are really lonely. Most bartenders will substantiate this fact. Is it not the contention of Whyte's *Organization Man* and Packard's *The Status Seekers* that when all is said and done, man is willing to pay the price of conformity not to be alone?

The need to make a difference to another person is so fundamental that a much greater proportion of our thoughts are involved with this than is ordinarily imagined.

In the novel *The Seeker,* Wheelis makes this clear: "We had created for each other an illusion, and by our presence gave it reality for a while. We fell in love, not with each other, but each with the image of himself in the other's eyes. These reflections acted and reacted, back and forth, cumulatively, and so expanded a nucleus of genuine affection into an illusion of overwhelming passion. At the file cabinet I saw something of eloquence and beauty in her face, and that was the real foundation upon which we built a fairy castle. For in that moment she happened to see my perception of her, found this image of herself pleasing, and began to think more highly of me for my discernment. My next perception discovered in her, therefore, not only the beauty already noticed, but her complimentary appraisal of me; whereupon I realized she must be a woman of extraordinary sensitivity. And when next she glanced at me she noticed this added element in my perception of her which led her again to revise upward her image of me. . . But she had looked, not into my heart, but into the mirror of my eyes and had seen there only an embellished image of herself. . . so I must conclude that what had so enchanted me about her was her appreciation of me. We were strangers looking into each other's eyes and *seeing only ourselves.*" [Italics mine] (Wheelis, 1960, pp. 40-42.)

When a person realizes that he does not have the ability to make a difference to anybody, he despairs, and in time this despair can lead to apathy and the false identity of anonymity.

As Camus said: "Like many men, they had no longer been able to endure anonymity, and that impatience had contributed to leading them to unfortunate extremities." (Camus, 1956, p. 26.) This may account for the person who walks into a train and says, "I will shoot the fifth person that enters." The Freudian analyst may conclude that it was his hostility to his father that made him decide to shoot that man, but while this concept may be technically true, it does not account for the man's false anonymous identity, nor the meaninglessness of his life.

Confirmation of Oneself

Just as important as making a difference to someone is having somebody know we are alive, in short, to acknowledge or confirm our existence. Martin Buber (1957) expressed this view eloquently in his article, *Distance and Relation.*

One of the most poignant statements made by patients relates to the fact that most of their material needs were met when they were children, but their real emotional needs were often ignored, neglected, or diverted. Confirmation by food and shelter alone was not enough. Often they report seeking beatings or punishment, holding their breath, or behaving in a provoking manner in order to get acknowledgment of some kind from significant others. A lonely person will start conversations with total strangers. How much effort at mere confirmation through the telephone people attempt daily defies measurement.

Recently in a Swedish film called, *The Doll,* a lonely man brings a store mannikin to his apartment and in fantasy ascribes to it the human qualities of a beautiful woman in order that it ask him questions about his day at work, and, more importantly, to confirm his existence.

One patient of mine reported that if she saw a single pencil, or nickel, or any object by itself, she had a strong need to fantasize another pencil, or nickel, or whatever, in order that these objects would not be alone. Her home was one in which she was essentially ignored and most of her needs were disregarded, so she desperately sought confirmation of herself. For many people, however, the only sad kind of confirmation is from a tail-wagging, happy-to-see-you dog.

Consider, too, how very important confirmation must be for a blind child. Indeed, psychologists report that if blind children don't get this confirmation from others, they will go to the extremes of inflicting physical pain on themselves. In a similar way a neglected wife will often drive her husband into a rage, even to the extent of provoking him to hit her, in order to get some reaction to herself.

But in a society that is becoming increasingly alienated it is precisely this lack or absence of a human other that causes pets and even machines to be substituted. I recently attended a conference given by the Academy of Television Arts and Sciences on the future of TV cassettes, and was appalled by the psychological dangers inherent in this new development; especially when the vice president of a large cable company calmly informed us that soon there would be a two-way contact from individual homes to a giant computer which would enable people to choose from 200,000 taped subjects. The potential for a kind of techno-dehumanization arising is alarming and would make George Orwell's big brother quite unnecessary. And what kind of confirmation are we needy human beings going to get from that computer?

Defining the Relationship

In any dyadic relationship there is always one person who defines the relationship whether this be done consciously or unconsciously. Obviously there are many ways in which the defining is done in a healthy fashion. For example, a school teacher clearly has to define his relationship to the pupils. This would only become a neurotic situation if the teacher were so despotic that he demanded total subservience from the children, or, the children from him.

Likewise, in therapy it is the therapist who defines his relationship with the patients. However, the relationship must be of basic equality of two people even though the roles are different. In *Of Human Bondage,* Maugham understood that the woman, Mildred, should not have been allowed to define the relationship with the man, Philip, but because he was strongly masochistic he allowed this self-destructive situation to continue, with the resulting conflict.

The goal of therapy is to allow the person to involve himself with naturalness in cooperative, mutual and "give and take" relationships. The British psychologist, Harry Guntrip, talks of the goals of human relationships most eloquently when he says, "A relationship between two fully mature, adult persons is one of equality, mutuality and spontaneity. It contains no element of complusion, no striving of either for superiority, no element of distrust or constraint . . . The two are 'on a level' and give and take freely . . . they seek nothing else but to enjoy each other for their intrinsic worth, fulfilling their own respective personalities in the process. There is an easy mutual giving and receiving. It is the relationship we have in mind when we think of 'love.' " (Guntrip, 1961, pp. 363-364.)

Very often in a love affair or marriage, one partner will define the other falsely, and if this is not corrected by the other person, it can result in a morbid dependency which leads to excessive jealousy, and anguished possessiveness which is rooted in ontological insecurity. If the person continues to be at the mercy of the other and unconsciously surrenders all power to him, this may result in the crumbling of the entire ego structure and lead to a schizophrenic breakdown.

The method used in Psycho-Imagination Therapy is very specifically geared to help people become strong enough not to allow others to define them falsely. As the sense of their true identity becomes clearer they are encouraged to subtly change the other person's evaluation of them, or, if this proves to be impossible, then they must discontinue the false relationship. (Laing, 1962, p. 91.)

In an asymmetrical relationship, in which one person is in a more dependent position, he might believe that he can improve the situation by resorting to ingratiation. E. E. Jones, K. J. Gergen and R. G. Jones (1963) explored the use of agreement to enhance one's power in their study, *Tactics of Ingratiation Among Leaders and Subordinates In A Status Hierarchy.* In an article in *Science*, based on this research, Jones states, *"Ingratiation,* like its sister term, *flattery,* is at least mildly pejorative in everyday usage. The word has connotations of dissimulation and deceit in social communication. Am I suggesting, then, that most of us are so concerned with the effects of our behavior on others that we deliberately engage in manipulative and deceitful tactics in order to gain their esteem? I do not know how one could ever obtain actuarial figures on this point, but I would argue — without great alarm — that all of us under appropriate circumstances do shape our social responses to increase our attractiveness to particular people. The scientific student of such response-shaping is unlikely to make much progress by interviews or naturalistic observation. In this particular area, I have learned through research experience that people are extremely likely to deceive themselves. Not only do they want to avoid publicizing the extent to which their responses to others are conditioned by approval-seeking motives, they work busily to protect themselves from awareness of the link between wanting to be liked and modifying one's behavior to this end." Jones concludes that often the ingratiator and his target person will form an unconscious autistic conspiracy which may be maintained by the most intricate interpersonal tactics. (Jones, 1965, p. 145.)

Unconscious Strategy

By unconscious strategy, I mean the manner by which the neurotic person copes, manipulates, repeats, controls, sustains neuroses, deceives himself, punishes himself or others, etc., without in the main being aware that he is doing this. And the word strategy in this case does not refer to a premeditated formula for action such as a military man might use in a campaign.

The unconscious strategy operates in a neurotic person to prevent undermining from someone else. This may take the form of defensive behavior such as inhibition, anger, avoidance, denial, reaction formation, phobias, withdrawal, or detachment syndromes. Or, it may take the form of controlling behavior, such as attack, provocation, insinuation, manipulation, destruction . . . which may indeed undermine the other.

Defensive behavior such as inhibitions, avoidance, denial or detachment in order to preserve the identity from being overwhelmed by other people is more generally known and written about. It is common to avoid situations in which we think we may lose our identity. The man who walks around the block for hours before he can face an interview for a job, fears the loss of his identity when accounting to the interviewer about his life. He would only feel secure in an interview, if, by chance, he senses the interviewer has doubts and weaknesses of his own. Fearing less than the loss of identity, in such a case he will function above his original expectancy.

On the other hand, the person who detaches himself when dealing with people, does so out of terror at an anticipated annihilation. Naturally the person he expects to annihilate him has no such intention and rarely suspects that he has aroused such fear. But the terror is so great for the detached person that he acts as if he is there, when he really feels "outside" at a safe distance. One patient remarked to me once that he felt he was looking at me through a telescope, although in reality he was only a few feet away.

But it is the person who uses the strategy of controlling behavior of others in order to preserve his own identity that is more difficult to understand. A typical example is that of a hard-driving, ambitious and successful man who seems outwardly sure of himself. But this facade often covers a compulsive need to run the lives of those around him.

One such man, who had separated from his wife in order "to find" himself, secretly set himself up in an apartment with another woman, yet went on visiting his wife because he could not bear for anyone else to have her, even if he wasn't sure that he wanted her. He really wanted all women as slaves, as his identity depended on being able to control them.

The parent who exercises rigid control over his family is not proceeding from a position of strength, but acts to protect his ego from being subjected to the will of others. The more rigid the discipline, the greater is the fear of being taken over by the "other." I once asked a man who was domineering in business and a bully in the home what he would least like to be called. His answer was, "Never call me henpecked!"

In some difficult marriages, one sees one of the partners using defensive behavior to sustain the identity, while the other will employ controlling behavior for the same reason. As an example of the former behavior, one patient of mine constantly claims to have heart attacks, and, of course, a condition of "helplessness" to prevent his wife from leaving him. He needs her strength and ability to make decisions. His unconscious strategy is his insulation against his expectancy that any woman would try to undermine him. In the course of therapy I will ask him the existential question, "Do you feel you will be taken over, or engulfed, by a woman?" This may alert him to the price he's paying by trying to control his wife by the unconscious strategy of sickness and helplessness.

But the wife also has an unconscious strategy, as she is interpenetratingly involved with him. She provokes her husband by flirting with other men at parties and then denying this behavior. So she pays the price for her relationship by the symptom of meaningless affairs. When asked the existential question, "Are you in constant competition with men?" her answer was "yes." By her unconscious strategy she is able to stay married, yet still compete with men who can never possess her. So, the "gruesome twosome" persists.

In this case both the partners have a well-developed neurosis; in other instances the interpenetration may have much less dire consequences. But it is my contention that if a person in therapy is not made aware of his unconscious strategies and those of others, and his stake in sustaining them, it may be impossible to help the patient to change.

Also the therapist must be aware of the patient's unconscious strategy in dealing with him. For example, one patient belittled what I considered a particularly effective session. When she did this several times, I sensed her unconscious strategy of minimizing nearly everything good. She came to realize, through existential questioning, that she was afraid of anyone swaying her thinking as her mother had done all her life.

I wish to stress here that there is no set way of using an existential approach to therapy. It must always be versatile and vary from one patient to the next. All of the therapist's intuitive imagination must flow with each particular patient's needs in order to fully enter into his inner ontological world. I hope to be able to demonstrate this in the following practical part of the book, which aims at revealing the *existential approach.* rather than any cut-and-dried technique or system. As Rollo May suggests, the therapy must be based on two questions: "What will best reveal the existence of this particular patient at this moment in his history? What will best illuminate his being-in-the-world?" (May, 1958, p. 78.)

For a more comprehensive examination of "Self-other" theory and the interpersonal theories, the reader is referred to Laing, R. D. *The Self and Others.* Chicago: Quadrangle Books, 1962; Laing, R. D. *The Divided Self.* Chicago: Quadrangle Books, 1960; Laing, R. D., Phillipson, H. and Lee, A. R. *Interpersonal Perception.* New York: Springer Publishing Company, 1966; and Sullivan, H. S. *The Interpersonal Theory of Psychiatry.* New York: W. W. Norton, 1953.

CHAPTER 2

The Imaginary Situation

"The picture is in the house next door."
"But there isn't any house next door."
"Then we'll build one."

Groucho Marx

"Imagination is not ... the obverse of reality, but affords, rather, a means of adaptation to reality."

Hinsie and Campbell, in
Psychiatric Dictionary

It was the realization that imagination lies at the central kernel of our consciousness that, many years ago, made me decide to research further in the use of this faculty as a tool in existential psychotherapy. For, as Kierkegaard maintained, "[Imagination] is not one faculty on a par with others, but, if one would so speak, it is the faculty *instar omnium* [for all faculties]. What feeling, knowledge, or will a man has, depends in the last resort upon what imagination he has, that is to say, upon how these things are reflected... Imagination is the possibility of all reflection, and the intensity of this medium is the possibility of the intensity of the self." (Kierkegaard, 1944, p. 46.)

What could be a clearer point? Surely if the imagination is the possibility of the intensity of the self, then why not use this imagination also to *reveal* to the patient his or her inner self and conflicts?

But first of all I started to further define the faculty of imagination. Rollo May concisely expresses Kant's view: "... not only does the world conform to our *intellectual* understanding as we actively form and reform the world in process of knowing it, but *imagination* and *emotions* play a critical role also. It is the *totality* of ourselves that understands, and not simply reason." (May, 1967, p. 11.)

Thus it would seem that one of the principal *functions* of imagination is that it is used to resolve the conflicts between the outer reality and the inner fantasy and can be thought of as the *modus vivendi* which harmonizes these opposing components.

To illustrate this, one patient of mine, a girl in her early thirties, Elizabeth, had an impossible relationship with a possessive mother who had ruled and scarred her life. When I asked her to imagine holding her mother's face in her hands, she was totally unable to do so and became quite hysterical at the suggestion. Much later in therapy, after she had worked with other imaginative situations which were easier for her to handle, and after she had gradually strengthened her ontological sense of self, I once more urged her, in her imagination, to hold her mother's face in her hands. This time she was able to do so — long enough for the highly critical look in the mother's eyes to change and soften towards her. I feel that this was a crucial turning point for this patient, because she was subsequently able to resolve her conflict about her mother, learn to "define the relationship" for herself, and start to live her own life at last.

At the beginning of therapy, some individuals may feel that they do not possess a vivid or intense imagination, possibly because they have doubts about the adequacy of their intellectual powers. Consequently, they may be amazed to discover that with proper guidance and encouragement, their imaginations flow easily.

I might ask them simply what they are doing for the rest of the day. After they have described what they plan to do, I point out that this was using their imagination. Or, I ask whether they save for the future. Usually this leads to a very definite description of the kind of future they desire, and once again, I stress, this is effective use of the imagination. Is there a person who has not daydreamed at some time in his life? Since everyone daydreams in one form or another, everyone is using imagination, whether they recognize it or not.

Armstrong (1963, p. 144) in a book entitled, *Shakespeare's Imagination*, says of Shakespeare that, "His daydreams, such as Philip the Bastard, are apt to indulge in *imaginary conversations* [italics mine] in which their lot is in favourable contrast with that of some person occupying an inferior position."

Are there not many among you who have experienced nightmares at one time in your life? Certainly this involves imagination regardless of the underlying reason for the nightmare. And it goes without contradiction, that everybody has reported dreaming about someone or something in their lifetime. I have never known anyone to doubt the existence of dreaming. Certainly without some form of imagination, dreaming would be impossible.

There are patients who have to know everything that may happen in advance, so that they can control their reactions and defend against the irrational fear of being taken over. This edge is something they cannot relinquish. The therapist must repeat again and again, "There is no right or wrong answer." Have him imagine himself in a situation in which he doesn't know what will happen in advance — stay with him, sharing his anxieties with him, and keep urging him to take the chance. Nearly all patients respond in a short time. With such a patient, one must suggest many competitive imaginary situations to make him more aware.

The person who needs to be the number one in anything he does has the same difficulty — needing advance information for his feeling of certainty. I suggest many imaginary situations in which competition is involved. This helps the person to involve himself in imagination, as well as providing therapy for his problem of overcompetitiveness.

It is inevitably the fears, anxieties, or frustration inherent in people's internal conflicts, which leads to the curtailment of an imaginary capacity, in order to shrink the boundaries of their self-hood to more manageable dimensions. It is precisely these dimensions which are revealed by the phenomenological approach to psychotherapy.

So, although each individual varies in intellect and background, nevertheless, imagination is available to all, albeit in a different form. This is very well illustrated in Ben Shahn's charming anecdote: "Some years ago, as I was laboriously planting a small maple tree in my front yard, cheering myself with visions of future cool drinks drunk in its future spreading shade, a neighbor of mine who was passing by stopped to watch me at work. He cleared his throat, 'D'you think it'll grow?' I condemned him in my mind as a fellow with no imagination. But after some years of reflection I realize he had just as much imagination as I. I am sure that, in his mind's eye, he could quite clearly see the tree a year hence standing dead in my front yard. Let's say that his imagination was other than mine — dour." (Shahn, 1967, p. 14.)

I maintain that it is only through the *active and conscious* use of imagination that one can begin to perceive the difference between one's world and that of others — and whether one's imagination will be tilted towards optimism, pessimism, or total despair. Proust was so acutely aware of the great diversity between each individual's inner perception of the world that he was able to comment on the fact that the only true voyage would not be to travel through a hundred different lands with the same pair of eyes, but to see the same land through a hundred different pairs of eyes.

One of the first imaginary situations with which I experimented was also used by Hanscarl Leuner and Carl Happich, and consisted of asking the patients to imagine themselves in a meadow (Assagioli, 1965). I assure you, I saw as many different meadows as Proust would have done through his hundred eyes. For instance, one patient, John, could only see a barren grey wilderness wherein he felt great anxiety. The next patient, Mary, admitted the meadow was green and lush, but she still felt isolated and alone there. Another patient was afraid of being attacked by wild animals.

Then, as Herbert Spiegelberg reaffirms, "We should remember from the very start that there are different kinds of imagination, not only the freely roaming variety but also the disciplined one, of which the scientific as well as the artistic imagination prove prime examples. Such disciplined imagination uses clues and is limited by rules. It is obvious that our new kind of phenomenological imagination subjects itself to this kind of controls." (Spiegelberg, 1964, p. 120.)

Perhaps it should be stressed here that it is not only the patients' imaginations which are being utilized, but also that of the therapist. He must flexibly exert his imagination to the utmost in order to enter the phenomenological world of his patient. Hans Kunz (1957, p. 150) describes this task of the therapist as "imaginatively thinking projection."

Likewise, Alberta Szalita, in her article *Reanalysis*, encourages this view when she suggests, ". . . 'a daring' is needed in reaching a patient and eliciting a response. I don't see any discrepancy in this kind of activity on the part of the analyst with the psychoanalytic tenets. It does not differ from the analysis of a dream. Perhaps that is why dream analysis is so useful; it gives a legitimate opportunity for the analyst to use his imagination." (Szalita, 1968, pp. 98-99.)

So, I proceeded with these *general* imaginative situations. The patients usually would be sitting up with their eyes open in order to keep the human dialogue flowing. Two examples out of countless possible general situations are as follows: I would ask a patient to imagine a cloud and tell me what shape it is, or to feel that they have strong telepathic powers and are in touch with someone in a foreign country. "What country would it be? Describe the person there. What thought would you send them, and what would they reply?" To this latter situation, one young man reported the country was Russia, and that the person with whom he was in contact was a peasant, bitterly burdened by his life of menial drab routine. This, in projection, showed how the patient felt about his own life and the frustrations of a dreary job.

Another recently divorced girl said she was in contact with a prostitute in Paris, who became a whore in order to get milk for her children. This immediately revealed her hitherto unadmitted anxiety about her own life and worry about her responsibility for her two children.

Situation

It gradually became apparent to me that although these general imaginary situations were useful indications of the particular *type* of imagination of the patient and gave clear clues as to certain ontological insecurities, with the growth potential this involves, at the same time, it still did not get at the main internal conflict areas.

It was then that I concentrated more on the concept of the *situation*. Sartre (1957) stresses that *man in situation* is of great interest to psychology, even though it is subordinate to phenomenology. That is, psychology is interested in man as he appears at his work, with his family, and in other situations. However, phenomenology takes precedence, as a definitive study of *man in situation* would have to take into account the concepts of man, the world, of being-in-the-world, and of situation. Hopefully, by stressing the *situation* in my work with patients and encouraging them in their *choice of action* within the situation, they would ultimately be helped to greater choice of action being-in-the-world.

Thus, although I had some interesting results from guiding a person in going into a house and telling me what he or she saw therein, far more was revealed when either I suggested introducing a significant "other" into the situation, or the patient did this for themselves. This way, I would urge the patient not only to tell me how he felt in the various parts of the house, but how he felt in relating to the other person in the situation.

It became increasingly urgent to develop a high degree of specificity – so much so, that many times either the imaginative situation, or the self-and-other existential question would relate so specifically to one particular patient that it would never be used again with anyone else.

Also, I found that, as a patient would become accustomed to this kind of therapy, it was less and less necessary to make any interpretations for him. With very specific cross-checking including not only the imaginative situation, but also the most-or-least method, the finish-the-sentence technique, and the self-and-other technique, it would be possible to help focus the patient to greater awareness, where he would be forced to face the truth *for himself.*

The following are just a few out of literally an infinite number of possible situations which, based on the clinical judgment of the therapist, may be used when suitable for a specific patient:

1. Imagine yourself taking a shower with your father. How would you feel? What would you say to him? What would he say to you? (Alternate this situation with mother, or siblings.)

2. Imagine yourself waking up as a baby. How would you feel? What would you do?

3. Imagine your father is standing next to you. Whisper something into his ear. What does he reply? (Vary this with whispering into mother's ear, or significant others.)

4. You are a necklace around your mother's neck. What do you feel? What do you want to do? Now your mother puts her hand on you. What do you do and what do you feel?

5. You awake in a field and there are footprints over your body. On what part of your body do the footprints appear? Whose footprints are they?

6. Imagine that there's a large blank screen on the wall. What do you see on it? Bring someone else onto it.

7. Imagine you are looking up at a balcony. Your father comes out and looks down at you. What does he say to you? What do you say to him? (Alternatives: mother, or significant others.)

As you can see, each imaginative situation has to be tried on for subjective size with each individual patient, as flexibility is more important than any system.

The responses to these situations are so vastly varied as to seem incredible at times. For example, I have asked patients to imagine unscrewing their heads, holding them in their hands, and telling me what they see inside. One man saw a large screw; and an older woman replied, "Nothing." One young man saw an orderly arrangement of brains like a maze; and a girl saw spiders in her head. One young woman, when I asked her to (IS)* imagine unscrewing her head and looking inside said:

♦ ". . . my head . . .

". . . oh boy, here comes the smut, Martha . . . actually, it really isn't that bad. My corridors are green, gold, beige, and warm. Most of my doors are open slightly, so I can peek into the room to see that everything's okay and pass on to the room I'm going to. A lot of my rooms are like Jim's . . . library rooms, sitting rooms, places to be comfortable and read, talk, lie on the carpet and stare at the ceiling. I have a white and apple-green bedroom with a big four poster bed, but the bed is white, so it isn't scary. It's very comfortable in my bedroom . . . sort of like a summer evening when I've been out running around all day in the country. I have a rose room which I go to when I'm down, because being surrounded with pale pink, or rather that lovely rose pink that you see in stained glass windows, is cool and quiet, and I don't have to think, just unwind. There is one room that I like a lot . . . it's a green and gold room where I do a lot of good work . . . writing, reading books, painting. Unfortunately, to get to this room I have to go throught the RED ROOM, which is simply revolting. The Red Room is big, dark, with ugly Gothic horror-film furniture, and candles . . . which cast shadows in corners and around the furniture. There's an enormous dark four poster bed which I never sleep in because there's a hand underneath it, and if I sleep and my arm falls over the side, or my leg sticks out under the covers, this hand will grab hold of me, and it's cold and clammy, and not at all nice. The room is hostile . . . it BREATHES nastiness and fear, and I hate it. So a while ago I decided to paint it white . . . all of it . . . starting with the walls. If it's white then I can go through it to my favorite room easily, although I'll never stay in it, because you can't change the atmosphere in a room just by painting it. But at least if it's white it'll be bearable. So I tried to paint it . . . but wherever I painted, no matter how many coats of white paint I put on, the red paint still showed, and sometimes while I'm painting I can see the red stuff oozing through the white paint like blood. Joe [the therapist] offered to come and help me with the painting, and even came up with a new formula paint, which is super thick and covers anything. So, there we were, painting away, and I still couldn't cover up the blood, so I looked across at Joe's bit of wall and it was ALL WHITE. I guess the blood wouldn't DARE come through on his paint. But it didn't make any difference to my painting . . . the red stuff still seeped through."

I then asked her (IS), "Imagine what you can see in my head."

♦ ". . .Joe's head . . .

". . . corridors . . . white on white in white. I walk quietly, although I'm perfectly comfortable. There's sort of a hush . . . like on the executive level of corporation buildings . . . but I know I'm free to open any door I like, and when I do . . . the rooms are rose mostly, though there are also gold and brown rooms, where I can walk in, close the door, and either be by myself, or Joe will come in and we'll talk and look out the window, which has a countryside view. My feeling in all of these rooms is wakefulness; I don't want to miss a minute being in Joe's rooms, simply

---

*Throughout the book I use the following abbreviations to identify examples of my four techniques of questioning. These are (IS) Imaginary Situation, (S&O) Self-and-Other question, (M/L) Most-or-Least method, and (FTS) Finish-the-Sentence approach.

because I'll be annoyed with myself if I do. A lot of the time Joe walks the corridors with me, and shows me into one of his rooms, and every time that happens, I find something that's absolutely mindblowing; like walking into a room and finding the answer to something that's been bothering me SCRAWLED in huge letters on the wall in front of me . . . then I have to laugh because the answer would be so simple . . . so obvious, that the fact that it's escaped me for so long is funny. When this happens, Joe stands by the door holding his pipe with a little smile on his face, then sometimes he leaves me alone in the room, other times we go back and walk some more in the corridor."

One interesting phenomenon that is sometimes encountered is that a patient will give one reaction to an imaginary situation, yet with a *variation* of the same situation, will have a contradictory reaction. When this occurs, it is wise to draw attention to this contradiction and often the patient will be able to focus very effectively on the reason for this.

Sometimes one will encounter some unexpected block with a patient. One girl who had been in therapy for some time and had been working successfully with imaginary situations, had expressed a fondness for birds, so I asked her to imagine a bird on her outstretched finger. To my surprise, she was incapable of doing so. I urged her to try again and once more she could not do so, adding, "I can't because it wouldn't be fair to the other bird." "O.K.," I said, (IS) "Imagine two birds." "Oh, I can do that," she replied, "I see two sparrows. They are identical and they are both chirping." (M/L) "Who is the fairest person in the world?" I asked. "Me," she smiled, "I am always being 'fair' to everyone. I am always aware of what the other person needs – but nobody is fair to me. You know, those birds made me realize that I have to be compulsively fair to people. I'm really angry at them for not being fair to me though. I'll show them – I am so much fairer than they are, that I'll always be the victor."

Transposed Elements

An imaginary situation which can be used is to have the patient imagine that he is an animal, or a flower, or an inanimate object. I will ask a patient, for instance, to imagine that he is a hummingbird. How does he feel as he approaches a flower? This may relate to sexual fears or inadequacies that the patient is loath to discuss directly.

In order to ascertain someone's feelings about his position in a group of people, I will ask him to imagine he is an apple in a box or barrel of other apples. How he feels by comparison with the other apples, and his exact location in the barrel, should give an indication of his relationship to his neighbors or colleagues at work.

Sometimes it will be more efficacious to use the image of a machine or other inanimate object for this transposition. With others it might be more fruitful to have them imagine that they are specific animals.

Mental Imagery

Another way of entering the phenomenological world of the patient is to ask him what image he can arouse when I say certain key words abstracted from his own statements. A question I might ask is, "What image do you imagine when I say, 'love'?" Other images to produce might be abandonment, loneliness, perfection, self-worth, conflict, shame, humiliation, closeness, or commitment. Still others might be images relating to time, such as, "you as a youth of ten, your mother at sixteen, or your father as a baby." These images, combined with an imaginary situation, enhance the possibility of effecting awareness in the patient.

The Cooperative Encounter

As I have become more experienced in using the specific imaginative situation as a tool in therapy, I also have endeavored to enrich and enliven the sessions with three other groups of questions — the self-and other questions, the most-or-least method, and the finish-the-sentence technique — which I will examine in the following chapters.

But here I would like to quote from a patient of mine, a girl in her early thirties, as she describes what this approach has meant to her: "Probably the worst feeling in therapy is to talk around in circles without being able to get at what is really wrong. Wasting so much time and getting more and more anxious without being able to pinpoint the problem. These are the times when the imaginary situation focuses my attention . . .

"I don't know whether it's because I lived in a pretend world in my childhood, so that this enables me to have my feelings in a productive but safe way. Sometimes those feelings that consciously I still want to hide from view will come out in an imaginary situation: then there is no hiding from them any more.

"Once I wanted to talk about a special feeling and I found it difficult because I was ashamed of it. So the therapist had me imagine making a 180 degree turn and talk about what I saw. There were people in a tunnel keeping me out in the cold with sticks. They were very angry and I wanted to be inside where it was warm. I wanted to belong to them. Then I was able to talk about my group therapy — how I had been feeling separate from about half of the group and feeling so special and superior.

"If I had not been able to use my imagination to get the realization of being special, I don't think I would have been able to talk about it, because I didn't like feeling that way. . .

"I think we forget in therapy, we spend so much time digging up the underground anger that we forget that underneath that anger is a whole new way of being. I want to go under the anger, not stop at just anger, and reach out for love and caring to give to these people."

So, with the help of the therapist's imaginary self-transposal into the phenomenological world of his patient and the use of the imaginary situation, one is able to form what Herbert Spiegelberg so aptly calls the cooperative encounter, when he writes, "Imaginative self-transposal may help again. But clearly more important is the cooperation of the patient on which the phenomenologist may now count and which he may develop and reinforce by the accepting and loving attitude which is at the heart .of any genuine encounter. True, he can only imagine the other's world, but he can now do so with the constant help of and check by his client." (Spiegelberg, 1964, p. 124.)

CHAPTER 3

Further Specific
Approaches to Therapy

"Rather abide at the center of your being; for the more you leave it, the less you learn."

Lao-tzu, 570 B. C.

"A self, every instant it exists, is in the process of becoming, for the self . . . is only that which is to become."

Soren Kierkegaard

In this chapter three other specific techniques will be shown that, with the imaginary situation, can be combined to help the therapist and the patient see his "being in the world." These techniques are: the Self-and-Other question (S&O), the Most-or-Least method (M/L), and the Finish-the-Sentence approach (FTS).

The Self-and-Other Questions

One other important way of eliciting the patient's conflict areas is by the use of existential questioning, or what I prefer to call the self-and-other questions. An existential question is that which elicits how a person views himself, and how he feels others define him. If it is used in conjunction with the imaginary situation, the existential question can be an effective tool.

In the course of clinical work, I found that some of these questions would seem applicable to nearly all patients, whereas others would occur to me spontaneously during a session and would not necessarily be relevant to any other individual.

One of the more general questions relating to the self is, "You can call me many things, but *never* refer to me as what?" The replies to this may be quite varied, including such answers as: "a failure," "a weak sister," "selfish," or "a lady." One middle-aged man who has a strong ambitious drive in his successful business and is a domineering bully at home, surprised me by answering, "candy ass." This clearly indicated that his bullying manner was a defense against being engulfed by others.

The manner in which these questions are presented to the patient is of the utmost importance. In essence the timing of the questions is critical and under no circumstances must they be asked routinely or as a series of test items. This would weaken the desired therapeutic effect. In one sense, the classical Freudian analyst stresses the emphasis on the correct "timing of an interpretation." But where my approach differs from the Freudian is that the self-and-other questions are posed without any predetermined answer in mind. I do not try to fit the patient in advance into any dogmatic theory or system of thought.

For example, with one patient I may feel it is appropriate to ask (S&O), "How do you make yourself aware to others when in group therapy?" From his answer, he probably will show me his inner consistency in functioning with others, in a way that is unique within his self-system. It is highly possible, that if I had followed a preconceived theory, I might have unwittingly tried to get a "desired" response and have missed the way he really sees himself in relation to others.

Furthermore, judgment must be used to decide whether the patient has the ego strength to handle certain questions at a particular time. For this, as always, there is no substitute for the skill that comes from experience. Indeed, in many sessions I might find it appropriate to ask a patient only one or two self-and-other questions. In another session where I have to be very supportive, perhaps none at all.

The Core of the Identity

There are literally hundreds of alternative questions, all designed to expose the specific sense of the core of one's identity — that self-being which Gerard Manley Hopkins so vividly described as: " . . . my self being, my consciousness and feeling of myself, that taste of myself, of *I* and *me* above and in all things, which is more distinctive than the taste of ale or alum, more distinctive than the smell of walnut-leaf or camphor . . ." (Hopkins, 1953, pp. 147-148.)

Sometimes I will ask a patient directly (S&O), "What is the core of your identity?" In response to this, one young, male patient replied: "My hands . . . I am only what I'm doing . . . If I am not doing anything, then I have no identity."

With another young man in his early twenties, in group therapy, I asked (S&O), "What do you sense as the body part core of your identity?" To which he replied, "The core of my identity is in the middle of my head. It's a cylinder made of a dense heavy material, not steel, but not fibrous. It's hard to get it out of the top of my head. When I put it into Paul's hand, it became very heavy. I did not want him to hold it. I don't like the feeling of Paul holding my core. I don't dislike Paul for holding it. But it is more the feeling of having to guard his moving off with my core. The feeling is having to be very alert. If Paul moved off with my core, I would leap after him, place both hands on it and jerk it up and away from his hand."

I continued (IS), "Imagine each of your parents on a balcony, with you below."

"My parents were on a balcony in a house we lived in, in Santa Clara. My father came out first. Stood looking down with his arms outstretched and his hands, palms down, gripping the balcony railing, looking down his nose at me. 'Here is the core of my identity, you can't have it. I won't give it to you. It's too hard for you to smash. You can't smash it. I won't let you. I block you out with it. It's mine, mine, mine, mine, totally mine.' I held it up in my line of vision, so that it blotted out my father's view. Joe, the only way to deal with my father is, blot him out, turn away from that measly son-of-a-bitch. My mother comes out and looks down at me. I feel I am something. Me holding up my identity. I feel me. My honest first reaction, Joe, was to turn my right shoulder and lift my back to them and swing around and walk away down the steps, never to see them again. But when you said, hold up my core, I felt the only way to do it, was to hold it up between us, block them out with it and then shout at them. Shout them down. To walk down a path, there is someone behind me. I can see — feel a sunny day, blue sky, and a mountain path."

(IS) "Who is behind you?" I asked.

"My father. My lousy father," he said.

To further focus the patient's obvious hostility toward his father, I asked (IS), "Imagine throwing a hand grenade at your father."

"To throw a grenade, the first one would almost kill him, the second would, and I want to throw a third, it feels good — but the first one really killed him. The second two turned into nice feelings. I have to screw the core of my identity on my cock and walk around with it. It would stay on.

"There is a lovely girl standing on the path with long blond hair. 'Come on, let's walk.' I could take her hand. I would feel apprehensive. But I want to do it. If she were really beautiful, it would be really hard. But I want to do it. If she were *really* beautiful, it would be really hard. But I would do it."

I asked a young woman the same question in individual therapy (S&O), "What body part can you, sensing yourself, feel as the core of your identity?"

♦ "My identity . . . the core of my being . . ."

I prompted: "Is . . . "

♦ "I think somewhere in the general area of my heart . . . covered up by layers of 'me.' It's like a gob-stopper . . . I don't know what you call gob-stoppers in America . . . we used to have them at home when I was little. They were huge candy balls . . . hard as iron, and easily filled up your mouth. There was no way in the world to bite through them . . . you just had to keep sucking until the outside wore down . . . and the people who made them were very clever . . . every layer licked off revealed another layer . . . of color. No matter what stage in the process of eating a gob-stopper . . . whenever you took it out of your mouth to look at it, it was a different color. But best of all, was the middle . . . and you had to be careful not to cheat and crunch through that last thin layer of candy . . . the middle was an anise seed. So the good part of eating a gob-stopper was having the anise seed there in your mouth, tasting of licorice, and finally biting through it with front teeth . . .

"I didn't do that very often . . . usually I'd work away at the gob-stopper until the anise seed was there, then I'd take the 'middle' out of my mouth, and put it away in a crystal and silver jar on my dressing table. I collected a lot of them . . . dried up and smelling good . . . but my mother threw them away, thinking, I suppose, that they were more of my rubbish.

"I can take my anise seed out . . . but I don't give it to anyone . . . although it was very hard to get it . . . I took it out and gave it to you, Dr. Shorr, and you took good care of it. Then you gave it back to me . . .

"That's my identity . . . my anise seed, covered up with layers of different colored me . . ."

Other responses to this specific question about the core of the identity have included: "my head," "my penis," "my vagina," "my heart," and many others.

Another question relating strictly to self-identity is, "What can you call your own?" One girl assured me that the only thing she felt was truly her own was the time she spent away from home. Another woman could only claim her bath. A wealthy, successful businessman thought about this for some time, then stated that he owned all material things, a house, a car and furnishings, but had never been given love.

Another revealing question is, "What is your experience in sharing?" One young man was distressed to realize that, although he acted generously towards people, he really was only putting on an artful act, because he wasn't really *feeling* generous; he could not risk a true sharing.

A young man who had had a very pampered childhood with exceptionally indulgent parents, admitted that he was not a good sharer. So, I asked him to imagine himself and his father not having eaten for days. (IS) "If there were ten pieces of meat, how many pieces would you give to your father?" I asked. "How many would you take?" After some time, the young man replied, "Oh well, I guess I'd steal two pieces, then I'd give us both four pieces each so that it would look like fifty-fifty." This reply enabled him to see his own concealed feelings about his interpersonal life and his strategy of surreptitiously sewing the edge over others while still managing to look good.

When a patient is able to respond with the full amount of feeling to the question about the core of his identity — when he is truly able to *feel* that his chest, head, penis, or heart are his core — then it is possible to test or check the degree of his defensiveness and his security operations by his ability to imagine handing the particular core of his identity to the therapist and how it would feel then. One woman who said the core of her identity was her heart, was hesitant when I asked her to imagine handing me her heart. Then she blurted out, "Well, maybe I could, but only for a second." She stretched out her hand towards me, then drew it back again quickly, saying, "Oh no, I can't give it to you. I'd be paralyzed. You know that's funny, because you're the one person in the world I trust, and yet I can't give you my heart."

Sometimes I will ask a patient what would be the core of their mother's identity, or their father, spouse or other significant person. Often this serves to reveal hidden feelings about the patient's relationship to the significant other.

Questions Relating Self to Others

In the previous section of this chapter I have shown how an existential self-and-other question can lead into an imaginary situation, but this can also operate in the other direction. What I hope to demonstrate in this book is how essential it is to use all these specific approaches — the imaginary situation, the self-and-other questions, the most-or-least questions, the finish-the-sentence method — not in any set *order,* but rather flexibly, to weave the tapestry of every individual's varied therapy.

An effective way of helping someone to define their relationships with others is to ask, "Whom are you accounting to?" or, "Who defines the relationship between you and your father?" (or any significant other). A closely related question to the last one, which can be used either as an alternative or as part of the cross-checking in another session with the same patient, is, "Do you know where you stand with your mother?" (or any appropriate significant other). With a very insecure patient it may be suitable to ask, "What did your parents endorse in you?" or even, "What did your parents *fail* to confirm in you?"

In all his work, Laing stresses the crucial need for a person to "make a difference" to someone — that everyone needs their existence confirmed by others being aware of them. In *The Self and Others,* he states, " . . . emptiness and futility can arise even when a person has put himself into his acts, and when these acts seem to have some point to him, if he has put himself into something and has been accorded no recognition by the other, if he has become convinced that he is not able to make any difference to anyone, no matter how much he puts himself into his acts." (Laing, 1962, p. 72.)

In order to get a phenomenological glimpse into a patient's inner world of emptiness or sense of futility, one can ask, "Do you make a difference to anybody?" or, "Do you come first with anyone?" One girl replied to the first question: "Only if I do everything the other person wants. If I show a need for anything, they will turn away from me." Several patients have reported that they only make a difference to people in the work situation, but never in a personal sense. One woman sadly commented, "I guess I make a difference to my cat . . . "

This also relates directly to sexuality, for, as Laing maintains, "Sexual experience is usually felt to be empty and pointless if the intrapersonal components of libidinal gratification are present in the absence of libidinal gratification in the other . . . Any theory of sexuality which makes the 'aim' of the sexual 'instinct' the achievement of closed uniorganismic orgasm, with the other, however selectively chosen, a mere object as means to this end, ignores what seems to be a basic human need to make a difference to another person." (Laing, 1962, p. 73.)

We will explore further the phenomenological approach to sexual problems in a succeeding chapter. However, I do sometimes ask a patient in the context of the self-and-other, "Whom do your sexual feelings belong to?" One girl was genuinely surprised when she answered spontaneously, "Certainly not to me!"

As therapy progresses with a patient and he, or she, becomes accustomed to these techniques, it is possible to use more complex questions, such as (S&O), "How would you drive someone crazy?" From this particular question one can surmise the undermining techniques which the parents used against that individual.

This may be presented in an exaggerated form, because the patient is talking about driving someone insane, but nevertheless the *methods* used are invariably the same as the unconscious strategy of his parents. For example, one patient said, "Oh, I'd show the person love for one day and then totally ignore him for several days afterwards." Another individual assured me he would drive someone crazy by sustained silence – by refusing to answer any questions at all.

Generally speaking, I would not use such a complex question at the outset of therapy. Certainly, I would hesitate to use the word "crazy" with any patient before sufficient rapport is established so that the word itself will not be threatening to him.

The Most-or-Least Method

The imaginary question, or the most-or-least method, serves to sharpen the awareness of a person's self-image and the concept of his basic attitudes and values. Typical of this category of type of question is, "What is the most immoral thing you can think of?" Or, for another patient, I might ask, "What is the most exciting part of your body?"

Often, a patient will assume a false identity allocated to him through the unconscious strategy of his parents. This can lead in two directions. The first is what Karen Horney (1945) refers to as "the idealized image," in which the person is constantly trying to live up to his image and needs the world to concur with it. The other direction is when a parent, or some significant other, gives a person a despised image. The person then may continuously strive unconsciously to throw off this false self and live up to his true potential.

One young man, in his mid-twenties, had been forced into most vigilant "unselfishness" by the unconscious strategy of his mother. When I asked him the imaginary question, "What was the most frequently repeated statement made to you by your mother?" he replied, " 'Don't be so selfish!' She was always telling me how selfish I was."

Consequently, he had become totally incapable of taking anything for himself in a healthy way, to the extent that when he had saved up for a much needed Honda, he felt obligated to give it to his girl friend. I found the most-or-least questions were most helpful to him, especially, "Who can see the selfishness in you the fastest?" or, "Who carries the greatest authority for you?"

In an effort to assist the patient to become aware of his own despised image or the rigid need to sustain the idealized image, and try to change it, the following kind of questions can be helpful:

"What is the most immoral thing a person can do?"

"What is the biggest lie you have ever told?"

"What is the most jealous you have ever been?"

"What was the most unfair demand put on you?"

"What was the most often repeated statement made to you by your mother (father)?"

If the answer to the latter question has been a continual harping on the child's shortcomings, this will become the despised image which may haunt him as intolerable all his life.

The other principal way in which this tool of the most-or-least question can be helpful is to reveal the guilt in a person. For, inevitably, either of the aspects of false identity is locked into guilt. If someone identifies with the despised false image then he feels guilty; if somebody falls short of the idealized image, the guilt will be compounded.

Questions such as (M/L), "What did your mother (father) despise in you the most?" and "What is the most distasteful thing about you?" can be a guide to the dimensions of a patient's guilt. Very important in this context could be, "What is the most shameful day of your life?" or "What is the most humiliating thing that ever happened to you?" In a sexual connotation, I sometimes will ask (M/L), "In whose presence would it be most (least) difficult to have sexual thoughts?"

The individual who has been sufficiently undermined by his significant others will be inclined to cling to his imposed false identity as a defense. This defense dynamic is a negative attempt at the maintenance of the false identity. The individual is truly stuck on the horns of a dilemma, for, although his wheels keep spinning, he gets nowhere. Engaged in this self-defeating behavior, he is only busily maintaining the same self-and-other syndrome. While on this treadmill he is preserving a neurotic conflict resolution.

The Finish-the-Sentence Technique

Since Jung, many psychologists and psychoanalysts have used word association tests — that is, having the patient respond to a list of standard words with the first word that occurs to him. Jung maintained that the slowness of response to certain words will reveal a blockage or area of difficulty which will indicate a complex of some kind.

Subsequently, many other investigators have used sentence completion tests for diagnosis of psychopathology. Julian Rotter was one of the first to use a sentence completion test in this way. Recently, Paul Daston has observed that word association tests are in the ascendancy. He also concurs with Murstein that the sentence completion method probably is the most valid of all the projective techniques in the literature. (Rabin, 1968.)

In my clinical experience, I have found that this particular method can uncover the more complex emotional blockages. However, it must still be stressed that this technique must only be woven into the fabric of the therapeutic dialogue at the appropriate moment. Several examples of this follow.

When I asked the young man what was the core of his identity (p. 22), he replied, "My hands ... I am only what I'm doing ... If I am not doing anything, then I have no identity." Following this, I might ask him to finish a sentence such as: "But for my father (or mother) I would have been _____ "; "My identity will suffer if I go towards _____ ; or "I feel most hostility towards_____ ."

The businessman (p. 24), when asked what he could call his own, replied: "All material things such as a house, furnishings, and a car, but never love." I then would ask him a question such as: "Sooner or later, people will find me _____ " or, "People will love me if I _____ ."

When I asked the young man (p. 24) what his experience of sharing was, he replied that he couldn't risk a true sharing with anyone, so he put on an artful act about his being generous. So I might confront him with this type of question: "My basic expectancy is ____ " or, "My best defense is ____ ."

Another patient, a girl in her late twenties, was being severely handicapped by guilt because of her mother who acts like a martyr. I might alert her to this by asking her to complete this sentence: "My best defense against martyrdom is ____ ."

The therapist may find that he will be surprised by the responses a patient may make to the question, "I deprive my wife (husband, father, mother, boss or other significant person) of the satisfaction of _____ ." The patient often is surprised, too. Some responses I have elicited are: "I deprive my wife of the satisfaction of **sex**, of **my attention**, of **the one thing she wants**, and of **being a saint**." Typical answers to the reversed question are: "My wife (husband, father, mother, boss or other significant person) deprives me of the satisfaction of **showing any weakness**, of **being smarter than she is**, of **being sexually excited**, of **her sensitivity**, or **about anything**." The patient also may be asked the question about any two other significant persons in his life, for example, "My father deprives my mother of the satisfaction of _____ ."

Years ago I would have been loath to ask a question that seemed like an item from a test, but this came about initially by accident, when I started to ask a woman patient, "The only good man is a ... " As I hesitated, searching for an appropriate word, she said vehemently, "... a eunuch!" After that I found it was both revealing and fruitful to enhance the fabric of the therapy by inserting Finish-the-Sentence questions at appropriate times. For it is precisely the spontaneity of the question and answer that makes it both phenomenologically accurate and full of feeling, usually surprising the patient by the degree of intensity as well as content.

I also have found the Finish-the-Sentence method useful with a patient who is quite amnesic about his childhood and who may have difficulty with an imaginative situation. An effective way to do this is to ask a patient to supply ten different endings to such a question as, "I strongly resent ____ ." Out of a list of such examples as: "stupidity," "my ulcer," "my boss," "my wife's back-seat driving," and "my family," I will ask the patient to pick the one item that he feels most strongly about, and to proceed further into his feelings and awareness.

Summary

I wish to emphasize that I do not recommend exclusive use of only these four techniques (Imaginary Situation, Self-and-Other, Most-or-Least, and Finish-the-Sentence). Some therapists are phobic about any specific approach other than those of the system, for, until recently, the non-directive technique allowed no deviations to arise from the patient's responses. The classic Freudian allows nothing but free associations and the Gestalt therapists disallow the past or any interpretations. However, I feel that one should interpret if it seems appropriate. Also, reflected statements of feeling or direct personal reactions can be valuable. While bearing in mind these four specific approaches, one must nevertheless remain one's authentic self – only then can one ask the patient to do likewise.

These four techniques enhance each other as they are combined and interwoven. Singly, they may be valuable but, in combination, the whole can be much greater than each of its parts. It is the *integration* of all the specific approaches within the framework of the individual's *phenomenology* that I am attempting to develop, so that he can achieve greater awareness of himself, thus opening the door to possible ways of change. Here, for example, are listed some possible ways that each of the four techniques can be utilized to make the patient aware of a single feeling reaction:

Finish-the-Sentence (FTS): Never call me ____ .

Self-and-Other (S&O): What image of yourself can you not allow?

Imaginary Situation (IS): 1) Picture yourself on a blank screen in a position in which you detest yourself.

2) You are walking down a street and a person your own age accuses you of something. What does he accuse you of and why?

Most-or-Least (M/L): What is the most detestable thing anyone can say about you?

CHAPTER 4

The Internal Conflicts

"The central, most pervasive condition for the development of motives and of psychopathology is conflict."

George S. Klein

"The neurotic person engulfed in a conflict is not free to choose. He is driven by equally compelling forces in opposite directions, neither of which he wants to follow."

Karen Horney

I t is not the purpose of this book to become involved in extensive theoretical discussion of the concept of conflict. There are many books that do just that.* My purpose in mentioning conflict is based on the pragmatic concept that people coming to therapy are in neurotic conflict and unconsciously go to great lengths to deny their conflicts. The normal person does not go to the limit to deny his conflicts; he can recognize them, accept them, and integrate them fairly well. The neurotic person has a great stake in keeping them hidden. Almost unknown to himself, the neurotic person, upon entering therapy, is caught between wanting to be aware of his conflicts and wanting not to be aware of them. These opposing tendencies are already in operation before he has entered therapy. The therapist must try to make him aware of them despite his resistance. As Wheelis says, "Each side of the conflict is likely to be a composite of many partial forces, each one of which has been structured into behavior, attitude, perception, value. Each component asserts itself, claims priority, insists that something else yield, accommodate." (Wheelis, 1969, p. 62.)

Why not utilize the bi-polar nature of neurotic conflict in the therapeutic procedure? Phenomenologically various answers are possible to the imaginary situation (IS), "Imagine closing your eyes and turning around 180 degrees and then imagine opening your eyes and seeing anything at all. What do you see?" On his first visit, one homosexual man said, "A woman's vagina, bleeding." He was quite surprised and shocked. I offered no interpretation. I asked him then (IS), "Imagine

---

*See Horney, Karen. *Our Inner Conflicts*, 1945; Klein, George S. *Perception, Motives, and Personality*, 1970; and Weisman, Avery D. *Existential Core of Psychoanalysis: Reality Sense and Responsibility*, 1965.

yourself in a ring with an opponent. Who is it? What would he look like? Who would win?" He answered, "Each of us is waiting for the other to move." He then offered his own interpretation. "I guess that's me, paralyzed." "Who is the opponent?" I asked. "My friend, Jim," he answered. "We love each other but are bored with each other and we're both caught." Thus, bi-polarization began to uncover conflict and expose it to both the patient and to me.

In using the bi-polarization concept of becoming aware of conflicts, I may ask a person (IS), "Imagine two large boxes. What person do you imagine in each box?" One man said, "My mother in one box and my girl friend, Rosalie, in the other box." "What does your mother say to Rosalie?" I asked. " 'Get out,' my mother says." "And what does Rosalie say to your mother?" I asked. " 'I won't go,' Rosalie says."

The methods are infinite to uncover the 180 degree variations. I may simply ask the patient (S&O), "Are there two parts of you at war?" Here is a patient's report of an experience in group therapy:

"Two Parts of Me in Combat"

♦ After Ray spoke about his feelings of illness, etc., I spoke about my own menstrual pains during my high school years, that had caused me to constantly go home from school. When I was home, I was alone, until she (mother) came home and took care of me. She was always concerned about me at these times.

Joe [the therapist] asked me to imagine a penis and my vagina on a set of scales, asking what would happen. I felt that my vagina would be so light, that it would raise up, thereby giving the penis the strength.

Joe asked what my vagina would be saying to the penis, and I replied, "Don't hurt me." The penis replied, "I won't," in my fantasy and feelings.

Joe then asked me what part of my body was in combat (or conflict) with my vagina? I immediately felt it was my anus. Joe asked me again (giving me the feeling that he wanted to know if I was positive). I really felt that the anus was combative. I spoke about my constant constipation since childhood, and how it affects my sexual experience, because I'm aware of some pain (often extreme) if I haven't emptied out. (Which I usually don't do.)

Joe asked me to describe the feeling of the combat and I felt that my intestines, etc., were blocking my vagina almost with a wall or something. This makes me feel that I can't relax and enjoy sex. Joe asked what was in there blocking me, and I felt there was wire of some sort. Joe asked if it was any specific type of wire and I said and felt it was "barbed wire." Barbed wire made me feel it was really hostile blockage, and suddenly I felt my mother was in my anus with one barbed wire. I felt angry at this discovery or awareness that she put barbed wire between my anus and vagina.

I felt (now feel) that it's no wonder I can't free my sexuality with that kind of conflict. The anus controls my vagina by not letting my womanly feelings come out. Joe asked me to do something about the barbed wire and my mother; to throw it out.

I threw it all out together, with the wind, feeling very angry. I told my mother to get out of my anus with that wire; to let me be free of that crap within. If I'm empty and free, Joe asked, can I then allow my sexual feelings to emerge, without fear, as a woman?

I, somewhere, said that I'd never had any peace in that constipation problem with my mother, because she always asked me if, "I was eliminating regularly." I said she still asked me in letters and on the phone. I felt strongly that if she dared ask me again, I would tell her that I was shitting right on her then.

I really felt that, and felt very pissed off, and angry about the entire situation. Somewhere in one discussion, I said I hated her because she always eliminated regularly and that I hated Walter too, because he did and I couldn't.

I also said my mother talked about my taking the pill now that I wasn't with Walter and I said that I explained it was to avoid surgery and that I wasn't going to be cut, unless my life would be on the line. I also mentioned that my mother's reply was that there's nothing wrong with surgery since she had a total hysterectomy at 37 or 38 years.

My mother wanted me to be a man, like her. She denied my female feelings and sexuality. Only when I realized this was true, and I rid my anus of my barbed wire, could I free my sexuality.

I really feel violently angry at my mother for this fucked-up mess of feelings.

Another way to elicit conflict areas is to ask the patient if he feels differently about his left hand and his right hand. One patient said, "My left hand is weak and my right is strong; my left hand is for women's approval, my right for the approval of men." In this case, I may urge him to have the conflicting parts fight, *i.e.*, the left and right hand. Who wins? Following is one patient's report about the conflict his hands revealed to him:

Joe [the therapist]: "How do you feel about your hands?"

Paul: "I don't know." (Resist, resist) "I think I would like to keep my right hand out in front."

Joe: "Why?"

Paul: "It seems a little safer. Maybe a little stronger." (My right hand felt more like a fist. It could make a fist. It could make a fist easier. My left hand is looser.)

Joe: "Can you hold your hands together?"

Paul: "My left hand feels more comfortable being held. It can't really hold my right hand *very* well. My right hand is strong. I feel like my right hand should straighten my left up to fly right. Make it not so soft. Maybe hit it a few times." (I hit it.)

Joe: "You have to punish it a little, huh?"

Paul: "Yeah ... I really feel like putting my left hand in my back pocket. It feels like it would be more comfortable back there."

Joe: "Well, go ahead if you want to."

Paul: (I immediately felt like I shouldn't. It wouldn't be being a man. I put it onto you that you would be feeling you were judging me with "go ahead and don't if you don't want to be a man.") "Oh, I really don't want to."

Joe: "Go ahead, you said you did."

Paul: "O.K." (And I put it in.)

Joe: "How does it feel?"

Paul: "Funny, it feels better. Like it is not in the way. It means I only have one arm, and I should not be able to function as well. But I feel that I can function better. My right hand knows more of what it is doing. My left hand is out of the way. That way I don't have to be confused as to how to act. There's no decision to make. I could function better cause I would know exactly what and how to do it." (Rather than just functioning better — more like defending myself better. That left side of me would hamper my defense.) (Incidents of my childhood flashed through my head about when I couldn't decide whether to use my right or left. The resulting confusion seemed to hinder a "perfect" performance. In sports I'm left-handed, but eat and write with my right.)

Joe: "Will you let me hold your left hand?"

Paul: (That immediately felt like an impossibility. And I couldn't really do it. I pulled my hand out but I couldn't give it to you.)

Joe: "Name your left hand. What is your left hand?"

Paul: "Clumsy, fuck up."

Joe: "You mean that the left hand is the one that has suffered, and been ridiculed, and hurt, and beat, and shed tears? And you are ashamed of it and have to hide it?"

Paul: "Yeah, that's exactly the way I feel. All those things are written on the back of my hand. All those crazy things I've done. All the stupid things I'm ashamed of. The pain, the crying, the craziness." (I really felt embarrassed and humiliated.)

Joe: "That's feeling guilty. Guilty and ashamed of who you are. That's part of you." (You gave me a lot of support.) "I won't ridicule you for that. I understand and accept that part of you." (That felt so good to me. I finally gave you my hand. It felt really good for a few seconds, but then it felt tense and good and then back and forth). " . . . If you keep seeing my hand as perfect, you'll keep me as a god, not as a human being who has also made mistakes."

Paul: (I really felt you as a flesh and blood human being who has also done some stupid, human, feeling things. It felt really good. I took my hand away.)

Joe: "Feeling guilty for that humanness is like beating a dog down all the time and then getting mad at him for feeling beat down and afraid. You're not responsible for feeling beaten. You're just human. You don't need to feel guilty for it. Accept it as you and be proud of it. You don't have to hide and defend it." (That felt so good to me. It was an awful lot of pressure released. Like it really is O.K. to be human. To make mistakes. To just let it be.)

Paul: "Let me hold your hand again." (I held it and it even felt better. I felt equally human. Your hand was strong and warm and so human, all at the same time.)

Joe: "Put your hands together now. Really make them together." (They felt so much *more* equal. Like they could work together comfortably. Not to have to cut that part of me off and feel guilty about it. And that part seems to include so much of my warmth, and compassion and understanding. No wonder I was so scared to walk into bars. Kill or be killed doesn't allow much room for tears, mistakes, pain, floundering, humanness, love, worth.)

A less directly personal and intimidating way to use the bi-polarization question is to focus on some seemingly unrelated object. "Imagine there are two different oranges on a table. Describe each." One patient said, "One is ugly, crinkly-skinned and decayed and the other one is healthy." "Give each one a name," I asked. "Evil and good, " he replied. I continued, "Have each orange say something to the other."

A good way to help the patient arrive at his own awareness of his conflicts is to ask him (IS) to imagine two different animals — any two different animals. Here is an example of one man's answers:

Therapist	Patient	
"Imagine any two different animals. What are they?"	"Fox"	"Snake"
"What adjective would you give to each?"	"Sleek"	"Slimy"
"What verb would you assign to each?"	"Running"	"Slithering"
"Now have each animal say something to the other."	"You'll never catch me."	I can kill you if I want to."
"If the fox and snake were in conflict, what would happen?"	"The snake would bide its time, and then when he had the fox in the right position he would strike."	
"Does the conflict between the snake and the fox have anything to do with your conflict?"	"I'll be damned! It sure does! It's me always waiting for the woman's approval before I will move towards her. I am angry at her for the power I give her."	

It is possible to ask a patient for two different birds, animals, or flowers, or even for two different animals of the same species, for example, two different zebras or anteaters. As the differences are imagined and the possible conflict of the animals is introduced, an awareness of the patient's own conflict is stimulated.

I try not to interpret, but offer more possible ways (by using the four techniques described in Chapters II and III) to have the patient begin to see it for himself. He is, by his answers, becoming aware of his neurotic conflict.

The effort is nearly always directed toward the discovery of the self versus self; self versus the other; or perhaps the "new" self versus the "old" self. If it is possible to use an approach that makes use of the 180 degree variation involved in neuroses, the "self" and the "other" can be immediately presented in opposition for viewing and awareness. At other times, one may use a "finish-the-sentence" or a "self-and-other" or a "most-or-least" question that allows the person (self) to include the "other" with whom he is in conflict.

I may ask him (FTS), "Never refer to you as ____ ." One man, after a great deal of time, sweating profusely and moving about a lot in his chair said, "Never call me a liar." It was probably one of the most difficult things he had ever said to anyone in his life. I then asked him (M/L), "Who is the biggest liar in the world?" and more easily this time, he said, "Me."

I invite the reader to now ask himself a seemingly simple question. Never refer to you as what? Take your time and being emotionally as honest as possible, answer the question with a single choice. It is my contention that, if truly answered, the reader will become aware of an image of himself that he has mobilized a great deal of defense against, and wishes the "other" person not to hold.

With another patient, in an early session, I asked him to (IS), "Imagine looking into a mirror and instead of seeing yourself, try to see someone else." His response was, "Someone like myself, a person with some talents . . . who never worked hard at developing. He is laughing at me and he says, 'I knew it wouldn't happen.' "

The imaginary situation in which the person is asked to imagine looking into a mirror and seeing someone other than himself elucidates some of the strongest feelings about persons with whom he has had the most conflicts. It is not uncommon for people to cry when becoming aware of seeing the other person. Of course, there is no absolute rule — but most reactions are strong. For example, strong feelings were elicited when I asked a young lady to close her eyes and (IS), "Imagine stretching your hands out and then imagine a person whom you would clasp with both the right and left hands." "My right hand, which has my fingernails bitten to the flesh, is clasping my husband. My left hand, which has my fingernails normally grown, is clasping my mother." "What does your right hand say to your husband?" I asked. "Stop picking on me,' " she said. "And, your husband's response back to you?" I said. "Why don't you shut up and go'," she said.

At other times, I might ask a person to imagine he is on a mountain and below him at a distance, are two armies, one to the left and the other to the right. What armies are they? What are their names? Who is the general of each and who wins? The answers are quite indicative of neurotic conflict and sometimes surprising to the patient.

At the beginning of therapy, as I am trying to make the patient become aware of his bi-polarized conflicts, I use those questions that I might like to ask nearly all patients. In a very short while, however, as the uniqueness of the individual unfolds, many other questions come to mind. I might ask him (IS), "Imagine the two most opposite things you can think of." I ask him to give me three or four of those. Or I might ask (IS), "Imagine you have a twin brother or sister. The two of you are going down a river in a boat. What happens and how do you feel?" Another question might be (IS), "Can you imagine two rooms in a house in another city? Describe each person in the rooms and have them say something to each other."

Or (IS), "Imagine walking down a street and you meet someone your own age and he accuses you of something. What does he accuse you of? What do you feel and do about it?"

Or (FTS), "Never let a man say I am ____ ," or (FTS), "If you don't watch out, I'll ____ ," or (FTS), "I experience conflict when I ____ ."

Obviously, the number of ways are infinite that can allow the person to begin to become aware of his internal conflicts. This is especially true in the earlier sessions. At a later point in this chapter, I will try to show that, as the patient becomes aware of his conflict, he will be more able also to see his defenses against the significant others. He may also become more aware of the nature of his neurotic conflict resolution and the possibility for healthy conflict resolution.

Usually, in the earlier sessions, awareness of the conflicts is achieved only at a primary level. However, this does not mean that more intense awareness may not appear in the early sessions. I remember, for example, when I asked a patient (IS), "Imagine telling a secret to a stranger in a train that you will never see again." He answered, "I'll tell him that I am a mama's boy. I'm indulged. I'm not masculine and I want to masturbate." Then without a word from me, he began to re-experience a traumatic incident of his mother sexually stimulating him and making him her "man." It was not difficult then to proceed to the awareness of his mother's strategies with him and his own strategies to counteract hers. It was even possible to go on to some focusing techniques to which he could respond rather easily. The focusing techniques will be discussed in full in the next chapter, but suffice it to say, it is not an approach that will generally be useful in the earlier sessions.

Also, trying to get at conflicts between the self and others and their polarities is something that may be always present at any phase of therapy. Some conflicts are resolved, leaving others yet still untouched to resolve. One person who said, "Never refer to me as a **weak sister**," in his opening session, answered after a few months of therapy, when asked the same question, "Never refer to me as **unfeeling**." Another man, when asked (IS), "Imagine turning 180 degrees. What do you see and feel?" answered, "The death mask and skeleton of my mother." Three months later, he answered the same question, "My mother's smiling face."

Here is the verbatim report of a woman who, earlier in her therapy, had conflicts about feeling that she was a little girl in a world of adults and was greatly concerned about assuming her rightful place and strength. At this point in her therapy, it is obvious that she wants the "others" in her life to be strong and assume their share of responsibility.

"Harry and Florence"

♦ Joe [the therapist] asked me to imagine I had two chipmunks on my hands. I did and named the chipmunk on my left hand, Harry, and the one on my right, Florence.

Harry was very beautiful and had a full bushy tail, but Florence was very drab and seemed nervous and skittish. Harry seemed content to sit and chatter to me, while Florence moved almost continuously around my hand. I was drawn to look at Harry, which seemed easy to do, but Florence demanded I look at her. I felt very impatient with her. Angry with her because I wanted only Harry. Every time I looked at Harry or talked to him, I felt Florence demanding me to pay attention to her.

I told Joe that I wanted to drop my hand out from underneath her. I did and she fell. I felt good. I let her run around for awhile next to me on the chair and then I put her on my left hand with Harry. She seemed very happy and contented. No demands for me to pay attention to her because she had Harry with her. She wasn't alone.

Joe asked me what this had to do with my life. I guessed that it was like me as a little girl with my parents. My father, who had been loving and at least was with me a lot, wasn't really a strong man. He was dependent on me, like I was the only thing worthwhile in his life. My mother made me feel that she was dependent on me as her extension to the world.

They both lived through me. I didn't mind with my father, because he was big and beautiful and loving and took me places with him and stood with me against my mother. Her, I detested with her begging and weakness and "poor me." My father didn't act like a strong, aggressive man. I'm not angry about that. I do see him as not being fair to me and that I had a right to be a child with him, not a grownup for him. I want men to act strong now. That must have been one reason for Hank and all the other unfeeling men who I thought were so strong.

I want Bruce to act strong and positive and sure of himself. I will accept him, hurting or upset or doubting, but I cannot stand the constant bitching, complaining and being a little cry baby boy. I want the men in group to act strong. I look to Joe to be strong and directive in group. It's all to make sure that the men are stronger than I am. I can be strong if there is a strong man also. I don't want to chance being strong myself unless there is a strong man, too.

As the conflicts are being made aware to the patient by such methods, the patient invariably mentions significant others as part of his internal conflicts. My experience indicates that parental figures and siblings are most often mentioned as the other person in the conflict. Occasionally, others are mentioned, such as spouse, boss, etc. It is possible to ask the patient to (IS), "Imagine your mother, wife, father, brother, sister, boss, etc., looking into a mirror. Who might they see, other than themselves? Have them say something to each other." Indeed, nearly all of the techniques for eliciting the conflict areas for the patient can be asked as if the significant other were answering and feeling the same situation as the patient.

Then one can ask (FTS), "My mind according to my mother is ____." " . . . **that it is stupid.**" The finish-the-sentence question (FTS), "My mother's mind according to me is ____," may be answered, " . . . **that she is totally prejudiced.**" I asked a patient who was constantly talking about his relationship with his mother to imagine (IS) his mother telling a secret to a stranger in the train. He was quite excited. He spoke of his mother's secret, " . . . that she really wanted to fuck Paul Newman and be free and wild in sex." But, then he added, "She never let me ever believe that."

The poignancy of the inner turmoil, churning, but going nowhere, was expressed by an obsessive-compulsive patient who had already spent five years in classical Freudian therapy. I was attempting to make him aware of his internal conflicts. My question and his reactions follow: Therapist: (IS) "Imagine two rooms in a house in another city and tell me whom you imagine in each room?"

♦ "I am in a long hallway walking toward the lighted other end. I walk hesitantly, something holds me back a little. It is my own small voice suggesting I go out and play, or go back to my own room and read or otherwise occupy myself for my own satisfaction. At the same time, I keep walking because of a need. At the other end, are my mother and father. They are talking. 'Rosie,' my father says, 'I know what is right, leave the boy alone.' My mother is not strong enough to know her own rights and not strong enough to fight. To fight my father means being put down by his logic. He will inundate her with words. My mother would like to punish me and make me toe the mark but my father says, 'What's the difference? Let him be.' My mother cannot get him to understand how difficult I am. I will go to my father and he will support me and give me his assurance that whatever I do is all right. Why should I do as my mother asks? It is more fun being angry at her. I can make her jump through hoops because she never really gets angry. She just keeps insisting and poking and nudging and when I figure the fun is about over, I may give in and do what she wants, but never happily. It is such a surprise to see Jay do something he is asked with a smile and an 'okay.' That is because I never did. The only time I smile and say okay is when protocol or father figure, or politics or situation demands that I be cooperative. My inside unvoiced response is always one of being intruded upon whatever the request. What is so difficult about going to the store or riding the bicycle to the station to pick up the papers – yet my response to my mother is always one of anger and fury and intrusion on me. So there at the end of the hallway are two of them in their room. Right now I'd like to go to my mother and say 'okay' – but my father will do something. He won't leave me alone with mother – if I have something to show her that I'm proud of, well first of all I don't think she will accept it. She will defer to my father, I can fantasize her looking at him for his approval. What I remember, like tying my shoelace or trying to write is a 'that's nice' but never an involvement. Why doesn't she take me in her arms and take my hand and show me how to write and think a little of me, instead of her shopping and her letters and phone calls and making everyone else in the world happy including herself? So I have the choice of the two rooms, mine – where I have to do my own thing and try to be happy or busy or content with MYSELF – or their room, where there is always an argument – not a fighting argument – a dirty, fucking, insidious, holier-than-thou correctness of my father and poor mommy gets the shit. She has no rights but she doesn't know it. She buries all the barbs he throws and rationalizes them into shopping or some busyness so that she does not get totally destroyed. And, of course, I join in the fun. What good would it do to cooperate with her, she won't change, she won't treat me like a human being – it has gone too far – a million times I promised my father to be good and I might even do it once, but my mother takes advantage of me. She is never satisfied with just one thing. If I go to the store for her, she will have something else for me to do – she is insatiable. Well, there in the room, my father welcomes me into bed. He will make me happy and show her what a good boy I am. He will read to me and have a surprise for me because I asked for it, and my mother will have her wheels spinning to figure out what she has to do in the house or in respect to a friend or someone she has to call — anyway, she will clear out. Then daddy and I will cuddle up and enjoy the conspiracy because we are together and have each other and don't need anyone else. Why should I go to my own room and be satisfied with myself when I can be with my father and we can be so happy together? Supposing I did go to my room — or if my father (or mother) told me to go out and play — it would only be temporary. There is no satisfaction. Only a momentary or temporary separation from my father. Okay, I go to my room. I look around. A project. Build something — always something I can show to him. But now, I would like to go to my room and do something for ME. Not to show anyone, just for me. Never happened. But what a good feeling, what a revelation if I did and my father said, 'That's nice, you did it for yourself, you must do things for yourself because that is where the real good feeling is, when *you* are satisfied — it is not important if I am satisfied, but are *you* happy with what you have done?' Never happened. No, instead he would say 'Julian, that is perfect, you are marvelous, you are a wonder, you are my boy, keep coming up with these things, and I will always adore you.' YOU BASTARD, what is mine? MINE!"

The immobilization of a person in conflict and the polarities of conflict were beautifully expressed by Shakespeare's *Hamlet*.

> ". . . Pray can I not,
> Though inclination be as sharp as will:
> My strong guilt defeats my strong intent;
> And, like a man to double business bound,
> I stand in pause where I shall first begin,
> And both neglect . . ."
>
> Hamlet, Act III, Scene 3

The Five Minute Life History

One simple method of dispensing with extensive regressive exploration into the unending events that a person might recall about his life is to ask him, in a time limit of three to five minutes to (IS) grow up from a baby in a baby's room. He will invariably recall those significant highlights that are emotionally charged for him and he will most certainly indicate how he has been defined by others. Here is an example of a five minute life history:*

♦ ". . . (Pause) Just a baby? I feel all alone as a baby. All alone in a cold room with no blankets and I can scream for blankets, but I don't think anybody cares to hear me or comes to me. And I just get a little older, feeling 'cold' like that is like I am supposed to be and hanging onto my Teddy bear for some kind of warmth. And I get a little older and I develop some kind of allergy, like I get hives and I am breaking out in a rash and then they figure I am allergic to the Teddy bear, so they take that away from me and they don't let me have any stuffed toys. That really happened, too. And then when I start getting old enough to wear dresses, they will take me out of the room and dress me up and then take me for a ride, both my father and my mother. And then like take me out in the sunlight and then take me places and then I get sick or my mother says I'm sick, so we have to go home. They

---

*From Debra's tape, Chapter IX, pp. 222-223.

take me into the bathroom and give me an enema and they put me back in my room and I hear them begin their fighting and I feel like they are fighting about me. And then I get old enough to go to school and they take me to the school and my father walks with me to school and I feel very, very alone at school. I don't seem to have anybody over to play with me or go any place to play with anybody else, like they expect me to be good alone in my room. (Pause) . . . And then after I start like getting old enough to go to school, I can hear them tell me that I have to do good in school and I have to have a lot of friends in school. My mother says to me, 'Why don't you have any friends and why aren't you making a lot of friends?' She and my father are fighting all the time over me and then when I start having to date with boys, when I am about 13, and I don't have any boyfriends and then she starts pushing me at boys. She starts getting involved in things that I'll be involved in boys, like clubs and pushing me to go to parties and asking me questions when I go to the parties like, 'Do the boys like me? And am I pretty, next to the other children? Do the boys want to kiss me?' And then my father goes away and I don't remember my father now and he is out of the house. There is just her and me. When I get old enough to go to high school, the same stuff. 'Why aren't you doing this? Why aren't you doing that?' And she looks so involved in what I am doing or what I am supposed to be doing. (Pause). . . If she would have just let me grow up inside that room until . . . I feel like I am getting so tall that I am hitting my head on the ceiling, but I don't have any of my things in the room and I don't even have my clothes in the room. It's like I just live in there, but I don't have anything in there and I feel like I am too big for that room and I am just too big to even sit in a chair in that room. My head keeps growing out through the ceiling, like I have to pull myself in and just huddle, sit in there to be big enough for it. The more I get to be my age now, I would be huge in that room growing, growing huge."

In addition, one can ask (M/L), "What are the two most significant events in your life?" Allow me to say that many a therapist may be surprised by the patient's answer. Often patients will respond to the points in their lives when a neurotic resolution was tightened for them or of those times in their lives when they have been able to broach some healthy conflict resolution. "When I first went to college away from home." "When I was in the army and I realized that sex was an open subject and that I didn't have to be guilty about it." "The time I went home after I flunked out of medical school to my mother's outstretched arms." Or, "At the age of ten when my father died and I had to be an adult." The possible answers are infinite and can serve as convenient points to reveal internal conflicts. This question has the added quality of limiting the patient's flow of talk towards the more central core problems. The patient's awareness of his defenses and the way he has coped with his conflicts become clearer. At all times, I urge the patient to express his feelings about these significant events. Mere reporting about these events without feeling must strongly be met on the part of the therapist with active redirection for feelings. (See following chapter on focusing techniques.)

Attitudes Towards Self-Help

One good way of assessing how the person feels about himself and his conflicts and what he will do about it, is to ask the patient (IS), "Imagine you are on top of a mountain and on a ledge below, *you* are also there. Now the *top you* lowers a rope to the *bottom you*. What will happen?" Some of the answers show great desire to help the bottom self up to the top where the top self is. Others have said that the top self will throw the rope to someone else on the bottom of the mountain, bypassing the ledge bottom self completely, leaving him stranded, and pull somebody else up. Some will indicate great reluctance on the part of the bottom self manifested by shifting his feet, digging his heels, or otherwise making it very difficult to be pulled up.

Here, the therapist and the patient have a fine method for viewing the patient's attitude towards allowing help. His hopelessness can be faced. His stake in maintaining his neurotic solution can be examined. Both can get at his self-destructiveness and try to deal with it at this juncture. Sometimes a patient can seem outwardly cooperative but in this imaginary situation he may indicate a powerful resistance. If this resistance is identified earlier in therapy and dealt with, many, many hours of time can be saved. More specific and detailed methods of handling resistance to self-help will be discussed in the next chapter on focusing techniques.

This type of imaginative situation can be used (with variations) at different phases of therapy. The attitude towards helping oneself may show marked differences between the earlier sessions and the later sessions. Variations of the situation which might be useful for repeated use are: 1) "Imagine *one you* in a boat and the *other you* in the ocean. The *you* in the boat throws *you* a line." 2) "Imagine *one* you at the top of a dry well and the *other* you at the bottom of a dry well. The *top* you throws the *bottom* you a rope. What happens?"

As Wheelis has said, "Some patients don't want to change, and when a therapist takes up the task of changing such a one he assumes a contest which the patient always wins. . . . [It] rests finally upon nothing more than the patient's will, upon his being able to say, 'This . . . is what I want to change.' " (Wheelis, 1969, p. 59.)

As Horney (1945) has suggested, we must attack the patient's hopelessness or his desire to dominate and control the therapist. The use of these imaginative situations to make us aware of his attitude towards self-help, combined with the therapist's help at the earlier sessions, give us a better chance to break this log jam.

One patient, for example, was asked (IS), "Imagine you are bound hand and foot, what would you feel and do?" She answered, "I would wait until somebody found me, but I don't really expect anyone to come." Her hopelessness had not been immediately apparent because of an outward cheeriness. I, then, tried some further focusing techniques in an attempt to break her despair.

It is not possible to list all the questions which might elicit the internal conflicts. Whether it be an imaginary situation, or a self-and-other question, or a finish-the-sentence approach, or perhaps a most-or-least question, the direction is towards enlightening both the patient and the therapist to the division within him.

Oscar Wilde once said, "A man is least himself when he speaks as himself. Give him a mask and he will speak the truth." This is an interesting concept since the reluctance of persons to reveal weaknesses and expose guilty feelings is common. But, there are more basic reasons for the reluctance to see the conflict in its full divisiveness. One is the terrible pain of conflict awareness too difficult to countenance; the second is the stake in holding on to the neurotic way of solving conflicts since other, more healthy ways seem almost impossible.

The techniques suggested for exposing internal conflicts are not test items read from a recipe book, standardized and capable of fitting a patient snugly into place. The patient varies and the ways of approaching him vary. The uniqueness of his patient will serve as a guide to the therapist in directing the process of revealing the internal conflicts.

These techniques should not be used until the patient feels the genuine acceptance of the therapist. When a question, especially one of the imaginative situations, reveals a major conflict, panic may result if the patient does not feel comfortable with his therapist. But, if the atmosphere is one of genuine acceptance, mutual exploration, and one human being relating warmly to another, the awareness of the internal conflicts need not be overwhelming.

One man, for example, saw in the imaginary situation of looking into a mirror, "half a green face of a woman." He became frightened and his hands began shaking. He was describing his own internal conflict. Caught between his enormous anger at his parents and his own self-hatred — neither direction in which he could let himself go — he creatively developed an alternative ghost-like creature with whom he could be in direct conflict. It was this ghost that knew he was evil. It was because of this ghost that he had to walk around feeling that he was Christlike in order to negate his evilness. At the moment of his reacting to this imaginary situation, he seemed to know he could "trust" himself and me to this secret self. Of course, the full awareness and all of the relevant consequences did not become clear until much later, but I am sure that my acceptance of him allowed it to come out despite his great difficulty.

In *Letters from Jenny*, Allport says, "In the drama *The Iceman Cometh*, Eugene O'Neill holds that a human being cannot live in full possession of the complete truth of life situation. The memory of pains, of injustice, and of guilt would be too searing to bear. Hence every mortal needs to defend himself through fictions and to engage in strategies of self-exculpation. These tricks of 'ego defense' (Freudian terminology) are necessary even if they are frequently incapacitating." (Allport, 1965, p. 185.)

Revival of Curiosity

The revival of curiosity in the patient is an important ingredient of change toward a more integrated personality. The person who has suppressed his curiosity is psychologically deadened. The great likelihood is that his natural curiosity has been thwarted by parental figures in his childhood. In short, when he was curious about things around him (and not only about sexuality) as a child, he was rebuffed and shamed. His neurotic solution was to conform to such a restriction.

How can the therapist revive curiosity in the patient? I attempt this by at first asking him (M/L), "About what are you most curious?" Sometimes, I may be quite directive, pushing for something about which the patient is curious. I might want to know if he is curious about me in any way. I look for the areas of curiosity that are flattened in him and ask him (IS), "Imagine you are in the home of a significant person alone for a weekend. What would you be interested in or curious about in that house?"

An appropriate self-and-other question is, "Are there marked differences in your curiosity level between things about men or about women?" A good question to ask a patient is (M/L), "What was the most vivid experience of your childhood?" Expanding his awareness by the use of imagination and the other techniques mentioned can help revive the patient's flattened curiosity and make him more aware and alive.

Dr. Szalita says, "A total lack of curiosity in the working of one's mind or that of other people is perhaps *more* morbid than an exaggerated curiosity in this direction." (Szalita, 1968, p. 99.)

Parent-Self Strategies and Self-Parent Strategies

Experience with Psycho-Imagination Therapy indicates that the patient, after the initial sessions, mentions parental figures in becoming aware of his internal conflicts. As a minor experiment at least a dozen times, I have purposefully *not mentioned* parental figures *in any* way at all for the first three sessions. Each patient has brought them up in one way or another without seemingly any suggestion from me. This and other experiences, especially from the results of the focusing techniques, only confirm the absolute importance of the parental-strategies upon the self and self-strategies to counteract the others. If the patient mentions his father, I then do not hesitate to have him *imagine* his father and himself in some situation, to see how the patient views himself and what definition of himself he has received from his father. Sometimes, I may ask him (IS), "Imagine you and your mother, father and brother in a lifeboat. What happens?" This situation usually reflects how he feels the parents have defined him and how the sibling rivalry defined him. Of course, how he defines them also becomes clearer.

Sometimes I will offer the finish-the-sentence question, "If I am strong, then my mother is ____." or, "If I am weak, then my mother is ____." One can also ask the self-and-other question, "What is the fiction of your father's (mother's, etc.) life?" or, "What is the frustration of your father's (mother's, etc.) life?" From his answers, the patient often is able to comprehend his own self-definition.

It also is possible to ask the most-or-least question, "Who is the most desirable man (or woman) according to your mother (or father, etc.)?" and, additionally, "What man does your mother despise the most of any man in the world?" Again, the patient's own answers can be used as a useful reference point as to his own self-definition.

The Parental-Self Strategies become quite clear during the following imaginative situation: "Imagine your mother (or father) is holding you on her palm and you are ten inches tall. Reverse the position so that your mother (or father) is ten inches on your palm. What do you feel and what do you do?" Another variation of the question is (IS), "Imagine your mother (or father or other) as a lawn swing and tell me how it feels to sit on them." On a feeling level this imaginary situation can be quite revealing and full of strongly expressed feelings. Of course, reversing the situation is just as revealing, with many strong feelings expressed.

Still another imaginative situation is to ask the patient (IS), "Imagine wheeling your father as a baby in a wheel carriage, or your mother, brother, sister, etc. What would you do and feel?" "Reverse the situation with each of them pushing you as a baby." "Suppose you were to push me (the therapist) as a baby in a wheel carriage?" "Reverse it again." The parent-child strategies often can become dramatically clear in such an imaginative situation.

Moreover, it is sometimes quite helpful for a feeling of awareness on the part of the patient when I have them (IS), "Imagine your mother and me (the therapist) dancing," or "Imagine your father and the therapist going to a football game." Of course, the imagining of various situations of the patient and the therapist, such as at a football game or in various social situations, contributes to an awareness of other authority-self strategies.

All of these and an infinite number of other possible phenomenological in-viewing show the patient how he is defining himself, how others are defining him, and what are his strategies to sustain or oppose such definitions.

Additionally, I may ask (IS), "Can you imagine you and your mother on a balance scale with each one of you on the scale?" One man answered, "I'd have to kick in perpetual motion to be sure that I was not higher on the scale than her." Another woman answered, "I'm heavier and I'll sink to the bottom and she'll be very high." "Tell me what your mother says to you?" I asked. She answered, "I'm ungrateful and why don't I help her to a better position." "And what do you say to her?" I said. "Right now, I just want to help you up there regardless of what you say," she answered.

Sometimes, I ask the most-or-least question, "What is the most difficult thing in the world for your mother or father to do?" "What is the most difficult thing in the world for you to do?" These might lead to the question (M/L), "What is the easiest for you to give: intellect, money, feelings or sex?" "What about your father? What would be easiest for him to give?" Of course, the reverse can be asked, "What is the most difficult for each to give?"

These questions, again, are convenient points for awareness of the patient's self-definition. They serve to reveal how he feels, how he is being defined by others, and how he defines others.

Interaction of the Head, Heart, Guts, Penis or Vagina

One of the best methods of eliciting the conflict areas is to ask the patient (IS), "Imagine what your head says to your heart." (IS), "What does your heart say to your guts?" (IS), "What do your guts say to your penis or vagina?" Of course, one then can pair off the head with the guts or sexual part, and back again from one part to the other, for a total of twelve interactions. One patient referred to this as an "anatomical journey," but my own clinical experience indicates that the various levels of the self are being expressed by the answers.

Most patients can respond readily with great awareness and often with surprise to themselves in a series of exploration. Here the unique phenomenology of the person can be viewed as perhaps in no other comparable in-viewing.

(IS) "What does your head say to your heart?" I asked one man, who answered, "Get bigger — feel more — become autonomous!" (IS) "What does your heart say to your guts?" I asked. He answered, "My guts are bigger than my heart, and I wish I were like you." (IS) "What do your guts say to your cock?" I asked. "My cock is as small as my heart ... Be a man — be dominant, be aggressive — be grown up." Then without urging from me, he continued, "My guts and my head are large. My heart and cock are small. I don't like it — it's incongruous. The heart and cock are discolored and are in formaldehyde. My head is stable and my guts are O.K. I feel O.K., about my strengths. I have been avoiding my heart and cock. I have been so busy allowing myself to believe in my own intelligence and my own guts — since I've been in therapy. Now that I finally got a job again, I know I have to allow my love and sexual feelings to come through." (IS) "What do your guts say to your heart?" He replied "Grow up — communicate — look for the link." In this way, the "anatomical journey" can help the patient become aware of his internal struggles.

In addition, the self-other struggle can be elucidated further, using the head, heart, guts, penis or vagina, in relation to another person's head, heart, guts, penis or vagina. I asked one man (M/L), "Which is the most difficult heart for your heart to talk to, in this world?" "To my father's heart," he answered. Without going into the details of the conflict of this young man, I merely wish to show that one can ask anyone to know what one's head will say to his girl friend's head, heart, guts or vagina. What will his heart say to the head, heart, guts, or vagina of his girl friend? What will his guts say to the head, heart, guts, and vagina of his girl friend? What does his penis say to his girl friend's head, heart, guts, and vagina?

The variety of possibilities is obvious, from any person to another, and from the other back to the person. "What does your penis say to your wife's vagina?" I may ask a couple in joint session with me. "What does your vagina say to your husband's penis?" The combinations are numerous and often times quite indicative of the enormous differences people may feel from one level of themselves to another level in another person.

I cannot imagine anyone who would not be aware of separate and unique differences between his head, heart, guts, penis or vagina and at least one other person's head, heart, guts, penis or vagina. The possibilities of the strength of the statement made from each direction and reversed, or the omission or block of feelings made in each direction and reversed, compellingly indicate conflicts in a clear and distinct manner.

The Saving Sense of Humor

In nearly all of these situations in which I am probing for an awareness of conflicts, I try to look for the humorous side, if indeed there is any. Sharp cynicism and strong sarcasm can help sustain conflict and fan the fires for further conflict. There are times in facing a conflict when it is better to turn to laughter than to attack. So, whenever a situation occurs in therapy in which the patient is responding to the imaginative situations and something funny occurs, I don't hesitate to laugh and to have the patient join in with me. Or, conversely, as he begins to laugh, I join in with him. Needless to say that laughing in such a context is not having fun at the patient's expense, but to change some of the directions to more positive ways. In some families, there was much humor, in others, humor was pathologically absent. Between the patient and myself, I hope we will always find time to laugh.

The Most Private Moment

Sometimes, I will ask a patient (M/L), "Imagine the most private moment that you can think of. Reserve the option not to tell me what it is, but tell me how you would feel if I were to appear on the scene." Private moments are not always in the sexual sphere. They may include incidents of intimacy and closeness with a loved one; fantasies of great achievements and acknowledgment, or of making a difference to someone important; and even accounts of the joy of taking a bath or other sensual experience. In any case, the reaction to this imaginary situation increases the patient's awareness of his conflicts, his attitudes toward authority and the degree of openness he can allow for himself. In reality, very few patients have chosen not to reveal the private moment.

Summary

I wish to state, that after a quarter of a century of therapy with patients, the best advice I can offer whenever the hazy, the foggy or the bewildering occur, is to ask directly, "What is the conflict — between what and what?" I keep probing until the patient expresses the conflict between his real identity and the false identity assigned to him by his significant others. If this is not understood by the patient, there is no real chance of his ever becoming aware of his neurotic conflict resolution or of what possibilities there are for a healthy conflict resolution. If it is not understood by the therapist, there is no real chance that he can use these techniques therapeutically and advantageously.

CHAPTER 5

The Focusing Techniques

"The undischarged, unreleased, or traumatic experiences are not repressed into the unconscious and there preserved, but rather are continued permanently in actual living, resisted, carried through to an ending or worked over into entirely new experiences."

Otto Rank

"The similarity of the nightmares of children and adults provides one of our most convincing pieces of evidence that the archaic fears, conflicts, and mental structures of early childhood may be preserved throughout the course of a person's life."

John E. Mack

The Traumatic Incidents

In the previous chapter, the Internal Conflicts were discussed, as well as the methods by which these conflicts might be made aware to the patient and the therapist. As the patient becomes aware of his conflicts, he invariably refers to specific traumatic incidents. This is especially true as he recognizes the unconscious strategies used by the significant others upon him and his own rigid defenses to survive them. When one observes the great mobilization of defenses, heightened anxiety, increased breathing, and other reactions in response to the self-and-other question, "What was the day of shame in your life?", it becomes clear that unless the resultant feelings are allowed out in a non-judgmental atmosphere and are refocused, the person will always condemn himself with these feelings.

It is not to torment the patient that I ask him to face the humiliations in his life. It is indeed an unpleasant task for him. But, unless he can find a way to reverse the self-condemnation, he stays self-condemned. I may ask a patient the most-or-least question, "About what do you feel most guilty?" The agony and self-punishing nature of his answer needs refocusing. A person is taught to feel guilty about certain standards of behavior. In time, the certainty of guilt becomes fixed.

If, in childhood, a boy asks his mother about his mysterious and prolonged erections, and his mother tells him to hide it and cries "shame," in time, every time he has an erection, he will feel guilty and be forced into secretive outlets. Eventually, for him, there is no doubt that sex is guilt and guilt is sex. This guilt needs to be eliminated. But, equally important, he needs to focus on confronting the guilt-inducer. And, in the focusing techniques discussed in this chapter, I ask him to do just that.

To the patient, it seems impossible that he will ever be free of the guilt feelings that have been induced by others. However, it is possible to completely eliminate the guilt feelings by releasing them, repeatedly focusing them, and confronting the significant others. The patient ultimately should be able to define for himself which actions are to be considered guilty. Some of the questions which can be used to uncover or release the traumatic feelings are:

(M/L) About what are you most humiliated in your life?

(M/L) What was the day of shame in your life?

(M/L) What was the guiltiest feeling in your life?

(M/L) What is the most immoral thing you have ever done?

(M/L) What is the most evil thing you have ever done?

Obviously, it is not always possible to ask such questions until sufficient rapport and trust has been developed between therapist and patient. This cannot be postured on the part of the therapist. Unless the therapist can truly feel non-judgmental, he should not attempt to elicit such strong reactions. I might, for example, ask a patient to remember a traumatic incident from the past in which he was humiliatingly laughed at, and to express the feelings about the incident on today's level. His sensitivity to being laughed at is faster then radar. If the therapist is not authentic in his acceptance of the patient, he will turn off faster than radar. The therapist, then, is no different from anyone else — the patient cannot trust his raw feelings to anybody — and, unfortunately, he must return again to his basic defenses, and therapy does not occur. If the therapist knows "in his guts" that he accepts the patient and allies himself against the original perpetrators of the neurosis, then regardless of the hesitations and tentativeness of the patient, in time, the patient will trust him.

The following verbatim account illustrates a woman's intense feelings while recalling a traumatic incident from her youth, in response to the question (M/L), "What was the most humiliating situation during your childhood?"

"I can picture my brother, Chris, now, sitting in his room at his desk, painting and listening to those Johnny Mathis albums. I must have been about 15 years old at that time. I slowly walked into his room feeling very affectionate, moody and wanting so much to communicate. But, as usual, Chris was too preoccupied to give me the time of day. I tried in my own way to give him what I felt inside, but I just *couldn't* get enough response. I tried and tried and tried, but the little response he did give me always felt like he was just pacifying me — rather than really giving wholeheartedly.

"I can't tell you how much I wanted him to include me in his thoughts — to share his emotions with me. Even to just hold me. Oh, that would have meant so *much* to me! There was something about Chris — a special tenderness that I felt. He was always so closed, so lost within himself that I could never get away from feeling left out, unimportant, and so rejected. I was confused why he didn't respond to me — why I couldn't get the responses that I wanted from him. All kinds of things went through my mind. Questions, questions, questions. Is it me? If so, what is it about me? What's wrong? He must not like me, nor really care about me . . . Never any answers. All I ever got out of my efforts was frustration and humiliation. And that goes pretty much for my whole family. And, because of this, it seemed to become more and more difficult for me to really express what I felt inside, in fear of no response . . .

"I felt like Chris didn't even see me — and when and if he ever did it was only critical. I could come or I could go and it wouldn't really matter one way or the other. For that matter, he didn't even really hear me or feel me. Not really!

"The relationship I always wanted with Chris was never really captured. The *few* times we shared warmth, love, affection and communication was so rare — and never lasting. And this is what I was starving for . . .

"And so, I slowly walked out of his room feeling totally neglected. All those feelings deep down inside just that much stronger and more assured. All alone, I left — empty. It was as if I'd failed to achieve what I really wanted, because somehow I believed that the real and earthy emotions were lost between us, and I was unable to reach them. I wanted something *real* and *lasting*. I was defeated again . . ."

Another patient, Helen, was able to feel the most angry feelings she ever had towards her father, when she recalled the traumatic incident of her father's hospitalization when she was a child. She remembered that her father dressed himself and said goodby to her many brothers, but not to her. She then paused, and cried bitterly. Through her tears, she sobbed her traumatic realization, "He never even spoke to me! I never heard him say my name — not even once." A few minutes later, between sobs, "He never spoke my name — he didn't know I was alive! No wonder I don't think any man will stay with me; my father didn't."

These devastating traumatic incidents may be in the patient's recent life, but in my experience, they are usually in the past, and in early childhood or adolescence. I attempt to bring them into the present to be dealt with at this time. But the traumatic incidents have to be *refelt* as if they were in the past, so that the understanding of refocusing the feeling toward the guilt-inducers can be clarified.

The traumatic incidents are points of fixation on which the patient's Neurotic Conflict Resolution is based. As evidence of this, consider the case of John, an adult male who was having sexual problems. I asked him (IS) to imagine holding his erection and screaming at his mother, "I'm not ashamed to have a cock! You are not right about sex — you are wrong about sex!" Even though the traumatic incident had occurred 25-30 years earlier, the resistance to do this was enormous. His mother had been dead for more than 25 years, yet seeing her face in front of him, he could not allow himself to feel. "I'm cutting off," he said. "I can't allow myself to say it, because it would destroy her." This patient was able to feel strong reaction to a business partner in the therapy situation and felt liberated by it. However, when it came to the fixated original trauma upon which his neurotic conflict resolution was based, he could not allow himself to be in touch with his feelings.

A few sessions later he was able to let his feelings come together and to let go of his hostility in full force, screaming specifically those statements I have already mentioned, and more. In essence, he felt liberated and said, "My feelings belong to me. What I feel is right for me, is up to me." The transfer over to sexual functioning was natural and positive. These things were involved:

1. The patient had chosen a neurotic conflict resolution and denied his real self.
2. In order to allow a healthy conflict resolution he had to allow himself to *feel* the separation from the other and to liberate himself in the direction of his real self.

The Focusing Techniques or Conflict Resolution

"As one grows older one either endorses, or tries to discard, the ways in which the others have defined one."

R. D. Laing

"Or one may try to tear out from oneself this 'alien' identity that one has been endowed with or condemned to, and create by one's own actions an identity for oneself . . ."

R. D. Laing

After the patient has recalled his traumatic incident, through his answers to the most-or-least questions, I help him to focus his feelings and to confront the perpetrators of his conflict. The techniques I use are varied, and new ones occur to me continuously as I apply these methods in my practice. Some of those that I have employed successfully are: 1) The Impossible Scream, 2) I Am Not – I Am, 3) Accuse the Accusers, 4) Talk in the Language of, 5) Your Face in My Hands – My Face in Your Hands, 6) Other Body Holding and Touching, 7) My Life or His, 8) Eyeball to Eyeball, 9) Transforming the Eyes of the Other, 10) Attending the Funeral, 11) Breaking the Log Jam, and 12) The Therapist's Scream. Doubtless, innumerable other confrontation situations are possible; the therapist again is urged to consider the individuality of his patient and to avoid using these focusing techniques in a cookbook manner.

The Impossible Scream

In the case of Helen (see page 51), after she recalled the traumatic incident of her father not bidding her goodby as he left home to be hospitalized, I used the focusing technique of The Impossible Scream. I asked her to (IS) imagine her father immediately in front of her and to tell me (M/L) what would be the most impossible thing to scream at him. Faced with this emotional task, she hesitated for awhile. I encouraged her to tell me the most impossible statement she might scream at her father. Then slowly, but powerfully, with her fists clenched, she focused a scream of a magnitude that unmistakably came from her core. Spurred by the release of the traumatic incident buried in her unconscious and the focusing of the confrontation with her father, she screamed, "I HATE YOU!" "I HATE YOU!" over and over again. She was Japanese and from a cultural background where anger at one's parents was indeed a sin. For her, "The Impossible Scream" was truly impossible.

Sometimes I have a feeling that the patient is not expressing an authentically impossible scream. Then, I may challenge him and urge him to give forth with his true feelings. There are times when the patient will admit that, as loud as the scream may sound, he is not feeling the scream. In time, it nearly always is possible for the therapist to be aware of those screams which are not authentic. From my experience with hundreds and hundreds of screams and with the awareness of the unconscious strategies involved, few patients indeed can pretend for very long. The real proof is, of course, the genuine feeling of liberation and freedom that follows. Repetition of The Impossible Scream is common if the complete feelings of liberation are not achieved the first time.

Occasionally, I have had patients hit a pillow as if it represented the mother, father, brother, or other significant person. There were times when this was very effective, but, often, it was not enough. Many times, I found patients were able to hit the pillow but were unable to scream The Impossible Scream. The liberation and real feeling of the person comes not only in the expression of the anger, but from very *specific* confrontations to the effect that the person is really saying, "I (self) am no longer going to be defined by you (other) in this way." In the patient's experience, the expression of anger usually only led to more guilt about such anger. That is why I try to be as specific as possible in The Impossible Scream confrontation. It is necessary to scream what will liberate, not just to scream anything.

I may ask the patient to scream (FTS), "How dare you ____ !" While he is screaming one scream, I may sense that an even more direct scream may be needed. I may suggest it to him. I may scream with him. My support usually is welcomed and, participating with him in his phenomenological world, I am just as interested in his scream as he is. Patients certainly sense this genuine interest.

I might suggest (FTS), "Don't you dare ____ ." I constantly urge the patient to express his real feelings.

Following is an excerpt from a tape recording of an actual therapy session, showing an application of The Impossible Scream in helping the patient become aware of an internal conflict.

Shorr: Is something wrong, Phil?

Phil: Well, I got very depressed this week. I can't really connect with it, but I can tie it with what's causing it, I think. This job situation that we had talked about. This is the only thing that I've come up with. I called the guy yesterday and I wasn't sure the last time I talked to him, he said the Tuesday after next – well, the next day was going to be Tuesday. It wasn't this Tuesday, but next Tuesday. So, I couldn't come to group and I felt very uncomfortable all the time, you know, but I felt that regardless of what kind of butterflies I had about this thing that I might as well do it. In the meantime, though, I was kind of glad that I didn't have to.

Shorr: You mean you felt relieved?

Phil: Well, a little. It was an area that I have been avoiding with Jack. And I told him what was happening and what I was up to and I tried to put together some of my feelings and tell him where I stood and what I wanted. We talked the night before last for about 45 minutes. We talked a little bit at lunch today. And I can't really come on strong and tell him what I want, but I'm trying to, and I got a fair amount out. Instead of figuring that he was handing me everything, I turned it around by asking for something. I'm tired of selling myself short.

Shorr: You mean you made some demands, huh?

Phil: Yeah, I did. I didn't make them as strongly as I would have liked to, but I don't know if that would have been realistic, either. I don't know really where I am yet, but it was good, it was a good feeling. After I had to talk with him two nights ago I felt a lot better when I went home. It really, really bolstered the depression. I guess it was all bottled up, you know.

Shorr: Oh, yes.

Phil: It didn't all go away, but it — I'd say most of it went away, at least temporarily, you know.

Shorr: (M/L) Well, what would have been the most impossible demand to make of your father?

Phil: I don't know. I . . . It would be to consider me as a person. Listen to what I have to say and, you know, react to me as a human being.

Shorr: (M/L) So, what would be the phrases you would like to say to him? In terms of the demand to your father. The most difficult phrases, what would they be? Can you say them out loud?

Phil: "Listen to me, I have something I want to tell you."

Shorr: Are you saying those with feeling, though?

Phil: No.

Shorr: Do you want to try it with feeling?

Phil: I don't know, I can't.

Shorr: Say the words or the phrase first.

Phil: "Don't tune me out, listen to me. I am important. As important as anybody else that you know."

Shorr: As important as anybody else you know?

Phil: I was going to say, "More important than anybody else you know."

Shorr: Can you now say that to him with feeling?

Phil: (Screams) "DON'T TUNE ME OUT. LISTEN TO ME. I'M IMPORTANT. THERE ISN'T ANYBODY ELSE THAT IS MORE IMPORTANT TO YOU."

Shorr: (FTS) I want _____ .

Phil: (Screams) "I WANT YOUR UNDIVIDED ATTENTION. I WANT YOU TO REACT TO ME."

Shorr: (FTS) I deserve _____ .

Phil: (Screams) "FEELINGS." This is going to take a little time to really get it worked up. I can kind of feel it, but I'm like blocking the feelings and I'm not coming on.

Shorr: Get closer. Which is harder, I deserve or I want? Speaking to him.

Phil: I want. Yeah, because if you deserve it you can build an argument for it, you can show why you deserve it. If you want it — on what grounds can you want something — just want it, just want it for yourself, just for me. Just cause I am . . .

Shorr: Start with "I want" then. Can you see him over there, can you see him in front of you?

Phil: It's hard for me to envision what he is today. And I can envision what he was before — I could remember him, like, but I can't really recall what he looks like during the period of time that we were really going through it.

Shorr: Try.

Phil: (Screams) "I WANT FEELINGS. I WANT YOUR TIME. I WANT YOU, NOT THE MATERIAL SHIT YOU ARE SO BUSY GATHERING. I WANT TO BE JUST ME. I DON'T WANT TO HAVE TO BE PERFECT ALL THE TIME." Shit! All the things that came into my mind — I could just remember — just as I said that — several incidents where, you know, I had to do things — you know, I was helping him, and the only way I would be allowed to do it is if I did it, like, perfectly. I remember things like when I went down to his place of business. It was during the war, and I was helping him do some jobs, you know, so I could have some time with my father. I wasn't allowed to do anything that was significant because I couldn't do it perfect enough. And the jobs that I had that I was capable of I had to do it perfect and if I didn't, it was pointed out, you know, where the flaws were.

Shorr: What do you think about it now? How do you feel?

Phil: Mad, damn it!

Shorr: What do you want to scream at him?

Phil: (Screams) "I'M ONLY A KID, JESUS CHRIST, YOU KNOW, I CAN'T DO EVERYTHING PERFECT, BUT AT LEAST ALLOW ME TO TRY."

Shorr: (FTS) Don't _____ . What do you want to scream starting with *don't* to him?

Phil: (Screams) "DON'T PUT ME DOWN ALL OF THE TIME. DON'T MAKE ME FEEL SECOND RATE ALL OF THE TIME." That's what he was doing. Oh, it just seems like such a long ways from what we started talking about to this, but it's not, is it?

Shorr: Do you see the connection?

Phil: Yeah, I see a lot of connections. How can I tell Jack what I want, you know, because I never could before. I could never tell anybody what the hell I wanted. Because before I could develop it, you know, into a feeling that I want something, they already took it away. It was gone. And I have to earn it — I have to deserve it. And the only way I can do that is by doing everything perfect. It's a pretty tough bill to fill. I wonder how some people manage to just come right out, you know. "That's what I want," you know, make their demands known. How in the hell can they do that? Because they are so far from my value of what they should be in order to come out blatantly and make a demand like that.

Shorr: You mean, you think you have even more going for you than they have going for themselves, and they can do it and you can't.

Phil: Yes! I mean, how do I compete with people like that? I can't ask for a goddam thing! Boy, that hurts! Because the way it feels is that everybody is getting their piece of the pie without earning it. And it's really the other way around. I'm not getting my piece of the pie because I'm not asking for it.

Shorr: O.K. How about the fact that you were just able to say that to your father? Does that make you feel better now when you talk to Jack?

Phil: I didn't even really think to say that that is what I want. I was sitting there at noon and saying to myself, "What is it that you are trying to say to him?" Which is a long ways, you know, which is a long ways from where I was. Whatever I was before. It's something that you have to . . . Well, in here and in group is — boy, talk about being indirect, I mean I didn't even know what in the hell I was asking for. I couldn't even formulate a thought on what I thought I deserved, much less just out and out ask because I wanted it. It doesn't mean he is going to give it to me, either. I couldn't make it that far today, but a hell of a lot closer. Yeah, I'm starting to feel it a little bit, too.

Shorr: You mean, the anger?

Phil: Yeah. God, I can just — it just seems incredible, Joe. Before I didn't even know that I should be angry. Why should I get angry when he was just doing his thing, that was the way it was. But I have rights, and one of the rights I have is to be angry with him for fucking me up like that. I can be angry. Years and years and years of hiding feelings, you know — don't let them out. I could get more of them out, but somehow I feel like time is compressed, you know, there isn't enough time.

Shorr: Not enough time?

Phil: Here. Because to get them out, they are not going to come out right away. I have to work at it. I've got to let it out.

Shorr: You let out some of it today.

Phil: There is a lot more I can feel is there.

Shorr: Yeah.

Phil: But it's not going . . .

Shorr: You are still holding the lid on some.

Phil: Yeah, I don't want to hold the lid on, but I can't take it off. I can only let the top off a little at a time — a little steam out, you know.

Shorr: Of course, you let some of it out that you would have never done before — that's a good thing. With "I want" and "I deserve."

Phil: I have never deserved anything and I never had the guts to want anything. I don't know if guts is the right word. It never occurred to me that, just because I wanted it, it's good enough.

One surprising thing is that when all the screaming is over, it usually does not leave the patient depleted, but rather exhilarated and excited. Most patients report feeling better, or perhaps, feeling free. The scream may have been waiting a lifetime for expression.

There are specific times when the fear of retaliation from the significant other may be seen clearly on the face and body of the patient. Words of encouragement must be expressed to the patient. Slowly, as he screams, he begins to face the fear of retaliation and overcomes this barrier. It takes time and patience, but the possible rewards are great.

On a smaller scale, when a patient is involved in a troubled situation with another person, I may ask, "Who is defining the situation between you and him?" He may answer that the other person is. "What do you want to yell at him?" I then urge him to yell at the other person. If the situation is of a more difficult nature, I may return to The Impossible Scream by asking, "What is the most impossible thing to scream at him?" In the long run, if the patient cannot develop a cooperative, mutual, or give-and-take relationship, he cannot let himself be defined in a way that is consistent with his real self-image.

I Am Not – I Am

In this technique, I ask the patient to imagine the person who is being confronted before him, and to scream at the person "I am not ____ ; I am____ ." I ask for as many pairs of nouns or adjectives as the patient will offer. Helen, who screamed at her father The Impossible Scream, "I HATE YOU! I HATE YOU!" (Page 52) was subsequently asked to scream at him (FTS) "I am not ____ ; I am ____ ." Her responses were:

"I AM NOT **TO BE IGNORED**; I AM **A PERSON**."

"I AM NOT **A THING**; I AM **A HUMAN BEING**."

"I AM NOT **NOTHING**; I AM **SOMEBODY**."

Accuse the Accusers

Here, the person who has been under a barrage of self-hate and powerlessness from certain accusers is told to imagine himself in a witness box, and to imagine the accusations that certain people are directing toward him. I then ask him to accuse the accusers. I urge him to scream at them in order to break his feelings of powerlessness and hopelessness. What he actually screams may be unique to him and the situation he is in. Sometimes it is an outgrowth of a prior imaginary situation that led into such an accusation. (See page 100 in Chapter VII.) There are other times when it may be helpful to use the "I Am Not – I Am" technique as part of the Accuse the Accusers. Of course, The Impossible Scream can be used if necessary.

There are numerous situations in which one can ask the patient to imagine himself with the significant other. Sometimes I have him imagine (IS) he is playing cards with someone who seems to define him, and this person accuses him of cheating when he actually is not cheating. It is up to the therapist to utilize as many situations as he can imagine which will help the patient define the relationship in his own behalf.

Talk in the Language of

Still another technique is to have the patient talk (IS) in the emotional language that is most meaningful to his current emotional state. For example, I may detect that a patient sighs frequently and seems to express self-pity and the feeling that everything is impossible. I ask him to talk in "impossible," or in "self-pity." I might strongly urge another patient to talk in "love," if that is the difficult thing to do. The possibilities are many, depending on the patient.

On the other hand, I may discourage a patient from talking in a language that contributes to his dependence or to continuation of his neurotic conflict resolution. I may not permit a patient to talk in "self-pity," for example. I tell him that I will stop him each and every time he talks in "self-pity." With still another patient, I will not allow him to talk "impossible," stopping him at every turn. I then will focus on talk in "strong," or whatever other attribute the patient needs to develop to achieve a healthy conflict resolution.

The following example provides a more in-depth understanding of "Talk in the Language of" technique. I asked a woman patient (S&O), "What strategies did you use against your parents to survive?" "The strategy of being a little girl," she said, "to avoid my father's deadly criticism." "Talk in 'little girl,' " I requested. She then proceeded to talk as a little girl for about a minute or two. "Talk in adult woman," I then requested. She talked in "adult woman" quite adequately. I then alternated back and forth, first as a "little girl" and then as an "adult." Eventually, a rather remarkable thing happened. Talking like a "little girl" became increasingly difficult for her until she absolutely refused to comply. However, talking as an "adult" was continued with ease.

Your Face In My Hands – My Face In Your Hands

A focusing technique that can lead to liberation is having the patient (IS) imagine that he is holding his mother's face in his hands. "What do you feel?" "What do you see?" "Now, say something to your mother." "What does she say to you?"

One woman could not keep her mother's face from looking away, as hard as she tried to hold the face. I forced her to imagine that she could make this happen with The Impossible Scream, "LOOK AT ME! LOOK AT ME!" She screamed until it did happen. For the first time in her life she felt a feeling of power in relation to her mother. Heretofore, she had felt certain that she indeed would have no effect on anybody. With the continued focusing of her hands on her mother's face in front of her, and the gut-level screams specifically and phenomenologically unique to her, she slowly but surely began to feel the liberation of her real self.

Additionally, holding the face of another person is especially difficult for those people who have problems with expressing feelings of intimacy. This is particularly true for those patients who have had forbidding, restricting parents. Here, the patient is put into a conflict between his or her desire for closeness and intimacy and the feeling of certain rejection. I have sometimes urged a patient, as a focusing technique, to put his or her hands on my face. The hesitancy and strong feelings can be agonizing to the patient. Once achieved, it is unquestionably liberating.

Variations of holding the face can be made by reversing the self and other, that is, having the parent holding the patient's face, or having myself hold the patient's face. Any variation has, as its key, that the specific purpose of the technique is one of focusing the patient's feelings and awareness toward conflict resolution.

Other Body Holding and Touching

Focusing for conflict resolution can be achieved by asking the patient to imagine (IS) holding the shoulder of his father, for example, while screaming The Impossible Scream. Alternately, what feelings can be focused if the situation were reversed? The patient also might be asked what he feels when he imagines (IS) the significant other touching his chest, heart, sexual parts, head, eyes, mouth, or any other appropriate body part.

One patient told me that imagining her father touching her stomach might upset her, but if he held his hand over her eyes it would "drive her crazy." This was an opportunity, at the point she was in therapy, for her to focus The Impossible Scream in an imaginary situation. Her father had been constantly characterized by her mother as a "dangerous man" and the patient had often been admonished not to "go near him." The temporary loss of sight resulting from his placing his hand over her eyes would have meant "not knowing where he was" and certainly incurring the disapproval of her mother. In the course of therapy, she discovered that her mother was afraid that the patient might be preferred by the father and had built a fabrication to prevent this. The Impossible Scream to the father was, "I TRUST YOU! I DON'T ALWAYS HAVE TO WATCH YOU!" It didn't really get "gut level" until three sessions later. When it did, her inordinate fear of men diminished and her own hidden desires to be the "man" (the safe sex in her view) were eliminated. She came to the realization that, " . . . it isn't really so bad to be a woman, after all."

My Life or His

I asked Brian (S&O), "How did your father give you confirmation of your existence?" He answered, "By being his loyal son — the chip off the old block. For my mother, I was a compliant, sweet boy."

Then I asked him to talk in "strong." He had great difficulty, and expressed that he felt that if he were to be "strong," he would be "evil," because he would be usurping his father and showing disloyalty. As a reaction, he had been acting in a sweet, compliant manner, hating himself in the process.

Here is his own statement: "Strength gives me an evil feeling, while compliance brings about self-hate, but not guilt. I was taught as a child that to be strong was to be disloyal – disloyal meaning being a separate self. I had to comply to avoid the murderous hate I had toward my father and mother, who always left me out. My father died, thus confirming my murder fantasy. So I had to become a saint.

"As a child of four, I would wait in a car while my mother shopped. I would imagine the butcher cutting her to bloody bits. I would be relieved when she came out alive. The core of my identity is a jungle animal, a killer. But hidden to avoid discovery. I never learned to love."

Then I asked him (IS) to imagine himself and his father late at night in a subway, with no other people around, and suddenly finding that his father is pushing him under the train. I asked him to imagine pushing his father, instead of his father pushing him.

He continued, "On a subway, late at night, my father and I are in a struggle for life as the train approaches. I throw him under the wheels in self-defense. My life or his. At first I felt weightlessness in the struggle, but then I planted my feet and threw him to save my life. Hate is my identity – love my disguise . . .

"The thing that gets me is that my father made me think I was a murderer for having justifiable anger. I had good reason to be angry at him. He was an Army hero, and beyond reproach, so my anger at his totalitarian tactics only made me feel disloyal – a killer and evil. This left me with only compliance or sainthood. There was no righteous anger – no room for an honest mistake. There was a futility about ever being right. Maybe killing in self-defense doesn't make you evil after all."

Eyeball to Eyeball

In this technique there is a confrontation, with the patient standing as if he is eyeball to eyeball with the person who is defining him. One can use The Impossible Scream. Alternately, a direct confrontation approach can be used. The patient is urged to *acknowledge* the shame or guilt he feels about some act, but accompanying the acknowledgment must be genuine feelings of expiation or relinquishment of the responsibility for the guilt. Some liberating statements to the other person are: "I won't feel guilty for you." "I have paid my price in suffering many times over." "I am no longer ashamed of myself."

Transforming the Eyes of the Other

In applying this technique, the patient is encouraged to stare into the eyes of the person whom he greatly fears, and stare until he can feel that he is transforming the eyes of the other from negative feelings to more positive ones.

One patient said, "I see two dark coals where her eyes are, and they are condemning me." I urged her (IS) to imagine staring at those eyes until they appeared non-condemning. "I can't bear to have her look at me that way," the patient answered. "Keep staring until you can transform them so that they are not condemning you," I strongly urged. She paused, then said, "O.K., I think I can do it now." After another long pause, she stated emphatically, "Yeah! I can do it. I feel better now." "What do you want to tell her?" I asked. " 'I DON'T HAVE TO BE ASHAMED OF MY SEXUALITY' " – (Pause) – " 'I AM NOT BAD.' "

I encouraged the patient to continue with I Am Not – I Am statements. She screamed, "I AM NOT **BAD** – I AM A **GOOD PERSON** 'I AM NOT **A TERRIBLE PERSON** – I AM **ALL RIGHT.**' 'I AM NOT **TERRIBLE** – I AM **GOOD ENOUGH.**'

Again, the focusing techniques are to be used in the specific context of the patient's neurotic conflict resolution, with an aim to achievement of a healthy conflict resolution. It would be useless and possibly dangerous to have a person engage in any of the focusing techniques without a clear awareness of the neurotic strategies that hold the patient in the same treadmill, and the alternatives to a healthy conflict resolution.

Attending the Funeral

Sometimes, for liberation to occur, one must have the patient imagine (IS) that he is attending the funeral of his father or some other significant person. Engaged in the feeling reactions of mourning and sorrow, the patient sometimes is able to let the separation from the "other" become complete. A new and separate dimension may emerge. The need to stick to the glue of being defined in the eyes of the other finally can be let go.

Breaking the Log Jam

In the previous chapter, I referred to hoeplessness and the patient's attitude towards self-help or receiving the therapist's help. (See page 41.) Several imaginary situations (IS) were used as examples to illustrate the possibility of uncovering the conflicts which might lead to these feelings. When the patient does indicate a feeling of "hopelessness," some ways in which the therapist might be able to help are:

1. Have the patient try to (IS) imagine that he has the strongest hands in the world. Make sure that he has the feeling. Now, have him (IS) imagine squeezing or tearing various things – starting from a telephone book to the neck of a lion. Again, I strongly urge you to be sure that he can *feel* this. If indeed he can, help him go through the experiencing of this strength. His powerlessness can start to change to a feeling of making a difference and inner powerfulness.

2. Have the patient (IS) imagine he has a railroad tie on his head and that he can feel its weight upon him. Now, have him imagine pushing the tie off his head onto the floor. Repeat it. Strive to help him achieve a feeling that he can fight his powerlessness.

3. Ask the patient to (IS) imagine he has a housewrecker's large steel ball and
    he can make it break brick buildings. The hostility released and the feeling
    of power may help to break the log jam.
4. Ask the patient to (IS) imagine driving a huge tank through various
    barriers and destroying everything in front of him. Feelings of powerful-
    ness may be achieved this way.

If the patient reports feeling better as a result of these experiences, I then try
to connect his strengthened feeling to specific *human* situations in which he has
been defined by others. I continue to try to focus on helping him change his
self-image and self-definition by using other appropriate focusing techniques.

Having the patient emotionally connect his strength in relation to *human*
experiences and the way he has been defined is of utmost importance. Otherwise,
the strengthening that may occur is not directed for change, and the techniques
suggested here become interesting but useless exercises.

The Therapist's Scream

The patient is brought to readiness to focus on change by: awareness of his
internal conflicts, the release of feeling connected with contributory traumatic
incidents, cognizance of the undermining strategies of behavior of the significant
others, and recognition of his own counter-reaction strategies. Specific approaches,
such as The Impossible Scream, have already been described. However, other
important components have not been described fully. These are such factors as:
guilt for screaming a gut-level truth, fear of the possible retaliation from the person
screamed at, and the need to make restitution or do penance for "daring" to change
the balance of the neurotic relationship.

The therapist's scream is on the side of the patient. He has to attack the
guilt-inducers and fight the fears of retaliation. The timing is related to the patient's
difficulty in getting to a gut-level response. Such statements as, "What the hell are
you feeling guilty about?", "What's the standard for such a guilt feeling?", and
"There's no guilt without a standard for guilt," are to be screamed in alliance with
and as a support to the patient's scream.

The possible therapist's screams relating to the fear of retaliation are as
follows:

"NOBODY IS GOING TO KILL YOU."
"THEY CAN'T DO ANYTHING TO YOU."
"YOU'VE DONE ENOUGH SUFFERING."
"YOU'VE DONE YOUR PENANCE."

Of course, this is not an exhaustive list. The statements used must be appropriate
and suitable for the particular phenomenological world of the patient. The more
the therapist is aware of significant strategies and counter-reaction strategies in his

patient, the better equipped he is to facilitate the process of bringing the patient to readiness for healthy conflict resolution.

Focusing in Depth

"People will continue to behave as they have always behaved unless something significant occurs to change them from that pattern of behavior."

Stieper & Wiener

"When a person changes in relation to another, the person not changing will tend to try to defeat or reduce the effect of the change."

Stieper & Wiener

The parental figure undermines the child unconsciously, usually in a subtle way, and rationalizes in an infinite variety of ways that what is being done is in the child's best interests. The combination of tactics indeed are so various that they defy cataloguing. It is true that similarities of strategies occur, but each neurotic undermining has its own special phenomenologically unique patterns.

The counter-reaction of the child to the undermining strategies of the parent is developed unconsciously, usually in a subtle fashion and in a rather desperate way to maintain some core of identity. Again, an infinite variety of ways may be used and, while certain similarities occur among persons, each counter-reaction of strategies has its own phenomenologically unique patterns.

Between the undermining parents and the counter-reacting child, a tenuous neurotic balance exists. Both sides of the balance have a stake in maintaining the structure at all costs. Each side pays its own price.

Just as a parent very often expresses great surprise and anger when it is suggested that he yield an undermining strategy, the patient in therapy also expresses surprise, anger and difficulty of sustaining awareness when he is made aware of his counter-reactions. This is called resistance. I have nearly three hundred answers to a questionnaire answered by patients on their very first visit, asking them to describe their chief or main psychological conflict. Not one person, no matter how psychologically sophisticated, has referred to the undermining tactics of the other and his counter-reacting strategies in return.

In the earlier sessions, I try to make the patient aware of his internal struggles by the methods I have already discussed. It is difficult for the person to allow awareness to occur at first. The *feeling* awareness (not the intellectual awareness) of the undermining strategies and his counter-reacting strategies are the most difficult for many patients. It is a slow climb to this feeling awareness. While the internal conflicts are made aware in the earlier sessions, it is the later sessions that allow for the depth feelings relating to these strategies.

As the patient experiences greater awareness of his conflicts, I try to make him aware of the original parental strategies and the counter-reaction strategies that are still in operation in his life. I ask him, for example, to (IS) imagine his mother yelling at him.

Patient: (Yelling, as if he were the mother) "WHY AREN'T YOU DOING MORE? NEVER MIND WHAT YOU ARE GOOD IN, WHAT ABOUT MATHEMATICS?"

Therapist: What does her yelling that do to you? (S&O) What's her strategy with you?

Patient: She wanted to do things, but couldn't — she did it through me — she set me up to feel I was superior and that I was the most brilliant student, the greatest leader of the group, and different from other children.

Therapist: (IS) Can you imagine yelling back at your mother?

Patient: Oh, no sweat, I'd yell over and over again, "LEAVE ME ALONE! LEAVE ME ALONE!"

Therapist: (S&O) What's your counter-reacting strategy with her?

Patient: Defiance after I was told to do things. I wouldn't do anything until I was pushed by others, but I never could succeed at it because I was defiant. I couldn't give them the credit — since they would be instrumental in my success, my success would belong to them. Also (Pause) everything that she is, is because I have made her that way.

Therapist: (S&O) Who does your strength belong to?

Patient: To her, I guess.

Therapist: (M/L) What was the most undermining thing your mother did to you?

Patient: Expected me to be brilliant for her without regard for me. I just wanted to be like everyone else — not *more* than everyone.

Therapist: Well, what is the conflict between — what and what — now that you know your mother's strategies and your counter-acting strategies?

Patient: Between being what she wanted and what I wanted. She wanted me to be number one and I wanted to be myself. So, I used defiance and superiority, and suppressed my natural self.

Therapist: How does that suppression of your natural self make you feel?

Patient: I feel sorry that I had to use defiance and superiority.

Therapist: Are you still suppressing your natural self?

Patient: Yes, I'm still acting superior in group and defiant to you — afraid you will demand brilliance of me.

Therapist: What do you want to yell at me?

Patient: "I'LL BE WHATEVER I WANT TO BE IN GROUP!"

Therapist: (IS) Now, imagine holding your mother's face in your hands. What do you want to yell at her?"

Patient: "I'LL BE ANYTHING I WANT TO BE!" . . . (Pause) "I DON'T HAVE TO BE ANY WAY YOU WANT ME TO BE!" . . . (After a long pause) "I AM NOT A FAILURE IF I'M NOT BRILLIANT — DON'T PUSH ME — I AM O.K. THE WAY I AM!" . . . (Pause) "I BELONG TO ME — I'M NOT YOUR LITTLE BOY!"

With constructive use of anger and with a specific direction achieved by his awareness of his own counter strategies, this patient ultimately was successful in changing a neurotic conflict resolution to a healthy conflict resolution.

Integration of Strengths

"There is substantial evidence that in effective psychotherapy the patient eventually incorporates into his own life style the facilitative conditions offered him in therapy. He is influenced by the significant sources of learning in therapy to become more open, understanding, and respectful of himself and others. Thus, what he is learning is new techniques of effective living."

Strupp, Fox, and Lessler

In the long run, there can be no compromise between the neurotic conflict resolution and the healthy conflict resolution. If a healthy conflict resolution is not achieved, the person does not define his psychological life. Achievement of healthy conflict resolution is not an easy task. The therapist doesn't wake up one morning and decide this might be a good day to attempt the focusing techniques with a patient. Many things must be taken into consideration. Among them are:

1. The general complexity of human nature, disallowing the possibility of merely following mechanical steps,
2. An assessment of the intensity of the conflicts,
3. The necessity of real awareness of the conflicts on the part of the patient,
4. The patient's own ego strength to allow the possibility of attempting change,
5. The love, compassion, understanding and trust of the therapist, who opts for change and trusts the patient's wish for change.

There is no sequential order for the above five points — they may come in any order — but all are necessary.

When a patient has involved himself in the focusing techniques, he almost always needs to integrate his change of behavior in life. One of the best places to demonstrate to himself that he can react differently and from his own core is, of course, group therapy. While this book does not concern itself with the use of Psycho-Imagination Therapy in group therapy, I can say that many of the focusing techniques can and do occur in group therapy. The interactions of the group members seem to be a valuable point of integration for the person attempting healthier methods of coping with his conflicts. It allows the possibility of strength and individual growth and the demonstration of new values for life.

Of course, all of life outside the therapy room, individual or group, serves as a point of integration for the new behavior. How gratifying it can be for a patient to say, "I didn't act that old stinky way any more, when I was as at Jim's house."

CHAPTER 6

Psycho-Imagination Therapy
and Problems of Sex

"He dares not take for fear of being taken."

Sarte of Giacometti

"All children are uncertain about their sexual role at first and each sex has a tendency to imitate the other. In other words, envy goes both ways."

Ruth Moulton

Since it is impossible in this book to be encyclopedic about neurotic problems which affect sexual behavior, I can only present *general* applications of Psycho-Imagination Therapy to such neuroses. As with the other internal conflicts discussed in Chaper IV, the neurotic conflict resolution is a result of the discrepancy between the individual's definition of himself and how he has been defined by his significant others. The person who displays sexual difficulties has been defined in a way by the other to prevent him from a wholehearted, free release of his sexuality and from the expression of the related feelings of intimacy. In short, he has been driven by guilt-induction, explicit or implicit, into a position of constriction, rigidity, or total inoperativeness. If a person has been falsely defined by the significant others as unworthy, as sissified (boys), as masculine (girls), or as evil, confusion exists. Again, he or she is in conflict between what he wishes to be and what he is said to be. The conflicts surrounding sexual feelings and activities are indeed the strongest any person might feel. Perhaps more than any other feelings, sexual feelings tend to pervade one's whole life, as Binswanger says, "... the power and significance of sexuality ... in shaping our relations to other human beings, shapes our *inner life-history*." (Binswanger, 1963, p. 158.)

In solving sexual problems, just as in any neurotic problem, the therapist is interested initially in the patient's internal conflicts. While some patients ca.1 become aware of the *non-sexual* internal conflicts in the initial phases of therapy, only a few can divulge immediately their internal conflicts about sexual matters. Since sexual conflicts deal with the most vulnerable, the most tender, the most shame-inducing, and the most guilty feelings, they are the most difficult to disclose to oneself and to others.

It must be stated, although it would seem obvious, that no sexual problem can have a healthy solution without the involvement of another person. Of course, the solution to a sexual problem can be neurotic, for example, masturbation, isolation or denial. But, if one thinks of a healthy conflict resolution, two people and their naturalness must be involved.

Existential Humanistic Problems of Sex

Man's two existential needs, the need to make a difference to someone and the need for acknowledgment or confirmation of his existence, are equally applicable to the sexual sphere as they are to other areas of life. Here, they manifest themselves in two pervasive concepts which underlie the individual's feelings about his sexuality. These concepts I have called "Allowable Sex" and "If I Can't Make a Difference to Someone."

Allowable Sex

Allowable sex refers to the sexual feelings which the person (self) feels safe in expressing to the real or imagined audience of his authority figures (others). Allowable sex is a concept that a child learns in his formative years. When the strategies of the parents are such that the child, in his counter strategies, must go in an opposing direction, an internal conflict results that is usually accompanied by feelings of isolation. A simplistic example is that of a child who will not cross a street even though it may appear quite safe to do so, or even if his friends are crossing, because of his internalized feelings of prohibition on the part of the parental figures. A similar mechanism controls non-allowability of sexual expression, except that, more often than not, the prohibition or disapproval by the parental figures in the sexual sphere is *implicit* rather than explicit.

Allowable sex (that which the individual feels is "all he deserves to be allowed" to express sexually) may occur, under certain specific conditions, with another person or it may take the form of a masturbation fantasy. When there is conflict between what he cannot keep himself from expressing sexually and what he feels is allowable from the authority standard, the individual is possessed by strong guilt feelings. This can completely undermine his system of self-worth.

While allowable sex generally changes with age and experience, it is possible for an individual to become fixated at a certain point, for example in the case of the voyeur. When a neurotic conflict resolution is made, the "treadmill" of the neurosis keeps the sexual problems at a generally fixed level. The patient's "allowable life" and his "allowable sex" are closely intertwined. The neurotic solution allows the person to say, "This is the way I am — this is my fate."

With greater awareness of his conflicts, the patient has a chance to liberate himself, not only from the false ideas about sex, but from the false ways in which he has been defined that forced him eventually into the sexual difficulty. In short, with the aid of the focusing techniques, he has the chance to opt for change.

If I Can't Make a Difference to Someone

This is the despairing cry of the man or woman whose sexual identity is of such little value to themselves that they settle for a counterfeit of the real thing. Usually these individuals have homosexual tendencies, but this is not always the case. One man went with a woman for more than a decade – sharing many extended experiences, yet was never allowed by her to engage in actual sexual intercourse. She controlled him. Seething underneath, he nevertheless accepted his denied state. Nobody explains this position better than Laing: "A man who despairs at his own power to make any difference to a woman may be prepared therefore to settle for a good counterfeit of the 'real' thing, deriving pleasure from the very complexity of the disillusionment and illusionment involved in the play of mutual indifference, meanness and generosity, helplessness and control." (Laing, 1962, p. 74.)

If one cannot make a difference to anyone, it is possible to become a tragic hero to oneself. If a person feels that he cannot effect a change in the other even if he gives fully and openly of himself sexually, he is involving himself in one of life's most frustrating experiences. On the other hand, one woman, because she could not accept the fact that she was a woman (like her mother) and really wanted to be a man (like her father), spent her sexual energies in arousing men, making them fall in love with her, but ultimately withholding from them. To make a difference to the other, in the sense of making some dent in a brick wall, became her greatest triumph. To allow the other person to feel that he made a difference to her in the same way became her greatest defeat. Genuine reciprocity then was truly impossible.

As Laing has stated so clearly: "So-called hysterical frigidity in a woman is often based on refusal to allow any man the triumph of 'giving' her satisfaction. Her frigidity is her triumph and her torment. The implication is, 'You can have your penis, your erection, your orgasm, but it doesn't make any difference to me.' And, indeed, existentially speaking, ability to have an erection, to ejaculate with an orgasm, is only a very limited aspect of being potent. It is potency without power to make a difference to the other. A man who complains of impotence is frequently a man who, analogously to the frigid hysterical woman, is determined not to give the woman the satisfaction of satisfying him." (Laing, 1962, pp. 73-74.)

Eliciting Internal Conflicts

The concept of internal conflicts and their bipolarization (see Chapter IV) is essentially the same for sexual problems, except for the specific sexual emphasis. When the patient starts to talk about sexual feelings and seems to be ready to allow himself to become aware of the conflicts involved, I may use certain questions to elicit them. I try to start with less specific questions and eventually go to the more specific sexual questions. Again, I must warn the reader that no two people react in the same way. I am suggesting a *general* approach; however, it must be in tune with the phenomenological world of the patient. The individual differences of each patient must be respected and heeded. My remarks should be used as a guide and certainly not as absolute.

Early general questions should have little or no sexual connotation and should permit considerable projection. A question I have found useful is (IS), "Imagine two large boxes and imagine a woman in one and a man in the other." The verbatim response of one thirty-five year old man follows:

Patient: It's a cardboard box. The woman is black — nude. The man is a kind of clinical man on a medical chart — non-descript — penis covered by a loin cloth. He's smoothed over a mannikin. The woman is handsome — fantastic breasts — sensuous woman — emerging out of the box.

Therapist: Have the man talk to the woman.

Patient: "Stand correctly. Be like me — mechanical — a robot on display."

Therapist: Now have the woman talk to the man.

Patient: She kind of laughs at him with writhing movements — jewelry on — necklace and bracelet.

Therapist: What adjective would you give each?

Patient: Man — robot; woman — sensuous. (Long pause) *I* am the robot!

Therapist: (IS) Now imagine that you and the woman are on a balance scale. Wha happens?

Patient: She is certain of her position. If I am myself, I outweigh her — we are even if I am a robot.

Therapist: (S&O) Who is your idealized image woman?

Patient: She's a beautiful, curvaceous woman who will give me the gift of he sexuality. (Pause) My job is to reciprocate, to perform perfectly and instantly fo her sexually. I fuck, therefore, I am . . . I am a robot, therefore, I'll fuck.

To the very same imaginary situation about the two large boxes containing man and woman in each, a woman patient replied as follows: "They are tw cardboard boxes — no labels on them. I am looking down at them. They are smalle than me. Half their bodies are out. It's my mother's kitchen. The lady has a 1930' skirt on — kind of plain. They are looking at each other." I asked her to have ther say something to each other. She responded, "No — nothing to say to each other. I then asked her what would happen if she were to leave. She replied, "They'd go i the box — they came out because of me." This particular woman put herself int the imaginary situation and could verbalize and feel her "observer" role in se> However, if I had started with a specific sexual question, her very detachmen about sex would have operated in making her resist the question.

Another question with no obvious sexual connotation is having the femal patient imagine (IS) a woman on horseback, riding on a trail where she meets a mai on horseback. One patient responded, "The woman is me. The man is vague. I an marking time just riding along kind of in the shade, but there is sun in the distance

I don't want to ride any farther. I don't want him at all. He couldn't be a gorgeous man for a romance or something – no, not that. I'm going off my horse and look for my mother – I might as well." This woman's conflict was between her loyalty to her mother and wanting to be a sexual woman to her husband.

Another *general* method of eliciting conflict areas is the "Directed Daydream" of Robert Desoille (1965). This method utilizes imaginative situations such as descending into a cave where one comes upon a witch, sorceress, wizard or a magician. However, while Desoille places great emphasis on symbols, I emphasize the internal conflicts that may be revealed. I asked a woman the question (IS), "Imagine that you are descending into a cave and you see a magician." Her reply was, "I see my husband, Ron. (Laughs) He waves his magic wand and his clothes come off and we have sex. (Pause) But it's the cave that I have to go through that's my problem – before I can have sex with him . . . (grunts and groans) . . . from the entrance. I have to cauterize my mother. I am standing in the middle. Ron is pulling me on one side and my mother is pulling me on the other side. I am angry towards Ron and my mother is angry towards me. I want to hold on to my mother's hand forever."

A fourth imaginary situation which is helpful in eliciting awareness of sexual feelings, is to ask the patient to imagine (IS) a balance scale with babies of the same sex on either side of the scale. A female patient's reply was, "If I am one of them, then I'm heavier. If it were two others, it would be even. I have to feel superior to girls. As a matter of fact, I can't stand girls."

As it appears that the patient can tolerate more pointed questions, I gradually proceed from the above general, projective imaginary situations into questions in which there is some sexual connotation. However, I limit these questions to situations dealing with animals or non-related people and in non-threatening contexts, until I am sure that the patient will accept more specific questions. I wish to stress again that each patient is unique; occasionally I feel I can ask a patient a specific, pointed question about his sexual feelings almost as soon as I've met him. But in general, the questioning should proceed from very general ones through slightly more sexually-oriented questions and finally to very specific questions relevant to the patient's phenomenological world. An example of an intermediate level of imaginary situations is to have the patient imagine (IS) two chipmunks – one on each hand – a male and a female. A woman's response follows: "They are both chewing an acorn – the girl is chewing away faster." I then suggested for her to imagine (IS) that the female was in heat. She replied, "Boy goes over to girl and he fucks her. He stays with her a long time. (Pause) I was O.K. (Pause) *I'm* her. She's being very proper-like. She enjoys it enough, but under control. (Pause) I must be labeled proper."

Other non-threatening questions with minimal overtones of sex are:

(IS) Imagine two rooms in a house, in another city. Then imagine a man in one room and a woman in the other. What would they say to each other and do?

(IS) Close your eyes and imagine your arms out holding a man or a woman.

A specific question to help expose the patient's phenomenological world of sexual feelings is to ask him (IS), "Imagine a sexual fantasy that a woman might have of you." This can elicit a clear, idealized image of how he feels he must act in relation to women and to the world. One man said, "She would want me to be a persuader of large crowds, of huge armies, and of large corporations." His enormous need to control the world and nearly everyone in it was evidenced by his response.

Either as a follow-up to the above imaginary situation or as a lead-in question at an appropriate place in the therapy session, I can ask the patient (FTS), "I have to prove to every woman that ____ ." Answers such as handsome, socially skillful, witty, charming, and "know how to handle head waiters" are quite common, illustrating the great demand for performance on the part of the male in our society.

Additional views of the patient's sexual feelings can be elicited by reversing the fantasy: (IS), "What is *your* masturbation fantasy of a woman?" One man answered, "The fantasy that arouses me is one in which I am undressed among a number of fully dressed girls and the humiliation excites me. Sometimes I imagine Amazonian women coming towards me and sexually overpowering me."

The comparable questions to a woman elicited the following response:

(IS) Imagine a sexual fantasy that a man might have of you? "It is that I'm beautiful, that he melts to my touch, that his excitement and passion are aroused as he touches my sexual parts. No other woman in the world can excite him and give him such pleasure. He knows that no other woman can love him with the depth of feeling that I can offer."

(FTS) I have to prove to every man that **"I'm the greatest; I'm indispensable."**

The Finish-the-Sentence technique is an appropriate lead-in question for exposing an awareness of the patient's feelings about the opposite sex. Expectancies about men (women) can be clarified with the following questions:

Common Responses

	Female	Male
(FTS) The only good man (woman) is a ____ .	A dead one, a eunuch, an old man, a kind man, a rich man.	A submissive one, loves me only, a giving woman, no such thing.
(FTS) Men (women), according to my mother, ____ .	Will use you sexually, are only necessary evils, are to be used for whatever you can get.	Would take you for everything, would be all-giving, are frivolous.

(FTS) Never let a man (woman) ____ .	Fall in love with you, use you.	Know what you are feeling, be important to you, become dependent on you.
(FTS) I want a man (woman) to prove to me that ____ .	He can love me without sex.	She won't use me, I'm the most important person in her life, she won't prefer another man.

The basic expectancies which an individual relates to sex and intimacy undeniably have their roots in the family interactions of the past. One woman said, in answer to the question (FTS), "Other women, according to my father, ____ ," "... were tramps, but I was a princess." Indeed, she tried to keep herself from men in a sexual way, and kept her purity and regality intact. This question obviously has many counterparts for both the male and the female patient: "(Other) women, according to my mother, ____ "; "(Other) men, according to my father, ____ "; "(Other) men, according to my mother, ____ "; or any significant others. Typical responses that I have elicited with these questions are:

Responses

	Female	Male
(FTS) According to my mother, women ____ .	Are beasts underneath, will never be true to you, can never be counted on.	Are sacred objects, are not as good as she is, are less than men.
(FTS) According to my father, men (women) ____ .	Were out to lay you, were not as nice as him, are only good to support you.	Are strange, are no good, only want security.

In addition to the Finish-the-Sentence method, any of the other three Psycho-Imagination Therapy techniques (Most-or-Least, Imaginary Situation, or Self-and-Other) can be used singly or in combination to evoke the patient's feelings about sex. A useful Most-or-Least question is (M/L), "Who is the most passive man in the world?" To which one young man promptly and with some facial glee responded, "Me." Then I continued:

Therapist: (M/L) Who is the most aggressive man in the world?

Patient: My father, absolutely!

Therapist: (IS) Imagine your mother sees a man and woman having intercourse.

Patient: Well, she'd make a remark about the political situation — oh, well, she might root for the underdog.

Therapist: (IS) Imagine your mother watching a tug of war between aggressive men and passive men.

Patient: She'd root for the passive men, because she wanted me to be passive.

Therapist: (IS) What sexual fantasy would a woman have of your father?

Patient: Oh, that he's strong and dominant or cruel, and she loves it.

Another imaginary situation which can be used to expose the phenomenological world of the patient is the desert island situation. (IS) "Imagine yourself on an island alone with a woman for an unknown time. How long will it be before sex will occur?" The patient invariably refers to how she (other) might think of him (self) and his attractiveness. He often also includes his and her fears and hesitancies, and all of the strategies back and forth that might be involved.

With a passive, dependent, male patient, I may ask the question (S&O), "Do you remember the first time you ever fought for yourself?" The patient might answer, "Never," or "Only once in my life." I then may ask (M/L) "What is the most risky kind of behavior you can take on your own behalf?" One patient replied, "Going to a party on a Saturday night." Naturally, I urged him to go and take that risk. Another patient returned from a meeting at an Eastern university, and told me he had taken the "Impossible Risk" by "picking up a girl at a bar with two other men competing for her." He felt he had broken his passivity cycle.

When I have a male patient who feels unfavorable comparison to other men, I may ask him (IS), "Imagine taking the initiative with *me*" or "Imagine anything you would like to compete about with me." If he hesitates, I reassure him that there will be no retaliation and that, win or lose, it will be fair. One young man took my challenge and engaged me in a handgripping contest, in which he won. His initial fear was enormous, but having done it — and finding I was not retaliating for losing — he allowed himself to experience a good feeling.

Another helpful imaginary situation is to ask the patient (IS), "Imagine going into a room where there are five women. Which woman are you most likely to come out with? What are her qualities?" One man said, "The most difficult one would be blue-eyed, Protestant and blonde. It would be easiest to come out of the room with either a black or a Jewish girl. With a blonde woman, I have to perform — to be what I think she wants me to be. I guess I feel superior to the black or Jewish girl, or the dark-haired girl, so I don't have to perform for them."

Later on in therapy, as he became much more aware of his mother (who was blonde, blue-eyed and Protestant) he was asked to focus (IS), "Imagine holding your mother's face in your hands and scream the most impossible phrase at her." He paused for several minutes and said, "This is too hard, Joe." I urged him on. Then he let go a scream, "I AM NOT YOUR PUPPET. I AM MY OWN MAN!" He said this over and over again. He cried for a moment, then he burst into hysterical laughter. "I feel better," he said.

Within a few weeks, he had dated and spent considerable time with a blonde, blue-eyed, Protestant girl, and for the first time in his life, he said, "I'm defining the situation and I am not performing."

There have been times when, after sufficient rapport between the patient and myself has been established, I ask him (IS), "Imagine you and your mother and father all nude on a bed. Now, imagine looking into your father's eyes." "Yeah, I can do that," a man said, "but I feel he'll kill me. I am afraid he'll think I am sexually interested in my mother. And my mother's eyes tell me she's afraid my father will think she's interested in me. Now, ain't that a mess?" "What are you going to do about it?" I asked. "I feel like yelling at them, "I AM NOT TAKING YOUR WOMAN AWAY FROM YOU, FATHER! HE'S YOUR MAN, MOTHER!' " "How do you feel now?" I inquired when he was through yelling. "O.K., I guess," was his relieved reply.

This man felt that any woman he might be interested in belonged to practically any other man who might show the slightest interest in the woman – just as his mother belonged to his father. His own feelings for his mother caused him such guilt that he renounced wanting a woman. Much work had already been done before this particular focusing experience. This facilitated the patient's acceptance of the question, his acknowledgment of his inner conflict, and his rapid movement toward resolution of his conflict.

I asked a woman the same question: (IS) "Imagine you and your mother and father in the nude in bed. Look into your father's eyes." "When I look into my father's eyes, I see he wants to fuck me. When I look into my mother's eyes, I see her own self-hate and (Pause) . . . it robs me of my womanhood. I feel that gives me a powerful little girl role. I have them both where I want them and I won't let go. I *have* to be asexual." (S&O) "Can you make a difference to a man?" I then asked. "No, because I have to be the center of the universe – egocentric (Groans)."

Another useful imaginary situation is to have the patient (IS) imagine nude photos of himself or herself taken at various ages and encourage the expression of his or her feelings about each photo.

A rather vivid question is (IS), "Imagine taking a shower with your father or mother." The phenomenological differences are great, but this particular imaginary situation probably stimulates the patient's own awareness as well as any I have used. One man said in reply to the shower question, "My father would have to go first and when my father finished, then I could shower," I urged him to *imagine* taking a shower together. "Well," he said, "he wouldn't even notice me."

"What would he say if he did look at your penis?" I asked.

"I wouldn't be able to get him to acknowledge it," he said.

"Make him acknowledge it," I said.

"O.K., I'd hold it up to him and yell, 'SEE, IT'S A GOOD ONE. I'M NOT ASHAMED OF IT! IF YOU'RE ASHAMED OF IT, THAT'S YOUR PROBLEM. I'M A MAN AND I'M GOING TO USE IT!' " he yelled.

Another question which is excellent to yield inner conflicts that relate to sexual feelings is (IS), "Imagine you are a hummingbird and you are going to extract nectar from a flower. What would you do and what would you feel?" Strom, a thirty-five year old male, answered this by saying, "I'd fly around and slowly put my beak into the flower and I'd find it closed. I'd fly around to many flowers and every time I'd try, the flower would be closed. I'd get tired and fly away somewhere else."

I asked him (FTS), "If I am sexy, I'll _____ ." He answered quickly and spontaneously, ". . . be punished." At this point I asked him (IS), "Imagine you are witnessing a rape." Slowly, with a contorted face, Strom started to talk about a traumatic incident that had occurred in his childhood. He described in detail what he had overheard in terror — his mother pleading with his father for him not to hurt her sexually. He re-experienced the entire incident, crying as his mother had and pleading as his father had. The re-enactment was detailed and dramatic. He became aware of his own feelings and fears. It became clear to him that he feared he would become his "cruel" father if he were to penetrate a woman sexually. As the re-enactment developed, he focused his powerful hostility on his mother's denial. More and more as he proceeded, his anger at his mother's denial and at her controlling behavior in making the father look like the cruel one, built up in him. Without any direction from me, he hurled attacking statements at his mother. On and on he yelled, screaming at his mother that it was she who had made sexual intercourse a dreaded, sadistic event. An excerpt from a subsequent passage in this patient's tape-recorded therapy session follows:

Strom: No, (Ugh) did my mother have tits? I can't imagine her having tits. She had them, but they were certainly something other than tits. They were, you know, here's something very interesting . . . (Pauses) (Chews loudly). It would have been so embarrassing for me — so traumatic for her — for me to even have recognized that she had tits, or enjoyed them. Or even just looking at them, or putting my head on them, or hold her or something when I was a kid. I just never did it. Instead, I found them repulsive. It's like now, my wife has small tits. Rather than be envious of other guys and desirous of another chick with big tits or something, or cheat on her, I make no reference in mind to tits at all. I just kinda eliminate them.

Therapist: (S&O) Why is it so difficult to imagine your mother having tits?

Strom: I just told you, because it would be difficult for her. The relationship would be incredibly difficult, even as a child, when she was a young woman. If I had given any credit to the fact that I wanted to sit on her lap and feel her soft belly or her tits, it would have been awful. She couldn't have handled it — it would have been *dirty*. She would have felt dirty and I would have consequently felt very dirty.

Therapist: (S&O) Is that why you had to deny the existence of her tits?

Strom: Well, I made her whole body repulsive, including her face and her hands and everything.

Therapist: (IS) How do you think she felt when a man's semen was inside of her vagina?

Strom: Terrible! I *heard* her feel terrible. I heard her when my father was trying to fuck her. She complained and she retched and she moaned. You would have thought she was on the verge of getting the electric chair. Oh, God, it was awful. Oh, Jesus, it was the most tragic, sick thing . . . and I just thought about some experiences I have had with Evelyn which parallel it. Boy, I should make a note of that, remind me to make a note of that after the tape. Don't forget! It is really incredibly important! My mother's awful, ugly virginity and my father's saying, "Oh, just a little, oh, just a little bit more – don't now, it's going to be all right." And her saying, "No, Jed, oh please, no, no more, Jed, oh please, Jed, stop!" Oh, it was just the fucking ugliest, *ugliest* kind of thing.

When asking a woman to imagine (IS) she is a flower and a hummingbird is alighting upon her, various answers that may directly relate to her sexual receptivity, or lack of it, can be elicited. The responses range from ". . . love the feeling of the hummingbird's beak getting its nectar," to ". . . somehow, the hummingbird just seems to hover over me and then goes on."

When I have asked the question (FTS), "I go to men for ____ ," or "I go to women for ____ ," I have elicited sexual conflict areas, as well as how the patient defines himself or feels he is being defined by others. "I go to women **for approval,** but I go to men **for acknowledgment of my being a man,**" was one man's answer. Another man said, "I go to men **for approval** and I go to women **for revenge.**

Again, I urge the reader to ask himself (FTS), "I go to men for ____ ," or "I go to women for ____ ." The awareness that can result from completely honest answers might be surprising. It will certainly illustrate, more vividly than I can do here, the depth of feeling and awareness that can be elicited from a patient.

Patients who have been involved in this kind of therapy respond readily to innumerable pointed and very personal imaginative situations even in group therapy. During one group session, I asked all the men in the group (IS) "Imagine a bird on your penis." One young man closed his eyes as he imagined and said, "Oh, my God, it's a Cardinal!" A woman in the group queried, "A Cardinal?" To which he spontaneously answered, "A red Cardinal." He began to cry for a monent, wiped the tears away, and said, "I'm angry at myself for having imagined such a bird. You all know how I struggled to come to this point, how I'd wanted to become a monk, a brother – something I never could really be – I'm too sexual for that."

(IS) "Imagine a Bluebird on your penis," I suggested. "Yeah," he laughed, "I can do that – that feels better. Ah, that feels good – that's what I really want to be . . ."

Some Internal Conflicts

This section does not pretend to exhaustively discuss internal conflicts related to sexuality. Its purpose is merely to demonstrate the method of applying Psycho-Imagination Therapy techniques in the context of some specific sexual conflicts that I have found prevalent among my patients. The reader is asked to recall that the aim of Psycho-Imagination Therapy is to help the patient become aware of the discrepancy between his definition of himself and the false definition his significant others hold of him. When this awareness is acute and when the patient's sense of his true identity becomes stronger, he can be helped to attempt to change the other person's definition of him.

To Whom Do Your Sexual Feelings Belong?

It is not easy for the person who feels at one with his sexual feelings to be understanding of those people who find it difficult to claim their sexual feelings as their own. In fact, it often is difficult for the patient who is experiencing a sexual conflict to admit to himself that his sexual feelings are not his own. When I ask the question (S&O), "To whom do your sexual feelings belong?" the answer is nearly always, ". . . to me, of course." But, upon reflection or in later phases of therapy, the patient becomes more aware of his feelings, and his answer to this question or related questions changes. For example, I might ask (S&O), "How much of your father still lives in you?" The patient may reply, "Seventy percent me; thirty, him." Or he might say, "Only when I deal with women am I like him; otherwise, not."

The realization that his feelings of sexuality are not entirely his own is often shocking to the patient. The focusing techniques may be useful in helping him separate out his own sexual identity. Basically, the patient should be helped to internalization of the feeling that he *can* make a difference to a woman and still allow himself to be his own man. Otherwise, he will continue to be what he thinks *she* wants and risk the loss of his sexual identity. This can lead to a feeling of sexual responsibility to a woman, perhaps to the point of being her only pleasure, and to the neglect of his own gratification. To become aware of the patient's feeling reactions in this area, I may ask (S&O), "What is your sexual responsibility to a woman?" The answers to this question often reveal the patient's feelings about the ownership of his own manhood and his own sexual identity.

Other questions that have been useful in eliciting feelings of sexual identity are:

(S&O) Whom does your penis or vagina belong to?

(S&O) To whom do your love feelings belong?

(S&O) To whom does your time belong?

(S&O) To whom does your life belong?

It is surprising how many patients have fragmented themselves and "sold" part of their feelings to the other, in order to survive.

Focus on Guilt

There is no guilt unless there is a standard for guilt. That behavior which is free and spontaneous in one family might be thought of as rigid and cause immobilization in another. In the undermining process of the individual by his significant others, guilt induction is fundamental. In time, introjection of the standard for guilt becomes fixed and any contrary behavior feels sneaky, anxiety-laden, and imbued with fear of exposure. To the individual, the standard for guilt which he acquires from the significant others seems beyond questioning. Doubt of the standard only leads to greater guilt, which leads to further compliance and "good" behavior. Finally, if the process does not allow a glimmer of protest, detachment results. The aim of therapy is to help the patient learn that it is ". . . a prerogative of man to become guilty – and his responsibility to overcome guilt." (Frankl, 1967, p. 139.)

The conflict between the natural expression of sexual feelings and the devious ways in which the individual was forced to express his sexuality often is symbolized in the "first lie about sex" reaction. When I ask the question (S&O), "What was your first lie about sex?" many patients respond with incidents from their childhood. A common incident involves playing the game of "doctor" or "discovery" with an adventurous playmate of the opposite sex. Invariably, when the child is found at this kind of play, he fabricates a lie to cover up something he senses is "wrong," even though he doesn't know why. Such incidents of childhood, involving the feeling of wrong-doing to an absolute authority standard, are capable of evoking pain or guilt feelings years later in the adult.

Sometimes the patient does not remember his first lie about sex but can recall some other significant incident. For example, one man replied, "I don't remember my first lie about sex, but I do remember the time I lied about being found in this girl's room at college, and the Dean wrote back to my parents. Boy, I had to talk my way out of that one!"

In my questioning, I am mainly interested in how guilt has been induced into the patient and the effect it has had in undermining him. In order to make the patient aware that guilt is perpetrated upon him by others, I make the directive statement, "There is no guilt without a standard for guilt." Then, as the patient mentions guilt, I keep asking directly, "Whose standard is it?" I may ask him to imagine himself (IS) "talking in guilt" or "talking in standards for guilt," until he becomes aware that his guilt was induced by the other and that he need feel guilty no longer.

Guilt can be present to such an overwhelming degree that it may cripple the individual's functioning and fragment his relations to the world. If the psycho-therapist can convince the patient of his non-judgmental attitude, he can elicit a truly honest disclosure of guilt feelings. The following actual transcript of a patient's statement about his guilt feelings illustrates the extraordinary trust this man must have had in his face-to-face contact with the therapist.

Therapist: (M/L) What do you feel most guilty about?

Patient: Oh, about a lot of things. Let's see . . . I am evil because I masturbated as a youth. I fantasized my mother cut to ribbons by a butcher. I was a no-good son, in that I did not support my mother after the death I wished for my father occurred. I asked a little girl to take my pants down when I was twelve. I participated in holding other guys' penises in my mouth and sticking them in asses when I was eleven. I went to a whore house for my first piece of ass. I called Shirley Blank a "goddam Jew" in front of Sheila Rosenthal, who was Jewish. I stood up Linda Monroe on the night of a dance she had asked me to. I lost my father's gun when I was four. I wasn't a good student after my father died. I stole a revolver from an empty house . . . I drank wine in a church office . . . I stole cigarettes from my mother . . . I broke windows and streetlights. I drank as a fifteen-year-old and from then on. I have had homosexual feelings at different times. I went to a movie and put my hand on the woman's leg next to me at fourteen. Many times I drank and went in search of older women and wooed them with poetry, and hated them after sex. I fantasize orgies and complete debauchery. I drove past an accident that had taken place and didn't stop. I went to whores in the Navy. I threw a girl out of a car who repulsed me – the car was parked. I witnessed a gang bang and didn't stop it. I hated my mother and do now – deeper down I hated my father and competed with him for my mother. I stopped seeing my grandmother before she died. I kicked holes in doors and walls in houses that I have lived in. I secretly hate and compete with people that I never express it to. I assume guilt for feeling human . . . for sleeping on my stomach . . . for smoking cigarettes . . . for drinking . . . for leaving work early or working at home. As a child I couldn't stand to cut the lawn or help around the house. When Howard Smith and I hadn't eaten in several days, I spent the remaining dime for food which I ate myself. I left Elisa (my first wife) as a boy and made her sad. I was a bad student after my father died. I was not grateful to people that said they liked me – I talked behind their backs. I almost killed a woman after drinking. I went on searches for evil when I was alone in a city. I drove a car dangerously. I failed to become a man. I spent for myself. I wanted Jim Brown's wife after he died. I called women late at night only for brutal sex or self-motivated sex. I was ashamed of the women I made love to. I don't work hard enough . . . I am a failure . . . I have never arrived. I feel superior but act inferior . . . or act superior. I don't allow feelings for others. I act and did act sadistic to women. I always wanted the other woman, with my friends . . . their wife or girl. I had an affair with a married woman. I never lived up to others' expectations . . . I was always a failure . . . or lucky.

Therapist; (S&O) What would others think if you went into a whore house?

Patient: My mother would approve; my father would condemn me; Elisa would have sent me to Purgatory; and grandmother would abandon me.

This man, despite the inordinate depth of his guilt, was able to remove the onus of self-blame and the pain of self-castigation by eventually becoming aware, through therapy, that he had no alternative but to act as he did under the circumstances of his tyrannical parents.

To Whom Are You Accounting?

Closely allied with guilt is, of course, accounting to the authority person. When a person, while he is engaged in sex, acts as though he is robbing a safe, we can be sure that his "lookout" for the police and his "getaway car" are not far away. One of the best questions for eliciting this reaction is (S&O), "In whose presence do you feel the greatest turn-off of your sexuality?" "In front of my mother," a twenty-year-old answered. "And, it's the same with Mary." (He and Mary were living together.) "Like, I get angry at Mary when I've been at a bar with the boys and she questions me because I'm a little late. It's like she's omniscient – she's everywhere, she can see all and knows I've done bad, regardless."

I asked this young man (IS), "Imagine walking into a room where your mother is and show her your erection." "My mother would gnash her teeth, her eyes would narrow and she would be seething. Yeah, like, I'd go up to her and say, 'This is my cock. It's a happy cock. It's good to fuck (Laughs) – you have the dirty mind, not me.' "

Another method of eliciting awareness of the patient's accountability to some authority figure is the question (IS), "Imagine yourself in a 'morality' witness box and accuse the accusers." Often this helps the patient learn to account to his own concept of morality and not to the concept of morality alien to his genuine feelings, which has been imposed on him by others.

Fantasy Father or Mother

When the real father is cruel, degrading, or physically abusive, a boy may find a fantasy father with whom to identify. The thought of the hated father is so reprehensible that the boy develops a reaction against being like the father in any way. This pushes him to look for confirmation in another father figure. If a real person is not available, such as a strong, kind teacher; a football coach; or an uncle, the child may turn to a father that exists only in fantasy. The fantasy may be so real to the boy that imaginary conversations may occur.

If the child's hatred for the father is reinforced by his observation of the father being cruel to the mother, the young boy may grow up with the feeling that he has to be gentle or passive towards a woman. It may be difficult for him to have strong pelvic movements during intercourse for fear of destroying the woman. An imaginary situation I have used with several passive patients is as follows: (IS) "Imagine you are having sex relations with a woman (on the floor) and imagine strong pelvic movements on your part." Some stubbornly cling to heightened passivity – but, usually, under strong urging from me, they are able to simulate the strong movements. When the patient becomes aware that kindness and gentleness are not contradictory to masculinity, he can allow his real strength to develop openly.

On the other hand, some men are passive because they have *become* their father in their sexual behavior. If they have identified with a weak, passive father, they may feel they can never be otherwise. If the passive father has a strongly controlling wife who operates from certainty, the young man also may fear castration. Such a man, Jim, spoke of his mother as a "Killer Whale," with whom he fought constantly.

Jim: Our arguing voices could be heard everywhere. I didn't know it then, but I was fighting for my life. She accused me of being selfish and thinking only of myself. My father was a defeated man who hid behind his newspaper. And my brother had already succumbed into his silent nature. She was after me, all right, but I fought with her and everyone. But, her insidious accusation of my being selfish persisted. I couldn't have sex with a girl because I'd just be *taking* what the girl was giving. I would have to make it fast – so fast that it was over almost instantly.

Therapist: (IS) Imagine your mother nude on the bed, and you, as an adolescent, entering the room.

Jim: I'd go in quietly, enter the bed and have sex with her fast enough that it would be over before she awakened. I feel that women will disappear or vanish from me if they know I want sex. I have to take what I want real fast.

Therapist: (IS) Have your penis talk to your mother's vagina. What does it say?

Jim: "You will kill me if you find me inside you."

Women also may have fantasy mothers or fathers. The prevalence of such fantasies is greater than one might expect, since usually such a fact is submerged by the patient and only emerges under direct questioning. If a young girl has a fantasy mother, as one young woman had made of her sewing teacher, she may unconsciously banish it from her awareness, for fear of her mother's detection and reprisal.

If the patient's identification with her mother is thorough, she may make a conflict resolution by "becoming her mother." In the case of one patient, the mother had been controlled by a cruel father, and the patient identified strongly with her. She reacted by denying her own spontaneous sexuality and, in turn, being sadistic to men. In therapy, I asked this woman (IS), "Imagine that you are a young girl during wartime who is going by train to a safe area, and you are leaving your mother behind."

Patient: I feel kind of, in a peculiar way, that there is nothing to lose – then I just feel the desire to grab onto her. Oh, hell, let the war take her away! Actually, I used to have a fantasy about my mother going to jail.

Therapist: (IS) Imagine holding your arms around a kind man after the train has gone some distance.

Patient: I don't want to hold a man – I want to hold off – it's my ugly way – that's all there is . . . All right! I'll try it again . . . (Pause) . . . I can do it! It's O.K.! . . . (Pause) . . . (Cries) . . . I don't know what I'm fighting . . . I can do it! . . . (Cries and sobs) . . . It feels good!

The Traumatic Incidents and the Rotten Part of Me

More traumatic incidents are offered by patients in the sexual realm than in any other area of interpersonal experience. The feelings of shame and humiliation related to these traumatic incidents are exceptionally strong, and the incidents usually are points in time that mark the beginning of a fixed neurotic conflict resolution.

One man gave the following account of (M/L) the most vivid sexual experience of his childhood. His enormous feelings of gratefulness to a woman and his feeling of permanent homage to her sent him into deep states of depression. The traumatic incident that helped fix his neurotic conflict resolution is as follows:

Patient: The dressing room was adjacent to the bathroom; the walls were painted a deep green, with white trim, and there were no windows in it that I remember. There was a soft deep-pile carpet on the dressing room floor, of a green that matched the walls. When my father bathed or showered, he would close the door that gave onto the bedroom from the dressing room, and leave open the door between the dressing room and the bathroom. He would turn on the shower, and both rooms would soon fill up with mist. There was a full-length mirror in the dressing room, and the mist would condense on it. We were effectively isolated from the rest of the world in the two misty rooms, and I remember feeling a rich sense of security and closeness with my father.

I was naked, as I remember, and my father was undressing to take his shower. Our bodies reflected as foggy images in the dressing room mirror. Perhaps it was the first time I had been allowed to participate; there seemed to be a sort of ritual about it. I loved my father, and was excited about the sense of oneness or of acceptance which my presence in this green, mist-filled room seemed to imply. Emotion and sensation – the thick, warm carpet under my feet, the warm mist from the shower – combined to make one of those moments which it would have been nice to enjoy and explore until all its goodness had been absorbed and added to my very *self*. The moment – the experience – was as integral to my existence as my arms or legs.

My father had taken off all his clothes except his undershorts, and I followed him in to the bathroom. Standing at the toilet, his own body towering over mine, he urinated. It was the first time I recall seeing his penis. The size of it was amazing to me. It was magnificent; my own, by contrast, was tiny and insignificant, hiding from the world behind its tiny foreskin. It was inconceivable that I should ever have a penis such as my father's and, awed, I reached out to touch it, to hold it. Whether he thrust my hand away or merely stopped me with a word, I don't remember, but I felt as though I had been stabbed – my feeling of closeness with him vanished and was replaced with a feeling of shame and valuelessness, and I began to cry. Having finished urinating, my father sat down on a low chair against the bathroom wall and read to me from a book, perhaps to comfort me. I sat in his lap, my naked legs across his, my back against his naked chest. It did something to reassure me. In a few minutes, however, he told me that I should go – that he had to shower. When I asked him why, he said it was because he was going out.

I told him I didn't want him to go, and he said that he had to, and that my mother was going as well. I felt as though I was being abandoned, and begged him not to go. He put me out in the dressing room and left me there, returning into the bathroom and shutting the door. It didn't seem to matter that I was crying. I must have decided to stay in the dressing room. I stood there, alone, naked and crying, so that he would know – upon emerging from the bathroom – how important it was for him to stay with me. When he came out, he would have to see how important it was; he could not fail to see it.

After a long time, the door to the bathroom opened and he came out, already partially dressed. He saw me and laughed, and said, "Are you still here?" I felt furious with him for a moment, but he picked me up. I wanted to ask him to help me – help me by staying home and being with me – to recapture what I had felt earlier, before the moment when he had not let me touch his penis. If he left, I would be alone and helpless: I would be *self*less.

At this moment, my mother – who had been out – came into the dressing room. My father, laughing, told her he had put me out of the bathroom while he took his shower, and that when he had emerged, I was still there. He told her this as if there were something amusing to it. I was crying again, begging them to stay. Laughingly, they patted my cheeks. I felt as though something very important had been lost, never to be recaptured. What actually occurred afterwards, I don't remember, except that they did, of course, go out wherever they were going. It was a terrible humiliation.

It must have been that at an early age I identified enormously with my father. He was my strength, my security. He lived *within* me, in a sense. A sense of oneness with the world came only through a sense of oneness with him. When he shamed me, rejecting my admiration for his penis, all access to strength – power – and security was denied, and I was reduced to nothing. I was between three and four at the time. At the moment I no longer need him to feel at one with myself or with the world, though from time to time the emptiness recurs. I should have left him to his shower and gone outside to explore my own world in the garden.

Therapist: (IS) What is the rotten part of your body, if you were to imagine sensing your whole body?

Patient: (Squirmed, paused for a long time) My pubic hair.

Therapist: (IS) Now, I want you to imagine handing your pubic hair into my hand.

Patient: O.K. (Laughed) I'll try. (Then he imagined with the full force of his feelings, grimacing as he handed me his pubic hair.)

Therapist: How do you feel?

Patient: How can you stand to hold it? It's ugly and dirty, and wiry, ooch . . .

Looking directly at him and holding my hand out as if I were really holding his pubic hair, I spoke of how I felt about him and especially my genuine regard for him and all of my positive feelings for him. It was difficult for him to accept this. "When I speak to you, I speak to your pubic hairs – they are one and the same," I said.

He sensed my genuineness towards him, and it was possible for him to relax his body. This ease triggered another incident from his early childhood that was traumatic in nature. His mother had noticed his erections when he was four or five and told him whenever his penis was "acting nasty" to come to her and she would make it "nice" again. When he did, she would put her hand on his penis, "making it" reduce in size. The disdain on his mother's face became introjected as "dirty," and somehow, this later was displaced to his pubic hair. He feared a woman would never accept his erection – rejection was certain. He became a voyeur who would look at women undressing while he masturbated at a barricaded distance, to avoid direct contact with women.

With the acceptance of his "rotten part," he seemed to change dramatically. He was able in a short time to move towards girls. Within a few months, after additional individual therapy combined with group experience, he could tolerate sexual contact with a woman. He had returned from his banishment.

As with males, often times women will feel that they are "rotten" and displace the feeling onto some body part. I asked one young woman (S&O), "What is the rotten part of you – from a feeling and sensing of your body?"

Patient: My mouth.

Therapist: Your mouth?

Patient: Without it, I'm nothing. It's my survival and shield. Without it, I would have been ignored by my father — it was only my screaming and my badgering him for hours until he responded that gave me any kind of identity.

Therapist: Can you imagine handing me your mouth?

Patient: No, definitely not, I'd have nothing.

With urging, she finally imagined handing her mouth into the palm of my hand. I looked at it as if it really were in the palm of my hand and then, looking directly at her, I told her exactly what I felt about her and the real core of her identity as I sensed it. She became self-conscious of my acceptance, trying to doubt me. Finally, she relinquished her doubts, realizing that she had known me long enough to be able to trust my authentic reaction. "Maybe I won't have to be so sarcastic, and cut the men down so badly," she said.

Defining the Relationship

Neurotic conflict resolution in the sexual area almost always involves a relationship with another person, except for masturbation in isolation. Many unhappy relationships are possible, both heterosexual and homosexual. It is not within the scope of this book to discuss exhaustively these relationships. Rather, this chapter aims to demonstrate the use of the techniques of Psycho-Imagination Therapy in helping a patient achieve awareness of the mechanisms contributing to the definition of the relationship and in helping him change the way in which he is being defined by himself and by the significant other.

The man with an exceptionally controlling mother may find that he must control the woman with whom he is involved and, additionally, cannot tolerate commitment of almost any sort. Even commitment to non-sexual activities, such as therapy, may be difficult for him, and he may "flee" if he feels the therapist is controlling in the slightest way. This man may relate to women who are masochistically inclined, who to him, at any rate, are "inferior," and who seem to know no end to their ability to accept rejection in the name of "love."

The reaction is identical in women who have been overly controlled by their mothers and who have an enormous fear of disapproval. They look for men who are passive, masochistic, or near homosexual in order to control them. They control lest they be controlled. With such men or women, I ask them (IS), "Imagine your mother (father or significant other) is carrying *you* up a mountain. Tell me all the feelings and events in the journey." It is usually difficult for such people to sustain the position of the *other* person controlling their journey. It is as if they are on top of a broken ferris wheel and about to lose control and fall. The therapist must participate in the journey with the patient, encouraging him to cope with the loss of control. Sometimes, I may have the patient (IS) imagine he is on *my* back and I am carrying him up a mountain, until he can accept the fact that he must relinquish the need to maintain control.

Some mothers seduce their boys in such an encompassing manner that, indeed, it is difficult for women to compete with their mothers when they become adult males. The patient may even be married, but no woman can give him the total all-out acceptance and ego trip his mother offered — the "She doesn't love me like my mom" reaction. Concurrently, with such a protective mother, the man probably never quite learned to compete with other boys on a masculine level. He demands that his "needs" be met by his wife as his mother used to do. His own sexual pleasure is primary, almost to the exclusion of the sexual awareness of the woman. Why can't a woman be like his mom — and give him all?

Steve, an impotent patient with a strong necessity to define the relationship with his wife, was suffering from the "She doesn't love me like my mom" syndrome. To help him become aware of his sexual attitudes, I asked him (IS), "Imagine you and your wife are at the bottom of a dry well and a rope is lowered from the top." Steve closed his eyes and gave this vivid, non-stop account of the situation he was imagining:

♦ Mary and I are at the bottom of the well — naked. It's early afternoon and warm — our nakedness feels exhilarating. We're caressing and stroking each other, and now I get a fantastic, pulsating erection. Mary is ready, too, but all of a sudden I catch sight of the rope — and the sight jerks me into reality. Here we are at the bottom of the well — and there is a way to get out!

Quickly, I show Mary how to climb the rope and she starts up. Instead of following, I just watch her — her long legs, her nice, curvaceous breasts with the nipples pointing straight outward, her beautiful, smooth skin. As she gets higher, I can see her pubic hair from below. What a wonderful sight — viewing my wife's cunt from underneath, wrapped around that clean, long and solid white rope. Once more I feel desire welling up inside me and my prick gets hard again. I feel like wrapping my hand around it and jacking off — but, no — I'll save it for the beautiful love that is to come.

As soon as Mary reaches the top, I grab onto the rope and start pulling myself up. When I get to the top, there she is — waiting for me. It's a lovely place! Beautiful, green meadows with pretty yellow and white daisies everywhere. I take Mary's hand, and as I do, I get one of the largest erections ever. I pull Mary down on the warm grass and we kiss and stroke each other. The lovely juice starts to flow from her pussy and, together, we put my hot, throbbing cock into her well-moistened pussy. Slide in — slide out. My pelvis takes control. We find each other's groove and continue on, moaning with pleasure. The pleasure is the sun, the earth, the world and the universe all rolled into one. I feel Mary increasing the pace — faster, faster — reaching for her climax. I'm reaching, too. Faster and faster! Then, all at once it happens! We scream like children — no, not children — children don't possess sensuousness.

As our screams decrease to moans, our bodies relax and we kiss and stroke and gradually drift off to sleep. As I fall off to sleep, images appear. There I am back at my parents' house. Dad is off to work, and I walk into the house and into the living room. There's mom in her usual house dress. Curiously though, I don't have on a stitch of clothes! I look down at my body. Jesus! Here I am in my parents' house, without any clothes on, and with the most enormous hard-on I can ever remember having.

I'm somewhat embarrassed as I look at my mother. She says, "That's all right. I understand." How *can* she understand? She can't know what's on my mind. This hard-on isn't for her!

She says, "You know, Steve, I haven't had a good fuck in such a long time. Your father is useless. He thinks that a cock is to pee through. Why don't you fuck me?" I'm flabbergasted! "What are you saying?" I gasp. She talks some more and gradually the idea is more palatable. Why not? She comes closer and starts stroking my dick. I get turned on and suggest we go in the bedroom. We lie down on the bed, both of us now completely naked, and begin stroking, caressing and fondling each other in earnest. She becomes very excited and – to my surprise – so do I. She slides up and down my cock with her hand. I suck on her boobs – now one, now the other, her nipples getting harder and harder. When I reach between her legs, I feel the juice flowing. It's time. I mount her and slide my cock in and start pumping and pumping! She does also, and our pace becomes furious. Harder and harder we push against each other. With each thrust I can feel the delicious taste of come and fuck! Finally, like a burst of lightning, we come and come and come! Who would have believed it – my mother, the most unbelievably fantastic fuck of all time!

Then I wake up. Someone is caressing my cock. I open my eyes and see that I am at home in bed with Mary. I can't look at her body the way I did at my mother's! I turn away. The hard-on that I woke up with gradually disappears as I feel my wife's touch.

Maintaining the Stake in the Neurotic Conflict Resolution

In probably no area of human interaction is there as strong a need to maintain the dyadic homeostasis as there is in sexual relationships. The stake to maintain the neurotic position is exceptionally strong and the motivation to change is more critical than in any other kind of problem.

Max Frisch, in his brilliant novel, *I'm Not Stiller,* which concerns itself with the problem of a man's identity, shows how fear can perpetuate an unfortunate sexual relationship:

"Looking at these two people from the outside, one has the impression that Julika and the vanished Stiller were suited to one another in an unfortunate manner. They needed each other because of their fear. Whether rightly or wrongly, the beautiful Julika harbored a secret fear that she was not a woman. And Stiller too, it seems, was at the time perpetually afraid of being somehow inadequate; one is struck by the frequency with which this man felt he had to apologize. Julika has no idea of the cause of his anxiety. In fact, Julika never mentions the word anxiety when she is talking about her wretched marriage with the vanished Stiller; but almost everything she says points to the fact that she felt she could only hold Stiller through his bad conscience, through his fear of failure. She obviously didn't credit herself with being able to satisfy a real, free man, so that he would stay with her. One gets the impression that Stiller, too, clung to her weakness; another woman, a healthy woman, would have demanded strength from him or cast him aside. Julika couldn't cast him aside – she lived by having a husband whom she could continually forgive." (Frisch, 1958, p.73.)

Julika's inability to cast her husband aside even though her marriage was "wretched" illustrates aptly the dilemma of so many patients, in both heterosexual and homosexual relationships. In many neurotic relationships the participants are morbidly dependent on each other, so much so that they *cannot* sever the relationship no matter how painful, humiliating or degrading it is. Before attempting to change the relationship, the therapist must be certain that the patient *wants* to change, for the stake in maintaining it may be an immovable force. Many times it would be disastrous to suggest severing the relationship. Above all, the therapist must keep in mind that the objective of Psycho-Imagination Therapy is specifically to *change the way in which the individual is being defined by the other.* However, to challenge the stake in the neurotic conflict resolution requires the maximum cooperation of the patient.

The Focusing Techniques

When it comes to sexual problems, the liberation of the neurotic conflict resolution by the use of the focusing techniques is essentially the same as with any neurotic conflict, but with greater emphasis on the sexual traumatic incidents and related feelings. Traumatic incidents that have sexual connotations are reported more often in therapy than most any other. Psycho-Imagination Therapy techniques which help the patient recall the full feeling of these sexual traumatic incidents are a natural bridge to any of the focusing techniques presented in detail in Chapter V. Several of these focusing techniques are specifically related to sexual conflicts in the remainder of this chapter.

One patient who had great difficulty in maintaining an erection when he was first with a woman, spoke of a vivid sexual trauma when he was a boy. After his feelings had been fully and dramatically expressed in response to a Most-or-Least question and an Imaginary Situation, there was a natural transition to the Focusing Technique, "Break the Log Jam," which allowed him to liberate himself. Here is an account of the relevant portions of the actual therapy session:

Therapist: (M/L) What was the most vivid sexual experience of your childhood?

Patient: I remember one night in particular. I was not feeling well, my stomach hurt, and because of this my mother let me get into bed with her. I was, I believe, twelve at the time. On several occasions before this I had stomach pains, and getting into bed with her seemed to make me feel better. I don't think she would touch me – I vaguely remember a back rub – hers or mine, I don't know. On that night, I remember lying next to her, my stomach in knots, when suddenly I felt her against me. Not just her body, but her Mons Veneris, her vagina, pushed against me, on the side of my knee, and I turned to look at her. She was smiling and I think she pulled back then, slowly, and I can remember my feeling confused, very confused because I didn't know what she wanted. Was I to return the contact, push back against her and risk a gesture that could be thought of as nearly incestuous, or was I to ignore it, pretend or even try to believe that it was merely a coincidence, a misinterpreted body angle? I felt, at the time, sexual. I did not know precisely the mechanics of sexual intercourse, but I did know that the part of her body that had pressed against me was for sex, was the female equivalent to my penis. I was excited, I wanted to push back, wanted to continue something – what I didn't know – but the overall feeling was one of self-doubt. Did my mother want me to return her overtures, if indeed they were overtures, or was I imagining everything? Was she totally unaware of her movement – unaware of my excitment? My reaction seemed governed by three possibilities. I could return her pressure and be received sexually, for what or to what I didn't know. I could return her pressure and find out that I was wrong, that I was misconstruing a harmless thing (a motherly thing) and actually initiating a "perversion," the results of which seemed to me catastrophic because *I could be wrong* – not because sex with my mother was a particularly bad or good thing. Or I could lie there, freeze, and ignore the whole thing. I wondered, am I right, she wants me to – am I wrong, she doesn't. The *indecision* seems so crushing, not what I missed, not what I should or shouldn't have done but the *inability to act at all.* It reduced me, even to less than a child, a living thing, but sexless, inert. She seemed for that short time – the whole event lasted only about a minute, maybe less – very young and very evil. She dared me, she challenged me and I could not act, but because I didn't know if *I* was right or wrong. I froze, then I went to sleep and late that night, awoke, and went to my own bed. I felt alone, maybe ashamed.

Therapist: (IS) Imagine your mother's vagina on the wall.

Patient: I can see my mother's vagina on the wall, before me. It is large, four feet high, hairless for some reason, with the lips tightly closed. It undulates. It is not menacing in an aggressive sense, but it is indestructable. It can absorb, like tar. I throw spears at it. They are absorbed, sucked into it. I cannot destroy it, nor even hurt it. Like an amoeba, it can regenerate itself.

Therapist: (Focusing Technique) (At this time I asked the patient to attempt to destroy the vagina, to do something to it that would make him feel powerful rather than powerless. I asked him to (IS) Imagine shooting it with a mortar, (IS) running over it with a steamroller, and (IS) running a train into it. But the vagina absorbed or repelled anything that attacked it. I then asked him to (IS) imagine himself and his mother in bed.)

Patient: I can think of my mother and me in bed. The image of the "seduction" episode comes to my mind. Her next to me, neither motherly, nor as an absolute lover, but slightly, ever so slightly, pressuring me. Smiling, daring me, maybe in a state of amused expectation – I am to be a lark.

Therapist: (Focusing Technique) (IS) Push her out of bed.

Patient: That idea has great appeal. Now I can act, I don't have to guess anymore, I can finally do *something.* (Pause) I don't want her – I want to be able to decide how to act. (Smiling, he pushed her out – hard.) I feel like a man! Not a boy – not a sexless thing! I did what *I* want! Now I can say, "Mother, I want to fuck you," or "Mother, I don't want to fuck you" – whatever I want to say.

Therapist: (Focusing Technique) (IS) Now destroy the vagina!

Patient: I can! With an axe! Look, it's not absorbing the axe! I'll sever it, then cut it into a hundred pieces! (Violently chops with imaginary axe) It's not bleeding, but it's dead!

The patient finally allowed himself choice in relation to his mother, and this liberated him. Heretofore, as long as a woman would bestow choice or "allow" him to be sexual, his sexual immobilization (resulting in no erection) continued. Now he felt powerful, and having the right to define the relationship with a woman, his sexual problem gradually disappeared.

Another patient, about twenty-eight years of age, was troubled by a great fear of developing cancer. At an appropriate time during a therapy session, I asked him (IS), "Imagine taking a shower with your mother." His answer was, "This is very difficult to tell you ... but when I take a shower, I always see my mother behind me — but I am afraid to look. I expect her to clobber me in some way."

In subsequent sessions, it became apparent to both of us that he felt extreme guilt in his relationship with his mother. At one point, he spoke of having to imagine making love to his mother before he could achieve orgasm with his wife. I then asked him to (IS) imagine sucking on his mother's breast. He closed his eyes and related an experience he said he had imagined many times. Then he said, "You know, she walked around in the nude very often, sometimes lying on the bed nude. She drove me wild."

(IS) "Imagine your mother seducing you," I said.

He then went on to a detailed step-by-step description of the imagined seduction. He writhed and groaned between his explanations. Then he stopped talking and began to cry.

When he stopped crying, I encouraged him to scream at his mother (Focusing Technique) "The Impossible Scream."

There was a long pause and, then, with a powerfully loud scream, he said, "YOU SEDUCED ME — YOU BASTARD! YOU WANTED ME SEXUALLY. YOU DIDN'T WANT DAD. YOU TANTALIZED ME AND MADE ME FEEL LIKE I WAS SOME SORT OF A SEXUAL MONSTER."

I continued with the Focusing Technique (FTS), "I am not ____ ."

"I AM NOT GUILTY. YOU DROVE ME WILD — WHAT ELSE COULD I HAVE DONE? I AM NOT GUILTY FOR BEING SEXUAL TOWARD YOU. I always thought it was me. I was too guilty to live. You were everything to me and yet I was a heinous monster for wanting to ball you. I made you my moral judge. I'VE PUNISHED MYSELF ENOUGH!"

His face was calm as he turned away from his mother and to me, "I feel completely free of guilt for the first time in my life."

(IS) "Imagine taking a shower with your mother now," I said.

"I am not afraid of her behind my back any more," he said.

A month earlier, this patient had responded to my question (IS), "Imagine you plant your heart in the earth. What does it grow to?" by saying, "A tree that's full of cancer." A few sessions after the focusing experience of the imagined seduction, I repeated the "plant the heart" imaginary situation. This time he said, "A strong tree, like an oak, and it's growing upward to the sky." His fear of cancer disappeared gradually at first and, in a short time, completely.

Again, as in Chapter V, I must caution the reader that the use of the focusing techniques should not be based on "whim" or on "desperation" when all else fails. The patient is *not* ready for the focusing techniques until he has grown sufficiently in his awareness of his conflicts, he has developed sufficient trust in the therapist, and he has demonstrated an obvious increase of ego strength in group therapy interactions. Other factors also affect the patient's eligibility for the experience of the focusing techniques. (See page 65, Chapter V.)

When using the focusing techniques for sexual conflicts, the therapist must be even more cautious. Despite the overwhelming change in our society to greater openness and less guilt about sexual matters, there is a strong residue of guilt about sex and resultant self-punishment in many individuals. Probably there are more negative moral judgments about things sexual than any other subject. When I ask the question (M/L), "What is the most immoral act you can think of?" the great majority of responses definitely are in regard to sexuality.

The need for caution in using these techniques is apparent from the types of personal threatening questions which are involved. In using the focusing technique, "Body Holding and Touching," I may ask the following question (under the appropriate conditions of therapeutic development):

(IS) Imagine sucking your mother's breast.

(IS) Imagine you are inside your mother's vagina.

(IS) Imagine you are inside your father's penis.

(IS) Imagine your father is in your vagina (penis).

(IS) Imagine your mother is in your vagina (penis).

What do you feel? What will you do?

If the patient is not ready for these questions, the therapist can inflict more damage than if he had allowed the patient to continue with his unresolved conflict.

I believe the therapist who is able to utilize these specific imaginary situations at the appropriate moments will find that the patient's responses will indicate feelings and experiences that relate to the totality of the interaction between himself and others and not merely to his sexual interactions.

CHAPTER 7

Use of Psycho-Imagination Therapy to Break "Impasse" in Therapy

"The problem is no longer 'Who am I?' but rather 'Even if I know who I am, can I have any influence, any significant impact on the world and the people around me?' "

Rollo May

"I wanted only to try to live in accord with the promptings which came from my true self. Why was that so very difficult?"

Herman Hesse

I had asked a colleague of mine, as a sort of exploratory experiment, to send me any one of his patients, with whom he had been using conventional psycho-therapy, for a session using psycho-imagination therapy techniques. The session was to be taped and Dr. X and I then were to listen to the tape together and discuss the session. I was attempting to assess the effectiveness of the psycho-imagination therapy techniques on a patient completely unknown to me. (As an added parameter, it so happened that the patient sent to me by Dr. X had reached an impasse in therapy with him. However, I was completely unaware of this fact until I met with Dr. X a few weeks later.)

In a week, I heard from a man who said that Dr. X had sent him to me for a session of some "wild questions." We made an appointment, and he arrived in a tee shirt and slacks, quite tall, muscular and very fast-talking. The only thing I knew about him in advance was his name — Hugh — and nothing more.

What follows is a complete transcript of the tape between this man and myself. A second column appears, which contains comments between Dr. X and myself from our discussion after hearing the tape of Hugh's session with me. These comments are juxtaposed next to the passage in the therapy to which they relate. The psycho-imagination therapy techniques are identified by the abbreviations (IS), (S&O), (M/L), and (FTS). Thus, the reader can see how these techniques are interwoven with supportive and interpretive remarks.

It should be pointed out that, because of the unusual situation, the psycho-imagination therapy techniques used were essentially those useful in revealing internal conflicts; the focusing techniques were used sparingly.

Therapy Tape

Shorr: (M/L) The first thing I was going to ask you is what is the easiest for you to give of the following four: money, sex, feelings, or intellect?

Hugh: Oh, intellect is much easier for me to give of the four.

Shorr: (M/L) And what is the most difficult?

Hugh: I guess either, I guess feelings or sex. Feelings, I guess!

Shorr: (IS) I want you to imagine that you are in a room and there is a thin wall and unidentifiable people are talking about you; they don't know that you are there. What are they saying about you?

Hugh: Well, they might start off by saying good things they'd seen on the surface, how I handle my job or how I conduct myself in places. But then they kind of have an uneasiness because they think there is something, like something not quite right, behind all the facade.

Shorr: Something not quite right? What would they actually be saying about you, Hugh?

Discussion by Doctors X and Shorr

Dr. X: What he brings out is that he has to look right because others always have more power than he does. They are always stronger and they can hurt him and manipulate him. And he always puts it in terms of power scenes, but what I think he really feels is that they have the power to make him feel good or bad about himself, to feel he exists or he doesn't exist. This is the kind of real power they have. And he doesn't feel it in himself. He *does* somewhat in the classroom – like he said he can give intellect easily, but feeling is hardest, then sex is next. He didn't talk about money. Although he is very tight – he is a terrible tight-wad.

Shorr: Yes, I can sense that.

Dr. X: Right. But he sees that the problem is more a matter of giving of himself and his feelings, and not the money thing so much.

Shorr: Well, I mean if you are tight with money, quite often you are going to be tight with feelings, too, as a defensive thing.

Hugh: Well, they might be saying they don't know whether they could really trust me because I seem to be all right, but sometimes it looks as though certain areas of my life are like vacant or not quite right in some way – like I'm too self-conscious or worried about myself.

Shorr: But you are telling me what you are saying about yourself – now what would they say about you? Do you get my point?

Hugh: Yes. (Pause) "I wonder what his sex life is like." (Pause) Well, actually, I don't think that the people I work with or the people I know would think about that, because everything seems to be all right, but I sort of imagine the fears I've got brought that out. Then . . . "There is just kind of an uneasiness about him that comes through in unguarded moments or something like that when he's not watching himself too carefully."

Shorr: (IS) Well, let's go on to another one then and maybe go back to that later, and that is if you were to look into a mirror (and this is kind of hard) – a full length mirror – but instead of seeing yourself you see somebody else. Whom would you see? Who comes to mind?

Hugh: I still see myself, but I'd see myself a lot better – the way I'd like to be here.

Shorr: No, but what I want you to do is to try to see if you can see somebody else. I know it is very hard, very difficult to do.

Hugh: Well, I'd see a good looking fellow who is sharp or sort of self-assured and sort of boyish-like and friendly — just the kind that girls would really dig.

Shorr: (M/L) Then who in this world do you think the girls dig more than anybody else? Any one person you can think of?

Hugh: No. I can think of a lot of types, a lot of . . .

Shorr: (M/L) Well, I want you to name somebody though — a specific person that girls dig most in the world.

Hugh: They all dig this physics teacher I work with.

Shorr: Physics teacher? Why do they dig him?

Hugh: Because he is well built, he's sure of himself and yet he's got — oh, like, I don't know — like, he's got some funny thoughts. He talks a lot about suicide and a lot of girls want to help him and get hooked in with him in some way.

Shorr: (S&O) So you think people like to help men that look in need?

Hugh: Well, if they are basically sure of themselves, but they can open up a bit and show that they really need a girl, or something like that.

Shorr: (M/L) Of all the people you know, or have known, who shows their needs the most in this world? (Pause) Who exposes their needs the most in this world?

Hugh: (Slight pause) I can't think of anyone that shows his needs.

Shorr: (M/L) Well, of all the people you know, if you can take a guess even — who do you think exposes their needs the most of anyone you've ever known?

Hugh: I guess Dr. X.

Shorr: You mean he's open about it?

Hugh: He's open and he goes after what he wants, but I haven't seen it like in a sex scene or anything like that. I just imagine that if he wanted somebody he would show it. (Pause) I just haven't had that much experience in seeing people actually showing their needs. I cut off when I see anything like that.

Shorr: You cut off?

Hugh: Yeah.

Shorr: You block out, you mean?

Hugh: I block it out like I don't see it. Well, there was a girl I used to know and she used to always show her needs — it would be all over her face and you could just see it. She didn't humiliate herself, but she showed it really strong — there was just no doubt about it.

Shorr: (IS) Now suppose you walked into a room and there was a girl who was showing and wanting sexual involvement, but showing her sexual needs, not all her other psychological needs, but ⟷ **Dr. X:** But I think the important thing I get from this is how much he needs to be pressed into exposing and taking a firmer position about himself and remaining with it, because he is aways

(Continued on next page)   *(Continued on next page)*

just pure sexual needs. You walk into that room and she's on the bed, in the nude, showing her sexual needs primarily. How would you feel?

Hugh: It would get me up-tight. I'd want to get out of there.

Shorr: You'd want to run?

Hugh: Yeah. Oh, I might — no I wouldn't run right away — I wouldn't want her to think I was frightened, so I'd try to play some kind of game where I'd look like I'd want her but yet I thought it was inappropriate or not right, so I'd come off looking O.K. — even though I'd hide the fact that I wouldn't want to do anything. No, I'd be afraid to try — it's not that I wouldn't want anything.

Shorr: You mean you'd want to try but you'd be afraid to?

Hugh: Yeah.

Shorr: (S&O) But most of all you would want to look right.

Hugh: Yeah. I'd want to get out of there, but I'd want to look right about it — like I was O.K., just that I decided, against my real wants and desires, that it would be best to leave.

Shorr: (IS) Now for a moment I want to switch over and I want you to imagine you are on the top of a mountain and you see in front of you a huge battle field, and there's an army on the left side and on the other side is another army. Now, using your imagination, I want you to name the two armies that you can see from the mountain. (Pause) Can you give them a name?

Hugh: Well, I'd say on the left I'd see a whole bunch of nutty kind of radicals — the ones who scream and holler and have a lot a hate even though they talk about love and everything. (Pause) I don't know, on the right I'd like to see some of these paranoiac right wingers.

(Continued on next page)

removing himself to a more rear guard position. Most of the time he actually doesn't even get into an assertive role of any kind, except in intellectual conflicts with people.

Shorr: Like, if he can't control it and dominate it, then he has to look right and look cool in a situation that he's not.

Dr. X: Yes, then he postures — he postures very well — he can posture with a girl like he is really all turned on. It's an interesting kind of convolution that he goes through. He really can be turned on by women, but he will not expose that to a woman — not the genuine basic feelings — so then what he does, he goes through like a series of numbers — he's anxious about it and frightened about exposing it and then he takes up a defensive posture of pretending that he is turned on. It's very reminiscent of the way Laing describes three different positions of the self. The real problem in therapy is really how to get him to feel safe about taking up the first position, the genuine position.

Shorr: I tried to get at the internal struggles with the two armies and other situations where one side has one adjective versus the other — stronger or weaker. Who wins or who doesn't win? But he gave them both equal power and they destroyed themselves. From there I switched on to other things.

Dr. X: Actually, I feel he is very resentful of anybody that takes a strong, intense emotional position. So he is very resentful of the radical left *and* of the radical right. At one time he used to ride around in his cars, years ago, with Nazi insignias on his car.

Shorr: Really, I didn't know that.

Dr. X: That's right. This was in his earlier years in college, and he used to take a certain delight in antagonizing

(Continued on next page)

I'd like to see them both just go out and kill each other off and yet, I'd like to see somebody win, so I don't know – it's a bad scene.

Shorr: It looks like no winner, huh?

Hugh: No winner, unless it's people I liked, or have shared the same ideas on one side. Then I'd like to see them win and just really humiliate and annihilate the other side, or the people I've disagreed with or argued with.

Shorr: (IS) Who would you put as general of each army?

Hugh: (Pause) I can't even think of one person. I just saw two masses going at each other without any leadership.

Shorr: (IS) Suppose you have to give, for all purposes here, a general, let's say, for each army, or whatever you want to call a leader.

Hugh: Oh, I think I'd like to see Johnson and Humphrey and McGovern and people like that on one side, all fighting McCarthy and a whole bunch of wilted lotus blossoms on the other side. Not to the point of being annihilated but just overwhelmed and maybe admit that they have been a little bit arrogant before.

Shorr: (IS) Now I want you to imagine that you are in a meadow. How does the meadow look to you?

people, you know, by having these insignias because there was still then some remnants of anti-Nazism and anti-Fascism. His father has at times taken a kind of rightist position – oh, he is not a real right-winger – I don't think his father is very political at all. But Hugh now has a kind of intense dislike for any militant political position. Right or left.

Shorr: The stronger the position that the other person takes the more it forces him into a position of defensiveness.

Dr. X: That's right. And real hostility about them. He would just like to see them all wiped out – any militant person – militant black . . .

Shorr: He doesn't want to let them know about it.

Dr. X: Oh, no. He won't. Well, he does with a couple of the people he rents rooms to in his house – who have been pretty left. He's had some pretty vociferous arguments with them. But ordinarily he doesn't – he stays away from these arguments. But he can with these people, because they are kind of inferior to him as he sees it; he has control over them through their low rental.

Shorr: The control is very, very important to him.

Hugh: Oh, I can see that real well. It's with mountains surrounding it, but way in a distance. The meadow is very high up in the mountains some place and very few people can get there. Sort of like my meadow – I go there and take the people I want and just sort of completely relax and lie down on the grass and try to get completely relaxed and get away from all kinds of nervousness and tension and all that kind of stuff.

Shorr: And you can feel real good and relaxed, huh?

Hugh: Yeah, I probably could. I'd like to try it.

Shorr: (IS) Can you try and just imagine that you are there, and be as relaxed as you know how?

Hugh: Yeah, I can be as relaxed as I know how, but in the back of my mind there would be all kinds of thoughts like what I'm going to do in the future – like I'd solve my problems and everything and maybe for a couple of hours I could just completely relax and take it in.

Shorr: And just lie in the grass, you mean, and relax?

Hugh: Yeah.

Shorr: (IS) Can you fall asleep?

Hugh: Oh yeah, I can easily fall asleep.

Shorr: (IS) Now, I want you to imagine a wild animal coming on the scene while you are in the meadow, by yourself there. Can you imagine a wild animal?

Hugh: Yeah.

Shorr: (IS) What wild animal do you imagine?

Hugh: Oh, I don't know — it's like a bear or tiger — a whole bunch of things just all wrapped in one — just a big mess.

Shorr: (M/L) But if you could pick one, which one would you pick?

Hugh: Well, I've never seen that many animals up close. It's got to be violent and powerful and move fast. I guess a bear would do, but it would have to be a super-deluxe bear though, really.

Shorr: A super-deluxe bear?

Hugh: Yeah. They seem too heavy and awkward and I want somebody to be a real menace.

Shorr: You'd want somebody to be a real menace?

Hugh: Yeah.

Shorr: You would demand this, in your imagination?

Hugh: I mean the kind of animal I would imagine coming at me. It wouldn't do me any good by imagining it would be a menace. A real slick, fast animal that had a tremendous amount of force.

Shorr: And you say this is a bear?

Hugh: Yeah. It's about the only kind of animal I can imagine in the mountains. It's got to be pretty agile, pretty fast on its feet.

Shorr: It sounds as though it is awfully big, too.

Hugh: Yeah, it's pretty big.

Shorr: (IS) Can you imagine this animal coming at you? Is that what you would do?

Hugh: Yeah, I can. I could either play a game or sort of pacify it in some way by acting harmless and everything, or I might be in a mood where I felt like I might want to challenge it, like, dominate it, or get mastery over it.

Shorr: Fine. (IS) Why don't you look into the eyes of that bear? Can you? Can you imagine the eyes of that bear?

Hugh: Yeah, it's frightened, too.

Shorr: (IS) (Focusing Tech.) Keep staring at his eyes . . . Can you imagine it now? Keep staring at them — until it seems like they are transformed into something else. Now what do the eyes look like?

Hugh: Well, it looks like my dad when he's in a rage and it looks like he's got some kind of sharp thing in his hand, raised to hit or strike.

Shorr: (IS) (Focusing Tech.) Now look into the bear's eyes until they are transformed into something *other* than that. (Pause) Can you imagine that?

Hugh: I can't really see anything, but I got a feeling like the thing had started to be friendly and I was sort of smiling at him.

Shorr: In other words, the eyes have changed?

Hugh: Well, I didn't actually see a change. I think I changed.

Shorr: Into friendliness? (IS) (Focusing Tech.) Now, I want you to imagine the bear changes into friendliness in its eyes. Can you do that?

Hugh: Yeah, I wouldn't know what to do, though.

Shorr: (IS) (Focusing Tech.) I want you to imagine, though, that it is so. Can you imagine that it's friendly — the eyes of the bear?

Hugh: Yeah, it's friendly and wants to be friendly but it looks like it expects something of me, like I am supposed to be responding to that friendliness.

Shorr: You mean it puts a demand upon you?

Hugh: Yeah.

Shorr: (IS) All right. I want you to do this, then — I want you to climb up on the bear and, uh . . .

Hugh: Ride it like a horse or dominate it you mean?

Shorr: (IS) Ride it like a horse and dominate it, as you say, and see if you can tell me how it feels to climb up to the mountain top and you are going along a direction and you are having a climb up the mountain top. Describe the countryside.

Hugh: I think the bear would get tired and wouldn't want to play that game.

Shorr: It's going to stop?

Hugh: Yeah. Like I couldn't get it to go along as long as I wanted. I just don't feel like it was giving me as long or as much as I wanted. Like half way up I couldn't even enjoy the trip thinking that any minute the bear would give up on that kind of game, he wouldn't really want to go on. So I couldn't really relax.

Shorr: (IS) O.K. Now what kind of a road do you see up — a path?

Hugh: Well, sort of rocky, then all of a sudden it gets real steep so some of it is straight up where you fall and come sliding down.

Shorr: (IS) Now I want you to imagine, though, that the road is passable up to the top. I mean, use your imagination and in a sense, like, force yourself, as you say, dominate the bear to go up that side of the mountain. (Pause) So that you don't fall back. Can you do that?

Hugh: Yeah, then the bear turns into a donkey or something.

Shorr: (IS) Now, as you are climbing up this path, what does the countryside look like now — now that you are able to go up?

Hugh: Well, it is just a little tiny, narrow road on one side and on the left side is a huge, steep bank, and on the right is another steep bank all the way down. It looks like it is miles down.

Shorr: (IS) What sort of vegetation do you see around there?

Hugh: Well, there are trees way in the background but, where we are, there is just nothing but rock and . . .

Shorr: (IS) But I want you to imagine that there is some sort of greenery where you are. Can you imagine that?

Hugh: All that comes to mind is like a path in the mountains, you know, where it's a dirt path and all around are trees and things hanging over.

Shorr: That's a lot easier to climb up that way. Isn't it?

Hugh: Yeah, you can just sort of take your time. You aren't under any pressure to get to the top.

Shorr: (IS) Now I want you to still think you are on the bear and . . .

Hugh: (Interrupts) It just reduces so tiny, that . . .

Shorr: What reduces so tiny?

Hugh: (In a very tired voice) The bear gets so tiny, it's not even any support any more.

Shorr: You mean you can't, or find it very difficult, to sustain the bear's size as it goes up the hill?

Hugh: Yeah, it gets to be the size of a dog and all I want to do is pet the little thing. I don't want to force it to do anything.

Shorr: (IS) Now can you imagine the bear back the way it was originally and . . .

Hugh: Yeah, it's coming right at me again.

Shorr: In other words, it's now a danger.

Hugh: Yeah.

Shorr: O.K., now (IS) I want you to imagine that you have a machine gun, and I want you to shoot that bear down. Can you imagine that?

Hugh: (In an eager voice) Oh yeah, that's a good feeling. I feel safe. I'd just shoot and have an inexhaustible supply of rounds and just keep shooting at it.

Shorr: (IS) What happens to the bear?

Hugh: Oh, it's already gone, I'm just worried about the other people coming at me now.

Shorr: Other people?

Hugh: Oh, from all sides they come after me for having killed something that was friendly, or an animal, or something.

Shorr: Who are these people?

Hugh: Oh, it just looks like a rabble or just irate citizens coming at me — just shoot them all down.

Shorr: O.K., (IS) now imagine that you ⟷ **Dr. X:** So, what I'm talking about is this
are in a courtroom and you are sitting in   repetitive theme where he is asked to be
the courtroom and a judge is there and a   angry, expresses the anger or rage, but

(Continued on next page)   *(Continued on next page)*

lawyer is accusing you of shooting that bear. How do you feel?

Hugh: Well, I feel sort of guilty and bad that people would think of me as that sort of person or that I would act that way when actually I feel inside I am not that way — I wish I hadn't killed the bear.

Shorr: (IS) (Focusing Tech.) Now I want you to imagine that you stand up in the box in the courtroom and you accuse the accusers — tell me what you say — I mean actually tell me — imagine that you are actually talking to them.

Hugh: I mean I'd rather, like, slip out — like, get on the floor real quickly — zoom out of the area and they would never catch me again.

Shorr: (IS) (Focusing Tech.) Hugh, I know what your feeling is, but I want you to stand up to your accusers — now speak to them as if you were actually talking to them — if you don't mind.

Hugh: Well, I'd say . . .

Shorr: (IS) (Focusing Tech.) Talk as if you were talking to them. Use first person.

Hugh: (Rather like a recitation, with little feeling) "I'm sorry I did it. I'll never do it again — I just was frightened — I didn't know what else to do — you have to understand that I'm just not an animal killer, and I hate all of you for taking that attitude that you are all so superior — you've probably done worse things than that — and you're accusing me."

then won't affirm himself about the rage. Like this courtroom scene. He will not actually defend himself in the attacking way; he has to rationalize, and this is very typical of him. Somehow he will present himself in some way with anger or other kinds of emotions — it doesn't seem to be with just anger at all. And then he removes his presence and he then postures, or he will then cater to the other and he just tunes into what the other person wants from him — he really loses his own impact presence. It's like he empties himself to another position. It's very, very typical of him. And when he does that, I expect him to be depressed. I mean, that what will come next will be that he will start to feel very unworthy — to feel he was doing this to protect himself because people had more power than he does. And that is what he was saying, that people have more power than he does. So he can't have an attacking position. He has to have a very defensive rationalizing position.

Shorr: The thing that struck me at that point, because I hadn't really seen or known anything about him at all except his name, was the fact that he always had to turn out to be right in a situation — look right to the world. That's what came to me at that point, not knowing anything else.

Shorr: (Focusing Tech.) That's a defensive answer — I want you to give me an attacking answer back to them without rationalizing — without . . .

Hugh: (Angrily) I know, but if I'm defending in court, I'm going to watch what I say.

Shorr: What's that?

Hugh: If I'm in a court situation, I'd watch what I say.

Shorr: Why?

Hugh: I'd have to win the thing that's all. (Pause) Oh, I can imagine myself getting violent, just screaming and hollering all kinds of . . .

Shorr: Why don't you do that?

Hugh: Creepy people.

Shorr: Yes. (IS) (Focusing Tech.) Attack your accusers.

Hugh: (Pause) It's like it is too much of a struggle — I wouldn't even bother with them. (This last in a disdainful tone)

Shorr: Yeah, but what happens to you by not struggling and not accusing the accusers when they are wrong? You obviously feel they are wrong.

Hugh: Yes, but then, they've still got more power so I'll just think to myself that I am right and try to sneak out of the situation.

Shorr: You still want to run.

Hugh: Well, not run. I feel better now. I want to stand to defend myself and handle that situation very well so that I get acquitted — there's no more turmoil to the whole thing — if I could get my hands on those people, I'd just pummel them.

Shorr: (S&O) In other words, you have two sets of things going?

Hugh: Yeah.

Shorr: One is the defense that makes you look all right . . .

Hugh: The practical thing, yeah, to get out of that bad situation.

Shorr: To look all right, and the other is your real feelings.

Hugh: Yeah.

Shorr: Which is to really attack the accusers because you did nothing wrong.

Hugh: (Hesitates) Yeah. (In a rather wondering tone)

Shorr: After all, if an animal was menacing you and you killed it, it certainly was not a thing that was a . . .

Hugh: Yeah, but I'd assume that I was wrong. Then when the rage comes out I'd feel that I was really right, but it wasn't that clear in my mind.

Shorr: (S&O) You mean that if there are situations in which there's a possibility of being right and wrong, you invariably choose the position that you are wrong?

Hugh: Yeah, I think I do and I try to find a sneaky way to get out of it, too.

Shorr: (M/L) Who is the sneakiest person you've ever known?

Hugh: I thought that my dad was pretty sneaky — now I'm beginning to think that my mother is pretty sneaky, too.

Shorr: (IS) Tell me this, if your dad would look into a full length mirror and he would see someone other than himself — which again is tough to do — who would he see?

Hugh: I thought that he might see me, which seems strange, but he might. Because he thinks of me as a success but he doesn't know some of the problems I've got. He might think that would be kind of nice, if I did some of the things that he wanted me to do. (Pause) I imagine that when my dad looks at himself he probably has creepy feelings, but then he probably sees himself better than he is, kind of, the image he makes up for himself.

Shorr: But he does see you other than himself?

Hugh: Oh, he did at first, but then I also think that he would see himself — sort of glorified or (pause) I'm not sure, really.

Shorr: (IS) I know it's a rather tough imaginative situation, but if you were to imagine your mother now looking in the mirror and she is to see someone other than herself, who does she see?

Hugh: Well, she really couldn't — all she'd see is just a sick blob. She really can't get out of herself that much.

Shorr: (IS) No, but if you try — it's a difficult one, I know, but try to see if you can imagine anyone that she might see other than herself. Who might it be?

Hugh: A young, slender woman who was very confident, who went out a lot, and did all kinds of things. (Pause) I really would see my mother seeing herself differently rather than another person. It would be, in effect, like another person, but it would be what she wanted to be, I guess.

Shorr: (IS) Now I want you to imagine two fighters in a ring. Can you imagine that?

Hugh: Yeah.

Shorr: (IS) All right now, can you describe the two fighters to me? Cause I don't know what you are seeing in your imagination.

Hugh: Oh, one is black and one is white — and maybe it's just because I saw the sports pages today for a fight. Muscular and powerful and sort of dumb looking. It looks like they have fast reflexes, though.

Shorr: (IS) Can you give an adjective for each of the fighters?

Hugh: Tough, that's all.

Shorr: Are they different adjectives, or do they both have the same adjectives?

Hugh: Well, the black man seems a little more intelligent, or with it some way.

Shorr: (IS) And who wins in this fight?

Hugh: Oh, I keep seeing the thing from the paper . . . I guess the white guy wins — somehow I can see he was stronger and he beat the other guy.

Shorr: (IS) In what round?

Hugh: Oh, I imagine the thing goes on a long time — it's not a real clearcut thing — they just give the decision to the white fighter.

Shorr: (M/L) Who carries the most authority in the world for you today? You understand what I mean by that?

Hugh: Well, I guess the chairman of my department. I mean from a practical level. (Pause) And about personal relations, I think Dr. X does. But I don't feel it very strongly, I'm just saying it.

Shorr: You don't feel that very strongly?

Hugh: No.

Shorr: (M/L) Who really carries the most authority for you in this world?

Hugh: I think I do. It's stubbornness or arrogance. I'm convinced that I'm right or at least that what I want I . . . oh, I don't know.

Shorr: (M/L) Who is the most dominant person you've ever known in your life?

Hugh: Well, I just can't imagine the past right now, but I think I am, but I . . . I really am.

Shorr: (M/L) Who is the most competitive person you've known in your life? ⟷

Hugh: Oh, that's me! (Definite tone)

Shorr: You are?

Hugh: Yeah.

Shorr: How do I know that? I mean, I'm essentially a stranger to you. How could you prove that to me so I can understand it? You know what I mean?

Dr. X: You know, he is physically very strong. He rides his bike way in from the West side all the way out to my office. He's got a racer. He can ride his bike 40 miles in a day. He's got muscles like iron. We've had a couple of physical scenes with him in group, where we put him on the floor and stepped on him because he was always talking about being stepped on. We just put him on the floor and people just stepped on him. Well, he was like a piece of iron. He just rigidified all of his muscles and just couldn't be hurt.

Shorr: I wonder why he has to be so strong . . . he's so weak, huh?

Hugh: Well, like when I'm on the road, ⟷ someone gets in front of me and I've got to fight that impulse all the time to get ahead of them to show them they had no right to get in front of me. I always wanted everything for myself. I wouldn't cut somebody's throat, but I would sure advance my own ends, by posing and doing all kinds of things like that.

Dr. X: Yes. He's so strong, he said, to be ready to defend himself against anything — anybody who would try to attack him or hurt him. He drives extremely defensively and paranoid on the road. It turns out to be pretty safe for him — I don't think he has ever had an accident.

Shorr: Posing?

Hugh: That's right.

Shorr: (S&O) Winning is more important than anything else on earth?

Hugh: Yeah.

Shorr: (M/L) Who do you most admire in this world?

Hugh: Well, I hate people who can go out and get what they want, but sometimes I think I wish I could be in their skin. Just do the same thing.

Shorr: Well, I doubt it.

Dr. X: But he's always jumping ahead of people and he's always watching out to see if you are trying to screw him on the road — that whole paranoic thing.

Shorr: You should engage him in a hand-squeezing contest or something. I've got a strong hand, but I don't know if I am as strong as he is.

Dr. X: I don't think I'm as strong as he is.

Shorr: I don't know if it would do any good.

Shorr: Like whom do you know? Or have ever known?

Hugh: (Pause) Well, some fellows who would just go out and grab girls and just go after what they wanted, or people who could just study for hours every day without getting all nervous about not being able to do it and just getting what they want — that's all.

Shorr: (S&O) If you have an argument with someone, do you have to win?

Hugh: Yeah. He couldn't change my viewpoints to win or anything.

Shorr: (S&O) Then, winning is the most important thing on earth.

Hugh: Yeah.

Shorr: (S&O) Sometimes, you sell your soul to win.

Hugh: (Pause) (Defensively) Yeah, I would, but I'd do it thinking to myself it would still be me, it wouldn't . . . I don't see it as selling my soul. I see it like cutting out from people when what we're arguing about is less important than something else going on.

Shorr: You mean the most important thing is to win — and therefore you can rationalize everything else away.

Hugh: Yes, but I'm also aware of the fact that I'm just cutting people off and putting distance between us and protecting myself. If I can win, at least I can go away looking good — you know? I can think faster, talk faster — I'd even use mean-type arguments sometimes. They would certainly have been unaware that I was sticking a knife in them.

Shorr: (M/L) So, who do you admire most in this world? If you can name one person.

Hugh: (Short pause) Well, I think I admire Johnson a lot. I accept some of his early stuff. He seems like a person who went ahead and did things and got things done.

Shorr: Regardless?

⟷ Dr. X: You brought out the fact that he has to win and I feel this is his way of winning — it's a way that he has construed — interpreted as a form of winning and . . .

Shorr: To deny need, you mean?

Dr. X: To deny his own wanting and needs. He doesn't deny some feelings — for example, anger — he's gotten freer with anger — I mean, he got quickly into an altercation with you. But the feelings that have to do with getting close, he absolutely fights off. The closest he comes is to feeling a certain sadness that he lacks this close contact, but even that is minimal. He will really fight that off, and I think he has this all developed out in a system that he wins by not doing. He describes this funny kind of analogy — he has a rope that goes around a pole and is tied around his own neck, and the harder he pulls on the rope to try and do something, the more he is pulling his own neck.

Shorr: That's the bind he's in.

Dr. X: And the more the group exhorts him, the more that I prod him, when I think he is close to real feeling, to help him express it, that's when he must fight. So we have come to the conclusion — the group has and I have — that we are not going to get into a competitive thing with him about expressing feelings. Well, we have been doing this for several months, and that is, we just leave it up to his own initiative — when he feels he can express and he knows

(Continued on next page)

(Continued on next page)

Hugh: Regardless, yeah.

Shorr: (M/L) Do you feel that accomplishment is the most important thing in the world?

Hugh: I act that way, but I don't really believe it.

Shorr: What do you believe?

Hugh: I'd like to get some warm relationships and really get some real love and affection from a girl. (Voice softens) I'd feel really at ease with myself about a thing like that.

that we are not going to push him, then he will. But he's now twisting it again by saying, well, we are waiting for him to do it. If we're waiting for him to do it, *he* is not going to initiate it because that would mean that he is admitting that for all these years he could have been doing it, you see. So he would be defeated again. (See pp. 110 and 127.)

Shorr: His competitiveness, I know. Waiting everyone out again.

Dr. X: So obviously we haven't yet cut through that competitive defense.

Shorr: (IS) If you had a two-sound tape recorder, you know, the kind where you can . . .
Hugh: Get sound on sound or something.

Shorr: (IS) But you can talk two ways into it — one, your feelings; and the other, your behavior in actions.

Hugh: (Quickly) Yeah, I could. My behavior in actions would show aggressiveness, but sort of toned down so that it doesn't offend people that it would be dangerous to offend, so to do it secretly — in a sneaky way. I know they would be crying out to get some of the good stuff — the stuff I really want.

Shorr: (S&O) So you approach people on a two-dimensional level — hoping that they really find out what your real motives are?

Hugh: Yeah, hoping that somehow I can break through and be nice. I get a real warm relationship going but then am never able to do it because . . . like I'm watching everything I'm doing and saying and I just can't relax enough.

Shorr: I mean you sound like you are eternally vigilant.

Hugh: Oh, yeah.

Shorr: Against what?

Hugh: (Pause) I don't know. It just seems that I have to be that way.

Shorr: (S&O) What should I never refer to you as, Hugh? Never call you what?

Hugh: Creepy or disgusting or . . . (Pause)

Shorr: Disgusting?

Hugh: Yeah.

Shorr: Never call you creepy?

Hugh: Never call me self-conscious. That's the thing that always used to bug me.

Shorr: Self-conscious?

Hugh: Yeah.

Shorr: You mean like shy and . . .

Hugh: Not just shy. It's sort of like that, but always being embarrassed about being shy or ill at ease. It's not so much being, as the . . . (Pause)

Shorr: As the appearance of it?

Hugh: Yeah, that horrible feeling of showing that you feel bad about it. Well, you could be shy and everything, and blush a little bit, but to me it seems that I have such a terrible image of the whole thing. That comes through more than anything else.

Shorr: In other words, you always want to appear cool? Is that what you are saying?

Hugh: Yes, I'd like to appear cool, but I wish I could let some of the embarrassment or naturalness out. I can't be natural, because I'm so afraid of looking . . . of showing anybody that I have this sort of creepy feeling about myself.

Shorr: In other words, if you were to let your feelings out, you are afraid that your feelings would look creepy to the world.

Hugh: Yeah, that's right.

Shorr: So, you have to put a guard on them?

Hugh: Yeah. And look cool. Yeah, that's it. I'm trying to get away from that a little bit.

Shorr: You sound like if you showed your real feelings, that people would assume that you were out of control or creepy?

Hugh: Yeah, or just excessive in some way.

Shorr: Excessive feelings?

Hugh: Yeah.

Shorr: (M/L) What is the most excessive feeling you have?

Hugh: It's that horrible sensation like maybe I'll be so humiliated it would be like hot water was poured all over me.

Shorr: Hot water was poured over you?

Hugh: Or boiling water or just . . .

Shorr: Who is going to pour that hot water over you?

Hugh: I mean that is just the sensation. I don't see anybody doing it. It's more like I'm doing it myself.

Shorr: To yourself?

Hugh: Yeah.

Shorr: (IS) And what happens to you if hot water were actually poured over you?

Hugh: Oh, I'd jump fast and get out of the way and minimize the damage and quickly put some burn salve on, or something, or get it taken care of or . . . it seems like I could handle that, really. I would get out of the way so it wouldn't get on my face. It would get on my arms or some place. It wouldn't be that terrible.

Shorr: (S&O) You seem to be so concerned about how you look to other people.

Hugh: Yeah.

Shorr: (S&O) Like you have got to look perfect all the time.

Hugh: Yeah.

Shorr: (S&O) No matter how embarrassing the situation, you've got to straighten it up like a gyroscopic instrument on a cord, that will always fly right.

Hugh: Yeah.

Shorr: What happens to you when you get a real drunk on?

Hugh: I can't get really that drunk. I can have eight or ten drinks ... No, sometimes when I get really tight I just forget myself a little bit and ... Actually I think — I don't know that I'd ever get — I mean I've gotten sort of close to people without really getting drunk.

Shorr: Is that kind of a convenient excuse to show your feelings?

Hugh: Yeah, it's like anything I do there, it is more, it's understandable — it can always be explained by having too much to drink.

Shorr: (M/L) What is your most favorite rationalization?

Hugh: I can't even think, how do you mean rationalization?

Shorr: Well, you seem to be so concerned about how you appear all the time to others, as you say. I wonder if you have a kind of a favorite rationalization you use to make it appear that you are cool? Or in control, or whatever you want to say?

Hugh: Well, with all the people I know I can always be cool enough so I don't really have to do anything. Sometimes I'm ... sometimes I feel awfully tired and low so I just say I'm not feeling well. I'll just say I'm not feeling well or I've got the flu or something like that.

Shorr: You mean you usually use some bodily ...

Hugh: Yeah, or something.

Shorr: (S&O) Are you a fake, Hugh?

Hugh: I feel I am most of the time.

Shorr: How do you feel about me asking you since, again, I hardly know you?

Hugh: It's sort of impersonal — I mean I don't ...

Shorr: It's O.K. with me then, huh?

Hugh: Yeah.

Shorr: Well, that's good. I'm glad, because I don't want you to feel I'm judging you in any way, and I'm glad you are honest. But you do feel like you are a fake, huh, at times?

Hugh: Yeah, but I wonder if I'm saying it right now like I really feel that I know I am a fake. I don't feel that embarrassed about it. I don't like it but ...

Shorr: (S&O) You mean you are still coming up gyroscopically right even when you tell me you are a fake?

Hugh: Yeah.

Shorr: In other words, you are always correcting, correcting, correcting, huh?

Hugh: Yeah. It's like I've got all these things going. I'm manipulating like a virtuoso and I've gotten pretty good at it, but it's not getting what I want, of course.

Shorr: You can't play that game forever?

Hugh: No.

Shorr: You're liable to get caught up with?

Hugh: No, no I never feel like I'd ever be caught up with. I feel like I could do it forever, but I feel like it would be too much of a burden. I'm tired of carrying all that weight around. It seems like . . .

Shorr: It's just not honest.

Hugh: Well, I don't care if it's honest or not. That doesn't bother me now. It's just not getting me what I want.

Shorr: (S&O) You mean you don't want to live on the defensive all the time. Vigilance all the time?

Hugh: Well, actually I enjoy manipulating things and doing it. It's just that I'm just not getting what I want. I realize that there is something else that I want more than that.

Shorr: Getting, not rewarding, huh?

Hugh: Yeah.

Shorr: Well, here is tough one. Now see if you can get this from your guts without giving me what you think I want, or playing it "right," which apparently, from what I gather you're saying so far, is that you are very skillful at playing things so correctly.

Hugh: Yeah, but I'm really trying though, to say the real stuff.

Shorr: Right, I think . . .

Hugh: Yeah, but I'd still like . . . I know that part of me still . . .

Shorr: You are caught in a conflict between wanting to say what you really feel — honestly, right? — and the vigilant game that you know you can play to keep you going.

Hugh: Yeah, but sometimes it gets so confused that I'm not really sure, in my own mind, what I really want.

Shorr: (M/L) O.K. This is why I'm going to ask you to do this. I want you to think of the most honest deep feeling you have — an honest gut feeling you have about anything in this world, but not intellectual — not about Johnson, McCarthy or Lotus Flowers, or God knows what else — but an honest feeling that you have about something and express it. The most honest — so it won't be diffused, it won't be confused — just let it come through.

Hugh: (Immediately) I just wish I could go to somebody that I liked or just (pause) tell them that I wanted them — I'd just cuddle up close and cry for a long time and have them reassure me.

Shorr: That's good. I'm glad you said that, Hugh. It ain't easy. But it's an honest, open feeling.

Hugh: Well, actually I say it's hard for me to say my feelings, but it's not *that* hard.

Shorr: You mean, you were still gyroscopically correcting?

Hugh: No, I was really saying the truth. This is terrible the way this has made the whole thing sound. I mean – part of this gyroscopic thing I have is convincing myself and other people that it's terribly hard and that I could never do it or something like that. I guess I know I could, but what I'm mad at about myself is that I say it is impossible and yet I know probably that if I just had the courage to do it, I could do it.

Shorr: You mean, it's very difficult to give up the game.

Hugh: Yeah. People would say, "Look, he could do it all along. We told you he could do it, and you wouldn't believe us."

Shorr: (S&O) And who would get the credit then?

Hugh: They would get the credit.

Shorr: So you would still be competing with them?

Hugh: Yeah.

Shorr: In other words, if you could do your own therapy, so to speak, on your own, and do it for you and you get . . .

Hugh: Not even therapy. I'd just have to have them think that I was like that all along and that for some reason, it just wasn't coming through.

Shorr: But it seems like you need the credit again. You've got to win again – even to getting to the point of complete honest feelings. You need the credit for having made that move for yourself, huh?

Hugh: Yes, but wait a minute – it would also be like I was really that way all along and it just wasn't coming out. That I hadn't really changed. I was just being more myself. I was really like that underneath. Just like the thing with the bear. I really was sorry for having to kill the bear even though it was attacking me or something like that – but I just felt frustrated. How could I ever make people believe that I wasn't the way I acted?

Shorr: (S&O) Were you ever believed as a child?

Hugh: I don't know for sure if I can remember it. Many times the significant things were. I came off looking worse than I was. Like at least I thought that I wasn't really the way I acted – some other thing took over. I did things that looked bad, but underneath I really wasn't that way. I just despaired of ever convincing people I wasn't that way – the way I appeared to be.

Shorr: It sounds like you were *not* believed or that you had a tremendous difficulty in proving to others that you were . . .

Hugh: Yes, that's true, but it's not the way I felt. I just felt that I did things and it wasn't the way they must have thought I was.

Shorr: (S&O) You mean there was disparity between . . . what and what?

Hugh: Well, between what I really wanted and what I did. Like I hit people even if I really wanted to be nice to them or something like that.

Shorr: (M/L) What is the most significant thing you've ever done?

Hugh: (Pause) I don't know. I really don't know!

Shorr: (M/L) What is the most significant thing you want to do in your life?

Hugh: I want to get married and have a lot of kids and just live in a big old-fashioned house with a big yard and everything.

Shorr: (IS) Now I want you to imagine that there is a girl and she has a sexual fantasy about you. What would that sexual fantasy be?

Hugh: Well, she would want me to want her and get real turned on by her and really be — really want her. She would probably imagine how groovy it would be if she could get me. We could be in love and do all kinds of things together.

Shorr: I'm not getting a sexual fantasy though, Hugh.

Hugh: (Quickly) Yes, well I don't want the sex thing. If it is just sex, then it turns me off completely. It seems like I would want a girl who would be real affectionate more than anything.

Shorr: (S&O) You want affection more than you want sex, even.

Hugh: Yes, if the whole affection thing comes after the sex, I couldn't function.

Shorr: Could you explain that a little further? I don't quite understand what you are saying.

Hugh: Well, if all of a sudden a girl wants me sexually then I'm just sure that I couldn't do anything. It seems like I have to perform first sexually, then she will give me the affection and everything I really want.

Shorr: In other words, if a girl had a pure sexual fantasy that . . .

Hugh: I just wouldn't even go around her.

Shorr: Because . . .

Hugh: Well, just because . . . I wouldn't — I'd feel inadequate and I wouldn't trust her and I just wouldn't want anything to do with that.

Shorr: (S&O) What proof do you have to give to a girl before you think it's O.K. to have sex with her?

Hugh: What proof?

Shorr: Yes.

Hugh: Well, I'd really have to want her instead of just going through the motions of having sex.

Shorr: Well, you said something in passing here a minute ago, you have to perform in some way before you felt it was right to have sex with her.

Hugh: No, the sex thing itself would be the performance.

Shorr: (S&O) How do you rate yourself in sexual performance?

Hugh: Well, I've never had sex really. (Long pause) I'd just be afraid to.

Shorr: Can you, however, for a moment *try* to think of a girl having a sexual fantasy about you — purely sexual — leaving all else out, if possible.

Hugh: Well, if you mean purely sexual, it seems like it would just be . . . I'd have to imagine that she was like grooving with me. It would be like she was getting a lot of satisfaction out of it. Then it wouldn't be just pure sex.

Shorr: (M/L) Who gets the most enjoyment from sex, the man or the woman?

Hugh: Oh, I don't know. I guess both, it all depends.

Shorr: What is your basic feeling?

Hugh: (Pause) It seems like the guy probably digs it more, but the girl would probably come along and enjoy it a lot, too.

Shorr: But more likely the man would enjoy it more?

Hugh: Yeah. Like something the girl gives.

Shorr: But she doesn't really get that much enjoyment out of it?

Hugh: Well, she gets enjoyment out of the fact that the man wants her.

Shorr: But not for sexuality and for herself alone?

Hugh: Yeah, but then when I see that . . . I hate girls that just get me up tight and just . . . it seems like they are greedy for it.

Shorr: Is it because they are greedy or is it because they demand performance from you?

Hugh: Well, they demand performance from me. If I could groove with that, I'd like a woman who's ready to go. That would be pretty great, I guess.

Shorr: (FTS) Finish the sentence, "I hate women because ____ ."

Hugh: (Pause) I hate women because they (pause) **demand too much.** No, that's not true — that's what I *feel*. Actually women are very giving, but I can't really accept it down on an emotional level.

Shorr: (FTS) From your guts, "I hate women because ____ ."

Hugh: I just hate them — I can't even say why. (Pause) **Because they make me feel inadequate.**

Shorr: (M/L) Who is the most adequate male you have known?

Hugh: I just never really ever thought about that. I just have a vague feeling.

Shorr: Who is it?

Hugh: People in general — guys in general seem like they are all adequate like that.

Shorr: You mean those that can ball real well?

Hugh: Yeah. But I think the guys that ball real well, I know that they are not really relating to girls, and are not getting that much out of it.

Shorr: (IS) Now suppose you go up to your mother — go up to her ear. I want you to imagine going up to her ear, and whisper something into her ear. Can you try that?

Hugh: Yeah, but I get contradictory things I might want to say.

Shorr: What do you want to say?

Hugh: I love her a whole lot, and I want to get close to her and get something from her, like a lot of affection and understanding.

Shorr: (IS) So tell me what you'd whisper. Just give me the word you'd whisper — in first person.

Hugh: Well, I'm so distant . . . I just get a creepy feeling that I don't want to do it. (Voice charged with emotion)

Shorr: (IS) Now whisper something into her ear. I know it is a little difficult. Can you do that?

Hugh: I really want to say . . . I just want to cry and have her comfort me (pause) but I really wouldn't want to say anything. I'd just want to give without even saying anything.

Shorr: (IS) Now, go up to your father's ear and whisper something into your father's ear

Hugh: I'd call him a dirty bastard! (Pause) Well, I don't know, sometimes I feel like I might be nicer to him.

Shorr: Do you have any brothers or sisters, Hugh?

Hugh: Yeah, I have a sister.

Shorr: (IS) Can you go up to your sister and whisper something into her ear?

Hugh: Well, I'm getting cut off on that one. (Voice emotional)

Shorr: This bothers you, this one, huh?

Hugh: Yeah, it bothers me because I can't let everything out.

Shorr: Why don't you?

Hugh: (Irritated) Because I can't, that's all.

Shorr: Well, suppose I force you, like, for our purposes.

Hugh: Yes, well I can hold out longer than you can. I don't like to get into that kind of thing where I . . .

Shorr: Why the hell are you in a contest with me, Hugh? You know this is to help you, not . . .

Hugh: (Irritated) I know it is to help. I realize that, but I . . .

Shorr: (S&O) You mean you'd rather beat me out in a contest involving withholding your emotion, huh?

Hugh: Yeah, but I didn't want to get into the thing where I would fight, because then I don't let the stuff out, because then I don't want to do it.

Shorr: (S&O) Then you have to win?

Hugh: Yeah.

Shorr: You get stubborn about it.

Hugh: Yeah, then I cut off my nose to spite my face.

(Continued on next page)

↔ **Dr. X:** I think his kind of nuclear problem with women is a very important part of his troubles. As an adolescent, he got involved with his sister — she would try to seduce him. She is just a couple of years younger than he is. She was apparently kind of precocious sexually. She is quite attractive and she appears to be a very naive adult, but apparently she learned to use that to cover over her sexuality, that was fairly out in the open. She tried to get him into sexual situations and he would respond to it up to a point and then he would cut off all of his feelings — so he got very practiced at that. And I think that is very relevant to what he does generally in the sexual spheres and actually in many spheres. So he has guilt feelings, not only towards her, but actually towards himself. He feels that he let himself down — that he should have followed through sexually all the way and have gone to bed with her, and fucked her. And if he had done that he then would have felt he had completed something. So for him to tell her now — to talk to her — is in some way to tell her this, "I wish I really fucked you." And to really admit that that was exactly what he wanted. For him to do that in the present is just impossible because he didn't do it then, and that's still where he is, and he is still trying to defend the fact that he didn't do that.

Shorr: What about the incest taboo — you know, with the sister?

(Continued on next page)

Shorr: O.K., how about relaxing and you know, after all, man, you really want to win and winning the right way, the healthy way for yourself, and you . . .

Hugh: I don't even see it as winning when I – there is no more person on top or bottom, when I can be open.

Shorr: Well, then, how about doing the most for yourself? You know? Like, man?

Hugh: Well, that kind of jargon turns me off when you use "man." It doesn't seem to be part of your whole background. I'm sure you don't use that at home with your wife or anything like that – it seems like jive talk you are putting on.

Shorr: Now it sounds like you are trying to put me down.

Hugh: Well, yeah.

Shorr: I use "man" once in awhile. I don't use it every minute, but I think what's more important, whether or not I use "man," is getting to your real feelings. Isn't it?

Hugh: Yeah. (Pause) (Quiet voice) I forgot the question we were on.

Shorr: I was asking you to whisper into your sister's ear. Let your real feelings come through, using first person.

Hugh: (Subdued tone) Oh boy . . . "I guess I'm just sorry that I can't be more open with you. I feel guilty about some of the things we did in the past. I tried to have sex or something like that. Wish I didn't have to play the role around you any more, I guess. Cause you are the only normal person in the family."

Shorr: (M/L) What do you feel most guilty about in your life, Hugh?

(Continued on next page)

Dr. X: Well, there was some of this – he told himself then – we talked about that – how it's kind of appropriate that an adolescent boy would feel that he shouldn't carry it through. And his mother did make certain intimations about him and his sister – suggesting that they were playing around and doing the wrong things. He has had in the past feelings that his mother wanted him sexually. He has been aware of this, but he has not really felt that she was very active about it. It was just that fantasy – it was like a passive attitude of hers. Mostly, he's felt that he treated her badly – like when you asked what would he whisper into his mother's ear and he would whisper into her ear that he really cared for her. (See p. 112 of therapy tape.) He now feels that she manipulated him. You know, she was an addict – barbiturate addict. She is extremely sick. She has been hospitalized sometimes for severe depression.

Shorr: Yes, he told me later in the tape.

Dr. X: Oh, he did? And he has always focused on his father as his enemy – generally. But he has, in the past year or so, begun to feel that his mother really sort of seduced him and manipulated him into a position where he was her caretaker, and conveyed to him that his father was always the enemy. So he sort of adopted this position from his mother and he feels that she used him, exploited him, and I think that is accurate – I mean, I think she really did do that.

Shorr: You mean, so he really cut his feelings off from manipulating women when they wanted the final consummation of sex, and that's like it is with girls, isn't it?

Dr. X: Exacly: I feel he really learned *that* with his sister in the actual behavior.

(Continued on next page)

Hugh: It's nothing I've ever done. I don't feel guilty about anything I've ever done. It's just that I feel sad that I didn't get some of the things I want.

Shorr: (S&O) You feel guilty about playing a role all the time?

Hugh: No, I don't feel guilty, I just feel sad.

Shorr: You mean you wish you could do something else?

Hugh: Yeah.

Shorr: (M/L) Who is the saddest person you have ever known?

Hugh: Oh, I guess my mother.

Shorr: (IS) I'm going to ask you a tough one now. I want you to imagine taking a shower with your mother. How would you feel?

Hugh: Well, it would be a creepy scene. If I'd just have to go through the motions of taking a shower and like watching. I just wouldn't feel at ease at all.

Shorr: (M/L) What would you be most concerned about?

Hugh: That she would be looking at me and thinking that I wasn't sexually developed enough . . . and wondering why I wasn't interested in her sexually or something like that.

Shorr: You mean it would be a demand upon you?

Hugh: Yeah.

Shorr: To be sexual or to look sexual?

Hugh: Yes, then she looks so sick and so self-conscious and without doing anything like that it just . . . uh . . . I just . . . it just gives me all kinds of creepy feelings, that's all.

Shorr: That word creepy comes up time and time again, huh?

Hugh: Yeah, I guess that must be my favorite word.

(Continued on next page)

Shorr: This happened quite often, you mean?

Dr. X: Oh yes, he and his sister for several years used to play around. I mean they used to get very hot – I mean, neck, and he would put his hand inside her blouse and he was really quite turned on. He masturbated and still does probably even to this day. Having this fantasy of going through the whole act with her. But with his mother I think he – I'm still not absolutely clear about and maybe this comes out later that his feeling toward his mother was largely pity – really pity – she was a sick person and he stood between her and his father. He would get her pills on the sly. You know, he would get her prescriptions for her from the physician and not tell the father. So he was kind of an intermediary.

Shorr: A pawn.

Dr. X: Exactly. And he never expressed – felt – the hostility about this – he never experienced it very much. But he also never experienced a really genuine, warm feeling towards an adequate person. The warm feelings he had were mostly those of pity – he's got to help her out because she's sick.

Shorr: Which he hates in himself – for anyone to pity him.

Dr. X: Exactly, right. He can't stand that. And he feels like he is the creep. That creep thing he talked about. (See pp. 102, 106, 115, and 144.)

Shorr: I can see now that I missed in not asking him his own masturbation fantasy – I don't think I did it on the tape. I should have picked it up on the sister, but I didn't because of the fact that he could talk easily about the mother and father but didn't about the sister, and sort of tailed off, and said, "I'm shut off in my feelings." Because this masturbation fantasy about his sister is short of

(Continued on next page)

Shorr: (M/L) Who is the creepiest person you have every known?

Hugh: Who is?

Shorr: Yes. That you can think of.

Hugh: I can imagine everybody as being basically creepy.

Shorr: Everybody?

Hugh: Yeah.

Shorr: Isn't there an honest guy in the world?

Hugh: Yeah, I know, but sometimes I think that everybody's . . . most people are fairly normal and I don't mind the fact that they have doubts of some aspects of their life that are a little bit troublesome or painful. The other times I see everybody as being creepy.

Shorr: (FTS) Finish the sentence, "My basic expectancy in the world is _____ ."

Hugh: Well, I, I really can't answer that because partly I'm sort of optimistic — like there is a lot of good things I can get, and the other part of me figures I'll never get them. It's like beyond my grasp. I see both of these in me, and they neutralize each other.

Shorr: (S&O) You sound like there are two parts of you at war all the time inside of you, huh?

Hugh: Yeah. The part that assumes that everything is going to work out in the worst possible way and yet sort of a naive child-like belief that things probably will work out and things will be great, just tremendously great.

Shorr: (IS) Suppose you took a shower with you father, how would you feel?

Hugh: I'd have the same feeling that he'd be looking at me thinking I was . . . that I had a small cock and just looked skinny . . . and he might be thinking what kind of girl would want something like that, except some old frump of a girl, who didn't know any better.

actual sexuality — he putting his hand in blouse — instead of actual intercourse itself.

Dr. X: But he would have all of the foreplay feelings and actions, too, with her. The thing that comes up over and over that I have a real stalemate about with him has to do with having him in a position where he will express a real genuine feeling — especially a feeling of wanting.

Shorr: The one thing that occurs to me is the emphasis on the foreplay with his sister. I think he must be great with foreplay with a woman sexually.

Dr. X: Oh, yes.

Shorr: And he's great with foreplay with people.

Dr. X: Absolutely.

Shorr: But when he gets to the point of closeness, then he . . .

Dr. X: He either cuts off or he pretends he is close, which is still cutting off, in a false position.

Shorr: The other thought which I had is that in therapy, if you can get him in a foreplay position where he is charming, he's great, he's witty, and he's moving along, and then get him to express a real feeling, you may have a chance to break him through. If he gets enough gratification from the foreplay. That's just a guess, I don't know. He's really tough to work on.

Dr. X: I've never had a more difficult person in therapy. Except a really psychotic person who is inaccessible.

Shorr: Yes, but those are the unreachable — but anyone who allows himself to be that reachable . . . The one thing I also noticed — when I ask some of my other patients a question and they don't say much, I am silent and my silence will force them to go on. But he wouldn't. And so I'd have to come up with another point.

Shorr: (IS) And suppose you took a shower with your sister, what would happen?

Hugh: (Pause) Oh, I don't know. (Pause) I just feel like I'm cutting off a lot of stuff right now.

Shorr: Just some real feelings you won't let come through, huh?

Hugh: Yeah.

Shorr: (S&O) Are you ashamed of your feelings?

Hugh: I don't know — they're just not coming out, that's all.

Shorr: You sounded pretty honest about the last couple with your mother and father. They weren't easy to talk about.

Hugh: It wasn't that painful. That's what worries me. It was a little bit painful, but it wasn't like it was wiping me out or anything.

Shorr: You mean, if you let your real feelings out you're just going to get wiped out and become a blob on the couch or something?

Hugh: Yeah.

Shorr: Is that what you are afraid of?

Hugh: Yeah, but then you probably realize that sometimes I am fairly honest and it doesn't seem to be quite as painful as I keep trying to tell everybody that it is going to be.

Shorr: Suppose I gave you a guarantee that no matter how much you let go — screamed, yelled . . .

Hugh: Oh, that doesn't do any good, because I wouldn't believe it — If you reassured me for a hundred years like Dr. X has I still can't . . .

Shorr: Still can't do it, huh? So that the worst part about telling me your feelings about you and your sister taking a shower is what? What she would say is ____ .

Hugh: I don't really care what she'd think. It's more what I think.

Shorr: (S&O) Do you care what anyone thinks about your cock?

Hugh: Well, that's one of the things that has bothered me.

Shorr: (S&O) What do you feel about your cock?

Hugh: Well, it isn't big enough . . . or that it's not going to work.

Shorr: (IS) I'll give you a real tough one, Hugh. Suppose you are in a room and you are standing in the nude. Now, two or three girls come in and they look at you. What are they thinking about you?

Hugh: Probably that my cock is too small.

Shorr: (IS) O.K., now you have an erection. Now what are they thinking about you?

Hugh: Well, I think they would think that was pretty good. (Laughs) Things like that, I get so hung up on that, that, well I just . . . well, if I did have an erection, then everything is all right. But I just can't get it.

Shorr: You can't get what?

Hugh: I can't get an erection. I'm not really turned on. Well, I've had sex with girls and I get a hard-on, but I'm just doing it, I'm not letting any emotions out. It's actually a painful experience.

Shorr: Painful?

Hugh: Yeah. It actually hurts.

Shorr: Physically hurts?

Hugh: Yeah. Physically hurts. Or sometimes it doesn't hurt, it's not even as good as masturbating, and afterwards I feel real low.

Shorr: Is it psychologically painful, too, or just physically painful?

Hugh: Well, it's just physically painful, because I cut off my emotions.

Shorr: You mean, your penis is out there and you're over here so to speak?

Hugh: Yeah. Like I'm thinking about something else while I'm doing it.

Shorr: You don't want to be connected with the penis feelings, huh?

Hugh: Well, I don't even think of it like that. I'm just not in the thing, I'm just performing and I'm thinking about something else – wondering how long it's all going to take, what I'm going to do the next day, or I'm just not in the scene, that's all.

Shorr: You can't let yourself groove in the sexual thing where all the sexual feelings take you over and just let yourself relax with it and go ahead with it, huh?

Hugh: No!

Shorr: (IS) Now I want you to imagine something that is kind of tough – as you know, I've said it before about many questions.

Hugh: (Irritated) Yeah, you keep saying it's tough every time. Everything is tough so, I mean, it's not going to make it any easier if you assure me every time that it's going to be tough. I'll just do the best I can with each question you give me.

Shorr: Now you sound angry.

Hugh: Well, I am angry because it seems like it's even harder for me when you preface everything with "It's going to be hard now." It seems like you are putting a bigger burden on me. Then I have to be more honest now or something like that. I'll just do the best I can, that's all.

Shorr: (S&O) In other words, you are ⟷ angry at anyone putting a demand on you.

Hugh: Yeah, and I'm not even so mad at them. I'm not really mad at you. I'm just mad at myself because then that makes the thing all super-charged, a big deal, and when I get like that I just get tied in a knot. I do absolutely nothing. Oh, I can perform, but it's not the real

Dr. X: The sense I have now is that what has to be made very clear to him is that he has to feel that he has the initiative in making any kinds of demands on me and feel that he can have a real influence over me, because he doesn't feel he makes a difference – really. That's what I'm getting out of this. That when the demand is made on him, you lose him, and that means that he has lost out on the

(Continued on next page)   *(Continued on next page)*

me. It feels much better if everything were low key, easy going, like, it would be much easier.

Shorr: All the time it's really a demand you put on yourself — almost . . .

Hugh: Yeah, I know that.

Shorr: (S&O) You can pick up anything the other person says and put a demand upon yourself that they are demanding this of you now, huh?

Hugh: Yeah, but recently I have been trying to work through that and not always turn everything to my disadvantage.

Shorr: (IS) I want you to talk to your penis. Say something to it, and if the penis could talk back, what would it say to you? Try that.

Hugh: I feel like I could call it a little bastard. (Long pause) I'm getting a little bit up tight and I just can't really think. (Long pause)

Shorr: You can't think because you are angry, Hugh.

Hugh: Yeah, I guess.

Shorr: And you're angry . . .

Hugh: I'd like to get out of that anger — it seems like I could relax a little bit and, yeah, I feel like I could just start pummeling people.

Shorr: Yeah, I thought so. I think you are goddam full of anger — anger, anger, anger — and you are goddam afraid that anybody should see it. Because you aren't a full man and therefore you aren't supposed to have the anger, are you? You have a small cock and therefore you are supposed to just lie there and look good all the time.

Hugh: Yeah.

Shorr: If they ever found out you had a small cock, they would kill you. They never would think of you as a man.

(Continued on next page)

struggle. I guess what it means to him to lose is to really feel that he is just very small and very inadequate and maybe, with a male especially, he feels sexually inadequate. He starts out with that feeling anyway, because he feels he has a small cock. So he has to have the initiative — it seems like that is what he needs.

Shorr: Dominate you in a way.

Dr. X: Yes. So he can experience control over the situation and set the tone.

Shorr: And he can allow the loss of the self-consciousness . . .

Dr. X: Yes. He always seems to feel like he's going to be tricked. Now if he opens himself up as he knows he could do — I think he is pretty close to control over that. I don't think it's really an unconscious act at this point. I mean there is some unconscious blocking, but . . .

Shorr: He's kind of self-conscious.

Dr. X: But he's got a fair amount of conscious control whether he's going to relate and emote at all. He feels, like he said earlier that, if he does, then others are going to say to him, in effect, "Well, you could have done this a long time ago and you have been holding out on us all of this time and you have been tricking us." (See page 110.) So he is afraid that people are going to see — I suppose it's a realistic kind of feeling — that they are going to see that he has been covering up all of this time. I mean this is what he has been doing. I don't think he has been in such control over it all of this time.

Shorr: Doesn't control always involve a concept of standard for what the control has to be? Because even when I say, "You don't have to," "you do," or whatever, I'm giving him a standard.

Dr. X: He's still got the standard inside of him.

(Continued on next page)

Hugh: No they wouldn't kill me, but I would be neutralized. All of this hollering and yelling and rage or imposing my will would just look ridiculous.

Shorr: In other words, you can't back yourself up because you have a small cock.

Hugh: Well, not only that, but because I don't perform in the sexual thing, you know. I can't do it.

Shorr: That's the determinant of a man?

Hugh: Yeah.

Shorr: (IS) Everything seems to come down to that. Suppose you have a ten-inch cock, normal, without even an erection. Now go into the world – what do you get?

Hugh: I guess I'd feel pretty cocky, wouldn't I? (Laughs)

Shorr: (Laughs) Well, we actually got a laugh out of you – great!

Hugh: I'm still mad at you.

Shorr: That's a demand, goddam it! Don't you see what I did? I said, "See, we got a laugh out of you." I did it on purpose. Meaning that from now on, I want you to laugh more. See the fucking demand I put on you?

Hugh: Yeah. I feel everybody . . .

Shorr: If *he* makes the standard. Is that what you mean if *he* makes the standard?

Dr. X: Yes, then he has to decide when to do it, and how much. And he has to judge whether that's acceptable to him or not.

Shorr: So, it has to be *his*, and not you saying, "I'll wait for you" because that means still you are telling him . . .

Dr. X: He's got to feel that he is the sole judge of the act – of his own act. He doesn't feel that.

Shorr: How do you make him feel like he is the sole judge of his act?

Dr. X: Yes, that's – I'm not clear.

Shorr: That's a rough one. He's so other-directed.

Dr. X: Yes. I think – and this is the part that's the real, the only problem – how could he realistically believe that no one is expecting anything out of him? That's living in an impossible world. It doesn't exist. In reality he is intellectually alert enough to know that that is an impossibility.

Shorr: I did it on purpose that time. I don't give a damn if you laugh more or not. I want you to get at what you have to get at. But I did that on purpose. I knew that by saying that, that I could press a button and I could get you to start laughing more. See what I mean? I press buttons, O.K.? I'm skilled at this; this is my work. I can press buttons and I know what to say that can make you do that. I can see that you will accommodate to me on almost anything that I'm going to say to you. Do you follow me?

Hugh: Yeah, but I can also say, on the other hand, if I were to start playing a game, I think I could hold my own with you. ⟷ **Shorr**: You will see some part during the tape where he says he could outposture me, so to speak. He could outlast me – like if the session were to go

(Continued on next page)   *(Continued on next page)*

Shorr: I'm sure you can. You can beat anybody in the fucking world, but what the hell is it going to do you?

Hugh: Yeah, that's something I'm beginning to wonder.

Shorr: You don't really win. You play the *game*, you win the *game*.

Hugh: Yeah, it's awfully hollow.

Shorr: Yes, especially when you leave — you know, "Oh great, I won that game, but shit!"

Hugh: No, I don't really feel good when I've won the game. It just seems that I just act that way.

on for a hundred years, he'd still outlast me. (See also p. 113.)

Dr. X: I think that's a wish — I don't think that is true.

Shorr: Yes, but that's what he said.

Dr. X: Yes, but I don't think that's true. But he believes that that is a real sign of strength in itself.

Shorr: Yes, but that's a false position — that's what Laing says.

Dr. X: Yes, exactly.

Shorr: As a defensive thing.

Shorr: Yeah, but I think that all roads lead to that small cock concept about yourself because you are not the man — the performing, feeling man. And, therefore, if you were president of the world, or the head of the United Nations, or the greatest man that ever lived, somewhere, someone is going to find out (probably a woman) that . . .

Hugh: I wouldn't let them find out, I'd just cut off. I wouldn't go near them.

Shorr: In the process of cutting off, you would . . .

Hugh: Well, I'd just be sitting there all by myself.

Shorr: It's like cutting off your cock. To spite yourself. You said, "to cut off my nose to spite myself." The second minute you were in here if you remember. (IS) I want you to imagine now, you know those steel balls, the kind that house wreckers use to break down brick buildings and stuff. Now for a moment . . .

Hugh: Yes, coming at my head.

Shorr: At your head?

Hugh: Yes, for a moment I saw it started to destroy a whole bunch of buildings, like a whole city — just smashing everything, and then I see the damn thing coming at my head.

Shorr: (IS) Now, I want you to be in charge of that particular thing. I want you to swing that ball at the buildings. Now try it.

Hugh: But, once I get the ball going at the buildings, then I'm getting myself into that violence scene where it's going to come back at me some way.

Shorr: (IS) (Focusing Tech.) Now, all right, I want you to attempt, through your imagination, not to have it come at you no matter what. Its automatic guard will defend you. It can't come back at you. You've got to break that building down. Keep smashing.

Hugh: Yeah, I keep it coming to me because I get inside of a huge, protected cabin like twenty feet of glass and steel and everything like that, so if it does come my way, it doesn't hit me.

Shorr: (IS) Can you imagine smashing the buildings down anyway? Even within that . . .

Hugh: Oh yeah, I could manipulate the levers and I can really get the ball to go.

Shorr: How does it feel breaking down those brick buildings? Can you get the feeling of it, now that you're safe?

Hugh: Yeah, I can just see them all falling to pieces.

Shorr: How does it feel though? Feel!

Hugh: Well, it feels like they deserved it. I feel good.

Shorr: Well, keep doing it! Even though you're in that glass encased thing.

Hugh: I'd feel much better if I could make huge bullet holes rather than having that damn ball coming at me.

Shorr: (IS) O.K., imagine that ball hitting you then. It hits you right in the face. Now what?

Hugh: Well, it hit me, but I'm still there.

Shorr: (IS) Let it hit you again. Let it hit you! (Pause) Is that what you are so goddam afraid of? Let it hit you.

Hugh: Yeah, it feels sort of good.

Shorr: (IS) Let it hit you some more. Tell me when you want it to stop and why.

Hugh: It feels like I've got to let it hit me for an awfully long time, though. (Pause)

Shorr: (IS) Now you have been hit for an awfully long time. Now what?

Hugh: Well, I just put it away.

Shorr: (S&O) How do you feel about yourself now?

Hugh: Uh, less frightened. Feels like sort of a good feeling.

Shorr: Do you feel better?

Hugh: Yeah, but it's dissipated real fast. It's just like I'd have to go through that time and time again. I felt good for a couple seconds afterwards, but . . .

Shorr: (IS) Why don't you take a large spear and just spear yourself right into your stomach. How do you feel?

Hugh: Oh, I can't even imagine it in my stomach. I'd rather stick it through my head.

Shorr: (IS) O.K., stick it through your head.

Hugh: Things always stick in my head.

Shorr: (S&O) Head, huh? Is your head at war with any other part of your body by any chance?

Hugh: Oh, it could be.

Shorr: (S&O) If you could match your head against any other part of your body, what do you think you would match it against?

Hugh: Just the physical part of my nature.

Shorr: You mean your drives, emotions, feelings.

Hugh: Yeah, the whole thing.

Shorr: Gonads, etc.

Hugh: Everything.

Shorr: So, it's either your head or your feelings.

Hugh: Yeah.

Shorr: It seems like you want to hit your head, and you don't want to be that intellectualized, controlled person, huh?

Hugh: Yeah.

Shorr: (IS) O.K., take the spear and hit your head with it. Now what? Or get it into your hand, whatever you want to do with it.

Hugh: It really doesn't hurt me though. I'm just the way I was before.

Shorr: (S&O) Nothing can touch your head?

Hugh:Yeah.

Shorr: (S&O) You can never relinquish your head? Like forty drinks and you will still be in control, huh?

Hugh: Yeah.

Shorr: (S&O) And a million bashes of that large steel ball and you'll still be in control?

Hugh: Yeah.

Shorr: (S&O) And if you let yourself go, what the hell is going to happen to you?

Hugh: I don't know.

Shorr: (IS) I want you to imagine that you can fly. Can you imagine that?

Hugh: Yes, if I could be sure that my power wouldn't suddenly stop or I'd just fall through space down to earth, something like that. I would like to fly if I felt like I could continue without falling. I mean, I'd hate to run out of power a mile over a city — you know?

Shorr: What is your power source?

Hugh: Well, I don't know. It just came from nowhere.

Shorr: (IS) Let's say I gave you permanent power — renewable so that it can never fail — can you imagine flying?

Hugh: Yeah, if I were positive, I guess I would have to fly around.

Shorr: You need that guarantee?

Hugh: I'd have to have a positive guarantee that the power isn't going to suddenly fail in some way.

Shorr: All right, you checked it out and you know that it's positively . . .

Hugh: Yes, but there's always one chance in a million.

Shorr: And you won't take that chance?

Hugh: (Pause) I might a little bit.

Shorr: Try it. Just for our purposes — try it — see what happens.

Hugh: (Immediately) I'd go out to the country first and just be a few feet off the ground . . .

Shorr: Come on — go a little higher — don't worry, you are not going to lose that power — I'm telling you.

Hugh: I can't believe it though.

Shorr: Well, try it!

Hugh: It seems like if I could believe that then my problems would be all over.

Shorr: (IS) O.K., go twenty feet high.

Hugh: Then I run into power lines.

Shorr: (IS) Get above the lines. This power is permanent. Imagine that.

Hugh: Well, I'd like to have a parachute on just to be double sure.

Shorr: (IS) Keep the line with the parachute then.

Hugh: But the parachute sort of negates my faith in the power. I always have a parachute or a way out.

Shorr: (IS) O.K., so just forget the parachute and stick with the power. (S&O) Who the hell do you trust in this world, Hugh?

Hugh: I don't trust anybody.

Shorr: You don't even trust Dr. X, do you?

Hugh: No, I have a few little flashes where I occasionally trust a little bit. Right now I don't feel like I trust anybody.

Shorr: What happens if you trust . . .

Hugh: I also feel that if I had everything, I ought to trust people so much — I would just trust them completely. I wouldn't — I would just fail to trust people.

Shorr: (S&O) Suppose you trust Dr. X completely. What happens? Does he take you over? Does he destroy you?

Hugh: No, no, I think I've begun to trust him enough so that he really wouldn't take over or try to control me or . . . I guess I'm mainly mad at myself because I can't trust him and I know I really should.

Shorr: (IS) O.K., let's assume that you finally trust Dr. X and he says that power is absolutely sufficient to fly. O.K., now start flying and go at great heights.

Hugh: Yeah, I'd be free of not believing any more — of suddenly getting doubts if the power would fail.

Shorr: In other words, that when the trust goes, the power fails.

Hugh: Yeah.

Shorr: And you can't trust anybody.

Hugh: Well, just the confidence in myself mainly. And that would disappear. Because my trusting him is my being at ease and trusting myself. I can't be sure I could really do that.

Shorr: (S&O) What is the price of trusting Dr. X?

Hugh: I can't really think. All I can really think is that I could really break down and cry – just let it all out. But all these problems with this wouldn't formulate them the same.

Shorr: (IS) It's like you would like to be a little boy for awhile and have him hold you, right?

Hugh: Yeah.

Shorr: Wouldn't that be nice?

Hugh: Oh yeah. It would be great!

Shorr: Then you could trust him, huh? He wouldn't be out to destroy you, or dominate you, or anything else, right?

Hugh: Or laugh, or any kind of unpleasant thing.

Shorr: Or ridicule you, or humiliate you?

Hugh: Yeah, yeah.

Shorr: And no defense necessary on your part, right?

Hugh: Yeah.

Shorr: You are O.K., just as you are?

Hugh: Yeah, without having to change anything about the way I feel, just feel exactly – be just what I am.

Shorr: Yeah, that's the only thing a person can be is what they are, huh?

Hugh: Yeah, I know that.

Shorr: You know all those words, huh?

Hugh: Yeah.

Shorr: (IS) But the real feeling is to allow yourself to be like a little boy, huh? And sink into his arms and let him hold you? And how does it feel?

Hugh: (Pause) It feels pretty good.

Shorr: It sounds like its awfully good.

Hugh: Yeah. (Barely audible)

Shorr: Wouldn't you like to cry right now?

Hugh: Yeah. I feel so sad. (Tearful voice) (Pause)

Shorr: Why don't you cry?

Hugh: Because I don't want somebody to tell me I was just . . .

Shorr: (S&O) You always have to do it on your own terms, huh?

Hugh: I didn't want the whole thing to come up where it's a ballyhoo. I just want to be myself.

Shorr: Good.

Hugh: Bypass all that stuff.

Shorr: It should be absolutely natural you mean?

Hugh: Absolutely natural. I'm not doing it because I think it's good for me or because anything – just do it. And I can also imagine that after crying a little bit, I'd want to play a little bit and have a good time.

Shorr: That's good. You give me a little trepidation if I try to encourage your naturalness – then it sounds like a demand upon you. Do you know what I mean, Hugh?

Hugh: Yeah, it just turns me off completely. I mean . . .

Shorr: Yeah, I see what it does. All I was trying to do is to encourage what you felt. I saw you feeling that way and I tried to encourage it, but I see you felt that fucking demand again.

Hugh: Yeah, but I was getting the thought that those things are in me.

Shorr: Who says they are not?

Hugh: I know this, but wait a minute, though. I know that you are not saying that they aren't there, but I feel as though it's because of some way you've done that. That how could you believe that those are really in me? That that's the way I really am or could be.

Shorr: Because you brought them up, not me.

Hugh: Brought what up?

Shorr: When I asked you what it felt like to be a little boy in Dr. X's arms, you *gave me* the feeling. I didn't make it. You could of said nothing at all. You could of shut off all together – they came from you.

Hugh: Yeah, but I still have that frustrating feeling that nobody would ever believe it. They still think that they had done it, that *they* had shown me the way to have nice feelings and everything. They'd never believe that that really didn't happen.

Shorr: And yet, that one, if we have to be intellectual for a moment. I just want to say it intellectually if nothing else. That was a feeling I did not demand of you nor anything but to support what you felt. I saw it and let it go. I encouraged your natural feeling. I don't . . .

Hugh: Yeah, all this talk, I just want to live with the feeling. (Sighs)

Shorr: Good, stay with the feeling. It's yours.

Hugh: (Laughing) I don't want anybody to tell me it's mine because it seems like if it is mine, you don't need to say it.

Shorr: Yes, there's always the entrapment on my part. Any time I encourage you – any time I encourage the feeling, it's, "Don't encourage me because it's really mine and I had it all the time." Right?

Hugh: Yeah.

Shorr: Like I should shut up. I'd be better off, right?

Hugh: Yeah, it seems like – no matter how nice you were, you couldn't win because I . . .

Shorr: Ha, ha, ha. O.K., why don't you just take it – take it and I'll keep quiet and you just let whatever feeling that is there come through. Fair enough? They won't be mine then. They'll be completely yours. I'll shut up.

Hugh: (Pause) I don't feel quite that strongly now. It seems like now I get a feeling, I keep thinking, "Well, next time it will go all the way, but this time I'm not ready yet." (Long pause) I guess maybe sometime I should get to the point where I can admit that other people can help me. I wouldn't have had these feelings if they hadn't been here and you hadn't asked questions. I've never gotten that close to my feelings – just all by myself. So, I'm glad that you did get that out of me. Otherwise, I'm just going to keep denying that anybody can help me. (Long pause) Now, it's going away again. (Long pause) I'm in a real bind because, I don't know, I'm just losing everything. (Long pause) I feel like you are waiting for me to do something or come up with some feelings. I'm just not going to do it.

Shorr: Does it become a demand again?

Hugh: Yeah.

Shorr: You put me in a double bind, don't you, Hugh?

Hugh: Yeah. You encourage me and then you just sit back and do nothing.

Shorr: Either way, I'm fucked. Ha, ha.

Hugh: It's like I'm sure it's all your fault. (Joking)

Shorr: Really, all I want you to do is, do your own thing.

Hugh: Yeah, but maybe I do need help from outside.

Dr. X: I'm not seeing him individually.

Shorr: You are not seeing him individually at all?

Dr. X: No.

Shorr: Oh, he is in two groups.

Dr. X: Yeah. Right.

Shorr: How does he work out in two groups?

$\longleftrightarrow$ **Dr. X:** Well, I think he is pulling the same stunts. He's useful to the group, because he is terribly frustrating, and he is paranoid, and he tells them all to go fuck themselves, or "I don't give a shit what you say to me," and "there's nothing you can do to help me." So this introduces the whole hostility dimension into the group more – although he doesn't demand anything of anybody – he doesn't actually intrude into people. He's very narcissistic but he's catalytic. So that's O.K. But as far as what he is getting out of it – I don't think he is getting anything out of it. He is in the same stalemate he was with me – but

Shorr: It's hard to accept it, huh?

Hugh: Yeah. Like I start to feel something like I want to prove to people that I did it on my own, but I really haven't been doing it on my own.

Shorr: You *are* really. What you just did with Dr. X, like melting into his arms. It's like what you really want and that you could call something your own and it wouldn't be taken away from you.

Hugh: Yeah.

Shorr: And just natural.

Hugh: Yeah, that would be great! (Long pause) I'm a little bit discouraged be-

(Continued on next page)

(Continued on next page)

cause I have gotten to this feeling before — lots of times — but it doesn't seem to go anywhere. I mean too definitely. I mean, I know in the overall picture, a lot of things have gotten out during my life, since I've started feeling these things.

Shorr: (S&O) This business of accepting help seems to be kind of basic here, huh?

Hugh: Yeah.

Shorr: Like, you got to do it yourself, then it's all right. And it's always been there anyway, huh?

Hugh: Yeah.

Shorr: I'm sure it has.

Hugh: It's just like I'm not going to give anybody the satisfaction of thinking that they can help me.

Shorr: (S&O) You're in a contest with Dr. X, aren't you? Or me, or anybody else?

Hugh: Oh, yeah.

Shorr: The horrible part is that you know intellectually, better than I, that I don't want to win.

Hugh: Yeah, but I'm still not going to give you that satisfaction.

Shorr: And you won't give me any satisfaction. Except to know that you are helped or something. But I think you think I go away and think, "Oh, boy, I really beat that bastard. I out-maneuvered him in that chess game," or something.

Hugh: No, I just — you have sort of a smug feeling that you were able to help me. Like it makes you feel good and I don't want you to get that good feeling. I mean . . . just the way I structure things in general, I can feel my dad would do that.

Shorr: (S&O) Did you do it with your dad?

Hugh: Yeah.

(Continued on next page)

we are in the same bind. I made up my mind that by June if we didn't — if nothing happened — I was going to find him another therapist. I thought of particularly a female — to get him to go to a woman therapist. Miranda Benson — do you know her? She is a psychiatrist and she is quite astute and especially non-demanding. In fact, I feel I can't realistically be that non-demanding with him, because that's not the way I am. And I think it's kind of phony to pretend to be something that I'm not. I'm not *too* demanding with him. I think the thing I haven't insisted on is simply expressing more feelings. Even though he accuses me of making a demand on him — I think that is the thing he has used to fend me off. Knowing that as a therapist I don't want to be the bad guy, you know, and be taking advantage, and all of that stuff. I noticed he tried that on you and it didn't work. (See pp. 118-121 of therapy tape.)

Shorr: Because I didn't have the stake in him that you have, I guess.

Dr. X: Yes, and maybe that's simply what I have to do — simply stick with where I am, which is that I am kind of demanding of him. I'm not as demanding of him as I used to be. I've been influenced by his double bind. I see the only way through for him — out of the woods — is that, when he is close to feelings, he should get closer to them, and be more expressive, and take the chances and the risks that he is always talking about.

Shorr: Keep questioning him, you mean?

Dr. X: Yes. I don't see any other way for me to do it. I simply have to be more persistent with him on that level, in that particular encounter, because that seems to be the crucial encounter with him.

Shorr: Have you ever thought of rejecting him?

(Continued on next page)

Shorr: How did that happen there?

Hugh: Well, I would never . . . He was always thinking there were things wrong with me and I was going to show him that I was perfectly all right.

Shorr: (S&O) You sound like you were in a horrible contest with him.

Hugh: Yeah. (Long pause)

Shorr: Very critical, huh?

Hugh: Yeah. He was.

Shorr: (S&O) And your best defense against it?

Hugh: Was to just look completely cool and calm and self-contained, and needing no help, or knowing exactly what I was doing and not let all those feelings of fright or all that stuff come out.

Shorr: (S&O) It sounds like the kind of central conflict of your life, with the old man, huh?

Hugh: Oh, yeah.

Shorr: I mean I knew nothing about you before I saw you so I just – something told me its got to be that more than anything. That and your feeling about your cock, which I think you probably will change soon. It really has no – I think it's more central to your father's criticism of you, which you centered upon your cock.

Hugh: Yes, I know, even before I ever got into therapy or anything like that, I knew all those things. That's the problem.

Shorr: Yeah. It's like you had to out think everything – out think everyone in front of you and everyone you dealt with to be sure you were on the cool side, or controlled side of things or one step ahead. But that smug satisfaction sounds again like your father. He'd really have it over you. If he could say something about you that was negative and he could prove it, and you'd have no defense, man, he'd really have you left to right, huh?

(Continued on next page)

Dr. X: Well, I *have* done that at times. I mean, I've had scenes with him where I've simply said, you know . . . Do you mean rejecting him and just kicking him out of therapy, or do you mean just for a session itself?

Shorr: Well, yes, even the whole therapy. It just seems ridiculous – he's just double binding everything, and there's no chance, and anything you say he's just counter-punching, and it's just a fucking game.

Dr. X: Yes, I've only done a little of that with him.

Shorr: And, maybe he'd just better go, that's all. I mean he pays you money – good-bye. And let it go at that. If he'll do better elsewhere – go ahead. And really put it to him. And make him face what he is so damn afraid of. That ultimate rejection. Then he has to come back.

Dr. X: That's certainly not far from what I've wanted to do.

Shorr: But you can't do that with patients.

Dr. X: Yeah, right.

Shorr: But he isn't a patient like most patients – you really can't do anything with him.

Dr. X: Have you ever had a patient like that?

Shorr: No, only the ones that are schizoid. They play the game so well – "I can't feel anything" – "I don't know what you just said" – "Tell me again" – "I don't hear it again." But not a patient who is that conscious of it – one who knows he does and still does it.

Dr. X: I think I really have to call his bluff, because he really is playing me in the sense that – I think you did hit the right sensitive nerve – he is playing me for the fact that I want to be the good guy and he can frustrate the shit out of me and I still won't kick him.

(Continued on next page)

Hugh: Yeah, but he'd also — it's not that simple, because there is another part of him that really wanted to be nice, but it was awfully hard for him to let it out and, like, he really would have helped me. It seems like he had to have you completely down, flat down and out before he could help you. (Pause) Before he could feel at ease enough with himself to be nice.

Shorr: And those would be rare, huh?

Hugh: What?

Shorr: His nice moments.

Hugh: Yeah.

Shorr: You couldn't trust it.

Hugh: No.

Shorr: Cause any time he was nice it might turn into something else right away, huh?

Hugh: Yeah, but you had to be completely defenseless around him and show all kinds of weakness. Then he would help or think he was helping.

Shorr: (S&O) In other words, he really wanted you to be as weak as hell before he'd help you, huh?

Hugh: Yes, but part of it was he was really frightened that maybe his kids would turn out badly. His sister had lost her mind. He's always been talking about that. (Pause) I think I'm getting disconnected — I'm just talking about him now.

Shorr: What I'm doing now, Hugh, is trying to avoid the double bind of demanding you feel a certain way, and/or my being quiet and letting you take the reins and go on yourself. In other words, I'm trying to be something other than your father was to you in reality, and hoping you'll see it. And if I am not a critical, dominating, know-it-all bastard, if you don't look at me that way, then you are not in contest with me.

(Continued on next page)

Shorr: Yes, but no therapist gets rid of his patients, you know, and you are such a nice guy.

Dr. X: Yes, I have done that with one or two patients who I couldn't stand because I couldn't get to them and all they were doing was just frustrating me. But he's been doing it in a somewhat more subtle way by pleading that he has this wooden leg. He frustrates me and then says, "Please feel sorry for me." "I've got this pain in my chest — I smoke too much." But he is still frustrating me.

(See p. 108, p. 134 and p. 136, for examples of this in the therapy tape.)

Shorr: And how! And just short of antagonizing you. He is so clever. Short of a total thing. But if you really told him he had to go somewhere else, and that is as much as you can do if he just persists in acting that way. If he says, "That's all I can do," just say, "Well, that's all *I* can do." And just call his bluff. It might be worth it. He either has to accede to the therapy or go, and I don't think he will go. I don't *think* that he will go, but that is always a chance that you have to take. But I don't think that he's so without a defense that he's going to go out and blow his head off, or something.

Dr. X: No, not at all. He's not like that. He's much too much in control.

Shorr: Control! His narcissism is too strong.

Dr. X: Right. He's got a very strong narcissism — very strong.

Shorr: Because I actually got to the point a few times where the intent of my voice was, "If you want to go, get the fuck out of here." And he just came right around. He didn't go out of the room or anything. Except to plead that he couldn't do any more — he was shut off. I just by-passed it then and let it go. (See p. 131 of therapy tape.)

(Continued on next page)

The other side of it is you don't have to be a kind of weak, sniveling, little child who lost all control of himself. It's like those two alternatives are the only ones open to you, and I think there is a third alternative. And therefore, if you can get to the point of seeing that or feeling that . . .

Hugh: Yeah, but I can't get there today. I feel that the hour's up and I'm just marking time now.

Shorr: Well, the hour isn't up — unless you wanted to go — I mean, it isn't up.

Hugh: I know, but I feel like . . .

Shorr: You don't want to go further you mean?

Hugh: No . . . like I'm just marking time now, it seems like . . .

Shorr: You are closed down, you mean.

Hugh: Yeah.

Shorr: Why did you close down? You have closed down hundreds of times before, right?

Hugh: Yeah.

Shorr: Here is another close-down.

Hugh: Yeah.

Shorr: Go into the close-down. Try to examine it.

Hugh: Well, I'm afraid of getting discouraged because I wasn't able to let out more feelings when I got closer to them — I don't want to go away with the feeling of defeat. It's like I'm closed down and any more stuff right now would just reinforce the whole close-down mechanism.

Shorr: O.K., since you have closed down hundreds of times, and you know why you close down . . .

Hugh: I *don't* know why I close down.

Shorr: You don't want to be defeated. You don't want to be unsuccessful. You don't want to be a failure.

(Continued on next page)

Dr. X: Actually he is no longer the real catalyst in either group, because there are other guys in the group who are pretty active. Yes, I think that is an important strategy. You get out of this the sense of the history of the real humiliating experiences with his father. With his mother if he had ever really expressed genuine feeling, other than the pity thing, he would probably have felt inappropriate. He probably, therefore, would have felt humiliated, but he would have felt that his genuine feelings were inappropriate with her because she was an invalid who couldn't deal with him on an equal level. So he had to just leave that out of the relationship. With the father, he knew. He got the vigilance at an early age and so he knew that, if he expressed genuine feelings, he would be ridiculed.

Shorr: Well, the humiliation has got to come from the father. That is the greatest fear. And the rejection has to come from the father.

Dr. X: With the mother it simply was that she was this fragile invalid and he just had to leave a lot of things out of their relationship.

Shorr: I asked him if I should dance with his mother and the answer is fantastic — yes, later on . . . and at the end of the tape. (See p. 141.) But I think maybe he has to face that ultimate rejection that he is so damn vigilantly guarding himself against all this time. I think therapy would begin when he comes back. When he goes, he'd have to come back on the terms of the feelings and not of the game.

Dr. X: On genuine participation.

Shorr: Yes. That's the only way. I don't think he really wants to go anywhere else. There is one part in there where I said, "Why don't you let yourself feel?" (See opposite column, this page.) He said he was afraid the session would be over.

(Continued on next page)

Hugh: Yeah, yeah, that's it, yeah. It would be easy to walk out of here and say I did pretty good. I got pretty close to the stuff without having to see the part of me that closes down. (Pause) It seems like that is so strong, so powerful, that that doesn't need any reinforcement.

Well, I said something like, "Go on." And he said, "Well, I feel closed down now." I prodded him to admit that he was holding back because he was afraid of being a failure — afraid of looking at the part of him that closes down.

Shorr: (S&O) And if I encourage you to break through further, it's a demand again, huh?

Hugh: Yes, but it seems like when you do do it — the question, or something, happens.

Shorr: (FTS) I am respected because _____ . Finish the sentence, please.

Hugh: Because I can run my life so well and manipulate all kinds of things to my advantage.

Shorr: (FTS) I am loved because ____ .

Hugh: I am loved because people think I have nice qualities, but then it never goes anywhere.

Shorr: (M/L) Now I want you to tell me the most private moment you can think of, but don't tell me what it is. In other words, you have an option to tell me about it or not to tell me about it. If you wish to tell me in time, fine. If you don't, you don't have to. You have that option. But I want you to think of the most private moment you can think of.

Hugh: Yeah, I can think of it.

Shorr: (IS) I suddenly appear at that private moment. You don't have to tell me what the private moment is, but tell me how you feel when I suddenly appear.

Hugh: Well, if the private moment is really the way I imagined it, you could come and I'd be glad to see you, and I'd smile and feel real warm towards you.

Shorr: (IS) Now how about if Dr. X came in? Would it be the same?

Hugh: Oh, I'd feel really warm. I'd just want to . . .

Shorr: Very happy, huh?

Hugh: Yeah, I'd want to be real nice to the guy.

Shorr: (IS) How about it if your old man came in?

Hugh: Well, let's see. (Pause) Well, I'd rather he came in afterwards and know what the private moment was, but not get close enough to see it. Intellectually knowing that it had happened but he would sort of talk about it on a superficial level — like make jokes or something — but not really see me right there.

Shorr: Now exercising your option, do you think you could tell me the private moment or not?

Hugh: Yeah, I know I could say it, but I want to be able to — I can always say or do anything if I . . .

Shorr: I mean you have the option, you don't have to if you don't want to.

Hugh: Yeah, I know, but what I'm trying to say is that I could just say it because I could steel myself up to it, but I'd like to be able to feel the moment and be able to say it, you know, if I want to.

Shorr: I wish you would, if I don't put you in a double bind as a demand. I wish you would for your own sake.

Hugh: (Long Pause) (Sigh) (Pause) Well, I just fell in love with a girl and had sex and it was real good and everything, and like afterwards we were just holding each other real happy, and he came in and . . . (Pause) I don't know how close I was to my feelings when I told you . . .

Shorr: I saw tears in your eyes.

Hugh: Yeah, I was thinking about the scene a little bit. How great it would be. I feel so — like all of the weight was off me, and life was really great.

Shorr: You make me feel really good to hear you say that.

Hugh: I don't know if I really believe it, though. Now I'm shut down again. It seems like I won't really believe it until I've actually seen it, you know.

Shorr: (M/L) What are the most tender feelings that you are capable of? Did I say that right? The tenderest feeling that you can . . .

Hugh: Yeah, it's like if you see a stray animal that has been beat up or is hungry or something like that. I'd feel real sad and want to do something for it, you know — make it feel all right. That's all I can really show.

Shorr: You'd take care of it and bring it back to life and stuff.

Hugh: Yeah, so it wouldn't feel so — it really racks me up when I see an animal that's scrounging around with nothing to eat, all frightened and not knowing what to do — like completely lost and hopeless and helpless and everything.

Shorr: Are you describing yourself, Hugh?

Hugh: Oh, yes, I know that.

Shorr: You are too smart to be fooled on any projections like that, huh?

Hugh: What do you mean, "too smart"? Well, I just know . . .

Shorr: You know it's you, huh?

Hugh: I know it's me — I don't have to say I'm smart for knowing it. I just always know that — I just, you know — it's obvious. That's the only kind of emotion I can show around people.

Shorr: (IS) Imagine you are a mouse who just came out of a hole. Tell me how you would feel.

Hugh: I'd get quickly back into the hole and protect myself.

Shorr: Against what?

Hugh: Anything could happen. I wouldn't want to come out of the hole until I had everything all safe and arranged so there's no more threats or anything. (Pause) Well, I can imagine the whole thing where I'd get in a real safe place that had an adequate food supply — no dangers, so I could go around wherever I was —

knowing I was perfectly safe, that I'd checked out *every* possibility, no cats, no danger of any kind.

Shorr: (IS) Now I want you to imagine that you are in a room that has a lot of those pads all around it — one of those padded rooms.

Hugh: Oh, that would make me furious because it would make me feel that people had put me there because I was some kind of nut. I would reject that whole image.

Shorr: O.K., you don't even want to try that one, huh?

Hugh: No, but if I could see why I was in that room. If the room were a room I had prepared myself, maybe I'd put padding there so that I could never get hurt if I bumped the wall. I'm not afraid of tripping or falling or anything, but . . .

Shorr: (IS) O.K., you prepare that room yourself and you go there because you want to go there. Now, what I'm really getting at is the fact that it is an isolated room from the world, in a sense . . . and now what I want you to do is act like you are going crazy.

Hugh: (Pause) (Yawn) Oh, I'd probably cry, scream and yell and just roll around the ground, bang and hit, and just go on for a long time, until I was too tired to do any more and I'd just go to sleep — and feel a lot better.

Shorr: Can you feel that when you are saying it or are you just saying it in the third person right now?

Hugh: I'm more like the third person.

Shorr: You have kind of withdrawn from the feelings now, huh?

Hugh: Yeah.

Shorr: Can you try to go into that one? Into that room you have created.

Hugh: I really feel like I've completely shut down. Any more is just like reinforcing all of that shutting down mechanism.

Shorr: Well then, how are you going to feel when you leave? Feel it now.

Hugh: I'd try to concentrate on the good things that happened.

Shorr: In other words, you've got all of your defenses up, not wanting to go ahead and feel some more.

Hugh: Yeah.

Shorr: Yet you have a pretty good opportunity right now.

Hugh: I know, that's another thing that makes me even more furious at myself. In fact, I smoke too much and I feel all uncomfortable inside, like I'm prevented physiologically from getting close to my feelings.

Shorr: Have you ever felt like screaming?

Hugh: Yeah, it's like I don't want to get into anything like that because I don't know how I could stop.

Shorr: I'll stop you. Why don't you try it?

Hugh: No, I don't want to scream. (Embarrassed tone)

Shorr: You are afraid of going out of control, huh?

Hugh: Well, I didn't think of that so much. I was thinking more of the fact that I couldn't really bring myself to scream as loud or as hard as I would feel that I would want to.

Shorr: Try.

Hugh: I just feel ridiculous.

Shorr: O.K., be ridiculous! It's about time you were ridiculous and not felt it was the end of the world.

Hugh: And not what?

Shorr: The end of the world. Or your vigilance is bent over and your guardedness and you have now been discovered as Mr. Dillinger in some goddam – like you are going to be shot down – Al Capone or something. I don't know what you are always afraid of – this goddam miserable person that they're going to discover. No one in the world is going to discover. Of course, you feel that, I guess. Come on – scream. I'll stop you if you get too violent.

Hugh: (Pause) It just makes me mad that I wasn't able to scream without having to go through all this rigmarole. (Pause) Why don't you count to three and I'll scream and I'll see if I can get a fresh start.

Shorr: O.K., one, two, three.

Hugh: (Screams loudly)

Shorr: How do you feel now?

Hugh: (Laughs) I don't think I feel much different. (Pause) I can't scream when I first felt it. It's like I waited until I felt safe about it.

Shorr: But it was quite a scream, I must tell you. I've heard a lot of screams and it was as good as any.

Hugh: I didn't want to do it at first because I figured my voice would crack and I thought it would sound ridiculous.

Shorr: Again, you're afraid you might sound ridiculous.

Hugh: Yeah.

Shorr: (M/L) Who is the most ridiculous person you have ever known?

Hugh: Oh, I don't know. I just never want to get that close to thinking about it.

Shorr: You sound like you are so afraid of being this ridiculous person. I wonder who in the hell this ridiculous person is, that you are so goddam afraid of being like.

Hugh: I don't know. I feel very uncomfortable when other people look ridiculous – like it's a threat.

Shorr: You mean a fellow makes a speech in front of the class or something and fumbles and . . .

Hugh: Yeah, I always want to make them feel better and pretend I haven't noticed – like I'm just getting out of the thing, you know. It would be really embarrassing for me.

Shorr: (IS) Now suppose that you were to walk up Park Avenue and your identity wouldn't necessarily be detrimental to you. I mean you wouldn't lose your position or whatever, but you walked up Park Avenue, like, in shorts and stripped to the waist and sort of supposedly looking ridiculous — what would happen? Could you do it?

Hugh: Well, maybe.

Shorr: Could wild horses make you do it?

Hugh: Yeah. (Pause)

Shorr: Then what? Would you just steel yourself for it and that's it?

Hugh: Well, I just had a feeling of freedom and I'd feel relaxed. I'd feel like I'd removed a problem.

Shorr: It sounds great!

Hugh: (Long pause, lit cigarette) I'm having a hard time breathing. I smoke too much. I just — my chest is all tight and — it's really an uncomfortable feeling. I was aware even while I was smoking, it was just putting up an obstacle.

Shorr: (IS) Now, imagine an elephant's foot on your chest. How does it feel?

Hugh: Well, just pressure and tight.

Shorr: (IS) (Focusing Tech.) Now, push that fucking elephant off. Move it away.

Hugh: I imagine myself pushing. I don't care how strong it is, I would push it away. I still have that tight feeling that comes from too much smoking, and my doctor told me I had to stop that because I was over constricting with nerves and everything, and nicotine is constricting — like my blood vessels and everything.

Shorr: How about just singing a loud note. Can you try that for a second to release the tension in your chest?

Hugh: Yes.

Shorr: Try it.

Hugh: (Sings a note)

Shorr: That's not very loud.

Hugh: The only thing I can imagine doing is getting up and talking and running something — like controlling a class — just getting under perfect control — just manipulating everything — every gesture, everything just perfectly. That's what gets me through the day some times — teaching.	**Shorr:** There is a part on the tape where he talks about his feelings with the class — where he feels the best. **Dr. X:** In class. **Shorr:** In class where he has complete control.
Shorr: It gives you a powerful feeling, huh?	**Dr. X:** Yes.
Hugh: Well, I don't feel powerful so much — other than sometimes the kids	**Shorr:** Where he could take the group over or something like that. **Dr. X:** Now *there* is a contradiction because in that situation, the class has

(Continued on next page)   *(Continued on next page)*

need complete domination – but more like I get out of that tightness and the rest of the day goes a little better.

Shorr: (IS) Now suppose that you are back in the meadow again and there's like twenty of these wild animals like tigers and lions . . .

Hugh: I'd feel like I'd want to get in a fight with them and just mess them up bad.

Shorr: Good.

Hugh: That I don't care what they did to me, I could still put a tremendous amount of injury and hurt on them.

Shorr: You have tremendous anger and hostility in you. You are so fucking angry at the fact that you have to be so terribly vigilant in your life – and so controlled and you really want to let all that damn control go.

expectations and that certainly is a demand.

Shorr: He's playing it so well – he's got them so controlled.

Dr. X: Of course, he is posturing in that situation – I mean it is a role.

Shorr: Because later on he feels badly – he says afterwards. He knows he can do it and be voted the best teacher and all that, but he doesn't feel any reward from it. (See page 143 of therapy tape.)

Dr. X: No. I think that when he would come to a point of relating to them as persons more, these kids, then I think he could feel it. But he doesn't relate to persons very much – once in a while the girl that he is attracted to.

Hugh: (Yawning) Yes, but I've been doing it so long.

Shorr: How old are you, Hugh?

Hugh: I am 35.

Shorr: That's a long time to hold it in, huh?

Hugh: Yeah, I know it. It seems like I'm getting near the time when . . . I've still got a lot of freedom to . . .

Shorr: Except you're not 21, so you're on a collision course to let that thing go.

Hugh: Yeah. If I were 21, I wouldn't worry about it like that. I have that horrible thing about time running out.

Shorr: Yeah, well, your time is running out, but how about letting your feelings through here – today.

Hugh: I really feel like I could . . .

Shorr: You mean you would like to go another year . . .

Hugh: No. I – the more tired I get – I think about time running out and it makes me feel more hopeless and helpless and everything.

Shorr: Bull shit! Because that's just a fucking rationalization. Because right now you can do something for yourself that will put yourself a year ahead, or six months ahead in therapy – in your whole life, more than therapy, because therapy *is* life.

Hugh: (Yawns)

Shorr: You like to yawn when you hear that, don't you?

Hugh: Yeah.

Shorr: You'd rather wait, wait, wait another year; wait another fucking year; wait a decade. You'll be 45 and you still won't know.

Hugh: Yeah, but this is a reinforcement. My desire is to walk out of here and to tell you to shove it, thinking that I just – that kind of stuff just doesn't seem to work.

Shorr: I wish the hell you *would* tell me to shove it. Maybe you would release something. At least that would be some feelings on your part.

Hugh: Yeah, but it still seems like a negative thing.

Shorr: It doesn't make any difference *what* it is as long as you get the fucking feelings out – negative, positive – it doesn't mean a damn thing. You've got a lid on everything.

Hugh: I'm really worried now whether or not I'm going downhill by prolonging this whole thing.

Shorr: I don't think you are going downhill.

Hugh: I'm going downhill if you are expecting me to open up and I'm not able to, and I go away with the feeling of . .. .

Shorr: Failure.

Hugh: Yeah.

Shorr: But that's not really the case.

Hugh: (Pause) How do you mean that's not the case? Have I done enough today that it makes it worthwhile?

Shorr: Oh, I think so, as far as that's concerned, but I think the fact is that there is no kind of . ... you make a judgment about the sequence of this thing, and how it has gone and how it is supposed to go. It's like that mouse, you know, who looked all around to see if all the cats were away and every possible danger was away, then it could come out. (See p. 133 of therapy tape.) Now the danger here is for me to have you react or feel your own . . .

Hugh: Yeah, I know, a lot of things you say, I'm just not following all of that stuff. I like to be just close to what I feel and no words about it.

Shorr: O.K.

Hugh: Yeah, but I don't know if I can get back to that feeling – feeling that I would like to be close, instead of the hopeless feeling about everything, whether it is the judgment of the failure, it is just the sadness, I am not getting it like I want to. I just seem to be so paralyzed. It seems like it sort of melts all of the rigidity in some way.

Shorr: Yeah, I know. Like you felt with Dr. X, in his arms, huh?

Hugh: Yeah.

Shorr: And the way you said earlier that you'd like to be with a girl in bed. You'd just like to melt into her.

Hugh: I didn't say that. I said it was like afterwards when we were holding each other. A calmer period, like, you know.

Shorr: (M/L) What is the greatest defense against your sadness?

Hugh: Oh, I'll do something to make myself more confident than I feel, or I'll buy some art objects, or buy something, especially something that has to come through the mail, so there is a delay and I keep waiting for it to come.

Shorr: Keep hoping?

Hugh: Yeah. (Pause)

Shorr: (M/L) Is that the most horrible feeling on earth to feel, is sadness?

Hugh: Yeah, it's pretty bad.

Shorr: Wanting?

Hugh: (Pause) I feel like I'm talking about another person. I can feel a little bit, but I don't know — all and all I've always got to find some way out of that feeling.

Shorr: If you get into it, what would happen, Hugh?

Hugh: I've really tried many times and sort of give into it and sort of try to cry, thinking there would be such a relief and everything, but I just can't bring myself to do it. I'll start smoking a lot . . .

Shorr: Is it mostly done in isolation?

Hugh:Well, yeah. I rent out rooms to people. I rented an old house and I rent out rooms. Often people are around. I guess I could just go in my room and shut the door.

Shorr: (S&O) What would happen if you showed the sadness to Dr. X? Alone, with him?

Hugh: I have a few times. It just seems like a little bit comes out but I can't let it all out.

Shorr: What would happen if you let it all out? Would you disappear?

Hugh: No, I wouldn't disappear, but it seems like I'd be clinging to him for hours and hours and hours, and go beyond the bounds of the session or something like that.

Shorr: So, what if it did?

Hugh: Well, I wish it would happen because I'm not really — I'm really not that worried, so I'd pay for five sessions and then I'd be much better off.

Shorr: Right.

Hugh: But I just — the trouble is in me more than . . .. .

Shorr: In other words, you need so much you're . . .

Hugh: It looks like I can never get it — it seems like I'd better keep away from it because I want it so much that it's just better not to get into it — because I could never get enough — I could *never* get enough.

Shorr: Is this what you want from a woman, too?

Hugh: Yeah, I could just never get enough. It seems like there just wouldn't be enough there. I need too much that has been denied for so long that it would just take an exorbitant amount — more than any person could really give me.

Shorr: Maybe you ought to start trying and see that there are people that can give.

Hugh: Yeah, I know all that, I just feel . . .

Shorr: (S&O) Is that the chance you have to take — the biggest chance — to show your needs and feelings? To know a person and find that they won't turn away after awhile?

Hugh: Yeah.

Shorr: (S&O) Do you always feel that you are going to be abandoned, Hugh?

Hugh: Oh, yeah, I'm convinced.

Shorr: What would happen if you were abandoned?

Hugh: I don't know, it would just turn out to be bad — the worst that you can imagine to happen. Not quite the *very* worst but so close to it that . . . Actually, I don't think I'm making any progress now. I feel it's just a waste.

Shorr: You mean, you understand all of this?

Hugh: I understand all this — it doesn't seem like I'm going to get anything by going over it. Cause I've been going to Dr. X for years, you know?

Shorr: How long have you been going to Dr. X?

Hugh: About six years.

Shorr: Have you learned anything new about yourself today?

Hugh: Well, I got closest — not closest, but close again — a little bit closer to how I feel, and more and more convinced and reinforced that that is where it's at — to get close to my feelings.

Shorr: (IS) Would you like to try one more thing though, and that is to look into your father's eyes. Can you try that?

Hugh: (Long pause) Ah, that's awfully hard. I mean not that I'm feeling all these things about it, but it makes it hard for me to look. It's just that it's hard for me to even think of it or to imagine it.

Shorr: See if you can look into his eyes. Try, and tell me what you feel when you see his eyes.

Hugh: Well, here is what worries me, I don't feel all of the things I feel I should feel.

Shorr: I don't care what you should feel, just tell me what you see when you look into his eyes. Should is unknown.

Hugh: It looks like there is some kind of fear. A sort of powerful fear that could just turn into violence at the least little thing.

Shorr: (IS) If you continue to stare into his eyes, can you transform them in any way? Can you imagiine your father a little boy?

Hugh: I've seen pictures of him as a little boy and he looks just the same.

Shorr: (IS) Can you imagine your father, a little boy, crying and coming up to you and hugging you?

Hugh: Yeah, I'd get down on my knees and really hug him and make him feel as good as I could.

Shorr: How would you feel about it?

Hugh: I'd feel real good!

Shorr: Stay with that feeling! Can you feel it?

Hugh: Yeah. (Pause)

Shorr: (IS) Now you are the father and raise him in the way you want him to be raised.

Hugh: Oh, yeah, I can imagine the whole thing.

Shorr: Like what?

Hugh: Well, I'd want to smooth over all of the rough spots. Not, I mean, not pamper, but take everything in a low key. Any kind of problems — when a person shows nervousness or fear or something like that — don't make a big thing of it, but sort of mute the whole thing, like, not getting so upset about it. And not making a person feel that upset about it. Like, it's a more normal thing and sometimes you feel frightened and sometimes you don't.

Shorr: You would give him complete acceptance then, huh?

Hugh: Yeah, complete acceptance.

Shorr: Non-criticalness, huh?

Hugh: Yeah.

Shorr: (IS) Can you *feel* that? If you were raising your father — he was the baby and you were raising him — you were the father?

Hugh: Yeah.

Shorr: Does it feel good?

Hugh: Yeah, it feels good, but I'm just barely in the scene, if you know what I mean.

Shorr: You can't get into it?

Hugh: No. I've got two dogs and I do the same thing for them. I don't ever want them to feel abandoned, or hurt, or upset, or nervous, or anything like that. (Pause) So, while I was leaning over my dad, there, I began to see one of my dogs that needs extra love. One of those high-strung dogs, you know.

Shorr: You gave it all the tender care you could, huh?

Hugh: Yes, but sometimes I just try to do things so the dog is . . . I mean, uh, not so many hangups and all of that stuff.

Shorr: (IS) Suppose you saw me dancing with your mother, what would you feel?

Hugh: Well, I'd say you were a miracle worker if you got my mother . . . (Laughing)

Shorr: Is she that bad?

Hugh: Yes, she can't even get out of bed.

(Continued on next page)

Dr. X: The miracle if you could dance with his mother. I got a flash that, in his relationship with his mother, this is exactly what he thought he was expected to be. Because obviously his father could not manage the mother at all. His father was very antagonistic to her and ridiculed her constantly for being a cripple and a dope addict and all that stuff, and the burden was on Hugh

(Continued on next page)

Shorr: You're kidding. You mean she's really that depressed all of the time?

Hugh: Yeah, her mother takes care of her, who is 80 some odd years old.

Shorr: You mean she's just really that ...

Hugh: Yeah, it's just a constant suffering, misery, victim – faced and tired by anguish, day in and day out.

Shorr: So if you saw me dancing with her, it really would be a miracle, huh?

Hugh: Yeah. (Laughing)

Shorr: Do you think she could actually, if I worked on her long enough and got her finally to dancing, that she'd actually let herself go enough to enjoy it? Or does she love her suffering too much?

Hugh: Well, I think she is in that bed too much, but I think in a way I'd actually be glad if my mother could get out of it. It's just that I've given up hope. I mean just no possibility of it, so ...

Shorr: (S&O) Do you feel very responsible for her?

Hugh: I used to feel that I had to do something – for years – a constant struggle to think of what I could do to get things to go better. Now, I sort of cut off completely from her, cause it's just a bad scene.

Shorr: Your grandmother still lives in the same house then, huh?

Hugh: Yeah. (Pause) What do you mean in the same house?

Shorr: What I was wondering – do you live alone or with your folks?

Hugh: No, I haven't lived at home for years.

Shorr: I had no idea, that's why I asked.

Hugh: No, I rent an old house that's been lived in for 89 years, and I rent out the rooms, and it gets my rent down to a reasonable level. No, they don't live too near here.

(Continued on next page)

to take care of her and make her healthy and, I suppose, wholesome. As a child he felt like that was his burden.

Shorr: Responsibility.

Dr. X: Responsibility to do all this for her, and I just imagine that he felt that this was what she wanted from him as well as what his father wanted from him. Although his father really didn't want him to take care of her very well. He just wanted ... He actually didn't enter into that aspect. He just, by being away from it, he just left it for Hugh to do it. There was no direct communication except when Hugh would get drugs for the mother secretly and things like this. He knew he had to avoid the father's vigilance. But the sense I have now is that, if he thought there was this much that he thought he had to accomplish, which is obviously impossible in relationship to his mother – nurturing her and so on – then he's never verbalized this. Except he said that women in general are expecting a lot from him. But he feels they are expecting normal things from him. Whereas, I think his mother was expecting a miracle and he couldn't produce it. Obviously. And, as a child, he probably had all kinds of unrealistic notions as to what he was supposed to be able to do.

Shorr: It would have taken an emotional miracle to move his mother.

Dr. X: Exactly, and nothing has ever moved her. She's been back in the hospital again and she's home a complete invalid. She's been declared vocationally unemployable and she collects social security before eligibility age, and some kind of public welfare benefits. She's considered totally dependent. The sense I have now is that he has transferred this to feeling women expect him to be a kind of miracle worker and that he is supposed to come across with all kinds of bountiful feelings.

Shorr: And sustain it.

(Continued on next page)

Shorr: (S&O) I see. Are you afraid of your department chairman you mentioned earlier? I know nothing about you; I just wondered.

Hugh: No, because I can play the role so well. He's very impressed and he gives me promotions and next year I come up for tenure, and he's assured me he's going to work very hard for it and there's no worry about it. No, I can manipulate things like that fairly well.

Shorr: In other words, the anxiety level at work is not that high.

Hugh: No, I can handle everything there. The trouble I have at work is that I realize that I'm just playing a role. It's like a burden. When I walk out to the parking lot, I sometimes wonder, after a successful day, what's the use, you know? What am I getting out of it for myself — except securing my income and job and everything like that.

Shorr: That doesn't give you any meaning, huh?

Hugh: No. And I joke with the students. They all like me and voted me best instructor. I give them parties and stuff, real friendly, and the girls get all turned on, and it never goes anywhere.

Shorr: (S&O) Do you date much?

Hugh: Well, no. Sometimes I do; sometimes I don't.

Shorr: Do you resent that question?

Hugh: No. I don't.

Shorr: (M/L) Are you most uptight in the dating scene? More than you are anywhere else? Where the girls are concerned?

Hugh: The trouble is I can play the role so well. The whole thing is like a performance. Then when it's time to ask your feelings on something, I don't — so I'm trying to really *feel* stuff.

Shorr: Do you hate the girl at that

(Continued on next page)

Dr. X: Exactly. So he's got a whole fictitious relationship there in which he is supposed to produce something that is extraordinary.

Shorr: Miraculous is really the word. It puts such tremendous pressure on him. If he lets go of his feelings at all, then he has to let go of them forever and make a total commitment.

Dr. X: So it fits in with his feelings that he should cut off.

Shorr: Maybe all women are potentially collapsible and depressive like his mother — sooner or later . . .

Dr. X: Yes, he does see that — that eventually women will need a very strong man and he's got to really support them. Yeah, he has verbalized that. But I don't think we've really established the relationship here between the sick situation with his mother (all the burden on him which he saw as inappropriate, but which he accepted even though he knew he couldn't fulfill it) and what he's doing now with women.

Shorr: You've got something there — a man who is either cruel or a miracle worker, huh?

Dr. X: Yes. He tried going all the way with his sister at fourteen or fifteen. I'm just suspecting that, I don't know that for a fact.

Shorr: The thought that I had was that his mother feared abandonment and his mother feared replacement. And that's probably why she went into this tremendous depression and immobilized invalid state. It was a guarantee against being abandoned. That's one side. The other side is that, if he's strong, then he has to be abandoned or he has the possibility of being replaced because when I said, "Do you feel that you are going to be abandoned?" he didn't even hesitate. (See p. 140.) Replacement and abandonment, and the other thing you

(Continued on next page)

point? For having been fooled by your performance?

Hugh: No — there must be some kind of rage there because I'm not going to give her anything.

Shorr: (S&O) Have you ever met any girl who saw through your performance?

Hugh: Yes, but it was only after awhile, and it was, like, I'd open up very carefully and she'd always be one step ahead of me, so I never really took that much of a risk. I never got the experience of confronting my embarrassment or anything like that.

Shorr: Sounds like she was, like, a therapist, huh? One step ahead of you and then you had to watch out.

Hugh: Yeah.

Shorr: You have to know in advance then, pretty much what's going to happen before you can . . .

Hugh: Yeah, I can't just go out and put myself on a limb and say something that might ruin the whole thing. Every girl I'm with, I think it's my last chance.

Shorr: (S&O) Do you feel you are always replaceable, is that it?

Hugh: Yeah, maybe I do, because if I don't do it right, they will find somebody who can just do it better. They're just not going to waste their time with some immature little creep.

Shorr: There we go again with "creep." (Laughs)

Hugh: (Laughs) Yeah, I knew you were going to do that when I said it.

Shorr: It's not criticism, I just . . .

Hugh: Yeah, I know, but I mean . . .

Shorr: Are you in group therapy, by the way?

Hugh: Yeah.

Shorr: (S&O) And let me ask you this

(Continued on next page)

said about the responsibility he would have to a woman, I think, are very key. I suppose he has faced the risk of abandonment by you and found that it didn't have all that deadly possibilities.

Dr. X: Maybe he has to face that. I'll come back to what you were saying about him, that he should get off the pot. Somehow he either has to come across with the real feelings that he seems capable of — I'm judging that he is capable of it — I think he is. And if he doesn't, he is forced to face the experience of having to leave me — be pushed out, actually, more than just leaving. But be pushed out and having to consider to weigh the whole thing by either going to someone else or not going at all. Or possibly having to admit to himself that he wants to come back.

Shorr: Well, you have already confronted him with the suggestion that he should get another therapist?

Dr. X: You see I didn't confront him in the context of making it very definitely clear and obvious to him — in the context of forcing him into a position that, "You've got to come through with some feelings and, if you don't, then you've got to get the hell out of here." I think that is the proper context.

Shorr: In other words, "I won't abandon you if you are strong, but I will abandon you if you are weak." His weakness is a guarantee against his abandonment, he feels — the helplessness . . .

Dr. X: Right, that is what he has been using so far — what his mother used. And that is an important parallel, I think. If he is strong, he will be rewarded for it.

Shorr: And he won't be abandoned for it. So confront him with the alternate possibility that he so expects. It's certainly worth a chance.

Dr. X: What?

(Continued on next page)

question. If Dr. X were to replace you with somebody in group therapy, what kind of a person should he replace you with?

Hugh: (Pause) Well, I don't know. Well, from some of the things that some of the women in the group say, they want a real active male who will sort of be a challenge to them and help them work at their own things. Of course, I play more like a little kid role, who needs protection. (Pause)

Shorr: You mean you'd like to be in some large woman's arms and sucking her . . .

Hugh: Oh, no, no − I can't even − that doesn't . . .

Shorr: That doesn't do anything for you, huh?

Hugh: No, I want some real cute young girl − that's what I feel I really want.

Shorr: A real good looking girl, huh?

Hugh: Yeah.

Shorr: Intelligent?

Hugh: Yeah, fairly intelligent.

Shorr: Perceptive?

Hugh: Well, I don't know, because I keep scoring different things. Sometimes I'm interested in the girls who are just exceptionally good looking, but are sort of dolls, like, and are aware of being good looking and want the man to come and be very appreciative and turned on by the fact that they are such adorable little creatures, you know. But probably what I basically want is some more mature, more understanding woman, but it seems like it's too far away.

Shorr: They wouldn't want you, is that it?

Hugh: Well, it just seems like too much of a demand. Too much showing of affection and stuff. Where some younger girl might be more on the surface. I

(Continued on next page)

Shorr: It certainly is worth the chance − but I guess he has enough strength to sustain himself.

Dr. X: Oh, yes, I think he does.

Shorr: His defense is so strong − he's actually a hell of a lot stronger than he will allow himself to be.

Dr. X: That's what I think.

Shorr: My guess, too. Yeah, I think he is strong enough to face it, but strength means abandonment − strength means isolation. The other way he can hold on to something, I guess.

Dr. X: I think he has never really had a crisis in therapy − with me − I think that I've avoided it with him.

Shorr: Well it's pretty hard for a therapist to precipitate a crisis if you have to be kind and nice and non-rejecting at the same time. I noticed when I said, "Bull shit, or you can go if you want to," he didn't (p. 138). I have the advantage that I don't have the investment in him that you have. Did you notice anything about the particular system of things that I was doing with him?

Dr. X: I thought that you got inside with him. I mean, you seemed to be able to ask him a question so that it was palatable to him. Considering how vigilant and defensive he is, he really was rather productive.

Shorr: Of course, I must add (it's not on the tape) that I did say I was going to play the tape for you. So I guess that it was important for him to perform. That probably adds to the ability − if you call this impasse therapy − it adds if you are going to say you are going to play this for the therapist. Then he's got to show up well, especially since he is a performance person. I didn't know that from the very beginning, or the second I saw him, but . . .

(Continued on next page)

mean it wouldn't be a real deep relationship — it might work into that, though.

Shorr: (S&O) The chance that you can't take, though, in a relationship with a woman, at first, is . . . what?

Hugh: Oh, the whole thing is so abstract I can't even — I'm just talking now.

Shorr: Yeah, I was wondering. We're close to the end of this, and I just wanted to hear what you'd say.

Hugh: Yeah, but I could say two or three different things. It would be all contradictory.

Shorr: How come?

Hugh: I don't even know where it's at for me around girls.

Shorr: You mean, intellectually you can't come up with the answer on it?

Hugh: No, I can't.

Shorr: (S&O) What about that replaceable factor? Can we go back to that for a moment?

Hugh: Yeah. I've never quite thought of that before but it seems like a sort of important thing. (Pause)

Shorr: (S&O) You mean you're guarding against that? You have to be a certain kind of way or else you will be replaced?

Hugh: Yeah.

Shorr: And maybe someone unidentifiable, or someone you don't even know — it might be actually, but . . .

Hugh: Yeah, just somebody better than me.

Shorr: Somebody better.

Hugh: Yeah, than me.

Shorr: (S&O) You're always on a kind of comparison — unfavorable comparison — that someone is better, huh?

Hugh: Yeah.

Shorr: Even if you don't know who the hell it is?

(Continued on next page)

Dr. X: I think you ought to hire yourself to do this for therapists with impasse, because it's got a lot to show there.

Shorr: What I'd really like to do is for you to hear the other patient's tape, because it shows a lot more of the things I was doing. Here I bog down into what I was doing five years ago or more — straight interacting, question/answer. I didn't give as many situations to get into. To get lost into.

Dr. X: But don't you find that he creates much more a sense of antagonism and friction when you are working with him, than other patients do?

Shorr: Well, I don't know if it's fair because he came as a guest and I don't think he would show it. He would just say, "I feel turned off" or "I'm not doing well enough at this point," but he gave the outward appearance of co-operativeness, because he knew how to play the game and he knew that I was your friend.

Dr. X: No, I don't mean that he was outward and direct about it, but when you say he got bogged down, I think that is something he does. I mean he is a very bright guy. He's very verbal, but still you get that feeling of being bogged down and that is something that he produces in people.

Shorr: Yeah, he wouldn't carry the ball.

Dr. X: No, not at all.

Shorr: Some of the people, I'll ask the question and they just go on and on and on, and stay with it, and add things, and add dimensions that I don't even know they are going to do, and I don't even ask questions.

Dr. X: And he doesn't do that, and that's how he is in relationships in the group.

Shorr: I can't get in the middle of his fantasy, because he never let himself go

(Continued on next page)

Hugh: Yeah.

Shorr: (S&O) And if you are really the better one would you believe it? Would you know it?

Hugh: Oh, I'm sure I wouldn't know it. No.

Shorr: That's the problem, huh?

Hugh: Yeah.

Shorr: To believe that. To believe you.

Hugh: Yeah.

Shorr: To believe Hugh Clemens does, as himself.

Hugh: Yeah, I think you better stop. I got a crook in the back just thinking about that.

Shorr: O.K., we'll stop then . . .

with his imagination long enough for me to get in the middle of it, as I can with other patients.

Dr. X: He's got a lot of fantasy, too. But he doesn't disclose it.

Shorr: No. He would stop. And because it is directive therapy which the whole thing is designed for, I would have to come in after awhile. I couldn't wait him out forever. I suppose I could if I wanted to, but . . . But with other patients, I participate in their fantasy — their going through houses and their opening doors, and what's happening now — I'm right with them through the whole fantasy. That's what I say. After I did it and I heard this second part — this last half hour — about a week later, I felt discouraged. What real value? It's what I said when I had lunch with you — like it was no miracle that I was performing. Diagnostically it gives you a lot — there is no question about that — you pick up cues, but . . .

Dr. X: Well, what would you do with him if you had him in therapy? Knowing what you know about him.

Shorr: The only thought — it's really not a good question, because . . .

Dr. X: It's what you would do and what I would do.

Shorr: First we have our own individual styles and temperaments. But I think I would test the abandonment out — and that strength doesn't get abandoned, strength doesn't mean isolation. And the other way he's actually isolated and abandoned anyway, but he feels he's always got that tit to suck on — to hold onto — that he won't be let go finally or replaced. Because the thing he gave the most spontaneous answer to of anything was that he will always feel or be abandoned. He was convinced. It was almost — he didn't even wait for a second to think about it. Like the others, he would think a little bit. And

(Continued on next page)

the replaceable factor. So I think that is
the chance that you have to take with
him, I would say. But it is a very unfair
question — how can anyone tell anyone
else? It's very hard. It's really presump-
tious to do it. These are thoughts —
these are ideas, but . . .

Dr. X: I think I'm going to try an intensive individual session with him at
first. First try pushing him much more
and see how he deals with that — how
that goes.

Shorr: You mean like almost getting
angry, and . . .

Dr. X: Having a real kind of showdown
thing on just getting him to express
feelings more, without the issue of ter-
minating with it and all that. I don't
think I'll get to that yet, but I think I'll
try an intensive session with him and try
to get him into more physical contacts
— to act out some of that fantasy. I'll
push him to do that and really create a
showdown around that. If that doesn't
work, then I'll get to the other.

Shorr: The other thought I had was — if
it was possible to set this up — is to get a
rope — a very difficultly knotted rope —
and let him unknot the rope as he is
talking to you, while he is doing the
therapy. To loosen some of that energy
away. I don't know how you could set
that up. It's a thought I've had before
with some other people — they are so
rigid, so vigilant. They get so much of
the tension out on the rope, then they
can let go of the other.

Dr. X: I had him bring his dogs into a
group session, and he did loosen up
some. (See p. 141 of therapy tape.) I
told him to bring them in again and he
wouldn't — he didn't. He didn't say he
wouldn't — he just didn't. I think the
dog thing had some of that element
because he was able — they were very
frisky, very restless dogs, and I think he

(Continued on next page)

has over-indulged them tremendously — they don't follow his orders at all — he doesn't order them around — I think you heard what he said about the dogs — he can give everything to them — and I think he gives them quite a bit. But he could talk about them and there was more feeling in the tone of the session from him. So I suggested he bring one of the dogs back with him. The group members thought it was a good idea. He didn't bring the dogs back and he gave us all of these excuses. So we didn't push him on it. We ought to push him on it.

[END OF TAPE]

Some time later Dr. X and I discussed what could be done to facilitate the process of therapy for Hugh. Dr. X decided that he would ask Hugh to leave therapy until he could return with the understanding that he allow himself to feel and express his feelings openly. While Hugh seemed disturbed, he reluctantly agreed to go. Six weeks later he returned to Dr. X. He said he was ready to expose his real feelings. Dr. X said that, if Hugh felt he could express his feelings, he would welcome him back, but if Hugh felt he couldn't allow himself to open up, he would refer Hugh elsewhere.

Hugh did return and worked through a great many of his feelings in therapy in about two months. Dr. X proceeded directly on the basis that, if Hugh wouldn't open up to his authentic feelings, he would indeed be replaced. He made this abundantly clear to Hugh.

In later conversation with me, Dr. X reported that the approach was effective. By urging Hugh to face his fear of being replaced, he was able to help Hugh finally accept that he would not be. Hugh then moved rapidly in resolving many of his conflicts, with a great deal of desire and self-assertion.

Although it was unplanned, the use of the psycho-imagination therapy techniques and the analysis of the taped session by Dr. X and myself gave us the awareness to break the "impasse" that confronted Hugh. With this patient at least, psycho-imagination therapy techniques succeeded in exposing the patient's conflicts and breaking an impasse in therapy. Perhaps it might be possible for therapists who use conventional therapy to utilize psycho-imagination therapy techniques to aid them in therapy impasse situations.

CHAPTER 8

Psycho-Imagination Therapy
in the Study of Therapy "Outcome"

"One learns more about a man from ten words which he speaks himself on his own behalf than from a ten hour eulogy by a friend. It does not matter so much what he says in those ten words; what really counts is the way in which he says them."

Robert Graves

This chapter is written with the intent of suggesting a possible method of outcome therapy, from an experiential standpoint; it does not pretend to be definitive. The method involves having the patient listen to and react to a tape-recording of his Psycho-Imagination Therapy session after an appropriate lapse of time. Although I have used this method with many of my own patients, I will present here a single case of a woman who was not my patient, but who had been sent to me by another therapist for a session in Psycho-Imagination Therapy. This woman listened to her tape after a lapse of two years, during which she continued to attend group sessions with her therapist. Since her initial session with me was essentially phenomenological, and her own later assessment was also phenomenological, I refer to the method as "phenomenological outcome assessment." Although certainly lacking in quantitative measurement, this method has been . enormously valuable to me and my patients. However, it should be viewed as only an additional possibility of outcome assessment, among all the other methods offered by psychologists and psychiatrists.

There are few problems in psychotherapy which are more difficult than assessment of outcome. As so ably stated by Gottschalk, *et al*, "The assessment of outcome with psychotherapy is difficult. Assessments made by the psychotherapist are likely to reflect his hopes for success or failure or predilections for one style of psychotherapy over another. Assessments by patients, through various types of self-ratings, are likely to be influenced by: 1) the desire to please or reward the therapist ..., 2) a tendency to suppress reporting symptoms or negative feelings ..." (Gottschalk, Mayerson and Gottlieb, 1967, p. 78.)

However, with the above in mind, I wish to present this case for two reasons:
(1) Further demonstration of patient-therapist interactions in Psycho-Imagination Therapy.
(2) Illustration of a case in which an attempt at phenomenological outcome assessment was successful in revealing both to the patient and the therapist the extent of progress the patient had made in two years.

Vicky was sent to me by Dr. Y, who had been her therapist for almost three years. I had discussed Psycho-Imagination Therapy with Dr. Y and he suggested that I record a session with Vicky, using some of my methods. Then he and I would listen to the tape to see what we could learn from the experience that might be useful in Vicky's therapy.

The force of events was such that we didn't hear Vicky's tape together. Instead, after she had been in therapy for about two years, we decided to let Vicky listen to her own tape (made with me) and react and comment into another tape in her privacy. Then Dr. Y listened to both the tape of the initial therapy session and the tape of Vicky's reactions on listening to her tape, and commented on his assessment of Vicky's progress.

When Vicky appeared in my office for our session of Psycho-Imagination Therapy, I was immediately struck by the contrast between her stylish appearance and her affectless manner and tone of voice. She was a well-dressed woman of about forty, very slightly overweight, moderately attractive, with reddish-brown hair. She appeared quite intelligent and unafraid; rather, her manner was listless and apathetic. The most striking difference to me between the Vicky I listened to in my office and the Vicky on the second tape was the change in her voice from apathy to vivaciousness and vitality.

The remainder of this chapter presents transcriptions of the two tapes. Vicky's comments appear in a right-hand column which is inserted at the exact points in the therapy transcription at which she interrupted the original tape to record her own reactions. Following the transcriptions of the two tapes are cogent abstracts from comments made by Dr. Y as he listened to both of the tapes.

Therapy Tape	**Vicky's Comments on Listening to Her Tape Two Years Later**
Shorr: Probably a little strange for you, huh? Talking to somebody else.	
Vicky: Yeah, it is.	
Shorr: Do you feel frightened at the idea?	
Vicky: I don't know if it's the apprehension.	

Shorr: Well, it should be. It's a horrible thing I'm going to do.

Vicky: Is it really?

Shorr: No. It's very easy, it really is. It's nothing more than any other conversational thing. I'm just going to ask you some questions and imaginative kinds of situations. The purpose, of course, is to see what you can learn from it. I'm doing this for the first time with somebody who is not my patient to see if it is helpful. The way it will be used is that Dr. Y and I probably will listen to the tape at some later point and maybe you'd like to listen to the tape with Dr. Y sometime, and see how it is. Hopefully it will be of value to you. I've found it of value with my patients. But this is the first time I've tried it with someone who isn't my patient. So I know it is a little strange, but what I'm asking you to do is just be as natural as you would in your own living room, even though I know nothing about your background or nothing about you except your name — not even your serial number. But in the course of our talking, I will have to ask you about yourself, naturally, in some way or another. You should feel free to reveal anything you wish because, as you know, you and Dr. Y will listen to it later. So I will be sort of catalytic, but not really a therapist as such. But maybe for just this period I'll be *sort* of a therapist to you, but not your therapist, not *the* therapist. The reason I'm saying this is because this is the first time I've done this myself.

Shorr: (S&O) Vicky, what shall I never call you? What shall I never refer to you as? In other words, I can call you anything I want, but the one thing I should never call you is what?

Vicky: I don't know. I never thought of that.

Shorr: Well, just try. (Pause, waiting for a response) Any idea about it?

Vicky: A descriptive phrase you mean, or a name?

Shorr: Anything. There's no right or wrong answers about all of these things. But, if you said I should never call you — what?

Vicky: Inadequate, I suppose, because anything that is related to inadequacy triggers me.

⟷ If I were answering that question now and I hadn't heard this tape, I would not want anyone to call me "red." I was thinking, while you asked me, that that would be my answer. But then you, Dr. Shorr, finished up by saying, "If I called you redhead, that wouldn't bother you, right?" And I answered that it wouldn't bother me. I was surprised because my original answer to that question was different. And I was also surprised that I called myself "inadequate." Somehow, I don't feel that way any more. Not just somehow — I *don't!* I'm sure it's still there, but I certainly wouldn't answer that question the way I answered it two years ago.

Shorr: Just the word "inadequacy" triggers you, huh?

Vicky: Well, I don't know, but it is the first thing that came into my mind.

Shorr: That's good. (S&O) I can call you redhead and that wouldn't bother you, right?

Vicky: No.

Shorr: (S&O) But if I said inadequate, you would get a feeling about it?

Vicky: If you called me inadequate, yes.

Shorr: You would get a feeling about it?

Vicky: Oh, yes.

Shorr: (IS) I want you to see if you can get an image of a tug of war. What comes to mind? The first thing that comes to mind.

Vicky: Isometrics. Isometric exercises.

Shorr: Good. Between what and what?

Vicky: I probably said that because I'm terribly conscious of weight at the moment. I have been for some time, and it's all kind of related.

Shorr: (IS) What do you see? What image do you see? What's doing the isometrics? In a visual image? (Pause, waiting for a response) Come on, you're doing fine. Are you nervous?

Vicky: No.

Shorr: Good.

Vicky: (Pause) I don't think of it as visual. Maybe I wasn't thinking when you said that it should be a visual image. It wasn't visual.

Shorr: All right, can you get a visual one now?

Vicky: Of isometrics?

Shorr: (IS) Of a tug of war. Can you visualize a tug of war? Just what do you see?

Vicky: I see children. I see young children tugging an equal amount on each side – tugging at this rope.

Shorr: (Pause) Are they boys and girls, or . . .

Vicky: Boys.

Shorr: (IS) Two groups of young boys, you mean? About how old would they be?

Vicky: About my son's age – eight. They seem evenly balanced.

Shorr: (IS) Now if you were on top of a large mountain and in front of you was a large area – a battlefield area – huge – can you conceive of two armies, one on each side? Can you get a visual image of that?

Vicky: Yes.

Shorr: (IS) Can you name each army? Give each a name, even if they are . . .

Vicky: A and B? (Questioning)

Shorr: A and B. (IS) Now can you give a general for each army? Like who would
(Continued on next page)

$\longleftrightarrow$ In reacting to this question, I named the armies in my head, before listening to the answer on the tape. And strangely, I named the armies in my head the same as I had two years ago. I named the generals as I did then. And, when it came to the question of who would win, I (in my head) said that the *good* army would win. I was impressed with the intellectual approach I had taken on the tape. It all sounded very heavy. Being the "good liberal" and saying that all war is bad and that neither army would win.

be the general of A and who would be
the general of B?

Vicky: General A and General B.

Shorr: (IS) Can you give an adjective to describe each army?

Vicky: Bad and good.

Shorr: (IS) And who wins?

Vicky: Neither one.

Shorr: You mean, they just fight to a draw?

Vicky: Because nobody wins.

Shorr: Nobody wins?

Vicky: Nobody wins.

Shorr: What do you mean nobody wins?

Vicky: Nobody wins in a war. Not really.

Shorr: (IS) Well, suppose you saw two prize fighters in a ring. What would they look like? (Long pause, waiting for response) Can you get a visual image of that? $\longleftrightarrow$ As to the prize fighting, I was trying to visualize it. I have the sculpture I just finished a month or so ago of a prize fighter — the head of a beaten-up, bald-headed, old man — his head was scarred so badly from fighting. And just now, in my head, I thought that both of them fighting, were really fighting themselves, and both of them would lose. Just like on the tape. So that would remain the same.

Vicky: Yes, they both seem unattractive. They seem heavily scarred and worn.

Shorr: (Long pause) (IS) Do you see them as different fighters or do they look alike to you?

Vicky: They both look alike to me. They look exactly alike.

Shorr: (IS) And you give them the same adjective — the descriptive adjective?

Vicky: No . . . oh!

Shorr: What? What came to mind?

Vicky: Well, I'm trying to think of what you are trying to do.

Shorr: It doesn't make any difference.

Vicky: In relation to the army thing — one was good, one was bad. Thinking back, I think of both of them as being bad.

Shorr: Both armies you mean?

Vicky: Yeah.

Shorr: And the prize fighters?

Vicky: Both fighters as being bad.

Shorr: (IS) You mean that they both have the same adjective to describe them.

Vicky: Right.

Shorr: (IS) And who is going to win that prize fight?

Vicky: I can't see that either one can win. Both of them lose.

Shorr: Both of them lose?

Vicky: Yes.

Shorr: (IS) Now here is kind of a tough one. I want you to imagine that you are looking into a mirror and instead of seeing yourself, you see somebody else. Who would you see?

Vicky: (Pause) My . . . a friend.

Shorr: A friend?

Vicky: Yes.

Shorr: Can you tell me who that friend is?

Vicky: Her name, you mean?

Shorr: Well, all right, it's all confidential, so . . .

Vicky: Her name is Sara.

Shorr: What sort of a person is she as far as you can see, or feel?

Vicky: She is very vital and very attractive. Physically attractive.

Shorr: (S&O) And how do you feel about her?

Vicky: She has been a friend of mine for a long time and we have been quite close. She was the one that was instrumental in my starting therapy. (Pause) I feel she is very dominant. I feel she is superior to me. (Long pause) Is that enough?

Shorr: (IS) Now, if *you* look into the mirror and see yourself — what do you see?

→ That's a hard question. I don't know that I could answer that now. I don't think I would answer it the same way. I still feel as strongly about my friend Sara as I did then. I don't know that there's been too much change in my attitude about feeling inferior to her. There still is an imbalance I haven't worked out yet.

Listening to the tape has worked a very strange reaction for me. Hearing my voice is very unsettling. It doesn't feel like me. It doesn't sound like me. It sounds so much like my sister, that I'm having a hard time relating to the tape — to the person on the tape. Because my sister's getting in the way. Somehow I feel there's a third person — or a fourth person, or whatever. The voice reminds me of my sister, Gerry. I am very fond of her — and have become more fond of her in later years. She is two years younger than I. She has so many qualities that I feel I lack. It's a very strange feeling — hearing this tape. Because it's like hearing her.

Another feeling I'm having in listening to this person is . . . my, how deadly she sounds. How awfully, awfully dull. This monotone. Not very alive. Actually, as I recall, that's the way I *did* feel and still do, a great deal of the time. But, certainly, I don't sound now anywhere near how I used to sound.

Vicky: I see all the reverse of what I just said of the other person, I guess.

Shorr: The reverse? Meaning what?

Vicky: Unattractive, unvital. (Pause) That's all.

Shorr: (M/L) Who is the most vital person you have ever known?

Vicky: (Long pause) I can't answer that — I don't know.

Shorr: (M/L) Who is the most alive person you have ever known?

Vicky: (Long pause) I think Dr. Y is perhaps that. (Pause) Yeah.

Shorr: (M/L) And who is the kind of deadest kind of person you have ever known?

Vicky: (Quickly) Me. That is the first thing that comes to mind.

Shorr: (Laughing) You said it so spontaneously that I wonder if the "dead" is valid.

Vicky: Yes, I don't know that. I'm speaking in feelings only.

Shorr: Good enough. Here is another kind of tough one. (IS) If you were to imagine two parts of your body — it can be any two parts of your body — and they were at war with each other — which two parts would you think were at war with each other? (Pause, waiting for response) I told you it was tough.

Vicky: (Pause) Could you say it again?

Shorr: Well, I know it is kind of a hard one, but if you could imagine parts of your body, like heart, lungs, kidney, or whatever it may be — any part of the body — and if you can think of two parts of the body that might be at war, which two would you think might be at war? (Long pause) Can you think of any?

Vicky: No.

Shorr: (M/L) Which two parts do you think are most in harmony — which two parts of your body?

Vicky: My hands are in harmony with each other, I feel.

Shorr: Your hands?

Vicky: But with each other.

Shorr: With each other? Meaning that one by itself is not?

Vicky: Right, they have to work together.

Shorr: (S&O) How do you feel about Dr. Y's hands?

Vicky: I've never been conscious of them. I've never thought about it.

Shorr: (S&O) What about Sara's hands?

Vicky: Neither. They don't have to use their hands to do what they do. I feel that I do. I feel that my hands ... That's interesting — that my hands are perhaps the only vital thing about me.

Shorr: Your hands? What makes them so vital?

Vicky: Because I can do things with them.

Shorr: What do you do with them?

Vicky: Oh, I can construct. I can create.

Shorr: What do you construct, Vicky?

⟷ I'm just about in the same area, right now. Not quite as much. But I still think things I can do with my own hands are ... it's still the most comfortable area. I've become more verbal through my participation in group therapy. And, therefore, I feel more comfortable in verbalizing my thoughts. But still it's scary ... it's not terribly comfortable for me. I've still got a lot of work to do on that.

Vicky: Oh, I can sew. I could sculpt — not very well. Nothing very well, but I can do things with them. I can build things.

Shorr: What do you build?

Vicky: Oh, I have in the past . . . (Pause) built fences, walls, furniture.

Shorr: Great, are you for hire, by the way?

Vicky: No.

Shorr: You said that so fast, too. Why?

Vicky: Because I don't think that I'm good enough.

Shorr: (S&O) And you think that that is the only thing that you are good for? Things with your hands?

Vicky: No. I don't know that that is the only thing that I am good for, but it's the only thing that I feel I can accomplish. It is the only area I feel comfortable in, I guess. Maybe that's it.

Shorr: You are not comfortable when you use your hands in construction or something like that?

Vicky: I *am* comfortable.

Shorr: You *are* comfortable. (S&O) But if I said to you, "Will you read this book by Schopenhauer and tell me what you think of it," what would you say?

Vicky: I would feel that I couldn't do it.

Shorr: You couldn't do it?

Vicky: No.

Shorr: (S&O) But Sara could do it.

Vicky: Oh, yes.

Shorr: But you can't? (Pause) (M/L) Well, what children's story most makes you cry when you hear it?

Vicky: Just about all of them, I think.

Shorr: All of them? You mean when you hear children's stories, you just start crying?

Vicky: Well, no. I can't really think of a child's story that would— I guess *Heidi* is the only one I can immediately think of.

Shorr: *Heidi*? Do you have any feelings about *Heidi*?

Vicky: It seems terribly familiar to me.

Shorr: Why does it seem familiar, Vicky?

Vicky: I think I must have read it a great many times when I was a child.

My reaction to talking about *Heidi* is that I now live on top of a hill and always have, almost. And that's the feeling I get when I think about *Heidi* — the freedom, being in the Alps, just being free and open. And that's what I love about my house. Because I'm way up high and I have lots and lots of windows and it feels very, very free. And I like that.

Shorr: And you can still get a feeling about it when you think about it, today?

Vicky: Yes.

Shorr: What is the feeling?

Vicky: I don't know what the feeling is. I just know it's a feeling.

Shorr: It can bring tears to your eyes?

Vicky: (Pause) No, no, I can't, right now . . . no.

Shorr: But do you think as a kid it did a lot?

Vicky: I think so.

Shorr: Who read it to you?

Vicky: I don't remember.

Shorr: (IS) Now you are in a room and you can hear unidentifiable voices who are speaking about you. They don't know that you are there and supposedly they can say anything about you that they wish, but they are unidentifiable — in other words, you don't know who they are. What are they saying about you?

↔ The reaction to the overall tape is that I'm starting to lose me as I am now, and starting to go with the feelings of the person I was two years ago. I'm finding that, listening to these questions, I'm starting to answer them almost identically the same. I'm losing my present feelings and going with the old feelings. Which I know is an area that I need work on — that I tend to not hold onto things. To let go and go with what else gives me a good feeling. I was answering in my head the same way — about the voices talking about me — as I did two years ago.

Vicky: (Pause) Well, I would first find it surprising that they were talking about me because I wouldn't think that the subject would warrant that much interest. Some might possibly be saying nice things, but generally I would think that most of them would be saying that — I can't think of the word. (Long pause) They would be mainly derogatory.

Shorr: Like what kinds of things? Can you be more specific, Vicky?

Vicky: Well, that she isn't a very interesting person or . . . (Pause) . . . I guess that is about it.

Shorr: (M/L) Who is the most interesting person you know?

Vicky: (Pause) I'm trying to think. I don't really know.

Shorr: (Long pause, waiting for some response) (M/L) If someone were to ask you who was really the most interesting person you've ever known or ever could think of, even — even if you've never known them personally — who would you think it would be?

Vicky: Including a public personage?

Shorr: Anybody.

Vicky: (Pause) There are so many — I can't really.

Shorr: Just the first one that comes to mind. There is no right or wrong, remember.

Vicky: No, I know.

Shorr: Well, what's holding you back on the thought? What goes through your mind?

Vicky: Well, first I have to decide if it's going to be a man or a woman. And I haven't decided which that should be. I think a man.

Shorr: Why a man?

Vicky: Because generally men are more interesting.

Shorr: (Pause, waiting for a response) (M/L) And if it were a woman, who would you find as the most interesting woman you can think of?

Vicky: (Quickly) I think I would have liked to have known Eleanor Roosevelt.

Shorr: (M/L) As a man, who would you pick?

Vicky: I think Adlai Stevenson.

Shorr: I certainly know who you voted for in the last election.

Vicky: Yeah. (Laughing)

Shorr: Now, if . . . how do you feel right now, by the way, are you a little more relaxed about this whole thing, or are you still . . .

Vicky: No, I'm relaxed — I was in the beginning. I . . .

Shorr: You see it's kind of harmless, easy going.

Vicky: Yeah.

Shorr: (IS) Now, I want you to imagine that you are tied up with a rope. Now, what do you feel and what would you do?

Vicky: (Long pause) I don't think I would do anything. I don't know. I would feel helpless.

Shorr: Well, what would you do?

Vicky: I would try to do as much as I could do. I would try to get the rope off. I would try to somehow do it. But if I found I couldn't, I wouldn't try any longer.

Shorr: Well, what would you do?

Vicky: I would just lay there.

Shorr: How long would you lay there?

Vicky: Forever, I guess.

Shorr: Forever?

⟷ Oh, my! *That* I had a different reaction to! I would *try*. I would try very, very, very, very hard. I would *not* lay there any more. I just would keep trying forever. I wouldn't lay there as I did. She — and now I feel the person on that tape isn't myself. She sounds just terribly, terribly dead. Like she's given up trying. She says that she will try, but I don't believe her. *I* would try. I would try to the very last bit of my strength.

Vicky: Yes, I would feel that way.

Shorr: (IS) Now I want you to imagine, Vicky, that you actually go through the whole feeling of ripping the cords away from you. Can you try that? You have to go through the whole feeling, using your imagination. Tell me what you feel as you do it. You must get the cords off of you or away from you. However you want to term it. (Long pause) Can you imagine that?

Vicky: Yes, but I have to imagine – in any situation that I'm in – I have to imagine why I have been tied up.

Shorr: O.K., then tell me why you have been tied up.

Vicky: I have been tied up by someone who has come in to rob my house or to attack my children. So I have to get loose to save *them*.

Shorr: (S&O) Who is more important in this world, you or your children?

Vicky: (Immediately) My children.

Shorr: (M/L) For whom do you have the most compassion in this world?

⟷ It seems like, each time I was asked a question, I'd have to figure it out intellectually and not tell you my first feelings. It seems like I would struggle for an answer, each time, to be *correct* rather than not caring in that vein, and giving my first feelings. Which is the way I would do it now. I would do it with feelings, more so than being so concerned with giving intellectually correct answers.

Vicky: (Pause) My children. (Pause) I'm not sure exactly what compassion means. I wasn't quite sure how to answer that question.

Shorr: How do you define it? I mean, use your own definition.

Vicky: Compassion ... sympathy. (Pause) Sympathy?

Shorr: Any way you want to look at it.

Vicky: Strong feelings. Strong feelings – I think more for my son than my daughter.

Shorr: You have two children, do you?

Vicky: Yes, a twelve-year-old girl and an eight-year-old boy.

Shorr: Eight-year-old boy. (S&O) And you have more compassion for whom did you say?

Vicky: I have more for my son now than I did – than I do – for my daughter.

Shorr: (IS) And if they were in a tug of war who would win? Your son or daughter?

Vicky: (Pause) That's hard to answer because I have all sorts of feelings of which one I would want to win and which one could logically win, or whether they would both lose. I don't know.

Shorr: They would both lose?

Vicky: I don't know. It would depend why they were doing it.

Shorr: (IS) Well, suppose it was just for fun. How would it be?

Vicky: I suppose my daughter would win, because I think she is much stronger, much larger. (Pause) But my son would be angry.

Shorr: What would he do?

Vicky: Oh, he would stomp about, and fling himself about, and be angry.

Shorr: (IS) Now, switching, I want you to imagine that you are on a TV quiz show. How do you feel? Do you get a feeling from that?

Vicky: Yes, ridiculous.

Shorr: Well, even if it was College Bowl or some high faluting kind of TV?

Vicky: Well, then I would feel terribly inadequate. Terribly.

Shorr: (IS) Now the quizmaster is asking you a question — like, name the kings of England in some century or other. How would you feel?

Vicky: I wouldn't be able to do it.

Shorr: You mean you would just blank out? Blush, or be embarrassed, or . . .

Vicky: Uh, yes. Embarrassed.

Shorr: What would you do? Just sort of wait it out until it was over?

Vicky: I would feel bad inside and try and . . . just wait it out.

Shorr: (IS) Now suppose you had Eleanor Roosevelt right here in this room. Can you ask her a question, please, Vicky — for the benefit of the radio audience, of course. (Long pause) What question would you like to ask her?

Vicky: (Pause) That is a hard one.

Shorr: You didn't think I was going to ask you an easy one, did you?

Vicky: No. (Laughs)

Shorr: I like to see you laugh, anyway.

Vicky: (Pause) I would like to know from her how to go about . . . being the person she is, or was. ⟷ I'm surprised that I sound as intellectually adequate as I sound. I mean, I sound quite passable in that area, and that's an area that I always thought I was so lacking in. And I don't sound too bad! I sound pretty good about some things.

Shorr: Especially what? What things about her, what qualities?

Vicky: Compassion, I suppose, comes to mind. Strong feelings about other people. Strong feelings to act, to be an activist. (Pause) That's all.

Shorr: (IS) And Mr. Stevenson? What would you ask him?

Vicky: (Long pause) I think I'd ask him just about the same thing.

Shorr: Mostly about the activist aspect? Is that what you mean?

Vicky: No, it is different with him. I don't quite know. It would be on a more intellectual level, but I don't know what I would ask him. (Pause) I don't know.

Shorr: Well, what would you ask him? (Long pause) Try to think of what you might.

Vicky: I'd like to know if he considers himself as much . . . if he really thinks of himself as large of an intellectual as everyone thinks he is. If he feels himself lacking in anything, and if so, where?

Shorr: (M/L) Who is the most intellectual person you have ever known? Not a public figure necessarily, but someone *you* have known?

Vicky: (Long pause) I don't believe I have really known one, really.

Shorr: You have never known an intellectual person?

Vicky: Well, yes, but . . . (Long pause)

Shorr: What are you stumped on?

Vicky: Those that come to mind, I can't quite term as being intellectual.

Shorr: Because . . . (Long pause, waiting for a response) What's an intellectual?

Vicky: I guess maybe I'm putting it on such a high level that it's hard for anybody to measure up to it. It seems to be the ultimate.

Shorr: (M/L) Well, what public figure or person you don't know would you consider the most intellectual?

Vicky: Adlai Stevenson would have been. (Pause)

Shorr: Anybody else?

Vicky: I suppose McCarthy.

Shorr: They seem to always be related to political thought, too, huh? Can you think of anyone who is intellectual who is not necessarily connected with political things or movements?

Vicky: I find it hard to think of any intellectuals in the entertainment business. And I'm not that aware any more of any other fields.

Shorr: What do you mean "any more"? You sound like at one time you were.

Vicky: (Long pause) I've got myself in a box . . . I can't think what I'm thinking. I don't know where I am.

Shorr: Am I pressuring you too much?

Vicky: No, no. I just – I'd like to go back and start over.

Shorr: Go ahead.

Vicky: I don't remember what the question was.

Shorr: Something about an intellectual other than related to political movements. You mentioned McCarthy and Stevenson.

Vicky: And can I think of any other area?

Shorr: Yes. Someone that would be considered intellectual.

Vicky: (Pause) I can't seem to think of anyone.

Shorr: (IS) All right, can you imagine that you are giving somebody an individual I.Q. test? You are the administrator of the test. Can you imagine that?

Vicky: Yes.

Shorr: (IS) Using your imagination, think of someone you are giving it to. Who would it be?

Vicky: My son.

Shorr: (IS) And what do you feel — as ⟷
you give him the test? Do you have a
strong feeling about that?

Vicky: Yeah, I feel that he is not going
to measure up . . . (Pause) . . . he's not
going to be . . . (Pause) . . . he's not
going to measure high enough because
he *is* my son — because he is a part of me
and therefore he is not able to . . .

Shorr: (S&O) Is he a part of you or an
extension of you?

Vicky: He is a part of me.

Shorr: (IS) What about your daughter?
If you were to give her an I.Q. test —
how would you feel?

Vicky: I feel that she would be more on
her own and she would be . . . it would
be more up to her what the outcome
would be.

The way I feel about my son now is
quite different from what I felt two
years ago. If I were giving him the I.Q.
test now, I would think that he would
do just fine. And it would have very
little to do with my being his mother. I
would think of him as being an individual, and he would do just fine because he's a very bright kid. And I feel
the same about my daughter, too. I feel
they are almost equal in taking tests —
they would do equally as well. And that
I would have had very little to do with
it. (Voice lowered, subdued tone)
Which is a put-down for me, too, I
suppose. Just the reverse from how I
feel.

Shorr: She has more control of the situation.

Vicky: That it wasn't foreordained, or whatever the word might be. That it wasn't
decided beforehand. But my son now, it is already decided what he will be.

Shorr: And you think he will be like you. Is that it?

Vicky: Right.

Shorr: (IS) And if I were administering an I.Q. test to you, how would you feel?

Vicky: (Long pause) That I wouldn't come out very well.

Shorr: (IS) Can you make up a lie about ⟷
yourself? Using your imagination. Just
make up a lie about yourself.

Vicky: Yes. (Long pause) I should tell
you what it is?

Shorr: Yes. Always tell me, because
that's what this is all about.

Vicky: (Pause) That I am very beautiful. (Long pause) That's it. (In a very
subdued tone)

Shorr: I gather there are some feelings
behind that. Am I right?

If I were to answer that question today I
would say the lie would be that I was
very young. Because I have a hang-up
about age, now. I'm surprised that two
years ago I didn't feel the same way. I
thought I would. I'm surprised that
there's an emphasis on beauty. I don't
feel that way any more.

Vicky: I don't know. (Long pause) It was the first thing that came to my mind.

Shorr: It sounds like you don't want to talk about it. Right?

Vicky: I don't know what to talk about. ⟷

Shorr: (Long pause) (M/L) What is the most absurd thing you can think of?

Vicky: (Long pause) I find it hard to think of anything absurd.

Shorr: (IS) O.K., now I want you to imagine that you are in a meadow. Can you imagine that?

Vicky: Yes.

That lady is dull, dull, dull! I'm getting very impatient with her. She sounds just so *dead*. She sounds so closed off and tight, in a cocoon, like she can't get loose. Those old ropes that were binding her earlier — she can't get loose of them. (See pp. 160-161.) She's terribly, terribly confined. I don't feel that way now.

Shorr: (IS) And tell me what it looks like. You have to use your imagination, of course. It's your meadow.

Vicky: (Immediately) It's a very pleasant place. It's a very warm day. It's a large, flat area with yellow daisies, I think, and there are trees — pine trees surrounding the meadow. It's a very bright day.

Shorr: It sounds very nice.

Vicky: It is.

Shorr: You feel good, huh?

Vicky: I feel very good. (No feeling in voice)

Shorr: (IS) Now, I'd like you to introduce a wild animal into the scene. Any wild animal at all. Just use your imagination. Which one would you introduce?

Vicky: (Immediately) A tiger.

Shorr: A tiger? And how do you feel about that tiger?

Vicky: I'm afraid of him. (Pause) He's going to hurt me.

Shorr: (IS) Now, assuming that he's not going to hurt you, I want you to imagine — this is again kind of tough — that you mount the tiger and you climb up a mountain, following a path, to the side of the meadow and going up the mountain. Now tell me how it feels and what you see all along the side as you go up the mountain riding on the tiger.

Vicky: (Pause) I can see the meadow, but it keeps getting farther and farther away, as we get higher. I'm a little bit afraid, but not terribly. I feel confident that the tiger can take care of us. And it just keeps getting farther and farther away and . . .

Shorr: What keeps getting farther and farther away, Vicky?

Vicky: The meadow. The meadow is far away now. It is just a little dot, at the very bottom. And we are straight up.

Shorr: Where are you now — at the top of the mountain?

Vicky: No, we can't seem to get there.

Shorr: Can't get to the top of the mountain?

Vicky: We just keep going. It just doesn't seem to . . .

Shorr: You mean endlessly?

Vicky: Yes.

Shorr: (IS) Now I want you to imagine though, that you do come to the top of the mountain. Can you try that?

Vicky: Yes.

Shorr: (IS) Now that you are at the top of the mountain, I want you to dismount — if you use such a term with a tiger — and now look all around you at the surrounding country. What do you see?

Vicky: (Pause) Well, we are on a very high mountain and it's very steep at the top. There is very little ground at the top. And looking down, it's very far away and I can see that little dot of a meadow, but just a dot.

Shorr: (IS) Can you see anything else?

Vicky: The rest of the ground at the bottom is green — a lot of green. And trees, a lot of trees. No houses, no cities, no people.

Shorr: (IS) Well, how do you feel right now at the top of that mountain?

Vicky: I feel very alone, but I feel very good.

Shorr: You feel alone, but good?

Vicky: Yes.

Shorr: Good because of why, Vicky?

Vicky: (Long pause) I'm not sure. It's kind of the same feeling I get — that I used to get when I lived alone before I was married. I lived on top of a mountain and I could look down. It's kind of the feeling I get now, living up in the hills and looking down. I just feel superior or I feel like I've — like here, where I am, I feel adequate. It's the only place it seems that I do feel this way.

Shorr: The security of your home?

Vicky: Right. I don't seem to feel it when I'm down there.

Shorr: You mean among people?

Vicky: Yes.

Shorr: (IS) Now, I want you to imagine, again, that you mount the tiger, but this time you do something — that's again kind of tough to imagine — you fly, you and the tiger. You, on the top of the tiger, can fly all around. Now tell me where you would fly to from the top of that mountain.

Vicky: (Pause) I think a sandy beach on a very warm ocean.

Shorr: (IS) And how does it feel?

Vicky: It feels good. (Pause) But there are no people. It's a deserted island.

Shorr: You are still alone then, huh?

Vicky: Yes.

Shorr: (IS) Now, I want you to imagine that you are on a crowded ferry boat — going across between any two points. How do you feel? Lots and lots of people.

Vicky: (Pause) I feel very much alone. I don't know anybody. I can't get to know anybody or they me.

Shorr: (IS) Let's assume that you get to know somebody on that ferry boat. Who might it be? If you had a choice, using your imagination, of anybody in the world. Introduce him into the ferry boat and make a friend of him or her. Who would it be?

Vicky: (Long pause) I can't think of anybody.

Shorr: (IS) Try to name just one person. (IS) You are on this crowded ferry boat and now I want you to name just one person that you can be a friend with or will be a friend with you.

Vicky: (Pause) I visualize the ferry being in New York for some reason. Between some two points in the New York harbor. And my first thought of the person is the mayor of New York.

Shorr: You mean Mayor Lindsay?

Vicky: Yeah.

Shorr: And he would be a friend of yours, huh?

Vicky: Yes. I imagine that it would be nice if he could be.

Shorr: (IS) And what would you be doing with him?

Vicky: Talking.

Shorr: (IS) Now he invites you to coffee on the upper deck at a table. How would you feel?

Vicky: Great.

Shorr: (IS) And then you go with him into the city of New York and he takes you to City Hall. How would you feel?

Vicky: I would feel fine.

Shorr: (IS) And that night he takes you to the Waldorf Astoria for dinner. How would you feel?

Vicky: I'd feel fine.

Shorr: (IS) And then you spend the night with him at the Waldorf Astoria. How would you feel?

⟷ I should react to that, but I'm not sure how to. I don't feel the same toward this man as I did two years ago. I'm annoyed with this person on the tape — that everything is fine, fine, fine, fine (Laughs) — with no variations in the "fines" and no ups or downs. Everything is just fine. Oh! It doesn't sound fine! I think the next morning, I would feel badly. Not that he — and I would also feel that he were a lesser man than I had thought. Not because he spent the time with *me*, but because he would have spent it with another woman other than his wife. I don't feel as self-deprecating as I used to.

Vicky: Fine.

Shorr: (IS) How would you feel in the morning?

Vicky: (Pause) I think that I would feel that he was a lesser person than I thought he was.

Shorr: Lesser?

Vicky: Yes.

Shorr: Why, what do you mean, Vicky?

Vicky: That he should be — everything I say sounds so terribly negative about me. I don't feel like doing it, but it seems to be the way I feel.

Shorr: Just say it as you feel it.

Vicky: I would feel that he were lesser than I had thought because he would have been wasting so much of his time with me.

Shorr: Whom *should* he have spent the night with, Vicky, dear?

Vicky: Well, the night or the whole time?

Shorr: Oh, the whole time.

Vicky: The whole time I think he could have been of more benefit to more people. Attending to his work.

Shorr: (S&O) Now, what do you think, if you were Mayor Lindsay, you'd think of you? Put yourself into his skin, so to speak.

Vicky: It's hard to do because I couldn't imagine why he would have to spend such a large portion of his important time with me.

Shorr: Maybe he just likes you.

Vicky: (Pause) That seems unlikely to me.

Shorr: But he can really turn you on, huh, Mayor Lindsay?

Vicky: Yes, I think he is a very vital person. Extremely energetic.

Shorr: You seem to like vital and energetic people, huh?

Vicky: Yes.

Shorr: He would be very good at isometrics, I suppose?

Vicky: Who — I? He?

Shorr: He or you. (Laughing)

Vicky: Well, isometrics doesn't take too much vitality. In fact, it's a lazy man's exercise, really.

Shorr: (IS) So Mayor Lindsay would be doing what?

Vicky: Oh, he would be jogging. He would be doing very active exercises.

Shorr: And you would be doing isometrics. Is that it?

Vicky: Yes, I have enough vitality to do that. (Laughs) No, I've tried them all.

Shorr: And given up on them, I suppose.

Vicky: The isometrics, yes. The jogging I keep going back to periodically. I belong to a gym, but I haven't been there for some weeks. But I have kept it up for several months at a time, daily. At this very moment, I have stopped going. I will go back, but I find it very difficult to stay at it.

Shorr: Is it a bore to you, or what?

Vicky: That, too, yes.

Shorr: (M/L) At what could you stick to the longest, do you think, of anything in your life, or in the world for that matter?

Vicky: Eating — it seems like.

Shorr: You mean you can start in the morning and not get finished until . . .

Vicky: Right, that's practically what the pattern has been recently.

Shorr: (IS) Now, I want you to imagine something rather tough — you really have to put yourself into it. Are you ready, Vicky? I want you to imagine that you are the most vital person in the world. Now tell me how you feel. Now, don't tell me that you can't do it, because you can. Come on.

Vicky: I feel fine.

Shorr: (IS) And what are you going to do today, Vicky? You are the most vital person in the world.

Vicky: I'm going to run through the ⟷ house and get it clean. Let's see, I'll set myself at 45 minutes — get the whole house done in 45 minutes. And then I'll have the rest of the day.

Shorr: (IS) What are you going to do?

Vicky: (Pause) I don't know. I think I'd like to get on an airplane for the day and go up to San Francisco.

Shorr: It sounds nice.

Vicky: And just go into all of the shops I wanted to and all of the art galleries I wanted to and come back.

Shorr: It sounds terrific. (IS) Take me along.

(Taken out of sequence from Vicky's later comments.) I'd like to speak about that trip that we talked about. I have been thinking about it. I was trying to fantasize to myself, if this same thing were given to me now, I would rush and get the house done in 45 minutes and then I would have the whole day ahead of me, and then what would I do? And then I got panicky because I really don't know what I want to do, and that seems to be an awful lot of my days. I have the time, and I don't really have anything to give me a great deal of pleasure or fulfillment. That's an area I guess I must work on.

Vicky: O.K. (No emotion)

Shorr: Does that frighten you?

Vicky: No.

Shorr: That wouldn't bother you, huh?

Vicky: What?

Shorr: That you took me along. You don't even know me or anything about me. You wouldn't be frightened of me?

Vicky: No.

Shorr: Why not? Because I know Dr. Y?

Vicky: (Pause) I suppose there's a part of that, yes.

Shorr: So you think that if I didn't know Dr. Y you still wouldn't be frightened of me?

Vicky: No, I don't think so.

Shorr: My, you're brave.

Vicky: Well, I'm not frightened. People don't really frighten me. I don't ever feel that I'm going to be harmed.

Shorr: (IS) Well, what would happen if I went up to San Francisco with you and you were this vital person? Would that be real easy? To be with me?

Vicky: Yeah.

Shorr: No problem?

Vicky: No.

Shorr: You wouldn't worry about any particular thing.

Vicky: No.

Shorr: (S&O) Would you think ahead and anticipate what this might be or where this might lead, or anything like that?

Vicky: No, I don't think I would – not if I were this vital person.

⟷ I took that same trip in fantasy, now. As a vital person, it would be glorious. It would be free, abandoned, glorious – just fantastic! As the person I am, and not as vital a person as I would like to be, I still think it would be glorious. I still think it would be fun. And I don't think I would be concerned about going with you, Dr. Shorr. I don't think I would be as concerned with your "finding me out" as I was. I don't think that's where it's at any more. (Laughing) I think I could last at least the couple of hours we would be there. Maybe for a couple of days, I would worry, but for a couple of hours, that would be O.K. And it would be a *lot* of fun.

Shorr: And if you are not the vital person?

Vicky: Then I might think . . .

Shorr: (S&O) What are you going to think? Tell me, Vicky. Since we are not going up there, you might as well tell me.

Vicky: (Long pause) I have a mixture of feelings of being afraid that I might be found out – that it might be misconstrued. That you might not want to go, but were going for other reasons. That I might feel that it was just too much of an effort to do. It wouldn't turn out the way I would like it to.

Shorr: What do you mean by that? How would you like it to work out?

Vicky: That it would be terribly pleasant.

Shorr: (M/L) What are you most afraid I might find out about you, Vicky? (Pause) You tell me. I won't tell anybody else.

Vicky: I don't know that it's anything that anybody might find out. It's no incident or . . .

Shorr: (Pause) What would you be afraid of? (IS) If we were in San Francisco for about three or four hours and just had lunch – now what?

Vicky: Well, that you might find me an uninteresting person and be disappointed with yourself that you would have used your time in this fashion.

Shorr: (S&O) With such a boring idiot, huh?

Vicky: Right.

Shorr: How great, glorious it is to know that you are a boring idiot.

Vicky: Yes. (Barely audible)

Shorr: Why did you smile when I said boring idiot? Because you know it is true?

Vicky: Because it is a facetious term. It isn't . . .

Shorr: Because you know that it is true, don't you?

Vicky: Not those words, no, not really.

Shorr: You are not really a boring idiot. Are you?

Vicky: No.

Shorr: What are you? (Pause) (S&O) Can you laugh about things? Can you be happy? Can you joke?

Vicky: Not as much as I would like to.

Shorr: But if I told you a good joke, would you laugh?

Vicky: It would depend upon the joke.

Shorr: There you go — what are you checking me out? You always make it hard for me to get along with you, don't you? I mean, if it wasn't really funny, you wouldn't laugh, would you?

Vicky: If *I* didn't think it was funny. It isn't a question of it's being funny.

Shorr: Oh. Can I tell you a joke?

Vicky: Yeah.

Shorr: It's a — it's kind of a funny. It's a guy that said, "I feel like I was Elizabeth Taylor's next husband. I know what to do, but will I be that interesting?"

Vicky: (Barely manages a laugh)

Shorr: Hey, is that funny?

Vicky: Yes.

Shorr: Good. I'm amazed, one would never know it. Can't you ever laugh like it comes from your guts?

Vicky: Almost never.

Shorr: Now try. That's what you're here for. Come on, I'll triple your fees. Anything. Can you try to laugh? From the guts, if you really had to?

Vicky: I don't think I can.

Shorr: That's a pretty good funny, you know? You won't hear that every day in the week. I don't make them up every day — just every couple of days.

Vicky: That is about as much as I can ever produce for a funny. It's never really allowed.

⟷ That's right. I do have trouble laughing. Well, no, that's not true — I have trouble laughing on demand. As I do have trouble doing most things on demand, or when I'm expected to do it. I laugh in group a lot. I find things quite funny there and I do laugh out loud. Watching

(Continued on next page)

a television show that is supposed to be funny, I never laugh — once in awhile, I do. But very, very seldom. With close friends I can laugh. I think I'm doing better in this. I *know* I am.

Shorr: You just wrinkled your face! That's all you did! Vicky, can't you laugh? No wonder I wouldn't take you to San Francisco — you wouldn't even laugh at my good jokes! That's what you expect, huh? (Pause) Did you ever hear of Moms Mabley? The negro. A woman. She said she married this older man — much older than she. Did you hear about that one? And Merv Griffin — it was on a Merv Griffin show — he asked her about was he still alive and she said, "No, he dead." And so he said to her, "Did you have a funeral, Moms?" She said, "No, I cremated him." Griffin said, "Well, why did you cremate him?" "Well, I wanted him warm once before he died."

Vicky: (Laughs)

Shorr: Gee, I got a snicker out of you that time. Hey, where is your husband these days? I haven't heard one mention in the whole hour of your husband.

Vicky: That's interesting.

Shorr: That's interesting?

Vicky: Yeah. He's very much a part of my life and I usually — most of the emphasis is on him in group. And yet, I haven't spoken of him in here.

Shorr: You say that in group therapy with Dr. Y you talk about your husband all of the time? Since I don't know, I have to ask.

Vicky: It seems like I do. Yes, it does seem like I do.

Shorr: (S&O) Why do you think you haven't mentioned him now? I heard about your daughter and your son and . . .

Vicky: He didn't seem to relate to anything that we were speaking of.

←→ It was interesting that we went the whole time without mentioning my husband. Very strange.

This is about the halfway point on the original tape and I've been walking around the house thinking about what I've heard and what I've said. And (laughs) I found myself falling into the same old pattern I used to have. Maybe it was because I was projecting back into that other person. But I was thinking, "Gee, I wonder if I'm reacting properly — if I'm doing a good enough job in my reactions to what I've been listening to? Am I doing it well enough?" Then I caught myself thinking that and I shrugged and said, "So, it's O.K.! I do as well as I can do. No problem." That's good!

Shorr: (M/L) Who do you think he would think is the most vital person in the world?

Vicky: Among his acquaintances, you mean?

Shorr: Yes.

Vicky: A man that he's — this insurance man that he has been involved with recently. (Pause) I think he might think that. I don't know.

Shorr: Is your husband in insurance or business?

Vicky: No, he is not. He's in printing.

Shorr: But you *are* surprised that you didn't mention him in the first hour?

Vicky: Yes.

Shorr: (S&O) By the way how do you feel about me?

Vicky: Very comfortable.

Shorr: What else do you feel?

Vicky: (Pause) That's the feeling I have.

Shorr: Well, that's good enough. (S&O) Do you have any other feelings? I know it's kind of strange. Talking about yourself very intimately to someone you don't know, right off the bat.

Vicky: I feel much easier about being able to do that since being in group. I don't know that I could have done it before, but now it doesn't seem strange at all. It seems quite easy to do.

Shorr: How long have you been in group with Dr. Y?

Vicky: About a year and a half.

Shorr: (S&O) It's a lot easier to talk about yourself now — reveal things about yourself now?

Vicky: Yes, not that I do. I don't very often do that with other people. It doesn't seem to be relevant.

Shorr: (S&O) How would you rate your participation in group? A lot of participation or very little? ⟷ I would like to comment on my participation in group. I certainly participate a great deal more now. I take a great many more chances than I used to. Even though I might be wrong, or think I might be, or am afraid I might be, I quite often will take the chance and say what I feel. I still don't participate as much as I would like to. It is still a difficult thing to do. But I think there has been great progress made.

Vicky: Very little. (Pause) It fluctuates. Sometimes there is more action than others. At the moment there is very little. It's not good at all right now.

Shorr: Is something happening right now? You said you didn't do jogging — you didn't do the other things.

Vicky: Yeah, I've had a very low period at the moment and I can't seem to work out of it. I don't seem to know how to. I have stopped doing the active things I was doing. I don't seem to be participating in group. I'm eating constantly. I'm fighting the weight constantly. I'm tired a lot. I sleep a lot. I *want* to sleep a lot.

Shorr: (M/L) Tell me, what is the angriest you have ever been in your life? ⟷ Well, *there's* a difference. I get angry a great deal and I get it out pretty fast. Certainly in group I do. And I do at home. Not all of that is good. I hadn't

Vicky: (Long pause) I can't remember any time that I have been . . .

(Continued on next page)   *(Continued on next page)*

Shorr: Well, you have been angry, haven't you?

Vicky: Oh, yes.

been able to handle, or to control it without submerging it or suppressing it. Now, I just get very angry and everybody knows it. I used to suppress it and just be sullen.

Shorr: Do you remember one angry time, then?

Vicky: (Pause) I can't seem to isolate the feeling of anger only. There are other things mixed in with it.

Shorr: Go ahead, tell me about it.

Vicky: It seems easier for me to remember things not in the too distant past. I can't seem to remember back too far. The incident I can think of now is something that happened not too long ago with my neighbor who is not on very good terms with me — she hasn't spoken to me for a number of years or we have not spoken together for a number of years. And she came up to me at a school function and accused me of damaging her son by not informing her of his actions. I had chosen not to tell her that he was doing something bad and instead let it go too far and then the police became involved. And then she found out about it. But she knew that I had known, but I hadn't informed her. And so therefore, I was at fault.

Shorr: You mean, she accused you of something?

Vicky: Yeah. She accused me of not acting. And I was both angry and guilty. On one hand it was just — her accusation was just. And yet I felt she was unjust. It was both feelings.

Shorr: So what did you do?

Vicky: I just took it.

Shorr: You mean, you didn't say a damn word?

Vicky: Yes. I finally did. I finally told her the reason that I hadn't told her was that I was afraid of her, and I had been. And I was not able to converse with her — not ever — not able to talk with her, because I was too afraid of her.

Shorr: And what did she say?

Vicky: She didn't seem to say anything. I can't remember exactly whether she answered that or whether I kept going. And I said that I was in therapy now, and that I was hoping that I could get some of this stuff straightened out. That I thought that she was right in her accusation — that I should have talked with her, but I was afraid to. That I was in therapy and I was hoping that I could find it easier to talk with her.

Shorr: Did she accept that?

Vicky: Yes, she did. She seemed pleased to hear that I was in therapy. She said that she was, too, now. And maybe we could . . .

Shorr: Members of the club, huh? (Laughing)

Vicky: (Not laughing) Yes, and maybe we could start over or something. So it ended on a relatively good note, but that was some months ago and she still hasn't made any overture, nor have I.

Shorr: (S&O) What was your father's fantasy about you? Can you think of your father having a fantasy about you?

↔ My answer to that question now would be, I would think my father had wanted a son, even though I was the first born. He never did have any sons — there were three girls. I still feel that he would have liked to have had a son and that I should have been the son. That is my feeling now. I don't know whether that has something to do with the fact that he is now gone. He died last summer. But I would have thought that I always had that feeling. I don't know why I didn't say it two years ago. It seems like a familiar feeling to me.

Vicky: (Slight pause) I find that difficult to think of. I was never that close, or have never been that close to my parents, to know what they really thought.

Shorr: (IS) Can you imagine what kind of fantasy he might have had about you?

Vicky: Oh, that I was all of the perfect things that he would have wanted in a child.

Shorr: Like what?

Vicky: Like brilliance and beauty and accomplishment

Shorr: Brilliance and beauty. Two b's, huh?

Vicky: Yeah, and accomplishment.

Shorr: (S&O) And accomplishment. The things you now talk about are the things you feel trouble you, huh? You're not beautiful enough? Not accomplished enough? And not brilliant enough? Was this more your father's fantasy or your mother's fantasy?

↔ No, my feeling, now, if I answered that question would be that it was my mother's fantasy. That I feel that it was she who had the aspirations and was disappointed. I don't think my father had these kinds of aspirations, but I think my mother did. And I think that it was she.

Vicky: No, I think my father's, not my mother's.

Shorr: Was your father himself rather brilliant, and accomplished?

Vicky: Not at all.

Shorr: What was he?

Vicky: He's still alive. But retired. He was in business.

Shorr: (S&O) What about your mother? Did she have a destiny for you in her own view of you, a fantasy of you?

Vicky: No, I don't feel that she did.

Shorr: Nothing at all?

Vicky: No.

Shorr: You mean, she just didn't care one way or another?

Vicky: I can't imagine — logically, I suppose she did — but I can't *feel* what her feelings were.

Shorr: (S&O) Well, what kind of confirmation of your existence did you get from your mother?

Vicky: (Long pause) It was not a good relationship. It was — I find it very difficult to remember myself as a child. I don't remember. I remember it was not happy — I did not feel happy.

Shorr: (S&O) But how did she confirm your existence, Vicky?

Vicky: I don't know what you mean by confirm my existence.

Shorr: How did she let you know that she thought you were there, that you were alive, that you were existing?

Vicky: By being angry, by criticizing, by doing all of the things I feel I am doing to my children.

Shorr: (S&O) And how did your father confirm you? How did he know that you existed, that you were alive?

Vicky: He was very volatile — a very warm, but explosive type person. My mother tended to be more brooding and more sullen.

Shorr: (S&O) What qualities did they endorse about you? The things that you had and that they liked about you? What qualities?

Vicky: (Immediately) I can't remember that they did.

Shorr: (S&O) What qualities did they not like about you?

Vicky: (Immediately) My willfulness. My — they thought I was self-centered and selfish.

Shorr: (M/L) Who is the most selfish person you know in this world? Right now?

Vicky: (Pause) I can't think of anyone.

Shorr: You don't know of any selfish people in this world?

Vicky: Oh, yes.

Shorr: Who do you think is the most selfish of those you know?

Vicky: (Pause) Children, I suppose, as a class, as a group.

Shorr: Do they want the most? They are egocentric, you mean?

Vicky: Yes.

Shorr: (S&O) How does your husband confirm your existence, and make you know that you are alive? (Pause) Know that you are there?

Vicky: I quite often feel that he doesn't know that I'm there. I quite often feel that I'm just a fixture.

Shorr: (S&O) And how do you confirm your husband and make him know that he is alive?

Vicky: (Immediately) Yeah, that's hard.

Shorr: What's hard?

Vicky: For me to do that.

Shorr: Why, why is that so hard?

Vicky: Because I can't feel close, I can't — I find closeness to be embarrassing, I guess.

Shorr: (M/L) To whom do you feel the closest in this world?

Vicky: I think my little boy.

Shorr: (S&O) Is it safe to feel close to children and not to adults?

Vicky: (Pause) I don't know. I hadn't thought about that. It's not really safe because it's such a temporal thing. He won't be here for very long — he won't be a child for very long.

Shorr: (S&O) And if an adult is close to you, it makes you defensive or wary?

Vicky: (Pause) I don't really know what the emotion is. Whether it's fear or whether it is . . . embarrassment certainly is some of it. Not knowing how to react or how to be warm.

Shorr: How to show warmth, you mean?

Vicky: How to show it. I don't know how to show it.

Shorr: (M/L) So, to whom are you the warmest?

Vicky: To my son.

Shorr: (M/L) And who is the warmest person you have ever known?

Vicky: (Pause) I really can't think of one person. Many people that have had warmth, but I can't think of one that I would say that they were a very warm person.

⟷ That passage is, of course, a very vital thing to me. How to be close. Throughout my time in group, I'm always asking how to, how to — because that has been my pattern. I buy a lot of how to books and put them together and manual things — how to. And I translate that into my therapy, also. I want to know how to feel close and it never has been satisfactorily explained to me. It comes out without anybody telling you or giving you a blueprint. I don't think that it is possible to tell you how to be close to people. It just happens through improving one's own self-image — becoming close to one's self. That seems to be what's been working with my husband and myself. We've become much closer in this past year than we ever were. Being able to communicate certainly has improved it. I have never been able to, or I never showed faith enough, perhaps, to expose myself. I seem to find, in therapy, a basis — or maybe that's not the word. But I'm not as vulnerable. I don't feel as vulnerable as I used to be and therefore I can take the chance. Whereas I wasn't able to before. I still feel close to my son — not as close as I used to, because he is growing away from me. I feel much closer to my friend, Sara, than I used to, because I have been able to contribute, whereas, before I didn't. I wouldn't allow her to get close to me. I didn't feel I could contribute, so I kept everything on the surface. Things are really great with her now.

Shorr: (S&O) Well, you have seen a lot of people who are warm. Who would you like to be like, or have the quality of warmth like someone you might know? Who might that be, that you have ever known?

Vicky: I think Sara has great warmth.

Shorr: (S&O) Can you show warmth to Sara?

Vicky: More so than I used to, yes. Yes, I can, a little bit more.

Shorr: But she can to you.

Vicky: Oh yes, she can.

Shorr: Does that embarrass you?

Vicky: Yeah, it does. But I can handle it better than I used to.

Shorr: Because of therapy, you mean?

Vicky: Right.

Shorr: (S&O) Now, which would embarrass you more – if I were to come and hug you as you are right now, or if I came into your bedroom and accidently found you in the nude? Which one would embarrass you more?

Vicky: (Pause) I think of them both as equally embarrassing.

Shorr: (S&O) Would you find it equally as embarrassing if your husband instead of me were to do it? If he hugged you clothed as you are now, and then walked into the room while you were in the nude?

Vicky: I think I would find it equally.

Shorr: You don't separate your husband from me then in that regard?

Vicky: No.

Shorr: (IS) May I ask you a tough question relating – can you imagine how it feels to have the semen of the man's penis in your vagina?

Vicky: (Long pause) I can't seem to separate it from the act itself. (Pause) It seems to be all part of it.

Shorr: (IS) Oh, and how does it feel? You aren't embarrassed by the question, are you?

Vicky: No.

Shorr: Good. How does it feel?

Vicky: It feels very warm. (Pause) It's a good feeling.

Shorr: (IS) Now, suppose that you are ⟷ I wish I could react to each one of these in a tower in a castle in the forest and segments differently than I did then. you are asleep, and a handsome prince But I don't seem to be able to. I'm comes up there to the tower and kisses finding myself very much in the same you, and you awaken. Take it from place on a lot of them. there – what would you feel and what would you do?

Vicky: (Pause) If I were the princess and I were not I? I would like to act out the whole fairy story. Being the one that the prince had been looking for and we discover each other and live happily ever after.

Shorr: It feels good, huh?

Vicky: Oh, yes.

Shorr: Can you speak two or three decibels above your present voice? How do you feel if you would? Can you speak loudly? Try it.

Vicky: Right now?

Shorr: Yes.

Vicky: What would I say?

Shorr: Oh, say the Constitution or the Preamble . . .

Vicky: I don't know the Constitution or the Preamble.

Shorr: Say anything, I don't care.

Vicky: (Not much louder) "Now I lay me down to sleep."

Shorr: Can you say it a little louder than that? In other words, I want you to say it as loud as you can. Don't be afraid. We are sort of sound proof.

Vicky: (Not much louder) "Now I lay me down to sleep, I pray the Lord my soul to keep." (Sounds exasperated)

Shorr: O.K., a couple more decibels higher than that.

Vicky: You mean louder?

Shorr: Louder, louder. Higher.

Vicky: You mean louder or higher?

Shorr: Both.

Vicky: Higher?

Shorr: Well, not necessarily. No, not higher — you are not an opera singer.

Vicky: (Quite loudly) "Four score and seven years ago our fathers . . ."

Shorr: (Focusing Technique) All right, now I want you to try something that's tough. I want you to try to scream a little.

Vicky: (Returns to normal, low, soft, ⟷ emotionless voice) That's hard.

Shorr: I know it's hard.

Vicky: I used to be an actress, or I tried to be. And I gave it up . . .

Shorr: Because you couldn't scream?

Vicky: Because I couldn't act.

Shorr: (Laughs) Well, don't act, just scream. Try to scream.

Vicky: (Joins in laughter momentarily) Part of the reason I say it is that it's hard for me to do this.

Shorr: I know it's hard, but I want to do something here. So try to scream.

This part — I remember this. This is the only part of the two-hour session that I can remember, almost in detail. That stayed with me. I didn't remember any of the other parts. This I remember vividly. It was the very hardest to do. I'm not really sure if I could do it now. I think I could. I'm not going to try now. I guess maybe I'll cop out. Maybe it's because of the neighbors. But, it was painful for me to listen to this part of the tape. Terribly painful. It really was the only painful part, because I could feel my resistance. My throat closed up almost like it did to her on the tape. It was just terribly, terribly painful!

Vicky: (Screams, but not very loudly)

Shorr: Ah, now you can do better than that. I know you can, Vicky. For me, do it for me, come on . . .

Vicky: (Quietly and without emotion) It's so hard for me to lose my inhibitions. It's very difficult.

Shorr: Yet, you seem to enjoy sex.

Vicky: Yeah.

Shorr: So, you can let your inhibitions out about sex, right?

Vicky: Yeah.

Shorr: Even with Mayor Lindsay that wasn't even *at all* involved. Good old Mayor Lindsay. He has all of the fun. There was no problem there, and not even any obvious embarrassment. But when I ask you to scream — that's much worse, huh? Come on, how about trying it?

Vicky: (Screams at about same intensity as previously)

Shorr: Give it all you've got, come on. It's important. It's your life.

Vicky: (Very subdued, barely audible) I feel terrible. I feel terrible.

Shorr: Come on, you are doing fine.

Vicky: (Screams, a little louder)

Shorr: Give it a couple more. Now, here is the thing. (IS) Your son has just hurt his leg playing ball and you've got to scream for a doctor down about a block. Come on. (Pause) He just hurt his leg. Come on.

Vicky: (Screams, about same intensity) (Coughs)

Shorr: Call the policeman.

Vicky: My throat closes up.

Shorr: Come on, try it.

Vicky: (Screams, not much louder)

Shorr: I want you to be as relaxed as you know how. Get all of the feeling out of your body — all the feelings out of your shoulders, arms, everything. Just as relaxed as you know how. Now, your boy is down on that floor and a block away is that policeman — call him!

Vicky: Help! (A little louder and with a little more feeling)

Shorr: (S&O) That's better. How do you feel now?

Vicky: (Pause) I feel I'm glad it's over. (Very subdued tone)

Shorr: (S&O) Do you feel silly?

Vicky: No, not now. Before I did.

Shorr: (S&O) Are you afraid of making a fool of yourself?

Vicky: Yeah — before.

Shorr: You see, you are so afraid of making a fool of yourself. For so little reason. (M/L) What is the fastest way that I can make a fool of you? Give me the job.

Vicky: Asking me to do things like that. (A little resentful)

Shorr: Yeah, but you did it. That wasn't so bad.

Vicky: Because I had to do it. (A little spirit in voice) I guess. (Subdued)

Shorr: Yeah, but don't you feel better for having done it?

Vicky: Not necessarily.

Shorr: But you haven't made a fool of yourself, have you?

Vicky: (Pause) No. Now that it's over, no.

Shorr: Now that it's over, you mean that before then it was?

Vicky: I think so, yes.

Shorr: (S&O) You were going to make a fool of yourself if you did scream.

Vicky: Yes, right.

Shorr: Now that you have screamed you haven't. What made the difference?

Vicky: I don't know. It doesn't make sense. (Quiet tone)

Shorr: What other kinds of things would give you the same feeling? Besides having you scream?

Vicky: That I should show a particular emotion.

Shorr: Mostly showing feelings, huh?

Vicky: I think, yeah.

Shorr: And warmth, intimacy and closeness are the tough ones, huh?

Vicky: Right. Right.

Shorr: (IS) If I put my hand on your shoulder, you would freeze right up?

Vicky: Oh, I think maybe I could handle that.

Shorr: Why is it that you can handle that and not — well, what would it be? What kind of bodily closeness shuts you down?

Vicky: (Pause) I think maybe the — holding hands perhaps does. Looking deep into the eyes does. Words that are intimate do.

Shorr: Anything that connects you to somebody else closely.

Vicky: Yeah.

Shorr: (IS) Now, I want you to imagine a pair of eyes — like on the wall over there. Whose eyes do you see? Using your imagination, whose eyes do you see?

Vicky: My husband's.

Shorr: (IS) And what do you see in his eyes? What do you see about them?

Vicky: He's not seeing.

Shorr: He's not seeing?

Vicky: No.

Shorr: What should he see?

Vicky: Me.

Shorr: And he is not seeing you, huh?

Vicky: No.

Shorr: (S&O) Are you letting him see you?

Vicky: Probably not.

Shorr: (IS) Why don't you go up and whisper something in his ear?

Vicky: I can't do that.

Shorr: Yes, you can. Try it. Come on, Vicky. That's what you're here for. (Pause) Whisper something in your husband's ear.

Vicky: (Long pause) "See me." (Very flatly, no emotion)

Shorr: (IS) And what do you think that he is whispering in your ear?

Vicky: (Pause) "Let's go to bed."

Shorr: (S&O) All he wants is sex. Is that what you mean?

Vicky: (Pause) That seems to be the only time he sees me. Yeah.

Shorr: (IS) Imagine you and your husband walking down an art gallery in San Francisco. What happens?

Vicky: He would be interested in seeing the — looking at the technique or some technical aspect of a painting rather than the aesthetic.

Shorr: And you would be more interested in the aesthetic?

Vicky: Yeah.

Shorr: (IS) Would he hold your hand?

Vicky: No.

Shorr: (IS) Let's suppose that he does hold your hand. How do you feel?

Vicky: I'd like it.

Shorr: But he wouldn't?

Vicky: No. I don't think he would.

Shorr: (IS) Would you reach over and hold his hand?

Vicky: It's possible I could if I were feeling particularly happy that day.

Shorr: (S&O) And how do you think he would accept it if you held his hand?

Vicky: And if I thought that he were — if I thought his mood would be receptive I would, but if I didn't think it would, then I wouldn't try, I wouldn't want the . . .

⟷ This is all familiar, even from right now. This much hasn't changed a great deal. I still tend to do the same things. I don't reach out very often. In fact, I think maybe my husband reaches out toward me more than I reach out toward him. In fact, I know he does. It's difficult for me to do it. I don't know if it's the fear of rejection. I imagine that that has a great deal to do with it, though.

Shorr: Humiliation of being turned down?

Vicky: Not so much that. I wouldn't want it to damage the spirit of the day. Any expediency . . . (Pause) My relationship with him is that I do things to make it as smooth as possible. To make the day as nice as possible.

Shorr: And if you held his hand, it might not make it so smooth?

Vicky: It might not if he were in a bad mood to begin with or in not such a good mood to begin with. He might become more irritable and therefore it might tend to lessen the day.

Shorr: You mean holding his hand makes him irritable?

Vicky: It doesn't sound like it when you say it that way. Logically, it wouldn't seem so.

Shorr: But it does, you mean?

Vicky: It seems like it could be. Anything can make him irritable. It seems like. If he wants to be irritable.

Shorr: (S&O) So you sort of stay clear?

Vicky: Yeah, as much as possible.

Shorr: Be a vacuum tube?

Vicky: Right.

Shorr: A self-contained unit, huh?

Vicky: Yes.

Shorr: (IS) Now what would happen if you walked down the museum with me and held my hand all of the way down? How would you feel?

Vicky: (Pause) It's funny, I can't seem to place you in San Francisco. I seem to place you here. I think my previous − or rather it seems that when I imagined my husband was in San Francisco, it seemed different there than it does here.*

Shorr: (IS) All right, you want to place me at the L. A. County Museum? I'll be very happy to go down and look at the gallery with you.

Vicky: I somehow feel things are more − I can be more free when I'm not in the same environment that I'm familiar with. I'm more familiar with this environment. If it were another city, I think maybe I could be freer.

Shorr: But not San Francisco.

Vicky: Oh, yes.

Shorr: Oh, if you went down to Museum Hall with me in San Francisco . . .

Vicky: Right, I could somehow be freer. I could feel freer.

Shorr: (IS) And you could hold my hand?

Vicky: Yes.

Shorr: (IS) And you wouldn't feel upset or anything?

Vicky: No.

---

*At this point in the tape, Vicky began speaking with a little more emotion in her voice and at a slightly louder level.

Shorr: (IS) Now, what would you whisper in my ear at the end of two hours looking at the pictures and stuff?

Vicky: "Let's have lunch." (No emotion)

Shorr: (Laughs) (IS) And what would I whisper in your ear?

Vicky: (Small laugh) "It's a good idea."

Shorr: (IS) Where would you like to go to lunch?

Vicky: In San Francisco, some place outside – it's a nice day.

Shorr: Sausalito?

Vicky: I'm not really that familiar with . . . oh, yes, I do, yes, I know where – an open-air restaurant.

Shorr: (S&O) Do you want me to pick the place or do you want to pick the place?

Vicky: I would like you to pick the place.

Shorr: I'll take you to a very nice place. Sausalito, overlooking the bay. How would you feel?

Vicky: Great.

Shorr: (IS) Afraid of anything?

Vicky: No.

Shorr: (S&O) With your husband you wouldn't be afraid of anything either, right?

Vicky: I might be afraid that his mood would change. I would be afraid that he would find something to make him distressed – something that would damage the day.

Shorr: He gets irritable about something every once in a while . . .

Vicky: He gets very irritable about many things.

Shorr: And then he's off for the day, huh? His mood is set for the rest of the day?

Vicky: No, not necessarily. It just damages . . . No, he seems to weather his moods much better than I. If he is irritable about something, he gets over it pretty fast. That's it. I hold onto it, I can't seem to let go of it. It takes time. It changes things for me and I can't pull myself back.

Shorr: (S&O) What makes you – I mean if I had a bad mood, then you would get a bad mood?

Vicky: Yes.

Shorr: (S&O) So your husband gets in ⟷ That was very well put. And it is still
a bad mood then you get in a bad   very true today. That I take my hus-
mood.   band's bad moods and hold onto them.
                                        He can get rid of them pretty fast, but I
Vicky: Right.   hold onto them. And it will spoil the
Shorr: And then it disrupts the whole   day and ruin the evening or something.
day for you?

Vicky: Right.

(Continued on next page)   *(Continued on next page)*

Shorr: You can't come back on the beam too readily?

Vicky: It's hard for me to, yes.

It's not as bad as it was two years ago, but it is still there. I let other people determine how I feel – quite often.

Shorr: (IS) But, since you know how fantastic I am and I'd be in a good mood, then you'd be in a good mood all day, right?

Vicky: That's about it.

Shorr: It would be all right?

Vicky: Right.

Shorr: "If only my husband was in a good mood all of the time, I would be fine."

Vicky: That's about where I put it, yeah. I know that that's not true logically, but that is the feeling I have.

Shorr: (S&O) Would you say that you ⟷ take the responsibility of the bad mood of the other person? As yours?

Vicky: (Pause) Maybe.

Shorr: (IS) Now let's say that you and I have been starving for about a week and we each have a fork in our hands and there's a piece of meat between the two of us. Who is going to get the meat? Or what is going to happen to that meat? You and I.

I don't understand the significance of what you said, Dr. Shorr. When you asked, do I then take the responsibility for the other person's bad mood. I'm not sure whether you mean, do I feel responsible for it. I don't know; I'll have to think about it.

Vicky: We would divide it.

Shorr: (IS) In other words, you divide it equally with me, I assume. And with your husband?

Vicky: I would suggest to him that he take it.

Shorr: And . . .

Vicky: I think he might.

Shorr: (IS) And how would you feel?

Vicky: (Pause) I would feel very, very sad.

Shorr: Confirmed in feeling that he really . . . what?

Vicky: That I wasn't deserving of it. (Almost inaudible)

Shorr: That what?

Vicky: I wasn't deserving of it.

Shorr: Wouldn't you be angry at him?

Vicky: No.

Shorr: (S&O) Isn't there anything that he does that makes you angry at him?

Vicky: (Quickly) Oh my, yes.

Shorr: Really? Like what?

Vicky: (Long pause) I guess I *am* angry when I'm in that situation that we just had. I think there was anger there, too.

Shorr: You felt the anger, huh?

Vicky: Yeah, I guess so.

Shorr: Two things — you didn't deserve it; that's why you gave it to him. The other thing is that you are angry as hell that he took it, huh?

Vicky: Right.

Shorr: (IS) And, of course, with the boy, you would give him the meat, I assume? The whole of it?

Vicky: Yes.

Shorr: (IS) And your daughter, too?

Vicky: I'm not sure what I would do with her. I think I would.

Shorr: (S&O) You seem to feel differently about your daughter than your son, huh?

Vicky: Yeah.

Shorr: (S&O) Is your daughter more like your husband to you?

Vicky: (Pause) No, she seems like not my daughter any more — she seems like an adult. She's only twelve, but she's very grown-up looking. I can't seem to feel . . . I don't seem to have the abandoned feeling with her that I used to have. That I have with my son.

Shorr: You mean the free feeling?

Vicky: The free feeling.

Shorr: (S&O) Are you competitive with your daughter?

Vicky: I'm not sure whether I am or not. I've been trying to think that out lately and I don't know. I think I am getting more so, yes.

Shorr: As she gets older you mean?

Vicky: Yes.

Shorr: (IS) So, what would happen with this piece of meat between you and your daughter?

Vicky: (Pause) No, I think that my mother feelings are still strong enough to offset the competitive feeling. I think that I would give it to her.

Shorr: (IS) And what would you whisper in Dr. Y's ear, by the way?

Vicky: (Slight pause) "Get me well." (No feeling)

Shorr: (M/L) Who has the greatest authority for you in the world today?

Vicky: My husband.

Shorr: Why is that?

Vicky: Because he is the one that holds all of the money. (Pause) Well, that is the feeling I have. (Strained voice, very softly)

Shorr: You have very strong feelings about that, huh?

Vicky: Yes.

Shorr: Would you like to cry?

Vicky: Right now?

Shorr: Yes.

Vicky: No.

Shorr: Did tears come to your eyes on that question?

Vicky: No, I don't think so.

Shorr: It's probably my bad eyes, huh? My eyes truly aren't that good. So, I thought you had a tear. (S&O) But it kind of struck you strong, huh? That he has the ultimate authority in your life?

Vicky: Yes.

Shorr: (S&O) It makes you angry?

Vicky: No, not really. I don't think that I would really like to have it myself. I had a fantasy last night. He didn't feel well after dinner and went to lay down. Which is terribly unusual for him to. do — he just does not do that. And I went into the bedroom and he was very quiet and I had fantasized that he was gone. I tried to live with that. I tried to feel how I would feel. I don't want to have the authority — I would rather that he have the authority. I don't want to be responsible. I guess that's it. I don't feel that I *can* be responsible.

Shorr: (S&O) There seems to be more to it than just that. You seem not to like part of that. Yielding all of that authority to him.

Vicky: No, I don't. I don't like feeling the way I do.

Shorr: Meaning what?

Vicky: Well, I wish that I didn't feel this way. I wish I felt more responsible, more adequate in handling things.

Shorr: (S&O) You sound like you are very dependent on your husband.

Vicky: I think I am.

Shorr: (S&O) Do you think he wants you to be so dependent upon him?

Vicky: (Pause) I'm not sure . . . I don't ⟷ It's interesting that this other tape was really know. He is a very unhappy person. Terribly unhappy in his work. Terribly frustrated. And wishes he . . .

Shorr: What does he do?

Vicky: Printing.

Shorr: Oh, that's right, you told me. I forgot.

Vicky: Terribly thwarted — terribly

(Continued on next page)

It's interesting that this other tape was done two years ago, because my husband said the other night in one of his usual terribly depressed moods — because it's even worse now than it used to be. Because business, of course, is bad. It's bad for everybody, but it's really, really bad right now. He was saying, "Gee, two years ago, when I was successful, when things were going O.K." And then he went on and on and

(Continued on next page)

frustrated, and wants to get out, but he can't financially get out, yet. Terribly beset by responsibility, and I'm one of the big ones. The family is – I don't know if he separates me from the children . . . Whether it's the three as a unit.

Shorr: (S&O) Is there some distinction between the financial responsibility and the authority therein, or is there another side? It sounds like you have to watch yourself in terms of him all of the time. Apart from the financial thing, I mean.

Vicky: (Pause) I don't know how to answer that.

Shorr: I just threw it open for something to think about, anyway. Of course, you and Dr. Y can go over that another time. I get the impression that your husband is the determiner, he defines the relationship.

Vicky: Yep.

Shorr: And you have very little to say. Let's say he was a millionaire tomorrow – he would still define the relationship. Or if you were a millionaire – independently wealthy. And some of this bothers you, apparently.

Vicky: Yeah.

Shorr: (S&O) Like you'd want to have more give and take.

on, and I felt like saying, "Hey, just a minute, what did you say back there, two years ago, you were successful? I lived through that period. I was right here. And I don't remember that you ever talked about being successful or anything being right. It seemed just as bad then as it is now." In retrospect, of course, everything *is* different. But he understood what I meant. But that is the way he is. I would think that after all of the time of hearing his depressions and bad-mouthing everything that I would get used to it and wouldn't hear. To a degree that is true. It's like the little boy calling wolf. And right now when there is a reality that has been sustained, I'm really not confronting the doctor with it because it's just the usual thing. Because he always is concerned to the very nth degree. I'm not sure about our relationship – whether he really does determine it. My learning in therapy really has a great deal to do with it. I can manipulate him by the way I behave. My behavior is a manipulation, and he reacts to that. So, I'm not totally innocent in determining the relationship. I've certainly had a great deal to do with it. And if it is bad, I share the responsibility.

Vicky: I would like it to be a little more equitable, yes.

Shorr: (S&O) And not walk on eggs all of the time.

Vicky: Right.

Shorr: (S&O) How would you drive someone crazy? Just for kicks.

Vicky: (Pause) I think coldness. Being cold and frigid. Unfeeling. Like I'm doing, like I am.

Shorr: (IS) Tell me, what if you would walk into a cave and you saw a sorcerer or a witch? What would you do and how would you feel?

Vicky: (Long pause) Empathy. That I would want to know how the witch . . . I wouldn't be afraid. I'd want to learn from the witch how to be a witch. So I could have those powers.

Shorr: To do what?

Vicky: To be powerful.

Shorr: To do what?

Vicky: To be whatever I want to be.

Shorr: To be what?

Vicky: To be happy? (Questioning tone)

Shorr: To be what?

Vicky: (Long pause) To be out of it. (Very strained voice)

Shorr: To be what? I'm going to push you to the wall until you tell me. Be more specific. To be what?

Vicky: (Pause) To be a woman, I suppose.

Shorr: Be what?

Vicky: To be a woman. (Angrily and loudly)

Shorr: Be more specific.

Vicky: How can I be more specific than that? (Flat tone)

Shorr: Well, being a woman – what does that mean to you? Everyone has their own view of what being a woman is.

Vicky: To be a warm, human being. To be alive. To be vital.

Shorr: Warm, vital, alive. (Pause) (IS) Now, go back to that meadow, huh? Do you remember that beautiful meadow with the yellow daisies, was it? (See page 165.) O.K., now I want you to really imagine – even if you have to close your eyes – but you don't have to if you don't want to. Imagine that you are as warm and vital and as alive as you can be in that meadow. You liked it there before, didn't you? Now, can you imagine that?

Vicky: Yeah.

Shorr: (IS) Now, I want you to introduce some man – any man on earth, other than anyone you might know. Just some man that you have never known before. Now, can you be warm, vital, and alive towards him?

Vicky: Yeah.

Shorr: And what do you do?

Vicky: I'm holding both of his hands and we are dancing.

Shorr: And how does it feel?

Vicky: It feels fine. And there are people around, too.

Shorr: Hey, that's great. And what are they doing?

Vicky: They are all smiling and everybody is very happy. (Strained voice)

Shorr: Great. (Pause) You are alive, and vital and you feel warm, huh?

Vicky: Yes.

Shorr: (IS) Then the people go away and it's late in the afternoon and you're still with this man up there. Now what happens?

Vicky: (Pause) I somehow feel that I would like to climb the mountain with him.

Shorr: (IS) Good, go ahead.

Vicky: (Very flat tone) And so we do. And we go all of the way up to the top. And we look down and we can see the people. And I don't know whether we are going to stay there or go down and join them.

Shorr: Well, how does it feel?

Vicky: It feels nice to be able to decide — to be able to do either one if we wanted to.

Shorr: It sounds mutual.

Vicky: (Pause) Yeah.

Shorr: And you feel good, huh?

Vicky: Yes.

Shorr: (IS) What feelings are you feeling?

Vicky: (Flatly) I'm feeling love. (Pause) I feel exhilaration, joy, abandonment. That's about it.   ⟷   This lady is putting me to sleep. I hear her saying that she feels all of these things, but I don't believe her. She is so dull, dull, dull! No animation! So "down" even when she is saying "up" words.

Shorr: Sounds good. How much joy can you stand? For how long?

Vicky: (Pause) I don't know — I'd like to find out.

Shorr: (Laughing) Checkmate — you beat me on that question. (IS) No, but, Vicky, if you thought about it and imagined it and felt it, how much joy could you allow yourself to have? If you felt joy for a long time, would you have to stop feeling it?

Vicky: I imagine that it would become — it wouldn't stay joy for a long time. It would tend to . . .

Shorr: Let's assume that it's sustained some. How much actual joy could you allow yourself to have?

Vicky: I don't know. (Strained voice)

Shorr: Could you let it go on for a day or two?

Vicky: I'd love to.

Shorr: Could you let it?

Vicky: I don't know that I could.

Shorr: (S&O) Do you deserve to?

Vicky: (Pause) Yeah, I do. (Quietly, not much emotion)

Shorr: (S&O) What do you deserve?

Vicky: I deserve having joy. I deserve it . . . I guess.

Shorr: Now, come on, don't guess. What do you deserve?

Vicky: (Pause) I don't know what I deserve. (Rather exasperated)

Shorr: (S&O) What do you deserve? Come on, come on, come on, Vicky. What do you deserve?

Vicky: (Pause) I deserve being happy, I think. (Quiet voice)

Shorr: What do you deserve without qualification?

Vicky: (Pause) Well, logically, I would think that I would deserve it, but feeling-wise . . .

Shorr: Feeling-wise, do you?

Vicky: Feeling-wise, I don't *feel* about that question.

Shorr: (FTS) Can you say "I deserve" and finish the sentence?

Vicky: I absolutely draw a blank on that.

Shorr: Try. (Pause) (FTS) "I deserve _____."

Vicky: I deserve **nothing.** (Flat, emotionless.)

Shorr: Come on. How about a positive answer?

Vicky: That's how I feel. (Strained voice)

Shorr: I know, but I want you to try a positive answer and see how it feels. End it with something positive.

⟷ I have a feeling of irritation with this person. Of — "Maybe you deserve all of the shit you can get, because that's the way you are behaving. Like you deserve to be shit on, and so that's what you are getting." And I'm really teed-off, annoyed, which is an area that I know is a bad area for me. I have little patience with something like this. She is really annoying me.

Vicky: (Pause) I feel that I deserve nothing because I felt that way as a child.

Shorr: What do you mean?

Vicky: I don't know exactly. I just have a faint glimmer of something.

Shorr: (IS) Do you have an image of something?

Vicky: Someone, or something, or somehow, something telling me that I didn't deserve . . .

Shorr: Because . . .

Vicky: Because I was bad.

Shorr: You were bad, huh?

Vicky: Yeah.

Shorr: What did you do that was so bad?

Vicky: I don't know.

Shorr: Did you masturbate?

Vicky: Not that I know of.

Shorr: So what the hell was so bad about what you did?

Vicky: I don't know what it was. I just get the feeling that I was told so often as a child that I didn't deserve.

Shorr: That you were bad?

Vicky: Yes, because I was bad. I was selfish.

Shorr: Selfish? It was really just the concept of selfishness — like bad character, you mean?

Vicky: Yeah.

Shorr: You were selfish, huh?

Vicky: Right.

Shorr: There wasn't anything that you really did. You didn't steal? Or . . .

Vicky: No, I can't remember that, no.

Shorr: You probably didn't, I would guess. This is just an outside guess. More like the quality of character assassination, huh? They said you were selfish, egocentric — all that kind of stuff. What else?

Vicky: That's all. (Barely audible)

Shorr: That was enough, huh? (S&O) So, if I said that you were selfish . . . (Pause, waiting for response) If I said, "I think you are a selfish bastard, Vicky," what would you say? What would you feel, rather?

Vicky: I would agree with you. (Small laugh)

Shorr: You *are* a selfish bastard?

Vicky: That was my first thought.

Shorr: O.K., you tell me why you agree with me. (Pause) (S&O) You are a parasite, is that it?

Vicky: Not really . . . uh . . .

Shorr: (S&O) Then you tell me why you are such a selfish bastard.

Vicky: It doesn't make sense when I answer the question, but it was the feeling I had.

Shorr: Right, stick to the feeling.

Vicky: I can't reply on the feeling. It was just enough to say that I was.

Shorr: Remember earlier when I asked you who was the most selfish person you have ever known? Remember you had a little trouble on that one? (See p. 176.)

Vicky: Yes.

Shorr: Can you come up with one now? (M/L) The most selfish person you have ever known?

Vicky: Yeah, *I* was.

Shorr: You were?

Vicky: *I* was.

Shorr: *You* were the most selfish person? (S&O) Will you please prove to me how you were the most selfish person?

Vicky: I don't think that I can prove it. (Flat tone)

Shorr: I'd *like* for you to prove it.

Vicky: I can't prove it. I'm just . . .

Shorr: (S&O) You want to be indicted without a trial? Is that it?

Vicky: Yes.

Shorr: Great. (Sarcastically) Now, come on. (S&O) You prove to me why you are so selfish, will you?

Vicky: Because I would only think of myself. I'm speaking of it as a child.

Shorr: Yeah, like what? Give me an example.

Vicky: Like, I didn't think of anybody else. Like my daughter does now. Like I was the only person around. Like nobody else was around – only me.

Shorr: Were you the only child?

Vicky: No, I have two younger sisters.

Shorr: (S&O) And if you had to share things with them, would you always take more than your share?

Vicky: I don't remember that, I just remember the feeling of . . .

Shorr: You really don't have any evidence to prove that you were the most selfish, huh?

Vicky: No.

Shorr: You were just accused of that. You picked it up as something about yourself. (S&O) Therefore, today, you don't deserve to have anything good go your way. Right?

Vicky: It would seem so. (Very subdued)

Shorr: (S&O) And therefore you have to accept shit if it is offered to you. Right? Because what the hell do you deserve? Right?

Vicky: Right.

Shorr: Great. (Sarcastically) Keep it up and you will go far in this world. (Pause) How do you feel now?

Vicky: Well, that I would like to think that were all true and that it would – it would get all solved, and all of my problems would disappear. Just knowing this.

Shorr: I think that it *is* true. Because you can make a kid feel selfish, if you want to.

Vicky: But maybe I was.

Shorr: Is there such a thing as *normal* selfishness?

Vicky: I guess so. I look at my daughter and think so.

Shorr: (IS) Now, if there was a pack of gum between you and your two younger sisters, would you take the gum away and not let them know that it was there?

Vicky: (Long pause) I suppose I could have.

Shorr: (IS) Do you think you would have?

Vicky: (Immediately) I suppose I would have.

Shorr: And then? The firing squad? What the hell are you condemning yourself for? Will you tell me?

Vicky: (With emotion, voice quavering) I don't know. I can't remember. (Recovers, voice normal) I seem to find it very difficult to remember.

Shorr: You don't have to remember. Even if . . . I *doubt* if you were selfish. But I think that you were condemned by an accusation from, perhaps your mother. I don't know. Or your father. I don't know how it was. It doesn't make any difference, really, so much. But this condemnation has stuck with you, and therefore you can't ask for anything that you deserve in this world. Because you feel you are really selfish. "What right do I have?" And then if you don't have a right, you say, "I know I don't have a right. Well, I'm really inadequate anyway. I'm not really very attractive anyway, and I haven't accomplished much." So you see, it just goes to show you. Right?

Vicky: Yeah.

Shorr: And you confirm it.

Vicky: Yeah.

Shorr: So, you can really be bright and attractive, but *you* would never believe it. As long as you don't deserve it. Since you feel you are so damn selfish anyway.

⟷ I'd like to react to the long analysis. This is the second time I've heard this part. The tape ran down when I worked on it last week, so I had to do it over. The first time I heard it and responded on the tape, I was very annoyed with you, Dr. Shorr, with your instant analysis. It sounded too pat, and I rejected it because it just came too fast, and I couldn't believe it. I wanted to believe it, but it seemed too good to be true, and I resented your saying it in such an instant fashion. This time, hearing it, I'm accepting it without the annoyance I felt with you, without the resentment I felt. It seems to make very good sense. I'm not able to feel this feeling that she describes as a child. I don't remember it now. Hearing the tape, I don't remember feeling that way as a child. I don't remember any of it. It's gone. I guess you were able to make me, or let me, feel it by getting into it gradually. Now I am not into it. It's come as a total surprise to me. But I do *like* the analysis. It certainly has explained a great many things.

Vicky: (Pause) Am I being selfish even if I were — was it terribly wrong of me?

Shorr: No, because it's just the way you feel about it. That's the way you were taught to feel about it. Just as if someone masturbates, they are taught that they are in league with the devil, or whatever, and then they begin to think that everything relating to masturbation and sexuality is so horrible and criminal. Naturally, later on, they are waiting for the authority person to attack them and find out what they are really like and then condemn them forever to the cell. As you allowed yourself to be tied up in that rope forever, you see? (See pp. 160-161.) Your resignation, your destiny anyway, for Miss Selfish of 1901, or something. Whatever it may be.

Vicky: 1925.

Shorr: Good! I'm *glad* you told me! That means you thought enough of yourself to *fight* for yourself to say that. It would be an insult to be 1901. Hey, good, you were *normally* selfish. That's great! There is such a thing as *normal* selfishness. (Pause) I think I will stop you, here.

Tell me how you felt about what we did today. I know it was the first time I've ever done this . . .

(Continued on next page)

⟷ I suppose I should react to the last part. I don't really know how to react to that. I can't delve my feelings on that. I think

(Continued on next page)

Vicky: I don't really know what this is. You know, I can't really define it or — I'm trying to assimilate your conclusions and it's very interesting. It's a concept that I've held to for so long, that it seems strange to be told that I don't have to think that. I've always taken it for granted.

Shorr: How did you feel about those imaginative situations that I gave you? Did they bother you in anyway?

Vicky: They didn't bother me. I felt inadequate coming up with a good enough answer for you. I mean, they seemed to aggravate my inadequacies.

Shorr: Even though there is really no such thing as a good or bad answer.

Vicky: Oh, but I felt that there should be — that the answer should be colorful, and elaborate and well defined, and I wasn't able to do this. So, I felt inadequate.

Shorr: If you were really inadequate you wouldn't even be so aware of what you were supposed to be inadequate about. You are too smart. (Laughing)

Vicky: (Laughing heartily) I wish I could be sure of that. I wish I could talk in feelings.

Shorr: Is there anything that you thought is different in the way we did this and the way you talk with Dr. Y?

Vicky: Well, I've really never talked with him. I've only been with him in group, and as you know, the group is much more fragmented. We don't get quite so intense with one person.

Shorr: So, you haven't really had individual sessions.

Vicky: No, I haven't. Other than my first session with him, which I don't even remember too well.

perhaps I'd better just comment on the entire thing right now. Unfortunately, I wish I had done this whole taping in one sitting, my listening to it and we recording my reactions in one session. I wasn't able to do that because my tape recorder, the batteries ran down, and I had to stop it and recharge the batteries for 24 hours. The 24 hours stretched into several days, unfortunately, and I've just now gotten back into it. So I'm having to just rely on my faulty memory in some respects. The last part, of course, is really very exciting to me now that I've gotten over my original annoyance. The analysis of my having been accused of being selfish and having built up this image of myself. It's perhaps the most important thing that I have gotten out of it. Another thing I got out was that I came over sounding much more intelligent and intellectual than I had imagined myself to be. I was pleased about that. I wasn't pleased at all about my lack of vitality. I think certainly that has improved. I feel more vital. I don't feel like that person sounded on the tape. And when I played my voice back to myself now in this second recording, it certainly sounds entirely different to me. Certainly two years of additional therapy has helped, but I could see that there were many, many areas that I didn't respond to because I was feeling very much the same as I did on the original tape, and certainly these are the areas I must continue to explore. I would like to have a copy of the tape. I would like to play it for myself, again. To remind myself of some of these things and to remind myself not to slip back into that old shitty pattern I used to have. Thank you, Dr. Shorr.

[END OF TAPE]

DR. Y's COMMENTS

I have worked with Vicky, in group psychotherapy, for almost three years. She entered therapy as a very self-protective, withdrawn person. She was distrustful, extremely sensitive, and very limited in communication. Her only statement on the initial information sheet was two words, "being uncommunicative." It was apparent, in her initial interview, that she had developed a neurotic skill to maintain this state. During this first interview she referred to her difficulty with her "self-centered husband, who only talks about his work." Her main area of contact with her husband seemed to be sexual. She spoke of her unhappiness with her husband as a "dark shadow" over her life. She felt he could never bring her the happiness she wanted from him.

Vicky's other major area of disturbance was in her relationship with her children. She felt she dominated them and often acted without regard for their feelings. In her severe criticism of her children, she believed she was like her mother, and she thought her husband acted very much like her father. It was her concern for her children that motivated her to begin therapy.

Vicky's participation in group was more introvertive than extrovertive for the first year of therapy. Her cries for help in regard to her children and her husband were expressed in the areas of weak ego function and lack of self-confidence. She exhibited this not only in group, but in her everyday life. She presented a picture of a person functioning with a great deal of inadequacy, to such a degree that the many adequate activities in her daily life were masked by her feelings of incompetence.

Initially she gained courage in group through another group member's progress or breakthrough. As time went on, she gained more courage and began participating more openly in the group. As current experiences and frustrations were brought into the setting to be worked with, she was able to increase her own participation and become involved with the concerns of other group members.

The group process has been eclectic in nature, with the major emphasis on feeling experience and awareness. A constant use of interpersonal behavior, awareness, interaction, insight, and emotional communication were facilitating functions within the group. Problem solving was a meaningful aspect of the therapy. At first the group met for an hour and a half, but recently sessions have been two hours once a week, averaging eight to nine members each week. Occasionally, new members have been added, while others have left or graduated from therapy.

Vicky has shown meaningful progress in group. Her level of communication has taken on a responsible character. She has gone from a person practically committed to "uncommunication" to one who, at present, almost goes too far in saying what she feels, often expressing intense anger very impulsively. In the area of emotional awareness, Vicky has a truer sense of her emotional being and has increased in ability to express her feelings honestly and openly. There are still some areas which cause her great difficulty. The major one is with her husband who, she states, has been an alcoholic most of their married life. This interpersonal relationship is difficult to evaluate, since there has been much reality in her life to cause some of these difficulties, especially in relationship to her husband's drinking. Her ego and self-confidence in certain circumstances still show degrees of malfunction.

I believe that Dr. Shorr's process has been beneficial to Vicky, especially in uncovering (for her own awareness as well as mine) specific areas of behavioral dysfunction. Listening to the tape, one gleans a better understanding of where she has been, as well as where she currently is, in her therapy. Various specific problems explored in this comprehensive investigation of Vicky's conflicts include the following:

- Her dissatisfaction about her relationship with her husband — her sense of dependency on him and constant looking to him for authority (pp. 172 and 184-188 of therapy tape) and the transference of this dependence to the therapist (p. 186). In earlier group sessions, Vicky did focus on her husband extensively, giving the impression that she really was getting nowhere with him. While she still has some difficulty with the relationship, she attests that it has never been better than in the past year (p. 177 of comment tape).

- The concern she felt about her disparate feelings for her son and daughter, her feelings of being threatened by her daughter (pp. 161, 164 and 186 of therapy tape). While Vicky emphasized the physical and intellectual superiority of her daughter, her chief problems with the child concerned the girl's assertive, aggressive and manipulative behavior. Two years later (p. 164 of comment tape), Vicky's relationship with her daughter seems to be on a more even keel.

- Her lack of ability to express feeling. This is manifested by her inability to scream (pp. 179 and 181), her inability to participate with feeling in group (p. 173), her inability to laugh (pp. 171 and 172), her ability to enjoy a trip only if she could fantasize herself as a vital person (p. 170), and her inability to handle closeness, desire, need, and exposure of herself (pp. 177-183).

Vicky has made her greatest progress in this area. She is a much more vital person. This is apparent at the very beginning of the comment tape, in the vitality of her voice. She is aware of it, too, as she comments that she would answer the questions more assertively now (p. 153), that she laughs more easily in some situations (p. 171), and that she would respond to the questions with much more feeling now (p. 161). This is very indicative of her change and progress in group. A major emphasis in her therapy has been to attempt to open up her feeling awareness and to help her express feelings in relation to other group members. Vicky's reaction on her comment tape (pp. 161 and 194-195) is more than awareness. It is really a true confrontation of herself and this other self that she sees several years back.

- Her disinterest in helping herself (pp. 160-161 of therapy tape, regarding situation of being tied up). The dramatic change in Vicky's feelings about freeing herself (p. 160 of comment tape) is indicative of her significant progress in this area.

- Her feelings of selfishness (pp. 176 and 191-194). Dr. Shorr's interpretation of the dynamics of this feeling made an obvious impression on Vicky (p. 194 of comment tape.) I like the idea that the culmination of this session results in the patient being left with a kind of positive therapeutic interplay.

- Her profound feelings of inadequacy in almost every area. On page 153 she expresses this feeling in general; on page 162 she is forced to face her feelings of intellectual inadequacy in the most exposed manner. Her revelation of being embarrassed and wanting to hide describes her early participation in group. She also had feelings of inability to measure up to her own self-imposed expectations (pp. 175 and 176) and feelings of inferiority to her friend in terms of intellectual ability and vitality (pp. 156, 157, 158, 177 and 178). Other manifestations of her conviction that she was inadequate are: her feelings about her physical beauty (pp. 156 and 164); her desire for more power (p. 188); the severe position she takes against herself as being a worthwhile companion (for Dr. Shorr, p. 170 and for Mayor Lindsay, p. 168) and her feelings of worthlessness, of deserving nothing (p. 191). The only area in which she felt adequate was in the use of her hands (pp. 157 and 158). This is the area in which she feels most vital and confident — interior decorating, art, and doing things around the house. Even Dr. Shorr's questioning of how good she is failed to shake her confidence in herself in this area.

While she has made some progress in this realm, Vicky realizes she still has work to do. She still feels that she doesn't quite measure up to Sara, although she does not feel as inferior as previously (p. 156 on comment tape). She allows herself a pleasant fantasy experience with Dr. Shorr (p. 170 of comment tape) but only for a short time. She is no longer concerned with her beauty, but has displaced the concern to age (p. 164 of comment tape). She is still unsure of herself — she is afraid of letting go of old patterns, for fear a demand will be made on her which she will not be able to meet (p. 159). She doesn't know what she wants out of life. She glosses over this (p. 169), preferring to think of it as an intellectual thing and evading the emotional responsibility of accepting the fact that this "no-goal" concept is the underlying reason for guarding and protecting herself. Additional probing questions and support might help her see this.

- Her need for attention (p. 195 of therapy tape). Here Vicky speaks about not getting this *intense* in group. I think she is not talking about *intensity* but *attention*. It is true that, while many intense and dynamic things happen in group, the kind of attention one receives in group is different from that possible in individual sessions.

These techniques of Psycho-Imagination Therapy have been helpful in eliciting areas we did not explore in group. Vicky needs this type of incisive probing which gets past her defenses and into her dynamics. She cooperates well, but one must dig to contact the life source in her. Dr. Shorr's technique, if it does not tap the source, at least leads us into pertinent areas of psychological concern.

To me a process like this — of hearing one's own tape — should not be taken lightly or be done without shared hearing with a skilled therapist, because there is danger of negative revelations. Vicky, upon hearing herself, realized that if she were to re-experience the original audio-tape sequence with Dr. Shorr, she would do it more on a feeling level than an intellectual one. I, as a therapist, get a better picture of her progress, an assessment of where she is now, and an awareness that might help me in guiding her through therapy to a healthy conflict resolution.

This process can be utilized in an organized, systematic, probing fashion, extending the revelations of personality dysfunction and possible changes. One, of necessity, would have to have a thorough grasp of psychodynamics, personality adjustment, and the process of personality change. In the hands of a skilled therapist, a vast array of these questions and imaginary situations would be useful in exploring many important areas. With a less skilled or less trained therapist, I would consider such an approach somewhat risky.

Another concern I would have is how thoroughly one would have to stay within the structure of Psycho-Imagination Therapy, or whether this would be only one aspect of a therapy procedure. If a therapist were to use this as a whole discipline, it seems to me he would have to learn it very thoroughly, at least to the point where he could become creative himself in developing specifically pertinent questions and imaginary situations.

My final concern with this procedure, as a method of outcome therapy, is that the patient might use certain important revelations as a definitive answer rather than as a springboard for extending learning into the disturbed area. Again, a skilled therapist can circumvent this.

In summary, I feel that this can be a valuable procedure to both the patient and the therapist in evaluating the outcome of therapy, provided that the therapist is well trained in the technique and is sensitive to the patient's possible further needs for support, interpretation, or more exploration as he listens to the tape.

CHAPTER 9

Upon Hearing One's Own
Audio Tapes of Therapy Sessions

". . . an event once recorded is re-presented and in the process becomes subject to conditions which did not hold for the original event, conditions which as a result transform the event."

Paul Blank

"For most of us memory and imagination are usually joined and can only arbitrarily be separated."

Leslie H. Farber

"Whatever the limitations of the instrument and the quality of the equipment, all recordings of an event have the effect of reinstating the original event in an absolute and naturalistic sense."

Paul Blank

The purpose of patients listening to their tapes is not usually outcome assessment (as illustrated in Chapter VIII), but evaluation of themselves in the process of therapy. This procedure can serve as a valuable guide to the therapist as to where he stands in relation to the patient and where the patient is in relation to him. An important dimension of Psycho-Imagination Therapy is how the patient defines himself and how he feels others define him. A tape of a therapy session has the ingredients of such an interpersonal evaluation. By reintroducing the original dialogue and then allowing the patient to impose his own unique opinions and impressions, we expand the range of possible exploration and growth.

Moreover, since contemporary man is increasingly being deprived of direct contacts with his fellow man, direct participation by reobserving oneself dispels the artificiality and mystery that is involved in much present-day communication. The tape says, "This is the way we really and naturalistically were during that session." Audio tape recordings have a reality about them that invites constructive criticism. With repeated playings at appropriate time intervals in therapy, we may experience even greater awareness of how we were, and where we are, and where we want to go.

An appraisal of the therapeutic experience is only possible when it is exposed to the light of objective evidence. Verbatim transcripts of audio tapes permit this type of objectivity to a far greater extent than do case reports, with their inherent capability for both conscious and unconscious bias.

I do not know of any studies that indicate differences in patient reactions in relation to differences in time lapse between the taped session and the subsequent hearing of the audio tape. My own experience is too limited to make any conclusions about such differences. Most of my patients have reacted to their tapes after a lapse of one year or longer from the time of the taped session, although I have included in this chapter two examples of much shorter lapses of time.

It must be noted that permission to tape the therapy session was obtained in all instances. Permission was given wholeheartedly, in most cases. Indeed, if there was the slightest resistance to the taping, I immediately dropped the idea.

The reactions of patients hearing their own audio tapes of a therapy session are phenomenologically various. One patient, Lyle, commented that Psycho-Imagination Therapy had helped him to greater awareness, while, for him, psychoanalytic therapy had not been able to do this. When I first saw Lyle, he had just been involved in pschotic episodes of self-destruction that had nearly cost him his life. The following verbatim comment was made after a lapse of two years from the taped session, during which time he had been in therapy with me.

♦ I feel that Psycho-Imagination Therapy has enabled me to get at my neurosis, whereas a purely analytical therapy did not work. The imaginary situations brought out the feelings from my unconscious and allowed me to look at them . . . forced me to face them in the presence and with the love of Joe [the therapist]. Where I could block memory of a dream, these situations acted like a dream on a conscious level. Once having the feeling, I could look at what it represented and tie it in to my present behavior. They also allowed me to carry out the fantasies of rage, sex, glory, etc., and showed me it was possible to feel good about myself if I let go of these fantasies and my past behavior and view of living. Having what I considered my hidden and most feared feelings come out in the presence of Joe made my first healthy connection with another human being, and I'm positive made my progress that much faster.

Lyle's comments after he had listened to his tape also included a statement of where he was now and where he intended to go. Listening to the tape gave him and me an opportunity to evaluate his past and present state and what remained to be done:

♦ I feel I have come about fifty percent of the way toward having my own life, and for me that's one hell of a distance! Where do I go from here and how do I get there? That question brings on a lot of anxiety. Up to this point in therapy most of my work has been in the direction of my father, and how he and his memory or myth fucked up my life. I now have the feeling that I stayed primarily in this direction because the feelings toward my mother were so intolerable to me and formed the basis for my feeling of being evil. I feel I now should look at these feelings both in private and in group. All the women I love bring on ambivalent feelings . . . not trusting their love being the strongest. Basically, it seems I must take my relationships with women out of fantasy and let reality be enough. I feel this has happened to a large degree in my relationships with men. I have faced my anger toward them, my competitive needs, and my need to be compliant to survive.

Women, on the other hand, I have told myself, were ducksoup. I knew how to handle them. Bullshit, I did. I played games and forced myself to believe I was accepted and loved by them. I had to be the most loved of all men in regard to women. But reality didn't allow this fantasy — couldn't allow it, as my idea of love didn't relate to real love. To change this area seems to be based on being allowed to make demands — feeling demands — and believe that I am not evil because of these demands. In private it seems to me a lot of work should be done on my feelings in the direction of my mother. My mother, my father and I are in a triangle. I feel different with men and women, and feel the more I am with them, the more I can bring on healthy growth and change. My allowing a feeling of equality with men — letting myself be with them and consequently letting them be — is also related to this triangle. I want to examine the triangle. See myself as I was and as I now am.

The following verbatim comment, unlike the preceding one, was made on listening to a tape of a session which had taken place only eight weeks previously. Larry is a 36-year-old man, an engineer by profession. His temperament is very controlled and non-spontaneous. He is fearful of authority and chose the strategy of being the "good, sincere boy" to survive his sadistic, impossible-to-please father. Social aggressiveness and self-assertiveness were extremely difficult for him. At the time of the taped Psycho-Imagination Therapy session, he had been in therapy for about four months.

♦ Well, I've just concluded listening to the tape. I don't know — it's almost like there has been very little emotional reaction to it and a lot of it seems like that's me and that isn't me. There are still some of the same feelings there and yet they are different. I had a difficult time really seeming to get with it. Speaking into a microphone is a little difficult, anyhow. I guess I felt there was some demand put on me — that something was expected of me — I had to listen to this tape and record some comments. And perhaps there was a feeling that I might not be able to do what is really required of me. Now I am saying — that really begins to feel like it — that somehow I'm not going to be doing the right thing. I guess that is a bit ridiculous, because I don't imagine that there really is a right thing. That any reaction I have to this whole thing is whatever my reaction is. It doesn't really have to be anything particular. But that sort of is an intellectual cop-out. The feeling is that I tried to do something and I didn't do well — failed, failed. I guess that's what it is. It's kind of funny that I still feel that kind of a demand because I don't think that it really exists. There isn't that demand for me from you to sit down and come back with something that is right on. The little bit of the "should" is coming in here. You know, that I should be able to do perhaps more. But the whole mood of this thing right now isn't one that I really like. I'm putting myself down, and I shouldn't, but it seems that relates to a lot of things that I do. I sort of put myself down unnecessarily. I guess I don't really have to. There will be enough people who will want to do it for me. But, on the other hand, there might be a few people that don't — that will accept you the way you are. It seems like a kind of a nice thought in a way. Like, I have tried so long to be something other than myself that it's almost impossible to let my own feelings come through and just be me — just do what I want to do.

Noreen is a 24-year-old detached girl with strong artistic talents. She has powerful fears of humiliation from people. Her neurotic strategy is to detach against this possibility, as well as from her own hostility. At the time of her tape,

after nine months in therapy, she was beginning to test her feelings with the risk of
being abandoned, and she was finding that she would not be. Her comments were
made on listening to her tape after a lapse of six weeks from the taped session.

◆ As I listened to this tape, it became very apparent to me how confused I am. I think
and I talk in a very confused manner. I felt as though I was talking more than
feeling. I was just going in circles — just repeating my confusion.

I feel that the dreams I gave you were not dreams at all, but rather they are realities
of my life. Now, if I were to dream of something solid, I would dream of myself as
a strong, decisive woman who has left behind all doubts and confusion. And if I
were to dream of something fascinating, I would dream of living a worldly life. In
other words, exposing myself to the many phases of life — traveling, dancing, art,
etc. Just really living a kind of independent, free type of life. To a much greater
degree than I have ever lived. To live each day to its fullest.

Strength is the most solid object I can think of. And the most solid feeling to have
is strength. The most solid man is a strong man. The most solid feelings I have ever
had are the strong feelings — the feelings of determination to get what I want, and
being decisive about getting those things.

The strongest feelings I revealed on this tape were those that I described of my guts
on a two-or three-foot island. That was great! I really feel that that is my attitude as
well as my feeling. To grow into something beautiful by using my creativity, or
whatever. I feel quite a bit of the real me came out in this part. I would want to
meet a man. A man who is strong, tender, warm, sensitive, and aware.

The other part which I feel very much is me, is when I told you I was made of
wood. I can't begin to tell you how much this is me. I feel this very deeply. It's as
clear as a picture that this is what I want. The immediate image I have of confusion
is like one of those toy soldiers that you wind up and it just goes every which way.
It has no direction.

But all in all, basically I feel that this tape has a lot of concrete material to offer.
The confusion I carry around with me is definitely holding me back — it is a
burden. But I am gradually becoming aware of this, and that in itself is a start.

One more thing I would like to add is that at times I get the feeling when I am
talking, that I am trying to convince the listener, rather than just being at ease with
what I have to say. There were also a few parts in the tape where my tone of voice
was that of a little girl, not of a woman. I feel like I have a very young sounding
voice. Well, I am very young, but I would like to sound more womanly. More at
ease, not so giggly, and just take my time, and really feel what I say, rather than
talking so much.

The following example is a verbatim report of a patient's spontaneous reaction
to the techniques of Psycho-Imagination Therapy during an actual session which
was being taped. Strom* is a 35-year-old man who had come to me for therapy at a
time when I was using the more traditional type of therapy. After many successive
and extended interruptions in treatment, occasioned by his being out of the area
for business reasons, Strom resumed treatment during the time when I had begun to
use techniques of Psycho-Imagination Therapy.

*See a short excerpt from Strom's tape in Chapter VI, pp. 75-77.

Strom was the son of a cruel, domineering father and a quiet, subtly domineering and castrating mother. His major problems involved paranoic ideas of persecution, devastating feelings of not belonging, a morbid fear of dependency, and a "special person" concept of himself that reinforced his feeling of non-belonging.

Strom had been in Psycho-Imagination Therapy with me for about two years (with interruptions) when this tape was made. We had covered many imaginative situations in a highly productive session. Suddenly, at about the three-quarters mark of the session, he stopped, stood up, leaned against the wall and volunteered the following:

♦ The reaction that just came to me is that I am very, very sorry that I didn't have the benefit of this ten years ago. I feel like a lot of the free association was not a waste of time, but that it was not nearly as concentrated as this. The asking of the questions seems to force me to look at what's on my mind, where free association doesn't and conversation doesn't. Sometimes when I just talk to you, it doesn't make me work as hard as your questions make me work. Because the questions are rigid; they don't allow for too much of *your* personality to enter in, or for my ability to side-track you, or your own ability to get side-tracked. A conversation for an hour, or just my free associating for an hour, doesn't point up problems or box me into myself the way the questions do.

I didn't notice any particular form that the questions had. Going over it now, it doesn't seem to me they had any particular progression to them. You know, whatever you had in mind when you wrote them all out, I wasn't aware of that when you asked them. But I was very aware when you asked me a whole group of questions. In the beginning, it kept making me look at and see my identity crises with people. After a while, it seemed like no matter what question you asked, that point just kept getting clearer and clearer and I couldn't duck it, even when I tried to duck it. It's still something about the form, the virginity of the questions having to be answered that made that come out.

Another big group of questions kept pointing up my whole sexual scene. And I don't think the questions were directed sexually, but it was just that once I got off on that, the questions and the answers were much more lucid and clear than just free associating.

The two big therapeutic things I got out of it were: 1) My fantastic need to assume such a similar role to my father's in the sex-world. Expecially when my neurosis doesn't demand acceptance in terms of identifying with or imitating him. After all, there are a lot of broads around for me and a lot of good sexual scenes, or even with my wife. (Laughs) 2) The other one was when you started asking about driving someone crazy. For a long time before that, in answering a lot of the questions, I saw myself as being a nice fellow. Yeah. (Laughs softly) About the meat, I said, "I'll share, I'll share." And in climbing the mountain, I thought, "Oh, yeah, don't hurt the billy goat, don't hurt the nanny goat." I seemed to me to be a pretty nice guy. Then you asked, "How would you drive a person crazy?" There was a reason why it was such a difficult question to answer. It was because I don't want to face the fact that I *do* frustrate my wife. Maybe not in an effort to drive her completely insane, but in an effort to keep her dependent by not letting her recognize that I **am frustrating her. Enough said.**

The next comment is striking because it depicts the way a borderline psychotic patient was able to assimilate and use the technique of *Imaginary Situation* in beginning to overcome his constant fantasizing. Charles entered therapy as a brilliant doctoral candidate in the sciences (which degree he subsequently earned). He spent six to ten hours a day pacing his small apartment while fantasizing grandiose acts of achievement and aggression. He had done this since childhood. He was extremely competitive and unable to trust anyone. The aim of his prodigious competition was to win a Nobel prize, or at least become the successful innovator of a billion dollar enterprise. With this burdensome level of aspiration, even his recognized superior capacities were put to a test beyond the capability of any human being.

Because Charles had been involved in such extensive fantasy living, it might be questionable whether the use of Psycho-Imagination Therapy techniques might serve to push him towards even greater flights of fantasy. But, in fact, the opposite was true. Here are Charles' verbatim written comments upon listening to an audio-taped session. I have included only the section of his comments dealing with the use of imaginary situations.

Imaginative Situations Or What Will Be, Will Be

♦ As I sit here, at the end of the tape, it seems that your imaginary situations have four main qualities for me. First, they allow me to escape authorities, both good ones and bad ones. Second, they are free and will go in whatever direction they go. I can no more make a happy one sad, or vice-versa, for an extended period of time, than I can fly to the moon. Third, really a consequence of the second point, they provide me with insights into my own feelings that I would not have otherwise. Finally, they really only take place in "safe" places; *i.e.*, your office or in group.

The escape from authorities lies in my total immersion into the situation. Not only do I avoid the inhibitions that my parents placed on me; but also, because of the extreme spontaneity I have, I don't try to out-guess you, either. It has only been recently that the advantage of the latter point struck me. Sometimes (rarely) I find I allow you, rather force you, to judge me. In an imaginary situation this factor is minimized.

Because of the way you suggest the original imaginary situation — and the way in which you modify its course — it retains free quality. Once it is started it just goes and goes until it runs down. *This, by the way, is different from the way in which my "normal" fantasies run. They go and go until I am fatigued.* [Italics mine] If they conclude an episode too soon, that episode just starts over. However, my usual fantasies also have this same lack of directability.

Somehow, when you interrupt my tale to get an expansion on some part of the action, I don't lose track of what I am feeling. In fact, the feeling is usually intensified because you are forcing me to confront some difficult element. How have you ever learned this non-directive control? *I seem to allow you to intensify my feelings, but not control what they basically are.* [Italics mine]

It is the intensification of my feelings which, I think, causes so many startling revelations to come forth during any imaginary situation. The course of events in one situation always provides much material for later discussion. The situations indicate where I am at very accurately. How this knowledge gets used to modify where I am at is quite another matter, or so it seems.

For me these situations can take place only in "safe" quarters, like your office or the group room. They either run down very quickly or degrade into my usual fantasy of glory, need for recognition, etc., depending on where I am. I haven't tried this experiment very often though, I just daydream in my normal way when I need to daydream some fantasy.

The remainder of the chapter presents a single case of an attractive, married woman of twenty-eight whose major presenting problems were sexual in nature and whose inner conflicts centered chiefly around a pervading feeling of responsibility to everyone she encountered, both in and out of the sexual realm, and feelings of never having grown out of the "little girl" stage. Debra had been in therapy about eighteen months when this session was taped. Her comments, made about a year and a half after the taped session, were both specific and general. The entire transcript of the therapy session is presented. Where appropriate, Debra's specific comments are juxtaposed to the relevant section of the therapy tape, in a second column.

Therapy Tape

Debra's Comments on Listening to Her Tape One and a Half Years Later

Shorr: (IS) If your mother were to look into a mirror and didn't see herself, but saw somebody else besides herself, whom would she see?

Debra: She would see me.

Shorr: (IS) And would she say anything to you?

Debra: Well, she would feel like I was a little girl and she would be telling me to be careful and not to hurt myself and not to do anything that is going to be dangerous. She would just be warning me all the time to take care of myself.

Shorr: (IS) Now if your aunt were to look into the mirror and see someone other than herself, whom would she see?

Debra: She would see (pause) a movie star.

In the first part, Joe gave me the question of looking in the mirror, as people not myself, and as my mother looking into the mirror and what would she see. The big thing seemed to me that I projected so much power to my aunt. She was such a fantastically domineering figure. The biggest difference now is that I don't really feel that way about my aunt. I feel that a lot of that was to protect my mother. To make it seem like my aunt was the bad guy all the time. And I really don't think she'd have that much control over me now. It's really different. I feel that possibly my aunt *wasn't* the ogre I made her into, and that maybe she even wanted to get close to me, and tried to get close to me, but that it was always me pushing *her*, away. I never trusted that *I* could have her as a mother. I wanted her

(Continued on next page)   *(Continued on next page)*

Shorr: A movie star?

Debra: Yeah, a very glamorous, regal looking, but very beautiful, very glamorous person and a real celebrity.

Shorr: (IS) Anyone you could name?

Debra: I can't think of anybody she would see that's a movie star or anything. Maybe not just a movie star but a celebrity like a very famous woman . . . like Jackie Kennedy — if she were in her late forties or fifties. Somebody who is very famous. Everyone would know if they saw her, instantly recognizable, a very commanding person.

Shorr: (IS) Now suppose your uncle were to look in the mirror and see someone other than himself; whom would he see?

Debra: (Pause) He would feel like a little old lady. Like a — the picture that came to my head was a little wizened orthodox rabbi . . . somebody small and tired looking.

Shorr: (IS) What about your cousin, Lisa? Whom would she see in the mirror other than herself?

Debra: Her mother (pause) as a very big woman.

Shorr: Anything else about it?

Debra: She would see her like my aunt would look in the mirror and see another woman. You know, a celebrity.

to be my mother, but she always belonged to the other people. And so it just confirmed all my feelings about being an orphan, about being the person in the house they didn't want. It gave me just a powerless feeling about my cousin, Charles. I felt powerless about my aunt, and I made her into this big huge monster for me to always do battle with. It seemed like I had to do battle with her all the time. I had to do my mother's battle. My mother never fought her. At least I fought her. It was really the only thing I ever did with my aunt. *Now* I feel that it's really too bad that that's all I could ever do with my aunt, because I really wanted her to be much more than just my enemy. I think I really must have identified a lot with her, and made her into an idealized mother. I hated her, too. I hated the fact that she never could belong to me. I hated my mother, although I hated my aunt out in front; I never hated my mother out in front. At least I could hate my aunt. She didn't collapse in front of me if I showed anger at her. What my mother would do if I showed anger at her was to just totally dissolve into a heap. So that it made me feel so shitty to be angry with her. At least, with my aunt, she was a big enough woman so that I could scream and yell and tell her to go to hell and that I hated her, and she didn't die on the spot. I think I felt that she respected me more.

Shorr: (IS) Uh, huh. How about your cousin, Charles, whom would he see other than himself if he looked in the mirror?

Debra: His mother (pause) as a more voluptuous woman.

Shorr: (IS) If you look into the mirror, other than yourself, whom do you see?

Debra: (Pause) I guess I would still see my aunt, but like an army officer.

Shorr: An army officer?

Debra: Yeah.

Shorr: That's interesting. (Laughs)

Debra: Kind of in a uniform, all boxed-up, all squared and hard looking.

Shorr: (IS) And does she say anything to you?

Debra: She would give me orders . . . like I was under her command. She would tell me to stand up straight and march in a line. "Don't deviate. Salute when I tell you. Don't smile." And pointing her finger at me and she was giving me orders.

Shorr: (IS) Now I want you to imagine a prostitute, and I want you to tell me what she sees in the mirror other than herself?

Debra: (Pauses for quite awhile) She sees a young, virginal, innocent, pure . . . she would see a young girl.

Shorr: (IS) What would she say to this young girl?

Debra: Look what could happen to you.

Shorr: (IS) I want you to see the customer of a prostitute, a male. He looks in the mirror and what does he see other than himself?

Debra: He sees something really ugly.

Shorr: You mean?

Debra: Well, like a monster, like Quasimodo, or something, utterly deformed.

Shorr: (IS) Is it a male or female that he sees?

Debra: Male.

Shorr: He sees a male?

Debra: Yeah. Like a deformed man pushed down and humped and dirty and hairy.

Shorr: (IS) Now you walk down the street and come to a house and you open the door. Now tell me what you see inside?

Debra: Nothing inside except a staircase, and it is very dark, brown, old. There is, like, a long corridor and there's a staircase right in front of you and then the corridor, like a hallway. It is very dark and there is a light way down at the end. Little rooms off . . .

Shorr: Little rooms?

Debra: Yeah, there's doors, I can see, like, doors.

←→ The next part is about going into a house. The first time I heard this, I cried. Like I couldn't stand the feelings. It hurt to listen to me — the sadness and the pain and the sound of my voice. It was like I really was in that house. And then going into the baby room. (See p. 211 of therapy tape.) At first I felt sad, because I could feel it was so grey and so lonely and unloved. But as I started listening to it now, two years later, I don't feel so sad. I feel more angry about the feeling I had to live with for so long. Of being a sad little orphan child. Now maybe that's the difference in two years. I don't feel like a sad little orphan child any more. I'm more mad at the me in that tape — the me who felt the pain was more important than anything.

Shorr: Is this all unfurnished, you say?

Debra: No . . . I don't know, I can't see any rooms, but it is just a staircase. It doesn't look like there is anybody in there.

Shorr: You mean you open the door and there you see a . . .?

Debra: A staircase on one side and a long hall on the other. And off the hall there are doors.

Shorr: But you don't know what is in the rooms?

Debra: No, they are closed doors.

Shorr: (IS) Now, I want you to imagine you climb the staircase. Where does it lead you and what do you see?

Debra: Like a big room upstairs . . . that's got windows and the curtains are drawn . . . and couches and a rug. It looks like a big, big, living room upstairs. But it has light in it, light from the windows. It is not so dark as the rest of the house and it has, like, coffee cups on the table like someone has been there, or is there.

Shorr: Who is there?

Debra: (Pause) Ben and you and Alice and some people from group . . . Nick. It's like you have been sitting around a table talking, and it's a nice place — it's got wood in it and the chairs are comfortable — not new.

Shorr: What do you feel?

Debra: Like I want to sit down and I want the people to come back and I want to be a part of that room. I even sort of feel like I live there, but it's like I have been away for a while.

Shorr: (IS) Can you imagine sitting down with the rest of the people?

Debra: Yeah.

Shorr: Then how do you feel?

Debra: I feel like it is my home.

Shorr: (IS) How do the people react to you?

Debra: Like I have been there the whole time, and we just sit down and have some coffee or something to eat, and then maybe we will all go and do our separate things in that room.

Shorr: This room is above the house?

Debra: Yeah, it is upstairs.

Shorr: And it is kind of well-lit?

Debra: Yeah, and it has a light in it.

Shorr: And it feels good all over?

Debra: It feels good.

Shorr: You are feeling acceptance . . . of belonging with people that you know and that you feel understand you?

Debra: Yeah, but I also feel like it is my home, I mean . . .

Shorr: It belongs to you?

Debra: Yeah.

Shorr: You actually own the home?

Debra: I belong to the upstairs. It's like that's my room and it is my house, Ben's and my house, and that's the place that's mine.

Shorr: (IS) Now I want you to imagine that you descend the steps and go down and go through that long corridor you described and go into the first room.

Debra: The first room I see?

Shorr: Yes.

Debra: O.K.

Shorr: (IS) Now what do you imagine you see?

Debra: It is a child's room, and it is very dark, and it is like somebody is sleeping in there. I feel like I have to tip-toe around. It's just very dark and grey, it's not like night-time dark, it is like closed-in dark, no windows. There is a crib there and there is a Teddy bear in the crib, but there are no lamps in the room and no lights. The frame of the crib is all up and there is just a sheet on the bed and no blanket, and there's a bureau by the door, but nothing on the top of it and no pictures on the wall. And I feel very sad, I feel sad in this room. I feel like somebody died in there.

Shorr: (IS) What do you imagine about that room, really?

Debra: Like somebody shut that room up. Like there was a death and that room has been closed up.

Shorr: (IS) Who died in that room?

Debra: A little girl.

Shorr: (IS) *Who* died in that room?

Debra: (Immediately) *I* did. From being closed up. There's no life in there, there's no pictures on the wall, and there's no color, and the only thing that's there is a Teddy bear sitting on the bed.

Shorr: (IS) How do you feel about that Teddy bear?

Debra: I feel better about that Teddy bear than anything in that room, but it is awfully old.

Shorr: (IS) Suppose you're that Teddy bear? How do you feel about its former occupant?

Debra: Sad. And like I have been left, too. Like the Teddy bear has been shut-up in that room, too, and it just got left and neglected and nobody cared about it.

Shorr: (IS) Now suppose you walk ⟷ The exercise room was kind of funny down into the next room and open the when I think of how much of my life door and walk in. What do you feel I've spent in trying to reduce, trying to there? change the shape of my body. How

Debra: It's all made out of metal. many gyms I have gone to, how many machines I've used. Like the outside of
Shorr: The room is made out of metal? my body reflected the inside.

Debra: It's a metal room. There is equipment, metal equipment — gadgets, like instruments of torture.

Shorr: Instruments of torture?

Debra: Yes, like gadgets for pushing and pulling, and a rack . . . (Long pause) It has a window with bars on it, like a jail.

Shorr: (IS) Who lived in that room?

Debra: (Pause) I don't think anybody lived in there, I just think people were taken there.

Shorr: (IS) Who was taken there?

Debra: I was.

Shorr: You were taken to that room?

Debra: Yes!

Shorr: For what purpose?

Debra: To be squashed and pulled and pushed and wrenched. ⟷

Shorr: Why?

Debra: Because they didn't want me.

Shorr: You mean they were trying to do away with you?

Debra: No, just manipulate me.

Shorr: For what purpose?

Debra: To make me do things right.

Shorr: What was right?

Debra: Make me be quiet, good, and not talk. (Long pause) Like a jail — a punishment room. It looks like an exercise room, too, where you do your daily exercises. It's a work room — work at being good.

⟷ The feeling I talked about, being squashed, pinched and pulled .. all to change the way I acted! All to change the way I appeared! I guess it's like the stuff I've been going through lately. "Accept me the way I am and don't try to change me. If you don't like me, then you don't like me, but don't ask me to change for you. Not change for you, but be a different person than the way I am." I feel like *someone* now, and I want to hang onto it, and I don't want anyone around who's going to try to mold me into a different way. Just like the torture machine would, or an exercise pulley, or whatever I imagined in that room.

Shorr: How do you feel about that room?

Debra: I want to get out of there.

Shorr: And do you?

Debra: Yeah, I can leave it now.

Shorr: (IS) And where do you go?

Debra: Down to the next room.

Shorr: And what do you see there?

Debra: It's got a light in front of it. It's a bedroom. It has two beds in it, and they have white bedspreads on, and it has a light on in it. (Long pause) But I feel like I'm sneaking in there. ⟷

⟷ I really remember the sneaky feeling of being in my parents' room. Not really ever my parents' room; it was my mother's room. I don't remember *ever* being in my parents' room. But I do remember sneaking downstairs when we lived with my aunt and going through my

(Continued on next page)   *(Continued on next page)*

Shorr: Sneaking?

Debra: Sneaking. I feel like I'm not supposed to be in there.

Shorr: (IS) Who, do you imagine, is supposed to be there?

mother's drawers, looking for *me*. I used to steal from her, too. She had a collection of silver dollars that I used to take. But mostly, I used to like to find things of me.

Debra: My mother and my father.

Shorr: (IS) Are they in there?

Debra: No, they're not in there, so I can go in there, but I have to be very careful and not leave any traces of myself.

Shorr: Why?

Debra: So they don't find out.

Shorr: Why is it so horrible if they find out?

Debra: Because I am not supposed to be in there, and then they would punish me.

Shorr: Why aren't you supposed to be in there?

Debra: Because I would be peeking.

Shorr: At what?

Debra: At them.

Shorr: (IS) What do you imagine them doing?

Debra: Living together.

Shorr: What's so horrible about that?

Debra: (Laughs) I don't know, it's just sneaky if I am in there. If I go in there and I'm not supposed to be in there when they are not there, then I'm trying to find something.

Shorr: (IS) What are you trying to find?

Debra: Pictures of me.

Shorr: (IS) What kind of pictures do you imagine?

Debra: Pictures of me as a little girl. Something of me, I want to look through the drawers and find *me*. Something of *me* in there, like they would keep something of me.

Shorr: Some remembrance of you?

Debra: Yeah, like something . . . like they might have kept a drawing that I made as a kid — anything. Like baby clothes, baby shoes, anything — my birth certificate. I want to look through their drawers and find it.

Shorr: You are looking to see if they have something there of you?

Debra: Yeah, that I was there, that I belonged to them, and that I have been a baby.

Shorr: That you existed?

Debra: Yeah, that I even lived. And I am afraid that I am going to get caught by them.

Shorr: (IS) Again, why is it so horrible to get caught by them?

Debra: I don't know. It is somehow, like, sneaking — you know, like waiting until they are gone because that is the only way I can go in there. And if they catch me, they will say that I didn't trust them.

Shorr: Do you?

Debra: No!

Shorr: (FTS) And you don't trust them mainly because ____ .

Debra: Because they don't have anything of me.

Shorr: (FTS) Because they ____ .

Debra: Because they wanted to put . . . they didn't want me around — they didn't want me to be there.

Shorr: (S&O) They didn't want you to exist?

Debra: No!

Shorr: You sound like you're an accident?

Debra: (Crying) I was. (Normal tone) At least that's what they told me. They told me that my mother had a child before me, a little girl who died in the hospital about a year before I was born, and the doctor told her she would never have another baby. Then they conceived me and I was, like, not supposed to happen.

Shorr: (S&O) Your mother never thought that you really should have existed even after you were born?

Debra: Well, she spent a lot of time telling me that I was yellow when I was born and that they gave her the wrong baby. Ha! Ha! (Sarcastically) A big joke!

Shorr: (S&O) You were just an accident and weren't wanted?

Debra: Yeah, I wasn't wanted, I was an accident. They had not planned on having another baby and they didn't even try. (Long pause) (Then, in a strained voice) Because they don't keep anything around to prove it, like I wasn't even there.

Shorr: (S&O) In searching for some source of identity to identify you in that room, what are you really searching for? What are you trying to prove, actually?

Debra: That I am alive. That I am, that I exist.

Shorr: (S&O) But who is the one that determines whether you exist or not?

Debra: Well, like, if I go in there and I am looking for things that prove me, *I* know that I am here. But, like, I want to have it to *show* somebody.

Shorr: Who do you want to show?

Debra: *Them!*

Shorr: (IS) Imagine you found your baby shoes; do you have to show them?

The first time I heard the tape and I played the part when I was trying to get my mother and father to see me, I just started to shake and I started crying. Ben came over and put his arms around me, and he kept on saying, "Don't cry about it. That isn't you any more. Get mad. Get mad." I started pounding my feet and my fists, and I started stamping the floor so hard that my legs ached afterwards. I couldn't tell whether I was more mad at me for wanting them to see me, or mad at them for never, ever, ever

(Continued on next page)

Debra: I want to show *them*.

Shorr: (IS) And what response would you get from them?

seeing me and that there's no hope that they ever will. And I don't want to need them to see me any more. I want to stand away from them because they're never going to. I don't even want my mother around. I just want her away.

Debra: They would say, "What are you doing in here? You're not supposed to be in here." And I would be in trouble for being in there.

Shorr: (IS) And what would you say?

Debra: "I have been looking for *me*, I have been looking for something of *me*. I want to see if you kept anything of *me*."

Shorr: (S&O) All you want to really do is prove that you existed?

Debra: Yeah, to *them*.

Shorr: (S&O) And if they say you existed, then you exist or did exist?

Debra: Yes!

Shorr: And if they don't recognize your existence?

Debra: But they don't, all they do is get mad at me for being in there.

Shorr: (S&O) Does that confirm your existence, their being mad at you? (Pause for reply) Is having them mad at you better than no existence or no identification?

Debra: Yes, because if they get mad at me at least they have to admit that I was in the room. (Pause) But if they get mad at me for being there, they are still mad at me like I was a little kid for being there.

Shorr: (S&O) How do you want to be known as or be recognized by them as?

Debra: As alive, as an adult.

Shorr: (IS) How can you force them to think of you as an adult?

Debra: If I hurt them.

Shorr: What do you mean "hurt them"?

Debra: If I am bigger than they are and if I hurt them — physically.

Shorr: (IS) Tell me exactly what you imagine?

Debra: Like, if I pound on them, and hurt them, and hit them with my hands. Like shaking, just seeing me and looking right at me. But not with anything else but my hands. I don't want to use anything.

⟷ The other thing that occurred to me, when I heard that part of the tape, is when I was trying to shake them and I wanted to do physical damage to them, this made me think of that dream I had when I wanted to pound Charles' head against the refrigerator door. I just wanted to pound his head, to *hurt* him ... Punish him for hurting me like that. I'd like to do the same thing to my mother. Bang her head against the wall.

Shorr: (Focusing Technique)(IS) Tell me what you say as you shake them.

Debra: (Yelling, with real feeling) "LOOK AT ME, LOOK AT ME, I'M HERE!"

Shorr: (IS) Now what do they do?

Debra: (Pause) They get mad at me for even touching them.

Shorr: (IS) But in spite of the fact that they are mad, you still continue until they *do* see you there.

Debra: That's right, so that I hurt them enough so they acknowledge I'm there.

Shorr: (IS) You can imagine doing that?

Debra: (Loudly, with feeling) Pinching them so hard that I would leave marks on them. And pulling at them and using my nails on their faces until they *know* I'm there.

Shorr: (IS) And how do they look, then, after you have finally got them?

Debra: Like I killed them. Like I have done something terrible. I mean, how could I dare to have hurt them, to put my marks on them. Like, I should be killed for doing that.

Shorr: (S&O) So what does that mean when you ask for people in this world to know you're alive and you have an identity? What does that mean then? How do you go about doing that?

Debra: I would just shake them.

⟷ It also seems to me that the whole part about the house and about trying to make people notice me and see me, and having to use really extreme anger, and feeling that I have to poke them and pinch them and violently do something to them physically, really reminds me of how I feel in group. Like when I had to go around the room saying something like, "How dare you ..." to everybody. And the reaction I had afterward was that I had hurt everyone so badly — that everything ' s ι was so devastating to people, tha, I shouldn't do that. I think that's where I get caught up in this conflict — there is still a lot of that inside me. It really isn't the group I want to notice or be affected by me. It is really, I guess, my mother, my father, my aunt, the whole chronicle of those people to be affected by me. I want to have weight — to be as strong as my aunt was. The power I gave my aunt — to have that power in myself. Then I wouldn't have to claw people. The feeling I have is that I'm bludgeoning them. I'm cracking them over the head with a heavy club. Because I do want to look at group and to be able to express other feelings about group — loving feelings about everybody in group from the ones I don't like, on down. I want to be able to make that choice. I still feel like I have so much of that other stuff to get out.

Shorr: (S&O) Otherwise they won't know that you are there?

Debra: I want to upset them, I want to hurt them, otherwise they *won't* know that I am there.

Shorr: Does that apply to other people?

Debra: Sure, it applies to people at work. I want to shake them, I want to upset them.

Shorr: And then they will know that you are there?

Debra: Yeah.

Shorr: And the price for all that shaking?

Debra: (Subdued tone) I am to be punished, to be sent away or punished.

Shorr: (S&O) What are you caught between? What conflict?

Debra: (Pause) Trying to get them to see me. Trying to get people who don't see me, to see me, at all possible cost to myself. And they are never going to. And, the other part that I feel nothing will ever become of it, but to be punished.

Shorr: (S&O) How then do you make yourself known to people?

Debra: By screaming at them.

Shorr: (S&O) How do you make yourself known to the group?

Debra: (Long pause) (Subdued tone) I don't know. I feel bad about the group. I feel best about the group when I'm (pause) reacting.

Shorr: Reacting? What do you mean?

Debra: Well, like somebody else ... I feel bad about the group. Like, last week when I acted like that, like, I felt really shitty.

Shorr: About what?

Debra: About myself, about the way I was acting.

Shorr: How were you acting?

Debra: Well, all the time before talking about being angry, you know, like I wasn't there. I was just answering questions, and I was being silly, and I was being out of line. And I feel good in the group when I just react to people.

Shorr: (S&O) Well, what quality is there, then, what emotional quality is there that makes you feel bad when you react to the group? (Pause for a reply) What difference is there when you feel good and bad about yourself in relation to the group?

Debra: When I feel there's nothing inside of my body. There's nothing inside of me, I feel very bad. And when I am just talking to talk — I feel very bad about that.

Shorr: You mean when you feel empty?

Debra: Yeah, I feel empty, just empty, just dead.

Shorr: (FTS) And you're just talking out of _____ ?

Debra: Out of ... out of answering a question or putting in my two cents.

Shorr: You mean without feelings, in other words?

Debra: I am totally without feelings.

Shorr: What makes you have this feeling that there is no feeling any more?

Debra: (Stutters) That, that, that nobody cares, nobody cares about me.

Shorr: Do you walk into the group feeling that nobody cares? Nobody cares whether you exist, like your parents?

Debra: (Very strained voice) Yeah, I guess I do.

Shorr: That is the basic feeling?

Debra: (Very strained voice) Yeah.

Shorr: (FTS) And they will only care if you ____ ?

Debra: (Voice still strained) **Well, they will only care if I have some kind of feeling inside of me.** If the feeling is about me, if it's about somebody else, but they would only care if I have, like, blood churning. But if I feel, like, dead and empty, nobody does care. (Pause) Like, I can only talk about achievement or something that I have no feelings about.

Shorr: (S&O) Now what conditions will make you feel like nothing when you walk into the group, and what conditions will make you feel like you are somebody when you walk into the group? Is it something within yourself prior to walking into the group, or does it happen while you are in the group?

Debra: I don't really, really know. But I know when I feel really bad it will be that way before I get there.

Shorr: "Bad," you use the word "bad"?

Debra: Yeah.

Shorr: (S&O) You are a bad person, is that it?

Debra: (Pause) It's just that I walk in feeling empty, dead . . .

Shorr: Like you were when you walked into your parents' room?

Debra: No, I felt . . . not empty and dead, then. I felt emptiness and deadness when I walked into the little girl's room.

Shorr: (S&O) So when you walk in as a little girl into the group, then you're empty and dead?

Debra: That's right!

⟷ When I try talking about the pain in group — being without feelings. I know we've talked a lot in group about the separation between my feelings, which are really there, and my way of talking about them. Something I remember when I first played the tape, you asked me about the best thing about the tape. (See p. 239 of therapy tape.) I said the best part was the last fifteen minutes when I was really talking in my own voice. Like substance in me. And I think that has something to do with what happens in group when I have to put the censor on and I have to protect people from whatever strength I might show. Yet I'm required to show strength, or I'm no good. That's where I get caught. Between being strong, which means to be superior and greater than everybody else — special, and not being strong, which makes me like my mother. I can't *stand* that, and that makes me have to fight the group — to maintain my own self. That's where I get caught with the fighting. When I feel ineffectual, that's when I have to fight for my identity. That is how I had it when I was a little girl and I was defiant to my aunt. I maintained it by being defiant and that said, "You're here, Debra, I can hear your voice." When I'm acting strong for myself, then I have to do it in spite of what someone else might say. If someone else criticizes me, I just have to say, "Well, maybe that's true, and there are areas that I have to work on, but this is the most I can do right now." And this is good.

Shorr: (S&O) And when you walk in saying, "I am somebody and I want to be known as somebody," then you're alive?

Debra: That's right. And then it doesn't seem to matter so much whether anybody loves me or cares about me. I really don't think about it that much.

Shorr: Because?

Debra: (Crying) Because I have some substance and I feel like I am alive. But when I feel empty and neglected and lost and dead, I am a little girl.

Shorr: (M/L) What is the fastest way to make you feel like a little girl?

Debra: (Long pause) The fastest way for me is to be with people that I feel don't accept me. I feel guilty — it's all mixed up — but it's like if I walk in after feeling . . . I can only tell you this way — I walked in Saturday morning feeling that way. The night before, Ben had played tennis with the fellow that lives next door, and they had people over. They were suppposed to come to dinner at our house, but they had a change of plans and didn't tell us about it. I was goddam pissed-off about it, because I had already planned dinner and they just trooped off with their friends and went to see a show. They didn't bother to invite us to see if we wanted to go along. They just passed us by. And I felt like I had just been shoved into the background. It was the same thing — just totally neglected.

Shorr: And ignored?

Debra: Yes, and ignored.

Shorr: Like mother and father in that room.

Debra: Yes, that's right.

Shorr: (S&O) Every time you feel neglected and ignored, you are nobody?

Debra: Yeah, that's right.

Shorr: And then the next situation that you come into, you are approaching them as if you are nobody?

Debra: That's right.

Shorr: And as a result . . .?

Debra: I act like it. (In strained voice) I have . . . I just . . . I feel abandoned, not worth shit, and ugly, and just not worth anything.

Shorr: (FTS) In other words, you have to force people into _____ ?

Debra: Into acknowledging me.

Shorr: (M/L) From whom do you find it the least difficult to get acknowledgment?

Debra: Ben.

Shorr: (Pause) So with Ben you're not the little girl.

Debra: Oh, I act that way sometimes, but I don't really feel like a little . . . I don't feel that terrible way with Ben. Sometimes I act like a little incompetent girl, but I don't feel empty and bad.

Shorr: (M/L) Well, whose recognition, today, do you most want to force . . . who do you want to force to acknowledge you? Who would you like to go up to the most in this world and force them to know that you are there and "acknowledge me"?

Debra: (Pause) The people that keep coming into my head are, like, older people, like the Johnsons.

Shorr: Your neighbors, you mean? They are older?

Debra: Yeah, especially she.

Shorr: The woman?

Debra: Especially Genevieve. I have a hard time with her.

Shorr: (IS) Imagine you are going up to her. How would you feel?

Debra: Well, I feel incompetent, you know. Like she is much better and everything than I am. That my opinions and feelings about things aren't worth anything.

Shorr: (Focusing Technique) (IS) But I want you to go up and imagine and tell me the words and feelings. *Force* her to acknowledge you.

Debra: (With much feeling) I just want to shout at her, "LOOK AT ME, I'M NOT FOURTEEN YEARS OLD, GENEVIEVE. I am twenty-eight and I have just as valid a reason for feeling the things that I do, as you do. I am not a little girl. You just never see me as anything but a little girl that lives next door. I can cook as well as you can. So I don't play golf, but I do my other things. I am just as good a business woman as you are, and I am just as good as you are. WHY DON'T YOU EVER SEE ME? WHY DON'T YOU RELAX WITH ME? Why are you always sitting there defending yourself against me? I always feel like I am bludgeoning you. Why can't you just relax with me? I'M NOT YOUR DAUGHTER. I AM YOUR NEXT DOOR NEIGHBOR. I'M A FULLY GROWN ADULT."

⟷ The section when I'm talking about Genevieve is really wild, because Genevieve and I have really gotten to be good friends, and it's a much more equal relationship. In fact, it's even kind of reversed. Genevieve is going through a lot of really bad things right now, and she comes to *me* and talks. Our relationship is just totally different. I'm not a little girl to her. When I stopped feeling like a little girl, like I was going to be put down by an older woman, she just opened up. She doesn't open up easily to women. She talks a lot about how she doesn't like women, and it's like she really loves me and I really love her. It's really neat right now. She has some problems with her kids and we talk. She knows that I think she has a lot of problems. I haven't really hidden that. I've been critical, and I've been more myself with an older woman than I have ever been with any older woman before. It's like we have a friendship where our ages really don't matter. And I know she loves Ben, and I love her husband. He's really a wild, sweet man and they've always been very good to me. But in the tape I sound like I felt that every older woman was down on me. Would never accept me as an adult — would always look at me like a little girl. That is what my mother would do. No matter if I was eighty, my mother would treat me like a little girl. A little incompetent girl whose opinions, ideas and talents were just kid stuff. "Some day you'll be able to do it better, but never as good as me."

Shorr: Now how do you feel?

Debra: Well, I felt better saying that.

Shorr: (IS) And what do you think would happen if you saw her again a few days later?

Debra: (Pause) I would have to keep vigilant.

Shorr: Like what?

Debra: Well, I would have to keep ready to say that at any time, I would have to repeat that.

Shorr: (IS) Now I want you to look into her eyes. What do you see?

Debra: (Long pause) They are just cool. They are just not accepting. They're competitive.

Shorr: (IS) I want you to keep staring into her eyes until you can see something else.

Debra: Well, if I say that over again, then I could make her eyes get softer.

Shorr: Yes.

Debra: Until her face smiles.

Shorr: Now how do *you* feel?

Debra: I feel better about her.

Shorr: (IS) What do her eyes look like now?

Debra: They are still nice, smiling.

Shorr: (IS) Now a few days go by and you see her again. Now how do you feel?

Debra: Fearful.

Shorr: Same as before?

Debra: No, different, I feel vigilant, I feel fearful that she is going to attack me for saying those things to her. Like, I have no right to say those things. I have no right to tell her that I am as equal as she is. I feel distrustful. Even if she doesn't put me down right away, it might be coming in a cynical, sarcastic way.

Shorr: (IS) Now look in her eyes again, what do you see?

Debra: I can still see her not being that way, but being a companion.

Shorr: So what you see in her eyes and the way she acts toward you at this point seem to be different?

Debra: Yeah. (Pause) Just like if I really look at her, she's not doing the things that I *feel* she is saying and doing. (Pause) She *doesn't* not acknowledge me. I know she does have some problems with me, but she did say to me when laughing at me for having an opinion on something, she said, "Oh, you do personalize everything, Debra." Then she looked at me again and said, "You know, sometimes I forget that at twenty-eight I *knew* what I was doing, that I wasn't a baby."

Shorr: In other words, she *is* giving you acknowledgement and recognition. Can you accept it?

Debra: That seems to be the part that ... I *can* sometimes but then, when she makes me mad, I can't. I can't say anything that seems to be ... I can't just say, "Hey, now, what the fuck, why didn't you tell us you were going out. You know, like, I had planned dinner." Now that's what I would *like* to be able to say. If I really felt that her eyes were smiling at me and they weren't out to punish me, then I could just say that.

Shorr: Yes.

Debra: She said, "I forget that at twenty-eight I knew what I was doing and I wasn't a baby." Except that, at the same time, she was really saying to me that sometimes *she* forgets that I am not a little girl. And she reacts to me more like she would to a daughter than she would to a peer. Which I am very hypersensitive about — anybody reacting to me like I am a little girl, whether it is me or them.

Shorr: It sounds like even though she is not regarding you as a little girl, you're still assuming that she must be, and you're always waiting for that.

Debra: Yes, I am always waiting for that. And I guess sometimes I talk about myself like I'm incompetent, or something, to reinforce that little girl feeling. When in truth, I am *not* incompetent, I am *certainly* not incompetent.

Shorr: You're not an incompetent person at all?

Debra: No!

Shorr: You're master of a lot of things, aren't you?

Debra: Yeah.

Shorr: (IS) Now I want you to go back to that baby room that you were in, in your house thing. Go back to that baby room. I want you, within a space of a minute or so, or just a few short minutes maybe, to find yourself going through the process of being a baby and accumulating the years into your present age. Do you know what I mean?

Debra: Yeah. I think so.

Shorr: (IS) Like growing up right in that room and telling me how you feel as you are doing it.

*****Debra**: (Pause) Just a baby? I feel all alone as a baby. All alone in a cold room with no blankets and I can scream for blankets, but I don't think anybody cares to hear me or comes to me. And I just get a little older, feeling "cold" like that is like I am supposed to be and hanging onto my Teddy bear for some kind of warmth. And I get a little older and I develop some kind of allergy, like I get hives and I am breaking out in a rash and then they figure I am allergic to the Teddy bear, so they take that away from me and they don't let me have any stuffed toys. That really happened, too. And then when I start getting old enough to wear dresses, they will take me out of the room and dress me up and then take me for a ride, both my father and my mother. And then like take me out in the sunlight and then take me places and then I get sick or my mother says I'm sick, so we have to go home. They take me into the bathroom and give me an enema and they put me back in my room and I hear them begin their fighting and I feel like they are fighting about me. And then I get old enough to go to school and they take me to the school and my father walks with me to school and I feel very, very alone at school. I don't seem to have anybody over to play with me or go any place to play with anybody else, like they expect me to be good alone in my room. (Pause) . . . And then after I start like getting old enough to go to school, I can hear them tell me that I have to do good in school and I have to have a lot of friends in school. My mother says to me, "Why don't you have any friends and why aren't you making a lot of friends?" She and my father are fighting all the time over me. And then when I start having to date with boys, when I am about 13, and I don't have any boyfriends and then she starts pushing me at boys. She starts getting involved in things that I'll be involved in boys, like clubs and pushing me to go to parties and asking me questions when I go to the parties like, "Do the boys like me? And am I pretty next to the other

---

*This passage is included as an example of a Five Minute Life History in Chapter IV, pp. 40-41.

children? Do the boys want to kiss me?" And then my father goes away and I don't remember my father now and he is out of the house. There is just her and me. When I get old enough to go to high school, the same stuff. "Why aren't you doing this? Why aren't you doing that?" And she looks so involved in what I am doing or what I am supposed to be doing. (Pause) . . . If she would have just let me grow up inside that room until . . .

I feel like I am getting so tall that I am hitting my head on the ceiling, but I don't have any of my things in the room and I don't even have any clothes in the room. It's like I just live in there, but I don't have anything in there and I feel like I am too big for that room and I am just too big to even sit in a chair in that room. My head keeps growing out through the ceiling, like I have to pull myself in and just huddle, sit in there to be big enough for it. The more I get to be my age now, I would be huge in that room growing, growing huge.	The part about going into the baby room. I loved it when I talked about my head growing too big for the room. That I was growing out of being a baby. I think that's the part I most identified with in the whole tape. It was beautiful. I was growing right in front of my eyes. Seeing myself grow like that was really neat. It was really beautiful. I really loved me when I heard that.

The symbol ⟷ appears between the two columns.

Shorr: But still in the room?

Debra: Yeah. (Long pause) Just like myself.

Shorr: (IS) How old are you now, as you are talking?

Debra: *My* age, ready to bust out.

Shorr: (Focusing Technique) (IS) Do it!

Debra: (With intense feeling) I just put my arms through the walls and my head up through the ceiling, kick the door down and bust out of it.

Shorr: Then what?

Debra: I would walk out and I would be in some sunlight! Walk out of that door, bust out of that door and walk into the front of that house! Open that door and let some air in there! Just have some air and some sunlight in there. Walk up those stairs. (Pause)

Shorr: And?

Debra: And I go up those stairs and I can be a person and have coffee, and I can talk to people and sit down in a chair that fits me, and eat and cook, and have children around and have people over.

Shorr: (IS) Now go back down to that baby room again. Now what do you see? You just did all that to it. You put your arms through it. Now what do you see?

Debra: I just see a tiny little gruddy [sic] shambles of kicked-in furniture, and busted-down door, and walls that have teeth marks on them from clawing, scratching and biting my way out of there. And I want to burn it, burn the whole downstairs of that house.

Shorr: And move the top portion?

Debra: And move the top portion and then put it on solid ground and make it my home.

Shorr: And you like that?

Debra: Yeah, that's how I feel. That's what I want to do, I want to make that top portion the bottom portion.

Shorr: The *whole* house?

Debra: Yes!

Shorr: (IS) Now you're in that new house as you want it, sunlit, and with people and children, just as you like it. Now think back about your aunt in another part of the town. What is she thinking about you?

Debra: "Look what she did! She just demolished the whole thing!" I think she feels afraid of me, like I am going to come over there and demolish her part.

Shorr: You feel like you want to do that?

Debra: Yeah, I want to ... No, I don't feel that way, but that's what *she* feels about me.

Shorr: I see. In other words, you really *wouldn't* do that?

Debra: No, I don't want to have anything to do with her.

Shorr: You feel free from her then?

Debra: Yeah, but I don't want to do that, but I think she feels that I want to do that.

Shorr: Uh huh.

Debra: I think that she is scared of me now. I really don't want to have anything to do with her. I just want to be in another part of town. I want to be in *my* things. I don't want to have anything to do with her. I don't want to *hear* from her, I don't want to *say* anything to her. I just don't want her. I don't need to burn her up, though.

Shorr: In other words, you don't *have* to get embroiled with her?

Debra: No!

Shorr: (IS) How about your mother, what is she saying as you are in your new house?

Debra: (Laughs) She is in that old house burning.

Shorr: And?

Debra: (Dramatically) Crying, "Oh, Debra, what did you do to me?"

Shorr: And?

Debra: And I feel pretty good about burning her up. (Vehemently) I don't want her anywhere near me, and the only way I can get rid of her is to just put her where she put me, inside of that house and burning up. ⟷ And somehow, it's really true. It's not my father I wanted to burn. He didn't put me in that room. My mother put me in the room. And when I could set fire to that house and move into my house — my home, it's like that was the best thing.

Shorr: (IS) And, now Charles?

Debra: (Vehemently) Put him in there, too. He can just burn with her. (More quietly) Lisa can stay over in the other part of town, she doesn't bother me.

Shorr: How do you feel right now?

Debra: I feel pretty good. (Laughs) (Therapist laughs, too)

Shorr: Liberated, huh?

Debra: (Laughing) I feel pretty damn good.

Shorr: Thinking back for a moment here, when I asked you to recapitulate your life in a few minutes, starting in the baby room. (M/L) What do you think was the most important thing that came out of it?

Debra: Busting out! The feeling that I was growing, that I didn't fit in there any more. That it was all "baby," that there wasn't any room in there for me any more. Like I was growing out of it. Then I had to bust out of it. I had to just claw the walls down to get out.

Shorr: (IS) Now you're in your new house, sunlit, nice. And this neighbor woman, Genevieve, comes in. How do you feel about her now?

Debra: Invite her in and give her a cup of coffee.

Shorr: Are you afraid of her?

Debra: No, I'm not afraid of her.

Shorr: Do you need her acknowledgment?

Debra: No, no, I just want her to be comfortable.

Shorr: Uh, huh. Do you feel good?

Debra: Yeah, I feel good about it. And I have anybody in the neighborhood in, but only the people I want around me now. I don't want any of the past people around me. In fact, I would just like them to live their own lives and stay there. But if they came and rang my doorbell, I would let them in and say "hello" to them, but I don't want to get involved in any of that any more. I don't want to have to prove to them that it is O.K. for me to have this place. If they want to come in and say "hello" to me, that's fine, and I'll give them a cup of coffee or whatever they want. And they can listen in, or they can join in and see my children and look at my paintings and my weavings or whatever I have around. Enjoy my home with me. But if they don't want to, then they are free to leave. They can just go and they can stay away forever. I don't want to write them; I don't want to call them; I don't want to see them; unless they come around me.

Shorr: (IS) Now go into group. How do you feel?

Debra: I feel good. I feel good going in like that and I feel like I don't need them to acknowledge me. I don't need them to say that I am O.K. I am all right. I can just react to them and be myself, and I don't need them to look down on me or look up to me, or say, "O.K., you're here." I don't have to worry about looking into someone's eyes and not being true. And I can laugh.

Shorr: (S&O) How would you give yourself confirmation?

Debra: By busting out of being a little girl.

Shorr: (FTS) Finish the sentence, "I am loved because ___."

Debra: I am happy.

Shorr: (FTS) "I am respected because _____ ."

Debra: I am a woman.

Shorr: (FTS) "Never refer to me as _____ ."

Debra: As little.

Shorr: A little girl?

Debra: A little girl, and call me "little girl."

Shorr: (IS) I want you to imagine that you're in any room, other than the ones we have talked about, and you can hear unidentifiable people speaking behind the wall. They don't know you are there. Now what are they saying about you?

Debra: I instantly got back to the room I grew up — not *that* room — but the *real* room where I was a young girl, in my aunt's house. And my aunt and my uncle are talking late at night and they are talking about . . . They are worrying about me. They are talking about me — how badly I'm doing, and how I am such a concern to them, and how I am making their life harder than it would have been — "Do we want this added responsibility of her? She doesn't fit in. She is being so difficult."

Shorr: And how do you feel?

Debra: I'm *mad*. I want to go in there and tell them they don't have to worry about me — not to worry about me. I mean, I am not going to *do* anything! I want to ask them specifically what I am doing that makes them worry so much about me? Or how I am an extra burden to them? I want to find out the reasons for what they are saying.

Shorr: Do you feel that that's resolved? The situation right now with your aunt and uncle?

Debra: Well the thought I had after I said that is, if they don't want to give me anything — they won't want to give me the specifics — tell me how I am really worrying them — then I will tell them, "O.K., Fuck you!" and walk out.

Shorr: You could do it?

Debra: I feel like I could do it, now.

Shorr: Uh, huh.

Debra: I could just say, "O.K., so that's what you want to do. Do it! I don't have to listen to you. I don't have to be afraid of what you are saying."

Shorr: And you would be free?

Debra: Yeah, and I would be free to just tell them to go fuck themselves, and just walk out — go and make my own life. To keep sitting in that room — being afraid to listen and afraid not to listen — I don't want to do that. I don't want to be afraid of overhearing something about me. I want to . . . if somebody is sitting there talking about me, O.K., that's the way they feel. O.K., so I am going to walk out. I don't have to sit there and listen. I am not trapped by them any more. I don't have to just sit there and be afraid of them, afraid they are going to kick me out. I can walk out. I can find my own people.

Shorr: (M/L) I want you to imagine the most private moment that you can think of, but don't tell me what it is, at least right now. You have the option to tell me, or you don't have to tell me at all. But imagine the most private moment you can think of. Don't tell me about it if you don't want to, it isn't important right now, anyway. But, imagine that *I* suddenly appear at that private moment. What do you feel? What do you do?

Debra: (Pause) (Giggles) I would invite you to sit down.

Shorr: How do you feel?

Debra: (Pause) I feel O.K. about it. I feel like I could share the private moment with you. I feel like, "Hey, Joe, what are you doing here?" I don't feel scared and I don't feel guilty. I feel like pulling you in, into my private moment.

Shorr: Exercising your option not to tell me, do you feel like you do not want to tell me?

Debra: Oh, no!

Shorr: I gathered the way you reacted that you wouldn't mind telling me?

Debra: No, no. I thought of being in bed at three o'clock in the morning with Ben, talking, laughing about something. Like, I would invite you to sit on the bed, and the three of us would just sort of talk.

Shorr: Very friendly?

Debra: Yes, very friendly. (Pause) We would share what we were laughing about with you. But very quietly, like it was just private.

Shorr: So I am not really intruding, then?

Debra: No, no, I didn't feel that way at all. (Laughs) The surprise would be, what are you doing in my house at three o'clock in the morning?

Shorr: (Laughs) But apart from the surprise, it is no invasion of your privacy or no intrusion?

Debra: No, no.

Shorr: And actually you like it mainly because there was a sharing?

Debra: Yeah.

Shorr: (IS) Now imagine that a man, any man other than those you know, has a sexual fantasy about you. What would it be?

Debra: (Long pause) That I would be like a sexy, not . . . like a sex kitten is the only thing that I keep thinking of. Like, I would be very cuddly and soft and excited, it would be fun and like an adventure. Playing a lot, but very exciting.

Shorr: This is the fantasy that a man would have about you?

Debra: Yeah.

Shorr: That you're playful, like a kitten?

Debra: Yeah, like a kitten. Funny, and fun.

Shorr: And fun?

Debra: And not serious and intense, but fun – playful.

Shorr: (IS) Now tell me how it feels if a man's semen is in your vagina?

Debra: (Pause) Wet, and it is after . . . (Very long pause) It feels good. It feels cool and I bring the blankets up over me and just feel relaxed.

Shorr: What else are you thinking? Your face looks deep in thought.

Debra: We feel drowsy. I would want him to be lying next to me, close to me, and maybe with his hands still on my stomach or something. I would want to sleep together. And I am also imagining that it's been pleasurable for me. Like it has been good for me, too. (Pause) Mostly, it is just being relaxed, and like I'd like to sleep now.

Shorr: (M/L) What is the most exciting time you have ever had?

Debra: (Pause) Oh, God, let's see. (Long pause) It isn't a good time. I mean it was when I was with that other man that we knew, Ben and I — the fellow that I worked with for awhile. I felt like I was sneaking and I felt like it was *all me*, and I was making big demands on him, but mostly it was a feeling of sneaking, and that it is a bad feeling.

Shorr: Yet it was very exciting?

Debra: Yeah, yeah, it was very exciting.

Shorr: So sneaking and exciting go together?

Debra: Yeah.

Shorr: Do you remember today you referred to sneaking? (See pp. 212-213.)

Debra: Yeah.

Shorr: Earlier?

Debra: Yeah, sneaking in my mother's and father's room to prove that I was alive.

Shorr: Does that tie-up with the man here?

Debra: Yes, I guess it must. (Pause) It was like I was talking about the semen in me and I was thinking of Ben, being with Ben. And when you say the excitement means sneaking, I think of cheating on Ben, betraying him. And that is what I did with my mother and father in that fantasy, too — not trusting that they would have things of me. So I would look for them and not find them, and know that they really didn't have anything of me, but that sneaky feeling of being afraid of getting caught.

Shorr: What makes it exciting?

Debra: The cheating must make it exciting and also being with somebody who I would cheat with — a bad guy. Somebody like Charles, who would put me down, who *thinks* of me as being a very easy . . . Who thought of me as, "Well, just give me enough time and of course I can get her to go to bed with me." But Charles, if he just kept trying and battered me down and kept trying, and trying, and trying, and finally I would really succumb to him — which is exactly what that guy did. He just kept day, after day, after day, trying to get me to go to bed with him, until I just gave up.

Shorr: Why did you give up?

Debra: I don't know. I did it impulsively and I didn't think I could go through with it, but then I felt trapped by it.

Shorr: Why?

Debra: Well, because he said, "I don't think you will do it." And I said, "Of course, I will."

Shorr: You mean before you went out, you discussed it?

Debra: No, at that time, he said he didn't think I'd go through with it and I knew he didn't think I'd go through with it.

Shorr: So then you really had an option?

Debra: It seemed to be part of the game that we were playing. I *had* an option, I know I did. I could have — I almost did say, "No, I am not going to do it" — but then I just felt victimized by the whole thing, too.

Shorr: But you seem to get some . . .

Debra: Some pleasure out of it, is right.

Shorr: Being the victim?

Debra: Being punished, or I wonder if the thought that I might be punished would be adding to it?

Shorr: Excitement and being punished go together? Cheating, excitement and punishment?

Debra: It is the cheating, excitement and being bad and dirty and being a bad person. That always goes along with the threat of being punished. Punishment is simple, though. Ben was always punishing me for things I didn't do, because all the time he was just sure that I was going to cheat on him — that I was going to betray him. He would accuse me every day of betraying him. He would accuse me even if I wasn't doing anything.

Shorr: (S&O) What was your mother's basic expectation about you?

Debra: (Pause) That I was *going* to do something. Unless she kept a pretty good watch on me, that I was *going* to do something, and that was exactly what Ben was giving me, too.

Shorr: (FTS) So according to your mother, you were going to _____ .

Debra: I was going to cheat, and I was going to be a whore, and I was going to get into trouble. Being bad, that I was destined to be bad. Born to be bad.

Shorr: (FTS) The only way you could prevent yourself from being bad was _____ .

Debra: To do nothing.

Shorr: And if you did anything?

Debra: To not to do it, for *me* not to do it, but to be done to.

Shorr: To be done to?

Debra: Yeah.

Shorr: What do you mean?

Debra: Well, I really wasn't bad if they were using me. If I was just being used, I wasn't really being as bad as if I had gone out of my way to take part in it.

Shorr: In other words, if you seduced the man . . .?

Debra: I would have really been bad.

Shorr: Then, of course, the vindication of what she said, you would have been bad, really horribly bad?

Debra: That's right!

Shorr: But if the man is using you?

Debra: Then I am only being involved in it. Then I am being used, and the victim, and then she could probably . . . well, then she would have felt sorry for me.

Shorr: Right, and then she would have been angry at the man?

Debra: Yeah, yeah, and would have punished him.

Shorr: So then you wouldn't have lost out with her?

Debra: No, no. So I get excited that way.

Shorr: You're permitted to get excited?

Debra: Yeah, if I am not losing her. If I am not putting her away, burning her up, or doing whatever I want to do to her. But if I get excited in a way for *me*, that's the time that I am killing her.

Shorr: (S&O) So every time that you have sex when you are the essential involved person or the leader, or the seducer, or you have the desire of sex, you are killing your mother?

Debra: I am killing her. I am letting her go and I am pushing her out of my life. And if I don't have any feeling, I mean if I don't have any excitement or there is no pleasure for me, that maintains and keeps her inside. That keeps my mother going. Then I don't ever pass her up, or push her away, or have something that she didn't have.

Shorr: (M/L) So the greatest guilt is what?

Debra: Is having sex.

Shorr: Having *anything* for you?

Debra: Yeah, having anything. Yeah, yeah, it's just having my life, my independent life, because it robs her of her life. She poured herself into me.

Shorr: She martyred herself for you?

Debra: That's right!

Shorr: She died for your sins?

Debra: That's right. (Laughs) She literally became a Christ.

Shorr: (Laughs) The first woman Christ?

Debra: (Giggles)

Shorr: (FTS) So therefore, it behooves you to ____ .

Debra: Keep her going. (Laughs) To drink and to do holy communion, so that she doesn't die. Because if I . . . and that keeps me being a little girl, too. Because I could only exist in her situation, as in the fantasy in that little room – in that little cell made for a little girl. But when I bust out of there, the first thing I want to do is to go to *my* place and I want to burn her place. I only want my place, and I don't want her anywhere near there.

Shorr: And if you burn her, then you can have sex and enjoy it, and sex could be yours?

Debra: That's right!

Shorr: Otherwise, it belongs to the man who victimized you and the only enjoyment and excitement allowed you?

Debra: That's right, it is sneaky and it is to cheat and still be a victim. It's all those men, it's all those men that I always felt I was sneaking and cheating and then, like, I could get excited in the beginning or something. At least I had that.

Shorr: But the excitement would go away and you wouldn't feel that much?

Debra: No!

Shorr: It still wasn't allowed for you? (FTS) Because if your mother knew that you had sexual excitement_____ .

Debra: She would die on the spot. Then I would *really* be a dirty, slob whore.

Shorr: (M/L) And who is the biggest, dirty, slob whore that you know?

Debra: Besides me?

Shorr: If you insist. (Jokingly)

Debra: (Laughs) Well, I am the dirtiest slob, slob whore that I know.

Shorr: But besides you?

Debra: Besides me? (Pause, then excitedly as if in revelation) Oh! Oh! Yes. I know now why I get that feeling about Alice. Like when she talks, you know, she just comes on about how much she is getting out of sex. I get this really squibbled-up feeling. And like Kristen, remember when she was talking in group about wanting sex three or four or five times a day? I just couldn't believe it. That's really terrible. It really made me embarrassed.

Shorr: Because?

Debra: Because I had so much desire, I couldn't stand it. To have excitement like that, that would be incredible. But if that was me, I would be the dirtiest thing in the world.

Shorr: You're dirty because you are killing your mother.

Debra: That's right!

Shorr: You're not dirty because you are sexual.

Debra: I am dirty because I am guilty, guilty!

Shorr: For killing your mother?

Debra: Yes, and loose, and hanging out all over, and dirty – yes, dirty . . .

$\longleftrightarrow$ The section about the sexual problems is really neat to listen to because I can't believe that only two years have gone by, and it's almost totally different now. I don't feel those feelings any more. I have orgasms. I can feel my whole being, being with Ben. I don't feel guilty about it. I don't punish myself afterwards. I'm being much more sexual, much more womanly, much more abandoned than I ever dreamed I could be. I used to think I was cold and that there was something wrong with me. Now I think I could even do it with my mother standing in the room. (Laughs)

Shorr: All the time you're involving yourself sexually, you are killing your mother. (IS) Can you imagine having one giant orgasm?

Debra: Well, that would be the end of it.

Shorr: You just destroyed her.

Debra: Well, it is just like : . . I totally blank out. I can't think of anything except my vagina, then. That's all I can think of, that's all I am really aware of.

Shorr: As what?

Debra: As me.

Shorr: You're just one large vagina, you mean?

Debra: Yeah, just pounding and pumping and . . . like it has a mind of its own.

Shorr: And what does it want to do?

Debra: Just fuck, that's all. Just get pleasure.

Shorr: (IS) If you could separate your vagina from you, then you wouldn't kill your mother?

Debra: (Subdued tone) No, I wouldn't. I don't know, Joe, whether I would.

Shorr: (IS) Suppose you sent your vagina over to Ben right now, you deliver it to Ben and he is fucking it. Does it kill your mother?

Debra: No, no, because that's not as important as . . . but, that's . . . you're right. If it's independent of my being, then it's just function and I have no feelings about it. But if it is part of me, then it is like a whole thing, all of me. That's what I want, it's not only just my vagina, but I want to feel my *body* with Ben's and I want to have my arms around him. I want to be there. I don't want to separate us. If I separate it, then I'm here, and I can judge that, and judging that is like being my mother.

Shorr: (IS) Now suppose you are a vagina, totally?

Debra: If I am totally a vagina, I would want more. I just don't want to stop. I don't want to stop short of my pleasure. I want the whole total thing.

Shorr: (IS) O.K., you walk into a room as a vagina. You are a vagina. You walk into a room and there's your mother. Now what do you do?

Debra: Oh, I just feel like closing up.

Shorr: And you shrink?

Debra: Shrink. Yeah, I just close up tight, and huddle, and pull everything in.

Shorr: (IS) And what does she say?

Debra: (Angrily) "What are you doing walking around looking like that? What do you think you are, you street-walker?"

Shorr: (IS) Now what do you want to tell her?

Debra: (Subdued tone) "I won't do it any more, mama."

Shorr: (Focusing Technique) Now what do *you want* to tell her?

Debra: (Angrily) I want to tell her to get the fuck out of the room.

Shorr: (Focusing Technique) Tell her!

Debra: (Screams) "GET THE FUCK OUT OF THE ROOM, MOTHER. GET OUT OF HERE NOW. IT'S MY LIFE, AND I AM *NOT* A STREET-WALKER."

Shorr: How do you feel right now?

Debra: (Subdued) I don't feel as good as I felt telling the other people. [See pp.220 (Genevieve) and 226 (aunt and uncle).]

Shorr: You mean other people, earlier?

Debra: Yeah. I still feel like I have to make it all right with her.

Shorr: (S&O) You still have to account to your mother?

Debra: Yeah. (Pause) I still feel like I have to hold back the feelings that are inside of me, because I will kill her if I let them out. Even if they are just verbal, I'll kill her with them. Like I have the power to annihilate her.

Shorr: With your pleasure?

Debra: Yeah . . . with me.

Shorr: With your sexual pleasure?

Debra: That's right. Which is part of me.

Shorr: Not if you eat and have pleasure.

Debra: No, no, then I would just get fat.

Shorr: Not if you have pleasure any other way?

Debra: No, no, no, no.

Shorr: (S&O) But, with sexual pleasure, you annihilate your mother?

Debra: That's right, I would just kill her. It's like she couldn't stand it, she would wither up and die.

Shorr: (S&O) And you're protecting her?

Debra: By not feeling, myself.

Shorr: But you are still protecting her, even at the price of your own sexual pleasure and existence?

Debra: Yes, I still make it nice for her. I don't . . .

Shorr: (IS) Look into her eyes. What do you see?

Debra: Milky, weepy, blue eyes saying, "Don't hurt me, don't hurt me." I really looked at her and made her my size, not a little, tiny, shrimpy thing. Make her my size and look into her eyes and say, "Mother, there's nothing in the world I can do to hurt you. There's nothing. I cannot hurt you. There's nothing that I *do* that hurts you." I can make her eyes tighten up and they can get angry at me, but her *angry* eyes don't bother me, it's those wishy, weak, "Don't hurt me" eyes, and I don't know what to say to those eyes.

Shorr: (Focusing Technique) (IS) I want you to keep staring at those eyes until you transform them into something else. Can you do that?

Debra: (Very long pause) I can transform them into marbles.

Shorr: Yes.

Debra: (Long pause) Mannikin marbles.

Shorr: Mannikin marbles?

Debra: Yeah, marble eyes in a mannikin.

Shorr: Now, how do you feel?

Debra: I feel better looking at them. I don't feel like I am going to hurt them. They are already dead.

Shorr: (IS) Keep staring at them.

Debra: I feel I could just push them out of the way and keep walking.

Shorr: (IS) Now you're a vagina again. How do you feel?

Debra: Kind of loose. (Pause) A little warm. (Long pause) I feel like I am suppposed to be this way.

Shorr: Earlier you were able to burn your mother up, and you felt free (See p. 224.) Now before, you were meeting your mother in a room as a vagina, and you told her to buzz-off, so to speak, and yet it didn't seem to make enough difference. (See p. 232.)

Debra: No, it doesn't.

Shorr: In other words, the only way you can really kill your mother and get her greatest disapproval is through sex?

Debra: Yes! But see, just pushing her away or telling her to go away, isn't . . . It's like, I guess, my feelings about her must be much more intense. I mean, the only way I could really get rid of her satisfyingly, and really feel good, would be to just burn her up.

Shorr: You felt good enough when you transformed her into a mannikin?

Debra: Yeah, I could do it, then.

Shorr: As long as she is dead?

Debra: Yeah, as long as she is dead, I felt . . . It's this alive, clinging, guilty, guilt-handing . . .

Shorr: Guilt-inducing.

Debra: Yes, making me feel guilty. Like, I have to take care of her. I can't stand it, and that's what makes me get all huddled up.

Shorr: In other words, you really can't have sex and feel free about sex, and enjoy it as an equal with the man, as long as your mother, or the influence of your mother, and your responsibility to her exists?

Debra: Yeah! That's right, because when I went up in that room and made that my home, I felt like an adult. But if I meet her, I go back to being a little kid, having to take care of her.

Shorr: Well, if you take care of her, you're not much of a kid, you must be more like . . .

Debra: (Interrupts) No, I am really not a kid. I'm more like an old woman, making her the kid.

Shorr: In other words, when you're responsible, you really are almost being like the husband?

Debra: Yeah. Or my aunt.

Shorr: Or your aunt?

Debra: Yeah.

Shorr: A controlling woman?

Debra: Yeah. I can't stand having to be leaned on by her, like she is some little ninny.

Shorr: In other words . . .

Debra: And that she is going to suck me if I do that.

Shorr: (IS) In other words, it's like having a little girl come into a room and seeing you in sexual intercourse. Your mother becomes the little girl, if you become the protector. And if she were to come into a room where you were having sexual intercourse with a man, as a little girl?

Debra: Oh, Jesus, I would have to cover up, and I would have to get away, and I would have to go to her. I would have to go to her, like she would be in pain or some kind of need. But I would have to take care of her. I would just shove the man away. If I were enjoying it, I would just get rid of it, and just cut it off right there if she came in.

Shorr: (FTS) So shutting off sexual functions is related mainly to ____ ?

Debra: My mother. My mother making me feel responsible for her.

Shorr: The word is "responsible."

Debra: Yeah!

Shorr: As long as you are a sexual woman who enjoys sexuality?

Debra: (In a definite tone) I am not responsible for anybody else.

Shorr: Yes.

Debra: It's like I couldn't stand to be responsible for anybody else. (Pause) It is certainly not anybody that is pulling on me. (Long pause)

Shorr: (IS) Suppose your mother is in Hong Kong and you're in Los Angeles having sex with a man where you're an equal partner in the situation. Now how do you feel? Is her influence still there?

Debra: Fuck, the telephone is going to ring.

Shorr: (Laughs) The telephone is going to ring. (Pause, waiting for a response)

Debra: Yeah, it is so strong, Joe.

Shorr: The telephone is going to ring and, of course . . .

Debra: It will be my mother. (Laughs heartily)

Shorr: (IS) It will be your mother and she is going to say . . .?

Debra: (Mimics mother's voice) "Debra, how are you doing, honey? I was just thinking about you, and I haven't heard from you for a long time. Are you O.K.?"

Shorr: (Pretends to be Debra) "I'm having sex, mother."

Debra: "Yeah, I'm fucking, mom."

Shorr: And she says?

Debra: (Outraged tone) "What?"

Shorr: And you say?

Debra: "Go to bed!"

Shorr: And then what?

Debra: She says, "Are you married?" Then I say, "Yes, mother. Goodbye."

Shorr: And now?

Debra: (Joyously) I want to go back and fuck.

Shorr: (IS) And can you have an orgasm?

Debra: Yes! If I could turn my mother off that easy! If I could just see her as being such a ninny. And not feel like I have to take care of her. That she's a stupid, idiot ninny who asked me such a stupid question. If I could just feel that I didn't have to be responsible for her!

Shorr: It sounds like the key word is "responsible."

Debra: Yeah!

Shorr: (M/L) Who are the people you have felt most responsible for in the world?

Debra: Oh, wow!

Shorr: Who?

Debra: My mother.

Shorr: And?

Debra: And my aunt, and my uncle, and Lisa, and Charles, and George, and every other stupid son-of-a-bitch that came into my life.

Shorr: The only kinds you seem to go towards.

Debra: Somebody that needs a great deal of support, and then I can't really give it openly, so *I* have to act like a ninny.

Shorr: Why can't you give it openly?

Debra: Because I am just supposed to be a jock-strap holder and hold up balls, so that they can go on and do great and wonderful things.

Shorr: And what about you?

Debra: "Just stay in the background, Debra, and keep your mouth shut, except in times when I ask you to talk."

Shorr: (S&O) And what can you ask for, then, in this world?

Debra: Nothing, like that, nothing. Just my little niche, just my little place in the history of all these people.

Shorr: (S&O) And so what kind of men do you have to collect?

Debra: Fuck-ups, failures, people that need a great deal of support. Very intelligent, very sensitive, very creative, but with no balls.

Shorr: And you provide the balls?

Debra: Yes.

Shorr: And tell them how great they are?

Debra: Yes, that's right! "Now, you really talented people, you really have something unusual." I remember telling Ben that he was going to be just great some day; he was made of such fine stuff. He said, "Oh, shut up!" (Laughs)

Shorr: (Laughs)

Debra: He said, "You know, I really don't need to hear that."

Shorr: So where are *you* with these kinds of people?

Debra: Jesus Christ!

Shorr: The people that you have to support?

Debra: I'm like underneath them, holding them up all the time.

Shorr: It gets pretty tiresome, doesn't it?

Debra: Yes, no wonder I loved Ayn Rand characters. They didn't do that.

Shorr: Right! And then when you have sex with such a man?

Debra: My God, what could be for me? It's all got to be for them, total supportive sex. No wonder I felt resentful.

Shorr: "Supportive sex." That's a new term. I have never heard that one; you just coined it. Should I give you credit or shall I call your mother in Hong Kong?

Debra: She'll ask you whom you're fucking. (Laughs)

Shorr: (Laughs) "I'm fucking your daughter."

Debra: "Are you married?"

Shorr: "No." (Laughs) What is she going to say?

Debra: She is going to say, "Then, stop that." (Laughs) "Stop that immediately or I'll call the police. Let me talk to Debra."

Shorr: In other words, "supportive sex" is for a man who wants sex, not whether you want it or not, but whether he wants it?

Debra: Yes, that's right. And he wants support, too, and kind of making him feel good and strong.

Shorr: Building up their masculinity?

Debra: Yeah, yeah, yeah, really. A human jock-strap. But see, in group, Michele did that with me. But, Joe, they all reversed it. They all said it was *me* that needed the support. But they did that to me ... it's like they reversed it. It was all the time I was standing there, totally nothing, like a post office — things going in and out. And all the time they said, "Oh, poor Debra, she needs all this support." But it was never ... I was always the one who was doing the holding up, making them feel good at my expense. And that's the kind of man I always looked for. Ben was that kind of man, too.

Shorr: The immediate demands upon you in dealing with another human being?

Debra: It is how much am I going to have to give to them?

Shorr: Great! (Sarcastically)

Debra: How much am I going to have to give you? Genevieve Johnson comes over; how much do I have to support her? How much do I have to make her feel that she is O.K.?

Shorr: What about someone that *is* O.K. and doesn't want that support from you? How do you feel then? Can you believe it?

Debra: No, I'd still try to give it. Ben is that way, now. I have all these little bromides saved for when he is hung-up. He just looks at me and says, "There's another one of your bromides, and they don't work, Debra."

Shorr: (S&O) If you can give "supportive sex," what can you take for yourself?

Debra: Credit for having given them pleasure, but nothing else.

Shorr: But not for you to have what you want?

Debra: No, no, not for me.

Shorr: So if you are masturbating a man, that's fine. Right?

Debra: Yeah. Yeah.

Shorr: But if you want to have sex for your own enjoyment?

Debra: Then I'd have to be non-supportive.

Shorr: And then you have lost your responsibility?

Debra: That's right, then I have robbed them.

Shorr: Of what they need. So you pick people who are in need, who need this support and you can't see another kind of person?

Debra: Yeah.

Shorr: But you somehow feel that they must exist in this world?

Debra: Yeah, but you know, Joe, it's like people I know . . . Alice doesn't need my support, and I'm not giving it to her so much, and we do just fine. Ben doesn't need my support any more, and we do better than just fine, now.

Shorr: So you're beginning to see . . .

Debra: That that's not what these people want. They don't want that from me. *You* don't want it from me in group. If somebody picks on you, you can damn well take care of them. If Nick gets angry with you, I don't have to sit there and say, "Oh, but Nick, you don't understand; it's really . . ." I don't have to defend you; I don't have to support you.

Shorr: I can take care of myself.

Debra: Yeah, you can take care of yourself.

Shorr: Therefore, if you don't have to feel responsible for me . . .?

Debra: It makes me feel free.

Shorr: To be you.

Debra: Yeah.

Shorr: And not to be afraid.

Debra: But it's scary.

Shorr: Because, deprived of your jock-strap role . . .

Debra: What do I have?

Shorr: What have you got? "I am nothing."

Debra: And that makes me, in a sense, come up. It makes me have to be me, and you told me you don't want a little girl.

Shorr: Right, therefore you can enjoy sex.

Debra: And I can have relationships with all sorts of people without having to jock-strap them through.

Shorr: Right. (S&O) So responsibility precedes most of your activities?

Debra: That's right!

Shorr: (S&O) And when the responsibility of the other person precedes your activity, there's self-negation.

Debra: Yeah, there's nothing.

Shorr: (S&O) When you negate yourself for a long enough time, there's no identity.

Debra: That's right, and I am just back in that little room.

Shorr: Until you can become another jock-strap as your only identity. And a jock-strap by itself . . .

Debra: (Laughs) It has no use. (Therapist laughs also) It's really quite a functional piece of equipment. (Laughing)

Shorr: (Laughing) It's quite a flexible elastic thing, but nowhere. So if you can eliminate your responsibility to the poor and the maimed and those you select ordinarily, then you can allow yourself to be yourself without self-negation. And what's more, you can say what you really feel, and can be yourself, and think of yourself first in a way different than the responsible way toward others. (Pause) Had enough for today?

Debra: Jesus! I don't mean Jesus, I mean (loudly) YES!

Shorr: (Laughs) In just a minute, because there's enough time — what do you think is the most important thing you got out of the session today?

Debra: There are two things. Again they are reconfirming — wanting to go to my own place, if I could bust out of that child room.

Shorr: Yes.

Debra: And then . . . really, the last fifteen minutes have just been saying in my own voice about this responsibility, this constant responsibility. It is a constant reflection of me and it all goes back to that little girl thing.

Shorr: (S&O) So that you can call yourself a woman with your own identity?

Debra: Me! That's right. And I won't have to feel guilty about it.

⟷ I think if I had to make a comment now about the most important part of the tape, I would choose the last part. The part about talking about being responsible, being the post office for my mother, being her representative on earth, and having to be so careful about myself all the time. (See pp. 236-239 of therapy tape.) I think probably that is the one most important thing I remember this time from hearing the tape. It seems to be the thing I got at, that was the most helpful. I'm still talking about it now. I also realized that this was a hard thing to do. I cried a lot during the first play of the tape. I really felt the loneliness and the sadness of that person. I didn't really feel it was me.

I feel older than that now, and bigger and stronger and more grown up. And happier. About a hundred percent happier than that person who made that tape. The difference in my voice seems to be like a non-tear in my voice, whereas then I seemed to be in mourning for something. I guess I really was

(Continued on next page)

sad almost all of the time and very unhappy. I really was having a hard time with almost everything.

I guess my biggest reaction to listening to the entire tape, even the second time, is that I really felt separated from this person who was talking. I really didn't feel like the same person. I couldn't believe how much has happened from the time of this tape to now. In fact, I wish I could talk to that person in the tape. It's like everything was such a big pain. I would talk about freedom, like burning the house down, the freedom that results from not being responsible for every single person in the world. I feel like it frees me so much. I can laugh; I can make jokes; I can dance around the room if I like.

[END OF TAPE]

CHAPTER 10

Summary

"Effectiveness is, moreover, as important in science as rigor. It is the reason for publication itself, since truth discovered but unrevealed is no good to anyone."

E. G. Boring

"And any *theory* not founded on the nature of being human is a lie and a betrayal of man."

R. D. Laing

The purpose of this book is to show a teachable, demonstrable method of psychotherapy. If the professional reader with clinical experience can learn to utilize the concepts and methods herein presented, then to that degree have I succeeded. But, I will have failed if the reader attempts to use this as a mechanical, recipe book, and worst of all, neglects to develop his own phenomenological understanding and awareness, and therapeutic creativity within the infinite varieties and range of human interaction.

Chessick's warning must be stressed and endorsed: "The therapist can become so absorbed in professional skills and techniques that his relationships with patients become depersonalized. Often the gestures of empathic communication are made, but the reality and the freshness of the meeting are lost and in their place an almost inevitable artificiality intrudes. When this occurs, it reflects a lack of vigilance on the part of the therapist; he loses part of his own humanity and slips into the habits of the bureaucrat, for routine is comfortable and apparently efficient." (Chessick, 1969, p. 114.)

Even though Psycho-Imagination Therapy involves an active directive approach in general, I must stress that it makes use of supportive measures when needed. It is extremely sensitive to where the patient is and takes into account the patient's resistances and hesitancies. For the patient is only human and very likely to have a tender ego structure. He only wants to know if it is possible to change and grow freely. No matter how active the therapist may be in helping the patient to achieve awareness, the patient is never to be manipulated. Free interchange and dialogue are paramount. Both the patient and the therapist must have full respect for each other. The patient (self) must feel the empathy and trust of the therapist (other) in a way different from the way in which the significant others in his early family

243

structure defined him. According to Guntrip, the ultimate aim of therapy is ". . . to help the patient to tolerate the conscious re-experiencing of his profoundly repressed and fundamentally weak infantile ego, which he has spent his life trying to disown in his struggle to feel adult." (Guntrip, 1961, p. 419.)

It is my firm belief that any method and technique of psychotherapy should be firmly rooted in a systematic theory of personality. In my opening chapter I have attempted to outline such a theory, operationally based on existential concepts and phenomenological foundations, blended with the interpersonal theory of Harry Stack Sullivan (1953). Throughout the book I have attempted to point out the connection between such a self-and-other personality theory and methods of conflict awareness and conflict resolution. Moreover, the emphasis is on the integration of imagination with the existential phenomenology and centeredness of the individual — imagination in the service of awareness and of the possibility of change.

As for the concept of imagination and the range of psychological and philosophical problems it encompasses, it is not possible within the scope of this book to examine this in depth. The integration of phenomenology and imagination in this book is bridged through the link of a psychotherapeutic process. For a full understanding of the role of imagination, the reader probably would do well to be aware of eidetic imagery, Jellinek's (1949) spontaneous imagery, the concept of imaginary companions, and the role of imagination in the development of a child as he progresses from sensorimotor stages into the characteristically human ability of abstract conceptualization — the ability to create a mental representation of an absent object.

There is perhaps no better statement on the integration of imagination and phenomenology than the one by C. M. Bowra, a professor of poetry at Harvard: "Most of us, when we use our imagination, are in the first place stirred by some alluring puzzle which calls for a solution, and in the second place enabled by our own creations in the mind to see much that was before dark or unintelligible. As our fancies take coherent shape, we see more clearly what has puzzled and perplexed us." (Bowra, 1961, p. 7.)

It is my hope that Psycho-Imagination Therapy can be used as both an investigative tool and as a therapeutic approach, with a minimum gap in its application. This has not always been true of other methods of therapy. Judd Marmor,* in a speech before the Group Psychotherapy Association said that the value of free association seems to be more as an investigative tool than as a valuable therapeutic technique. Others, such as Strupp (1967, p. 149), have spoken of the wide hiatus between psychoanalytic theory and psychoanalytic therapy. In Chapter VII, Psycho-Imagination Therapy techniques were used in an investigative manner, as Doctor X and I attempted to explore the reasons for Hugh's impasse in therapy

---

*January 13, 1971, Los Angeles.

and possible approaches to resolving the impasse. Throughout the book I have attempted to demonstrate Psycho-Imagination Therapy as a means of making the person more aware of the core of his identity, his internal conflicts and his neurotic conflict resolution. I have tried to show how, with the aid of the focusing techniques, this type of therapy can effect healthy conflict resolution.

Psycho-Imagination Therapy can yield a wealth of information revealing the patient's conflict areas and attitudes towards help, as well as other assessments. Naturally, if the reader were to listen to the audio tape of a session, he would gain even greater knowledge about the patient than from reading the transcript. No amount of editing can convey the tone of voice, hesitancies, and other mannerisms that reveal so much about the patient.

At the present time Psycho-Imagination Therapy has been used mainly with neurotic populations and with a few depressed and schizoid patients. I have not worked extensively with psychotic patients, although this may be attempted in the future. I *have* used the techniques extensively in group therapy, although I have reported very little of those experiences here; I felt it was not possible within the scope of this book to give sufficient separate emphasis which the group experience deserves. Colleagues have suggested that Psycho-Imagination Therapy might be useful with alcoholics and drug addicts. I hope to make such an attempt.

While I have not emphasized dreams in this book, I do not wish to give the impression that I regard them as unimportant. Dreams are vivid indicators of a person's phenomenological world. I am not averse to dream interpretation if it enhances the patient's awareness of his conflicts and feeling awareness of himself in relation to others. Making the patient imagine he is the various parts of people in the dream and saying something to the other parts or persons as well as feeling like the parts or persons, makes the dream come to life, as in Gestalt therapy techniques. Additionally, I may ask the patient to imagine that he is the part or person in the dream and have him interact imaginatively with people outside the dream who are significant to him. I nearly always ask what conflict the dream indicates — between what and what? Moreover, does the dream indicate interpersonal strategies for our awareness? What aspects of conflict resolution does the dream reveal? Dreams and the awareness of their meanings add perspective to the therapy. As Eckhardt (1969, p. 11) so ably states: "Ethical issues implicitly permeate therapeutic discussions. Dreams are often amazing for their succinctness in posing moral questions . . . All we can do is point the finger. It is an activity that hopes to know."

Since this book emphasizes therapeutic approaches, it might be assumed that discussions of values, life-meaning, and choices are to be neglected. Nothing could be further from the truth. If, during a session, the Psycho-Imagination Therapy techniques lead into the possibility of a changed value system, or of a new approach to meanings, perspectives, and choices, such discussions should be a natural development. It is such a human dialogue that humanizes the use of specific techniques.

It is of immense importance that, for the growth and expanding awareness of the therapist, he ask himself the same questions and imaginary situations that he proposes to the patient. With both the patient and the therapist attempting the feeling response to the same question or situation (not, of course, simultaneously), greater authenticity is bound to occur.

Within the scope of a book such as this one everything seems possible, and yet no author can ever cover the infinite range of problems and questions that human interaction can pose. To emphasize technique and method means to limit theoretical emphasis. Yet any technique not rooted in a firm theoretical basis of man is valueless. The complexities are so enormous that one investigator remarked that in a two-hour videotape of a patient and therapist interaction he had the potential of several hundred research projects. Of necessity, then, certain problems of the therapeutic interaction must be omitted, while others are included.

It is from my failures in therapy that I grew. One becomes discouraged by knowing a great deal about the psychology of interaction and not being able to implement this to a therapeutic conclusion. One can be fooled by patients, even manipulated by them in their stake to remain neurotic. Horney spoke of a patient who always came poorly dressed to her sessions. Quite by accident, Horney encountered this patient on another occasion and was stunned to see her very smartly dressed. When confronted with this disparity, the patient said she felt Horney would abandon her if she were strong, and furthermore, why should she give Horney the satisfaction of having helped her? Max Frisch, in his novel *I'm Not Stiller*, refers to people who do not wish to be responsible for their own lives:

". . . it was time Julika stopped seeing her own behavior towards her husband, and towards people in general, as only a reaction, never regarding herself as an initiator, in other words it was time she stopped wallowing in infantile innocence."
and
"Anyone who is always seeing himself as a victim, it seems to me, never gets wise to himself, and that's not healthy. Cause and effect are never divided between two people . . . It just strikes me that you explain everything you do or don't do by something your husband has or has not done." (Frisch, 1958, pp. 114-115.)

Yet, despite this point, I believe it is still the responsibility of the therapist to be able to find ways and means to help a patient beyond all his resistances and manipulations. It is possible to blame the failure on the transference relationship. This too often is a convenient defense. Sometimes, those who emphasize transference reactions neglect the encounter ". . . within which, and only within which, transference has genuine meaning. *Transference is to be understood as the distortion of encounter.* Since there was no norm of human encounter in psychoanalysis and no adequate place for the I-Thou relationship, there was bound to be an oversimplifying and watering down of love relationships." (May, 1964, p. 29.) The therapeutic encounter fights against the two people in the room becoming distant shadows. Change occurs in both persons, however minutely, in a genuine encounter. Unless the therapist is open to change the patient will not be, either.

In summary, I wish to present the following beliefs:

1. Whenever possible, taping of sessions should be utilized for the growth of and re-evaluation by the therapist and the patient.

2. Does imagination have a "reality" to the patient? After all, it might be argued that it is only imagination and, although the person may have a strong experience in imagination, he will probably discount it if he realizes it is not an actual experience. Therapeutic experience, however, strongly rejects this argument. The direction of the experienced imagination becomes individualized to that person. Here is one example, among countless I have observed: A patient indicated that he felt the core of his identity was his heart. When I asked him to imagine handing me his heart, he moved his body forward and suddenly spread his hand out desperately lest he drop it. He said, with feeling, "My heart is so large it will fall on the floor." He was surprised by the experience and remarked that he never would have believed that he could have experienced such a reaction. His awareness of his heart's vulnerability needed no interpretation from me. As William James said, "Each world *whilst it is attended to* is real after its own fashion . . ." (James, 1890, p. 293.)

3. Psycho-Imagination Therapy gives Sullivan's term "participant observer" a dimension of intensity that I hadn't encountered in using conventional methods of therapy. It seemingly takes more of the resources of the therapist and patient. There are fewer "dead" spots in the sessions. The therapist not only listens but also experiences the patient's communications at many different levels.

4. The therapist has greater opportunities for creativity, seeking the appropriate self-and-other questions, finish-the-sentence questions, most-or-least questions and the imaginary situations to stimulate the patient to responses and reactions. Instead of the patient trying to fit into a prescribed theory of therapy, the therapist is trying to envisage and assess the unique system of the individual. It is phenomenology in action.

5. Not unlike other approaches, the assessment of the "ego strength" of the patient is extremely important. In Psycho-Imagination Therapy this need at times may be heightened. For an adequate assessment of ego strength, there is no substitute for actual experience with patients and the knowledge of human dynamics.

6. With the appropriate use of focusing techniques, mobilization of the constructive forces within the individual can be energized on his own behalf. Liberating a person from an alien identity allows him to be what we are all hopefully striving to be — more human — namely, ourselves.

REFERENCES

Allport, Gordon W. Editor. *Letters From Jenny*. New York: Harcourt, Brace and World, 1965.

Armstrong, Edward. *Shakespeare's Imagination*. Lincoln, Nebraska: University of Nebraska Press, 1963.

Assagioli, Roberto. *Psychosynthesis: A Manual of Principles and Techniques*. New York: Hobbs, Dorman and Co., 1965.

*Barcai, Avner. "But who listens" — Therapeutic value of replayed tape recorded interviews. *American Journal of Psychotherapy*, April 1967, *21*(2), 286-294.

Bellow, Saul. *Herzog*. New York: Viking Press, 1961.

Binswanger, Ludwig. *Being-in-the-World*. New York: Harper Torchbooks, 1963.

Blank, Paul. Reproducing the moment: the image in the event. *Review of Existential Psychology and Psychiatry*, Spring 1966, *6*(2), 105-119.

Bowra, C. M. *The Romantic Imagination*. New York: Oxford University Press, 1961.

*Brée, Germaine. Editor. *Camus*. Englewood Cliffs, New Jersey: Prentice-Hall, 1962.

Buber, Martin, Distance and relation. *Psychiatry*, May 1957, *20*(2), 97-104.

*Buhler, Charlotte. *Values in Psychotherapy*. Glencoe, Illinois: The Free Press, 1962.

Camus, Albert. *The Fall*. New York: Random House, 1956.

Chessick, Richard D. *How Psychotherapy Heals*. New York: Science House, 1969.

*Crampton, Martha. The use of mental imagery in psychosynthesis. *Journal of Humanistic Psychology*, Fall 1969, *9*(2), 139-153.

Desoille, Robert. The directed daydream. *The Bulletin of the Los Angeles Societe de Recherches Psychotherapiques de Langue Francaise*, May 1965, *3*(2), 27-42.

*Eckhardt, Marianne H. Alienation and the secret self. *The American Journal of Psychoanalysis*, 1961, *21*(2), 219-226.

Eckhardt, Marianne H. Therapeutic perspectives. *Contemporary Psychoanalysis*, Fall 1969, *6*(1), 1-12.

*Eron, L. D. and Callahan, R. *The Relation of Theory to Practice in Psychotherapy*. Chicago: Aldine Publishing Company, 1969.

Farber, Leslie H. Introduction to the proceedings of the AEPP conference: The phenomenology of tape recording and films in psychotherapy. *Review of Existential Psychology and Psychiatry*, Spring 1966, *6*(2), 100-104.

*Ferenczi, Sándor. *Final Contributions to the Problems and Methods of Psychoanalysis*. New York: Basic Books, 1955.

*Foa, Uriel G. Convergences in the analysis of the structure of interpersonal behavior. *Psychological Review*, Sept. 1961, *68*(5), 341-353.

Frankl, Viktor E. Logotherapy and existentialism. *Psychotherapy: Theory, Research and Practice*, August 1967, *4*(3), 138-142.

*Frankl, Viktor E. Self-transcendence as a human phenomenon. *Journal of Humanistic Psychology*, Fall 1966, *6*(2), 97-106.

*Frenkel, Richard E. Psychotherapeutic reconstruction of the traumatic amnesic period by the mirror image projective technique. *Journal of Existentialism*, Summer 1964, *5*(17), 77-96.

---

*These are sources which are not referred to in the text.

*Freud, Sigmund. *Recommendations to Physicians Practicing Psycho-Analysis* (1912). London: Hogarth Press, 1958, Standard Edition, Volume XII.

*Freud, Sigmund. *Therapy and Technique*. New York: Collier Books, 1963.

Frisch, Max. *I'm Not Stiller*. New York: Vintage Books, 1958.

*Garner, H. H. The confrontation problem-solving technique: Developing a psychotherapeutic focus. *American Journal of Psychotherapy*, Jan. 1970, *24*(1), 27-48.

*Gendlin, Eugene T. A theory of personality change. Chapter in Worchel, P. and Byrne, D. *Personality Change*. New York: John Wiley & Sons, 1964.

*Gerard, Robert. *Psychosynthesis, A Psychotherapy for the Whole Man*. Greenville, Delaware: Psychosynthesis Research Foundation, 1964.

Gottschalk, Louis; Mayerson, Peter; and Gottlieb, Anthony A. Prediction and evaluation of outcome in an emergency brief psychotherapy clinic. *The Journal of Nervous and Mental Disease*, February 1967, *144*(2), 77-96.

Guntrip, Harry. *Personality Structure and Human Interaction*. New York: International Universities Press, 1961.

*Guntrip, Harry. *Schizoid Phenomena, Object Relations and the Self*. New York: International Universities Press, 1969.

*Hammer, M. The directed daydream technique. *Psychotherapy: Theory, Research and Practice*, 1967, *4*(4), 173-181.

Hesse, Herman. *Demian*. New York: Harper and Row, 1965.

Hinsie, Leland E. and Campbell, Robert J. *Psychiatric Dictionary*. New York: Oxford University Press, 1970.

Hopkins, G. M. In Gardner, W. H. Editor, *Poems and Prose of Gerard Manley Hopkins*. London: Penguin Books, 1953.

Hora, Thomas. Existential psychotherapy. Chapter in Masserman, Jules. Editor. *Current Psychiatric Therapies*. New York: Grune and Stratton, 1962, Volume 2.

Horney, Karen. *Our Inner Conflicts*. New York: W. W. Norton Company, 1945.

*Horowitz, Mardi. *Image Formation and Cognition*. New York: Appleton Century Crofts, 1970.

*Horowitz, Mardi. Visual thought images in psychotherapy. *American Journal of Psychotherapy*, Jan. 1968, *22*(1), 55-59.

Jackson, Don. The question of family homeostasis. *Psychiatric Quarterly*, 1957, *31*(1) (Supplement), 79-90.

*Jackson, Don. The study of the family. *Family Process*, March 1965, *4*(1), 1-20.

James, William. *Principles of Psychology*. Volume II. New York: Henry Holt and Co., 1890.

Jellinek, Augusta. Spontaneous imagery: a new psychotherapeutic approach. *American Journal of Psychotherapy*, July 1949, *3*(3), 372-391.

Jones, Edward E. Conformity as a tactic of ingratiation. *Science*, 9 July 1965, *149*(3680), 144-150.

Jones, E. E.; Gergen, K. J.; and Jones, R. G. Tactics of ingratiation among leaders and subordinates in a status hierarchy. *Psychological Monographs*, 1963. *77*(3), Whole No. 566, 1-20.

*Jung, Carl. *Contributions to Analytical Psychology*. New York: Harcourt and Brace, 1928.

*Jung, Carl. *Modern Man in Search of a Soul*. New York: Harcourt and Brace, 1939.

Kierkegaard, Soren. *The Sickness Unto Death*. Translated by Walter Lowrie. Princeton: Princeton University Press, 1944.

Klein, George S. *Perception, Motives, and Personality.* New York: Alfred A. Knopf, 1970.

Kunz, Hans. *Ueber den Sinn und die Grenzen Psychologischer Erkenntnis.* Stuggart: Ernst Klett, 1957.

*Laing, R. D. *The Divided Self.* Chicago: Quadrangle Books, 1960.

*Laing, R. D. *The Politics of Experience.* New York: Pantheon Books, 1967.

Laing, R. D. *The Self and Others.* Chicago: Quadrangle Books, 1962.

Laing, R. D.; Phillipson, H.; and Lee, A. R. *Interpersonal Perception.* New York: Springer Publishing Co., 1966.

Leuner, Hanscarl. Guided affective imagery (GAI). A method of intensive psychotherapy. *American Journal of Psychotherapy,* Jan. 1969, *23*(1), 4-22.

Mack, John E. *Nightmares and Human Conflict.* Boston: Little, Brown and Company, 1970.

*MacLeod, Robert B. The phenomenological approach to social psychology. *Psychological Review,* July 1947, *54*(4), 193-210.

Maugham, Somerset. *Of Human Bondage.* New York: Doubleday, 1936.

May, Rollo, Contributions of existential psychotherapy. Introduction to May, R.; Angel, E.; and Ellenberger, H. F. *Existence.* New York: Basic Books, 1958.

*May, Rollo. Dangers in the relation of existentialism to psychotherapy. *Review of Existential Psychology and Psychiatry,* Winter 1963, *3*(1), 5-10.

May, Rollo. Introduction to Gudeman, Howard E. The phenomenology of delusions. *Review of Existential Psychology and Psychiatry,* Fall 1966, *6*(3), 196-197.

May, Rollo. On the phenomenological bases of psychotherapy. *Review of Existential Psychology and Psychiatry,* Winter 1964, *4*(1), 22-36.

May, Rollo. Passion for form. *Review of Existential Psychology and Psychiatry,* Winter 1967, *7*(1), 6-12.

Mezvinsky, Shirley. *The Edge.* New York: Doubleday, 1965.

Moulton, Ruth. A survey and reevaluation of the concept of penis envy. *Contemporary Psychoanalysis,* Fall 1970, *7*(1), 84-104.

Packard, Vance. *The Status Seekers.* New York: David McKay Co, 1959.

*Perls, F. S. *Ego, Hunger and Aggression.* New York: Vintage Books, 1969.

Rabin, A. I. Editor. *Projective Techniques in Personality Assessment: A Modern Introduction.* New York: Springer, 1968.

Rank, Otto. *Will Therapy.* New York: Alfred Knopf, 1936.

*Richardson, Alan. *Mental Imagery.* New York: Springer Publishing Co., 1969.

*Sanford, Edward F. An acoustic mirror in psychotherapy. *American Journal of Psychotherapy,* Oct. 1969, *23*(4), 681-695.

Sartre, Jean-Paul. *Being and Nothingness.* London: Metfaun and Co., 1957.

*Sartre, Jean-Paul. *Existential Psychoanalysis.* Chicago: Henry Regnery Co., 1953.

*Sartre, Jean-Paul. *Situations.* New York: George Braziller, 1965.

*Sartre, Jean-Paul. *The Psychology of Imagination.* New York: Citadel Press, 1963.

*Searles, H. F. The effort to drive the other person crazy — an element in the aetiology and psychotherapy of schizophrenia. *British Journal of Medical Psychology,* 1959, *32*(1), 1-18.

Shahn, Ben. Imagination and intention. *Review of Existential Psychology and Psychiatry,* Winter 1967, *7*(1), 13-17.

*Shapiro, David L. The significance of the visual image in psychotherapy. *Psychotherapy: Theory, Research and Practice,* Winter 1970, *7*(4), 209-212.

*Shorr, Joseph E. The existential question and the imaginary situation as therapy. *Existential Psychiatry,* Winter 1967, *6*(24), 443-462.

Spiegelberg, Herbert. Phenomenology through vicarious experience. Chapter in Straus, Erwin. Editor. *Phenomenology: Pure and Applied*. Pittsburgh: Duquesne University Press, 1964.

*Stern, E. Mark. Mirror-dialogue approach to the treatment of a borderline psychosis. *Journal of Existential Psychiatry*, Winter 1964, *4*(15), 207-218.

Stieper, Donald R., and Wiener, Daniel N. *Dimensions of Psychotherapy*. Chicago: Aldine Publishing Co., 1965.

*Straus, Erwin W. Editor.*Phenomenology, Pure and Applied*. Pittsburgh: Duquesne University Press, 1964.

Strupp, Hans. Who needs intrapsychic factors in clinical psychology*Psychotherapy: Theory, Research and Practice*, Nov. 1967, *4*(4), 145-150.

*Strupp, Hans and Bergin, Allen. Some empirical and conceptual bases for coordinated research in psychotherapy: A critical review of issues, trends, and evidence. *International Journal of Psychiatry*, 1967, *7*(2), 18-90.

Strupp, Hans H.; Fox, Ronald E.; and Lessler, Ken. *Patients View Their Psychotherapy*. Baltimore: Johns Hopkins Press, 1969.

Sullivan, Harry S., *The Interpersonal Theory of Psychiatry*. New York: W. W. Norton, 1953.

*Swingle, Paul. Editor. *The Structure of Conflict*. New York: Academic Press, 1970.

Szalita, Alberta B. Reanalysis. *Contemporary Psychoanalysis*, Spring 1968, *4*(2), 83-102.

*Tart, Charles T. Editor. *Altered States of Consciousness*. New York: John Wiley, 1969.

*Tillich, Paul. *The Courage To Be*. New Haven: Yale University Press, 1952.

Vespe, Raymond. Ontological analysis and synthesis in existential psychotherapy. *Existential Psychiatry*, Summer-Fall 1969, *7*(26-27), 83-92.

*Watzlawick, P.; Beavin, J.; and Jackson, D. *Pragmatics of Human Communication*. New York: W. W. Norton Co., Inc., 1967.

Weisman, Avery D. *The Existential Core of Psychoanalysis: Reality Sense and Responsibility*. Boston: Little, Brown and Company, 1965.

*Werner, Heinz and Kaplan, Bernard. *Symbol Formation*. New York: John Wiley and Co., 1963.

Wheelis, Allen. How people change. *Commentary*, May 1969, 56-66.

Wheelis, Allen. *The Quest for Identity*. New York: W. W. Norton and Co., 1958.

Wheelis, Allen. *The Seeker*. New York: Random House, 1960.

Whyte, William H. *Organization Man*. New York: Simon and Schuster, 1956.

Will, Otto A. Schizophrenia and the psycho-therapeutic field. *Contemporary Psychoanalysis*, Fall 1964, *1*(1), 1-29.

Section II

Psychotherapy Through Imagery

CHAPTER 11

Imagination and Psychotherapy

Man's imagination is as infinite as the universe: it knows no bounds, has no known limitations. The awareness of discovered imagination is awesome; even more awesome are those discoveries which have yet to be revealed beyond existing frontiers.

Man has always been intrigued by his imagination. Throughout the history of human thought it has variously been granted great prominence or relegated to virtual insignificance. The concept of imagination has been utilized as an explanation of human behavior, as an agent of causality. Montaigne felt that it was responsible for the contagious effects of human emotion; it was the source of physical, emotional and mental disease — even death; it produced manifestations which other men might have attributed to magic; it was the cause of conspicuous physical phenomena, capable even of transforming the one sex to the other. In the history of psychotherapy, imagination has played many roles with diverse implications. As early as 1784, as a result of the enormous conflict surrounding the veracity of Anton Mesmer and his concept of "animal magnetism," the king appointed a commission of inquiry enlisting members of the Academic Sciences and the Academie de Medecine; another commission was formed among the Society Royale. Benjamin Franklin, at that time the American Ambassador and a foremost scientist of his time, deliberated the matter and concluded that no evidence could be found for the physical existence of any "magnetic fluid" at all — and finally the effects of Mesmer's hypnotic technique were ascribed to imagination.

In the same century, an Italian, named Muratori, wrote a treatise called "On the Power of Human Imagination," which gained wide currency. Muratori's concept of imagination comprised dreams, visions, delusions, *idées fixes*, phobias, and somnambulism. This last subject became the central focus of all contemporary discussions dealing with imagination; stories were often told of people who while apparently asleep would write, swim rivers, walk over rooftops — people whose lives would be critically endangered if they were suddenly awakened. These stories were widely believed at the time and, remarkably, persist to this day. Somnambulism became the purest example of imagination's marvelous workings, and it was inevitable that interest in this phenomenon should spread to other fields, including the arts. An early sample and a classic one is Shakespeare's unforgettable portrait of Lady Macbeth as she walks Dunsinane Castle by night, recounting scenes of her murderous role and giving herself confessional.

During the nineteenth century, actions once attributed to imagination were deemed the products of suggestion or autosuggestion, and it was not until the twentieth century that imagination and imagery were redefined and revitalized by Freud, Jung and Forenczi. In America, the use of imagination and imagery as psychotherapeutic tools followed a difficult path, however; and we are fortunate that in recent time, the concept of imagination has gained respectability.

Prior to the twenties, Titchener of Cornell worked for a time with problems related to imagination, such as introspection. Later, J. B. Watson, America's first star of behaviorism, turned the direction of human psychological investigation away from a concern with man's inner images – his daydreams, his dreams, his fanciful ruminations – and toward concepts of conditioning. It was only the psychoanalysts of the period who viewed the fantasies and dreams of their patients as relevant areas of imagery investigation. These dreams and fantasies were personalized between the patient and the analyst, and it was primarily the dream which was of interest. "Free Association," the technique of reporting everything one thought, neglected the full range of imagination itself in that it required the patient to turn his flow of thought into verbal reporting. The free use of imagination was not encouraged since, to many analysts, it reeked of resistance; the patient was usually guided back to his verbalization. Slips of the tongue which were undoubtedly related to the unconscious were considered merely as slips in the verbal reporting. A patient's imaginings of feelings for the analyst were viewed as transference reactions and usually not explored beyond that point. Freud, however, as early as 1892, attempted a "concentration technique" in which the patient reclined on a couch and Freud placed his hand on the patient's forehead, pressing firmly.

Freud described his technique in the following manner:

"I inform the patient that, a moment later, I shall apply pressure to his forehead, and I assure him that, all the time the pressure lasts, he will see before him a recollection in the form occurring to him; and I pledge him to communicate this picture or ideal to me, whatever it may be. He is not to keep it to himself because he may happen to think it is not what is wanted, nor the right thing, or because it would be too disagreeable for him to say it. There is to be no criticism of it, no reticence, either for emotional reasons or because it is judged unimportant . . . Having said this, I press for a few seconds on the forehead of the patient as he lies in front of me; I then leave go and ask quietly, as though there were no questions of a disappointment: "What did you see?" or, "What occurred to you?"

This procedure has taught me much and has also invariably achieved its aim. Today I can no longer do without it." (Breuer, J. and Freud, S., 1953, p. 270.)

Freud was enthusiastic about his technique: "My expectations were fulfilled; I was set free from hypnotism. . . . Hypnosis had screened from view an interplay of force which now came in sight and the understanding of which gave a solid formation to my theory." (Freud, S., 1959, p. 29.) This was in the year 1892.

"Freud's emphasis on the visual elements may clearly be seen in the precedence of terms: '. . . he will see before him . . . a picture or will have it in his thought . . .' and, 'What did you see?' or 'What occurred to you?' and again, 'Things that are brought to light from the deeper strata are also recognized and acknowledged, but only after considerable hesitations and doubts. Visual memory-images are of course more difficult to disavow than the memory-traces of mere trains of thought." (Breuer, J. and Freud, S., 1953, p. 299.)

After a while, Freud abandoned the technique: While initially an expedient, it could lead to increased resistance and difficult transference reactions later in treatment. In an article titled, "The Relation of the Poet to Daydreaming," published in 1908, Freud showed an embarrassing intransigence in declaring, "We can begin by saying that happy people never make fantasies, only unsatisfied ones. Unsatisfied wishes are the driving power behind fantasies; every separate fantasy contains the fulfillment of a wish, and improves on unsatisfactory reality." (Freud, S., 1963, p. 37.)

Freud notwithstanding, imagination is not the compensatory obverse of reality but man's way of organizing reality from his imaginings of the past and into the future. The simplest demonstration of this is to ask a person how many doors there were in the house he lived in as a child. I think you will see, if you ask yourself that question, that you will begin to visualize the image of the house itself, the stairs, the rooms, etc., as you begin your count. In this way, you are organizing the reality of the past into the present. If you are asked to imagine a house you have never seen, it is still the imagination of houses seen in the past that is brought to bear in your visual representation of the house, whatever you may imagine. Even if you were to imagine a house without any doors at all, you bring to such a visual image imagined feelings of your past. It goes without saying, then, that one cannot engage in imagination − or even disallow imagination − without involving experience from the past. Imagination is a way of organizing one's world, utilizing the past to assist in making sense of the present. Rollo May stated it as clearly as one could possibly imagine when he said, " . . . you can live without a father who accepts you, but you cannot live without a world that makes sense to you." (1967, p. 8.)

Dr. Jerome L. Singer, who has devoted a great deal of investigation to the role of imagery and cognition, has made a statement about Freud which warrants full examination. " . . . Freud may have errored in not insisting on imagery alone rather than allowing patients to shift to free verbal association. He might have gotten more powerful uncovering more rapidly from his earlier technique. Undoubtedly individual practitioners have sensed the importance of fostering greater emphasis on concrete imagery by patients and have found themselves impatient with the apparent glibness or defensiveness that often characterizes verbal free association." (Singer, 1971, p. 9.)

One can only imagine what enormous changes would have occurred in the field of psychotherapy if Freud had proceeded with "Free Imagery." This is not to deny credit to the concept of "Active Imagination" and Carl Jung who fostered it; throughout his life, Jung investigated the most subtle recesses of imagination and had important influences on European intellectual life.

On December 12, 1913, Jung began his own self-analysis, resorting to the technique of provoking the upsurge of unconscious imagery and its overflowing into consciousness. He recorded his dreams daily; he also wrote down stories, forcing himself to take them in any direction his imagination went. He imagined himself digging into the earth and into underground galleries and caves where he encountered many kinds of strange figures. Then, according to Ellenberger, " . . . he had to examine carefully each image from the unconscious and to translate it, insofar as this was possible, into the language of the consciousness." (Ellenberger, 1972, p. 67.) This led Jung to this technique of "Active Imagination."

Jung suggested that the contents of the unconscious are presented in conscious form as images. Since the unconscious is divided into its personal and collective aspects, so are its images. Those that are based on the remnants of the innumerably repeated, universal experiences of primitive man are referred to as "primordial images" to distinguish them from the "personal images" which are peculiar to each individual. These primordial images, or inherited patterns of thought, correspond closely to universal symbolisms. They are identical or similar among all people and are easily to be found in the unconscious of the present day human being. A half century ago, Forenczi, the most innovative of the Freudians, asked his patients to "fabricate" a fantasy if they could not readily imagine one; that is, tell " . . . all that comes into their mind without regard for objective reality." He sometimes offered fantasies which he felt the patients *should* have been experiencing until the process took over within them.

Forenczi claimed his "forced fantasies" to have an unquestionable analytical value because they brought about the production or reproduction of scenes quite unexpected by either patient or analyst (" . . . which leave an indelible impression on the mind of the patient") that aided perceptibly in advancing the analytical work; important also because " . . . they furnish a proof that the patient is, generally speaking, capable of such psychical productions of which he thought himself free, so that they give us a grasp of deeper research into the unconscious." (Healy, Bronner and Bowers, 1930, p. 476.)

Historically, the psychoanalysts have not been kind to the function of "images" which may spontaneously emerge in the course of psychoanalysis.

They have labeled such imagery as manifestations of regression or resistance; images, like symbols, they say, are defenses and pose an alternative to the verbalization and ideation of the ego. At best — according to this line of reasoning — images are screens memories (i.e., what a memory conceals); in short, they defend against revealing the unconscious conflicts and lead to decreased communication. Recently, however, Horowitz (1970) has indicated that some psychoanalysts are now paying more attention to the images created by the patient.

In 1955, Fromm wrote a little publicized paper in which he voices a plea for moving beyond the conventional, free association procedure into the therapist-initiated situations. This is to be experienced by the patient in a vivid, alive way. His advice to analysts is for them to make fullest use of their own imagination, and suggest active imagery methods to improve the flow of the patient's free associations. Alberta Szalita in her fine article "Reanalysis," dealing with the reanalysis of unsuccessful psychoanalysis of persons, strongly suggests "a daring" is needed to reach a patient and elicit a response. "I don't see any discrepancy in this kind of activity on the part of the analyst with the psychoanalytical tenets. It does not differ from the analysis of a dream. Perhaps that is why dream analysis is so useful in that it gives a legitimate opportunity for the analyst *to use, his imagination.*" (Szalita, 1968, p. 98-99.)

Freud believed fantasy and imagination to be related to the person's defenses. Even Anna Freud (1946) considered fantasy a defense mechanism. That the imagination might have an adaptive function was not stressed by psychoanalysts until Hartman in 1958 and then only with minimal knowledge of his publications. By and large, American psychologists have tended to regard reverie and imagination as unproductive, impractical, and completely unempirical.

The return of the *image* in American psychology in the last half decade has oddly enough been given great impetus by the same theoretical framework which delayed its emergence, namely, the present day behaviorists, heirs to the tradition of J. B. Watson. The emphasis is on visualization during systematic desensitization of the patient to "bad" images related to disturbing symptoms. The patient's production of vivid imagery is a critical feature of desensitization therapy as he learns to respond to increasingly difficult images to which he has phobic feelings. Aversive conditioning for persons with so-called deviant sexual fantasies is also accomplished by shocking the person in a painful manner, as he responds to images or pictures of unacceptable sex partners or objects and rewarded for imagery involving acceptable sexual fantasies.

Still another variation with more powerful negative imagery is the "Implosive Therapy" of Stampfl (1967) who has the patient vividly imagining the worst possible consequences of a particular fear or obsession (e.g., being arrested and paraded before a jeering panel, being horribly crushed under a subway train's wheels, or covering him with slime and vomit, etc.). The anxiety is gradually extinguished as he repeatedly faces the horrible scenes since, in reality, there is no actual consequence.

To the dynamically oriented and to those therapists of the humanistic emphasis, this smacks of torture and the neglect of human values. Although the behaviorists have now helped to reintroduce the image in therapy, it is not with a keen interest in the patient's inner experiences or fantasies and unconscious processes are generally rejected, uninvestigated.

The Gestalt therapists have made much use of imagination, mainly in conjunction with the patient's dreams, but have limited the possibility of the interpretative value of images and shown disinterest in the imagination as it relates to the patients' past lives. Those doing Psychodrama — especially in the role reversal technique — make use of imagination but the systematic emphasis on imagery, as such, is lacking.

Imagination must not be considered indefinable or cast aside as too vague a subject for examination. Ordinarily, it is thought that imagination is the sole property of writers, musicians, painters, and the like. No prejudice is further from fact. While imagination as a psychological function of the human mind will perhaps never be understood in its entirety, it is not a process reserved for a few creative persons. All of us have imagination, and all of us need imagination for our living, whether we be dull or bright. As the famous American artist Ben Shahn has stated:

"Imagination supplies the banalities of life as well as the inspirations. Imagination is the total conscious life of each one of us. Without it, neither you nor I could make his way to the parked car, or recognize it when he arrives there. Without it, we could not dress ourselves in the morning nor find our way to the breakfast table nor know what we are eating or what was said to us by the morning paper. Without it, we would recognize nothing at all. This seems axiomatic." (Shahn, 1967, p. 14.)

The universality of imagination in each of us as an organizing principle of life is evident. The use of imagination as man's way of adapting in an autonomous manner is even more clearly demonstrated when it is used as a preparation for action. Dr. Salvatore R. Maddi, writing for the Nebraska Symposium on "Motivation," has clearly described imagination used to try out possibilities for future action:

"So the adolescent boy who fantasized making love to a beautiful classmate finds that he begins to think about her, experience her, and interact with her in a more intimate fashion, even though he is frightened to death of sexual confrontation. But the subtle changes that take place in his actual interactions with her, express well the manner in which imagination is a preparation for action. Perhaps she has similar fantasies of him which lead her to avoid him without any apparent reason, while at the same time, she subtly encourages him. Let them be alone together in some unexpectedly secure circumstance, or let another sexual partner loom up to cause jealousy, and the love and attraction they prepared for in their fantasy may find sudden if frightening expression. Similar circumstances befalling two young people who had not fantasized about each other in such fashion might not have had any effect on action at all. What I am saying is that the function of imagination as preparation for action is so potent, and natural, that even fear of consequences cannot demolish it entirely." (Maddi, 1970, p. 151.)

That individual or group psychotherapy sessions should have as part of their process the rehearsal of anticipated and imaged events would appear to be the logical outgrowth of Maddi's thinking. There is the strong possibility of developing general principles about his own dynamics as the patient imagines himself in various situations. Despite the obvious complexities the images permit us to *see,* and perhaps the better we are acquainted with our imagery, the better able we will be to shift toward a new, healthy imagery.

Most American psychologists and psychiatrists are well acquainted with the names of Freud, Adler, Jung, Horney, Rogers, Sullivan and R. D. Laing and could probably relate some incident involving each of these distinguished theoreticians; they could imagine Freud or the others in their minds — how they looked, how they acted. A great many European psychotherapists, contrary to popular belief, are not solely influenced by Freud or Jung but draw heavily from the work of men such as Desoille, Hanscarl Leuner, Carl Happich, Assagioli, Fretigny, Virel, Bachelard, etc., — fellow European investigators who have shared an interest in using "Imagery" and "Imagination" in their psychotherapeutic experience. And, while over the last five years they have sponored annual meetings, such as the International Societies for the Study of Mental Imagery, I would hazard that few American psychotherapists have been at all influenced by them. It is not possible here to make a thorough examination of their procedures, but it is important to emphasize that it is not the patient's verbal reports but rather his imagination which forms the basis for aiding him to reveal and "work through" his conflicts. Good results have been reported, strongly suggesting that the verbal is not a necessity in psychological change.

The one European name that stands above all in the use of imagination in relation to psychotherapy is that of Desoille. While he was indeed a pioneer in the development of such methods, it is a little-known fact that he himself was first influenced by a physicist named E. Caslant (1927). As early as 1927, Caslant began experimenting with people; he would ask them to imagine themselves rising up into space and observe the ease or difficulty with which they rose; he would ask them to overcome such obstacles as they had imagined by using suggestions of various sorts, such as, " . . . use a sword to cut through that web." These imaginary trips in verticality were an attempt on

Caslant's part to find a method of studying clairvoyance and paranormal abilities.

Desoille is neither a psychologist or a psychiatrist, but an engineer. He personally got in touch with Caslant and was present at some of his sittings. He then tried the method himself, and what started as an entertaining psychological study grew into a considerable psychotherapeutic practice. It must be noted, however, that he initially began working with essentially normal subjects, with the neurotic ones coming later. From Caslant's original notion, Desoille (1965) developed the more involved technique called *rêve éviellé,* or what is known in English as the guided affective imagery technique (GAI). It served as a point of reference for nearly all the psychotherapeutic developments evolving later which employed imagery as a prime mode of approach. It is a method that limits formal analysis of the imagery, suggesting rather that many problems can indeed be worked through by means of that type of symbolic combat, amelioration or transformation which takes place in imagery.

The philosophical roots of psychoanalysis were provided by Freud himself; with the concept of psychic determinism, and the matrix of the triplicity of the Ego, Id and Superego, this philosophical system was uniquely his own. Jung, too, insofar as his concept of the "collective unconscious" is concerned, provided his own philosophical base. A comparable philosophical base but one with emphasis on imagination and imagery was represented by a non-psychotherapist, the highly regarded phenomenologist Gaston Bachelard. A former physicist like Caslant, Bachelard more than forty years ago began an intensive study of man's imagination and his symbolism. When he became the Sorbonne's professor for history and the Philosophy of the Sciences, he pioneered in the exploration of Desoille's two books on the "Rêve Eveillé in Psychotherapy." His appreciation of the importance of Desoille's discoveries as they related to general psychology and psychotherapy was set forth in his book, *The Air and the Dreams,* written in 1943.

Bachelard breaks with the more traditional psychological method of introspection by calling to our attention with a wealth of evidence of fact that the world of things is our home and thus contains the images of human intimacy. A man almost unknown to behavioral scientists in America, Bachelard was something of an armchair philosopher, delving into the symbolism of fire, water, earth and light. The psychology of the crackling fire in the grate, the quiet lake and the restless breakers, the flight of the jubilant lark, the earth calling men to labor, caves temptingly leading to adventure, the black dampness of the tomb — all of these were a part of his philosophical journey, and man's innate capacity for generating imagery and symbolism is a critically important feature of his work.

Singer, referring to Bachelard says, "For the Western European clinician, therefore, the detailed exploration of the intra-psychic or the direct use of imagery have had an acceptance and meaning that is even wider ranging than the classical psychoanalytic influences of Freud in America." (Singer, 1971, p. 14.)

Along with the increased awareness of imagination and imagery, the last decade saw a growing emphasis on phenomenology: the study of how a person sees his world. To my way of thinking, phenomenology requires of a person that he use his imagination as the vehicle by which to ready himself for all that he uniquely perceives, anticipates, defends and acts upon; events to come (as stated on an earlier page) are "rehearsed" in advance of their actual occurrence; a person imagines how it *will be*, thereby preparing for whatever action may result. Thus seen, the increased awareness of phenomenology has been no accident; its integration with the concept and use of imagination was a palpable necessity. Our world of images reflects and represents our being-in-the-world and we can only understand man as an individual, and as a part of mankind, when we grasp the imagery of his existence.

The phenomenologists, and especially R. D. Laing (1962) in *The Self and Others*, have applied imagery to interpersonal relationships. "How does Jim think Mary thinks, that Jim thinks of her?" – This is the kind of interpenetrating imaginativeness that humans are constantly engaged in; and to Laing, the use of imagination in this manner provides the sinews of human interaction. How a person views himself, how he views the other person, how he imagines the other person views him, and, even more essential, how he has learned to be defined by others who have raised him – these are all questions basic to phenomenology. A further concern of major importance is the conflict between how a person imagines himself to be and how he is *told* to be by his parents: to Laing this is the basis of human conflict. It is certainly the origin of bipolarization in neurotic conflict.

I would like to submit the following poem which shows this point beautifully. This was written by one of my own patients:

He loves me for who he thinks I am
but,
who he thinks I am
is not who I am.
Therefore,
it's hard for me to be who I am
when we're together,
because I think I have to be
who he thinks I am.
Of course, I don't know exactly
who it is he thinks I am.
I just know it isn't who I am.
Who am I?
Well . . .
Who I am is something I recognize
when someone tells me
who I am *not*.
At least, I *think* that's *not* who I am.
Maybe who I am *not*
is who I *am*.
If that's who I am . . .
My gawd! He really loves me!

In *Psycho-Imagination Therapy* by Shorr (1972), extensive use is made of the Imaginary Situation ("IS"), in order to elicit the internal bipolarized conflicts of the patient. Imaginary Situations are also used to help the patient focus on changing his self-definition.

With the increased emphasis on phenomenology and the singularity of each person's "world," imagination as a function of the mind has gained new importance for both "viewing" and therapy. At the very least, its use has returned from ostracism and despite the varied shadings of opinion which have greeted it, there is little doubt that it is here to stay, providing, as it does, an invaluable leverage to man's potential.

Idealized Image/Despised Image and False Position

Karen Horney (1950), in developing the concept of the idealized image and the despised image, did not essentially involve the patient actively in imagery; nonetheless, she helped clarify how one can arrive at those forms of self-image which neurotically tend to propel us. If we agree with Laing's concept of an attributed identity – an alien identity in sharp bipolarized contrast to one's real identity – it is to this identity that Horney's concepts are most applicable. The person who is indeed falsely defined by others may make enormous steps toward becoming or appearing quite the opposite of that definition. The image he would want the world to have of him, and to which vigilantly he lends all his efforts to maintain, may be idealized as, for example, the best kind of mother or father, or the most competent performer, etc. In his or her heart of hearts, of course, the person may not *feel* that way at all, and the vigilance against this idealized image from being "seen through" is constant; if it were to be seen through, it would make the person depressed and anxious. At best, that image is a front line, a generally unconscious "good person" defense against the introjected, unacceptable person within; it is an attempt to maintain one's position in the world, but the position is false — one operates in a compensating manner, busily sustaining a neurotic conflict resolution. In general, I would say that the greater the idealized image, the greater the security operations necessary to perpetuate it.

If I were to ask a patient to (IS) imagine your most idealized image of yourself, I believe one would note greater anxiety in the imagery of those people whose idealized image is far greater than their attributed identity. To my way of thinking, when a person is operating essentially from his *true* identity, the need for an idealized image becomes more realistic and the disparity between his idealized image and real self-image is minimal: the possibilities for feeling in false or untenable positions are considerably diminished; depression and anxiety would be lessened as well.

If one falls victim to all the negative attributions ascribed to him by the "significant persons" of his life, if he becomes defined by them, he may come to feel that he is in his "despised image." Add a large dash of guilt, and one soon believes he *is* the rotten self. Disclosure and exposure are feared as never before; security operations may go to the extreme, involving even isolation and detachment. I once asked a patient to (IS) imagine a person other than himself if he were to look into a mirror. He answered that he saw a werewolf. As he continued, he realized the meaning of what he imagined seeing: the werewolf was the despised image that he didn't want the world to know about. He had accepted his false definition as if it were, indeed, him. Subsequently, he was able to change this "alien identity" he had internalized. Another man, who was unemployed, stayed in his apartment during normal working hours so that nobody would see how "rotten" he was. Isolation and detachment were companions to his "despised image."

While Horney did not use concrete imagery to make the patient aware of these self-concept images, her contribution to the understanding of the dynamics of self-imagery is outstanding and brilliant. Especially is this true of her concept of the "search for glory" and the role of imagination in its development. She describes the subtle unconscious use of imagination by people prone to such a search, showing how such people may use their imagination against themselves. "The more injurious work of imagination concerns the subtle and comprehensive distortions of reality which he is not aware of fabricating. The idealized image is not created in a single act of creation; once produced, it needs continued attention. For its actualization, the person must put in incessant labor by way of falsifying reality. He must turn his needs into virtues or into more than justified expectations. He must turn his intentions to be honest or considerate into the fact of being honest or considerate. The bright ideas he has for a paper make him a great scholar. His potentialities turn into factual achievements. Knowing the 'right' moral values makes him a virtuous person – often, indeed a kind of moral genius. And of course, his imagination must work overtime to discard all the disturbing evidence to the contrary." (Horney, 1950, p. 33-34.)

Reaching Out for Meaning

Our minds need to make meaning of some kind out of our life experience, and the capacity to do so has sustained men in the darkest of circumstances. Frankl's "search for meaning" sustained him by the use, among other things, of the imagery of the future of a manuscript he kept hidden in his coat while he was kept in a Nazi concentration camp. Man's concept of imagery of paradise – be it derivative of Persian, Hebrew or Christian thought – has sustained him throughout history; his images of utopia and other concepts of his future have given him similar meaning and hope. Such reaching out for meaning with the aid of imagination is perfectly illustrated by a story told in Romain Gary's novel *The Roots of Heaven.*

"In a German concentration camp during the war, the French prisoners are becoming increasingly demoralized; they are on a down staircase. A man called Robert devises a way to arrest the decline. He suggests that they imagine an invisible girl in the billet. If one of them swears or farts, he must bow and apologize to the 'girl'; when they undress, they must hang up a blanket so she can't see them. Oddly enough, this absurd game works: they enter into the spirit of the thing, and morale suddenly rises. The Germans become suspicious of the men and by eavesdropping, they found out about the invisible girl. The Commandant fancies himself a psychologist. He goes along to the billet with two guards, and tells the men: 'I know you have a girl here. That is forbidden. Tomorrow I shall come here with these guards and you will hand her over to me. She will be taken to the local brothel for German officers'. When he was gone, the men were dismayed; they know that if they 'hand her over', they won't be able to recreate her. The next day, the Commandant appears with his two soldiers. Robert, as the spokesman, says, 'We have decided not to hand her over'. And the Commandant knows he is beaten: nothing he can do can force them to hand her over. Robert is arrested and placed in solitary confinement; they all think they've seen the last of him, but weeks later, he reappears, very thin and worn. He explains that he has found the way to resist solitary confinement – their game with the invisible girl has taught him that the imagination is the power to reach out to other realities, realities not physically present. He had kept himself from breaking down by imagining great herds of elephants trampling over endless plains . . ." (Gary, 1958, p.159.)

With increasing frequency, greater numbers of people refer to their lives as being meaningless. This applies to the general public and especially to patients seeking help. "What's It All About Alfie?," the name of a recent popular song, sums up the problem neatly. But, one may wonder, perhaps it is merely the fashionable attitude in this age of existential thinking, this age of the absurd. Edith Weisskopf-Joelson (1972) undertook a very detailed study of 500 undergraduates, requiring them to write an extensive autobiography; she found that when five clinical psychologists rated the autobiographies for a "life devoid of meaning," 147 of the students were thus classified. The interjudge realiability was 92%. The 147 comprised 96 males and 51 females, she found, and set out to interview each one. After listening to the taped interviews, she concluded that three operational divisions existed:

1. "I have thoughts, wishes and daydreams, but they are in no way related to external reality. I am disinterested in what goes on around me. I cannot produce the mixture between fantasy and reality which makes life meaningful."

2. Some claimed that their lives seemed meaningless in the sense that they lacked explanations and interpretations with regard to themselves in the world in which they lived. Establishing connections and explanations lacked integration.

3. Some felt their lives lacked meaning in the sense that they had no purpose or goal. The goal of going to the bathroom to wash one's hands does not add meaning to one's life.

Endorsing life with meaning requires a relatively comprehensive long-term goal that embraces large parts of life. The goal-directed person integrates various aspects of life with the others, then integrates the whole thus created with goals to be reached. As is evident, approximately 30% of the students were judged to be leading a life devoid of meaning. My own observation is that the percentage would be higher still if one were to include, amongst one's sample group, people in assembly line work, certain kinds of sales work, etc.

Tangentially, Weisskopf-Joelson states, "People tend to focus on meaning more often when they feel it is absent than when they feel it is present." (p. 260.) In a further step, the imagery of the 147 was tested by asking them to react to ambiguous material in the Thematic Apperception Test; the result was a bimodal distribution:

1. They either produced fantasy without paying attention to reality.

OR:

2. They focused on reality without producing fantasy. (They were reality-bound to the point of being talented, but were unable to be creative because they could not "let themselves go.")

By contrast, the control group produces a bell-shaped distribution of their imagery, tending to achieve an integration between fantasy and reality. I refer to this detailed study both to show how important imagery can be in judging meaninglessness in people's lives. In *Psycho-Imagination Therapy* (1972), I have asked patients to finish the sentence: "My whole life is based on proving that _____." Or, "My whole life is based on denying that _____."

One need only to ask oneself these questions in private to see the marked emphasis on goal, meaning and direction which emerges as one attempts to finish each sentence.

The Image in Psychotherapy

An image may appear to a person in the form of hallucination, in a dream, in a daydream, as an unbidden image, in the presence of another person, in a particular situation, in a particular position, etc. These "nonverbal memory representations" are unique to that individual and even should they be fully reported, the listener cannot fully confirm that he has seen the identical image. As with dreams, a therapist may repeatedly inquire into the minutest details and still fall short of congruity. While absolute congruity may be impossible with the use of imagery and imagination – given consistent accuracy on the patient's part in reporting them – still the therapist for all practical purposes may come close enough to seeing what the patient himself is seeing. We do know now that a word may arouse an image and an image may arouse a word; further, the more concrete the word, the more easily is the image aroused. Conversely, the more abstract words do not arouse images easily. The task in psychotherapy is for both patient and therapist to assign meanings to the images and to relate this process to the possibility of new awareness and, hopefully, change.

Allan Paivio (1972) has demonstrated from a strictly experimental point of view that imagery or imagination in the human mind operates synchronically; that is, any part of an image can be elicited instantly without apparent loss of intensity.

For example, if you are asked to imagine entering a room you are familiar with, you may report first what you see to the left of that room; when asked what you see in the middle, or to its right, the one image can be seen as readily as any other. All images synchronize and interchange upon the request of the person who is asking about them, whereas a poem or verbal report can be recited forwards, but backwards only with extreme difficulty. The image of White-House takes one-half less retrievable space than the verbal abstraction of Basic-Truth; White-House is seen as a single image while Basic-Truth requires two separate sequences. Hence, to verbal material which must follow sequential patterns to make sense, Paivio assigns the concept of sequentiality. One need only ask a person to remember the middle line of a long poem, or to repeat the poem backwards to demonstrate this. Imagery, on the other hand, can occur between and among many images synchronously.

Each emotion appears to have its characteristic projection gestalt. We may speak of waves of anger coming over us, the lassitude of grief, gut reactions of hate, the lighteners of joy, and so on. These are more than figures of speech: there appear to be clear, separate virtual images that correspond to the specific emotion. Manfred Clynes (1973), who has studied emotions with an eye toward scientific reductionism, concludes this very pertinent example of emotion and the sensory image it encompasses.

"To take a particular example, the emotion of love is often felt together with a sensation of a kind of flow. Flow implies space. But it is not a static but flowing spatial experience. The direction flow is sensed, generally, from central regions of the body outward, towards the limbs, or generally outward. Yet, that sensation does not mean that at such a time, there really is an actual corresponding, substantive flow outwards; rather, this is a sensory projection. Although there is a sensation of outward flow, nothing really leaves the center and moves outward, but the sensation of flow persists without any corresponding redistribution of a substance. It is thus in the nature of a virtual sensory image. This particular virtual spatial sensory image is characteristic of love." (Clynes, 1973, p. 106.)

In psychotherapy, it can be quite advantageous to use imagery and imagination to make a person more aware of his internal state and conflicts. The flow should be quicker and easier than with other methods because of the wide variety of possibilities eligible for recall or imagining. Verbal reports, developing in sequence, must of necessity be slower. As a result, it is certain from clinical experience that asking a patient to (IS) imagine placing a flower between his mother's breasts will elicit much more feeling-material and association-material than merely asking him how attracted he is to his mother. Since one inch of imagery may elicit a yard of associative imagery (or the old Hollingsworth term of redintegration) pure verbal association may be of limited value. We need not relegate the verbal process to the scrap-heap, however; rather, it can be used contemporaneously with imagery to yield a cohesive logic and internal consistency to the psychotherapeutic process. But the patient's unique way of sensing, seeing, or feeling through the use of imagery does not usually produce the same degree of defensiveness that occurs in more traditional verbalized reports. Meaning that can be conveyed or received by imagery and imagination may have more impact than that gained from verbal insights alone.

Szalita cites the experience of one of her patients who sensed a wavering quality to the design on the ceiling of the therapist's office; aware that this was a faulty image, the patient's emotional response was to see it as an "aggressive witch." (1958, p. 60.) Spiegel makes a similar point with one of her patients, writing, "For instance, Raymond, a young man with recurrent schizoaffective relations and paranoid trends, tested himself for improvement early in one episode by noting his percepts on looking at photographs in a pictorial magazine. Sometimes the faces wavered out of the page, coming alive and mocking him with their eyes, and he recognizes that he was still sick; when they subsided into the page and became inert again, he 'knew' he was better. In the height of his elation, he did not challenge his erroneous percepts and delusional interferences."

Spiegel continues her observations: "With the stirrings evoked in psychotherapy, the patient often experiences not only a sense that dreaming is activated but also more favorable imagery."

With the lifting of depression, imagery returns. Indeed, in the writer's experience, one of the heralding symbols is the rebirth of nature, the growth of trees, of new leaves. Mr. Harry W., as his mood of depression gave way to zest in living in going around and meeting people, said, "Trees are soft, green, round. Trees, when you lie under them and look up at the sky, are especially nice. They always move a little and generally there are little clouds – and green of course. The green of trees is always very soft." (Spiegel, 1959, p. 944.)

Reference to the imagination of therapists is not ordinarily referred to in psychotherapeutic literature. Frank Barron in his book "Creativity and Personal Freedom," makes an important connection between forethought and imagination.

"When we say that a therapist's skill has increased, we mean partly that he has learned how he affects the patient, and that he is able to produce desired effects deliberately, with forethought. Forethought requires some degree of imagination, so that is imagination which determines scope in therapy. Because the therapist can imagine, he can understand; and, understanding, he can take action to affect. If the therapist has imagination, no personality is alien to him." (Barron, 1968, p. 81.)

The imagery of the therapist as he imagines the imagery of the patient can help to "see" what the patient imagines. Commonly shared images, as one patient expressed to me; "Do you remember the image of the peach in my head?" "Yes," I said. "I remember what meaning it had for you at the time. Do you have any idea why you have the imagery now again?" Such examples are now commonplace for me and my patients and their imagery is as much a part of them as any aspect of them. The more I share their imagery, the more I understand them and the more they feel understood. Greater empathy is thus assured.

There is no doubt that the patient's imagery may set off imagery in the therapist. This associated imagery or even reminiscent imagery may add clues and further meaning in a more sharpened participant-observer relationship. It is my opinion that imagery lends itself for greater possibility of participation than verbal reports.

Klinger (1971) has found that the content of imagery is positively related to a person's self-concept and holds fairly consistently for many kinds of thematic content regardless of whether society supports or punishes a type of behavior. This may make us believe that if imagery can be used adequately in therapy, we indeed may have a "royal road to the person."

Image and Psychosis

The importance of the image in psychosis is probably greater than in any form of human behavior, as a means of communication by the individual as well as a means of understanding psychotic behavior for the therapist. And a vast subject it is. The schizophrenic has sometimes been described as having "cancer of the imagination." The incomprehensibility of psychotic images, of hallucinations, of fragmented and bizarre images haunts the therapist as he hopefully looks to bring meaning and help to his patient. But there are infinite styles and intensities to the patient's use of imagery; meanings are elusive, the therapist's skills are challenged.

It is not uncommon for psychotic patients to hallucinate God's voice. One woman said that it afforded her greater comfort than did her less constant image of her therapist. In another instance, a young man much troubled by object loss and separation was greatly preoccupied with the notion that objects photographed in a certain way might be preserved forever. Burnham, Gladstone and Gibson summarize the role of imagery among psychotics:

Some patients approach the problem of object inconsistence and separation anxiety by attempting not only to avoid actual contact with the doctor but also to shut out any image or thought of him. One woman who for months had striven to maintain a facade of self-sufficiency, finally acknowledged to her doctor, "You've gotten under my skin; I hate you for it. You don't bother me so much when you are here. It's when you are not here and I can't get you out of my mind that I hate you most. I was sure I could get along without you and take care of myself. I feel that by letting you become important, I have lost my strength and have lost part of myself." Another patient said, " I don't know your name and I certainly don't want to think of you as my doctor. That would mean I might lose you."

On the other hand, patients may prefer their image of the doctor over his actual presence, saying, for instance, "I can be more certain of my picture of you than I can of you. I can talk to you more easily when I'm not with you." This would appear to be variant of eidetic imagery in persons who are fixated midway between the poles of narcissism and object-relatedness, and for whom a vivid image is in some ways more satisfying than the actual object in the real world. They may attain a pseudo-consistence of the object image by systematically excluding badness from the image. Such a purified image can be more readily maintained in the absence of actual object contacts which inevitably arouse some bad feelings which would spoil the good image. One woman told her doctor, "I know that my image of you will never leave me, but you as a person might leave me. When I think of you as a real person, I get sick."

The mental images of dead persons may be cherished as defenses against separation anxiety. One young woman with severe separation anxiety, clung to an image of her grandfather, who, she was convinced, was the only person who had ever loved her; she vividly recalled that as a child she had pleaded with him at his deathbed, not to leave her. Years later, a boyfriend kissed her goodnight one evening, and as he turned to leave, she suddenly perceived him as changed into an old man. (Burnham, Gladstone and Gibson, 1969, p. 294.)

As one can readily see, the vast and uncharted area of the imagination in relation to psychosis is sometimes comprehensible; more often, however – at least to this point in time – it is beyond our fullest grasp. Especially is this true of fragmented images, hallucinations and delusions. Increased imaginative activity plus living in the fantasy he creates is a common function of the schizophrenic. However, to my knowledge, the active use of imagery and imagination in the treatment of psychotics has so far escaped the literature of our science, even though the importance of its role is undeniable. (That is, besides art.)

Two Schools of Thought on Imagery

Theoretical concepts dealing with imagery fall into two distinct categories, such as the proposal of David L. Shapiro (1970). On the one hand, we have Freud's frame of reference. One proponent of this approach, Kanzer (1958), speaks of visual images coming into consciousness; according to him these visual images have no feelings or movement connected with them, but serve to dissipate the disturbing idea of which engendered them. The image itself remains "an island of resistance." This attitude, while perhaps resembling psychoanalytic procedure, is not accompanied by an insight. In it, the image is taken to be an alternative to the verbalization of ideas, invariably screening the impulses directed towards the analyst as transference resistances. Just as in dreams and in symptom formation, the patient may choose unimportant objects as the subject matter of the image to avoid, the really central and commanding object: the analyst himself or transference reactions. According to this point of view, images are essentially interruptions of the main flow of ideas, motivated by resistance. At best they represent thoughts submerged at the moment. Those who hold to this school of thought are beginning to recognize that the analyst's interpretations may, in turn, give rise to imagery, and they contend that these images are the condensations of inner impulses; if the analyst pays attention to the images, he will merely contact those psychic processes attempting to elude detection.

No mention is made of the possibility that listening to a patient's free association may lead to imagery on the part of the analyst, or the further possibility that such imagery (rather than thought processes) on the part of the analyst might be countertransference resistance. Finally, if a patient free associates and sets off the analyst to indulge in imagery of his own, does the process not imply blockage on the part of the analyst and consequent impairment of the free flow of analytical interpretation?

Fisher (1957), in an experimental period of free imagery, observed a striking similarity to the imagery of dreams. This, of course, suggested that the same resistances found in dreams of submerged thought must be found in the imagery of a patient as well. Warren (1961) speaks of spontaneous imagery arising from free association as representing a regressive state which is more in the nature of narcissistically cathected representations than the — to him — more trustworthy verbalizations. Imagery, he says, satisfies id and superego drives while verbalization is more in line with ego functions and the desire to communicate. Freud (1923) said that thinking in pictures is an "incomplete form of becoming conscious." The visual image represented the return to the "concrete subject matter of things," consequently making the underlying impulses far more difficult to communicate. He suggested that associations to the images be obtained, summarizing that at best the visual image is to be conceived as a screen memory, an innocuous picture represented to screen displaced feelings.

By and large, this point of view conceives of imagery as dynamically similar to dreams in that both are presumably brought about by topographical regression, but dissimilar from them in that the plastic representation is more evident, there is less distortion than in dreams, and the relations to preceding material are often clearer.

The work of Brenman, Gill and Knight (1954) makes comparable observations in discussing the depth of hypnotic trances. "Going deeper" may increase the flow of imagery. These dynamics are very similar to what has been described for the image: a compromise formation like both a defense and a symptom. For instance, going deeper may at one and the same time gratify a passive longing for the therapist and defend against the recognition of that passive longing, since the deeper one goes, the less voluntary control one feels that one has over what one is doing.

By way of review, then, the first point of view, stemming from Freud, concentrates on imagery as screen memories, i.e., what a memory conceals. As in dream work, the emphasis is on the latent content and what it conceals rather than on the manifest content and what it might reveal.

The second point of view stems essentially from the work of Desoille, Leuner and Assagioli; it sees the visual image — in part because of its primitive form — as the direct voice of the unconscious, an expression of the impulse itself rather than a defense against the impulse. This symbolic experience, according to Hammer (1967), is totally transparent requiring no analysis or insight to understand it. It is a level of symbol-making consciousness lying between the conscious and the unconscious; it is the "point of departure for all creative production and healing processes." In this realm of symbols, meetings with unrecognized aspects of the self enable "spontaneous healing through the *transformation* of symbols." The therapist can and does manipulate these symbols, giving some direction and maintaining a degree of control of the patient's fantasy. The therapist may suggest scenes which have symbolic and therapeutic importance related to the basic difficulties in the individual's intrapsychic or interpersonal functioning. According to Hammer, whatever is psychically unresolved will, in the description of the scene, manifest itself through symbolic visual forms and resolve itself at a symbolic level independent of conscious control. The induced visions contain meaningful symbols analogous to dream symbols, but the "psychodynamic organization of affect is projected into such visualizations more clearly than in dreams."

In such procedure, the recall of early memories that hold great affect for the patient is almost totally deemphasized and rarely introduced, since the patient is symbolically dealing with the therapist-directed imaginary situations.

Reyher (1963) used a technique he calls "free imagery" or "emergent uncovering" to make similar points. He asks patients to close their eyes and report such visual images and sensations as occur to them. In 1968, he notes, "As repressed material emerges, it generally becomes represented symbolically, and, as the symbolism breaks down, marked blocking and resistance occurs along with the activation of anxiety and/or symptoms." He goes on to maintain that it is the very appearance of these symptoms which obviates the need for interpretation: the patient directly experiences the effects connected with an image that has been stirred up.

Kubie (1943) advocated hypnotic reverie as an adjunct to a standard psychoanalytical procedure and asserts that it adds more flow of free associations, intense feelings with little distortion.

Reiff and Scheerer (1959), in a study of hypnotic age regression, speak of remembering as the transformation of a previous experience according to ego structures and present schemata. The theoretical difference between the psychoanalytic concept of early memories being a screen for deeply repressed conflicts and the Adlerian idea that the early memory represents a good deal about the person's core-conflicts and the way he structures his life is one which still hangs on unresolved.

Thus, as in memory phenomena as well as in those of visual imagery, there are two very distinct approaches; namely, what memories and images conceal vs. what they reveal. This applies to symbols as well. Analysts such as Jones state with special vigor that one symbolizes only that which could not be expressed, i.e., that which one has deeply repressed, while Silberer (1951) maintained that conflicts were more a conscious level (e.g., the need to work versus the need to sleep) and were almost subject to symbolic representation. Again, interest is divided between what the symbol conceals and what the symbol reveals.

CHAPTER 12

Imagery and the Internal Conflicts

A person's inner conflict is brought about by the opposition of two strong and incompatible forces, neither of which can be satisfied without exacting pain, fear, guilt, or some other emotional penalty. From an existential viewpoint, this definition is an abstraction and also, to be sure, something of an oversimplification. No single conflict encompasses the multitudinous fears and wishes that, each with an urgency of its own, swirl about in one's mind. Perhaps the most reliable method to determine the roots of any given conflict is to relate the conflict to the way in which the parental structure has defined the patient, and to the idealized image the patient feels bound to maintain. The difference between how a patient feels he *should* be and how he really *wants* to be can easily produce a gnawing conflict. A natural and spontaneous act may feel degrading and worthless if it violates an "ideal" form of introjected behavior.

It is well known that all of us, in attempting to resolve our conflicts, oscillate between one polarity of experience and the other. Performance, trial and error, interior dialogue which weighs possible alternative acts — we are constantly bringing these elements to bear on our behavior. When the polarization is rigid, immutable, we feel duly stymied, deadlocked.

A crisis situation may rekindle conflicts arrested and/or unresolved during earlier times. At such a point the "usual" ways of responding to the realities of the world may break down, giving rise to a host of symptoms. Too, there occur transition periods in everyone's development which are referred to as "identity crises," during which he is expected to change his identity in the course of solving the unique problems which confront him at the time. These periods add and magnify conflict.

Ordinarily, most of us can say with a good degree of awareness, "I am ambivalent about that man (or woman)." But most people do not nearly so easily accept *the fascination for frightening events:* feelings of disgust preceding temptation, love disguised as hate, tenderness concealing a wish to destroy (or, for that matter, Harold Lloyd movies showing him perched precariously on high ledges). Weisman (1965) believes that the prevalence of such antithetical affects is far more common in ordinary life than is usually recognized; such feelings fan the fires of conflict and confusion. To know these antithetical feelings within oneself, these ambivalences, is to begin to recognize the complementary opposites within experience. To be in conflict is a powerful part of experience and not just an interesting concept for abstract discussion.

Gardner Murphy defines the problem of conflict in human existence when he states: "Most tragedy, whether in the grand style or in the petty style of the daily suffering of common man or woman, is a matter of a personality divided against itself. The awareness of conflict in oneself may be a major basis for self-reproof or self-pity, and the failure to become aware of it when it is strong regularly gives rise to inexplicable behavior." (Murphy, 1938, p. 296.)

In psychotherapy it is inescapable that both patient and therapist should be constantly concerned with the discovery and definition of conflict. To resolve the conflicts, one must first be aware of them. As George S. Klein states, "The central, most pervasive condition for the development of motives and of psychopathology is conflict." (Klein, 1970, p.21.) It is axiomatic, then, that neurotic conflict involves equally compelling forces in opposite directions, *neither side of which wants to move.* The therapist must aid the patient to become aware of this, and guide him in ways to overcome the stalemate.

Psycho-Imagination Therapy, inevitably, places great emphasis on the awareness of conflict. If the therapeutic situation is without movement and the patient seems lost, we must ask the question: Between what divisive aspects of himself is the patient caught, or, between what polarized aspects of himself and others? And it is precisely at such a time that certain useful techniques can be used to advantage: the Imaginary Situation (IS), Finish-the-Sentence (FTS), Most-or-Least question (M/L), and the Self-and-Other question (S&O). The responses to the techniques will assist markedly in illustrating the strategies of the "other" as used against the "self" and the counterreaction strategies of the "self" in dealing with the "other."

As the patient and therapist proceed to clarify existing conflicts, twin approaches are maintained: the phenomenological and the dialogical. They are not mutually exclusive, since most of the time it may be possible for a person to explore his interior life and still maintain a dialogue with the therapist.

Barron makes the point rather sharply: "Conflict in many instances is generative of new solutions rather than a disabling form of stasis. The real question is this: Can an internal dialogue take place between conflicting forces in such a fashion that the speakers do not simply repeat themselves but that occasionally something new gets said?" (Barron, 1968, p. 233.)

Dual Imagery

A rather remarkable phenomenon appears to occur when a person is asked to imagine two *different* forces, dolls, trees, animals, impulses, etc., and then to contrast each of them in line with the projected imagery. In the great majority of the reported imagery (but not all), there appears to be some form of bipolarization between them. This can be better demonstrated when one asks the imager to assign an adjective to each of the two images. The adjectives may reflect opposite forces of some kind. To enhance the opposing or contrasting forces, one can ask the person to imagine one of the images speaking to the other images, then to imagine the answer back to the first image from the second image. Again, this can be reversed with the second image speaking to the first image and the first image's remarks back.

Dual imagery is so fertile that from here it is possible to develop it in many directions. I will demonstrate a few directions:

First image	*Second image*
the person	
Statement to person from image	Statement to person from image

Another direction:

First image	*Second image*
the person	
Statement from person to image	Statement from person to image

Another direction:

Suggest that the first and second image walk down a road together (or appear together in some way) and become aware of what their interaction appears to be.

Another direction:

First image	*Second image*
the person	
(M/L) The most unlikely (or difficult) statement from the image to the person.	(M/L) The most unlikely (or difficult) statement from the image to the person.

Another direction:

First image	*Second image*
the person	
Statement from the image to a significant person in the person's life	Statement from the image to a significant person in the person's life
or	*or*
Statement from the significant person in the person's life to the image	Statement from the significant person in the person's life to the image

or	*or*
Statement from the therapist to the image	Statement from the therapist to the image
or	*or*
Statement from the image to the therapist	Statement from the image to the therapist

Experience with Dual Imagery as a means of discovering areas of conflict and expanded awareness seems to fall into the following general groupings:

1. Those that compare two images of *things*: two rocking chairs, two tables, two rooms, two bathtubs, two houses, etc.
2. Those that compare two images that *are alive but not human*: two flowers, two trees, two animals, etc.
3. Those that compare two images that *are human*: two women, two men, two children, etc.
4. Those that compare the person in relation to *forces or impulses*. Those include (IS) above you is a force. What you feel and do, etc. (IS) You awake from sleeping in a field at night and there are footsteps over your body. Over what part of your body are the footsteps and whose are they? Or (IS) you walk down a road and somebody taps you on the shoulder, etc.
5. Those that compare *two of you*: (IS) you are in a cave. You are also outside the cave. Call to yourself. Or (IS) you are in a boat in the ocean and you are also in the water. Throw a rope from the you in the boat to the you in the water, etc.
6. Those that compare *two body parts of one person*: (IS) imagine what your heart says to your head. (IS) What does the left side of your brain say to the right side of your brain, etc.
7. Those that compare *body parts of one person to another person*: (IS) what does your heart say to the heart of another person, etc.? (IS) What does the heart of the other person say to your heart, etc.?
8. Those that compare *differences in physical space directions*: (IS) you walk down a shallow river and you see something different on each side. Or, (IS) you look ahead and see something; then turning, what do you see, etc.?
9. *Combined categories* of dual imagery: (IS) imagine two different animals in a human situation, or any other possible combination of dual imagery conceptions that may occur creatively in the operational use of imagery that seems to help delineate conflict areas.

In asking a person to image two bipolarized images together and then to imagine them as one image, great difficulty is experienced by the person as he attempts this. Some persons protest and say it is impossible. One person brought the two images together and then exploded them in his imagery so that they would disappear. Apparently, the more bipolarized the dual images the more difficult it is to imagine them in a unitary manner.

In the use of dual imagery with detached or schizoid persons, I have observed changes in their imagery when the detachment lifts. What appeared in detachment as dull and limited seems to enlarge and expand and become more vivid. At other times, with some detached people, one of the dual images has upon examination revealed itself as the "secret self" of that person.

At this point I would like to illustrate some of these directions. A simplified example is to ask a patient (IS) to imagine any two different animals and have them walk down a road together. The patient might continue describing the animals and their "adventures" for quite a time, but at a certain point I would attempt a dialogue so that we can both arrive at awareness of his conflict and its meaning. The dialogue is not initiated for its own sake but to assist the patient in revealing to me and to himself the "what" of his imaginary experience so that he may eventually be able to get at the meaning of his conflicts. This can be true of any imaginary situation posed to a patient. I once asked a woman (IS) to imagine that she was wearing two different earrings and to describe them:

Joan: One is a large looped earring – the other is a pearl earring.

Shorr: (IS) Do you get a further image for each?

Joan: The large looped one gives me an image of me in a slit dress – sexy as hell.

Shorr: What about the pearl earring?

Joan: I get an image of the Virgin Mary.

Shorr: (IS) If you were to imagine the two of them together on a table, what would you see?

Joan: They would hide from each other. I don't think the loop earring wants to be seen by the pearl. . . . It's a battle between the good and evil . . . I've had this relationship with this man, and my husband doesn't know about it.

In learning the language of Psycho-Imagination Therapy, it is best that any given question be integrated into the fabric of the therapeutic procedure. One who picks an individual question at random "to see how it works" may do so, so long as he returns to the particular line of development that tends to elicit the internal conflicts and leads to the focusing techniques and conflict resolution. In this way we can avoid strict computer-like selection of questions, allow for the individual's intuition without straying from that particular individual's unique patterns. My own experience indicates that when a person is involving his imagination in visualizing and feeling, we should allow him to continue the imagery and the reporting of the experience until it seems that he can imagine it no further. In short, it is best not to hurry the patient on to another direction while there is an in-depth exploration of the one at hand. While Psycho-Imagination Therapy is an active therapeutic approach, there is always room for silence, for just plain listening, interpretation, support, human understanding and warmth.

Above all, it must not be assumed that when a person responds strongly to his or her imagery and feelings the answer will conform to the therapist's preconceived interpretation unless further complementary questions and imagery corroborate it. I remember being certain that a response a man had given me in his imagery was definitely related to a sexual problem and continued with this certainty for several minutes before his direction turned away from my expectancy and, to my surprise, revealed that he was referring to feelings of fear of his own death. It was indeed a lesson to me: never *assume.*

The combination of imagery situations together with other techniques and their possible sequence is primarily guided by the direction taken by the patient's early responses. *What is he or she revealing for examination? What is he or she willing to face? Where is he or she going? What is he or she ready for? What does he or she appear to deny?* For the therapist these questions and their tentative conclusions lead to further use of imaginary situations and other approaches that suggest new directions and the working through of unresolved areas of the patient's life. The process of Psycho-Imagination Therapy aims at an integration of imagery sequences with dialogue, in which the dialogue combines reminiscences of feeling and meaning. Findings of a more factual nature are not rejected, but blended, rather, with the other constituents into a picture of the whole existence much the way a good novel or biography brings the central character to life for the reader.

I am reminded of what Freud said in 1895 when he was using the concentration technique to elicit patients' imagery: "The one advantage that we gain is of learning from the results of this procedure the *direction* in which we have to conduct our inquiries and the things we have to insist upon the patient." (Breuer and Freud, 1953, p. 272.) It is my experience that, truly, when imagery is used to reveal the internal conflicts of the patient, the "direction in which we have to conduct our inquiries" becomes clearer. Moreover, as Binswanger has suggested, in our encounters with a patient we must be aware of him as "Thou." His case studies and other writings indicate the actual power of *love*, analysis and imagination combined to break through fragmented and distorted images so as to enable us to see persons *wholly.*

It is an interesting fact of observation that when a patient is asked to imagine two "different" people, animals, things, impulses, etc., and then asked to compare them or have them interact or speak to each other, a delineation of the internal conflict becomes clearer. Clearer, too, becomes the significance of meaning of the conflict. As an example, suppose I ask the patient to (IS) imagine two *different* animals and give an adjective for each. Then I may ask him to imagine one of the animals saying something to the other and the emotional response of each. I might then want to know which would win if they had a fight – or what would happen if the two animals were to walk down a road together. I would then inquire if this imaginary sequence had any relationship to the life of the patient himself. While not all of these dyadic or bipolarized imaginary situations reveal the deepest of a patient's conflicts immediately, one must be alert to those which – especially in the initial stages of therapy – evoke the greatest effect: often it's best to switch to other material until the patient is ready to return to them.

These dual imaginary situations are not standard or constant, though I have found certain specific ones to be very useful. There are countless possibilities, of course, and the variation is infinite. I may ask (IS) for two images and that the images interact, then ask the patient to express his feelings about the interaction. For example, when I asked one man to (IS) imagine an animal from his head, he said, "a fox," and when I asked him to imagine an animal out of his guts he said, "a snake." When I had him imagine the fox and the snake walk down a road together, he said, "The snake would constantly try to choke the fox to death — but would always fail." When I asked what he thought the image meant, he offered, "My feelings are rotten; I am afraid of my feelings — they will hurt people — so I have to be like a fox in my mind, thinking quickly, selecting my thoughts to be what I think I should be — I'll hurt people with my feelings."

Although asking a patient to imagine two different animals may seem a simple avenue into the patient's internal conflicts, complexities are frequent and may not always be obvious. For example, one woman gave the following answer to a dual IS:

Bird . . . . . . *Image* . . . . Fish
Free . . . . . . *Adjective* . . . . . . Free—but confined to water

"We really live in the same
surroundings." (*Spoke first*)

"Yeah, I feel you are right." (*Response*)

"I am Zeus, you are Neptune—
we are powerful—king of
different areas.(*Spoke first*)

"Yeah, I agree." (*Response*)

When asked if this answer related to her own conflict, she replied, "The bird says, 'I have it better than you; I can fly through the air.' The fish, however, says 'I can fly through the water and I'm gorgeous.' " She continued, "They both compete well in their own areas." And as she continued to talk she came to realize that direct competition was the most difficult thing for her to contemplate. "If I can be best in jacks (the child's game) because of very special eyesight, I would feel okay, because there would be very few others who would want to compete with me."

She then recalled a reading group in the first grade in which she had intentionally failed in order not to be one of the best readers. Her conflict was to serve her idealized image of being well liked but nonthreatening to her peers. When she was given the same (IS) six weeks later, she offered a different image this time:

Sloth . . . . . . *Image* . . . . Black Leopard
Stationary . . . *Adjective* . . . . Active

"Do you need anything?" (*Spoke first*)

(*Response*) "No, I can handle it."

(*Spoke first*) "You seem ambitious today—
    you must have something to do."

"Nothing unusual—just going about
my day." (*Response*)

"I identify with the sloth," she said, "because I go along with things – I really want to be a leopard and move fast and do things."

When one compares this response to the previous imagery, it is clear that some barriers had been removed, making it possible for her to face her conflicts.

It is apparent that the imaginary situation is useful in telling both patient and therapist to what point the patient has progressed, or where he appears to be, or even that it seems he is not ready to proceed ahead. One approach that can be utilized is the "repeated imaginary situation," i.e., repeating an imaginary situation that was used earlier in the therapy – one which elicited strong responses – and comparing the more recent response with the prior one(s).

An extremely useful imaginary situation is one in which patients are asked to imagine themselves on stage as *two of themselves* and then to describe each. When asked, additionally, to say something to each other, many aspects of the self versus the self become more evident; many feelings are exposed as the differences between the "selves" are described. There are instances, however, when the two people on stage are so separate that no communication is possible between them. Too, there are those persons who live so much within their own ego-boundaries that they may have difficulty separating the two. This was true of the patient who said, "Those are two of me on stage and we are making love to each." From this point it was possible to see his internal conflicts when he expressed his feelings in relation to an imagined audience.

As one can see, there are many directions in which this question can be pointed. Often, the answers can indicate the person's false position versus the solid position. Further, it affords the possibility of making comparisons between how a patient views himself (that is, self versus self) during the ongoing course of therapy. An example of this was the patient – an actor by profession – who answered as follows: "I am both of them – one of *me* is sitting in the corner on my haunches, eyes to the ground, looking up furtively to see my other *me* standing guard duty, looking out of a trench window for signs of the enemy." At quite a later point in therapy I asked him the same imaginary situation and this time he responded, "One is directing the other in an acting part. The other has great confidence in his ability to act a truly great part about real people's lives."

The same situation is equally useful as a method of eliciting the internal conflicts and then gradually extending the scope of response to include other people. For example, one man answered the imaginary situation in the following way:

"The Two Me's"

1. Immaculately dressed — brings to this performance years of fine training in the French horn — about to crack from the strain.

2. I'm not dressed up — like I hit the bottom — I lost everything — like I burnt acid in me to get rid of all the shit — I do what I do.

I then had him imagine a statement that he might make to me (Shorr) from each of his "Me's."

"I shake your hand — I say, 'Dr. Shorr, I hope that you enjoy this fine performance.

"Hello, Joe — I am really glad to see you."

He then suggested an imaginary situation in which he was receiving an "Emmy" for his playing and what he would say to his mother from each of his two "Me's."

"Mom, you stuck by me — I really hope I can make a better life for you."

"This is beautiful to win."

Continuing, he said, "The first me talks and is taken in by a martyred mother. The second one is free. I can no longer be defined by my mother as 'her own.' I won't be affected by her subtle martyrdom. She's like an adhesion; wherever I go she sticks to me ... etc."

Not only was he able to elicit and recognize the conflict within him but by extending the imaginary situation to significant people in his life, he was able to view their influence upon him — to see how they defined him.

One woman responded to the same imaginary situation in these words: "There is myself, as one and another woman on the stage. We are in a play by Strindberg called *The Stronger*, in which two women are in love with the same man. However, one woman says nothing and the other woman does all the talking. It's a half-hour play in which the audience decides the fate of the women. Which part will I play? Which is really the stronger?" She then added, "Why can't people be like the Navajos who play basketball and never keep score? I guess I am caught in a scene of whether to compete or not to compete in this shitty world. Maybe I think my strength would devastate others."

In such dual imaginary situations we often elicit negative self-images in conflict with positive self-images. Sometimes it's possible to draw forth historical self-concepts in conflict with a contemporary self-concept. "Seeing" the conflict may come about through the use of an infinite variety of imaginary situations (or Finish-the-Sentence statements, or Most-or-Least questions, or Self-and-Other questions). All individuals are different, and we as therapists must try to approach each person via that question which seems most useful and appropriate as we continue to develop the ability to "see" what each patient "sees." While some questions might have been posed to nearly everyone, some are applicable to one person only and perhaps to no other person again. Certainly and unequivocally, there are imagery responses that belong *only* to that specific person and no other; I am reminded of an example that demonstrates the point. In response to the imaginary situation (IS) "Imagine two different animals in two different human situations," a twenty-two-year-old woman replied:

1. A groundhog going shopping. It's on all fours and looks at everything around — goes by other people — ladies don't like him and they gossip and talk behind his back — but he goes on shopping.

2. Black rabbit at a circus — big arena. He's sitting in one of the box seats but people don't know he's a rabbit. He gets up for popcorn and still no one knows he's a rabbit — even when he leaves, the parking attendant doesn't know he's a rabbit.

When I asked her an adjective for each human situation, she gave:

Pushy   **Ignored**

I then asked her to conduct a conversation between the two human situations:

"Don't get in my way or I'll run you over with my shopping cart." (*Spoke first*)

"I can get out of your way." (*Response*)

"No, I can claw you with my sharp claws." (*Response*)

"Get out of my way. I can jump on you because I've got big feet." (*Spoke first*)

When I asked her if the two images had any meaning to her, she said, "They are both me — I feel masculine as the groundhog, because my father made me his 'boy' and trained me to ride horses and drive trucks. My older brother was a disappointment to my father so I became my father's 'boy.' I never could be like my mother who was ineffective and weak. As I got older I wanted to be a woman. I don't like to be frilly and weak, and yet I don't want to be another Barbara Stanwyck with a black whip. I like men sexually. But it seems I'm nowhere; I go unnoticed like the black rabbit. I am a female all right, but I can't be weak like my mother or masculine like I was raised to be. Can I be the woman I want to be?"

It's possible to ask a patient for two different birds, animals, or flowers, or even for two different animals of the same species, for example, two different zebras or ant-eaters. As the differences emerge through the use of the imagination and as the possible conflict between the animals is introduced, an awareness of the patient's own conflict is stimulated.

I try not to interpret; I try to offer more possible ways for the patient to see it for himself. He is, by his answers, becoming aware of his neurotic conflict. The effort is nearly always directed toward the discovery of the *self versus self, self versus the other*, or perhaps the *"new" self versus the "old" self*. If it is possible to use an approach that exploits the 180° polarity in neuroses, the "self" and the "other" can be quickly presented, their opposition immediately available for recognition and study. At other times one may use a "Finish-the-Sentence," or a "Self-and-Other," or a "Most-or-Least" question which permits the person (self) to include the "other" with whom he is in conflict.

In terms of revealing what an individual may feel to be pressuring him and his reactions to that pressure, a particularly useful imaginary situation is: (IS) "Above you and behind you is a force; describe your feelings." Some people sense a force above and an additional one from behind; others report a single force from both directions. My experience indicates that this force is most commonly nonhuman in nature; it might be a "large piece of steel," "a hurricane," "a devil," etc. But, of course, there are those patients who refer at once to a human force: a father, a mother, etc. My own procedure is to eventually ask the patient to humanize the force. One man, in answer to the initial question, said that the force was a large magnet which was holding him in its power; it was fifty feet above the chair in which he was sitting. I then asked him to (IS) humanize the force. The answer, drawn from his imagination, was: "The magnet is my own arms holding me up there. It's my own intellectual control that I won't let go of."

As you can see, equally important as the definition of the "force" itself is the individual's particular reaction to that force. One man felt that there was a huge chunk of steel pushing into his back, and while he felt that he was permitting it to do so, he was not letting the force control him. When asked to humanize the force, it proved to be his subtly coercive father as well as his own subtle counterreaction to his father. Another man said of the force, "It's my wife, I feel her controlling me, she pulls me, and I pull against her." A young woman described the force as "power-energy all around me — I have to open my eyes for it to be part of me — it's me against the world." Still another man said the force was "a large block of granite, very heavy. It's just there, in a way it is pushing me, wherever I go, it's there. Same position in relation to me no matter how I move." When I asked him to (IS) humanize the force, he answered, "People that I don't have control over — like a fellow at work who pretends to be boss, who is a co-worker really." In this particular case I was able in time to have him focus his real feelings toward this co-worker. "Get fucked!" he screamed at the imagined image of the co-worker.

There is an additional component to this particular imaginary situation which is worth noting. Often a person will describe the force as supernatural, and it may be that what some people refer to as God is closely related to such a sense of force. When those people who respond that the force is God are asked to humanize the force, it is the person who carries the most authority for them that is invariably mentioned.

When a person has resolved some of his internal conflicts, the dual imagery situation will not appear as radically bipolarized — the essential differences between the two images may be minimal. A fifty-year-old man who had resolved a host of problems, and who seemed very much at ease in comparison to his state of tension earlier in therapy, was asked to (IS) imagine something different in each hand. His right hand held a rose and his left hand held Indian beads. I asked him to have each of these say something to him. The remarks from both objects were gentle, aesthetically warm; his remarks back to the objects were of a similar tone. I then asked him to bring both objects together. He did, placed them over his heart, and seemed to flow in a most relaxed fashion with the peacefulness of the imagery. This was enormously different from his reaction eight months earlier, when I had asked him to (IS) "Imagine someone on either side of you, and have them say something to you." To one side of him he had visualized his grandmother, to the other, his mother; they tugged at him until he was ragged.

The "new" image (and other comparable ones in similar IS exploration) showed little of the original bipolarization, little of the original conflict and greater integration.

One can also pose to a patient what I call Reverse Time Imagery. In such an exercise the person is asked to imagine a situation at the present point in time and then asked to imagine what his imagery to the same situation might have been five years ago, or even last year. I asked one man to (IS) imagine a field, and build something in the middle of it. His response was, "A teahouse where you can see the sun and there is lots of music and food." When asked to retrogress five years in time, he said, "I would have imagined a tall office building, and I would have seen myself walking through it, very sweaty."

If verified by other elements of the patient's development, reverse time imagery provides a viable rule of thumb for measurement of the person's change.

It's beyond our scope to explore all possible bipolarized or dual imagery situations which might elicit conflict areas; I have included only a few in any detailed form merely to demonstrate the technique. But, in brief, one might ask, (IS) imagine your right leg is standing on something and your left leg is standing on something else; (IS) animal out of head and gut; (IS) an image of the day and an image of the night; (IS) ascending upwards into the air and descending down into the sea; (IS) an image within you and an image outside of you; (IS) an image of the past and an image of the present; (IS) an image in front of you and an image in back of you; (IS) imagine looking into a mirror and seeing someone other than yourself and have a conversation; (IS) imagine kissing yourself; (IS) imagine two caves and then imagine a different person in each; (IS) imagine who you would hold with your right hand, then your left hand.

The number and variation of such imaginary situations are infinite. It is for you to experience them and perhaps create new ones for your own use.

Transference Indications

At times, a dual imagery situation may bear directly on transference reactions between the patient and the therapist. A young woman, Joan, who was quite reserved and who appeared outwardly cautious in her first meeting with me, offered the following response to the question (IS), imagine an animal out of your head and an animal out of your guts:

"Imagining an animal from my head, I say a raccoon. The raccoon has a mask on his face and looks as if he is blindfolded, but he can of course see past the mask. He also has long claws which he uses to tear apart shellfish. I am like the raccoon in that I felt the need for a mask. Where you could not see in but I could see out. Like the raccoon, I am frightened easily, yet with claws am ready to protect myself. I feel threatened by you as if you were annoyed with me because I wasn't open enough with you or giving the right answers. The rabbit from my guts was trembling as I felt on the inside. It was small and cute. I despise the word cute, because it seems trite and degrading. If something is cute, it is young, weak, and merely appeals to someone's fancy. When someone tells me I'm cute, I get very defensive as if they are trying to manipulate me 'nicely.' My animals walk down the road together amiably because they have to stay together or it seems like they would be destroyed. It is as if my body and mind united to defend me from you."

I then asked her to imagine (IS) any two faces. She imagined seeing Barbra Streisand's face and then mine. She offers the following:

"The two faces of you and Barbra Streisand annoy me because it is me and not Barbra. Yet, I can see, hear and listen to the things she says as if the person Barbra has said them. Yet they are my things I had been thinking about earlier. She feels that she has some need for your help, yet she could do without it and still go on with her career and be successful. Eventually, she would wonder whether she did the right thing and sometimes wish she would have finished with it.

"Some of the reasons I am frightened or wary of you is because you force me to think out situations without doing any of the work for me. Since I don't feel close to you or secure with you, I am left on my own without someone to at least back me up. It is the feeling of being dumped into the middle of a crowd of strangers by you and then merely watch what I do instead of coming over to me or allowing me to come over and talk to you.

"Trusting is hard for me because I'm not sure of what it all means. When one trusts, they leave themselves open to all kinds of pain, ridicule, humiliation and also to a heavy load of responsibility. How far should one trust? Who determines where to stop trusting and why? What happens when I fail in a trust of someone else's? How should I determine when to not trust a person anymore? What are the advantages of trusting? In this situation, trusting would be good because I could accomplish more with you than if I didn't trust, yet if I allow myself to trust you, will I slip and trust others that shouldn't be trusted? Then when they break my trust, will I become more bitter as I have in the past? These are some of the questions that I need to find answers for before I trust. I don't trust because I am afraid, but I don't like my life being ruled by fear. That is why I come here.

"When I trust, I reveal very private feelings that I'm not always sure of. Most people I have trusted take these things and use them against me later when I am not in the same frame of mind. Such an instance would be telling a person that I want to be less hostile with someone. Later when I slip and am hostile toward that person I was working on, the first person throws what I've said into my face. It is as if they are saying, 'See, you are a liar and don't mean the things you say.'"

This response came at the beginning of her therapy and alerted me to her very powerful need to trust me; it revealed all the cautions and emotional brakes she had applied to herself. Further, the need to understand the meaning of imagery was exceedingly important to her; she did not want to feel she was "lost" in a maze of her own imagery. Accordingly, from that point on, I emphasized the meaning of her remarks and their possible interpretations and did not proceed until I felt that meaning was quite clear. In short, I was there for her when she needed me. In time, I felt less and less remote to her; in time I became more real to her and she learned to trust me.

Sexual Conflicts

(IS) Walk into a room and you will notice a *hole* in the floor; now look through it and tell me what you see. In most instances the imagery responses to this imaginary situation are related to how a person feels about sex, how he senses sexuality, and how he deals with sexual relationships. One man said, "It's a dark room with old-fashioned floorboards − like an attic − dust around − there is a nude woman − it excites me − all I want to do is fuck and nothing else − just meat − no feelings − she's a tough looking chick." Well, as one might suspect, this man had great difficulty expressing tender feelings toward women and wanted to control them.

Another man, who was very frightened of sexual involvement, responded to the same (IS) in the following way: ". . . dark, and (it) gets darker the longer I look − people are swimming or floating in oil − they are vertical − I feel troubled − I might fall in and become one of them − I really envy these people."

Let me repeat that I do not at once push for interpretation or meaning; the responses may serve merely as starting points for mutual exploration, detailed analysis often postponed until a later time and even then with different direction. Still, for the majority of people who do not experience overwhelming difficulty in answering the initial question, it is possible to go further. One person, having imagined the room and the hole in the floor, said that upon looking down through it he saw a bridge swinging back and forth beneath. "How far down is it?" I asked him. "A thousand feet," he answered. "Gee, it's far." And without further prompting he recalled an incident in very early life in which a governess had seduced him in a hammock.

One woman in her thirties gave the following response to the same initial imaginary situation: "(I go) into a room that looks like a modernistic castle. I am looking through a square hole. It's a winding square staircase all rosewood — beautiful gorgeous rosewood — it's a room that opens to the sea — high ceilings with books I haven't yet read. Fireplace — fur comfortably squared over traditional hearth — aesthetically pleasing to get down."

I then asked her to (IS) imagine going down a round staircase, to which she replied, "I go down and down endlessly like an Escher painting to nowhere." Following this I asked her to imagine (IS) a staircase that turned square corners periodically (inspired by her own response). She answered, "It changes so much — it becomes more narrow — at each intersection there is a window or painting — at each window, there is a nothingness wherever there is a painting — they are mixed up and it doesn't make any sense. They are always pretty and impressionistic — then it becomes narrower and the paintings become narrower."

I then asked (M/L): "What is your most frequently repeated relationship with men?" She replied, "Forming the relationship and then dominating it — I had hoped my present relationship would be different. The more I control the relationships, the less happy they become." Then she volunteered, "I guess the squared steps are like my relationships with men as I control the things that will happen."

This imaginary situation is not one to be suggested or taken too lightly, and adequate caution must be employed to ascertain which direction one should take in developing it further. Verification and cross-checking must be used frequently, since we are interested in knowing:

1. How the person defines himself in relation to the opposite sex.
2. How he feels the opposite sex defines him.
3. The specific conflicts involved.
4. His or her readiness to face the conflicts.
5. Finally, the degree to which he or she fears judgment on the part of the therapist or others with regard to his or her sexual attitudes.

I am reminded of a time when I had asked one of my groups (IS): "Imagine looking through a hole in the floor; tell me what you see." And one man answered, "I see a clerk as she is filing all the papers in an orderly neat manner in filing cabinets — keeping it very clean and neat." It was embarrassing to him to hear that this imaginary situation relates to sexual things, and he recoiled from therapy. This reinforces the fact that blanket interpretations are sometimes hazardous, often needless. It is best to use them primarily as a guide for further exploration.

To the same imaginary situation, a woman of twenty-six responded, "It's not very big — the hole isn't — I couldn't get down there because I'm much larger. I see dirt there — ah! — it looks like the Grand Canyon — I can only get one arm in it —

but when I get close to it, it's granite and like the Grand Canyon. There are little people in it, or they are very far away. They have their arms up because they want something — all crowded together — they want out of there. I can't reach them — every time I try, I can't look or I will turn into their size. But, if . . . I kind of concentrate on what I want — I have to look away disinterested and stick out my arm — but I am not sure what they want . . . (Pause)."

Shorr: (S&O) What is your responsibility to them?

Jane: A lot. What do you want? But I can't look. If they saw me as big as me, they would be afraid. If I look I'll shrivel into their size. That's why I have to do it sneakily, like.

Shorr: (IS) Can you go down in there?

Jane: Only if I am little and I don't know if I can get up again. Well, unless I arranged it in advance as the big person. Then I could return — I'd have to have the edge. I must arrange it in advance. They seem kind of hostile. They ain't happy to see me. I'd have to find out what they want. I'd move through them and around them. They don't mind me being there — but I have to justify my presence. I have to help them or make them feel better. I don't want to stay long. My advance plan is for them to want to get out. But, I find they are not too unhappy. I'm stuck. They must be getting something out of it — but I'm getting nothing. There is nothing for me to do. Everybody has got the market cornered.

Shorr: (IS) Imagine your father looking at you.

Jane: He wants my support — he loves me, yet, but, I am paternal to him — not him to me. I have to organize things for him. Just be there.

Shorr: (IS) Imagine your mother looking at you.

Jane: What does she want? A calculated move. I'm apprehensive. Make waves or what? I don't know nothing but arguments — discord.

Shorr: (IS) Imagine Bernie (boyfriend) looking at you.

Jane: . . . More like my mother — yet I'm not sure. He can't take me seriously. He's got to be cold — I want him not to be warm. If he's nice, I don't know what to do — I get sarcastic and push him away. I need the edge. I don't want to fall for anyone or have them fall for me. If I give them a helping hand, they fall for me — then I crush them. It's to get out of it. They bring up sex, marriage or love, not necessarily in that order. (She laughs at that remark.) I run from them.

Another man gave the following account in response to the same imaginary situation: "I walked down the trap door which opened into the room below. The room is bare except for a carpet on the floor. There are four paneled walls. My feeling is that the room is my life and I must furnish it. After looking around for awhile, I first put in a very large round table with a white linen tablecloth. Next came a *very large* three-tiered layer cake all white with much icing, having hundreds of blue, burning candles on it. The cake was thick and took up the full diameter of the table. Next I very strongly threw a naked girl into the birthday cake on her back and she squished into the cake. I jumped onto her (she landed with her legs spread apart) and started fucking her. We fucked until we got tired and lay breathing hard for a few minutes. We both got hungry. I remember first sticking my mouth and face full into the cake and biting the cake and getting my face covered with cake and icing, still clutching the girl, with my cock inside her. It was great. Every time I think of this fantasy, I laugh. It is the neatest, best, cleanest, greatest fantasy I ever had. And you can believe I fully intend to try it in reality!

"It's hard furnishing that room. I feel that I can furnish it any way I like. The carpet is kind of Persian. The walls are wide paneled oak. I would furnish it first with my family (my group) (this included my friend, the doctor). Each one will have a bit of my birthday cake. I want them to. I have feelings about each one and how individually each would react to eating my cake.

"Next, I will have a banquet buffet and I have feelings how each person would react at the buffet.

"Next, I would open the door and let the rest of the world eat at my buffet. They would come in a few at a time.

"I still must furnish the room, Joe, and it's difficult right this moment.

Lest the reader misinterpret the use of the imaginary situation of the hole in the floor and what one sees and feels when one looks through it, I must add that it is one I just find very useful.

There are countless others including dual imagery, such as (IS), Imagine two different vaginas or penises or two different women's faces or two different men on a platform, or imagine taking a shower with one's father, etc. These and many others can help point to the sexual conflicts and serve as valuable reference points for further exploration and eventual focus for change.

The Three Boxes

An imaginary situation that very often reveals the inner and outer phases of the personality with a view to the person's defenses and conflicts is a seemingly simple question: (IS) Imagine three boxes inside of each other; imagine removing them, and arrange them in front of you; then imagine something in each box. My experience indicates that patients have to "work through" the extrication of the boxes as well as the process of arranging them; invariably, though (but not *quite* always), the greatest effort is involved with opening the boxes and seeing into them. Results from this imaginary situation indicate the following generalizations:

1. The largest box indicates the outer conception of the personality – the veneer or style with which the patient deals with the world.
2. The middle box relates to the person's defenses – the barriers inside him.
3. The smallest box seems to relate to the person's core, or center aspect of himself.

Or so it *seems;* I have no intention of implying that we are dealing with an infallible absolute. One man, when offered this imaginary situation, allowed his imagery to flow and said, "I'm putting the middle box over my head. The large

box is full of cobwebs and is stale and dark. The middle box is over my head –
it rests on my shoulders. I want to hide – it's a neutralizer – it keeps the old stuff
from coming in. It really acts as a buffer from getting into my heart. That's where
the heart is, in the small box. At first I thought it was a carefully protected jewel
resting in purple velvet, but it's really my heart."

Another patient, a woman, had a remarkable set of responses to the same
imaginary situation:

1. "Large box – it's bigger than me. I'm inside of it like a playhouse. I'm the
kid – pictures on the side – just a brown box with just a washing machine – it's
dark.

2. "Now I've grown bigger, I'm not a kid anymore. I see rows of male organs
– like a movie I saw once where there was a thing you held. I guess you call it
a stem and you touched people with it and it gave 1–8 on a scale intensity of pain
or 1–8 intensity of pleasure. If I touched you with it, you'd be subservient to me
because you'd have so much pleasure. (Pause) I dump those male organs out.
They are like a box of little steaks you buy in the store. They all roll out downhill.

3. "Then the little box. It's most different from the others. This one has no
lid, a jewelry box all tied up in a ribbon. I untie it. In tissue paper inside is my
mother's heart and it's still beating and I snip at it and it squirts out some stuff.
It's frightening. (Pause) As I stand there, the snipped part grows in the air and
wants to grab you like a Venus fly trap. I think it's an embrace, not a strangula-
tion. I stand there to find out. It comes around my neck. I cannot let on that I'm
afraid. I offer her a bargain. I say, 'You want my body?' I am caught. I just remain
there talking – trying to get out of it. Can I make a good enough bargain to keep
it from strangling me? I see money certainly won't help. It must need something.
I'll have to figure it out and try and get it."

When I asked her how this related to her life, she replied: "They call me 'the
kid' at work. I come off like I'm easy going with no responsibilities. The first box
is like my apartment – small and I'm the only one there. The second box stumps
me, but when I think of what I see in the small box, it begins to make sense. My
mother accused me all my life of trying to be sexual with my father. She was
skinny as a rail and had absolutely no breasts. I was afraid to touch my father
– because he belonged to her. I am afraid to touch any man because he belongs
to some other woman. I can only have the man nobody wants. I guess I really
have to show her how contemptuous of men's organs I am – so I roll them down
the hill."

To add an additional dimension, I have asked a person to imagine that he *is*
what he imagines in each box. One man saw a mouse in the small box. I asked
him then to imagine he was the mouse and to Finish-the-Sentence, I am _____
_____. I feel _____. He answered, "I am *weak*. I am *frightened*." This
helped crystallize meaning for both of us.

Katherine, a thirty-five-year-old woman, when offered the three boxes, responded, "Three boxes of graduating size stacked like a pyramid. When empty, which they never are, the boxes easily slide one into the other so they could appear to be one box.

"In the largest, which is a magic box, is an endless complete wardrobe from all the best couturiers around the world, from all the greatest, funkiest boutiques everywhere. Everything is characteristically fit for me. When these clothes wear out, the magic box, systematically is a black, flowing, swishy, slinky, silky, clingy, marvelously comfortable thing.

"The second box is very pretty. It is red and white striped – shiny – with a sleek laquered lid – black. When opened, it holds sweet, succulent fruit – much tropical variety – papaya, Kiwi, guava, lychee – as well as all the familiar favorites. The fruit is clean and glowing. It is nicely snuggled in a fine piece of white linen. Nestled amongst the fruit is a silver knife which invites us to sample the contents of the box.

"The third box – the inner one – has a sole telegram in it which reads:

LOVED YOUR TAPES STOP RETURNING THEM SHORTLY
     STOP CONTRACT TO FOLLOW

The telegram is from a large city."

After I suggested the possible meaning of the three boxes, she then continued:

"The largest box – the one with the wardrobe – the magic box – is representative of the way I present myself to the world. Or how I would LIKE to do that, perhaps. I seek 'comfortable' relationships. I seek beauty, grace. My being I want to be understood as characteristically, individually me. This individuality I would like to have it magically, systematically, naturally produced without my thinking about it – that's the magic part of the box.

"The middle box – the red and white striped one – is the box which connects the outer box to the inner one. Therefore, the contents of this box tie together my outer self with my inner one. The succulent fruit is indicative of a quest for survival. Further, a kind of survival which is happy, pretty, delicious, good, healthful, and sharing. A sense of aesthetic is always some sort of yearning for knowledge of other places, and cultures and people.

"The smallest box is the one with the telegram in it, and represents the core of my personality, at this point in time anyway. I would like to have valid recognition for whatever it is that I might do or create. I would like it to be meaningful and satisfying.

Occasionally, a person may invest the largest and middle boxes with imagery of a "healthy" nature, then discover a seemingly incongruous image associated with the smaller one. One man reported what seemed like healthy imagery in the large and middle boxes, then saw a tranquilizer in the small one. Similarly, another man saw apparently healthy imagery in the largest box and the medium-sized one – then reported that the small one contained a ferocious possum-cat which ripped at everything in front of it. As our dialogue revolved around this point, powerful areas of conflict and bad feelings were revealed.

One young lady appeared to have seemingly healthy responses to the small box: ". . . a million little things in it – filled with wonderful things in an endless array. I feel gay and joyful. I am chock full of neat things." The middle box, too, was unperturbing: "A beautiful, unique Easter lily. I am full. I feel strong and giving." But, in the large box, she imagined a bedroom, to which she added, "I feel lonely. I am not full enough." This seemed to indicate loneliness and an unshared life, despite her developing strength. It also paralleled a point in time when she knew she had to leave group therapy (in which she practically "grew up all over again") and was faced with a sense of genuine loss as well as other, good feelings. The large box represented her conflict over having to leave group therapy.

Some Additional Thoughts on the Three Boxes

In doing clinical work involving imagery, some sort of trial and error creativity takes place. Sometimes an image will occur to me that suggests it may reveal a specific aspect of personality or characteristic behavior. At other times there is specific information I require and I intuitively create an imaginary situation which may elicit the desired material. It is beyond my own capacities to set up an experimental design in advance of clinically using an imaginary situation to determine what specific kinds of imageries purport to reveal about a person. Of course, once several hundred persons are asked to do the same imaginary situation, their reported images can be examined for commonalities of themes or conflicts with an idea towards possible empirical validation. The whole process rests initially on an intuitive framework based on clinical experience.

In determining subjective meaning, consensual validation between myself, as therapist, and the patient, was the general procedure used. When the patient and I reached total agreement we could then assume that the imagery production was, indeed, indicating particular meanings. This procedure was then repeated with hundreds of persons on each imaginary situation offered. In time, after hundreds of records of one image production were reviewed, certain unmistakable patterns emerged that appeared with extremely high consistency and reliability.

In all attempts at subjective meaning in the use of imagery it is the patient who leads the discussion and makes the connections that are necessary to effect such conclusions. The therapist takes an essentially non-directive position, allowing the patient to explore possible meanings until he or she is satisfied with the likely meaning. With thoroughly studied patients, agreement from the therapist as to subjective meaning occurs an extremely high proportion of times.

In teaching a class in Imagery and Human Growth at UCLA in 1972, it occurred to me that the Russian type dolls with succeedingly smaller sizes inside the other, sometimes having four or five dolls inside the larger doll, might reveal succeeding layers of personality. It was at best a construct with a possible logical basis.

Experience with the Russian dolls didn't seem to reveal very much. No general consistency of responses emerged. In fact, my idea seemed to bog down and the students became bored. I persisted, and modified my approach into using three boxes. This time I attempted to use three separate boxes in succeedingly smaller sizes. Eventually I chose a large box, a medium-sized box, and a small box. Each person was asked what he or she imagined was in each box. What would they reveal?

I collected "three boxes" responses from hundreds of people. As I examined the responses I began trial and error thinking and observation. After months of study and observation of patients' responses, it seemed that the large box was showing how the person appeared in his or her interaction with the social environment. The middle box took longer to make sense to me. After months of study and observation of patients' responses, the small box appeared to represent the inner core of the person, or so it seemed. Still, it was trial-and-error creativity.

A few weeks went by. It occurred to me, why not ask the imager to imagine that he or she *was* whatever he or she imagined was in the boxes, and then finish certain sentences. Out of this came: I feel _____; The adjective that best describes me is _____; I wish _____ _____; I must _____; I need _____ _____; I secretly _____; I will _____ _____; Never refer to me as _____. Then clearer than ever came the meaning of the three boxes. Now the middle box emerged in concept as the coping and defense mechanism between the large box and the small box. What I had anticipated about the large and small boxes was confirmed.

Several thousand persons have now done the three boxes! Remarkably, it seems this special imagery has had an exceptionally high consistency to reveal what by trial and error I, in consensual validation with patients, discovered it might reveal.

The Three Doors

Soon my mind wandered to other possibilities. Would three balls, three windows, three doors, or three anything give us the same kind of delineations of meaning and personality information?

I attempted some of these other imaginary situations upon myself. Certain confusions seemed to occur. Perhaps I was trying too hard or knew what I was looking for. Clear categories of interpretation did not seem to emerge. I then decided to try it on others in my training classes and with patients.

The three doors seemed to yield the most information in my trial and error activity. For, in asking a person to imagine three doors (left, right, and center) and then to imagine opening each and to report what he or she saw, did and felt, one concept clearly emerged. In about 98% of the persons asked, the center door could be subsequently interpreted through consensual validation to reveal concepts and dynamics about sexual matters or about relationships with the opposite sex.

Similar to dream work, the manifest content of the center door imagery may not be explicitly sexual. Subjective meaning can become clearer from the dialogue and subsequent imagery associations to the center door imagery. However, one will be surprised by a fairly large number of specific sexual references and references to actual persons with whom the imager is intimately involved.

The right and left doors could yield much material. Here indeed were observable psychological phenomena. But, subjective meaning and interpretation of these doors was not easy to determine. In fact, no clear-cut patterns of meaning emerged at first. I tried collecting hundreds of three-door responses, but my intuitive judgment yielded confusion. I thought many times, There is certainly a great deal of material here, but what does it mean?

For the next year I would periodically return to this "three door" image, but it was only the center door that could reveal meaningful material. The meaning of the right and left doors eluded me – or perhaps there was no special meaning to them at all.

One day I tried the image with one patient and something sparked in my mind. The material I was getting in the left door in combination with the center door was the essence or the nucleus of that person's *central* conflict. The right door was presenting some form of *resolution* to the conflict or some aspect of a hoped-of future.

I felt elated. And I collected further records of the three doors. Soon my elation was jolted, for I had come across two persons who reversed the proceedings. The right door revealed what I had found in others as occurring in only the left door. It seemed amazing to me. Right or left handedness made no difference, and neither were there any sex differences.

I found that five persons in approximately fifteen reversed the left/right doors and their meaning. Once I became alerted to this possible reversal, I would proceed to gather vital personality information that had previously escaped me.

It is my opinion that what will be revealed in the left door, in combination with the center and right doors, will contain many of the central aspects of that person's conflicts, styles, and defenses. But for clarity, it must be stated that sometimes the left door will reveal the core conflict of the person. This may be reversed in some people so that the right door reveals the core conflict. The resolution of the conflict then appears in the other door. Once the pattern can be seen, valuable material results.

The Three Gates

Another imaginary situation that contains the "three" is titled "The Three Gates." In this image subjects are asked to imagine three gates in a row, one behind the other, and to open each in turn and then report what they see, do and feel.

Again, I collected hundreds of responses from patients to this imaginary situation. Again, consensual validation between myself and the patients ensued.

After several months, certain patterns became clear. In about 90% of the persons responding to the three gates imaginary situation, the first and second gate responses led into the deeper levels of the unconscious of the person, that then seemed to be revealed from what they saw, did and felt as they entered the third gate.

With hundreds of respondents, it now seems clear that a highly reliable view of the person's unconscious can be observed from the patient's responses to the opening of the third gate. This seems to be true in 90% of the respondents. About 5% of the persons reverse this and give the first gate the same prominence that ordinarily appears in the third gate. Ordinary observation of the responses can quickly orient the interpreter to the point (first or third gate) that reveals the deepest levels of the unconscious.

There is a very small group of persons that go past the third gate to a fourth gate before revealing heavily unconscious material. Only actual experience with one's own imagery and that of others will yield the clarity I believe exists in the "Three Gates" imagery.

The Four Walls

One of the most complex imaginary situations to ask a person is to imagine (IS) "You are in the center of four walls, each wall being ten feet by ten feet and you are to imagine something on each wall." The reference to complexity is based on the experience that no recognizable definite, conceptual framework is evident from the clinical data and that generalizations cannot be made from the material in the other imagery productions. Despite this, on an individual phenomenological basis, the "Four Walls," as an imaginary situation, can be more enlightening for specific individuals as any I have been able to observe.

My original contention was that there was imagery that could comprehend the being-in-this-world of an individual. Indeed, for some persons, this is an adequate explanation and does quite verifiably represent the person's "world view." The usual symbolic predictability of the front view being the future and the back view being the past does not always seem to apply in this imaginary situation. No specific pattern of predictability seems to occur in contrasting right and left sides. Yet, despite the lack of symbolic predictability, the material elicited can be of the most unique and meaningful and sometimes the most powerful of any imagery.

Reminiscent imagery is one direction to which this imaginary situation can lead. Imagery that reveals undetected conflict may be seen on some of the walls. To develop this kind of imagery, I may ask at which wall one would care to spend the most time and which wall one would care to spend the least time.

As the imagery is experienced, one wall may be more emotionally charged than the others. It is possible to ask the person (IS): "Imagine entering the wall and then to continue the imagery." This may serve to clarify conflicts, significant areas of defenses as well as characteristic styles of behavior of himself and those he may include in the imagery. The variations are enormous and the therapist must be prepared to use his own creativity as the patient's imagery leads to points of heretofore undetected conflicts and feelings. It may be necessary to leave the four walls and go onto other areas of exploration if the patient develops his own directions of intensity.

Hazel, a twenty-four-year-old woman, responded to the four walls, in the following sequence:

At the Left: A forest with lots of tall trees and greenery.
Statement the Imagery Makes to You: "Come inside and find me."
In the Front: Big canvas painting with some splattering on it.
Statement from the Imagery: "You are always waving back and forth."
On the Right: Something splattered against the wall almost black.
Statement from the Imagery: "You're dead."
Behind Me: A little box like a peephole.
Statement from the Imagery: "I'm going to frustrate you."

She then said, "I keep looking forward to that canvas – the one with the splattering on it."

When I asked her at which wall she would like to spend the most time, it was at the left with the forest and trees. She said she would spend the least time in the one behind her where there was a little box with the peephole.

I then asked her to (IS) "Enter the right wall." She responded: "I see a long box like a coffin in pastel satin inside (she laughs strongly) with a light shining over it. I'm always a martyr. My mother called me a martyr and said I was too dramatic. Mother could drop dead from one of her epileptic convulsions. I was always afraid of what we children would do if she did, and what my responsibility would be if it did happen. Also I get a view of my grandfather's funeral."

Following this, she entered the Left Wall and said, "It's cool and refreshing. It's full of potential. I'm going to find new things. I'll find a cabin. It gives me feelings of growth and growing."

When I asked her to enter the Front Wall, she imagined, "My life the way it's been. To draw circles extending out. Like I used crayons when I was a kid – I would draw wavy lines over the page. It's like my life crossing lines – wavy – going from the Chicano life into other ways of life."

The strongest imagery occurred when I asked her to (IS) "Enter the Rear Wall." At first she couldn't and said all she could do is look through the peephole. A few moments later, she said, "I can do it now," and she imagined entering the Rear Wall. "I see a kitchen table that's bright, but it's dark all around it. It reminds me of the table we had in our kitchen. Sometimes it looks big. It's the old-fashioned chrome kind with dishes on it. Silverware and food in bowls. Now it changes to one setting. I walk up to it and sit down and look to the left to a door. It's dark behind there and it leads to my old bedroom. My door never opened all the way so you could see and hear things secretly. We could never say what we really thought. It was the house my mother and father got divorced in. I remember now suddenly my high school days. They were dreadfully unhappy. Mother was sick there. She has epilepsy. When she had seizures, I was blamed. I remember painting the four rooms to cover up the misery. It's a house I cried in a lot and got slapped around in. I was told how I must behave. My father lectured me about becoming a lesbian, because my aunt was and I liked her. I never knew what a lesbian was. My aunt, who was one, moved to San Francisco, and when I threatened to leave, they thought I would join her. I'm not a lesbian, but they kept thinking I was going to be one because I liked my aunt's freedom."

I find that usually one wall (which I cannot predict in advance) will be most emotionally charged and lead to powerful uncovering of reminiscent imagery co-mingled with present-day experiences. It can lead to the awareness of historical self-images. Significant people in a person's life may be revealed without interrogation. It can be most comprehensive for some persons and narrow in scope for others, but nearly always a rich source of meaningful material.

Body Routes to Conflicts

Imagining the inside of one's head can be used to elicit awareness of conflict and defenses. One man answered the question (IS): "Imagine entering your own head and tell me what you see and feel." Here is his report.

"As I enter my mind, (head) I see this complex array of machinery working with clocklike efficiency. Parts connected to parts, all interrelated. It seems to be an incredible precision factory except that I notice in one small corner there is a piece of machinery not working, just closed down.

"I try to start the machinery, but it won't work; the parts are all clogged and rusted. I'm going to clean them but seem to have a great deal of difficulty. It's as though it's too big a job and I want to give up. Finally, I ask someone for advice about repairing the machinery and he tells me to drop the parts in muriatic acid, to strip and clean them, which I do. I also polish all the brass parts, install new bands, overhaul the motor, but still I'm not happy, except in a localized way, still no satisfaction. Why not? The machinery is all fixed and in fine order. It's a magnificent sight, the pieces all fit and work together. Why no lasting joy with this? Is it something I did, but not me? I build houses; am I a builder? I'm a musical soul; but not a practicing musician? I collect antiques, but am I just a dilettante?"

In the realm of imaginary situations there is also the possibility for interbody journey, in which body parts travel and communicate between one person and another or between the patient and an other. An example might be, "What does your heart say to the heart of your girlfriend, and what does her heart say to yours?" One can include the head, heart, guts, penis, vagina and relate them to any conflict in the whole spectrum of possibilities. The following is an example of how a young woman responded at length to this form of imaginary situation – an interaction between her body parts and those of her parents:

1. My head would say to my mother's head: "I'm strong and I know how to compete with men on their terms. I won't be weak like you."
2. Heart to heart: "Look at yourself, mom. Become your whole self. Don't allow everyone to destroy your heart."
3. Guts to guts: "Don't play martyr with me. Give up trying to manipulate me. I'm tired of it."
4. Vagina to vagina: "I'm alive and healthy and like to be sexual. It's great!"
1. My mother's head to mine: "Straighten up, think of what people say, think of your reputation. Go to school. . . ."
2. Her heart to mine: "I need you, I love you, I am afraid for you. Let me and your father protect you.
3. Her guts to mine: "You must be cautious, the world is a frightening place, be afraid."
4. Her vagina to mine: "We are prisoner. This is the only part of a woman men like, watch out for them."
1. My head to my father's head: "I can compete with you and do well. I am as good as you."
2. My heart to his heart: "What are you doing? Are you crazy? You are hurting everyone you love. Stop it!"
3. My guts to his guts: "I'm not afraid of you any more."
4. My vagina to his penis: "Stay away from me! Learn to love your wife."
1. His head to mine: "You are sharp but need a lot of refining. Learn from me how to talk logically and be able to get your point across."
2. His heart to my heart: "Be careful, don't get hurt. I can't stand to see you hurt, because then I hurt too."
3. His gust to mine: "Enjoy life, do all you can, learn all you can. Don't be like your mother.
4. His penis to my vagina: "It would say nothing overtly, but subtly indicate that it was there, just there, not going to do anything but be omnipresent."

Other questions are available too, such as (IS): "Sense your body from your head to your toes; what is the body part core of your identity?" The body part mentioned may be the one which is most protected against – the one which the patient feels to be most "him" or most "her." Indeed, this may very well be the "centeredness" that Rollo May refers to when he says, "I assume that this person, like all beings, is centered on himself, and an attack on this centeredness is an attack on his existence. He is here in my office because this centeredness has broken down or is precariously threatened. Neurosis, then, is seen not as a deviation from my particular theories of what a person ought to be, but precisely as the method the individual uses to preserve his own centeredness, his own existence." (May, 1964, p. 22.)

Situation and Imagery

The concept of being-in-the-world, or man's sense of himself in his surroundings, always involves a *situation*. As long as he occupies space, he is in a situation. Ask yourself where you are right now, and you will be in your home, in school, in bed, etc. The use of the imaginary situation (IS) as part of the psychotherapeutic process is a natural product of this concept. For example, one can ask a person to (IS) imagine his favorite room in the house; then one can ask him to imagine himself in that room with his father. The possibilities of response are countless, the combinations endless; the results depend, of course, upon the reported responses as well as on the therapist's guidance and his own imagination. It is the hope of Psycho-Imagination Therapy to strengthen the role of the situation, to encourage patients in their *choice of actions* within the situation, and ultimately lead them to greater choice and freedom in their being-in-the-world.

Too, if one asks a person to imagine himself in a situation, it is also possible to be aware of his hesitancies, doubts, freedom, fears, anxieties, etc., as he imagines his feelings and actions in that situational context, be he alone in it or accompanied by an imagined "other."

By way of demonstrating the permutations of situations, we arrive at the following list:

1. In some instances, the self is alone in a situation.
2. Then there are those instances in which the self is imagined in combination with an "other" in a situation.
3. There are those instances in which the self imagines only the other in a situation.
4. Then there is the self who imagines the other imagining the self in a situation.
5. And the self may imagine an other imagining yet a different other in a situation.
6. Finally, the self imagining the other imagining a different other who is imagining about the self in a situation.

On the Use of Imagination and Imagery

It is better to have the patient close his eyes or focus on a spot on the wall. All of us have been with people who, while sitting with us, have become engaged in mind-wandering; you have probably mind-wandered yourself. It is generally noticeable in that the mind-wanderer will be focusing his eyes on one spot. If he were not fighting social decorum, he would prefer mind-wandering with his eyes closed; therefore, I suggest that the patient close his eyes when he is asked to imagine something. I personally prefer the patient to sit in a reclining chair; a person in a horizontal position has greater avenue to imaginery than when he is vertical; when not using imagery, the chair can be returned to its erect position.

While the relationship of the patient and the therapist is basic, since we are both interacting upon each other, the use of imagination in the therapy should not detract from the establishment and enhancement of this relationship. As therapists, we must assist the patient's exploration but the actual direction of any imagery situation rests with the patient's responses and feelings. The more the imaginary situation illustrates the conflicts and strong reactions with the patient, the less necessary are interpretations that might ring of psychoanalytical pontification.

The patient has greater responsibility for his daydreams and for his responses to imaginary situations than for his dreams over which he has no control. So when he imagines a response to an imaginary situation and is "surprised" by his imaginery, he is quite aware that it came from himself and, thus, unquestionably relates to him. Certainly whether he is the participant or the observer in the imagery is important. When a combination of different imaginary situations is offered the person, the responses are more and more illustrative of his inner world of experience.

Through *imagination* we can help reveal the person's *conflicts* as a way of seeing together. The therapist and patient can share the experience. The *pain* and *anguish* are expressed for both to feel as the patient involves himself in imaginary situations. Certain *resistances* are seen by the *difficulties, hesitancies* and *blocks* expressed in imagination. Certain *vital memories* are *recalled* as a result of *association* to specific *imagery. Parental strategies* are revealed in imaginary situations, as well as the patient's *counterreaction strategies* to the parent. Transference reactions with the therapist are revealed by reaction to specific *imaginary* situations. Thus, imagination is in the *awareness of conflict.*

Predicting Imagery

To predict the reported imagery production in another person one has encountered for the first time would be virtually impossible. Yet, when two persons, intimately involved, are asked to predict each other's imagery reported separately and privately, surprising results may occur. For example, I have asked married couples each privately and silently to imagine five consecutive images and then to write them down on paper. I then asked each partner to predict the imagery of the other. A bimodal distribution of predictions seems to occur. That is, some couples were able to predict a good many of each other's imageries while others seemed to have little awareness of the other's imagery. The results of the dialogue that follows when a couple reveals their own imagery to their partner can be of great therapeutic value. It can heighten the degree of awareness for the person and the partner. Increased communication invariably results because the partner is seeing the other through his or her way of viewing the world. Even those who are poor at predicting the other's imagery now have a chance for awareness of the other heretofore overlooked viewpoint.

On the Manner and Style of Imagery

Not only do people differ in their responses to various imaginary situations, but there are countless variations of observable body reactions as well. Some patients have particularly strong reactions; they may laugh or cry as they imagine, yet show very little body movement. Others may move their arms or legs as they experience certain strong imagined feelings, but invariably – if my observation is correct – not until after the *felt* experience of the imagination. To one man, asked (IS) to imagine himself struggling out of a giant web, it seemed that he was involved in violent, muscle-exhausting movement; but despite all his loud grunts and groans, there was little large-scale activity of his body at all.

Each person seems to develop a style of his own as he involves himself in imagery and imagination. Some continue their imagery without requiring further stimulus from me, while others will rarely enlarge upon their imagery unless urged. It is precisely when a person seems to change an established "style" of response that I want to check further for possible significance. One man who seldom opened his eyes during imaginary situations finds it difficult to close his eyes when imagining his mother.

Then there are times when a person may report vivid and terrifying imagery without indicating any feelings which match the intensity of that which he is imagining. This may sometimes be due to the patient's having so internalized his imagery that he does not show the overt signs of his terror; at such points my experience indicates that it is best to ask the person for his feelings, to assess his intensity without stopping the flow of imagery. I once asked a man to (IS) imagine two chipmunks, one on each hand. He said that they both came up to his eyes and scratched them out. It was to me an obviously terrifying sequence of imagery, yet his reporting of it was neutral as reciting the time of day. Asking him to finish the sentence (FTS) "I am afraid to see _____" at once brought his body into rapid movement as he squirmed and finally answered, "My penis."

Thus, a feeling may yield an image and an image may yield a feeling. The more congruent the feeling and the image, the more impact, meaning and awareness.

Occurring less often is the phenomenon of the patient's thoughts being different from what his or her imagery reveals. I remember asking Clara, a young woman, to imagine (IS) walking up to herself and seeing herself asleep. She expressed an immediate thought, "I would wake her up." Then she added, "But I see her sleeping and I let her continue to sleep. I guess my head says one thing and my real me says another thing."

This phenomenon can sometimes be evoked when one asks the person to imagine a situation that involves sexuality. If the person shows embarrassment, he may instantly make a remark (many times quite funny) that precedes the actual imagery production. In such cases, the person is quite aware that the thought is a mild defense against what he fears his imagery may reveal.

Phenomenology

Merely stating that each person is unique is useless, unless one respects the specific uniqueness. Phenomenology is a way of revealing and respecting this uniqueness. When a person is confronted by imagines, statements and imaginary situations, he is the only one in the world to "see and feel" them *that particular way*. For example, asking a person to (IS) imagine being nude in bed with his nude mother and father will elicit solely that individual's unique and special reaction. One need only ask this of a patient to verify the point.

While parental admonition invariably contains a frequent or occasional "Don't say that," or even a "Don't think that," it rarely prohibits a child to "Imagine that . . ." It is common in the experience of children and adolescents as well as adults to have "unbidden images" and imaginary situations come to mind. Essentially, the phenomenologist asks the questions "What?," "Whence?" and "Wherefore?" and all later questions are guided by the answers to the first.

From the Universal to the Specific

There are those imaginary situations which are seemingly general, neutral or noncontroversial, such as (IS) imagine some clouds, what color they are, etc. There is no spefificity – the person must organize the imaginative sequence with very little to go on. From this point, one can increase the details of the given imaginary situation and still arrive at a more or less generalized image. A further example might be to imagine (IS) that above you and behind you there is a force; what do you imagine it is and what does it do? Or, (IS) imagine looking through a telescope and tell me what you visualize; then turn around 180° and tell me what you imagine you see through another telescope stationed there. Or, (IS) imagine you have telepathic powers and you can imagine someone in a foreign country; tell me what they are thinking and in what country you imagine them to be. There are a hundred other examples, but suffice it to say that the initial emphasis is on the universal or the general, with a gradual shift toward specificity. There is, of course, no perfect scale by which to calibrate increments of specificity, but if I should ask a patient to close his eyes and (IS) imagine my face in front of him and imagine my saying something to him, then I am indeed getting quite specific. After a good trusting relationship is developed between the therapist and the patient, the therapist can offer specific imaginations very directly without encountering a great deal of defensiveness.

One woman who had made considerable progress in her therapy and had expressed a strong desire to work on her sexual problem found it relatively easy to accept an imaginary situation which would have been an impossible assignment months before, i.e., imagine (IS) entering your father's penis. A though imaginary situation, undoubtedly, but she accepted it well and despite a certain obvious anxiety, she attempted to allow her imagination to operate.

One may frequently be surprised by some individuals who respond to the most specific imaginary situations in the earliest moments of therapy. Their readiness is apparent in their attitude and in the degree of involvement; they seem open, too.

Spontaneous Imagery

The most common form of imagery in man is spontaneous and arises before our "inner eyes" without any apparent stimulus from any specific source. Augusta Jellinek, originator of the term "spontaneous imagery," put it most aptly when she stated, "These images are experiences as they would originate independently as though we were only spectators and not the source of these productions." (Jellinek, 1949, p. 372.) Anyone who has asked a person to "just imagine anything that comes to you," with no regard for direction or specific content, will know that surprises never cease for the person imagining, who may express discovery, amusement or shock and for the therapist himself, who may be quite astonished by the unexpected nature of the imagery. Most frequently the imagery seems to flow into a continuous stream of scenes and actions. It is quite likely, from observations, that verbal reporting of spontaneous imagery, when uninterrupted and prolonged, provides the same function of release as painting or similar diversions. Nearly everyone is able to describe adequately his imagery, and these word pictures are usually much more complete, much more open to meaning and awareness of unconscious processes than other, more "artistic" means of expression and exploration.

As a person grows to trust his spontaneous imagery during the therapeutic dialogue and beings to see meaning and direction from it, he can begin to trust his spontaneous imagery when he is outside the therapy situation and can begin to derive his own meanings and directions. These "waking dreams" allow the person to consciously observe and interpret his own productions. We are likely to remember our imagery with greater clarity than our dreams; indeed, there are some people who claim to never remember dreaming who may suddenly report having dreamed after having been involved in spontaneous imagery for a time, such is its impact.

Directed Imagery

Directed imagery intends for the patient to react to images presented to him. This does not mean that the patient's spontaneity is sacrificed, however; the directed image may very well serve as a springboard for continuous spontaneous imagery. In essence, no matter how direct the therapist's suggested image may be, he does not suggest the entire imaginary sequence. He may offer direction whenever he feels it is needed, and if the patient offers a spontaneous scene, he would certainly regard it as an appropriate point for further study by imagery. Directed imagery by no means takes the patient's responsibility for his own image productions away from him.

Horowitz and Becker found in studies of intrusive thinking "that the specificity of instructions for reporting visual images increases the tendency to form as well as to report images." (Horowitz and Becker, 1971, p. 39.) As such, directed imagery has certain obvious advantages for the therapeutic production of images.

Nonsymbolic Imagery

"Imagine you are casting a fishing line into a river and tell me what you will come up with," I asked Tommy, a thirty-five-year-old man. He answered, "My grandfather's law books," and began to talk about his conflict with authority and his fear of being "caught," even though he had done nothing to be caught for. It is with such an example that I introduce those images that elicit conflict from a nonsymbolic imaginary situation. These imaginary situations are countless; they are often enormously indicative of a patient's internal conflicts as the image is unveiled and the concomitant feelings explored. This is not to say that such imaginary situations cannot yield some form of symbol, or that they are devoid of all symbolism. If I were to ask (IS): "Imagine that you are drunk; say something to your wife," a patient might imagine, in response, that terrible monsters are descending upon him. There might be no direct reference to his wife at all, but the symbolism is palpable. Clearly it is impossible to draw any absolute line of demarcation between the symbolic and the nonsymbolic, but my experience indicates that there is a category of nonsymbolic questions which tend to evoke imagery of a generally nonsymbolic nature; in asking a person to (IS) imagine a hoax he might play on someone, it is rare indeed to get a symbolic answer: a specific, concrete image is virtually always elicited.

The important aspects of imagery are the mode of its use in the therapeutic process, the degree to which it affords awareness of the patient's internal conflicts, its value as a tool by means of which to focus the need for change. Past experience, the continual use of imagery vis-a-vis patients and their responses – these will fashion my selection of image-questions whether they be symbolic or nonsymbolic. Within each patient lies the kernel of image possibilities. Within the therapist lies the kernel of intuitive application, plus the knowledge of human dynamics and psychopathology. Moreover, while I stress here the use of imagery, the reader should not be ignorant of the Finish-the-Sentence technique, the Most-or-Least question, or the Self-and-Other question, all of which can be introduced as needed.

One of the nonsymbolic imaginary situations that I find useful is (IS): "Imagine you are a baby in a baby's room and that in the space of three to five minutes you grow to your present age." This exercise affords the person a chance to view his development, the strategies of significant people in his life, and his own counterraction strategies. Critical points of identity development and conflict resolution may be illustrated. It is rare that the person will not want to break out at some point and leave the room. Those patients who cannot, or don't want to, are troubled by other areas of conflict resolution which need to be examined further.

(IS) Imagine carrying yourself up a mountain, or imagine various people carrying you up a mountain; relate all the connected feelings. This imaginary situation is helpful in revealing a patient's awareness; should the roles in the IS be reversed, further feelings are elicited; invariably the responses are nonsymbolic.

Included in the domain of nonsymbolic imagery are those imaginary situations in which one is asked to imagine holding or touching another person, or being touched *by* another. When I once asked a woman to (IS) imagine her father's hand on her back, she shrieked, "Oh, I can't stand that!" leading to an exploration of her relationship to men. Further, the imagery may be related to body focusing, i.e., (IS) imagine whispering something in your father's ear; then imagine him whispering something into your ear. Once again, the number of similar imaginary situations is vast, the answers almost always nonsymbolic. Jerome L. Singer (1965), in his book *Daydreaming,* reports on a daydreaming exercise of his own device, a fairly extensive personal experiment. In observing and collating his results, he concluded that ". . . the more general trend, however, was for the occurrence of memories or fantasies that were not specifically symbolic in content." My own experience tends to confirm his view: most imagery reported by patients is nonsymbolic. But be that as it may, clearly it is what one *does* with the imagery – how one uses it to help the patient – that really matters.

Symbolic Imagery

The history of symbolic imagery can be traced back to the work of Caslant, Desoille, Leuner, Assagioli, and – to be sure – Freud and Jung. It might be expedient (but perhaps overly simplistic) to say that symbolic images are those which are representational of certain people in the patient's life or certain elements of his life without his awareness that that is what they signify.

As Gendlin (1962) and others have shown, the act of symbolizing is a creation of meaning out of experiencing. It is a formation of an organized pattern which comprehends and clarifies what might be diffuse, plural, or a combination of different elements. The Guided Affective Imagery of Leuner uses ten standard imaginary situations; they are presented to the patient in order to elicit symbolic aspects of conflict. He offers, for example, (IS) imagine a swamp in the corner of a field and imagine something coming out of it. Should the patient imagine some sort of monster or dragon, the therapist will aid him fight the creature by direct confrontation, offering all sorts of aid to the patient to help him win; possible methods involve exhausting the monster, feeding it, or engaging in other neutralizing procedures. It is from the symbolic process of confronting the monster and successfully destroying or neutralizing it that an improvement in life situations springs. The monster may very well represent a father figure in the patient's life, but his possibility is ordinarily left unmentioned as the patient proceeds through the symbolic imagery of the situation.

My own experience leads me to conclude that symbolic figures are frequently translated into nonsymbolic ones. Assagioli (1965) quotes a case history of Robert Gerard in which the patient was instructed to imagine that he was descending to the bottom of the ocean. As he descended he was attacked by the image of a powerful octopus. The therapist asked him to visualize rising to the surface and taking the octopus with him. Upon reaching the surface, the octopus seemed to change into the face of the patient's mother; this revealed the extent to which she was at the root of the neurosis.

I include symbolic imagery in this discussion both for the evaluation and definition of internal conflicts as well as for focusing change. My experience indicates that the use of symbolic imagery alone is insufficient to deal with all the needs and problems of a patient new to therapy. The complexities of human dynamics are so vast, so fantastically different, that effective treatment demands the integration of symbolic *and* nonsymbolic imagery within the fabric of the therapeutic dialogue. Symbolic imagery alone falls short, does not allow the patient to leave his session with the awareness and insight necessary to permit him to cope in his day-to-day functioning. My own experience with imagery impels me to utilize as many forms of imagery as may be necessary to reeducate the patient, to help him deal with and resolve his conflicts. One of the advantages that symbolic imagery provides is a decreased ego-involvement on the part of the patient as he engages himself with the imagery. *Increased* ego-involvement within the context of the imaginary situation, however, does not necessarily handicap the patient, especially as it often leads to conflict resolution – as the focusing techniques. For example, in the following chapter which deals with focusing, a man in the course of therapy is asked to imagine himself in his mother's vagina and fight his way out, this as a means of breaking his feelings of castration. He succeeds, with a very positive result. Ego-involvement was certainly at a maximum and the symbolism at a minimum, but the technique was a powerful and effective avenue for change, nonetheless.

A given imaginary situation may produce either symbolic or nonsymbolic imagery. Take the following example: (IS) Imagine something behind you and something in front of you. One woman saw her mother behind her in a rage, and her husband in front of her, smiling. There was nothing symbolic about her imagery and we were able to proceed from that point to certain specific awareness.

Yet a man, when asked the same question, imagined a very comprehensive symbolic imagery which he fought through in a symbolic manner. No psychologist has yet been able to predict which type of imagery will occur to any given person engaged in any given imaginary situation.

Here is a written report of the man describing his symbolic imagery session:

"I went into Joe Shorr's feeling better than I had ever felt – than I have felt in a long, long time, feeling very positive from the previous group session, for many reasons. I came in basically feeling terrific. We discussed all the good things and some of the progress, and so on, and what the previous group perhaps represented. Then he gave me the imagery of 'there is someone in front of me and someone in back of me.' I immediately saw someone with an erected penis in back of me – nude – a woman – a nude woman in front of me and I was nude. And I got very nervous and fought the image and tried to change it. It was very hard at first to change it. And it took me a few beats. Then finally I did change it – it reeked with the phallic situation, homosexuality and so on, and that scared me, so I got away from that and saw myself on a large, open plain, like a desert, and in front of me was an old kind of covered wagon – a western wagon – crickety thing, and I was walking towards it as it was going in front of me. And then a jet airplane – the nose of a jet airplane came and prodded me towards it. It kept pushing me, pushing me, making me go faster and faster, as though it wanted me to make more progress. So I stopped and I told Joe that, and he said, 'Let's get back to the other one.' So I went back into it, and he asked me to turn around and to see who the man in back of me was, and when I turned around, I couldn't tell. It was all very dark and it was like there were black strips – he was covered like a mummy, but very sloppily covered And I looked and I tried and tried to figure it out – who that person might be. And I couldn't do it. I told him it was just total darkness. It was like I didn't see anything at all, but I knew something and someone was there. So he asked me to tear away the strips of whatever that was there and – oh, no – before he said that, he said, 'Put a flashlight on the thing,' to find out what it was. I couldn't figure out whose face was there and so then I put the flashlight on it and I saw strips of 35 mm film, so it was like the guy – the person – was encased like the mummy, with film, so then he told me to clear away the strips of film to see who was underneath it. When I did, I saw a large sword, a very pointed, very dramatic and beautiful sword, and sort of surprised me. It was sitting on a pedestal and on the pedestal was a dried prune and a walnut, and I told him and we were both a little confused about that. So then I stayed with the imagery and all of a sudden, the point of the sword started tilting towards me and it caught me underneath the chin, and I said, 'What the fuck is this?' and then all of a sudden a hand came into frame and he lifted me high in the air and I was hanging by the point of the sword tucked underneath my chin. And when I took a better look at who it was, it was like a mythological God. It had a helmet on, like Mercury without the wings. It was a huge person, like in metal or whatever. It was a cross between Father Neptune – or Neptune – and Mercury. The face had a beard and so on – there was nothing – I couldn't really define the face. I tried to figure out who it was and I couldn't. And all of a sudden, Joe asked me to deal with it – or Joe asked me to give it a name and I felt like I was in a cartoon strip and then all of a sudden – oh! and then the thing had a two-foot erection4his penis was two feet long. And the name I saw – I called him God. I called it God, and then Joe later asked me to find – to put another name across its chest, although I didn't see it clearly, but what came out was 'King' – K.I.N.G. King. And the chest was throbbing, very big and powerful and proud. Then I had to deal with the thing a little more, and blood was coming out of my chin from the point of the sword and I looked very small up on top of the sword – the person was a giant. And so I started to deal with it, trying to get down, and he took the sword and flicked his wrist and sent me flying, and I got clobbered against the wall, as though I was very impotent and had no chance against this monster. And then I said, 'Well, I don't like that, so let me do it again.' So he flipped me again on the – from the point of the sword and I went sailing, and before I hit the wall, I – I made a hole in the wall for myself, or I allowed a hole to be there and I went soaring into the universe, and Joe later said, '. . . went soaring into oblivion.' I think that's what he said. So what I had – it was – uh – dark, I was flying through space, it was dark with the sky and the stars and so on. And so I stopped and was very confused and – I was confused about how I could've walked in there so happy, so positive and so much enjoying the seeming progress, and so Joe, realizing it was important for me to get back at this big fucker, made me deal with coming back to deal with it and so I flew back – flew myself back – and I saw myself coming towards him from far – from high above – and my feet – I came down feet first and then I belted him in the head, then knocked him over. And as he fell, it built and built and built, like I was an animal – a vicious animal – and I started punching the shit out of him. I – uh – I went and broke his cock over my knee and I took my knee and I started belting him in the side of the face – in front of the face – his nose – with my knee and my fist – I kept pounding and punching – I kicked his body several times – I took my knee and I – I squashed it into and rammed it into his groin – I – I beat him mercilessly – I just didn't stop – I kept on going – and – and then in reality as I was sitting in the chair relating this or seeing this, the impulse was such that even my foot kicked out once, – my whole body was tense and I was uptight and I wanted to, like, scream and I felt a need – I even expressed it – I told Joe I wish there was something, like a huge, stand-up bag that I could keep belting now – I felt the need to want to punch and punch and punch and punch. And as I said, a couple of times my body jerked – and I felt like kicking out or punching or whatever it was I did. And, God, I wanted to kill this thing – I – how I wanted to kill it – I kept at it and I kept at it and I just – this son-of-a-bitch wouldn't die. Then I went and I stomped on his eyes and two geysers came up and again it was like – it was like rendering me impotent, it just threw me up in the air with these two gushes and whatever fluid was coming out of his eyes and I couldn't get down off of it and I knew I had to, so I finally broke loose and I jumped – I was about twenty, thirty feet high, and I jumped off that geyser that was holding me up there, and I jumped on his stomach, and that hurt him – and I kept up and I – I just kept it up and I went and grabbed his sword and – oh – and then his tongue – I – he started flicking his tongue out or something and I started clawing at it and then – and my hands wouldn't do anything – so I started biting and I was biting his tongue and spitting out the pieces. I kept telling Joe how much I wanted this thing to die – I wanted to kill it – I wanted to kill it desperately and he told me to get at the heart – go get his heart – rip his heart out and I tried and I started clawing away at his chest and I couldn't get to it to – uh – I couldn't break open his chest and uh – and uh – oh, his chest turned – as I was beginning to make progress, his chest turned into metal – into iron – it was like he had one of those iron chest protectors on. So again I was rendered helpless. I couldn't make headway with this prick, so I kept going and kept going and I finally went and I grabbed – I knew I had to kill it and I went and grabbed his sword and I – the thing – you know – it was – boy – it was trying to get away from me and it was almost getting away from me after all the pummelling I did, the son-of-a-bitch – and I was squeezing his throat – I was squeezing his throat. He uh – no, no – uh, yeah – right, and he started crawling away from me, so I went and grabbed his sword and I – uh – went for his heart and finally it pierced his heart and – uh, he let up a roar that was just incredible. The sword pierced the iron and went into his heart and out of it came a black – a gush of black fluid like that which comes from a squid – the ink from a squid – uh – but it was a huge, like an atomic mushroom blast, that's what – it was all black and gray. And his face came closer and closer to me – it was roaring, it was like he was still coming fucking after me, he didn't stop, then I jumped down and I made sure I missed his mouth, of course, and I jumped on his neck and – uh – evidently the weight of that finally got him, and I went down with him and it was like we were falling twenty stories, and he came down with a crash, and again I started kicking and punching and fucking, kneeing the son-of-a-bitch – I – I hated him, I wanted to kill him so and I – he still would not die, after all of this. And – um – I had his throat – that's what it was – I had his throat and while I was squeezing his throat, he could barely breathe – his tongue came out and that's when I started biting his tongue and spitting out the pieces, while I was squeezing his throat, and he still wouldn't die, so I took his sword, and I – uh – sliced his neck and I – uh – severed his head and his head came off. And the bod – while the body was still just moving around a little, the fuckin' head was still coming at me – uh – uh – I mean it wouldn't stop, so I didn't know what to do – oh, and then I punched its eyes – oh, I looked at its eyes and there were – they were black with fire in it – and – uh – then I remember telling Joe it was like watching a Saturday cartoon – uh – on TV – and then I took some implement, I don't know what exactly, and I started scraping out of his skull – the base of his skull – uh – the head – all the stuffing – all the stuff that was inside his skull, I started pulling out like you pull stuffing from a turkey and I did that and the fucking head still looked at me and still started coming at me so then I took his flesh and skin and I started ripping it off his skull – and – uh – there was – uh – that, and – that still didn't stop him. It was as though he were still alive and I was still ineffectual in terms of destroying and killing this thing, and then finally all I had left was the skull, and bare – bare-boned skull, and I said 'Okay, that should do it, hopefully,' and then I put it on a shelf, and then all of a sudden it started moving and there was – there was Joel Grey – uh – with the same makeup he had on in "CABA-RET" and he slid the skull across – uh – that was hiding his face; and there he was, smiling at me and then he brought the skull back in front of his face to cover it and I felt again that I had lost, that I had no chance to win against this fucker – uh – I am now consciously aware – I am not going to be put – the – the thing is, I'm ready to do battle and I wanna – I want to kill – I want to get all that hostility – that hatred that I have in me – uh – for these – all these years, well – I will kill him. I will win. I do win. I am me."

The point I am making is this: the same imagery situation might have produced nonsymbolic imagery – the image of the patient's boss, the patient's sister, etc. Both possibilities can exist. If symbolic imagery is produced, I will attempt methods of resolution using symbolic imagery. With specific nonsymbolic imagery I may use some of the focusing techniques, or an interior dialogue psychodrama resolution.

Dreams

Looking back historically we find that soon after Freud abandoned his "concentration technique" of eliciting patients' imagery, he published his monumental work, *The Interpretation of Dreams*. Rather than negating the imagery, the book elevated its value to a new plateau. Still, wider possibilities remained unexplored, and Jung's preoccupation with active imagery essentially involved dream work.

While the major emphasis of this discussion has to this point been on waking imagery, I welcome and encourage patients to remember and report their dreams.

Images from our dreams are pictures of our conflicts and intimacies and basically
reflect what we think of ourselves and what we really think of others. Beyond
doubt, they are a useful guide to the internal conflicts of the person. Dreams as
such are a complex and varied phenomena, and I can only limit my discussion
to a few points.

Psycho-Imagination Therapy approaches dreams from several viewpoints. The
first is simple, relating as it does to those dreams that have clear and obvious
meaning which can be shared by patient and therapist. The second approach
encompasses any or several of the four basic techniques generally used in Psycho-
Imagination Therapy, with prime focus on meaning, direction, and conflict, i.e.,
what the dream signifies, what mode of experience or behavior conflicts with
other possible options.

The Most-or-Least technique may be brought into play with regard to a given
element of the dream or even in regard to the "title" of the dream. One person
gave the title of her dream as "The Train." I then asked her to tell me (M/L)
the most unlikely person to be on the train. She answered, "My father" (who
played no part at all in the dream). She then reflected that she ". . . never did
anything with him as a youngster." The dream, in this light, began to make sense
to her, and she connected it to her present behavior with her boyfriend. Also, the
phrase "to please" appeared in her dream several times. On the basis, I inquired
(M/L) who was the most difficult person for her to please, and (M/L) who was
the easiest person to please. At this point, she experienced a flash of anger at her
boyfriend for the difficulties he had set up to be pleased by anything she did. In
a way this cleared the path for her; she became aware of how she was being
defined by him and resolved to take action.

Her dream involved a train ride in the course of which she was trying to please
her boyfriend Frank. He did not seem to respond to her, did not seem to know
how to handle himself in the social situation of the dining car, etc. She was
frustrated as she tried to buttress his self-confidence and overlook his lack of
sophistication. I asked her to imagine (IS) two different trains, using dual imagery. She gave this response:

1. Very streamlined – sleek,   2. Big chuggy – old fashioned like
   sophisticated.   my mother.

She then volunteered that she was the sleek train and her boyfriend was the
unsophisticated, big, chuggy train, just as she had always felt about her mother.
The meaning of this did not escape her, nor did her boyfriend escape her feelings
of anger.

Sometimes one may ask for a title to a dream; after getting it, one can then
ask (M/L) for the most *opposite* title. This may or may not provide clarification
as to meaning, and can sometimes serve to refine the feelings connected with the

dream.

Many dreams naturally indicate some internal conflict. We must try to recognize the elements in opposition and ask the person to contrast these elements. It is helpful to ask where the dream took place (the "setting" of the dream itself); often one location has greater emotional significance than another. It also seems to me a good idea to ask the patient to imagine the people in the dream, and to imagine what they might say to him or her. Then I ask the patient to "guess" the names of the unidentifiable persons in the dream. The "guessed" names may relate strongly not only to the dream, but to the patient's life.

I agree with Jung's suggestion that in the therapy session the dream be "continued" beyond its actual termination, that the patient be encouraged to imagine the consequences that might occur from this further development of the "story." At times I will ask the patient to imagine any one of the dream's personae speaking directly to me, the therapist, and then to imagine what I might say in reply.

The reminiscences of imagery evolving from a dream indicates residual feelings and conflict; thus, a springboard is provided for further imaginary situations. Furthermore, asking the patient to imagine that he himself is each of the various parts of the dream (as the Gestalt therapists are fond of emphasizing) is beyond question a valuable approach. I suggest additional scrutiny of meaning and interpretation.

What follows is a dialogue in which a patient, Kenneth, reported one of his dreams to me. My own comments are inserted parenthetically throughout his report.

"I dreamt I was in the living room of a house with another man. He had a large bag of marijuana and I had a small one. I knew that someone was coming to get the stuff. The other man and I hid our bags and he left. Then I dreamt that a 'gangster-type' came into the living room and asked me for the stuff. I quickly gave him mine, but panicked for a second because I couldn't remember where the other bag was. Then I remembered it was hidden under the cushions of the couch. Very relieved, I found it and gave it to him. He told me that they would still have to kill me because I knew too much. I told him it was OK and that I wouldn't tell anyone, but he said I would still have to be killed. He disappeared and in came the 'killer.' He was thin, with shoulder-length black hair, and good looking He came at me making hand movements that appeared to be ballet-like. He was also wearing some type of costume which I vividly remember was white with colored polka dots. He came at me and I grabbed his arms. I remember trying to twist them with no apparent effect on him and getting frustrated at the thought that he must be double-jointed. I then started scratching him which seemed to have an effect on him. However, he backed away and revealed that he possessed fingernails several inches long and gave me a look as if to say that if scratching was what I wanted, he could do it in spades. I then remember deciding to charge at him, no matter what happened, so I put my head down and charged at him. I got in close to him, picked him up, turned him upside down and bashed his head into the ground.

"In discussing this dream with Joe, the following came out: 1) When asked to name the dream, I immediately thought of the title "Rebirth." 2) The most obvious meaning of the dream (certainly as to its conclusion) was that in my pretherapy days, I probably would have given up any hope of fighting the killer and chosen the easier way out of just letting him kill me. Now, as a result of therapy and, as evidenced by various little incidents in recent months, I decided not to be afraid of what might happen (putting my head down and taking my chances) and to fight back even though this required more effort than allowing him to kill me."

(I asked him the Self-and-Other question: What choice did you have in the dream? I also asked him for imagery of the small bag, and what it would say to the large bag.)

Small Bag	Large Bag
"I want to be as big and cool as you."	"You're OK. You're fairly cool – but not one of the 'in' group or one of us."

He volunteered, "I have always been on the periphery – never an outcast – not completely accepted as a true inner group."

3) "When asked to think of the person *most opposite* to me in the dream, I couldn't think of anyone right off, and then I flashed on 'old Jews' which I'm sure included but was not limited to my father. To me, historically, 'old Jews' are weak, can't fight back and are therefore killed at the killer's whim. I'm sure that despite my rebirth in the dream, I still see myself as an 'old Jew' to a certain degree."

(I asked him the Finish-the-Sentence: Old Jews _____; to which he said, "never fight and play dead.")

4) "One of the most interesting insights was the interpretation of the movements of the killer. In describing the dream, I referred to them as ballet movements, but in the subsequent discussion, I realized that they were the type of hand movements made in karate routine. This fit perfectly into the 'masculinity measured by strength and toughness' trip that I guess I'm still into, wherein I've many times fantasized being proficient at karate and how impressive (especially to women) that would be; I actually once started karate lessons but quit shortly thereafter."

(I asked him to (IS) imagine the name of the killer. To which he answered, "Steve." "Steve" led him to associate the name "Doug" a few seconds later. I then asked him to (IS) imagine Doug and himself on a balance scale when he became aware that Doug was the trim man who was divorcing the woman whom Kenneth, a lawyer, was representing.)

5) "The last, most nebulous and therefore, most frustrating, recollection was the attempt to determine who the man was that had the large bag in the beginning of the dream. I finally decided it was the husband of a client of mine in a divorce case. What was frustrating is that this man does not, at least consciously, impress me; I have never thought of, or have any present desire to be like him. The only thing Joe and I could think of was that, by virtue of being a relatively good-looking, trim man for his age (early forties), he represented the attractive, self-confident man I would like to appear as."

Depth Imagery

A depth reaction can be viewed from many directions. A person may have a deep set of reactions to just the mere presence of the therapist. I have also observed intensive emotional reactions to a mildly reflected statement in the Rogerian fashion. Furthermore, one cannot help but observe enormous individual differences of intense emotional reactions to the same imaginary situation. But, there are certain imaginary situations that nearly always elicit a profoundly deep set of reactions, no matter who the patient may be.

These highly emotionally charged imaginary situations should be employed with caution and with some awareness of where the patient is and what he appears ready to face. Needless to say, at these times the mutual trust between patient and therapist should be at its optimum. Support and therapist encouragement may be of vital importance during such imagery sequences.

One can ask, for example, the imaginary situation (IS): Imagine that you are a child and you are crying; now imagine your mother and father 'licking' away the tears.

In all but a very few instances very powerful reactions will emerge. Some people do not wish to cope with their strong reaction and say such things as "I'll punch her out" or "I'll hit him in the teeth." For the majority of the persons the imagery continues with surprise, horror, anger, shame or love and tender feelings. What becomes clearer is the way in which the mother or father defined the patient and how he began to define himself. Sharp differences between the actions of the mother and the father are frequently noted.

I ask you to imagine the following response is being related by a twenty-seven-year-old woman and then ask what your reactions might be.

"My mother is licking my tears and as they drop from her tongue, they fall on my breasts and vagina and burn holes into them until there is nothing left of me."

Or the response of a forty-five-year-old man:

"My father licks all my tears just as they emerge. He is determined not to have mercy. He then proceeds to lick me all over my body including my asshole. The obliging bastard."

I am certain that you cannot fail to note the intensity and the depth of the feeling presented.

One young woman, Wilma, reported the imagery in a halting manner. She was breathing very heavily and sighing frequently. Here is her report of her depth reaction:

"Imagining one of my parents licking my tears is impossible with my father. It is only possible with my mother if I am a baby who isn't aware of what is going on. Then she would really have to be in a really different mood than I've ever seen her. My mother is very clean. From her I have learned to cringe when sleeping in anyone else's bed unless they have freshly laundered sheets. She can't even handle it when I lick a spoon, after trying whatever is in a cooking pot, and putting it back in the pot. Even though the heat would kill any germs. My mother would be able to hold me closely but I couldn't handle it also if she licked my tears unless I was an incoherent baby. In some ways I have forcibly gone against her. I allow my cat to eat off my plate. My friends and my younger brother are welcomed to share my glass or silverware, plate or food. Besides my mother just doesn't get that close physically. We can go up and hug her easily. When she plays with my brother or me (a year ago or before) she would tickle us or hold us so we couldn't get away. But as a rule she isn't overly affectionate. To touch us, she does things like holding one of our faces to the light to look for blemishes. When she does this it doesn't feel like she is being critical. It is more of a way for her to be physical with us, I think.

"With my father it was impossible to imagine it because even if I were a tiny incoherent baby. I guess I couldn't imagine it because I always have such a strong feeling that he would be sexual and not just tender and loving. The feeling is that he gains out of any touch instead of giving. He is taking and getting a thrill off me that he has no right to. I always feel powerless with feelings of being taken – that is another reason I used to not want to be a woman. As a woman I feel very powerless or am reduced to the level of a child, who, of course, has no power. When a man looks at me or says things I always feel anger because I have no means to stop him from visually raping me. That is usually what it feels like when men 'look me over.' Usually, if I am feeling especially hateful, I try to outstare them. Of course, from my mother I learned that when men look you over that they are mentally raping you. Maybe not. She probably never said it that directly but the feeling came from her. The words probably just came from someone else. She doesn't trust any men. I, of course, went against her about the age of 16 or so. I started going over to a guy's apartment, calling them and just wholeheartedly trusting them. In fact, I went overboard. I would trust anyone that gave me half a chance. Immediately I would do anything for them and give of myself till I was eventually knocked down, every time. It's interesting the spectrum I've gone through. From complete trust to no trust and a lot of hate and suspicion. I am aware that my worst area for mistrust and terrible feelings are towards Mexicans and old men. They only take for themselves. They can't give as far as I am concerned, of course, it's far too generalized. There are probably some who are quite giving but it just is too hard to get past my feelings to find out. It also seems like these two groups are the most attracted to me of all men. So I also hate it because I want to be wanted by young liberal longhairs who don't want me."

As each of these persons continued in their imagery it led to reminiscent imagery of crucial incidents in their lives. Awareness of the self image versus the prescribed image was sharply focused. The intensity serves as a natural bridge to the focusing procedures to change the person's self-concept to a more authentic position from the previous false position.

Other imaginary situations that nearly always elicit a depth reaction are as follows:

1. Wake up as a baby. What do you feel and do?
2. You are in a cave and you are to call for help from your mother or father.
3. Take a shower with your mother or father.
4. You are in a playpen with your mother and father and you are all one year old.
5. Father or mother beating you up.
6. Look into a mirror, but instead of seeing yourself imagine someone else. Speak to each other.
7. Your mother or father walks into a room and finds you dead on the bed.

Again, it would be wrong to assume that certain imagery produces profound feeling reactions and the others have little or no effect. Experience with imagery indicates that strong emotional reactions can come with any image if the patient is ready to face something difficult within himself even if certain seemingly nonemotional imagery, such as a train or sled, is presented. Such a train or sled may be associated with guilt and shame feelings and would then need to be dealt with.

My own references to depth imagery here emphasizes those imaginery situations that seem to almost always elicit powerful reactions. Clinical judgment must be exercised in their use. They are most effective in impasse situations and other points in therapy where the clinical judgment of the therapist comes into play.

CHAPTER 13

Imagery and the Self Image

Man's preoccupation with his self image is as ancient as recorded history and as contemporary as this moment. It is unlikely that anyone has better expressed this concern than Robert Burns in "To a Louse":

O wad some power the giftie gie us
To see ourselves as others see us!

Defining the self has presented problems for professionals, and in 1978 an entire conference at Northeastern University in Boston was devoted to this task.

The concept of self is an elusive one which includes self-control, self-knowledge, self-esteem, etc. It is essentially a self-system that has as its main concern security operations to prevent anxiety in interpersonal relationships, as H. S. Sullivan suggests.

Currently psychotherapists have presented formulations that view cognitions about oneself as vital mediators in the maintenance and modification of behavior; and in social psychological theories involving attribution, cognitive dissonance, and self awareness. Understanding how attitudes about the self are developed and maintained has thus become increasingly important.

Since the self is such an elusive concept, how can we actually be concerned about it? The answer lies in the fact that all of us have a theory about ourselves, about what kind of person we are. Our self-concept, whether it be as competent or incompetent, attractive or repulsive, honest or dishonest, worthy or unworthy, has an enormous effect on our behavior and thoughts. There is considerable evidence to support the belief that each of us has a self system – a set of attitudes towards ourselves, (Gorden and Gergin, 1968). We define ourselves by this self-system, yet our perceptions of how others see us is inextricably bound to our own self-definition. Harry Stack Sullivan (1953) stated that even when we are alone, our thinking, images, and behavior always relate to other people, real or imaginary.

A compelling aspect of the phenomenology of human experience is the sense of individuality and continuity that psychologists refer to as the self. By means of introspection and the observations of what others feel, say and do, each person gradually evokes a notion of who he is, and how he resembles and differs from other people.

When people are asked how they know that they possess certain characteristics, a typical answer is that they have learned about them from other people. A

319

more formal theoretical statement of this view has been articulated by the influential school of thought known as "symbolic interactionism." This theory proffers the idea of a "looking glass self" and asserts that one's self-concept is a reflection of one's perceptions about how one appears to others. This assertion has received widespread professional acceptance and is intoned with catechistic regularity in many leading texts on social behavior (e.g., Raven and Rubin, 1976; D. J. Schneider, 1976; Secord and Backman, 1974).

Social philosophers and psychologists of the late 19th century such as Peirce (1868), James (1890), and Baldwin (1897) were precursors of symbolic interactionism in their emphasis on the self as a product and reflection of social life (Gordon and Gergen, 1968; Ziller, 1973). Cooley (1902), generally credited as the first interactionist, developed the idea of the looking glass self. He posited that the self is inseparable from social life and necessarily involves some reference to others. This process of social reference results in the looking glass self: "A self idea of this sort seems to have three principle elements: the imagination of our appearance to the other person; the imagination of his judgment of that appearance; and some sort of self-feeling, such as pride or mortification." According to Cooley, from early childhood our concepts of self develop from seeing how others respond to us: "In the presence of one whom we feel to be of importance, there is a tendency to enter into and adopt, by sympathy, his judgment of ourself" (p. 175). Mead (1934), the major theorist of symbolic interactionism, amplified and expanded the view of the self as a product of social interaction: "The individual experiences himself as such, not directly, but only indirectly, from the particular standpoints of other individuals of the same group or from the generalized standpoint of the social group as a whole to which he belongs" (p. 138). Essential to the genesis of the self is the development of the ability to take the role of the other and particularly to perceive the attitude of the other toward the perceiver. Mead's looking glass self is reflective not only of significant others, as Cooley suggested, but of a generalized other, that is, one's whole sociocultural environment. More recently, Kinch (1963) has summarized and systematized symbolic interactionist self theory by noting that it basically involves an interrelation of four components: our self-concept, our perception of others' attitudes and responses to us, the actual attitudes and responses of others to us, and our behavior.

The notion of an ideal self – what one would like or feels constrained to be – can also be posited. McDougall (1932), for example, described a "self-regarding sentiment" and stressed the active process of comparison that goes on between the actual and the ideal self. Socialization, according to McDougall, is in part the resultant of a continuously more effective and encompassing reconciliation of these two selves. Allport (1961), in his concept of the proprium, sought to bring together seven facets of selfhood, including the bodily self, continuity, self-esteem, extension, imagination, rational coping, and goal-directed or propriate striving. The degree to which these facets of the self are harmoniously integrated will determine the degree to which an individual becomes what he or she is capable of becoming.

To this I must add William James' (1890) little-reported concept of a growing awareness in the developing child of the disparity between what one wants and what the world is prepared to give.

I have already discussed the role of Karen Horney with her concept of Idealized Image and Despised Image in chapter one. I would like to re-emphasize that I have found her concepts of inestimable value.

The self is such a vast subject that it would be beyond the scope of one chapter even to introduce the subject properly. I have been attempting to give cogent highlights, but many volumes would be needed to be comprehensive. There is, however, one element of the relationship of the body to self in infancy that I would like to include before proceeding to the imagery processes and self.

As Gardner Murphy (1947) suggests, very little is known regarding individual variations in the early experience of the self. We can say that variations in intelligence make for variations in the complexity of the experience involved; among imbeciles, for example, we should expect the recognition of body boundaries to be retarded. Conversely, the early acquisition of an appropriate body vocabulary seems to accelerate the growth of self-awareness.

E. L. Horowitz has made profound observations with case studies of the localization of the self in early childhood which throw considerable light on the process by which consciousness of self grows:

> Joan, aged 3 years 8 months, was interviewed in the presence of her mother. Questions aimed at the discovery of the attitude of the child toward the inanimate objects about her revealed some concepts startling to the interrogator. The conversation developed somewhat as follows: "Who are you?" "Joan." (The child was well known to the interviewer and the question was designed to serve as a baseline.) "Who is Joan?" "Me." "Is this Joan (pointing and touching bed alongside)? "Is this?" "No." Touching the various objects as we proceeded, we drew such responses as: slipper-no, sweater-no, leg-no, head-no, body-yes, neck-no, etc. She seemed to localize Joan quite definitely in the abdomen and lower thorax; the back was not Joan, appendages and head were described as hers, but not her.
>
> This experience surprised us somewhat, and days later we were discussing it with a friend in a store when in walked a strange youngster, and we proceeded to demonstrate the phenomenon. Conversation yielded that the child's name was Lena; Lena was three years old (accuracy unchecked). Lena localized herself at first in the body. As we continued exploring, in order to check the consistency of the response, Lena appeared in her lower right jaw. She was not in the hand, arm, or

leg, nor in the eye, head, nor other (left) side. Lena seemed fixed in the lower right jaw. The definiteness of this localization may be indicated by her petulant response when we touched her right cheekbone and asked, "Is this Lena?" What is the matter with you? I told you three times this (pointing to lower right jaw) is me."

The following day, five days after the original exploration, a retest was made of Joan and she was found to be still in the same place, the belly and lower chest, but not in head, neck, arms, legs, nor back, nor dress, nor shoes.

Barbara, Joan's sister, at the age of 2 years 6 months, localized herself in the mouth region. The gesture indicating where Barbara is was this: hand across the mouth covering the chin and opened mouth, with the fingertips resting on the edges of the upper incisors. A pinch on the calf of her leg hurt "my leg," but not Barbara herself.

Mona, aged 4 years and 2 months, said not "Mona" but "my leg," "my head," though she had pointed to head as "me;" later she indicated her body. After a while, when asked in peek-a-boo fashion, "Where is Mona?" she tapped her head.

Doubtless the area in which the self is localized depends both on the way in which adults emphasize selfhood by touching and pointing and also upon the vital importance of the region from the child's point of view.

This, at least, is case study proof in infancy of the existence of a body part core of a person's identity which I have referred to in my work in body imagery (Singer and Pope, 1978).

The many aspects of self in development cannot be included because of the enormous scope of the subject. Suffice it to say we know the self is in constant flux from infancy, through early adolescence, to adulthood, and into old age. That it has historical and developmental processes makes it possible for us to think in terms of changes that may occur within life and therapy.

Imagery as Self-observation

All awareness of ourselves is subjective; as a result, we often turn our attention inward, attempting to know and to understand ourselves. In a general sense, the self may be revealed by self reference test items such as Gough and Heilbrun's Adjective Check Test (1965), or by introspective reporting.

Investigators have attempted to assess contrasts between the real and idealized selves, or aspects of the self, with ways in which their congruence or discongruencies can be measured. Many attempts to assess these differences (Wylie, 1974) make use of methods such as the Q sort (Butler, 1968; Butler and Haigh, 1954), the semantic differential (Pervin and Lilly, 1967), the interpersonal check list (Leary, 1957), and the Minnesota Multiphasic Personality Test (Rosen, 1956).

It is my contention, however, that the self may be even better revealed to the individual (especially in therapy) through the use of visual imagery as a form of *self-observation*. Self-observation in the make-believe play of children substantiates this point. For example, pretending is so common among children that we all readily accept it. As children develop, they practice a variety of make-believe selves and roles. Gradually, they learn to differentiate themselves from the surrounding world and to see the many options within themselves, a greater range of trial selves. This is indeed a form of self-observation. These differentiations ultimately become the basis of the more solid and separate self.

Our self-image may be the single most important concept in our consciousness. Right from the beginning it is not neutral, but evaluative. The child develops judgments about himself through such self-observation.

Throughout our lives, we require an accurate and acceptable self-image, and toward this end, we are constantly exploring, redefining, and evaluating ourselves. Great novels and dramas have been written about these struggles for self-knowledge and self-acceptance. However, the problem is basic and universal in human experience, and not confined to just a heroic few.

Thus, time after time in our interactions with others, we are recognizable as the same person. We maintain a coherency and consistency both for others and ourselves. If for some reason we step out of character, present another image, we may startle or puzzle others or even ourselves. It may very well be that whatever we do in maintaining and enhancing this self is the prime activity of our existence. And so we observe ourselves and expend much of our energy protecting our self-image.

It is my contention that a person's self-image can be revealed to him through interpersonal feedback of various kinds, but any method that allows some form of contemplative self-observation can lead to superior knowledge of himself. The imaginings and images a person continuously has going on in his consciousness is probably the best starting point.

One can elicit a person's self-image by asking that person to imagine himself or herself in various imaginary situations. Such use of imagery has the capacity to add new dimensions of understanding to self-awareness. While any imaginary situation is capable of revealing a person's self-image, I have found specific kinds of self-image imagery that at times surprise the observer. Although we can gather perceptual information about our own self-image by actually looking into a mirror or by seeing video tapes of ourselves, we often gain even greater dimension and depth by the use of imagined mirror images which may elicit reminiscent imagery or unconscious material.

Mirror Images

To start, we might ask a person to *imagine* looking into a mirror. Then the person is asked to report what he or she sees, does, and feels. Many people experience such mirror images quite differently from the actual perception in a mirror. Closing one's eyes and allowing oneself the free flow of visual imagery can release certain unconscious factors that may bypass ordinary censorship. Some persons see only fragments of themselves. Others have difficulty in seeing their faces at all. There are still others who say they appear much younger or older than in the imagery. Also, concomitant feelings covering a broad range of feelings may be expressed by the imager, such as disgust, regret, pleasure, or shame.

Not all people find it easy to actually look into a *real* mirror. Facing oneself is not easy for some persons. I knew one man who for a period of ten years had not dared to look at himself in a mirror. He avoided any reflections of himself at all times. He was so enmeshed in shame and self-hatred that he couldn't face himself. Then one day I passed an actual mirror to persons in group therapy and had each person report his/her reactions upon seeing him/herself. This man, after working through many of his shameful feelings in prior therapeutic time, slowly, with great trepidation and sweat, peeked at himself, and after several long minutes he "saw" himself in the mirror. With tears he rejoiced in his new-found face.

There are those persons who not only have difficulty in seeing their faces in actual mirrors, but also in imaginary situations while closing their eyes. Invariably there is shame and guilt at the basis of this reluctance. When the shame is dealt with, a change in the imagery occurs, allowing the person more expansive behavior rather than punitive behavior.

Here is a verbatim report of a man who had difficulty seeing his own face, and the subsequent changes.

> During most of therapy when I was asked to imagine myself in a situation, it was nearly impossible for me to visualize my face. I could always see a body, but the only way I could struggle to see my face was to imagine shaving in the morning and therefore looking at myself in an actual situation.
>
> When asked to see myself in a room, I saw a body sitting at the end of a bed, but to see the face was extremely difficult if not impossible. This caused me a great deal of frustrated feelings at the time.
>
> Recently when asked to imagine myself sitting in my own lap, I was able to do it with great ease. At this moment, I am able to do it. This change startled me at first, and then I felt almost overwhelmed with happiness because I could see myself. It felt like I existed – to myself – and that seemed to mean more to me than existing to someone else.

In the same dimension, yet still utilizing the imagined mirror, a woman responding to the identical imaginary situation gives the following account:

> The mirror is very big, gilt-framed, and old-fashioned; I think it's out of the 1800s. I'm very, very small compared to the mirror. The impression I get is that I'm Alice in Wonderland and I've been shrunk in size after eating the cake that says "Eat me."
>
> I can't see myself in that mirror. Instead, the mirror is like a window (looking glass?) that looks out into Wonderland. The Cheshire Cat is on the other side of the glass, grinning at me. It's a secretive, tantalizing grin which seems to say: "If you're ready, come inside. This is where you can find out about yourself. So if you're ready to make the trip, come on in."

It showed her ambivalence to openly explore her unconscious life in therapy and her desire to do so at the same time. Old-fashioned attitudes, probably about sex and morality, is a very likely interpretation. The Cheshire Cat may be myself as her therapist.

In time, as she reexamined this imagery sequence after several months of therapy, she agreed with the tentative interpretation I had offered earlier.

Another imaginary situation that makes use of an imagined mirror image is asking persons to imagine themselves looking at themselves at their present age, then five years hence, then ten years hence, and more if desired, in five-year increments. The response to this imagery sequence can be strongly emotional in anticipation of the future, and relates to the projections of the self-image attitudes towards aging and other related feelings can be thus elicited.

In one of the most profound imaginary situations and also one of the earliest I developed, the person is asked to imagine looking into a mirror. However, instead of seeing himself, as he would ordinarily do, the person is asked to imagine seeing someone else. My experience with hundreds of responses to this imaginary situation indicates that the "other" person seen invariably is an important person in the imager's life. Sometimes it is another part or self of the same person. It is not uncommon for strong feelings to emerge such as crying or sadness or joy. When the person is asked to say something to the "other" person, expressions of love or statements of hatred are often forthcoming. When the person is asked to imagine what the "other" person may say in return, strong feelings of anger or joy may also be elicited. It is also not uncommon for reminiscent imagery to occur.

What follows is an example of this imaginary situation by the same woman who saw herself in the imagined mirror and saw herself as shrunken like an Alice in Wonderland character:

> I'm looking into a very big, old-fashioned mirror, gilt-framed, probably from the 1800s. In the mirror I see a small figure of a Civil War

soldier. He and his horse are standing alone in the middle of a dirt road. The soldier doesn't know where the rest of his company is, and he's not quite sure where the battle is going on. He just leads his horse down the road in this deserted area in the countryside. He's feeling cut off and detached from the rest of his company, and lonely. It's like he and his horse have to go it alone.

In dialogue with this woman the "other" person was her detached self, the part of her that felt different and apart from her peers and groups of peers.

Still another useful imaginary situation that utilizes the imagined mirror image is to ask a person to imagine looking into a mirror, then imagine the most difficult thing to say to himself (M/L). Very few persons fail to have a strong reaction to this imaginary situation. Aspects of the unconscious and current concerns tend to combine to elicit aspects of self-hate, self-denial, or acts one feels one should and will do. Forcing the person into a most-or-least situation (in this case "most") limits the choice of possibilities.

Most of the time, as adults, we accept our identities without much question. It takes some unusual circumstance to focus attention on our self-image. For example, coming out of an anesthetic, we wonder who and where we are. Being alone in a foreign country can make us very aware of ourselves.

An anthropologist who had lived for a year in a small village in the New Guinea highlands told me how he awakened one morning not quite sure of who he was. Months of living among a small group of people, whose lifestyle and language were totally alien to him, had disoriented him and had triggered self-doubts. He found himself staring into his mirror, feeling his face and body. He kept repeating his name in order to convince himself of his own identity.

The image of one's self in a mirror is often a serviceable way of reality testing. Some people, when asked to see themselves in a mirror, ask, "Is that really me?" They often become angry or annoyed with themselves because they see a reflection they do not like – they are too fat, too ugly, too awkward. Seeing the disliked reflection may create a "reality" that will lead to some action for change.

The mirror does not always tell the truth – it reflects our image as we perceive it. We glance into it to see if we are properly dressed, we check our grooming, but we do not usually really look at ourselves. An unexpected reflection in a shop window or in a mirrored wall may give us a moment's pause until we recognize that image as ourself. For a fleeting instant, we look at ourselves as a stranger and may see someone who differs from the picture in our mind.

Sigmund Freud tells a story of traveling in a railroad compartment and looking up to see what appeared to be a stranger in front of him. A moment later he realized that he was seeing his own reflection in the glass partition.

The mirror also validates us as a person:

The crystal spies on us. If within the four walls of a bedroom a mirror stares, I'm no longer alone. There is someone there. In the dawn, reflections mutely stage a show.

Jorge Luis Borges

Looking at Yourself Looking at Yourself

One of the most effective therapeutic imaginary situations is to ask a person to imagine (IS) that you are looking at yourself looking at yourself looking at your "self." Initially I thought that this particular imagery would be too fragmented, that it might possibly upset some people. Continual use of this imaginary situation has proved my suspicion groundless even though patients' reactions have been profound.

There is no consistent theme that can universalize all people's reactions to this imaginary situation. The variations in reactions are enormous, appearing particularly unique to each person. In some instances the first self (or the one that is being observed by the second self) may be the one that is deeply involved with a host of conflicts and negative feelings. At other times the second self may be the target person involved in conflict and negative feelings. The third self, or overobserver, generally does not have the severity of negative reactions, but his position in the triplicity opens up perspectives sometimes not seen before.

One man, for example, in response to this imaginary situation gave the following response:

> The first Edward is well dressed, articulate, sincere, from a good family – he is hollow – he wears a mask – his body is taut – eyes are not focusing.
> The second Edward is defiant, insecure, lonely, angry, hostile, with sarcastic humor.
> The third Edward is grounded on earth – follows his own intuition and feelings.
> The first me is all the levels of expectation demanded of me. "Be this, Edward, be that, Edward." I don't like the first me but I don't say to everyone I don't want to be him, but I slip into my Edward Two and remain defiant and sarcastic. I operate mainly here. When I go to gatherings of my family I feel I am supposed to go as Edward the First (that's funny). And I play the role but I secretely operate from Edward the Second and defiance. It's the Edward the Third I really want to be because that would be rooted in my own standards and I can give up secretely defying the world.

Here is one woman's response to this imaginary situation:

The first me is standing straight. As I look to the second me I notice she is half-way bent over. The third me is bent over on the ground.
I feel like a loser. I want to stay straight. The straightened one is unconscious – going through life without awareness. The second has some awareness but is not a total failure. The third me represents failure, or the knowledge that I've failed. I haven't done anything in my life.

My own experience indicates that despite the fact that there are three "selves" involved there rarely occurs a dissociating effect; rather an enlargement of perspectives. As a means of viewing the self-image of a person, it has proved to be an excellent technique of imagery involvement.

Area of a Circle

One of the most unique pictures of how a person views himself in relation to the world is to ask the imaginary situation (IS): Imagine yourself in an area the shape of a circle. What do you do, see and feel?

In a sense, the person responding is probably referring to his "life space." While "life space" is not subject to an absolute definition, it may very well refer to how the person sees himself in the world and to the pressures of the environmental forces upon him. If he feels especially cramped and cornered, it may well relate to the pressures upon him that he strongly feels are impinging on him. Other persons may feel quite expansive in the center of the circle and display mastery of the area. Obviously, the variety of responses of individuals is virtually endless.

Often I may ask the person if he can leave the circle. Again, the answer hinges on how the person feels about himself in his self-image in relation to life forces. In interpersonal thinking, these function contemporaneously. Some persons can leave the circle or not as they wish. This suggests freedom. Others feel constricted and trapped. If one can focus strongly, asking the reluctant person to make himself leave the circle, it is possible to elicit clues as to his style of approach and the conceptualization of the environmental forces that he is coping with.

Here is the response given to this imaginary situation by a 24-year-old female patient during a therapy session:

Patient: I am on an island. There is grass and trees. There is lots of water. I am sitting and looking out. I am isolated. I am not helpless. I am lonely. I didn't choose to be there.
Therapist: Can you leave?
Patient: Yes, there is a boat. A row boat.
Therapist: What do you think it means?
Patient: I'm lonely and isolated. I can only get away by myself. I want to get off the island.

A 40-year-old transsexual gave the following response to the "circle" image:

Patient: A stage – a theatre in the round. I'd be entertaining, singing. I feel overwhelmed.

Therapist: Can you leave?

Patient: Yes – at a given time at the end of the performance. I feel really terrific.

One other response given to this imaginary situation was as follows:

Patient: I saw myself as though I had a view of earth in space – getting down to what is important – getting all the distractions away – but very isolated and scared. Empty space that had to be filled – the old isolation – now instead of filling it with trivia, fill it with substance.

The Intimate Self

Perhaps there is no more private experience than that of the person experiencing himself. Nobody else may know what the individual is experiencing unless each individual decides to share the experience. Even if we observe a person engaged in violence, it is virtually impossible to know what is going on inside the person involved. So, the self has the power to be experienced in its own isolation and uniqueness. Is it true, as Neitche suggests, that "Finally one experiences only oneself?"

Nevertheless, there are certain imaginary situations that indicate an extremely high degree of intimacy. One is to ask the person to imagine holding his face with his hands, and to say what he feels, sees and does. Attitudes of attraction and niceness vary with no feelings or actual revulsion. Attitudes of the closeness and intimacy factors can often be revealed in this way.

Another imaginary situation that yields clues of experiencing oneself and also includes elements of self-confrontation is the situation in which the person is asked to imagine walking in a lightly wooded area where you see a hotel. Walk through the lobby, up the staircase, and enter a room where you see yourself. The person is then asked, what do you see yourself doing? Then speak to that other person and have that other person speak back.

This sequence of self confrontation through imagery and imagination may often lead to unexpected reactions. Some persons experience feeling shame or isolation or the feeling of being lost. Sometimes very tender or good feelings may be expressed. Secret feelings are not uncommon. It appears to be another way of revealing the intimate self.

The Double

Sometimes we do not need the mirror image. We create it internally. Freud and Rank refer to the concept of a "double." Rank saw the double as an insurance against the destruction of the ego, "an energetic denial of the power of death." Freud, too, believed the double was invented "as a preservation against extinction" or a protection against loss. He tells of a child who dealt with a brief separation from his mother by making his own image alternately appear and disappear in a mirror.

Association with others is necessary for validating and expanding the perception of the self by the self. They are our mirrors. When there are no human others to serve as mirrors, as in the case of those living in isolation, we invest our surroundings with imagined personalities: the prospector and his mule illustrate this need. By interacting with his mule as if it were human, the lonely prospector was able to experience many aspects of himself which could not be called forth in solitude. He used the animal as a mirror when he imagined the mule discussing and describing his actions at length. Prisoners in extended solitary confinement have been known to play the same game with spiders.

Children use imaginary companions to mirror themselves also. They fantasize other children, or animals, or adults. The imaginary companion becomes real for them and provides the feedback necessary for developing the self-image as well as a rehearsal for interactions with others. One child I know of was so convinced of the reality of her imagined friend that whenever she was taken to a restaurant, she ordered food for her imaginary companion.

There is a phenomenon called "Doppelganger" or "autoscopy," a visual hallucination in which the other person is recognized as being oneself. Usually the Doppelganger apparition appears without warning and takes the form of a mirror image of the viewer, facing him and just beyond arm's reach. It is life-sized, but very often only the face or head are seen. Generally the image is transparent. A few cases have been reported where a person's double followed him around permanently, like a shadow. Experiences reported by normal people involve isolated episodes of short duration, which occurred during times of stress or fatigue.

The concept of the phantom "double" has perturbed humankind since ancient times. It appears in folklore and fairy stories throughout the world and is prevalent in the religious beliefs of many primitive societies. Shamans and witches cultivate and control their doubles. The shaman double may be dispatched to round up the erring spirit of the patient, or to bring back news of events in far-off places. Some Australian aborigines believe that a man's soul leaves his body after his death and then joins the double in the ancestral cave. The appearance of one's double is common when death is in sight. It is only a small step to presume the double is a harbinger of doom. There is an old German folk belief that Doppelganger is a sign of imminent death.

The idea of meeting one's double has had a morbid fascination for many creative artists. The list of distinguished writers who have described autoscopic phenomena in this way includes Guy de Maupassant, Oscar Wilde, Franz Kafka, Edgar Allan Poe, John Steinbeck, and Feodor Dostoevsky.

Goethe, a very stable personality, once met himself on the road riding a horse. Shelley, considered to be a much less balanced person, was walking near the leaning tower of Pisa when he was approached by a figure in a long cloak whose face was concealed by a hood. The figure advanced to within a few feet of the poet before raising his hood. Shelley was terrified to find that it was himself. "Are you satisfied? (Siete sodisfatto?)" inquired his double.

The self image comes to us in an infinite variety of forms, and the Doppelganger is one of the most unusual. There is a long history of the mystical nature of seeing one's double. It is not considered to be as common today as it once was – or else we just don't seem to talk about it as freely as our ancestors did.

In an illuminating way, when persons are asked to see two of themselves, attitudes toward the self are revealed. One of the methods involves seeing oneself, as: (IS) There are two of you and one of you is looking at the other you through a keyhole. What do you see, do and feel? Clinical experience with this imaginary situation indicates that it reveals some aspects of the most private and often secret aspect of the self as seen by the imager. Strong feelings and surprise may be an associative reaction. Attitudes of self-acceptance or non-acceptance, shame, or self-revulsion may emerge. This self observation may reveal conflicts and styles of defenses heretofore concealed from the imager.

Sometimes, one can eliminate obsessive components of excessive verbiage if one is to ask the person to imagine (IS): There are two of you. Both of you are sitting opposite each other in an easy chair. Have a dialogue.

Not only obsessive persons can be helped to clarify their feelings, since all of us will refine our statements as the dialogue ensues.

These two imaginary situations help us "see ourselves" and "talk to ourselves."

A further use of the "two of you" is when a person is asked to imagine (IS): There are two of you. Imagine one of you is sitting on the lap of the other you. The following is the response of one woman:

> The two me's are posed in a lovely impressionistic sculpture made of smooth, polished, gleaming stone. The first me is adult-sized and is sitting in a chair. The second me is child-size and is sitting on the lap of the first me. The child-me is facing the adult-me and has its arms around the adult-me's neck. The adult-me also has its arms around the child-me's body. The child-me doesn't want to face the world, but rather turns inward to the "safe harbor" offered by the adult-me. The adult-me is tender and protective of the child-me. It's a very nurturing scene, like the epitome of mother-child love.
>
> I guess this shows my desire for an idealized nurturing love relationship. It's something I don't have with another person right now, so I try to give it to myself as best I can. Not trusting other people, the adult-me shields the child-me from the painful realities I'm not facing. It reminds me of my childhood, when I would handle my own emotional hurts rather than share them with an adult or a friend.

Others in the same dimension are: (IS) Imagine hugging yourself; kissing yourself; or holding yourself up. One other is (IS): There are two of you and one is entering the body of the other. Here is an example of a response to this type of image:

> I pictured entering into my body as if I were swimming into a body
> horizontal to mine. I cut it open with my hands like opening a loaf of
> bread. Then I lifted it up and crawled in. It was a doughy consistency.
> Then I began to put myself on – placing my arm in my arm, etc. It felt
> tight – like a glove that was too snug. I remembered then how once I was
> laying by a pool when I was seventeen and thought no one could hurt
> me because I was inside and my outside would protect me.

Images of this type often help attitudes of self-acceptance or non-acceptance,
shame, or self-revulsion to emerge. Such self-observation may reveal conflicts and
styles of defenses heretofore concealed from the imager.

There are those self-images that are combined with rich reminiscent images
when persons are asked to imagine themselves in a child's playground. The
following is a response of a 30-year-old man:

> I see all the kids running around. It's recess. A teacher is standing off
> at a distance. I feel different from everybody else. They're feeling one
> thing, and I'm feeling something else. When I play it's an act. I don't
> enjoy it. I think I should. I just can't. I think it's stupid. I feel like I am
> in prison. I run from one place to another. I start throwing stones. I hit
> someone. Then I run away. I want to run and hide in a ravine. (Patient
> then cried.) I'm scared.

Asking a person to imagine himself in a classroom has a similar effect.

Experience indicates that self-image imagery may offer clarity and many times
it may be thrust upon you. Whether or not you realize it, if one is to do all of
the images suggested in this chapter one will likely see that he possesses a series
of principles for organizing the way in which he sees himself and the world
around him.

On occasion there is a shift in self-definition from an old to a newer way of
viewing oneself. Self-image imagery may offer clarity in such cases.

Self-image imagery may well offer a unique opportunity for revealing as well
as understanding the self-image through self-observation.

CHAPTER 14

Imagery and the Focusing Approaches

In the long run it is not enough for a person to be aware of his inner conflicts: a change must be made in the way he defines himself. The resolution of an internal conflict is more important than a mere solution; sleeping pills offer a solution to insomnia, taking a vacation offers a solution to an unpleasant situation, but in neither case is the actual problem resolved. Superficial solutions are easily conceived and more easily prescribed, but it is the duty of the therapist to ignore such temptations and deal constructively with the problem itself, however difficult it may be to liberate a person from a neurotic conflict resolution.

The focusing approaches are designed to free the patient from a deadlocked position in his psychological life. Suppression, avoidance, distortion and withdrawal provide avenues to sustain conflict and escape from resolution; approaches must be implemented to provide healthier, more positive avenues. As their cornerstone, these approaches depend upon the concept of self-definition. It is essential that the patient be assisted in changing his self-image and in combating the inclination to let others define him falsely. It requires little effort for the neurotic person to be placed in false positions, and the focusing techniques provide a starting point for the patient's inner resources to work for him in fighting these uncomfortable and painful situations.

Interior Dialogue/Cathartic Imagery

In order to demonstrate the focusing approaches, I am presenting a portion of a taped discussion with a twenty-five-year-old man, Arly, who had been in therapy for about six months. The discussion involves interior dialogues between Arly and his mother, as he imagined they might take place, during which he confronts her with the purpose of changing his self-image. Essentially, the method makes use of cathartic imagery though it also includes use of the "impossible scream" and powerful expressions of anger feelings — a valid force in liberating the individual from a negative self-image. Let me emphasize that these techniques — imagery in interior dialogue, body touching and holding, body focusing and task imagery — are not employed capriciously. Clinical judgment is required to assess the ego strength of the patient, to determine whether the patient is *ready* to mobilize his forces against an archaic bastion of defenses. The therapist must also align himself on the side of the positive forces, consistent with the patient's true identity; obviously, it

333

is only when the trust of the therapist is secured that the individual can allow himself to be free to face elements of his life which have heretofore seemed overwhelming.

Arly: Um, I feel sort of like a something is expected of me — something I should be *giving* more than I should be doing, and all the ploys she used on me, it reminds me — remember that time in group when I said I went real stiff? — somehow that all related in there, like I could associate it with dear old mom and me and stiffness.

Shorr: (S&O) What were some of the ploys she used on you?

Arly: Mom? Well, mainly just faking the sadness and hurt and not being able to make it, I mean — it's like I know all that in terms of her.

Shorr: Faking sadness — clueing you in, sucking you in.

Arly: Yeh, I never, you know what — I never even thought about it. I mean, I always associated sadness with her as being genuine, this is the first time I've ever said faking.

Shorr: Yeh, it slipped out?

Arly: Yeh, how about that, not a bad slip, huh?

Shorr: (Focus) (IS) No. Okay now, your mother faked sadness; I want you to imagine pointing your finger at her face.

Arly: Okay, I'm imagining, do you want me to say something?

Shorr: (Focus) Yeh, what are you going to say?

Arly: (Focus) (Angrily) QUIT FAKING YOUR SADNESS OR I'LL PUNCH YOU IN THE MOUTH — (Laugh) I'd like to belt her one.

Shorr: You're pretty angry, huh?

Arly: Yeh.

Shorr: 'Cause you were taken.

Arly: Yeh.

Shorr: She seduced you with fake sadness, therefore it behooved you to _____ . And it's your responsibility to _____ .

Arly: To be there all the time to make sure she didn't wither up and die of fake sadness, hum, (Sigh) so that, hum. . . . .

Shorr: (FTS) So I have to convince every woman that _____ .

Arly: (Sigh) That I'll always be there.

Shorr: (FTS) Every woman has to convince you that _____

Arly: (Sigh) Um, that she is incapable of making it without me.

Shorr: How do those two jive?

Arly: Oh, they jive real well unfortunately, yeh. . . . .

Shorr: (IS) Do you want to go through that scene again where your mother comes on with a fake sadness, try to imagine it, she coming on toward you now with a fake sadness of some kind, now you react to that.

Arly: (Sigh, sigh) It's hard to react, it's hard to picture, the only reaction I have, I mean I'm not even sure that I can picture it — or it's just to hit her in the stomach.

Shorr: Well, how do you feel after you do that?

Arly: Yeh — Wow! I just had like a strange flash, as I was hitting my mother I could almost see my father like a shadow in the background, you know, like he's coming into focus too, so I had to let him have it on the jaw.

Shorr: (Focus Scream) Yeh, and what do you want to scream at him?

Arly: I'm not sure, just "get away," you know, it's like I could punch the — if I — like I can picture punching them both toward the door and just closing the door and locking it.

Shorr: (IS) Okay, just imagine closing the door.

Arly: Well I, well I can still hear them banging on the door.

Shorr: You have to get rid of them you mean?

Arly: Yeh — it's guilt you know.

Shorr: What are they screaming at you?

Arly: Don't shut us out or something like that.

Shorr: (IS) (Focus) And how about you screaming at them with "How dare you" — What would you say to them?

Arly: (Sigh, sigh) Um, (Loud) HOW DARE YOU PLACE SUCH A TERRIBLE DEMAND ON ME.

Shorr: (Focus) (FTS) I don't need _____ .

Arly: God, I don't need YOUR PROTECTION, I don't even know what that means but, but it's, it's sure in there someplace.

Shorr: Is it hard to scream at them?

Arly: (Sigh) Hum, no, I think I could do it.

Shorr: All right.

Arly: (Yelling Loud) I DON'T NEED YOUR PROTECTION — I think that was my dad, my mom's still there —

Shorr: (Focus) (FTS) I am not_____ .

Arly: (Loud) I AM NOT YOUR LITTLE BOY ANYMORE AND YOU DON'T NEED MY PROTECTION (Quieter) YOU DON'T NEED MY PROTECTION (Sigh)

Shorr: Do you feel better?

Arly: No, still feel a. . . .

Shorr: Still hooked into it?

Arly: Yeh, like I want her to go away and I, I guess I'm surprised cause I don't — I wasn't feeling very hooked into her either, you know. I'm pissed off that I still, have some hangups that I thought I got rid of. It really bugs the shit out of me. (Sigh)

Shorr: And she still persists.

Arly: Um, seems like it, everything started feeling better the last few weeks, much more aggressive and full and everything and (Laugh) I still feel these kinds of shadows of mom or whatever you call them.

Shorr: Well, what is it you want to do to get rid of her then?

Arly: I don't know, kill her I guess, would be the best way, but if I could do that without (Laugh) feeling guilty, which is the problem.

Shorr: Yeh, would you like to just put her away separately and go your own direction?

Arly: Yeh, that would be fine.

Shorr: Where would you like to put her?

Arly: Well, it's hard to do, that's what it is, it's like going my own direction is, almost comes out in terms of something like distance instead of, (Sigh) you know, not like I don't want to see her anymore, I just want to be free of her, it's the only way I can —

Shorr: How can you become free of her?

Arly: That's the thing, I mean . . .

Shorr: (S&O) What is your obligation to your mother?

Arly: It's still to be there, (hum), nuts!

Shorr: What do you owe her?

Arly: I don't owe her anything.

Shorr: Except your life.

Arly: (Laugh) Oh yeh, you know about that.

Shorr: That's no little item.

Arly: Yeh — shit.

Shorr: (Focus) (FTS) How about I don't owe you _____.

Arly: I DON'T OWE YOU ANYTHING, NOTHING. (Laugh) I'm having this fantasy of me with a double-barreled shotgun and her right there and it's like, if I pull the trigger, it's like I'll blow her away but I'm not sure what the after-effects will be. Well, I'll see what happens. (Sigh) (Long Pause)

Shorr: Did you do it?

Arly: Yeh, I did it but I don't trust it, it's like I don't see her anymore but I've got the feeling she's still lurking around back here someplace, like I —

Shorr: (IS) Could you put her in a net?

Arly: Put her in a net?

Shorr: Yeh.

Arly: Okay.

Shorr: (IS) Then hang her from sort of a crane.

Arly: (Laugh — Sigh) All right, this is hard to do, okay, all right I'm on the edge of this chasm and I take the crane and I put the net on the other side, it's like there's no way she can get back and I leave it there — a — okay, that wasn't too hard, now comes the hard part, and that's like walk away. I'm walking and I can hear her yelling like "Don't leave me" (Sigh) and suddenly I see my father standing alongside of her and he's waving to me and I feel very sad about the whole thing but —

Shorr: How will you break your responsibility to them, how will you break their guilt induction to you?

Arly: How? I don't know, it's like I just feel like if I can just keep walking —

Shorr: How about — what do you want to scream at them — can they take care of themselves?

Arly: Um.

Shorr: Can they get along without you very well?

Arly: Well, that's, that's where it's at, isn't it?

Shorr: Can they take care of themselves?

Arly: (Sigh) Yeh, they can take care of themselves.

Shorr: Tell them that. (Focus)

Arly: Okay. (Firmly) YOU CAN TAKE CARE OF YOURSELVES, YOU CAN

CONTROL YOUR OWN DESTINIES AND YOU – YOU'VE GOT TO DO FOR YOURSELVES, I CAN'T DO IT FOR YOU.

Shorr: (Focus) (FTS) I am not responsible _____.

Arly: (Focus) I'M NOT RESPONSIBLE FOR YOU, FOR TAKING CARE OF YOU, FOR SEEING THAT YOU SURVIVE, FOR BEING THERE AT YOUR HOURS OF NEED ALL THE TIME, FOR (Sigh) FOR SEEING THAT YOU MAKE IT FROM DAY TO DAY, FOR SEEING THAT IT ISN'T TOO HARD FOR YOU TO WORK, YOU KNOW THAT WORK ISN'T SUCH A DRAG. IF YOU DON'T DIG IT THEN GET OUT YOURSELVES. Um. (Sigh)

Shorr: (Focus) How about (FTS) I am not your caretaker _____ .

Arly: Ouch, I AM NOT YOUR CARETAKER.

Shorr: Are you really saying that from your gut?

Arly: I'm trying. (Slightly Firmer) I AM NOT YOUR CARETAKER.

Shorr: Doesn't sound from the gut.

Arly: (Laugh) It doesn't, but it sounds pretty close. (Exhale, exhale, exhale) (Firmly) MOTHER YOU CAN SURVIVE ON YOUR OWN, I AM NOT GOING TO TAKE CARE OF YOU ANYMORE, YOU'RE GOING TO, YOU MAKE IT BY YOURSELF, I'VE GOT MY OWN LIFE TO LIVE. Whew.

Shorr: Don't explain it, just state the position and act on it, don't prove it, just state it and that's it.

Arly: (Focus) I'M NOT GOING TO BE RESPONSIBLE FOR YOU ANYMORE.

Shorr: Well that really sounded like that came from the depths of your core.

Arly: Yeh, I'm still mad – (Laugh) – I feel better though, I'm still pissed off. Oh, this is like a shaker. Whew, I mean I see where freedom lies, I really see it so – I'm just (Loud) *pissed,* I'm tired of being where I'm at, I just want to be completely and unequivocally free. I mean I knew something was bugging me and I didn't know what it was, now I know but I don't feel completely free but at least I know where it's at, like, all the strings are not clipped – most of them are though. (Sigh)

R. D. Laing said: " . . . as one grows older, one either endorses or tries to discard the ways in which the others have defined one." And, " . . . or one may try to tear out from oneself this 'alien' identity that one has been endowed with or condemned to and create by one's own actions an identity for oneself . . . " (Laing, 1962, p. 84.) These quotes serve as a basis of the theory to help the patient change his 'alien' identity to his "true" identity. One patient referred to a day of shame in his life, giving the following account:

"I was in terrible shape in the bathroom. I was barely twelve years old and all my brothers who were older were laughing at me as I retched and twisted, holding my stomach in pain. They didn't believe me. They thought it was an act. I felt so powerless to have anyone believe me. For this had happened countless times before. I once came home with a bloody nose from a fight at school and they wanted to know, "Where did you get the ketchup, baby?" On this particular day that I remember lying and squirming on the bathroom floor, my mother joined in and said sarcastically, "Leave the little baby alone!" In time I was able to crawl onto my bed and cried all night in pain, feeling so alone and unbelieved. I felt powerless like this again and again. How long would a kid go on with everyone laughing at him like he was just a sick baby?"

The patient was twenty-six years old when he related this emotion-charged account of his day of shame. Although he felt a certain humiliation in revealing such a terrible event in his life, he had been in therapy long enough to trust me; looking at my accepting and compassionate face as he concluded his talk, he felt relieved and seemed ready to deal with the agonizing "sick baby" concept.

When a patient has recalled a traumatic incident, together with its attendant feelings, I may urge him or her to utilize some interior dialogue which I will then suggest. Sometimes it may involve *The Impossible Scream* in which I ask the patient to (IS) imagine his mother or father in front of him and then ask (M/L) what would be the most difficult thing to scream at them. The patient usually responds with hesitation to this emotional task, but I persist in encouraging; I would not have initiated the procedure if I had not been certain of the patient's "readiness" to redefine himself. Further, I am willing to accept his feelings of rejection and humiliation, and this acceptance helps bridge whatever difficulties he may have in expressing anger. During that period in which a patient is growing up, the expression of anger toward significant people causes him to feel guilt, subject to retaliation; thus, the therapist's support and encouragement is of special help.

The twenty-six-year-old man described above was asked to (IS) imagine his brothers in front of him and to express (M/L) the most difficult thing to say to them. Slowly, but with great strength, he clenched his fists, focused a scream of considerable magnitude which came unmistakably from his core. "*I am not a sissy!*" he screamed, "*I am not a sissy! I am a man! Man! Man! You bastards!* I put my hand on his shoulder for reassurance. He seemed shaken but relieved, having indeed faced that which he had thought to be totally impossible.

It is worth reiterating that specific techniques should be used within the precise context of each individual's neurotic conflict resolution, with the aim of achieving a *healthy* conflict resolution. It would be useless and perhaps perilous to have a patient engage randomly in any of the focusing techniques if one did not have a clear awareness of the neurotic strategies which enchain him to his neurotic treadmill.

A focusing approach involving the interior dialogue was of particular help in dealing with a puritanically raised young man who had become obsessed by his "proper" behavior. I had him (IS) imagine himself walking down Wilshire Boulevard wheeling his wife in a baby carriage and answering to a number of men who were asking him why he was doing such a thing. Initially, his responses to them were expository, to the point of begging their permission to be allowed to continue pushing his wife along in the carriage. While quite patently not a reality situation, it evoked great fears and accountability. I had him repeat the sequence three of four times before he could tell the men to "fuck off." When he did this, he blushed markedly and hid his head in his hands, and when I asked him why he was reacting so strongly, he remarked, "I never said 'fuck' before in front of my wife."

The use of an obscenity was not important in and of itself; what was essential was to liberate him from his puritanical mold. At first he felt there was no possible alternative, then through imagery he allowed himself to feel a new way of behavior. Gradually, as a consequence of his therapeutic experience, a definitive and healthy change occurred in his life at home.

(IS) Imagine yourself in the gondola of a ferris wheel with members of your family; the gondola is stuck at the top for a long time. This imaginary situation often reveals a fear of heights, a loss of control; but more importantly, within the imagined interplay between the family members, it discloses heretofore unrecognized intimacies and hostilities. It is helpful both as a delineator of internal conflicts and as a focusing technique, especially powerful when the patient is ready to confront the situation. At times patients have imagined the experience of throwing various members of their families out of the gondola entirely. Combined with the liberating screams of (FTS) I am not_____; (FTS) I am_____; or (FTS) How dare you_____, it has often helped free patients from false definitions imposed on them by significant others. A patient's development can often be gauged by the therapist and revealed to the patient himself, if this technique is used in the early phases of therapy and then again later on — first to highlight internal conflicts and later as a focusing approach. Sometimes, however, a patient will at once involve himself with it as if it were a focusing approach, though I do not recommend its use as such in the early stages.

Clearly, there are other comparable imaginary situations which offer the possibilities of cathartic focusing for change.

Resistance and Imagery

It is commonly agreed that the censorship over imagery is less than in verbal reporting. It should not be automatically assumed, however, that imagery productions are relatively free of resistance. Diversionary imagery may occur. An example of this was a man who was engaged in imagery, exposing strong feelings of shame about his "cowardly" approach to people. As the imagery expanded, he noted images of food and guessed he must be hungry. In subsequent imagery sequences, he himself began to become aware of food images as being diversionary images. In time, as this would occur, he would smile and say, "I know I must be resisting. I'm getting those food images again."

Another man was asked to imagine his father hitting him. While he was a vivid imager, this seemed like an impossibility for him, despite continued attempts at imagining this situation. In time and with repeated focusing, as his self-confidence grew, he was able to visualize his father as a cartoon figure. This, too, was an atypical imagery for him and it persisted in subsequent sessions.

In time, when he seemed more ready to face his real feelings towards his father, his imagery lost the cartoon character and he visualized his father as a flesh and blood person. The expression of his strongly repressed hostility and the ability to truly visualize his father appeared to coincide in time. As his self-image became more positive and he was able to overcome his guilt feelings at having marked hostility towards his father, the resistance to related imagery about himself and his father disappeared.

Another form of resistance occurs in certain people when they are seemingly ashamed that they are revealing immature imagery and that would result in my possibly mocking them.

Here is the report of a young woman and her resistance to imagery that she thought would cause me to laugh at her. I had asked her to (IS) "Imagine someone standing behind you."

"Standing behind me, I saw George Segal. He placed both of his hands on my shoulders. It was a very warm comfortable feeling. Then as I turned in the chair to face him, he became angry. The next thing I knew, we were standing on a street corner and he was yelling at me. I couldn't figure out why I had made him so angry. He shouted, 'I've had it up to here!' For the life of me I don't know what he was referring to. At this point I also realized that I had the old feeling again of you and your desk being a long ways away from me. Suddenly, George took my hand and stormed across the street and into his car. I asked him again why he was mad at me but I only got a 'I've had it!' back. We drove down to the beach and went into the house. He seemed to be mellowing a bit. He came over to me, took both my hands and sat down on the couch with me. 'I'm sorry but I want our things for just us. If you want to share things with Dr. Shorr, fine, but not our private things.' This was probably the hardest fantasy for me to relate to you. It is one of 'my' fantasies I have when I'm by myself. I feel like a little girl who is dreaming yet none of them can come true. I am afraid of you laughing at me and thinking I am just a child. I had the feeling that George Segal is also another side of me that got mad because I was revealing things that are too personal."

This led to a discussion of "shame" in her life. Both her parents and her religious training made her feel shameful about her sexual daydreams. In time, she realized I felt no shame towards her for such fantasies and, on the contrary, I felt they were quite understandable in her present condition of loneliness. This served to make it a "natural" imagery for her and later on, she did not view me at a telescopic distance.

Transformation of Imagery

The directed daydream technique, used almost exclusively in Europe by Leuner in Germany, Desoille in France, Assagioli in Italy, has been reintroduced by Max Hammer (1967) in the United States as an effective means of psychotherapy in dealing with the unresolved conflicts of childhood treated in symbolic terms. The patient brings his symbolic conflicts into the open to deal with them. As Hammer says, "In a sense, the patient is asked to enter 'hell' in order to conquer the 'fiendish demons.' This meeting with unrecognized aspects of himself brings about spontaneous healing through various symbols. . . . Symbolic experience requires no analysis or intellectual insight for therapist effect, although such insight may be used adjunctively." (Hammer, 1967, p. 173.)

Hammer suggests that this type of visualization is autochthonous, i.e., largely independent of conscious control. Typical scenes are introduced, all having symbolic value in which the patient is asked to visualize himself in a meadow, in a house, in a cave, forest and climbing a mountain.

The emphasis is away from dialogue and conversation that might occur in a normal waking state, since it is felt this detracts from the free expression of feelings. The technique operates best when the patient is in a deeply relaxed or hypnoidal state.

Theoretically, the assumption is made that the use of this procedure facilitates the process of extinction of those harmful reflex responses which, "though relevant to the conflict, are active only in the patient's imagination and are not being reinforced by the patient's current reality situation. Through this process, we help the patient to develop new dynamic patterns which he will subsequently transfer from the realm of imagination to reality." (Hammer, 1967, p. 174.)

One of the techniques is the active approach of Symbol Confrontation, in which the p atient is asked to face, for example, a big snake that he imagines coming out of a sw amp. The therapist suggests to the patient to stare into the eyes of the snake until the snake is transformed into a bird, later into a mammal and finally the threatening mother figure stands in front of him, showing that the original symbol was a mother derivative. The end result of successful confrontation is strengthening of the ego.

Other suggested techniques are the Principle of Feeding, The Principle of Exhausting and Killing, the Principle of Magic Fluids and the Principle of Reconciliation. All of these principles stress the transformation of symbols through visualization into better symbols with which the patient is much more comfortable. The work of transforming the symbols, with the support of the therapist, is therapeutic.

Keith Johnsgard (1969) has utilized symbol confrontation in a recurrent nightmare with dramatic success by reexperiencing the nightmare.

My own experience utilizing these methods has found them to be quite helpful. However, there are times when certain patients do not seem to have the readiness to respond to symbolic confrontation, and rapport in this direction seems difficult. The hypnoidal state, while readily accepted by some patients, is resisted by others who wish more of a dialogue and conversation. With these patients, I will attempt task imagery which may not be as highly symbolic. I will discuss task imagery in the next section.

While Symbolic Confrontation techniques are designed to deemphasize analytic understanding, again my experience indicates that many patients in "working through" imagery get more benefit if insight and understanding are combined with the imagery sequence. In general, task imagery offers more of this possibility. In any case, however, one must conclude that transformation of imagery can have a highly therapeutic effect. Transformation of nonsymbolic or concrete imagery can have a powerful therapeutic effect just as the transformation of symbolic imagery can. What appears to be basic is that a person can find better ways of dealing with conflicted areas by transforming, reexperiencing or redoing imagery whether it be symbolic or concrete imagery.

Task Imagery

Certain imagery situations useful for focusing involve the patient mastering a piece of work or action, and I refer to this approach as task imagery. Invariably they involve the redoing or reexperiencing of the imagery. An example would be to ask a patient to (IS) imagine climbing 1,000 steps to the top. As the patient undertakes the imaginary task, he often reveals a particular style or attitude of approach, doubts or feelings or mastery, his need for power − or the absence of such a need. He might meet other people in his ascent; they might exhibit certain feelings about each other; he might meet someone at the top. To be sure, there are those persons who cannot go more than ninety percent up; others take the steps two at a time to the very top in no time at all. One woman got to the top readily enough, then held her hands high above her head and spoke of meeting the archangel Gabriel and a host of other angels, all of whom clamored for her to perform. It is often surprising for patients as they describe what happens to them and the dynamic stresses they feel. Repressed feelings may emerge; the degree of hopelessness or optimism in a patient's life is seen, together with distortions of reality should they exist.

Another imaginary situation would be (IS) imagine building a bridge across a gorge to the other side. The ways of imagining such a task are infinite, often revelatory of the patient's attitudes toward himself and the world. One man said he would build a bridge, and a very good bridge − but when he finished he imagined that a flood would wash it away. The meaning was that he could operate very well under great challenge, but once the challenge has passed, his interest diminished.

Another man, Hank, responded to the same imaginary situation by saying, "I'm getting the shit beat out of me while I'm building it but I continue on with it. I start out from one side and it's all right for a while and then I fall into the gorge. I come up anyway, like a cartoon character. I throw a rope to the other side and swing over but I slam up against the other side. I'm battered but I make it up the side, but I don't complete the bridge. I do something I set my mind on, no matter what the cost. I guess I'm masochistic."

The reader will see how readily task imagery reveals the patient's internal conflicts, his style and manner of approach, his defenses and fears; also that it serves as a vehicle for focusing a changed self-concept in the "working through" of the imaginary task. The important ingredient following the initial flow of imagery is to reexperience or redo the imagery in a manner that leads to a possible healthy conflict resolution.

One man, after prolonged imagery, could not get himself to the top of the 1,000 steps; remained at the 995th, clutching desperately to hold on. I urged him upward, supported him until he could get the courage to climb to the top. Working at the problems with palpable intensity, he was able to strengthen himself in his struggle against always being "second best." His greatest conflict was to succeed — without alienating others in the process. To complete successfully and still be well liked kept him always in the second position. His resistance to get to the top was enormous. "I can be best man on the second team," was his constant statement. In working through task imagery he seemed to be able to change sufficiently to assume a "first" position in his professional work. If his involvement with the task imagery had been anything less than assiduous, the change would probably not have taken place. That I supported him during his arduous struggle helped him accept the fact that he could succeed without incurring dislike.

A very intensive exercise in task imagery (for most people, but not all) involves (IS) walking out of a plane wreck. Some people respond with very little emotion; even if they imagine all of the other passengers to have been killed, they may appear remarkably uninvolved. Others are guilt-ridden and may cry. One woman was so overwrought with guilt that she sobbed uncontrollably for a time. Her imagery was that all the other people in the plane had been killed, and to her this made her responsible for their deaths. This was traced back to an interior dialogue between her and her mother, her mother having constantly made her feel strongly responsible for any aches and pains, no matter how minor, which she (the mother) experienced. Even with this recognition, it was some time before the young woman was able to utilize an impossible scream (FTS), "I am not rotten!" (FTS) "I am good!" The Task imagery brought to a sharp focus the "certainty" of her rottenness, and the impossible scream liberated her from the false designation.

The variations to this particular imagery situation are remarkable. Some patients would have flown the imaginary plane themselves; others would have their loved ones with them; others might be in a foreign country; others yet will imagine walking away from the plane wreck to start a new life after experiencing such a close call with death. At the very least, one can gain insight to a patient's attitude toward death.

Task imagery affords the possibility of a patient's facing himself and then attempting to change his self-concept. When I ask (IS) imagine yourself in a tank of the foulest liquid you can think of; describe the liquid; what are you going to do? — we are probably dealing with a well-ingrained feeling of rottenness if the patient finds it difficult to get out of the tank after describing the foul liquid in all its terrible aspects. The therapist must be alert to helping and urging the individual not to be submerged by his rottenness. It is sometimes nothing short of amazing to observe people's obstinacy in refusing to leave the tank, refusing to take a hot shower (or a cold one, for that matter) and remove from themselves all of that foul liquid. One woman wanted to drink the liquid and just stay there in the tank until the hangover was gone.

This imaginary situation is not offered indiscriminately to everyone, but to persons who stubbornly cling to a rotten self-image despite the efforts of the therapist and/or other members of a therapy group. Such a woman was Beulah. She was made to feel "rotten and worse" by a mother who related to her in a snobbish and superior way. She actually felt she was too rotten to allow for change. When I asked her the abovementioned situation, she reported this reaction:

"It's all menstrual stuff – like before Kotex was invented – it's blood and mucous – it's sickening. I do not know what to do." At this point I urged her to fight being drowned by the stuff. She paused, muttered something and then appeared to want to stay in the stuff. I continued to urge her to fight. Several minutes went by, during which she persisted in her silence. Finally she spoke very quietly:

"There is a plug in the tank and I'm going to let it all go out. (Long pause) Now I'm going to take a hose until it's chlorine fresh. I'm going to get perfume and pour it over me and the whole tank – I'm going to fill it with clear blue spring water and let the kids swim in it. I suddenly see a meadow beyond the tank. I can feel a relief of pressure in my head."

At the next meeting of her therapy group, she surprisingly initiated talk without being asked and seemed to exhibit behavior of a positive form she had never shown before. When she was bypassed by the group discussion (as she often had been) she fought it by asserting herself. She challenged anyone who referred to her as a "sourpuss." Her readiness (albeit initially reluctant) to do the task imagery and then actually fight her way out of her rottenness seemed to have a direct bearing on her changed behavior.

Asking a person to (IS) imagine himself in jail; imagine breaking out serves as another useful focusing approach as well as a method of assessing the individual's style, his behavior characteristics. Some people refuse to leave the prison, representing as it does their neurotic conflict resolution. Such people must constantly be urged to make the effort to leave. Among other information available from responses to this imaginary situation is each person's characteristic way of coping with conflict.

A large number of patients – unfamiliar with the realities of prison – refer to movies they've seen which deal with the subject. Nonetheless, the imagery is a product of their own choice and no less significant. One man said he would hide under his cell mattress until six p.m. The guard, arriving with food, would not see him, would leave the cell door open and run for help, at which point the patient (the "prisoner") would escape down a long hall and out the back exit to the prison. When asked what was characteristic about his imagery, the patient replied, "It's me, all right. I hide in life. I'm the old observer himself. I won't confront – and I guess I do run out on people."

I made him revisualize the incident in such a way that it would involve direct confrontation. He imposed strictures upon himself in visualizing any form of confrontation, however, and balked, saying, "I just can't." But I urged him on, and slowly, with great trepidation, he imagined " . . . rushing the guard when he came in with the food. I knocked him out. I then went through the long hall and out the back. Somehow I don't care as much as I did the first time because in the long run they will find me innocent."

How a person feels as he leaves the prison, where he goes from there, what he feels as to his innocence or guilt — these become especially important. Theresa, a twenty-seven-year-old woman, pole vaulted herself over the wall to freedom while in the recreation yard of her imagined prison. But once she had gotten her freedom, her anxiety was noticeable. "I have to run," she said, "but I can't go through life running. The thing is, I always get caught. Somebody is going to catch me. I can't say I'm innocent because even if I were, they would still condemn me. Some people would sympathize but there is nothing they can do about it. Someone would find out."

I then said, (IS) "You are in court now. Look for the person who would find you out and condemn you." The sequence of imagery which ensued led eventually to Theresa's violent condemnation of her father. From there we made use of cathartic imagery directed towards the father.

As you can see, many dimensions can be unfolded from such an imaginary situation, leading to the possibility of focusing for change.

A particularly powerful example of task imagery involves (IS), imagine yourself as a fetus about to birth. Well? — Some people seem not to want to give birth to themselves; others relate directly to their own birth from their mothers' uterus and express some of their strongest feelings, imagining their parents' respective attitudes to the event. The awareness that they were unwanted may emerge. Still other patients react with hostility as they imagine the task; it was one man's desire to " . . . crawl on all fours away from my parents so that they never can find me."

A common reaction is the sense of being born anew, with new possibilities in life. But beyond these typical examples, the spectrum of response is limitless; rarely does the task fail to evoke strong feelings; and as with other forms of imagery, this one can lead to a sequence of other imagery or reminiscence, allowing finally a focusing for change.

Here are other examples of task imagery:

(IS) Imagine going down the road and doing something worthwhile.

(IS) Imagine cleaning an oily, scaly piece of metal.

(IS) Imagine starting at ten inches of height and growing to your present size.

(IS) Imagine walking into a middle of a field and then build something.

(IS) Imagine walking down a road and confront a stranger.

(IS) Imagine hacking a road through a dense forest.

(IS) Imagine working your way through a web with a sword.

(IS) Imagine a huge wave is coming over you. You are to get free and safe.

(IS) Back up and go through a paper wall.

All of these and many more are helpful and offer the patient the possibility of working for change. But it must be remembered that the patient must be *ready* to focus for change. The elements determining this readiness are the patient's awareness of his internal conflicts; the release of feeling connected with contributory traumatic incidents; cognizance of the undermining strategies of behavior of the significant others; and recognition of his own counterreaction strategies.

The Repetition of Imagery

In repeating the same imaginary situation with a person, one can attempt to increase the intensity of the desired response, focusing for greater feeling response each time. This is especially true when the feeling response seems devoid of affect. In repeating the same imaginary situation, one may offer the instruction to "say something with more feeling." An example of this was asking a man "to imagine two different rocking chairs and then to imagine somebody different in each." He imagined an old man in one rocking chair and a young man in the other. I then instructed him to make a statement to each of the men. He started with an abstract statement in his initial response. His second response was a factual statement about the furniture. I repeated the imaginary situation urging him to make an emotional statement to each man. This time, he was more feeling in his statement and expressed some concern about "the older man's son who was lost in Vietnam." From this initial feeling spark more profound expression of feelings emerged.

Body Touching and Holding

Sheila, a twenty-nine-year-old woman, often spoke of the anger she felt at herself for being just like her fragile martyred mother. "Oh! I hate myself for being like that." she would repeatedly lament. I asked her to (IS) imagine holding her mother's face in her hands. She did this, holding her hands as if she felt her mother's face between them. After a long silence she started to cry. "It's very hard to do," she said, "I'll get her sickness. I feel really threatened by touching her – I feel unclean."

She was then asked to reverse the imaginary situation and picture her mother holding *her* face. Responding slowly, Sheila said, "I don't get feelings that way. I can feel her playing the game, that gentle fragile way of hers. I feel like stone between her fingers. I feel dead until she stops. I have to turn off so that I'm not susceptible."

From this point on, I tried to focus for her to separate from her mother by using the (M/L) question: "What is the most difficult thing to say to your mother?" Her immediate answer was, "See me." She was then guided to the impossible scream, "I am not _____ ; I am _____." After a long hesitation she was able to respond, "I am not *you*. I am *me*." It was necessary to repeat this at subsequent sessions until she was able to reach the feelings that would establish her autonomy.

This focusing procedure is very valuable both in individual and group therapy; it is a powerful instrument in breaking intimate deadlocks or gaining access to areas where guilt is especially strong. It may also elicit the most tender and gentle feelings or provide a focus for the softening of feelings which some patients may badly need.

Here is a report submitted by a thirty-six-year-old woman who describes her experience in body touching and holding:

"I was talking about being ashamed of my vagina. Ashamed of its being wet. Wishing to hide it. Pretend like it wasn't there. Disown it. Avoid it. Joe asked me who did my vagina belong to. I said, 'My mother.' Then Joe said something about my telling my mother that my vagina didn't belong to her; it belonged to me. Or in other words, told me to find a way to make it mine — take it back from my mother.

"I had my hand on my vagina (over my clothes) and I started trying to get it back. Each time I spoke, it came out in a begging, pleading tone even though the words were, 'It's mine, it belongs to me.' I struggled over and over and each time Joe kept saying you're begging, saying it again and over again. You're begging — louder.

"It became a frantic exchange between me, Joe and my mother. Just as it seemed I wasn't going to make it, I think Joe reversed things and I felt closer to the ownership than I knew, and the suggestion of relinquishing it triggered the floodgates — from the depths of my being, perhaps my vagina, or up through my stomach, chest, throat, and mouth. I started to scream at my mother. I could *feel* for the first time the full change of resentment, anguish, rage, hatred, abuse and pain as I called her vicious, evil, hideous bitch and on and on and I kicked and bashed the walls with all the strength I had and rolled in anger and agony on the couch. Then I remember yelling and pronouncing, 'It's mine, you hear, it's mine, it belongs to me.' the shrillness gone from my voice and deeper resonating tones coming out. It was the first time I can remember feeling whole and unfragmented since early childhood. I could sense my own presence and being. That afternoon after my session was the first time in many years that I'd driven the car unafraid. I drove happily about the town feeling that I belonged and *was*. That I was master of myself and not needing to grasp and gasp for confirmation from every person and object in the world that I passed."

Body Focusing

History records countless cases of people who were accused of being "obsessed" or who claimed to be "possessed." Invariably accompanying such claims and accusations were statements relating to the person's body; it was assumed that being "possessed" by the devil, God, evil spirits, involved some foreign presence within the body. It was (and is, if you're a believer in that sort of thing) as if the person no longer owned his own body (or parts of it) — as if some outside force or presence had not only occupied it but taken control of it.

As often as not (but primarily in more recent times) these cases were attributed to psychosis. Ignorance regarding such a condition resulted not infrequently in the isolation or ostracism of the person afflicted lest by touching him other people become similarly "possessed."

Normal people, of course, and even neurotic individuals do not become victims of these forms of illness in the course of everyday events. But in my experience over the years with hundreds of neurotic people it has not been uncommon for me to hear that a patient "senses" or "feels" a part of his body (or all of it) to belong to parental figures, if not demonic forces. When a person feels little or no identity of his own or if he operates constantly from a false position, he may make bodily identifications with a strong parental figure and incorporate that figure internally. Seidenberg (1969) reports a case of an individual who was completely dominated by his mother and by the feeling that "he was owned by his mother." The patient talked of a "protoplasmic bridge between them." Shutz (1967) used guided daydreams to help explore "one's own body" in the case of a woman who had excruciating pains in her stomach. He asked her to imagine herself as being very small, then to enter her own stomach. In the course of her journey through her body she encountered many imagined obstacles, and with the aid of the therapist was encouraged to overcome the obstacles. A considerable improvement in her physical health and social relations was reported.

The phenomenological aspects of people who report similar "possession" are various and unique. A question I ask is, (IS) Imagine your body as a whole; now see if you can sense the part of your body in which your mother or father resides. Most patients are not overly surprised by the suggestion and respond quite naturally. Imagination is the vehicle by means of which such associations can be made, leading ultimately to therapeutic experience and change.

Below is the verbatim account of the use of imagination in this context. The patient's symptoms in this case included inarticulation and speech hesitancy. He was thirty-one years old.

Shorr: (IS) In what part of your body does your mother reside?

Bob: In my vocal cords.

Shorr: (IS) I want you to imagine that you are entering her body.

Bob: I enter through her vagina — I go up under rising water — through the intestinal area and glands. (Long Pause)

Shorr: Why are you frowning?

Bob: Well the truth is, my first image was to enter her mouth — but I was afraid I'd be stretching her jaws apart — that's repulsive and ugly, like tearing it apart.

Shorr: (IS) Try to enter the mouth anyway.

Bob: O.K. I'll try — I'm standing on the back of her tongue, looking around — I slide off the tongue into the vocal cords. It looks like a prison. I am a prisoner of the vocal cords. In fact, I am an enemy of the vocal cords. They should recognize I'm not an enemy. Now they appear more like they are alive and they are not steel bars. They can move.

Shorr: (IS) Pluck the cords as if they were harp strings.

Bob: O.K. − good music − but I'm still a prisoner.

Shorr: (S&O) How can you define your vocal cords so that they don't define you?

Bob: I can fight back.

Shorr: O.K., fight back.

Bob: (Long Pause) How do you fight back? I am tickling the base of each vocal cord and uncontrollably each one is opening up − so I can get out − I run up the tongue and I jump out of the mouth to freedom.

Shorr: Now how do you feel about your own vocal cords?

Bob: I can define them and then show me how it works. I can say anything I want to, whenever I want to.

Shorr: (S&O) Keep defining them.

Bob: They are nothing but my servants, they are only mechanisms of sound.

Shorr: (Focus Scream) Try screaming "I have the final authority over you."

Bob: (Focus) I HAVE THE FINAL AUTHORITY OVER YOU − (Continues Normal Tone) −. They are nothing but a bunch of vibrations. They can't think, they will not define me. They are my prisoner.

Shorr: I get the feeling you gave the vocal cords a separate identity.

Bob: It became alive and told me what I can say or what I can't say. Like my mother, "Never say anything wrong to anyone or they would leave you" − that's my conflict.

Shorr: (IS) Enter your mother's body again.

Bob: Through the mouth. All I feel is revenge; this is what you did to me − now I'm going to show you what it feels like. (Pause) It deprived me of my hostility towards her. I couldn't liberate from her person. I had to be perfect or I could expect the worst.

Imagine in What Part of Your Body Your Mother Resides

The following is a report of a patient, Jim, in group therapy. He includes a running account of the events leading into the group experience, his experiencing of his mother in his stomach, and his efforts to liberate himself from her influence.

"I don't really remember too well what actually happened. I know that I had been suffering from extreme stomach pains for two days. Everything had been going extremely well in school for three weeks. Karen and I had just had the best two weeks of our relationship. For the first time in my life, I felt protective, social, myself, and in love with Karen at the same time. My fantasy of a "sunshiny winter afternoon" was coming true every day. I felt like everything was going well, except for some unknown reason, my neck and shoulders were tightening up harder than steel − more than I had ever known.

"Back to the stomach pain. At first I thought I had the flu. But I had extreme pains that were very high in my stomach. At the same time, I felt like vomiting, but I couldn't. I even stuck my finger down my throat and I couldn't, I wouldn't vomit.

"Tuesday morning, I went to work. I talked to Helen before I left and she said it sounded like I had an ulcer. Right then I got extremely depressed, angry, tearful and alone. I went home and I was really angry. I felt shitty (guilty) for having an ulcer. I felt shitty that I was still so uptight and fighting and unproductive as to have an ulcer. I was also really mad and untrustful of group and my last two years in it. I went back and forth, from guilt and anger.

"Then I called Bill (group member). The *one* thing I remember from the conversation was him saying, 'I care that you are in such pain' — and 'I really like being around you and Karen when you're happy.' When I got off the phone, I was wide open. I cried by myself and for myself without hesitation. For the first time, I let my guts hurt and I cried without any thoughts or judgments. I then felt like I wanted to cry "mommy." I wanted someone to love me and take care of me. I wanted a mother. But I knew I didn't want *my* mother. And it made me angry to realize I never had a mother.

"When Karen came home, I was very aware of not wanting to show her my feelings. But I had called and asked her to come home. That was pretty hard to ask for. If I ever let it out to my mother, she used it for her false motherings and to shrink my cock and consume my balls.

"By the time I got to group, my stomach was really hurting and I explained that everything was good but I was dying of pain."

Shorr: What part of you hurts?

Jim: My stomach. Right in the middle of my guts.

Shorr: Can you hand that part to someone? ("When Dr. Shorr asked that, all I could do was cry. He asked me several times and it seemed impossible. It seemed it would be giving the most vulnerable and dearest part of me away.")

Gwen: (Group Member) No wonder it hurts so much. It always hurt you and you were always alone with it.

Jim: What bothers me is that I never got anything with my pain, and I'm not now.

John: (Group Member) You must have gotten something.

Jim: Yes, I got to stay home. I didn't have to go to school and compulsively achieve. I got protection against my father. I didn't have to feel alone at school with the kids. I felt like I got some love. Even though it was being used to manipulate me into taking care of her. She had a way in, through my pain, and I had a way in with my pain.

Shorr: (S&O) Who does your stomach belong to?

Jim: To me. It's a good stomach. Good color on the outside. But the inside is all jumbled.

Shorr: (IS) Give that part a name.

Jim: Me.

John: How does the rest of your body feel?

Jim: Fine. It's all mine.

John: Then your stomach must not be yours.

Jim: No, it's not. It's the shit part of me.

Shorr: (IS) In what body part does your mother reside?

Jim: In my stomach.

John: Isn't it true that you still want your mother and you want to call to her?

Jim: Yes, no — I want a mother, but I don't want mine.

Shorr: (Focus) (IS) Reach in and grab her out.

Jim: She's in there with tentacles — it is all around me of — (Pause) all through my meat.

Shorr: (Focus) (IS) Rip her out. She's scared of you.

Jim: That's really true. That makes a difference. She's god damned scared of me. I scream at her and she shrinks like a sea urchin. I'm not really the scared one, she is. (I remember the dream where I jacked off on my mother and then I screamed I was going to kill her.) I pulled her out with my right hand, and held her there and talked about her. She was like a huge, sickly cancer cell. I talked a lot about her, and the more I talked, the more she was back in my stomach and the more my stomach hurt.

Shorr: (Focus) (IS) Rip her out and throw her in the fire (a dream I had about the ending of the world). Scream at her and tell her to get out.

Jim: For a long time I didn't feel like I could. I just couldn't reach in and get her out. I decided to stand up and try it. I had to. My stomach hurt so bad. I couldn't let her stay in. Thinking of her as scared of me helped. But I still couldn't do it.

Group Member: You won't be alone — we're all here.

Shorr: I'll be right here.

Jim: I know you all love me and you'll be here. But I'm afraid once I scream, I won't be able to call for you anymore when I really need you. (This feeling is the same feeling when I get sick and am scared that I'm all alone and I wouldn't get any help if I really needed it.)

Shorr: You won't have to call for me. I'll be right here with you, anyway. (That did it.)

Jim: AND THEN I SCREAMED. I SCREAMED WITH ALL MY MIGHT. WITH ALL MY PAIN FOR MY WHOLE LIFE. WITH ALL MY ANGER FOR MY WHOLE LIFE. WITH ALL MY GUTS. I SCREAMED FOR HER TO GET OUT. I SCREAMED FROM MY GUTS. WITHOUT ANY HESITATION. I SCREAMED FOR MYSELF. 'CAUSE I WANT TO LIVE FOR ME. 'CAUSE I DESERVE FOR ME. AND SHE GOT OUT. YOU'RE DAMN STRAIGHT SHE GOT OUT. AND SHE CAN NEVER GET BACK IN. SHE'S SCARED. I KNOW NOW. I KNOW IN MY GUTS. I KNOW WHO I AM. I KNOW MY STRENGTH. AND I KNOW HER WEAK, SADISTIC, INHUMAN GAME. I DON'T NEED IT. I DON'T NEED YOU. I'LL NEVER NEED YOU. SHE'S GONE.

"As soon as I screamed, I bent over and clenched my fists. I felt like I was screaming to hell and back. Dr. Shorr straightened me up and told me I didn't have to bend over. She couldn't get back in now. He hugged me and protected my stomach with his belly. It felt good, I really needed the warmth. I don't really remember what happened after that. I was shaking a lot and Dr. Shorr stayed next to me and hugged me and sat down next to me. He really cared. And he was really there. And I didn't have to call for him. And I looked up and people really looked human and warm. And especially the women looked different. I guess not so much like my mother. They looked human and fleshy. My stomach actually felt like it had a wound in it. But it was a clean fleshy wound. And now it can grow back together with me. It's mine."

Several months have passed since that group session, and the patient has shown considerable change; he is much calmer and there has been a marked decrease in his strong suspiciousness. His own analysis, verified in time, suggested that he felt accountable for his behavior to his mother, behaved according to her standards and felt great guilt if he did not. Since she was "inside" him, the accounting system was acute and ever present. Just as the paranoid person is defined by nearly everyone he meets, this man on a lesser scale was defined by his mother and substitute mother figures.

Lest the reader misinterpret that the mother is the only target person, the same question can be asked emphasizing "in which part of your body does your father reside." Whether the question involves the mother or father would depend upon the prior communication and feelings of the patient as well as other prior imagery. Of course, in some instances, both parents can be imagined.

One man, Lester, when asked, "In which part of your body does your father reside?" responded as follows:

Lester: In my brain, sitting on it like it's got handlebars. He's up there trying to pull my head. He's the size of a mouse and exerts lots of pressure. I want to move my head in the other direction. I'll show the son-of-a-bitch. But he has the power to stop me.

Shorr: Try to imagine putting your hand into your head and try to get him out.

Lester: OK. (Pause) I can do it. It's like a snail and I step on it. But it jumps up like a rubber ball. I get a knife and cut it in many pieces. Then I throw it on the street and cars run over it. That feels better. (Pause) I can now walk down a street tossing my head high. My own hands go onto the handlebars and I hold on to it like it's a motorcycle. I feel in control. I feel I am my own master.

It is possible to reveal feelings of self in relation to the other by imagining entering the body of the other and then imagining the other entering one's own body. Many deep feelings may be revealed, numerous aspects of the interrelationship brought to light. Here is a verbatim example of such an imagined journey on the part of a twenty-four-year-old woman; she was ordinarily detached, not too verbal:

"I enter my father's body through his stomach. His stomach is thickly congested with fog. Blindly feeling my way through the fog, I find a safe deposit box. Inside it is filled with cobwebs. At the bottom of this box lies my father's heart. What a terrifying sight! His heart is dark brown and it's dead. I can't stand to look at it. It's revolting! It's morbid! It's rotten! I say to his heart that all of my life I have been most curious to know what you are all about. I've *always* felt that there was something much deeper about yourself that you have never exposed. Now I am looking at it before my eyes. Only a man with a dead heart would have to live off of the lives of others. And only a man with a dead heart would use his daughter for his own means and at the same time try to suffocate me from my own sense of self. Inducing in me what you couldn't accept in yourself – that *you* are the rotten person, not me. Of course, my father's heart could not reply – it's dead.

"And – my father enters *my* body through my guts. He feels threatened and frightened by the echoes of truth that the depths of my guts reveal. My guts are echoing to him that I am *not* what he has tried to make me. I will not accept responsibility for his own rottenness. My father cannot bear the pain that it brings him, so he violently fights back with sudden anger as he intellectually and physically makes every effort to degenerate me with his degeneracy. When he finds my heart, he is overwhelmed by its intensity. It is bright red, healthy and well endowed with warmth, human depth, and a great eagerness to *live*. My father's reaction to my heart is disapproval. He cannot afford to accept it. If he accepts my heart, then he has to accept his own rottenness. I don't feel that my father could say anything to my heart – he would merely deny it."

I asked a woman of thirty-five to (IS) imagine entering your mother's body. Her immediate answer was, "Her womb – I just go in – it's dark in there and round and I fall asleep." I then asked her to (IS) have a dream while she was sleeping there. She reported her imagined dream as follows:

"I see colors, dark, red and purple. There are cubes glistening and bouncing all over. I am slipping over them all and I build a little house with them – I build a little igloo – it's all snow everywhere I look – it's crisp and cold and I have a fur coat on. I walk around in the snow and lie in the snow and Mona (her dog) is with me. I ski down a hill into a green valley – old Western town appears – it's one of those old Western bawdy towns – I take off my coat and have on a dance-hall dress – I get on stage and dance – the applause is terrific – I have a boyfriend who owns the club. It's a great dream!"

Shorr: You feel good?

Vicky: Who wouldn't feel good in their mother's womb? Even now when I'm in trouble I cry for her. Mama, Mama. I have lots in that womb. I can have lots of freedom. I can be a hooker, singer, dancer and a child. *The womb is the door to the world.*

Shorr: Can you visualize a sign in the womb?

Vicky: HERE YOU ARE.

"Responsibility is taken over by the womb. You see, my mother was authority. I felt safe with her. I let her be responsible in allowing her that power. I was not preparing myself for life. I started to look for things to be dependent on like drugs and men – a cozy place because it meant dependence. I walked away from my mother at seventeen — and then to drugs — then to people who took care of me. (Pause) Like I get into bed — then the tube will take care of my mind — I know there are trees out there but I won't go — I want to go but I won't — it is as if my mother said, 'Thou shalt not be without me!"

One man of twenty-eight had talked about having a "filter" inside of him that constantly prevented his feelings from coming through; the filter made him "switch up" to his head from his reactions. If his wife reprimanded him for playing chess for hours with his friend, his immediate reaction was anger, but he transferred it "to my brain, by a filter inside of me" and answered her with an innocuous remark.

I then asked him, (IS) "In what part of your body does the filter reside?"

Gene: In my chest — as a round filter, right around my heart, like a.big basket. I see it as somewhat overloaded. It needs cleaning. It doesn't seem to be working in conflict with anything around it.

Shorr: What does the heart feel?

Gene: Some kind of pressure. The heart is able to do very little except to maintain itself.

Shorr: What material is the basket made of?

Gene: Made of wood, very finely constructed high-quality wood — it's actually immobile right now.

Shorr: Is there anything you can do to change that structure?

Gene: Not really unless I concentrate.

Shorr: Imagine entering your body and go to the heart area.

Gene: It's very large. It's got to be ten times larger than me. The heart is five times bigger than me. I can walk right through this basket thing. It's quite easy to do. But when I get inside the basket the heart stops. (Long Pause) It gets very dark. I am staying there pretty scared because I am pretty small compared to all this.

Shorr: Can you get the strength to break the basket (Focus) and eliminate it out of your system?

Gene: I might falter.

Shorr: Try to.

Gene: Oh! I'm not big enough. In order to do it I'd have to be big enough — I'm only one-half as tall as the basket. (Pause) O.K. — I can imagine myself as tall as the basket. It's extremely heavy. It's not made of wood, it's made of iron — (Pause) I manage to tip it over. My heart wasn't beating until now — now it's started again.

Shorr: Can you go inside your heart?

Gene: I can't go in my heart. I'm sorry for my heart. That's strange. I would hurt it if I went inside. (Pause) I'm standing there.

Shorr: Say something to your heart.

Gene: Why haven't you grown bigger?

Shorr: Your heart answers.

Gene: Because you haven't taken this basket away from me. Now that you have entered me *I will open up and show you what's inside of me.* It's immaculately clean. That's saying a lot (Laughs) — immaculately clean for my whole heart. It's a very good feeling. It's a very good heart. We have a very good thing going there. The basket wasn't doing much good at all.

Shorr: (S&O) Who does your heart belong to?
Gene: It belongs to me. It's having a lot of trouble with the basket. But it's a good heart. It looks at me and says, "Quit screwing around."

One young woman, Clara, was asked, (IS) "In what part of your body does your anger reside?" Her reply was as follows:

"My anger is the central part of my being — a central core of hot carbon. It's solid and static inside me. In fact, all my feelings are contained in that carbon rod — it's hard to imagine the good feelings apart from the anger.

"It takes a special effort to separate the anger from the other feelings, but I can imagine them sort of falling off the rod as little black specks, and I'm left with a strong carbon rod with little piles of soft black specks around it.

"I want to take the carbon rod out of me — but it's too hot to touch — I've got to use tongs to extract it.

"I can take it out but there's no place to put it. It's glowing red hot — then white. Joe says to put it in a furnace, but that won't help. It only acts as fuel for the furnace — it won't be destroyed.

"I can destroy it with water — simple, but effective.

"But there's still this hollow inside me where the anger was. It's hard to fill it with good feelings — but I can. I feel guarded, as if it weren't possible to be rid of my anger. The good feelings fill me very slowly. There's an insecure feeling of lightness (vs. the dense, heavy rod) — a floaty feeling that I don't really exist. If I can drink the cool water of a fresh stream — that makes me feel more real — but then there's the feeling that the stream isn't real. I'm not really convinced."

In time as therapy continued, she was able to develop a better self-concept; and one might say she "filled up her body with good feelings" instead of her "hot carbon."

I Enter My Own Body

Another man describing his journey on entering his own body:

"I enter my head through my nose. I go up just under the surface of my skull. I don't like my head. It keeps playing tricks on me. It won't cooperate with my body. Hey head, you're ridiculous. Why don't you just pack it up? One minute you're a peach, and the next minute you're concrete. I'm tired of your game. It looks like you're going to keep it up for awhile though. You've really helped me survive, but god damn it, the war is over. You are another General Patton. In the face of danger you can turn my eyes to cold steel and take anything on. I thank you. But now it's time for something more. You don't seem to help me much when it comes to warmth and love and soft things. I guess I can't blame you too much, after what we've gone through in the last twenty-six years. It was a long battle, wasn't it? Hey, I think we made it! You protected my heart pretty well. But now it's time to live and I need you to relax a bit and slowly come along with me. I'll be easy with you though. I know how you get going in vicious circles and then you panic. Just take it slowly. In fact, why don't you just take a vacation and let the feelings take over for awhile. I want you to keep one eye open though, 'cause I'm still a little tender. And my heart hasn't seen a hell of a lot of sunlight yet. Slowly, slowly, slowly, with lots of love and care. Friends? Friends. I travel down the back of my neck. God, it's uptight. You need to relax neck. I give you the same advice I gave my head. It's all okay. It's time to feel good. I travel down my throat and into my chest. My chest is kind of a traffic jam right now. I would imagine just like after the war in New York City. There still seems to be a lot of tears and anger running right down the middle. Those motherfuckers never loved me for one minute. And now I know it. I have called the game. It's still kind'of hard to accept those feelings all the way. I've always felt so god damn isolated. No wonder. The more alone, the harder I tried, the more I sold myself, the more alone I was. Those fucking assholes. And that fucking cunt of a mother of mine. She never squeezed me once or told me she loved me. She didn't love me. She didn't, she didn't, she didn't. I can feel the tears and anger in my chest right now. I think it's going to have to come out in group. I'm just so tired, I need a rest. But it has to come out pretty soon, and be done with it. I go over to my heart and that feels much better. My heart is round and red and plump and just really full. What a beautiful heart. It's thumping away, and alive, and so full of love that it looks like a little kid's cheeks full of air. It is soft and strong at the same time, and it's full of hugs and kisses and dreams of sunshine and really loving myself. I think that dream is pretty close now, at least I know that now I have a chance for it. It's hard for me to picture, but I feel like there is a possibility of a slow sunshiny life that is really enjoyable. As soon as I think about that I get scared and the old head starts in with 'How am I going to do it, and what do I have to do now, and what to achieve. That's what I have to stop. I guess it's going to take some time and practice. Maybe some just sitting around.' The next dream in my heart includes a woman. I'm in my house. It's been a slow day and sunny. My back hurts a little and I'm enjoyably tired from maybe building something or from gardening. I get into bed and there are small paned windows completely covering three sides of the room. There's a hill behind the house and there's no curtains on the window. A couple of the windows are open inward and it's kind of warm out. My wife comes in and she looks out the window and just stands quietly for a minute, and I know she's happy and smiling. She's pleasantly tired, too. She has been excited all day. She's been excited about some project she has going, and she's most warmly excited about being pregnant. And I've been so excited my heart is twice its normal size and still growing. And my head feels like a peach. Anyway, she slowly gets undressed and I can faintly make out the silhouette of her beautiful body. She lets down her hair and she's soft and simple and earthy and beautiful. She comes over and just sits down on the edge of the bed next to me and she says, 'Golly, I love you so very much.' And I say, 'God I love you.' And we just stay right where we are for a second and just really love each other and just let the warmth flow all over us and fill up the room. Then she just hugs me and climbs in bed and we hug each other so tight and so warm and so naked.

"That's what's in my heart, and it's so beautiful. When I think about it I start to figure out 'what to do' and it screws me up. I just want to let it be. That's the kind of life I want to have.

"There's a direct line running from my heart to my penis and balls. When I just go ahead and let my heart feel good, my cock and balls feel so full and just kind of natural, like they're really my cock and balls and really belong to me. When I woke up this morning, I looked at my cock, and it really looked nice to me. Really mine and natural and just the right size. I looked at my cock for a long time and if I may say, it even looked sexy and sexual to me. For the first time I realized that a woman could really want to make love to me in a really feeling and hungry way. Imagine that – a woman with her feelings wanting my body just as much as I wanted her. That sounds far out. When my heart and my cock can feel that way, baby, I'm making hay – you might say.

"There also seems to be a direct connection from my heart to my head. When my heart swells up, my head feels so much lighter and it can dream and create and laugh too.

"Right now it feels like all these things can happen, but they don't seem really together. They are all there, but they don't seem to be able to flow. I think the flow might have a lot to do with just sitting back for a change and climbing into my stomach and not worry about things. And when my stomach says, 'Hey, I REALLY want to taste some of that,' go ahead and taste some. It's okay, and if I don't like it I don't have to be discouraged. I can crawl right back into my stomach and just be. I'm afraid it won't just happen though. And that's what I've always done; I've been responsible to do something more if I wanted something to happen or if I wanted to be loved. My stomach is real hungry, but I can't force-feed it. I would rather sit back and be hungry and just get one little thing at a time than eat what everybody else is eating.

"Who knows, maybe I could really let someone love me and love them back and do what I want, and feel good and feel slowly, all at the same time. If that's not the way the world really is, then I think I'll stay in fantasy for as long as I can."

I Enter Your Journey

Sharon reports feelings of desperation for her boyfriend, filled with fear that he will abandon her. When she is with him, she can only think of what to do that will please him so that he will stay.

In previous discussions she had become aware of how little she mattered to her father – she made no difference to him. I asked her what was the (M/L) most difficult thing to say to her father. She answered, with great difficulty, "You are weak; you can't see me." At that point she became faint and asked to lie down on the couch. I told her to do so.

(S&O) "How did you punish your father?" I asked. Her reply was that she would be angry at him for his peculiar breathing, and then leave the room to punish him for it. Nobody else apparently thought her father's breathing was peculiar.

Shorr: (IS) Where does your anger reside in you?

Sharon: In my chest.

Shorr: (IS) Can you enter your chest and go to it?

Sharon: (Sobbing) Yes, I go in and there is a large steel plate and it's very wide.

Shorr: I want you to use the largest blowtorch you can think of and melt it down.

Sharon: (She continues sobbing and moves her hands as if she is using the blowtorch) Yeah, I can do it — but it takes a long time.

Shorr: Take all the time you need.

Sharon: (Long Pause) I've melted it down.

Shorr: What do you see?

Sharon: I see a bright blue sky and fields.

Shorr: Can you walk into it?

Sharon: No, I can't. (Sobs some more)

Shorr: Let me come with you.

Sharon: (After another pause) O.K., but it's sloping out there. There's a large mound and then a steep slope. I'll fall.

Shorr: I'm holding your hand. Let's build a bridge from that mound. I'll help you build it.

Sharon: It goes to another place, but there is a lot less slope. Then another bridge, then flat fields.

Shorr: You come across a pool of spring water and drink some of it.

Sharon: I want to bathe in it.

Shorr: Go ahead and enjoy yourself.

Sharon: All right. But will you go away?

Shorr: No, I'll just sit here and watch you. I won't go away.

Sharon: (Pause) I'm bathing and I look over at you and you are writing.

Shorr: Enjoy the water. I'll be here.

Sharon: I can't believe you're not going. (Pause) I'm letting myself enjoy the water and it feels good.

Shorr: How do you feel?

Sharon: Very good. Maybe I can believe men won't abandon me.

Good Guts Vs. Bad Guts

Some patients are so thoroughly convinced that they are their alien identity — that they are rotten in (or *to*) their core — that only after a loving relationship with the therapist can they finally allow themselves to examine this so-called rotten core.

Shorr: (IS) Can you sense or imagine a body part of you that is rotten?

Murray: My penis. (Pause) No — guts — yes, a sinking body feeling comes over me. My guts — for a moment I thought my penis, then I decided my guts are the worst part of me. My penis is O.K.

Shorr: Why guts? (Long Pause)

Murray: They're rotten — (Pause) — It's very hard to say. It's that they're — (Pause) — putrid. That word is very difficult to say.

Shorr: Can you hand them to me using your imagination?

Murray: (Pause) – I don't know. It seems easy and yet – I know I have to make sure I do it with my feelings. (Long Pause – Murray, after several half-attempts, reaches across belly and scoops out 'guts.' Holds them down, not wanting to expose them to full light by holding them up.)

Shorr: What did you see?

Murray: They're – (Pause) – slimy – (Pause) – putrid. They're not good.

Shorr: Can you hand them to me?

Murray: Well – (Pause) – I'm feeling anxious. (Then very reluctantly hands them over to Shorr after making several false starts. Shorr holds them with care.)

Shorr: Do you know what I see?

Murray: No.

Shorr: I see good guts. They are brave, strong, courageous, healthy, loveable, loving. They're not putrid at all. This is a case of the good guts vs. the bad guts. (We both laughed.) You have very good guts. Can you see them this way?

Murray: Well – (Pause) – (Starts smiling – anxious look starts to fade) – I don't know.

Shorr: Here, hold them. (Passes guts back to Murray.)

Murray: (Holds guts a little nervously while examining them.) I guess they're OK.

Shorr: Can you put them back?

Murray: (Slowly lowers them into his belly and carefully seals them in. Suddenly he starts patting his tummy. At first gently, then more vigorously.) I like this. These feel good. I like them.

Shorr: You have good guts – everyone does naturally. You were taught that they were bad guts. What do you think that the bad guts did for you?

Murray: They – (Long Pause) – they prevented intimacy. I couldn't have any close contact or people would discover how rotten I was. I had to compete and keep control of every situation to retain my secret. I feared discovery of my rottenness – my inadequacy.

As will be seen later, many of the focusing techniques may occur in group therapy. The interaction of the group members seems to be a valuable point of integration for the person attempting healthier methods of coping with his conflicts; it allows the possibility of strength, of individual growth, and the demonstration of new life values. Of course, all of life outside the therapy room (whether the therapy is individual or group) serves as a point of integration for the new behavior.

Liberation From the Body of the Other

This young man felt castrated, duty-bound and obligated to his mother. He feared women could enslave him if he didn't perform. Coupled with this was a constant suspicion that women were about to entrap him. He would become circular in his self-accusations; first, that they were regarding him only as a problem and not as himself, and second, that they wanted him but didn't care about his .

problems. There was no way he imagined a woman could please him, no way he could please himself.

In the course of a session, the strong enveloping hold which his mother exerted on him became clearer and clearer. The imaginary situation (IS) "Imagine entering your mother's vagina and fight your way out" was presented to him. So embarrassed and ashamed was he that he could not do the imagery in front of me. Here is the verbatim audiotape of the imaginary situation which he finally managed to complete in his own apartment.

(There is one minute or so of silence – clattering noises – heavy breathing.) "I feel embarrassed doing this – don't know if I can do it – (Sigh) – it's really scary – I guess I'm afraid of the ridicule for even doing this right now – Joe asked me Friday to – crawl into my mother's vagina – and come back out again – and I feel like I'm in there (Sigh) – and it's – it's like all of therapy – coming back into a circle again – it's like it it's really the life, it's life or death struggle to be here or not to be here (Slight Chuckle) – and we talked about it Friday – the overwhelming feeling was – that I was embarrassed to do it even with Joe – it's like really a baby. (Sigh) We talked this morning and it's really being the castrated man – it's living in my mother's vagina – the incredible power she had over me – and it's embarrassing, every fucking thing I've been through – it's like (Slight Chuckle) it's all been kind of a survival thing, like getting rid of the paranoia – at least getting my mother out of my body – keeping her out there – but it has to go beyond that, it has to be me living my life with my balls – (Sigh) – there's a, this imaginary situation brings together like the whole shot, it's – well – that's life – finish the sentence, 'Never refer to me as,' it would still be – 'Never refer to me as the baby,' and (Sigh) the way my mother related to me was keeping me as a baby, keeping me as hers – and (Sigh) what I did back was, the way I punished her was – 'Okay, I'll be a baby – but you won't get any more of me – so I'll go ahead and relate to you as a baby,' (Sigh) which is how she got her hate out of me – she would keep me that way – all I would show her was my 'baby' – and all I will show a woman to this day is my 'baby' so that I don't get taken over – it's like she could take me over as a baby and I would relate to her and I went along with that, that was fine but I'll be damned if I'll let you take the real Steve over, I'll be damned if I'll let you have my balls – but, that neurotic conflict resolution screws me in the end – because I still relate as the baby – the other part of it was the humiliation from my brothers and from my father – it's like as I imagine myself, not actually doing it but as I imagine what would happen, me fighting out of the womb – it's like it's the most difficult thing that I've ever done – at the same time as I imagine myself doing it – the thing that – one of the things that is just so fucking impossible about it – is that as I'm fighting out – as I'm fighting not to be the baby – as I'm fighting to be the fucking man I am – it's like my brothers and my father are laughing and ridiculing and still calling me baby – no matter that I'm beating my way out with machetes or – or flame throwers or whatever the hell I'm using; it's like they're still laughing at me as the baby — and that's the way they related to me as a kid — (Sigh) my imagination says that even, it's like I fight my way out of my mother's vagina — and it's like then they're still there and it's like having fought my way out and being a man — which none of them are, I feel — it's like then I threaten the hell out of them — and I imagine violence coming from them because they're so damn threatened at that point — at the same time I guess actually doing it I might find that the strength I have and the power I have, I might threaten the hell out of them so much that I might not even have to worry about them — in the end — Sooo (Sigh) that's where it's at, being a baby with my mother — my father and my brothers always referred to me as a baby. I always felt like a fucking baby, no matter what I do — it's like in the end I will always be the baby — and that feels really fucking alone — it's like it doesn't work for me anymore — to be the baby — just talking right now, I was feeling really self-conscious about sitting here in my own room talking to a tape recorder, but it feels better, like being here alone, because of the fucking humiliation — it's like that would get me into a bind of not even being able to move, not knowing which way to go no matter what. I would be a baby — I go to my mother and that's a baby, I try and fight out of it and that's a baby, and like the constant ridicule, the constant laughing, the constant humiliation, the thing of laying on the bathroom floor, the time I fainted — it's like that was the total humiliation, and at that point it's like it didn't make any difference anymore — (Sigh) — (Sounds of Crying) — Ooh — (Sigh) (Sniff) — the dreams that I had last night — had some incredible dreams — one of them was of Lucille Heatherton — and like I hadn't even been able to remember her face but in the dream last night her face was right there, exactly as her face is — about the whole thing with her and Logan — the other dream was that my brother was giving me a blow job and that's the point that I feel I've gotten to, it's like — hopeless with a woman — and yet realizing what's going on now, the hopelessness is kind of — I feel like there's something I can do about it — I forget the other dream, (Deep Breath) — (Sighing) — well anyway I guess that's enough for the dreams, those dreams themselves, it's like, (Sigh) it's the part of me I guess I've always been afraid of — it's like, finally the impotence I feel like — Jesus Christ — you know, I would rather be a homosexual than — than a — no, I wouldn't be (Slight Snicker) — that's the way it feels — feels castrated, feels helpless — (Sighing) — I don't know, but a — (Loud Sigh) — this is really hard — my a — sitting here with my eyes closed I can imagine being in the womb — (Chuckle) — I'm really scared to do this — (Sighing) — it's like my feeling is — it's like I'm laying down in the womb — and if I'm just laying there not making a move, or not standing up for myself or not being the man that I am — not being sexual or not being — competitive or anything else, like as long as I don't make any problem — I'm okay — I — I mean not okay but — I won't get the retaliation — it's like as soon as I start to make a move — it's like the retaliation is going to be there — the — the picture I have is an — it's like as soon as (Voice Cracks) I — or I start to get up and press into the meat of her womb or whatever it is — inside of her vagina, it's like it's going to smother me to death, it's going to clamp down on me and it's like once I make my move it's going to be all or nothing — and it's like, it's going to be the battle of my life — (Sigh) — it's humiliating (Teary Voice) — it's humiliating — (Sigh) — I don't know if I can do it right now without support of some kind, I feel like I have the support, it's like (Sniff — Sigh) talking to Joe this morning, Joe will be there — aah — I can call all sorts of people if I want to — maybe I really do have to do it on my own — (Sighing) — I don't know maybe I'll just — (Clatter Noise) no, no, like this has to be for me — (Sighing) — it's like I'll be god damned if I'm going to go through this again — it's like it's got to be for me my way — there's no way to perform this anymore — only perform is to get the recognition and make sure that I don't get the humiliation instead — those sons-of-bitches — (Sigh) — (Sniff) (Voice — sound of crying) This is a — I was thinking the other night — it's like with the humiliated — with warmth — when I used to have it, it's like any kind of feeling, it's true it was any kind of feeling but the more specifically — the feeling that they humiliated the most in me was the warmth — it's like they — they couldn't stand the warmth and joy is included in there — the time I was skipping down the driveway and I got the ridicule for the joy that I was feeling — it's like that's when I shut it off, there was no way that I was going to feel warmth in that family — um — it's so incredible, it's like it takes some of their power away, I guess even — even thinking about that (Sighing — aaah) just like they weren't men at all (Slight Chuckle) — I remember my father used to watch television and if any kind of — if any kind of sad scene, a movie, or a love scene, or any kind of feeling that would bring feeling out in, in the rest of people in the family, my father would sit there and he would have to laugh and make jokes and ridicule until the scene was over. I mean it was so fucking threatening to him to have any kind of feeling go — it's like — feelings were to be ridiculed and humiliated — the only other, the only time, I mean (Deep Breath, Sigh) it's like I say warmth, it was (Voice — Snicker) still humiliation, I mean it wasn't warmth at all, but the only time my father even really touched me, in a semblance of anything, but it was just a bunch of bullshit and that was that I was crying on the floor as a little kid — he picked me up in the rocking chair and I was like about probably four years old or something like that, and he said, 'Poor, poor baby' and made me stay there — he grabbed onto me and wouldn't let me go and just humiliated me for crying — (Chuckle) and that was the only touch I ever got from my father except for, for getting hit or, or swung on — (Sniff) — just kind of like to break that humiliation, to break the babyness — always a fucking battle, am I a baby, am I a man, am I a fag, do I have balls, can I make it with a woman — (Sighing) — it's like no matter what — it's fighting my way out of the vagina — (Sigh) — Joe asked me — it's like I've been saying, you know, like the girls at school, it's like they're babies, they're, they're — they're not for me, they're not enough or something, they're not mature enough — and he asked me if my mother was a baby, well I didn't answer it right then, but yeah my mother, my mother was really a baby and that was the one way she really got to me, it's like the only thing I identified as warmth as a kid was my, was my mother's babyness, her, her, her martyrdom, her inability to fight back, her helplessness, her, her just laying down and taking it all, and it's like, it's like I would − fight her battle for her − I would scream at her, 'Why in the fuck don't you, you know, get what you want or something like that'; (Sighing) − it's like my, you know, it's like my own battles (Sighing) − why in the hell couldn't I get what I wanted − (Sigh) − she was a baby and that's, and, and I guess her tears, her babyness is, is what I identified with − as being some sort of feeling, I mean that's the way I felt − to my mother − I was her sick comrade, in her sickness − but I don't think I need to go on anymore with that (Big Breath) (With a teary voice) − I will go ahead and try it − I don't know how many of my feelings I got in here right now (Big Sigh) − I'm pretty much there I guess → pretty much laying down in her fucking womb − (Sniff) − I think I'll lay on − I think I'll lay down on the bed − (Sigh) − god damn son-of-a-bitch − (Long Sigh) − begins to feel so, so fucking difficult, feels so fucking difficult − (Sigh) − I don't know what's going to happen − it's like once I start I don't know what's going to happen − I don't know what tools I need but I guess I can have any tools I want − just feel like the fucking meat is just going to surround me, it's like, no matter what, it's like it can crush anything, it's, that it's just, the retaliation is just incredible − (Aaagh − Sighing) − (Big Sigh) − (Sniff) − (Clatter on the mike) − (Big Sigh) − (Big Sigh) − (Sniff) − that's funny, I got a big machete − it's like there's meat on the other end (Chuckle) − I'm afraid, and just keeps coming down, I wish I could just be tight around me − (Heavy Breathing − Sigh) − (Angrily) fucking cunt − she sucked me in, she sucked me all the way in and that's where the fuck I've been − (Sigh) − GOD DAMN YOU − (Heavy breathing − few seconds) − keep it screaming, it's what they want in there, it's like the helplessness and the powerlessness to, to scream and be crazy, it's like that didn't work all I got was humiliation − (Sigh) − FUCK YOU, YOU FUCKING CUNT − (Sigh) − you horrible evil bitch − you slimy shit − (Sigh) − I'm just so scared − (Sigh) − just have to take my time with it − (Big Sigh) − (Sigh) − so afraid of the humiliation − shameful to be a man that's what I'm saying, it's shameful to be a man − (Sigh) − (Sniff) − I'll sit up in the chair − (Noise of walking and noise of the mike) − (Sigh) − SWISH − (Sigh) − track of blood comes trickling down − it's like it's starting to envelop me − SWOOSH − (Sigh) − it pulls back a little bit − then it starts coming down − I stand up − (Sigh) − I have a little bit of room − it, like it's closing in right around me − (Sigh) − SWISH − SWISH − (Sigh) − as long as I slash at it − I can keep my room anyway − keep the room right around me − (Sigh) − I'll use the flame thrower just to, just to singe it back, just to burn it, just to make it pull back − SWOOOOOO − SWOOOOOO − SWOOOOOO − SWOOOOOO − SWOOOOOO − SWOOOOOO − (Sigh) − Oh balls (Agonized Voice) − Ooooooh − (Sigh) − (Breathing heavily while talking) − it's pulled back, I don't know what direction to go in now, I don't know which way is out, it's like everything is sealed up − I feel it's in front of me, I feel like the pathway is — feel like it's in front of me — (Sigh) — take one step forward — it's like there I am, it's like there's just a fucking wall of meat in front of me — (Sigh) — I feel real weak in my knees — (Sigh) — take a long, like a long spear — (Sniff) — god it's hot, it's a hot spear, it's like the ends — a red hot — right on into the fucking wall — it pulls back a little bit, it's like I can see there's the slit, there's the opening (Sigh) — (Sniff) — and I just keep poking and poking and it opens up a little bit — it's like I can see the opening, can't see any light, can't see the light but I can see an opening — (Sigh) — (Sniff) — like I see a tunnel, I see a tunnel there — (Sigh) — I don't know if I want to climb into that or not but I got this — it's like the womb is like seared, it's like seared open — (Sigh) — (Stronger Voice) — I'm coming out — fuck all of you, fuck you man, I'm coming out — god damn I'm coming out, you're not stopping me now — you're not stopping me — (Sigh) — (Sigh) — Joe's out there — Joe's out there — (Sniff) — (Sigh) — Joe's out there — (Sigh) — all I got to do is make my way out — (Sigh) — (Sniff) — I can do it, I know I can do it, I can't do it right now but I know I can do it, I know I can do it — (Sigh) — (Sniff) — (Sigh) — just as I take one step, this just starts the stuff just fucking closing in on me again — like all over around my neck and my back — (Sniff) — (Sigh) — SWISH — take a slice out — SWISH — (Sigh) — cuts the meat all up and down the sides — SWISH — just *whack* the meat away, just *whack* the meat away, just WHACK it away — it's not closing in so much — I'm scared of having my feelings, I don't know, I don't know right now — I'm just feeling — (Sigh) — I don't know if I can do it ‑‑‑‑‑‑‑ see, (Sniff) ‑‑‑‑‑‑‑ said it before, don't want to perform it — I don't want to perform it — (Sigh) — I don't want to perform (Sigh) — I got to do it — (Sounds of throwing up) (Tape went dead) — I feel my cock — like I can have my cock for me, I'm having my cock for me — fucking bitch — (Sigh) — (Louder Voice) — my cock for me — my cock for me — MY COCK FOR ME — MINE — IT'S MY COCK — (Sigh) just get it out — SWISH — SWISHHH — SWISHHH — SWISH — SWISH — SWISH — SWISHHHH — SWISH — SWISHHH — SWISHHHHHH — (Lots of foot noise during this) — SWISHHH — SWISHHHHHHHH — SWISHHHHHHHHH — SWISHHHHHHHHH — SWISHHHHHHHHH — SWISHHHHHHHHH — SWISHHHHHHH — SWISHHHHHHHHHH — SWISHHHHHHHHHH — (Sigh) — SWISHHHHHHHH — (Heavy breathing for one minute) — I don't know where I am — I feel like I'm on the outside — it's like I can see her cunt from the outside — I don't know where I am with it — feel like I can use the fucking flame thrower and like just burn it up — swooooo — ugly fucking cunt — looks like her vagina just ripped open — try and stand up now — (Sigh) — (Sigh) — (Sigh) — she's lying down, she's little — all the fucking shit all my whole fucking life — I'll get the machete — SWISH — SWISH — SWISH — SWISH — (Sigh) — SWISH — I just want to cut it to pieces — SWISH — (SIGH) — fucking ugly cunt — (Sigh) — (Sigh) — (Sigh) — I want Joe's arm around me — put your arm around me Joe — (Prior line said with sad voice) ‑‑ I can see your face — I don't even know if I need your help or not — (Sigh) — but it's okay I

guess if I have to do more, I have to do more I don't know — I've held myself inside
— I don't know if I got out the old things or not, feel like I'm on the outside but
don't know if I went through it or not, I don't know if I can trust myself or not —
(Sigh) — (Sigh) — try and see her face at least, she's dead — she's just dead,
she's . . . dead, it prided me, didn't surround me but it, but any way I cut, it's okay
— (Sigh) — put your hand on my shoulder (Sad Voice) — (Sigh) — you (Chuckle)
have a nice face — (Loud Exhale) — I'm scared I'm still back in there — (Sigh) — I
don't know — I must be — (Sigh — Sigh — Sigh — Sigh) I don't know — (Sounds of
walking) — don't think I've quite made it out — feel like I got into the, like I got
into the canal, like, the vagina itself is closed up tight on the end — it's like I can go
in the canal and not be smothered like I thought I would be — I'm stronger, I'm a
fuck of a lot stronger than I thought I was — (Sigh) — it's like, it's like I'm still in
the canal — at least I got — anyway I begin feeling sexual just like, just like getting
to the, to the, to the, vagina itself, it's like the outer genitals makes me feel sexual,
even to cut it up makes me feel sexual, like to cut her vagina up and have my cock
— yeah — I'll make a slash crossways — SWISH — yeah, just kind of makes it open
up a little bit, see light out there and there's Joe grinning out there — I can't, it's
not wide enough yet — (Sigh) — I just start slashing the sides of it and just cutting
meat off, just, just, cutting meat out — SWISH — SWISH — cutting across the top
and on the sides and just whacking it, cutting hunks of meat out — just cutting it
out, it's like behind me is just pus, shit, just — evil as — cutting and cutting —
SWISH — (Sigh) — it's like it's open, like the vagina's open — I put a bar across the
opening, one at the top and one at the bottom to make sure it stays open, just
stand there (Sigh) — I turn around and look back — it's just ugly and black, dark in
there, what a horrible place to have lived — it's horrible — and it's not even
powerful — just like a vacant hole — turn back around — and here's the opening and
all I have to do is step out — Joe's sitting there laughing, 'Come on Steve' — says all
you do is step out — Oh yeah, I won't worry about my brothers and my father
being out there someplace right now, 'cause they could destroy me — (Stronger
Voice) — I ain't no fucking baby no more, I'm not a baby — I can have my feelings,
and I can hack my own way out, I can be a man, I don't need to live around in a
fucking vagina, I don't need you, I don't need your vagina anymore, I don't need
your fucking vagina — I don't need your god damn womb, I don't need what you
told me was love — I don't need my own fucking tears — I don't need my own
impotence — I don't need to feel sorry for you, feel sorry for your own fucking self
— you felt sorry for yourself your whole life and died that way, you died of cancer
— a death well deserved — I'm a man with my own fucking cock and I'm going to
use it and it's going to be happy and strong and my balls are going to hang between
my legs, and you guys, you can, you can laugh and you can ridicule and you can sit
there and slop in that fucking vagina and hate each other and kill one another —
and suck off of her dead pussy — evil sons-of-bitches — you're no men — you're
weak, you're weak, you're really weak — you're the babies and I thought you were

men — fuck you — it's like I push that opening of the vagina with my hands, I push it open — it went away — step out — (Sigh) — feel like I got balls right now (Sigh) to here, like I'm stepping out, turn around — let it close — it's an ugly vagina — it's like the vagina's still not as tight at least, feels like my shoulders are getting bigger — my chest is expanding a little bit — (Sigh) — pull myself out — (Sigh) — I'm growing up bigger — (Sigh) — I'm a man, I'm a man with balls, I'm a god damn man — fucking a — I don't need to be in your vagina, I don't need to be there no more, I don't need to be in your vagina — I don't need your vagina — I don't need to be a baby — I need to be a man — need to feel good about my balls and my cock — don't need to feel ashamed, don't need to feel like I have a little cock — I got a nice cock, I got a nice big cock — and balls that are mine — and I can fuck with them, feel good about them natural, not uptight, not embarrassed, not feel like a little kid, not humiliated — you fucking old man, you don't even know what a cock is — you got a fucking angry cock — you got a weak cock, it's limp — you gonna all live together, you fucking cunt and you fucking sons-of-bitches — live together, I don't need you, I don't need you at all anymore and I don't need to be crazy, I don't need to be in an impotent rage all the time either — I can have Steve — I want to love a woman of my own choice — and I don't have her right now but that's all right — I don't want what you guys have — I want my balls and my cock first of all and I got 'em — anybody want to argue about it, any fucking brothers want to argue about it — want to try laughing — aah you're scared shitless aren't you — you want to try something, come on — beat the fucking shit out of you — I don't need no machete for you guys either — come on you chickenshits, you laughed while I was in there, now laugh that I'm out, come on — what's wrong, can't you do it — yeh, turn your tail, run back in there and hide, hide in the vagina, go ahead, go back in there then you can laugh in there, you can laugh your hearts out — cry for yourself — sick people, you're sick, you're really sick — and I thought I was the only one who was sick — I got feelings my whole life and a hell of a lot of strength and I played baby instead, it was the only way I knew how — you can take it from me, fuckers, you can all go wallow in your own puke and your own shit, I'm sick of it — (Sounds of walking about) — (Clattering noise) — (Sighing — aaah) — I feel sick to my stomach, I feel like I want to throw up — I'm so sick of 'em all — I can see them all around the vagina — they're all little and they're all crazy, like little midgets — I feel just really sick — I want it all out of me, all of it — yaaaaaaagh — yaaaaaagh — (Coughs) — (Sounds of throwing up for approximately one minute) — (Sniff) — (Sigh) — feels like one of them is caught in my throat — which one — Ron, good old Ron, you weak son-of-a-bitch, you shit (Sounds of throwing up four times) — it won't come out and I reach in and (Sounds of throwing up) (Sighing — Saying, aaah — oohh — aaggg) — Yaaaaag, it's out — ooooooh — ooooooh — (Sighing — ooooooooooh) — ooooooooh — (Sigh) — Sigh) — ooooh — (Sounds of throwing up) — (Sigh) — (Sigh) — oh that feels better — (Sighing — aaah) — wallow in the puke you shits, wallow in your puke — (Sniff) — (Sigh) — OOOOHH —

(Sniff) – (Sigh) – (Sigh) – (Sniff) – now I need to wipe them up and put them in the toilet (Sounds of walking away) – (and return) – (Cough) – (Sounds of wiping up) – (Sniff) – (Sigh) – (Sigh) – (Sigh) – (Sigh) – (Sigh) – (Sounds of walking) – (Toilet flushing) – (Loud cough) – (Walking back) – (Sniff) – (Sigh) – (Sigh) . . . . (Clatter noise – walking to door) – (Sigh) – in fact there's light outside, looks nice outside – it's beautiful (Noise) – (Sigh) – fresh air, a glass of cold water – (Sighing deep – oooooh) – another one – (Exhale) – and another one from a brook, aaah with the cold breeze and trees and people – my friends – hot sun, cold water – (Sigh) – (Sigh) – (Sigh) – (Sigh) – (Sigh) – that tree outside my window is beautiful – it's what I love, mountains and a blue sky and the trees and the grass, it's so beautiful out – it's mine and I don't have to be alone – I've got me – I don't think I'll ever go back into the vagina I'm scared I will – I'm scared I'll go back in – I don't think I want to, I don't want to, I don't want to go, I don't ever want to go back in – not unless I want to wallow in shit and pus and puke with them – I got no reason to go back in – (Sigh) –––– it's like it's so new for me to be myself – and I'm not even sure where I'm at right now – I'm not sure what it's like to be me and not be so afraid of humiliation – I feel like I can calm down now – and still be me, it's like I can laugh but I can be calm or I can be angry and I can be calm, like I can have all my feelings and be calm – like some inner strength, a core of strength. I can feel my cock like a core right now – like my cock and my balls and my whole crotch are like coming right up the middle of me into my chest – especially my balls ------- (Sniff) ---------- (Noise) ---------- that's enough for now ----------."

In the months which followed this rather powerful imagery experience, a marked change in Steve's feelings took place. He reported feeling more masculine, less inclined to anticipate his former "obligatory" mode of behavior towards women. Occasionally, he still experienced "entrapment" feelings in his relationships with women, but the likelihood of any real entrapment was appreciably diminished. Being defined by women and being without a choice were conditions of decreasing probability. Steve had become freer and enjoyed a more positive self-image.

CHAPTER 15

Imagery and Dialogue

I have audiotaped several hundred hours of sessions between myself and patients, utilizing the methods set forth in the previous chapters. About a year ago I attempted a videotape of myself and a woman named Lynne who had been in group therapy with another therapist but had now been out of direct contact with therapy for several years. Lynne had heard of some of my methods from her previous therapist (who is my colleague) and expressed interest in doing a videotape. Of course, I was interested too. She had appeared on TV years ago and expressed no self-consciousness about the possibility of videotaping a therapy session. What follows is a verbatim record of the audio portion of the videotape. Other than what I have mentioned, I knew nothing more of her than her name.

In choosing this session, I am aware that it is limited insofar as it could not possibly cover each and every point encompassed in the preceding chapters. The reader is asked to be aware that this is only *one* session and essentially the beginning session between me and Lynne. The range of possibilities is vast and I could only attend to the subject which arose in this session. There are no *typical* sessions, as each session takes on the feelings and attitudes of the people involved. The reader should be also aware that a printed text of necessity leaves out many nuances, voice changes, physical movements and other nonverbal manifestations of the session.

A year or so after the videotape was made I asked Lynne to return, listen, and comment about the tape at any point she wished. (She volunteered to inform me that she had been too busy to get any therapy in the last year.)

Spaced below the text are her comments, taped one year after the original recording.

(A note to the reader. From previous experience with patient-therapist printed texts accompanied by patient comments, it seems clearer if the reader would read the entire patient-therapist text first and then read the patient comments second, in that order.)

Shorr: How do you feel, Lynne, coming here?
Lynne: Oh, I guess I feel all right about it, just a little bit shook up at first.
Shorr: Shook up? You mean . . .
Lynne: Well, you know, I think my getting lost really was a sort of a — I mean I tried not to get lost.
Shorr: Before you came here, you mean?
Lynne: I really tried because I was afraid of getting lost for the simple reason that this is sort of a strange thing for me to go back to. I have avoided, tried to avoid being in front of a camera altogether.

Shorr: Well, we're on the camera right now. How does it feel?

Lynne: Well, that's fine. Hi there. (Laughs looking into camera)

Shorr: Good. Where can we start? How should I not refer to you? In other words I can refer to you in any way but what's one way you would not want me to refer to you as?

Lynne: I don't think that at this moment that there is anyway. There was awhile that I would have resented being referred to as Lynne in any way because I consider that a part of a dead past and I think at this moment I . . .

Shorr: (S&O) Well, what about what quality would you now not want to be referred to as, any quality you can think of?

Lynne: You mean in order that you are going to avoid it or in order that . . .

Shorr: No, if I said to you (FTS) never refer to you as whatever quality that would be.

Lynne: Well, I think an actress.

Shorr: That's the worst?

Lynne: Uh huh. That's sort of − oh, I guess that's sort of like saying you're bad. I'm free associating right now. But it's like saying you're bad and you're insecure and you're not loved. Now that makes me feel like crying. (Pause)

Shorr: (M/L) Who is the most unloved person that you know of?

Lynne: My mother and me. And I don't particularly like my mother at all.

Shorr: I want you to try something. I want you to − it might be that you close your eyes or focus at a point with your eyes opened and I want you to imagine something − O.K.?

Lynne: Will this be pleasant or unpleasant?

It's very significant, I think, that I forgot all about having said anything like that even though I felt that − it's interesting because I actually never did want to be an actress; however, lately as I progress in therapy, I feel that there wouldn't be much . . . oh, phoniness in acting. I think it's more or less a betrayal of the truth as you see it. That's strange because at one point I had to use the cobalt treatment for cancer on my face and I was just petrified − absolutely petrified of the machine even though there was no pain whatsoever associated with it and I think the crushing very possibly could have been pressured into anything.

On the part where I say I feel the pressure is my mother. Oh, I think it's amusing that I say that I'm blending with it because I really actually don't feel that at this moment. That I would want to be a part of my mother − she is more like a child that has to be taken care of and I am more of a grown-up, but, oh, I don't know − I guess I could humor the child but I don't feel it's all that threatening anymore.

On the mention of the people that I have used through the telescope, they were sort of tied into one another. Only recently, I have begun to feel that there might be a possibility of my being open to other people and accepting them, therefore accepting myself. At the brink of the recording I feel I was less able to accept myself or feel that I would be receptive or open to other people.

Shorr: Well, I'll tell you and you will imagine whatever you wish — let your own imagination go as it will.

Lynne: O.K.

Shorr: I don't have a preconceived idea — you just let your imagination roam — O.K.?

Lynne: O.K.

Shorr: (IS) I want you to imagine that above you and behind you is a force — now you try to imagine that force.

Lynne: What kind of force is it?

Shorr: That's what I want you to do. Using your imagination.

Lynne: Well, I see it as a crushing force.

Shorr: A crushing force.

Lynne: Sort of, if there were heavy, you know, one of those radioactive machines that they use for cancer — one over here and one behind me and they are both trying to crush me and I'm resisting them.

Shorr: You are resisting them. Now what I want you to do — still imagining (IS) — see if you can imagine that particular thing you mentioned as the force — humanize it in some way. In other words, give it human form if you possibly can. Use your imagination and let it be your guide.

Lynne: Well, I don't have to imagine very hard, it just came to me immediately — my mother.

Shorr: She is pushing you, you mean?

Lynne: The pressure.

Shorr: Pressuring you?

Lynne: Both pressures. They are sort of me and my mother combined. They are one in the same. I am my mother and my mother is me.

Shorr: And you are resisting as you said that.

Lynne: All of a sudden I'm not so much — I'm blending with it. I guess that would be the word — blending.

Shorr: You're just letting it happen to you, you mean?

Lynne: I'm accepting it, rather than trying to hold back from it.

Shorr: How do you feel about accepting it?

Lynne: Good! It feels like, well, to hell with it, you know. It's not a thing — it's something that I have imagined; therefore, I can release it. I can make it what I

On the part where I see the other telescope and I see the people that hate one another. It's rather strange that I say that people hate one another because perhaps at that point it was me hating myself and also me probably hating other people at their ability to communicate with one another.

On the part — I look through a mirror and I see a picture of my mother when she was about seventeen or twenty — uh, it's rather interesting that I see her looking gentle because most of the time, every time I can remember my mother, I see her looking annoyed and angry and displeased. So, well, I'm not too sure but I think that maybe the gentleness which I feel I have a lot of but I don't feel my mother is a very gentle person.

wanted to make it. I mean, it could be flowers falling or it could be anything, but it doesn't have to be dangerous.

Shorr: Now, what I want you to do is try to imagine something else. (IS) I want you to imagine that you are looking through a telescope and tell me what you see using your imagination as your guide.

Lynne: Oh, the first thing was the stars and the planets and then I see, well, maybe a never-never land.

Shorr: A never-never land? What does it look like?

Lynne: It's blue, a very beautiful blue and green and the people are happy and they are sort of tied into one another.

Shorr: You like that, huh?

Lynne: It makes me feel like crying. It's sad because it's like it's not going to happen. I've imagined that.

Shorr: (IS) Now what I want you to do is imagine turning around completely 180° and there you find another telescope that looks away from the one you just looked through.

Lynne: Oh, that's bad.

Shorr: What is it?

Lynne: Oh, it's like people are today. There's hate and dirty and dirty — the air is dirty and everything around it is nasty — there is no love maybe even worse than today — sort of at a time when there is no love at all, and people hate only — that's all they do is hate and destroy — they don't understand — they don't know anything. It's just black and gray and hateful.

Shorr: (IS) Now I want you to imagine — switching to another one — that you look into a mirror and instead of seeing yourself which you would of course see, try to imagine somebody else other than yourself. Whom do you see?

Lynne: I see another me.

Shorr: No, but if you were to see someone other than yourself — of course, you would normally see yourself, but to imagine someone other than yourself.

Lynne: Would it be someone I like or don't like?

Shorr: It could be anybody, see I don't have the answers.

Lynne: Well, the picture that comes to my mind is this picture of my mother when she was about sixteen and she posed for some kind of hair ad and she's got very long, long, black wavy hair and she's got very soft, dark eyes and she's smiling and she looks very gentle in that picture.

Shorr: And she was sixteen at the time?

Lynne: She looks (Pause) — and gentle in an appealing way.

Shorr: (IS) Now I want you to say something to your mother that you see in the mirror — the image you've just seen — say something to her.

On the part where I talk to my mother through the mirror and I hear her saying when I ask her what happened, I hear her saying I don't understand. It's rather reminiscing of my behavior when things get too much pressure for me and I can't handle them for me to say that I am mixed up or I don't understand — there's quite a great deal of similarity here that perhaps it is more me saying that I don't understand, or that I am mixed up, than my mother.

Lynne: I don't think I can.

Shorr: Try.

Lynne: This is very hard. Well, I could ask her what happened. You want me to talk to her?

Shorr: What does she say back?

Lynne: She doesn't know.

Shorr: What does she say, what is her statement to you back?

Lynne: I don't know. Or she could say in Italian, *"No capisco"* — I don't understand. I don't know why I am throwing in the Italian but that's coming to me.

Shorr: *No caprisco?*

Lynne: *No capisco* — I don't understand — it's a smile and everything but yea, I put this up — I don't understand, it's like I could say to her, why don't you accept me and she would still say I don't understand.

Shorr: No capisco.

Lynne: She threw another language in — Spanish — *non comprendo* — it wouldn't matter — it would always be confusion. It would be something that I — I try to reach but I can't because what I am reaching for — it's such confusion.

Shorr: That's the way she dealt with you, you mean, with confusion. And so when you talk to her now in the mirror — even though she is sixteen years old at the time — the image you got you feel a lot of confusion. Now I want you — we'll go back I'm sure to this again but now I want you for a moment to switch to another thing and that is — I want you to imagine two animals — any two at all — there is no right or wrong about any of these as you know.

Lynne: The same kind of animals?

Shorr: (IS) No, any two different kind of animals I should say. Just whatever comes to your mind.

Lynne: A cat.

Shorr: (IS) And another one. A different one.

Lynne: A parrot.

Shorr: A cat and a parrot. (IS) Now can you give me an adjective for each of the animals.

Lynne: Cat's love, loving.

Shorr: Loving.

Lynne: The parrot's bickering.

Shorr: Now here's what I want you to do. (IS) I want you to imagine a statement that would come from the parrot if it spoke first to the cat.

Lynne: Cat nasty, nasty, nasty.

Shorr: (IS) O.K. Now one from the cat back answering that.

Lynne: Oh, that's O.K., I don't care what you say.

On the part where I feel the confusion in my mother when I look at her through the mirror. It's rather strange again that the confusion actually was created by my mother but I create my own confusion, it appears to me, when I can't deal with something on an emotional level or I can't understand it. There's quite a great deal of similarity here.

Shorr: (IS) Now if the cat were to speak first to the parrot what would it say?

Lynne: I wonder if you are a friend or an enemy.

Shorr: (IS) And the parrot would say back?

Lynne: I don't like you, I don't like you.

Shorr: (IS) Now if the cat and the parrot were to fight, who would win?

Lynne: The parrot.

Shorr: Why is that?

Lynne: 'Cause it would punch out the eyes of the cat.

Shorr: The eyes.

Lynne: And the cat couldn't see.

Shorr: Now this thing between the cat and the parrot — does that remind you about anything in your own life perhaps?

Lynne: My childhood.

Shorr: Your childhood. How's that?

Lynne: Oh, my mother bought me a parrot and it was always getting into trouble and I picked out an alley cat and I loved the cat and she gave it away. You got any Kleenex's?

Shorr: Yes, right in front of you. Sorry . . . you had a very strong reaction to that, huh?

Lynne: It's like all my rights were taken away.

Shorr: (IS) I'd like you to imagine a house in another city — one perhaps you have never seen before, and then try to imagine two rooms in that house. And after you have done that, now try to put a person in each of these rooms that you have imagined. Can you do it?

Lynne: I'm trying, it's hard to imagine a house that I have never seen before.

Shorr: Take your time.

Lynne: O.K.

Shorr: (IS) Can you see the two rooms?

Lynne: There are two separate parts of the house. One is sort of white and peaceful with pretty music — soft. And the other is dark, dreary with no music — it's just empty, it's kind of creepy feeling. It's not horrifying, it's so empty in there, it's so dark.

Shorr: (IS) Can you think of a person in that room?

Lynne: My mother.

Shorr: (IS) Who is in the other room?

Lynne: I am.

Shorr: (IS) Now can — if you had a telephone connected, could you say something to her on the telephone?

On the part between the cat and the parrot, it's interesting that I say, well, the parrot would win because it would punch out the eyes of the cat. Uh, my mother is constantly talking about birds punching the eyes of cats and so forth, and I see this as the cat being nonthreatening and a loving figure and the parrot possibly doing a mother symbol or a bickering and angry symbol of some sort.

Lynne: No, I wouldn't want to talk to her.

Shorr: I see. Does she say anything to you?

Lynne: Well, if she did she would take away the white room. It's just like the telephone would wreck the whole.

Shorr: You mean, as long as you could keep them separate you could survive it?

Lynne: Uh huh.

Shorr: Can you finish the sentence? (FTS) My mother defined me as _____. What word comes to mind?

Lynne: My mother defined me as a *machine.*

Shorr: As masheen? What does that mean?

Lynne: A machine to fulfill . . .

Shorr: Oh, a machine, I'm sorry. I thought you were giving me another Italian word.

Lynne: A machine to fulfill her needs. Not a human being.

Shorr: Just an automaton, you mean. Just a functioning automaton to do as she, as she . . .

Lynne: A doll would be better.

Shorr: Even a doll, huh?

Lynne: A doll that, that can be dressed up, and fixed up and made to look pretty, that has no feelings. You can do anything you want with the doll.

Shorr: At twelve years old I would assume then that that's the way you defined yourself then? The way you just described.

Lynne: At twenty I did.

Shorr: Even at twenty. And how about today in your heart of hearts. Finish the sentence (FTS) I define myself as a _____.

When I imagined the two rooms and I imagined the dark room where my mother is and there is a telephone there and I feel she might call me or I might call her and I feel that she would take away the good feeling and the beautiful room I am in: I feel this is sort of a reflection of a fact, whenever I have done anything, even though my mother says that she is happy that I did it, she asks in such a manner as to make me feel that I didn't do anything very good or to bring about something or say something or insinuate something by the tone of her voice and by this tone of her voice and by this tone sort of take away everything I have gained. I don't think I buy this package anymore, however, oh, I think I'm a little afraid of it. Actually, in the part where I say I won't be allowed to grow even though it is in imagination, I still wouldn't be allowed to grow by my mother. Uh, in that I feel I have grown, however, if I let her get in the picture I wouldn't grow at all. I can feel it very strongly as a part of the saying that kept me back all of the time from really developing all of the time as a human being. I could function in the theatre as a doll, not as a full-fledged performer – it's pretty dull. I think at this point perhaps there is more of a freedom about me than there ever has been even though I still look at my mother in that particular relationship with a deep sorrow now because I don't ever think it will be a workable relationship. She will constantly see me as a little child or a doll and I just can't let it bother me. I have my own life to lead and that's about it.

Lynne: A growing human being.

Shorr: That sounds good.

Lynne: I'm not even frightened about growing. It was kind of interesting but I cannot tie up to that other because if I do it's going to — I've got to remain separated because if I tie up it's going to bring me down. I won't be allowed to grow. Even though I know this is imagination the threat in any way you look at it is there that if I accept anything she says I might as well vegetate. And I don't think I would accept it anymore anyway.

Shorr: Now, I want you to do something — (IS) go to another room completely away from the house you have just mentioned — you are just there by yourself and you walk into a room and in the center of the room is a hole — now I want you to look through the hole, again using your imagination of course as your guide, and tell me what you see with the imagination as you look through the hole in the floor.

Lynne: Well, the first thing that I imagined immediately was like a snake pit. The hole is full of rising snakes and it's slimy and it's — maybe the snakes turn into — into crazy women, maybe even men. They are all locked up down there.

Shorr: (IS) How would it feel if you went down into that pit?

Lynne: Part of me feels that I would be afraid and part of me feels that maybe there could be something I could give, but it's such a big test.

Shorr: It's more than you care to get into, huh?

Lynne: Well, not more than I care to, more than I'm ready to at the moment.

Shorr: (M/L) Who is the most giving person you have ever known?

Lynne: I'd really have to search for that.

Shorr: It's O.K.

Lynne: Maybe my grandmother. Yes — my grandmother.

Shorr: (M/L) Who is the least giving person you have ever known?

Lynne: My mother. But my grandmother would be my father's mother. My grandmother was just a delight to be with. She used to wrestle around with me and pretend she was asleep and then I'd go up to bite her nose and she'd come awake, she wasn't really asleep, and she'd wrestle around with me and she had a good mind and everything was pleasant around her.

Shorr: It sounds like a lot of fun, and happy times, huh?

Lynne: But my mother was there and she made things bad.

Shorr: (S&O) How did your grandmother define you as?

On the part where I remember my grandmother and I remember wrestling with her when she pretends she is asleep and she really isn't and so forth. As I go back now and think about it, I think that was really — I was about three at the time — when we went back to Germany I must have been about nine — but it seems to me with my grandmother I had a real deep human contact — a sense of touch and feeling and enjoyment. And about the only time I did have a sense of contact and being just close to someone for a long, long time. Since then, I hadn't had any and I'm just beginning to recapture that feeling of touching and being close to somebody, but just barely.

Lynne: Somebody she loved. Every time I say love, I think I'm going to cry. I do, as a matter of fact. Wait a minute.

Shorr: Good. (IS) Now if you had telepathic powers so that you could tell what a person in a foreign country was thinking or feeling using your imagination, tell me who the person would be plus what country it's in and what they are feeling or thinking.

Lynne: It would be Spain. And they would be very brave and a lot of fun.

Shorr: You are thinking of a particular person?

Lynne: Yes, a Spanish dancer and, come to think of it, she was also very giving.

Shorr: Someone you've known, I take it.

Lynne: When I was a little girl and she was full of fun. My mother didn't like her either.

Shorr: Your mother didn't seem to like anybody.

Lynne: No — anybody that likes me. That love me. There was a fight for possession there and if they loved me and then I like the, like the Spanish woman — she was a Spanish dancer and she had dogs and animals and I like animals, and I used to want to spend weeks up there and I asked to go there for weeks to stay and my mother would — well, one of the times I went that's when she gave my kitten away and then she kept saying that's no good for you, you shouldn't go there — and it was very happy, very happy. She was married to a Canadian and he was happy too and somehow or other they appeared to be my mother and father but friends too. It was fun there.

Shorr: (IS) Now if you were to imagine yourself on a balance scale — like they use in chemistry or weights — a balance scale and on one side you are standing and on the other side is your father. Tell me what you'd imagine you'd feel and do and so forth.

Lynne: He would weight me down. In other words, his weight would be so heavy that he would bring me down — I mean, I would be up but his weight would be so heavy that I couldn't balance it. He wouldn't do anything; he wouldn't try anything but the weight would be so heavy for me to try to keep those scales even. I couldn't do it.

Shorr: (IS) Could you say something to him?

Lynne: Oh yes. I like my father.

Shorr: (IS) What would you say to him? Can you give me the statement?

Lynne: Yea, I would say, why can't you help me?

Shorr: (IS) And what would he say back?

On looking back on the Spanish dancer and her husband the Canadian man, perhaps when I think of where some formative good feelings began besides my grandmother I think they would have been instrumental in giving me some healthy feeling versus the awful crappy feeling I was getting at home and I think possibly, oh, I can only feel kind of sorry for my mother that she could not give any love to me. She could give me things but never love, and therefore she constantly must have felt threatened when I found someone that could give love and I could give love in return. And I guess she did feel that I could not give her any real love or communicate with her too well.

Lynne: Well you know how your mother is.

Shorr: And how would you feel to that?

Lynne: Rejected.

Shorr: (IS) Now I want you to imagine you are on a train — perhaps in a foreign country — and you are sitting next to a stranger — whom you never see again and I want you to imagine that you tell him a secret — since you won't see him again that you tell him a secret — and tell me what that secret is, using your imagination again.

Lynne: I have to pick a secret first. It's very hard to reach that stranger. I have to make him warm first — approachable.

Shorr: You mean he is not responsive to you?

Lynne: He's a shadow.

Shorr: (IS) Well, how would you go about making him warm toward you then?

Lynne: I was thinking of sex. (Ha, Ha) That's my old hangup. I couldn't talk to him.

Shorr: (IS) How old do you imagine him to be, Lynne?

Lynne: He's about — oh, maybe fortyish. But he's not real defined. I can't make up a definition for him. That's where my problem comes. I . . .

Shorr: (IS) Now I want you to imagine holding his face in your hands and looking straight at his face. Could you get a better definition of him? Could you imagine doing that?

Lynne: He is a ballet dancer. He's all made up in sort of — oh, arched eyebrows and heavy makeup and sad lips — like a clown but not really a clown, he's really more like a satyr. His hair is all curled up and his ears are pointed, and I can't figure out whether he is wicked or evil or good or he is just teasing.

Shorr: You just can't figure him out at all, huh?

Lynne: No — he's . . .

Shorr: (IS) What happens when you hold his face in your hands though?

Lynne: Oh, he smiles. I guess the closest I can come to the stranger is somebody I know or used to know. He was a sculptor named Vito and he had that kind of a face. His eyes gleamed. There was a gleam in his eyes all of the time and he smiled, but you could never be sure whether he liked you or not. But that doesn't matter, I can like him — can't I?

It's interesting when I meet the stranger I'm sitting next to the stranger in the train and at first I see him only as a shadow and I can't reach him and then the fact that I should use sex as the only way in which I could reach him. In the past I used this — this is my only means of communication with anyone. Uh, and it was a bad hangup just trying to communicate with people or feel in touch with people through sex. Since then, I think that I am able to communicate with people through touch and complete warmth and giving but not necessarily calling it sex except perhaps with my husband where I think he's sort of hesitant of touching me in a friendly manner and I — although I used to approach him and hug him and so forth in a friendly manner, I freeze now when I'm close to him because I think I'm going to be rejected — now I don't know how much of this is my own feeling and how much of it is the actual rejection I may be getting from him — I have sort of half a mind to think right now it's probably fifty-fifty and that I'm not really opening up all that much myself.

Shorr: Yea.

Lynne: I'll try to like him.

Shorr: But what is it you want to say to him before you tell him the secret? I want you to say something to him. (M/L) What would be the most difficult thing to say to him? To speak to him?

Lynne: That's kind of hard to do.

Shorr: I know. It's not easy.

Lynne: The most difficult. Maybe that I would like to be a Bohemian like him.

Shorr: Why would that be so difficult to say?

Lynne: Because being a Bohemian then means you have no responsibilities and you sort of paint and draw and act or do whatever you want to do — but you sort of feel like I would be letting somebody down.

Shorr: (S&O) Who would you be letting down if you were a Bohemian? Or you felt free about things?

Lynne: My parents, I guess.

Shorr: So what is this secret you want to tell Vito in this case?

Lynne: That I want to be free like him. Sort of . . .

Shorr: (IS) Try saying that to him — like you are holding his face — and say it freely — don't be afraid — just let it out.

Lynne: Vito, I would like to be free like you.

Shorr: Do you have any feeling behind that? Or are you just saying it?

Lynne: It's sort of a strange feeling.

Shorr: Come on — go ahead — say it.

Lynne: It's good and it's sad.

Shorr: (Focus) Try to say it and mean it and not be afraid of any retaliation. Just say it — just be it.

Lynne: VITO — I WOULD LIKE TO BE FREE LIKE YOU.

Shorr: More feeling this time?

Lynne: And then I could — I COULD DO SOME GOOD THINGS, maybe.

Shorr: You like saying that, don't you? Gee, say it again.

Lynne: Hmmmm.

Shorr: Too much? How do you feel right now?

Lynne: Good!

Shorr: I'm glad.

Lynne: Just give me a minute to . . .

Shorr: Oh, sure.

Lynne: It feels very good, like I — I could really be something different.

It's interesting when I finally do hold the stranger's face in my hands I disguise it still further by making him or putting him in the wild ballet makeup which further confused my seeing anything in his face, and it looks to me as if I'm also seeing him as a clown, perhaps. Uh, I think this is a tool by which I keep myself from actually being in contact with a stranger.

Shorr: (Focus) Right now I'd like you to try, Lynne — I'd like you to try that again. And this time, you know, scream it out. Have your guts — give your guts.

Lynne: O.K., give me a minute.

Shorr: Sure — take your time. This is no rush. We may be on the tape but we're not — we're not interested in a performance — you know we just want your real feelings.

Lynne: I know.

Shorr: I know you know.

Lynne: This should get some interesting feelings this way. It surprised me.

Shorr: I'm glad.

Lynne: It really does. 'Cause I get a lot of insight when — it's very interesting. O.K., I'll try it again. I don't know . . .

Shorr: (Focus) But this time I want you to let it come from your guts and don't be afraid — like I'm here and no retaliation is going to happen. Just say that to Vito — let it out.

Lynne: VITO — I WOULD LIKE TO BE FREE AND JUST BE ABLE TO DO ANYTHING I WANTED TO DO. That's painful.

Shorr: (Focus) Could you get even louder — like more from your guts — like from — from your guts and . . .

Lynne: I'm trying just as hard as I . . .

My goodness, When I'm talking to Vito the sculpturer or thinking of him or holding his — the stranger's face and the hands and thinking of Vito — it just occurred to me that Vito was quite a giving person and he appeared to like me even though I couldn't at the time whether I like him or not or he likes me or not. Uh, he did an awful lot of things for me and he accepted me a hundred percent. I think the problem was I couldn't quite accept him a hundred percent, but he did quite a bit for me in many ways. I think because of Vito, that I finally went to see Shapiro — it was — it was a Doctor. . . . that was going to Vito's sculpturing class and I think it was him that I finally got Shapiro's number and started going there. So, actually Vito was the start of a brand new life for me and he was completely altruistic I think in his own Bohemian manner — he was quite a likable guy as a matter of fact. I remember him as great fun when I tell Vito that I would like to do some good things like he does and I felt like crying and I cried up a time even to this day I still feel that I would like to be much freer than I am now. I would like to be a completely giving person so that I could do something for other people. At the present moment I feel like I'm sort of on the borderline between being giving and not giving. Sort of on a seesaw, but I think I probably will get to the point where I am more giving. I did notice a thing in my voice that when I talk at any time and I am afraid or in connection with my mother or father in any way my voice is very much that of a little girl and that when I talk to Vito with understanding and emotion my voice is that of a mature woman. It's rather indicative of the feeling there. If I am my mother and father's daughter, then I must remain a little confused girl — if I am a grown-up outgoing woman — well, if I ever get there it is a feeling that is both likable and at the same time where the fear is fearsome because it would mean that whatever I decide or do I would have to take full responsibility for it.

Shorr: (Focus) I know it's very difficult — I'm just pushing you — like don't be afraid — let it out.

Lynne: VITO, I WOULD LIKE TO BE FREE — I WOULD LIKE TO DO ANYTHING I WANTED TO DO IN LIFE.

Shorr: That's good.

Lynne: That makes me feel like crying.

Shorr: That's all right. Cry all you want — feel free to cry — if you want to cry. But you felt it a lot more.

Lynne: It is so sad because being free is such a good thing why should it be so sad.

Shorr: You pose a very philosophical question. I couldn't agree with you more.

Lynne: If you were free you could — you could give. When you are not afraid, you can give of yourself.

Shorr: And when you are free you can also accept good things.

Lynne: True.

Shorr: Not only give, but accept that which is good.

Lynne: I think giving is important.

Shorr: Sure.

Lynne: I think you have to have plenty to give a great deal. I've never done so and it's sad that I haven't done it.

Shorr: Well, let me ask you this question, Lynne. (S&O) Who does your giving belong to? A strange question maybe.

Lynne: It's never belonged to me.

Shorr: Who does it belong to?

Lynne: Oh, it goes back to my mother I guess. I remember when I was five years old and there was a benefit for poor children who didn't have anything and so everybody had given these beautiful dolls — all kinds of things for these poor children and my mother and this other lady took me over to look at the toys and they asked me to pick something for myself and I said I didn't want anything for myself because it wasn't for me — it was for the poor children and somehow or other I wound up with this big doll and I hated it because I was depriving some poor kid. They were forcing me to take it instead of enjoying the giving.

Shorr: You mean, they were encouraging selfishness, I gather?

On the part about being free so that I could accept things and give — that's rather strange — I had a point to make here and I sort of blocked it out altogether. It must be meaningful but I had a very definite point to make and I just can't seem to remember what it was. I'll go back to the tape.

The part about the doll at the benefit that was supposed to be given to the poor children and instead my mother and my teacher actually, my first grade teacher that was what it was, wanted me to take it and I did take it even though I had said I didn't want to take it. It's quite vivid in my mind when I think back how I felt this was completely unfair and I could no longer feel that my favorite teacher, her name was Elema, or my mother could ever be fair about anything again. It was sort of a complete disenchantment at that time. I think it may have been a deepening of the feeling that I just could not trust anybody.

Lynne: I didn't want it. I realized at five years old that it was wrong and I knew that I didn't want to do it and that I didn't want that doll and what they were doing was wrong, but they were deciding − I had no choice. I felt rotten because it wasn't a very human thing to do It was worse than selfishness − it was cruel.

Shorr: (S&O) What were the rules in your family for owning things − what was the mother's rule for that or the father's?

Lynne: No rules.

Shorr: The unspoken rule, I mean.

Lynne: Oh I guess everything was my mother's. We did everything to please her − dad wouldn't make a move if my mother didn't approve and I guess we were all afraid of her wrath or more than the wrath was the silent disapproval of − we'd get − both my dad and I kept trying to manipulate ourselves around my mother so that we could not escape punishment because we get it one way or another anyway − to get the least possible. And then my dad depended on me so much that I had to do all of the protecting of him. Even at a young age I had to look out for him − and that was too much for a man. You don't do that to a child.

Shorr: (S&O) Let me switch for a moment and ask you what was your way of punishing your mother?

Lynne: I didn't want to punish her, but I could stop her and I would stop her by getting sick. 'Cause when I got sick then she couldn't touch me.

Shorr: That was your protection and you punished her − she had to take care of you?

Lynne: Yea, I guess it was a form of punishment. I never felt very revengeful towards her, it was more like I wanted her to get off my back − I was so busy protecting myself I didn't have time to get mad − which was later in life that I got mad at her. And then I just couldn't hold a grudge against her.

Shorr: (IS) Now I want you to imagine your mother looking at herself in the mirror − seeing herself. Now what I want you to imagine is the most difficult thing that she could say to herself. The most difficult thing for her to say to herself.

Lynne: You want me to be my mother?

Shorr: (IS) Yea − I want you to imagine you are her and tell me what you imagine if she were to look into the mirror and see herself − what the most difficult thing for her to say to herself would be.

On the part where my dad and I are trying to manipulate ourselves around my mother so we can at least get the least possible punishment. It's sort of, well, it brings to mind my own behavior in my life where I've sort of learned or being conditioned I suppose, to sense the other person's level of wrath or whatever and go by that. In other words, always do get a feeling of the other person and then react or behave accordingly. Not react the way I really wanted to react but react in the manner in which I hear or feel the other person will want me to react.

On the part where I could keep my mother from reacting towards me by getting sick. It's rather strange that even today when the pressures at work are too heavy or the pressures around me are too heavy I will invariably come down with a heavy, heavy cold and will have to stay home in bed with medicine and so forth. It's almost as if I have been conditioned to avoid pressure by getting sick.

Lynne: I'm ignorant.

Shorr: Now switching – (IS) what is the most difficult thing for you to say to yourself if you were to look in the mirror and see yourself?

Lynne: That I'm smart.

Shorr: That's the most difficult, huh? (IS) Now I want you to imagine that you are sleeping in a field overnight or something and then in the morning you were awakened and you saw footprints on your body. Now I want you to tell me on what part of your body you imagine the footprints to be on.

Lynne: Oh, on my belly.

Shorr: (IS) And whose footprints would they be?

Lynne: At first they were big – they became little all of a sudden. They were a baby's. Baby's.

Shorr: A baby's, a baby's footprints?

Lynne: I feel sad because I've never been pregnant. Maybe that's what made me imagine that. That's sad.

Shorr: (IS) Now I want you to imagine again two large boxes, and using your imagination, I want you to . . .

Lynne: Wait a second!

Shorr: You want to take your time – sure.

Lynne: Well, I just want to wipe my nose, I . . .

Shorr: O.K.

Lynne: I seem to open all of this meaningful material – I choked up a little bit here. Can I have a cigarette while . . .

Shorr: Why, sure.

Lynne: This is just absolutely incredible –

Shorr: You like it, huh?

Lynne: But it's like having fast therapy. These things are many things I've never thought of for a long time. O.K.

Shorr: You ready?

Lynne: Uh huh.

Shorr: (IS) O.K. Now I want you to imagine two large boxes – now using your imagination again I want you to imagine two different men – one in each box.

It's amusing when I go over the part where my mother looks at herself in the mirror and says or I say she says she's ignorant and then I look at myself in the mirror and I say I'm smart. Even to this day I can't quite – even though I know it intellectually, I can't feel that I am smart. It's not so much a feeling of snobbery or feeling that being better than others, but a feeling that I would be able to perhaps do things for others or better than most people; therefore, I would be able to help others and help them help themselves because of my knowledge and ability to understand almost ahead of time how they are going to react or feel about things. That's almost as if I were saying on that part of the tape that I got smart by learning to side-step my mother or predict ahead of time what my mother's reactions to things were going to be, and I got pretty nimble-minded about reacting to other people's emotions or coming emotions or whatever.

Lynne: What kind of boxes are they?

Shorr: That's up to you again, Lynne, you can . . .

Lynne: Well, you know I think of hearse, or funeral boxes.

Shorr: Coffin.

Lynne: Coffins – I couldn't even think of the word.

Shorr: (IS) Now can you imagine a man in each one?

Lynne: My dad would be in one.

Shorr: And the other?

Lynne: Billy.

Shorr: I don't know who Billy is.

Lynne: Oh, he is somebody I loved many, many years ago. He died. And they are two people I basically liked. One is dead and the other isn't. The other is old. And I guess someday he is going to go. That's kind of sad but I guess he would be happier if he did.

Shorr: (IS) Now switching again. I want you to imagine you are in a room and there is a hole in the room looking into the next room over – now look through that hole and tell me what you see there.

Lynne: It's a Bacchanalian feast (Laughing).

Shorr: Well, that's nice.

Lynne: People are like the old Roman days, they are having a ball – they really are – they are having fun though – at first I thought it may be just a, a sexy Bacchanalian feast but it really isn't. It's them drinking wine and dancing and – somebody is sculpturing and somebody is painting – oh, somebody may be reading fortunes, but everybody is doing their thing.

Shorr: (IS) How would you like to go through the wall and join them? Can you do that?

Lynne: I would, but I wouldn't belong.

Shorr: Why not?

Lynne: 'Cause I'm not all that happy.

Shorr: (IS) No, but I want you to imagine that you are a part of it. Can you try?

Lynne: O.K.

Shorr: Just let yourself be part of it.

Lynne: That's hard. O.K. I go in there and I dance.

Shorr: (IS) Good. Can you let yourself relax and enjoy it?

On the part where I imagined the footprints on my belly to be a baby's, uh, even to this day it has quite an emotional impact and I think that perhaps, well, my husband and I have been talking about it but perhaps maybe we ought to adopt some older children or something like that. I have a very big need to give to children and I rather enjoy them. At least I think I do. I, we would not have known how much until I try it.

The hearse or coffin, it's still painful to this day. I think maybe it was a deep meaningful relationship and I have not been able to have such a relationship since that time. Hearing the tape – it does make me very sad remembering.

Lynne: Uh huh.

Shorr: Are you a part of it? You belong there — stay there.

Lynne: I can't.

Shorr: (Focus) Now I want you to stay there.

Lynne: It's very hard.

Shorr: Why don't you belong there?

Lynne: Something drags me back.

Shorr: Who drags you back?

Lynne: Things I have to do I guess. My mother, duty . . . so many things.

Shorr: So how long do you think you could stay there?

Lynne: A minute.

Shorr: (Focus) Just a minute? Now I want you to try and stay there a couple of minutes. Come on — you imagine it. Stay with it.

Lynne: Oh, that is so hard.

Shorr: You allow two minutes — now go ahead — at least.

Lynne: O.K., I am dancing.

Shorr: Come on — you are free — let it happen.

Lynne: And I find some other dancers — a fellow, and we are dancing.

Shorr: Good.

Lynne: And he tosses me in the air and I go up and down and . . .

Shorr: Terrific!

Lynne: Like a ballet dancer. And I enjoy moving.

Shorr: That's good — stay with it.

Lynne: And then all of a sudden we are Shakespearean actors.

Shorr: That's nice.

Lynne: And I'm doing a wicked, wicked woman — Macbeth maybe — Lady Macbeth — I'm having a ball — the meaner the better. It's such fun to do bad people. I mean to pretend that you are doing bad people. And then, on the other hand, we could also be doing Romeo and Juliet and she is so naive and so nice. Or then I could be painting something — oh, I know — I'd be writing poetry and I'd be writing about older things that shouldn't be so.

Shorr: That shouldn't be what?

Lynne: So. Why? It would be very good poetry.

It's funny, but the memory of looking through the hole and seeing the Bacchanalian feast makes me feel like crying. Maybe it's because I've never been able to really enjoy myself at anything quite yet. Maybe someday I will.

The part where I imagine myself in that room and I'm writing poetry makes me feel like crying because when I was very little I wrote quite a bit and as the years went by I wrote from time to time and I like my poetry, but I just enjoyed doing it and as I got older it seems that I just, oh, just let it go by the side like I did everything else that was important to me. I just couldn't hang on to any good feelings, maybe I will someday.

Shorr: It sounds beautiful.

Lynne: It would have such – and on the other hand it would be critical – it would have to be. That it would be nice to be. Oh, and I'd have a cat there and it would be the most beautiful cat and I could write poetry and have the cat there. And that's nice.

Shorr: See, you stayed with that a long time, and you enjoyed it. And it wasn't so bad at that, because you allowed it.

Lynne: I haven't written poetry since I was – many, many years ago I wrote poetry when I was a kid. And – this is most enjoyable.

Shorr: Thank you. We can start again now.

Lynne: O.K. I imagine – when my cigarette starts to run out and you'll let me know. (Laughing)

Shorr: We'll have to get you some new ones. (Pause) Now I want you – you feel O.K.?

Lynne: Oh fine, this is great – I feel so much better – I feel like I could do things really.

Shorr: Good.

Lynne: You know it's – every time I think I could do things I start to feel like I'm going to cry.

Shorr: (IS) Well, now I want you to imagine sensing your body from your head to your toe – I want you to imagine . . .

Lynne: You want me to keep my eyes closed or . . . .

Shorr: Yea, you seem to do quite well that way, but . . .

Lynne: O.K.

Shorr: You can do that or you can focus on some distant object or something, but whatever you want.

Lynne: O.K. Well, we'll try it this way. (She closes her eyes)

Shorr: (IS) OK. Now sensing your body from your head to your toe, I want you to sense the body core part of your identity. The body part core of your identity – from your head to your toe. What do you sense?

Lynne: Oh, I sense it's . . . .

Shorr: (IS) Where is it though – what body part?

Lynne: It's – well, it's hard to pinpoint because it flows out. It could be my mind, my head. It started with my heart, my chest.

Shorr: Well, if you had to pick one part that was the body core part – body part core center of your identity?

Lynne: My eyes.

On the part where I'm centering on the body core and I center on the eyes, it appears as if the maturing in the voice keeps increasing as there is a feeling of security – having been an actress I am very conscious of the voice – and it is really amazing how when you think of the little girl your voice is like a little girl and as you, you grow or mature or become more reassured within yourself, you're more centered within yourself, your voice becomes much nicer really, much more like a, an instrument. As a vibrating instrument rather than a squeak.

Shorr: Your eyes.

Lynne: It's like a camera.

Shorr: Your eyes are, huh?

Lynne: Uh huh. It's like you are flowing out through your eyes. You're — the whole person flows out and it's good.

Shorr: You like it?

Lynne: Yes. Because you can contact — I mean I feel this or . . .

Shorr: Looking into somebody's eyes you can make the contact.

Lynne: Clear contact.

Shorr: But that's the center of you — I mean if you think of your body from head to toe that is the body part core center is your eyes. (IS) What would you say is the body part core center of your mother, for example?

Lynne: Her vagina.

Shorr: Unmistakably.

Lynne: Oh, yes.

Shorr: There was no hesitation on that.

Lynne: A demanding vagina. It would even try to suck me back into the womb.

Shorr: If she could. Are you ready for this? Closing your eyes this time.

Lynne: Sure.

Shorr: (IS) I want you to imagine what you just said.

Lynne: Being sucked in?

Shorr: (IS) Yes — into her vagina.

Lynne: I don't want to.

Shorr: (IS) I don't want you to either, but I want you to get out of it. I want you to imagine being in there and fighting your way out. Can you try that?

Lynne: No, if I get in there I get trapped.

Shorr: (Focus) Now I want you to get in there and this time I want you to focus getting out — for example, if you want any help of any kind — if you want a sword or if you want any kind of help at all — let me know and I'll let you have it so that you can come out — I want you to fight out of there.

Lynne: That's tough.

Shorr: It's not easy.

Lynne: If I get in there — I'll feel myself in there in a minute — and it's — I want to get out.

Shorr: (IS) O.K., what do you want to get out — do you want a big knife, or a . . .

The part where the body core of my mother's, the vagina, that would try to suck me back into the womb reminds me of an oil painting that I did, oh, in about my fourth or fifth year in therapy when I started to realize that I could be free, slightly free anyway at that point. I did an oil painting of this mother and child and the mother is a dark figure that encompasses the child and the child is trying to reach out of the darkness into the lighted area. Instead of a picture that I painted in, oh, I guess it was a couple of hours it went so fast it must be meaningful.

Lynne: No, no.

Shorr: (IS) What are you going to use to get out — anything, or do you just want to use your own power?

Lynne: My own power.

Shorr: (IS) O.K., now I want you to imagine getting out. Would you go through the motions and feeling of getting out of your mother's vagina.

Lynne: She's fighting me — she's tightening up.

Shorr: (Focus) I want you to get through. I want you to get out. Don't let her win.

Lynne: It's like I get my head out and she chokes me.

Shorr: (Focus) Now I want you to use your arms and flail and push and no matter what, get out of there. Don't let her win.

Lynne: I got it.

Shorr: Where are you now?

Lynne: Floating somewhere.

Shorr: You like where you are now? Stay with the feeling.

Lynne: It's like the feeling when I was writing poetry.

Shorr: It feels good?

Lynne: Uh huh.

Shorr: (IS) That's fine. Now I want you to imagine that you are standing on top of a dry well — then I want you to imagine another you which is identical to you but that you is in the bottom of the well and one at the top which is also you — equally — no difference at all — one is at the bottom of the dry well and one is at the top of the dry well, but the one at the top has a rope that is lowered to the bottom. Now tell me what happens — what would happen?

Lynne: The one at the top would try to get the rope to the one at the bottom. The one at the bottom wouldn't want to grab it. I wouldn't want to help her up.

Shorr: (IS) What would happen then?

Lynne: That's hard. I think I'd rather leave her down there.

Shorr: You don't like her?

Lynne: She's too much like my mother. The one on the top is the person I want to keep.

Shorr: (IS) Could you put a boulder over that hole?

Lynne: No, I wouldn't do that either.

Shorr: Just leave her there and go away you mean?

Lynne: Let her work her way out.

Shorr: But the one on top goes away happy?

Lynne: Uh huh. I don't want any part of the other one. She can work her way out

---

It is interesting that when I have the two me's — the one in the bottom of the well and the one on top with the rope — I try to get rid of the one part of me that is like my mother. It's interesting to me because consciously whenever I have acted or reacted in any manner at all there was similar to that of my mother. I would try to reject it and when I would give in and behave just like my mother, I would absolutely be thoroughly and completely disgusted with myself.

of it — and that feels good.

Shorr: Now finish the sentence (FTS) the only good woman is a _____ .

Lynne: *Bright* woman.

Shorr: (FTS) And the only good man is a _____ .

Lynne: *Good* man. That's free association.

Shorr: Whatever comes to your mind — that's fine. (IS) Suppose that you imagine that you went into a cage — well, I'll change it — a cave instead of a cage.

Lynne: Why not a cage?

Shorr: Why — did you have a thought on that? What was it?

Lynne: I was going to my own cage where my animals are.

Shorr: Oh, you have animals now?

Lynne: I raise Siamese Bluepoints — and I was going to go in there and . . .

Shorr: And have fun.

Lynne: Uh huh.

Shorr: Good.

Lynne: They are fun. I like animals — especially cats. Especially Siamese — they are so proud and beautiful. But maybe that doesn't fit with what you wanted.

Shorr: No that's fine. (IS) I want you to imagine that you go into a cave and when you walk into the cave at some distance you find a magician standing there — now tell me what you feel or do about the magician and your feelings.

Lynne; Well, I watch him.

Shorr: Yea . . .

Lynne: I want him to do something very special, but I don't know what.

Shorr: (IS) What do you imagine that might be?

Lynne: I don't know.

Shorr: (IS) Well, use your imagination — anything at all.

Lynne: Even if it is impossible?

Shorr: (IS) Sure. If you are using your imagination.

Lynne: Take me back to when I was twelve. No, no take me back when I was five. O.K.

Shorr: Sure.

Lynne: I could tell people what I think of them instead of keeping my mouth shut.

Shorr: You remember some incident, I gather.

On the part where I have to finish the sentence the only good woman is the bad woman and the only good man is the good man. It's very interesting in associating the bad women with good — I don't know at this point whether it's me that's supposed to be bad or my mother. There is a dichotomy here — on the other hand, the man part of course would be my father and my father would be good. Good mostly because he would stand my mother and he would not try to make waves and a person that tries to make waves in a way, as I do sometimes I guess, would be a, a bad person. Oh, no it doesn't make any sense because you have to make waves if you want anything done in this world.

Lynne: It's not just one, it's everything. It's when I — my mother came to me with some note some little boy had written to me about how crazy he was about me — I didn't even know who the little boy was — but I thought it was kinda nice — but she made somethin' dirty out of it. And she had the maid walk me to school every day from that day on. Like I was being guarded. And I'd say mother — ah shut up — mind your own business and let me go. And she'd stand there and she wouldn't know what to do.

Shorr: You could speak up to her then, huh?

Lynne: Uh huh. Because I wouldn't give a damn. Let her have a temper tantrum. I want to be a little girl.

Shorr: And you've done nothing wrong.

Lynne: I just want to be a little girl.

Shorr: You weren't a dirty little girl, were you?

Lynne: I'd be a happy little girl. In spite of her.

Shorr: Good. Now when you were twenty you say you still felt this kind of thing she put onto you. You said earlier, I believe, that at twenty you still felt that — that pressure she put onto you. She defined you as nothing, as an automaton, as a doll.

Lynne: That's why she wanted — she said she did not want me to be an actress but everything she did made me feel that I had to be an actress.

Shorr: You mean she defined you as an actress?

Lynne: I don't think I ever defined myself as a actress. Oh, I could.

Shorr: But that's what she wanted you to be?

Lynne: I defined myself more as a — oh, I guess writer or somebody that worked with — you know, I'm very bad with words but I still like it.

Shorr: So it was her that defined you as an actress, huh?_

Lynne: I'd rather write the plays and the books.

Shorr: If you were to speak to your mother right now — as you remember her — and you finish the sentence that "I am not." How would you finish the sentence? (FTS)

Lynne: I am not bad.

Shorr: Yea, and if you said I am to her, how would you finish that sentence? (FTS)

Lynne: I am very good.

Shorr: (Focus) Now, suppose you said that to her very loudly — like imagine she's in front of you. Can you close your eyes and imagine that she is right in front of you and I want you to say that "I am not . . . " and finish it and then say "I am . . . " and finish it.

On the part where I say that I like cats and I'd like to be in a cage with my studs. It's rather strange, you know, my liking cats because actually this is the only similarity I have to my mother — she loves cats.

On the part where I say to my mother I am good, very good and I am not bad, I formed a mental block again. This particular area seems to be conducive to mental blocks.

Lynne: MOTHER, I AM NOT BAD – IT'S ALL IN YOUR THOUGHTS – NOT MINE. BECAUSE I AM VERY GOOD.

Shorr: And "I am . . . "

Lynne: VERY GOOD.

Shorr: No, but I want you to say it without trying to convince her – just say it as you feel it – that's what you are and that's what you are, period. I am not . . .

Lynne: I would have to grow up for that.

Shorr: Well, I want you to do it right now. Where you are right now, but imagining your mother right in front of you, and I want you to say that as you are right now, Lynne.

Lynne: Me?

Shorr: You! "I am not . . . " to her. Now I want you to speak to her now. (IS) Can you imaginé her in front of you?

Lynne: Yea, we'd have an argument.

Shorr: (IS) No, but I want you to imagine her in front of you.

Lynne: O.K.

Shorr: And I want you to say nothing more than however you finish it. I am not – you finish it – I am . . .

Lynne: I am not bad.

Shorr: (FTS) I am _____.

Lynne: I am very good.

Shorr: (Focus) Now I want you to say it with a lot more anger in it and a lot more conviction and not proving anything to her.

Lynne: I can't be angry with her. I feel sorry for her. I feel so sorry for her.

Shorr: But nevertheless I still want you to try that, Lynne.

Lynne: That would be cruel.

Shorr: It would be cruel? For you to say I'm not a bad person – I am a good person, is a cruel statement? Doesn't sound very cruel to me.

Lynne: No, it isn't.

Shorr: O.K., let's try it then. Don't protect her.

Lynne: I am protecting her.

Shorr: O.K., don't protect her.

Lynne: MOTHER, I AM NOT BAD. I AM VERY GOOD.

Shorr: Now, I want it more from your guts. I want it to come out with – with a little scream – with a . . .

On the part where I am telling my mother that I am not bad, I am very, very good, it's rather strange that any time I've ever been angry, not only at my mother, but at anyone, I most of the time have tried not to release that anger in order to what I thought, was protect the other person. Actually, what I think that it was, was avoiding rejection, possibly more fear of rejection, than consideration for the other person so much.

Lynne: I'm giving you as much as I can.

Shorr: I know, but I want to try it again. I want it from your guts out to her — don't protect her.

Lynne: MOTHER, I AM NOT BAD — I AM VERY, VERY GOOD.

Shorr: (Focus) O.K., let's try it again, and this time really more from your guts — don't be afraid to be — to let it out — don't protect her — she will not wither — now let it out!

Lynne: Oh, I'm trying as hard as I can.

Shorr: I know — it's not easy. But don't protect her. Yield that protection.

Lynne: MOTHER, I AM NOT BAD — I AM VERY VERY GOOD. (Screaming)

Shorr: How do you feel?

Lynne: That scares me.

Shorr: But how do you feel?

Lynne: Tired.

Shorr: Is there a good feeling, though?

Lynne: Yea, but being angry always wears me out.

Shorr: Yea. Also protecting the person to whom you are angry I think wears you out a little bit more. As a matter of fact, you'd feel very good if you didn't protect her and just let the thing out.

Lynne: Or anybody else.

Shorr: All you are saying is that I am a good person — I am not a bad person. Now one would think that you are saying the most horrible thing on earth — you were saying the most critical devastating remark on earth and obviously it isn't.

Lynne: Sure is silly, isn't it?

Shorr: Before you let up, how about trying it once more?

Lynne: Oh!

Shorr: With all the feeling. Yea, that's right, get comfortable and — but really get your guts into it — but don't protect her — liberate yourself from that definition of you that she put on you.

Lynne: It's hard to do.

Shorr: It's not easy.

Lynne: (Screaming) MOTHER, I AM NOT BAD — I AM VERY, VERY GOOD. That's as hard as I can do.

Shorr: Are you begging her to — are you begging her to acknowledge that you are good? Are you begging her?

Lynne: No.

Shorr: That you separated from her?

Lynne: Oh, I think I separated from her way back in the womb scene.

On the body — core center of my father when I mention it there it is his hands and how kind they were. It seems to me that any time that I have ever gone out with a man I have always noticed his hands and no matter what else he looked like, if his hands were gentle or looked gentle and they reminded me of my father, then I would immediately like the man. It was a ready connection there — the hands.

Shorr: Good, O.K., this is really a statement of you of your own identity. That's fine. (IS) I wanted to go back to asking you about the body core, you know, of your father — what would you pick up as that?

Lynne: I don't know — he's hard to pick out — 'cause there's sort of a definite — indefinite sort of a — hands.

Shorr: Hands.

Lynne: Gentle.

Shorr: (IS) That was the core of his identity?

Lynne: Gentle, gentle hands. Like you would expect a priest or Jesus Christ maybe or somebody like that.

Shorr: (IS) In other words, when he put his hands upon you, it felt very good.

Lynne: Well, it was really the way he used them. I used to as a little kid look at his hands and thought how kind they were but everything else about him was kind of — oh, I hate to say this — wishy-washy. He was afraid of my mother. Can I have a cigarette?

Shorr: Oh sure. It was just that screaming that was holding you back for a moment.

Lynne: That's hard, that screaming bit.

Shorr: Yea. (S&O) What is your responsibility to your father?

Lynne: Protecting him.

Shorr: (S&O) And what is your responsibility to men?

Lynne: You mean to all men?

Shorr: Well, those whom you have known, of course.

Lynne: Protecting them. Yea, I'm a big protector. Particularly men.

Shorr: (S&O) What is your sexual responsibility to men?

Lynne: None.

Shorr: (S&O) What is a man's responsibility to you?

Lynne: None.

Shorr: But how do you protect them exactly?

Lynne: Oh, first thing that comes to mind is being smarter and wiser and making things in life easier for them — like I did for my father.

Shorr: Now, do men do that in return for you? I mean, do they make things easier for you and protect you?

On the part where I relate to protecting my father and also protecting men in general, I can relate at this moment to the fact that I was making things so darn easy for my husband that I was practically making him into a vegetable and it wasn't until, oh, I guess November of the year before last that, oh, I would think it was right after this tape, uh, that uh, no, that was February of '72, anyway, about a year ago, I just decided that I wasn't going to protect my husband anymore. I was going to let him take the pension and just accept him for what he was. He could do what he wanted to, but I wasn't going to be responsible for him and amazingly enough he suddenly grew up and got a job and got himself all involved in growing up, so I guess actually by protecting them I was kind of doing the same thing that my mother was doing to me — making him helpless.

Lynne: Has anybody ever done that − I'm trying to think. I can't think who. No, anybody who had made anything easier for me has demanded something. So they haven't made things easier.

Shorr: And you have demanded very little? Were you protecting these men?

Lynne: No, I demanded.

Shorr: I don't quite understand what you are saying. You protected them, but you also demanded.

Lynne: I think I demanded that they behave according to my ideals of what a man should be.

Shorr: Which is?

Lynne: My father.

Shorr: Helpless, wishy-washy, and giving you the role protector − that gives you a purpose.

Lynne: Well, I think it's more the only pattern I ever learned.

Shorr: What would you like to be then? If you give up the protection − the protection racket − what would you do?

Lynne: Oh, I'd like to be free and just − just be free − I guess I don't like marriage very much.

Shorr: But could you have a man protect you? Could you have that?

Lynne: Not very well.

Shorr: You wouldn't know how to accept it you mean?

Lynne: This may sound funny, but I don't think a man lives that can protect me.

Shorr: Why not?

Lynne: Because that's the way I feel.

Shorr: But what is there in your life that's so difficult for a man not to protect?

Lynne: I can take care of myself.

Shorr: Yea. What would you want then from a man?

Lynne: I first thought of Ed's Stud Service. (Laughing) It's awful.

Shorr: Why is that awful?

Lynne: Well . . ._

On the part where I am talking about the helpless wishy-washy type of man that I protect it's − darn it, I blanked out again. Let's see if I can remember it now. Oh, yes, the helpless wishy-washy type of man, well, when my husband started to go out and be quite aggressive and work in the work place and do fairly well, uh, that's another scene that started to throw me out in the open − one of them was the fact that I got my masters degree − the other my husband became independent so he could go out and earn his living, and the third was that the library where I work was not − I had problems there and things weren't allowed to grow the way they should. So, therefore, I was completely surrounded and am at the present time by the problems where I have really no way out really and I can find no excuse for anything except to look within myself and find the answer within myself, within my own growth, and I think all of these situations have helped although by accepting a more agressive male now, I find myself feeling more insecure and more uncomfortable, but I think it has been a step in the right direction.

Shorr: Would you want something more though?

Lynne: Oh, I suppose I would want somebody I could talk to.

Shorr: Is that too much to ask for?

Lynne: Yes.

Shorr: You mean you have to give up your protection racket if you do that?

Lynne: I suppose.

Shorr: You can't protect somebody and start talking about yourself. You wouldn't be listening.

Lynne: I don't listen anyway.

Shorr: You don't?

Lynne: Not on a man/woman relationship, I don't think I do.

Shorr: You don't hear what the guy says, you mean?

Lynne: I don't think so. I feel very deeply that I don't think I hear. It's kind of kooky.

Shorr: It sounds a little contradictory. You say you are very protective of a man — at the same time you don't give to a man.

Lynne: I don't give to anybody.

Shorr: You mean your protection is a way of not giving?

Lynne: Probably.

Shorr: I want you to finish the sentence. (FTS) My whole life is based on proving that _____ .

Lynne: That *I can take care of myself.* Very much so. Alone.

Shorr: So what do you need a man for?

Lynne: You know, a thought just struck me. Wouldn't it be marvelous if you were back in the cave days and women were the ones that drag men with their hair (Laughing) and they did everything and they drag the men and say "come on." Now it's your turn.

Shorr: I think the way you talked earlier your mother would be very good in that role.

Lynne: Yea, I think I've learned a lot. I haven't learned any other roles.

Shorr: What would happen if a man really took care of you? Thought about you, protected you?

Lynne: I wouldn't like it.

Shorr: What would happen?

Lynne: I would feel guilty.

Shorr: Why?

On the part right after I say I would like stud service from a man and then I go into saying that I don't listen in a man/woman relationship. This is very interesting that this is the first time that I, well, it's taken me completely by surprise because I didn't realize that I recognize the fact subconsciously that I wasn't listening in a man/woman relationship. I mean it comes like out of the blue, and when I come to think about it, it's terribly quite right in relationship to sex that there is no listening on my part, and it's something I didn't realize until just now.

Lynne: I don't know. I'm free associating – I would feel guilty.

Shorr: Yea, I believe what you are saying, it's just that the standard – what is the standard?

Lynne: It's not standard – it's just a feeling thing. I would feel I'd have to pay him back in kind. I couldn't owe him anything – if he did too much for me, I would owe him something and if I owed him something I would have to work so hard to repay him. Like I worked with my mother. We paid her all of the time and it was just too much – I mean . . .

Shorr: You mean she constantly obligated you to her.

Lynne: Uh huh.

Shorr: And you were constantly in bondage. It was always impossible to feel a man would not want to obligate you and put you into bondage.

Lynne: True.

Shorr: (S&O) They really take you over and engulf you – the closeness of a relationship.

Lynne: I never looked at it that way before, but it's true. So I couldn't unless I was able to take without feeling I had to return twofold.

Shorr: Now, in other words, if your husband came home one day and he found – and he said why aren't you doing my socks right.

Lynne: Oh well, I wouldn't bother with that.

Shorr: Oh, what kind . . .

Lynne: That's – that's a feminine – I resent feminine roles.

Shorr: (S&O) What kind of criticism you know that your husband might put upon you would you really feel bad about?

Lynne: Oh, maybe by not thinking intelligently. Or doing something dumb.

Shorr: Something relating to brain power, you mean?

Lynne: Uh huh.

Shorr: (IS) Suppose you imagine a penis on a balance scale on one side and a vagina on the other.

Lynne: Oh, the vagina would be way too heavy for the penis.

Shorr: (IS) If the vagina could speak – could make a statement to the penis – what would it be?

Lynne: I've got you under my power.

Shorr: (IS) What does the penis say?

Lynne: It would be helpless.

Shorr: And how would you feel?

Lynne: (Ha, ha) I feel like laughing.

It is so interesting that when I am talking about being protective towards men I bring out the fact that I don't like women that are overprotected or that maybe I am jealous of them. Uh, it's sort of a dichotomy I think in that as a child I was brought up to feel that the only role for a woman was to be the one protected and sheltered and so forth, at least that's what my mother told me. But then, on the other hand, she gave me boys' toys to play with and encouraged aggressiveness – so, I guess there is sort of a dichotomist picture right here.

Shorr: Why?

Lynne: I don't know. I don't seem to have much of a picture of men. It's like women are the amazons. The old accomplishers, the achievers.

Shorr: They are the strong ones?

Lynne: I don't like women that are all protected — maybe in general there are some of them — I don't know. I've never liked them. I wouldn't know how to act if I was protected.

Shorr: What do I do next then? Is that what you'd be saying?

Lynne: I would be suspicious — I know I would think there is something that he wants.

Shorr: And usually it's . . . ?

Lynne: Oh, usually it's sex or if it's not sex then it's something I can do — some kind of help he wants.

Shorr: (S&O) Nobody would like you for yourself alone, huh?

Lynne: That's a hard one, but that's the way I feel.

Shorr: What do you have to do for me so I'd like you — just like that when you don't know me very well but what would you have to do for me so I'd like you?

Lynne: Oh, I'm here so you'd have to like me.

Shorr: Because you're doing something I want you to do.

Lynne: Right.

Shorr: Now you've paid your obligation so you're all right.

Lynne: So I feel O.K.

Shorr: You're O.K.

Lynne: Yea.

Shorr: So each time you have to earn your position with . . .

Lynne: Right.

Shorr: You don't know where you are at any one time if you're not earning it, huh? What do I do next? It puts you in a real bind — constant. Incessant activity, huh?

Lynne: Pressure.

Shorr: The pressure.

Lynne: There's a lot to think of it there. I hope I don't forget it. That's like somebody that's kind of trained. That's the way I am. And they trained me to automatically react to anybody doing anything for me — I automatically repay him twice in kind. And so I'm conditioned.

Shorr: Well, what about the sexual part of it then? Do you have the obligation of going that way too? Who is sex for, the woman or the man?

It's interesting in the part where the father's brought out that I have to earn everything, that I can't just take anything for free, everything has to be earned, and that at work in particular lately I have gotten more and more to the point where I feel guilty if I am not rushing around always doing something. Actually, part of me is saying, well, what for, I'm not interested in helping the library, then why should I try to knock myself out which I hate. If I have this attitude at this point then, the attitude I had before, is always having to pay back for everything double.

Lynne: Uh, women use it to achieve a purpose. If sex could be right the way I'd imagine it to be, it would be a mutual thing, but it hardly ever is. As I can think of it.

Shorr: What do you mean?

Lynne: In the past somebody always has something to gain — maybe me — maybe demanded something and I paid him back — I'm talking about work — you know . . .

Shorr: Uh huh.

Lynne: And the days I was in show business. Or maybe that's why sex and marriage is kind of there's nothing to prove so there's no — I mean the women can do the conquering sometimes too but if you do it just for the sake of conquering or for the sake of proving a point — there was one guy I had sex with that wasn't proving anything.

Shorr: What was there about him that was different?

Lynne: He was strong. And yet he was weak. But he wasn't all that weak. He could top me intellectually and yet he was in my business — in show business at the time and I would say something with most of the time he would accept something I'd say. He could say something to top me and I had my mind about it, but he would do it in such a way that he wasn't humiliating me. He was conversing with me. I like him.

Shorr: (S&O) So what kind of a contest are you in with men?

Lynne: Oh, about the same contest I am with anything else.

Shorr: Uh huh. (IS) Using your imagination, how does it feel to have the semen of a man in your vagina?

Lynne: Not very much.

Shorr: Not very much?

Lynne: No.

Shorr: What do you mean by that?

Lynne: In the past I wanted to have a baby and I never did. So what is the purpose of the semen? You can't do something.

Shorr: Finish the sentence. (FTS) I hate men because _____ .

Lynne; (Laughing) A crazy thought came through me — because *they masturbate.*

Shorr: You hate that because they masturbate — because they're not . . .

Lynne: That's crazy.

Shorr: What do you get out of that?

Lynne: I don't know, that's what came to my mind.

It's kind of interesting in the part where I am talking about the penis and the mechanism of the penis and how it operates and how I was telling this one ex about it. Actually, I think I got, I don't know why, but I've got my men mixed up. I think the one that I'm referring to, I think I'm referring to, who's a very interesting man, not mentally, but physically, and the man that I actually told him about, told about the physiological reaction of the penis and an erection and all that was actually another person for I'm — I don't know whether it's on purpose or not — I'm confusing two men and making two men one.

Shorr: Because they're not giving you their semen?

Lynne: No – I'm not all that semen crazy unless it comes to cats – when you get a breeding thing going. I don't know why it leaves me, uh.

Shorr: You hate men because they masturbate, you said.

Lynne: I mean that's the feeling I had at that moment – it was a free association type thing.

Shorr: Fine.

Lynne: I don't know where it came from.

Shorr: Fine. I mean have you seen men masturbate? Have you had some experience along that line?

Lynne: Yea, my – one of my ex's – my ex-husbands – I thought he was kind of a pig. There was nothing – he wasn't even very exciting – I'll tell you what it was. I could look at him with a clinical eye – detached – just figure out how the mechanism of the penis worked physiologically. That's what you can think of. (Laughing) I remember one time I told him that and how his mechanism worked just when he had an erection. It didn't bother him but I thought it was kind of stupid afterwards. He didn't much like it. But I was interested – in the physiological aspect of it.

Shorr: Like clinically and detached apart from the feeling part.

Lynne: Yes. That must – I must have been doing something there because it was so clinical.

Shorr: (FTS) I hate women because _____. How would you finish that?

Lynne: I don't – I – I can't finish that. *Maybe they are helpless.*

Shorr: You hate women who are helpless, you mean?

Lynne: Because they are helpless. Not me, though.

Shorr: Now I want you to use your imagination again for a moment. I want you to close your eyes again. (IS) I want you to imagine entering your father's body – using your imagination – where do you enter?

Lynne: His heart.

Shorr: And what happens?

Lynne: He gets frightened. I don't know.

Shorr: Why should he be frightened?

Lynne: I don't know. Maybe it's because every time I wanted him to do something for me he would have a heart attack or something and so I guess he got frightened.

Shorr: You felt responsible for the heart attack?

Lynne: I didn't hurt him much. I let mother work on him. You see, I'm a buffer. Sort of like a thing between two people.

Shorr: You mean when the real chips fell, you let your mother take over.

Lynne: Well, I acted as a shield for my father so if she wouldn't hit him too hard emotionally. I'd take the hurt and the pain and the brunt.

It is strange, but at the mention of my father and how he is the dummy or teach me to bear things. I suddenly get very tired, it's a weariness – almost as if I just wanted to lay down and go to sleep. I'm just exhausted.

Shorr: (IS) Now, if you could imagine the opposite now — again using your imagination — if your father were to enter your body . . .

Lynne: I can just see minds, heads, brains.

Shorr: But where does he enter?

Lynne: Brain.

Shorr: He's in your brain and what does he do there?

Lynne: He teaches maybe.

Shorr: What does he tell you?

Lynne: He tells me to bear things.

Shorr: To tolerate things, you mean?

Lynne: To be kind.

Shorr: And how do you feel about that?

Lynne: Well, it's all right — not all the time — but it's all right — it's not bad.

Shorr: You mean you like that — what your father told you to do when he enters your head?

Lynne: I mean it's not unpleasant. Except it's too altruistic. It's too . . .

Shorr: It denies you a lot — it denies you of your individuality you mean? So what would you tell your father?

Lynne: You can't be kind and good all of the time. And you've got to tell my mother to knock it off.

Shorr: Be strong. You bastard.

Lynne: I once told him this and he had a heart attack.

Shorr: The next day!

Lynne: The next week.

Shorr: And you were responsible. So you protect men rather than tell them to be strong because they will die on you — they will disappear — is that it?

Lynne: I suppose. That is so funny.

Shorr: If you were to stand with your right hand and your left hand like this, you know, outstretched . . .

Lynne: Uh huh.

Shorr: (IS) Who would you hold with your right hand and who would you hold with your left hand?

Lynne: A person?

Shorr: Uh huh..

Lynne: I don't think I'd want to hold anybody.

Shorr: But if you were to imagine that you did, who would you hold with your right hand and who would you hold with your left hand?

On this part about my father — it has been altruistic and all this must have some heavy emotional content because I feel rather upset about it. I remember him as, well, I remember from what my mother has said that when I was a young child he was sort of a playboy, but that's what my mother said, but anyway I think this has something to do with my feelings towards my father. I can't quite figure out how I am reacting to this, but it's sort of an upset feeling.

Lynne: It has to be a human being?

Shorr: Yea.

Lynne: Oh shucks. O.K., let me think. Oh, I guess it would have to be my mother and father.

Shorr: But you fight doing it, huh?

Lynne: What?

Shorr: You fight doing the whole thing?

Lynne: Yes.

Shorr: You don't want to imagine that. O.K. (IS) Put your hands down and I want you to imagine a blank piece of paper in front of you and using your imagination I want you to imagine on the left side there is a word and on the right side is a word. Now you tell me what the word you imagined is.

Lynne: Fuck-it.

Shorr: What do you think you are talking about really when you say that?

Lynne: Everything.

Shorr: The world, you mean?

Lynne: Uhmmm. I guess I must be bitter. But then I think it's a healthy word. It expresses a lot of − not dirty word − it expresses a lot of good, healthy emotions.

Shorr: When you say that it means you don't have to be what?

Lynne: You don't have to take a lot of crap.

Shorr: Which is what you do a lot of.

Lynne: Yea − my whole life.

Shorr: (M/L) What's the most difficult thing to say to anybody?

Lynne: I love you. Well, you can say it and not mean it. But to really feel it − this is very hard.

Shorr: Have you said it much in your life?

Lynne: Not with feelings. Not meaning it. I meant it sort of haphazardly − but not 100%.

Shorr: You never really felt that real love towards anyone − anybody.

Lynne: Yea, I guess I did towards Billy − it was so long ago and I was such a young thing I guess I must of meant it. And then I got punished − I mean he died.

Shorr: Billy is who? I don't know.

Lynne: He was somebody that I knew when I was twenty-five and he died of cancer two years later. My mother hated him. It's the only time I opposed her. I think that was the beginning of my starting to do things, but it was so painful because it was painful that he died and it was painful that I had to accept her afterwards as a substitute. I had to fall back on her again. While he was alive I didn't have to. He was a little stronger than her, I think.

Shorr: That was the first time you were actually able to oppose your mother, huh?

Lynne: Uh huh. The first time.

It's interesting that when I talk about my father always getting a heart attack that I get upset, almost as if I were going to have some kind of a stroke or heart attack or something like that − almost as if I were he.

Shorr: (M/L) What is easiest for you to give: sex, money, intellect or feeling?

Lynne: Intellect.

Shorr: That is the easiest?

Lynne: Easy, very easy.

Shorr: And the most difficult?

Lynne: You mean good sex or any sex?

Shorr: Whatever you — you tell me.

Lynne: I mean any sex — that's no problem, but I mean really to give feelings in sex to give it . . .

Shorr: That would be the most difficult?

Lynne: Very.

Shorr: I take it then — you say it's never happened that much, huh?

Lynne: It only happened that one time because I could admire the guy. It wasn't Billy — it was this guy and we weren't in any way tied up — I mean it was the kind of thing that — like ships passing in the night. He didn't owe me anything. It's one of the few times that I could be half free, I think.

Shorr: No obligations.

Lynne: No. It was a strange incident.

Shorr: It didn't last very long I take it.

Lynne: About two months.

Shorr: What happened?

Lynne: We passed.

Shorr: In the night. (IS) Now, if you were to imagine your mother and father nude in the bed.

Lynne: That's a hard one.

Shorr: (IS) And then in addition to that you are in there — all three of you there in the bed in the nude.

Lynne: Oh, my mother would be looking at me.

Shorr: (IS) Now I want you to imagine that you look at your father — what would happen?

Lynne: Nothing.

Shorr: What would your mother do?

Lynne: Nothing.

Shorr: How would you feel?

Lynne: Nothing.

Shorr: Nothing at all? I mean the situation would just be completely without any feeling at all? You wouldn't be afraid, frightened, or waiting for your mother to

---

It's interesting that after I mention Billy's death and how painful it was that I had to have at that time some kind of a substitute — I couldn't just stand alone — I had to have somebody to lean on. I didn't realize how much I was leaning on my mother and she was letting me and I suppose I resented that, but it's an interesting point. This whole sequence about my father and Billy is quite painful.

criticize you or something?

Lynne: Yea, yea, I guess I would.

Shorr: I had to remind you – how come? That she might criticize you.

Lynne: Because I'm moving away from her, I think.

Shorr: (M/L) What was the single most undermining sentence that your mother would repeat to you?

Lynne: Sex is dirty – I guess.

Shorr: What about her?

Lynne: Oh, don't do it – I'll do it for you.

Shorr: Anything you mean. Not just the sex, of course.

Lynne: Anything, I mean.

Shorr: She took over, you mean?

Lynne: Yea, that was the worst part, I guess. It wasn't so much that sex is dirty. I think it was if I go in the kitchen to do something when I was a young girl – don't do it – you won't do it right – I'll do it. Or no matter what I wanted to do she did it.

Shorr: So how did she define you that way? As . . .

Lynne: As a doll.

Shorr: This helpless doll.

Lynne: The only thing/duty I had – I had to look pretty. I had to be admired by people – I didn't have to say anything – I had to just be admired by people. That made her very happy. But I had to be a nonentity, like a doll, I guess.

Shorr: Who demands that of you today – that you just be a doll or nonentity?

Lynne: Nobody – since I got out of show business.

Shorr: That was like being a doll, you mean? Or being . . .

Lynne: I had to be a doll – I had to be pretty and I had to be – look good – and now I don't have to look good.

Shorr: (M/L) What is your greatest concern when you are with a man?

Lynne: That's a hard one. Ridicule, I guess. I would be afraid of ridicule.

Shorr: Now, finish this sentence. (FTS) I have to prove that every man is

_____.

Lynne: *Stupid.*

Shorr: (FTS) And every man has to prove that I am _____.

Lynne: *Smart* was the word, but I don't know why it came out.

Shorr: And who carries the greatest authority in the world for you today?

Lynne: I would say the two women premiers.

Shorr: You mean like Ghandi and Meir?

Lynne: Yea. They appear to be very good leaders. They don't do anything half-assed.

It is interesting that when I mention the part about my mother saying that she wouldn't let me go into the kitchen, she'd do it all for me and to tell me don't do it, I'll do it for you, that actually at that point I sound just like my mother or the way my mother used to sound when she was talking to me at the time.

Shorr: Like the men do.

Lynne: If they do something – they do it – if it's bad or good, they do it.

Shorr: Like the men do?

Lynne: Yea. Men always.

Shorr: Not to mention names.

Lynne: Well, men are always all over – take the American presidents – practically all of them have done things half-assed. I mean, they always find a way out.

Shorr: But these other, they have stood up and fought the war and done the things that are necessary.

Lynne: They have done things. They, they – bad or good – they have stood by their beliefs and done things.

Shorr: Finish the sentence. (FTS) Why can't a man be _____.

Lynne: A leader.

Shorr: Now I want you to try something a little different – switching – (IS) I want you to imagine handing your heart into my palm.

Lynne: Oh, that's easy.

Shorr: Let's see.

Lynne: O.K.

Shorr: I have it now – it's in my palm.

Lynne: It's all right – I trust you.

Shorr: Why do you trust me?

Lynne: Because I like you.

Shorr: But I'm a man.

Lynne: No you're not!

Shorr: But I'm a . . .

Lynne: Psychologist.

Shorr: So I'm not the wishy-washy man.

Lynne: Yea, clinician or person that has a clinical approach. A psychologist is not a man or a woman.

Shorr: In other words, you cannot give me a sexual gender?

Lynne: No.

Shorr: But if you were.

Lynne: I couldn't give you a sexual gender.

Shorr: If you were to, it would be dangerous?

Lynne: Yea.

Shorr: Then I would have to be just an ordinary half-assed, indecisive man. As long as I have my title and all that I'm . . .

It's kind of interesting that since – in the part where I am mentioning about the American presidents and about the two women premiers – since then I have felt that Nixon, for example, is a very decisive person. Right or wrong he certainly did, does do decisive things and this may be a change in my attitude towards men – I don't know.

Lynne: No, not only your title − I have to approve of you.

Shorr: O.K., you approve of me.

Lynne: Like you and Shapiro, I sort of . . . O.K.

Shorr: A clinician.

Lynne: I mean, I've met psychologists I couldn't stand so they were men.

Shorr: (IS) Suppose though that I were to give you my heart into your palm.

Lynne: I don't want it.

Shorr: If I were to, what would you do?

Lynne: Give it right back to you.

Shorr: Why?

Lynne: Because you are not supposed to.

Shorr: The obligation is so great, or is it just the prohibition of such a thing?

Lynne: I wouldn't know what I'd do with it.

Shorr: (IS) Suppose it is just any man that gives you his heart − what would you do with it.

Lynne: I don't think I'd want it. It would be too embarrassing.

Shorr: (IS) And what about your heart − can you hand that to anybody?

Lynne: I suppose − half-assedly.

Shorr: Like a little bit but not really vulnerable feelings you want to have?

Lynne: Yea. Sort of.

Shorr: What is your idea of a good time?

Lynne: Doing something constructive.

Shorr: Like what?

Lynne: Oh, I guess creating something. Oh! When I directed the company show and I had all these people under me working for me and I did a good thing − it was very good − I had a good time − it was work but it was fun work.

Shorr: (IS) Can you imagine a bird on your head − what would it be?

Lynne: . . . bluebird.

Shorr: (IS) Can you imagine an animal coming out of your stomach.

Lynne: A cat. It's silly.

Shorr: You seem to have a lot going for cats. You like them.

Lynne: They are smart − nobody can fool them.

Shorr: Tell me − how smart are you, Lynne?

Lynne: When not panicky, I'm smart − when panicky, I'm dumb.

Shorr: (M/L) Who is the smartest woman you have ever known?

Lynne: My mother appears to be pretty smart in her own dumb way.

It's funny that my relating psychologist to a non sex type of. . . .Well, there's many walls up if we could − if we weren't role playing. If we were in a regular clinical picture let's say we would have a greater tendency to be more careful as to what we say, but in − by role playing and pretending we can be less guarded and therefore get into the actual therapy situation much faster and work through some problems a lot faster than you would through the old therapy methods.

Shorr: What do you mean by that?

Lynne: Cunning is the word. Not smart.

Shorr: (M/L) What was the most cunning thing she ever did?

Lynne: Oh, I guess trap me and my father and she is helpless — there is a dichotomy there. Maybe by being helpless she is being most cunning — my mom never does anything for nothing.

Shorr: She's really manipulative, huh?

Lynne: Yes. That's the word. I guess I learned that from her.

Shorr: You regard yourself as manipulative, huh?

Lynne: Something — I don't particularly like it very much but there it is.

Shorr: It's a living, huh — instead of anything else it's a living. What do you do for a living — I'm a manipulator. (Laughing) "If I don't manipulate well somebody is going to manipulate me."

Lynne: That's about the gist of it. It would be nice if everybody could exist by accepting – I would like to think that would be kinda nice but it's kind of hard to find. That kind of a thing.

Shorr: (S&O) If you aren't manipulating, do you turn into your father or something like that?

Lynne: Probably — altruistic, and a dreamer and sort of . . .

Shorr: Then you could be used or taken advantage of — but rather than that you want to revert back to . . .

Lynne: I'm many people. Under certain given circumstances I can be extremely giving at that moment 'cause I felt that that particular party was, well, like when I was taking psychology I helped a few people and I wasn't being manipulative then — but I could help them because I was playing a role and when I was being an actress I was being a manipulator. And now I'm a librarian and I can be kind of clinical about my work 'cause it's information and so forth — occasionally when I get involved in something where I want to gain a point I manipulate. Now with my husband, I don't know what I'd do. I really don't. It's a strange relationship — it's not bad — it's not great. But I think the cats keep us together because we have so much in common, with the cats.

Shorr: Do you have a lot of cats?

Lynne: Yes.

Shorr: It appears we have to stop our talk now. Thank you for coming.

Lynne: Thanks. I enjoyed it.

Extensive use of imagery, comingled with dialogue, suggests that it can be a valuable source of awareness of the person's neurotic conflicts. Patients tend to react to the integration of imagery with dialogue so that the naturalness of the interchange is not affected.

On the part where I am talking about the relationship with my husband is sort of interesting that as time goes by I can see both of us sort of growing — for greater give and take — as we go along. In other words, the more honest I become it appears to me the more honest he becomes — maybe it's just me. I don't know.

CHAPTER 16

Imagery and Group Therapy

In the last decade group therapy has become an integral part of the treatment of emotionally disturbed individuals and while some therapists regard it as a secondary method, others believe in it as the approach *par excellence.* To my way of thinking, group and individual therapy should complement and enhance each other; ideally, a patient should experience both. This does not always occur, unfortunately. Beyond the financial considerations, some people are hesitant about confrontation with other patients, and others fear exposure. If a patient has an especially weakened sense of identity, or "core," his fears may be aggravated by the group situation; when feelings of rottenness have engulfed the self-image, the prospect of group therapy may become unbearable. In such cases, individual treatment must proceed until there is a change in self-definition; this change, combined with a trust in the therapist, will finally allow for direct contact with the group.

How a person has been defined by others during his formative years, the degree to which he feels "condemned" to his alien identity, his efforts to define himself in a manner more consistent with his true identity — these issues constitute the very kernel of Psycho-Imagination Therapy. Therapy — individual or group — is an invaluable catalyst in the patient's forging of a new identity. It must help him become aware of the conflicts between the alien identity and the true (albeit inchoate or emerging) identity; it must help him recognize the strategies that were used by significant others upon him and the counterreaction strategies he used to survive them.

As patient and therapist become aware of central conflicts — invariably between what the patient really feels and the way he feels he *should* feel — group therapy provides a place where the conflicts can be seen in neurotic solution. It provides expanded awareness of the conflicts and their neurotic conflict resolutions. Neurotic conflict resolutions are effectually a treadmill to nowhere, and the experience and interaction afforded by the group situation will open avenues to *healthy* conflict resolution, to a new (true) self-definition. It will, hopefully, permit the patient to be nothing less than *himself.*

It is Rollo May who best expresses the neurotic's struggle to maintain his centeredness and the fear of what interaction with others involves: " . . . he sat nervously smoking in my waiting room; he now looks at me with mingled suspicion and hope, an effort towards openness fighting in him against the life-old tendency to withdraw behind a stockade and hold me out. The struggle is understandable, for participating always involves risk; if he or any organism goes out too far, he will lose his own centeredness, his identity." (May, 1964, p. 176.)

Laing and Buber have pointed out that man basically needs to feel a confirmation of his existence from the other and equally to feel that he makes a difference to an other. Too often in contemporary life does man desperately search for confirmation, with only the meagerest of results. As Arthur Miller said in discussing contemporary writers, "Society in effect is a deaf machine; and they feel themselves competing with machines which have stolen the imagination of men." (Miller, 1966, p. 16.)

In the contemporary world, success often bears little relationship to fulfillment. "Can I make a difference to someone?" poses an existential safari for modern man, one which often leads to loneliness, purposelessness and powerlessness. For, to quote Rollo May again, contemporary man is prone to ask, "Even if I know who I am, can I have an effect on the world?" (May, 1964, p. 176.)

Our age is one of conformity, of the "other"-directed man; one finds it difficult to project one's uniqueness, one's authentic feelings; one offers up his own identity for the sake of social belonging and acceptance. Ostracism is the ultimate terrible position and to guard against it, meanings and values are borrowed from somebody else's meanings and values. Direct and open interchange, direct experiencing of other human beings and the world have become increasingly infrequent. Max Frisch in *I'm Not Stiller,* comments brilliantly on the subject: "We live in an age of reproduction. Most of what makes up our personal picture of the world we have seen with our own eyes, but not on the spot: our knowledge comes to us from a distance, we are tele-viewers, tele-hearers, tele-knowers. One need never have left this little town to have Hitler's voice still ringing in one's ears, to have seen the Shah of Persia from a distance of three yards, and to know how the monsoon howls over the Himalayas or what it looks like six hundred fathoms beneath the sea. Anyone can know of these things nowadays. Does it mean I have never been to the bottom of the sea? Or even (like the Swiss) almost up Mount Everest?

"And it's just the same with the inner life of man. Anyone can know about it nowadays. How the devil am I to prove to my counsel that I don't know my murderous impulses through C. G. Jung, jealousy through Marcel Proust, Spain through Hemingway, Paris through Ernst Junger, Switzerland through Mark Twain, Mexico through Graham Greene, my fear of death through Bernanos and the inability ever to reach my destination through Kafka, and all sorts of other things through Thomas Mann? It's true, you need never have read these authorities, you can absorb them through your friends, who also live all their experiences second-hand." (Frisch, 1958, p. 151-152.)

Group therapy provides direct and open contact for people. They can say what they feel, whether it be "right" or "wrong." Each group member can confirm the existence of any other group member and they his. A patient can begin to feel he makes a difference to the group as a whole and to each member individually. He comes to realize that he need not sell his soul in order to belong.

With the increased emphasis on immediate solutions to problems and the growth of computerization, dehumanization has become the vogue; less fashionable are the concepts of intimacy and growth, shared experience. It is precisely this lack of prolonged and loving intimacy that invariably catapults a person into neurotic behavior. Instant intimacy, instant love, the substitution of sheer encounter for real conflict resolution — all of these may leave the patient in a state of confusion, opened and raw, but basically no more solid than before in his centeredness or ability to trust other human beings.

There has come to be extensive use of imagery techniques in encounter groups, marathons, T-groups, sensitivity training, and related approaches which, according to Jerome L. Singer "can only be described as a national craze rather than as a systematic new treatment method." (Singer, 1971, p. 24.) Bach (1954) used group fantasy early in his work, but by and large the explosive burgeoning of imagery in group therapy (adapted from Leuner and Desoille, with a heavy overlay of Moreno's psychodramatic approach) is rather recent — part of the games technique that pervades the encounter movement. Alexander (1969) strongly suggested that the nuclei of the most commonly employed methods are outgrowths of children's play, used to expedite the breaking down of formalities and evasions inherent in the regular verbal interchanges among adults.

I suppose that as a counterreaction to the rigidities and inflexibilities of the more traditionally psychotherapeutic approaches, imagery was a natural development. But as Singer (1971) says, "The almost wild, unsystematic application of these methods in unselected groups (often organized by relatively untrained persons with little background in psychopathology and no special clinical training) must ultimately be a subject of professional, if not national, concern." (Singer, 1971, p. 24.)

When a person lacks adequate means to develop new inner strengths, a massive attack on his defenses may lead to precipitous decisions or greater entrenchment into himself. His self-image, already negative, may be made worse. He may leave one of these modish encounter situations without the tools needed to provide awareness of his basic conflicts; he may find that such "instant" precepts as he has acquired have little application to his everyday life. The transitory sense of intimacy disappears, leaving him alone and unhappy, without a sense of belonging.

In an on-going group, the patient finds it difficult to get away with duplicity and inauthentic behavior; he also acquires a viable view of the therapist, seeing how he behaves with him both individually and in the group situation. Given a chance to observe him thus, there is the opportunity to dissociate him from significant parental figures. This in itself may strengthen a patient's desire to solve his conflicts and liberate himself from a false identity.

Psycho-Imagination group therapy emphasizes the patient's self-definition and the degree to which his self-concept permits or constricts his behavior vis-a-vis the other group members. His awareness of how others in the group define him becomes crystallized. He is encouraged to be as truly himself as possible. The therapist is open and receptive, the atmosphere nonjudgmental. Furthermore, the group can become the arena for reenactment of old family interactions which molded the patient's false positions and negative self-image. By the process of interaction, transference reactions are brought to the surface. "Transference prevents each member from being able to accept another by conferring traits upon him which originally stood in the way of a full relationship to a member of his original family." (Wolf and Schwartz 1968, p. 27.) A minimum of restriction is maintained on the group interaction so that each patient's indifference, detachment or other withdrawal tactics can be observed, as well as the more easily detected forms of hostility.

The modes and techniques of imagery in group and individual therapy are so numerous and diverse that they can hardly be exhausted. Though I have participated in group therapy for more than two and a half decades, the groups that I work with now would seem foreign to people who were in my groups even five years ago. Therapy has been an evolving, growing, joyous and painful process for me as well as for my patients. There is so much to know and experience. At times, my own mistakes, my own lack of awareness, have hindered the growth of the groups. But with the development of Psycho-Imagination theories, with the improvement in imagery techniques, my ability to help the group patients has grown considerably. I am constantly looking forward to learning, participating, giving to the growth of the group and its members.

Perhaps the key word in group therapy is "interaction" between the group members — amongst whom I include myself. Without the possibility for spontaneous and unrestricted interaction, group therapy would be of little benefit. Here are some of the forms of interaction possible in the group therapy situation:

1. Nonverbal interaction of feelings. Some silent members may be strongly affected by other members' reactions without reacting verbally.
2. Testing the expression of certain feelings in interaction. Such feelings may be the expression of the near-impossible for that person: he may just put his toes in the water to "love" and "anger."
3. Interaction of the inauthentic, competitive and controlling feelings used to sustain the stake in the neurotic interactions.
4. Those interactions from the core of the person, genuine and authentic, designed to define him as his true identity: "I am not to be defined this way; I am to be defined *this* way."
5. Interactions that relate to and are intended to affect the therapist — perhaps provoking him, or testing his trust and understanding.
6. Interactions that spark awareness which heretofore had been unconscious to that person.
7. Interactions of a more cognitive nature — to clarify concepts of values and meanings — or just plain information.
8. Interactions involving touching and holding or stroking.

The Internal Conflicts

The overall purpose of interaction within the group is to help each and every patient become aware of his or her conflicts and then take the risks inherent in focusing for change. While, broadly speaking, nearly all of the approaches suggested for individual therapy can be utilized in group therapy, there are several factors that must be taken into account. First, groups involve interaction between men and women together; some patients find it considerably easier to express feelings and imagery to members of the same sex and almost impossible to make the same statements to members of the opposite sex. This is especially true with problems of masculinity and femininity. Overcoming this kind of reluctance, permitting oneself the free flow of imagery and emotional expression without the feeling that one is bizarre or weird is a barometer of the patient's growth.

Second, the factor of peer competition, which, while not always evident in one-to-one therapy, may surface as a host of symptoms in group contact. But the disclosure of such feelings and the coping with their source can be attained. Too, basic trust of authority figures and basic trust of one's peers are areas which may be subjected to considerable emotion and conflict within the group setting. By example, by identification, by stimulating one another, by giving increasingly free play to their fantasies, dreams, imagination and unconscious productions, co-patients often afford the conflicted group member a chance to develop and nurture the courage for new alternatives.

The use of imagery in group therapy may take the following directions:

1. Imagery within the person subjectively experienced.
2. All the persons in the group engaging in imagery about a single member.
3. That member's reactions and imagery in response to the other's imagery.
4. One person engaging in imagery about every other person in rotation.
5. All of the other people, then, emerging in imagery about the one person in return-reaction imagery.
6. All of the persons engaging in imagery about the therapist at various points in his past or present life (or the future).
7. The therapist engaging in imagery about each of the group members at various points in their past or present lives (or the future).
8. All of the persons interacting in imagery without any directed consecutiveness, but yet having its own internal consistency in the sequences of reactions, depending upon the emotions generated and depending upon the particular group.

While the main thrust of this discussion involves imagery, it would be unwise to assume that imagery is the sole method used in group therapy. I have found that the "Finish the Sentence" questions can also be of invaluable help as "group starters." Among these "FTS's" are:

1. The more I know you the more I _____.
2. I cannot give you _____.
3. The most difficult thing to tell you is _____.
4. If only you would _____.
5. I like you best for your _____.
6. The adjective that describes you best is _____.
7. Sooner or later you will find me _____.
8. Never refer to me as _____.
9. I will not allow you to define me as _____.
10. My best defense against you is _____.
11. I have to prove to every woman or man _____.
12. Your strongest point is _____.

There are countless other "Finish the Sentence" approaches that can be used. Not only are they useful group starters, but they can also be used at any time in the group interaction for the purpose of clarifying reactions and feelings. They may also very well serve as leads into imagery if they result in particularly strong reactions. There are times, especially in the focusing approaches, that certain imagery may lead *back* to an appropriate "Finish the Sentence" question, as in Cathartic Imagery. The possibilities are extremely varied and can be created effectively at almost any moment of feeling and interaction.

Dual Imagery

One way to utilize dual imagery is to pose to the group as a whole an imaginary situation, such as (IS): "Imagine something inside of you and something outside of you." Follow this up by going around the room, asking each person to state his imagery. Eventually, key in on one person, with the group free to interact, and develop the imagery further for him to enhance his awareness and encourage liberation from old archaic ways. Sometimes, as we go around, the imagery of one individual may be so strong and compelling that we may not get a chance to include everyone's in-depth reaction. There is no way of absolutely anticipating such strong imagery with certainty. I remember once asking the group to (IS) "Imagine, above you and behind you, there is a force." As I went around, one woman began to cry and seemed to be badly frightened. It was not her turn, but I switched to her as soon as possible. She then described a very panicky awareness of her mother's being "above" her. Her mother died when she was four years old and the imagery had reactivated a terrible sense of guilt and conflict over her imagined responsibility for her mother's death. The group's support and reassurance were very helpful, and she was slowly able to break through her responsibility, conflict and guilt.

A further use of dual imagery might be for each person in the group to react to a single patient, as in (IS): "Imagine standing on Steve's shoulders — how would it feel and what do you imagine will happen?" Bipolarization of feelings and conflicts may be indicated between the central person of the situation and each of the other members in the group. For example, John's response was, "I can't get on Steve's shoulders because my heels would dig into his shoulders and hurt him. I will be too much of a burden on him." I then asked Steve (IS) what he would feel if John were standing on *his* shoulders. "I'd be in competition with him," Steve said, "I'd have to show him I can carry him with ease and never flinch even for a second. I can never show another man I'm weak. That's unmasculine."

As the group members take turns giving their imagery to standing on Steve's shoulders, and as he responds to them, it will be quickly revealed with whom he is in greatest conflict among them. At any one point in time a sequence of intense interaction may occur between two persons, or among several. The emphasis, to reiterate, is on helping the individual to become aware of his internal conflicts, his negative self-image, his other self-definitions, and the difference between how he defines himself and how others define him. This awareness may serve to engender in him the strength to attempt behaving differently, more in line with his "true" identity. If, as a result of the reactions to an imaginary situation, anyone in the group is being defined falsely, he or she must of course be encouraged (by me as well as the other group members) to assert himself or herself and insist, "You cannot define me that way."

The possibilities for situations in which one person may be centrally imagined by the others are countless. The therapist may ask, for example (IS): "Imagine sitting on Mary, as if she were a chair, and describe the feelings." The answers may bring to light feelings and conflicts which might remain submerged and undetectable in the course of ordinary verbal interchange. The therapist expects, for example, that Mary's imagery reactions to each of the other person's imagery may clarify her conflicts with that individual. Transferred reactions may be made sharper. As one man said about Steve, "Sitting on you is like sitting on my father — it's really like sitting on Spartacus' spike."

Other examples along similar dual imagery lines would involve the following (IS):

1. Imagine lying on a person as if he were a mattress.
2. Imagine standing on each other's chest or back.
3. Then reverse positions and people. Ask John to imagine what he thinks another person, Bill, will imagine if Bill were to be involved with yet another person, Theresa.
4. Imagine kissing a group member. His or her reactions in return.
5. Imagine what the hands of one group member would say to the hands of another group member. His or her reactions in return.
6. Imagine staring at the back or chest of a group member and imagine something. His or her reaction in return.
7. Imagine the eyes of one person saying something to the eyes of another person. His or her reaction in return.
8. Imagine something in the lap of a group member. His or her reaction in return.

Such combinations are quite various and are often a rich source of hidden reactions, frequently unsuspected by the person who does the imagining.

An additional use of dual imagery would be to ask each person in the group (IS): "Silently imagine two different musical instruments and imagine each musical instrument saying something to Jack; imagine what Jack says back to each instrument." Then one can ask each person in turn to report his dual imagery, sharing it with the rest of the group. The individual's awareness of the meanings of his own imagery production become clearer as reactions and interactions proceed. Surprise at one's own imagery and the imagery of the others is common. The feedback of reaction and the comparison of imagery may help clarify meanings and awareness of conflicts within each individual.

In this kind of dual imagery the numbers of imaginary situations are legion (give or take a little). Samples mentioned in Chapter II can be utilized, plus many others. The creativity of the therapist may be drawn to develop new examples. I have used (IS): "Imagine walking down a road; somebody taps you on the shoulder." I then proceed around the room asking each person to report his imagery and allow for interaction from all the group members. Other examples would be (IS): "Imagine a word on your chest and a word on your back; or, (IS) Imagine two different rocking chairs with different people in each — now have each person say something to the other;" or, (IS) "Imagine the left side of your brain and then imagine the right side of your brain."

Additionally, it is possible to ask a group member to go around the group whispering a statement into the left ear of each person and then to whisper something in their right ear. Reverse the interaction among the members of the group, allowing for the meanings to develop as the interactions occur. The results may illustrate the conflicts over intimacy as well as the bipolarized feelings each may have towards a particular person and that person's reaction in return.

In a personal conversation, Marylin Lovell reported working with institutional psychotics and has been able to get some startling results when she combined dual imagery with psychodrama. For example, she reports asking one psychotic man who rarely spoke to imagine (IS) any two different animals. Apparently finding it easier to imagine two different animals than to respond to a directly personal question, he surprisingly responded readily and offered: "A large German shepherd dog and a small poodle dog." He was then asked to imagine that he was the larger dog and was asked to say something to the smaller dog. In the psychodrama he was able to very forcibly shout at the smaller dog although he was previously extremely quiet and taciturn. With him (and with numerous others) such use of the dual imagery combined with psychodrama seems to have a highly therapeutic effect and, indeed, staff observers agree that it had great catalytic value.

With neurotic people in group therapy it is also possible to combine imagery with some form of psychodrama to help increase patient awareness of internal conflicts. I asked one man to (IS) imagine two different animals and he visualized a

Koala bear and a panther. I then asked him to imagine that he was the Koala bear and then to make a statement as the Koala bear to each group member. When he had finished I asked him to imagine he *was* the panther and then to make a statement to each group member as the panther. Without going into the details of his responses, I can say that this experience was highly therapeutic and effective both for him as well as the other group members.

Needless to say, such combined use of imagery and psychodrama can be utilized with effectiveness in other imaginary situations, in addition to dual imagery, such as Task Imagery and the like. The group therapy setting helps focus and crystallize the reactions for greater awareness and therapeutic change.

Group Imagery

Group imagery, in which the entire group is simultaneously presented an imaginary situation, permits participation of each person's imagination for a time, and then the imagery is shared by all.

One of the imaginary situations that can be used is (IS): "Imagine you are all in prison and then imagine that we all find a way out." The responses are sometimes quite individualized, seeming to disregard the group nature of the imagery, as in "I didn't want to get out; it was dangerous to get out. The way I would get out was to become an honor prisoner and I would get a job in the workshop and make a bulletproof jacket. One night I would make a run for it and get out. Even though the guards shot at me, they couldn't hurt me and I get away." Another man said, "I'd make a deal with the warden through my lawyers and the court in order to get me free. It would be a deal. I would give them information they wanted in exchange for my freedom." Other patients visualize the entire group lining up as a single, powerful unit and killing the guards in order to escape together.

Occasionally, one person's imagery may trigger off an awareness of a particular characteristic of himself and his style of life. One overindulged patient said he realized he really didn't care about anybody else's being in prison. "I am only interested in myself,' he said adding, "Boy, that's hard to say." He had exposed his excessive self-involvement and narcissism to the group and was waiting for the counterreaction. There was a negative reaction to his remarks, forcing him to face up to his self-involvement, his pseudo-caring of others. In a sense this imagery served to invite the other group members to force him to stand up to his conflict. Apparently, he didn't want to get away with such behavior in the future. In this case, his own need to expose himself forced him to cope with the conflict.

Imagery in which the entire group participates may start from an imaginary situation such as (IS): "We are all in a stagecoach and we are going on a journey. What do you imagine will happen to us as we go?" Again, this is a good starting point for interaction, especially designed to see how others view us and how we view them.

Other group imagery situations that can further sharpen interaction and awareness of conflicts are (IS): "Imagine the entire group is part of a circus – what part would each of you take?," or (IS) "We are all stuck on the elevator near the top of a very tall building," or (IS) "We are all stuck on an island for an indefinite time – what would you do and feel?" or (IS) "We are all forced to spend a winter in the frozen north in a very large hut."

In addition, one can ask a person to go around the group and (IS) imagine a bird on the head of each group member and their reactions back to him. Or ask each group member (IS) to cast a fishing rod into a river and then to see what you come up with. This again serves as a vehicle for reactions, interactions and awareness of conflicts.

I must emphasize again that group sessions are not so structured that imagery is the only function involved. Anything may be brought up at any time: a particularly traumatic situation or decision a person is involved with; carryover reactions from previous sessions; thoughts and feelings people have had about some of the others in the days between group meetings. Also included may be such awareness and feelings as patients have gleaned from individual sessions and wish to bring up spontaneously in the group situations. Nothing, certainly, should deter spontaneous behavior unless the spontaneous behavior is used as a cover-up for some difficult internal conflict. To keep the structure and the spontaneity of the group unfettered is a fine goal for any group therapist.

For all its beneficial aspects, group therapy does not always offer the most expedient determination of a patient's readiness to deal with the focusing approaches or what conflicts he is ready to face. In group therapy, each person is in a "different place" – his own awareness and plateau of growth; certain patients may require a great deal of clinical intuition and readiness for the unexpected on the part of the therapist which might not be necessary in a dyadic situation. I believe that the therapist should offer support when patients are facing heightened awareness of conflicts, and in the focusing approaches, I discourage wherever possible the extended one-to-one involvement between myself and a patient without the group members being involved. I encourage group support and find it an invaluable aid in helping a specific person through a "tough" spot. But clearly there are instances in which this is not possible or advisable.

Utilizing the Creative Imagery of the Patient

With patients that have been experienced in the use of imagery, it is a natural bridge to have them be the originator of imagery with each other. In order to facilitate the process, I asked the first, third, fifth, seventh and ninth person in the room to ask the second, fourth, sixth, eighth and tenth person an imaginary situation in rotation and have each person respond with his or her imagery. The first person asks the second person to respond with his or her imagery, then the entire group participates. Then the third person asks the fourth person an imaginary situation and as he or she responds again, the group participates. This continues until the entire group is involved in a similar manner. Of course, one can reverse the procedure by asking the second person to ask the first person an imaginary situation with group participation, etc.

What follows is a portion of an audio tape of ten people in a group where this creative procedure is developed. It is difficult in printed form alone to indicate all of the nuances, voice sounds and the gestures that can be seen in visual and auditory observation. The reader should realize that I am emphasizing the creative use of the patient's imagery and it is beyond us to explore in depth the conflicts of ten people. It is my judgment that this procedure serves to intensify the interaction among the group members and that many images developed in this session were referred to in many subsequent sessions.

Shorr: I want you to try something that's a little different. I want the first, third, fifth, seventh and ninth person to think of an imaginary situation. I want you to create one and ask the person next to you an imaginary situation.

Martha: Like the thing on each side?

(All talking)

Shorr: Anything, but you have to use your own — I don't want you to use one I would use. You would use any one you want to.

Larry: That's really wild. (Laughs)

Nancy: Use one of Shorr's old ones and ask Robert to imagine so-and-so, is that right?

Shorr: You can use any, but not necessarily one of mine. You ask anything you want to, using your own imagination.

(Everyone laughs and talks)

Nora: Robert, imagine "your wife as two women. . . ."

Robert: That's tough.

Shorr: Well, you think about that, Robert.

Robert: Oh, oh, I'm supposed to think about it?

Shorr: And go back to it.

Nina: Ah, somebody commissions you to do a mural on a wall and what do you paint on the wall?

Arly: Do I think about this now or do I . . . ?

Shorr: Think about it and then we'll go back to it.

Roberta: I'll give you what I have.

Shorr: Let me hear you. (Roberta was speaking very low)

Roberta: Ah, there is a large grizzly bear in your left hand and your other hand is full of rice.

Nora: A hand full of what?

Larry: Rice (Laughing) Jesus.

Roberta: Dick, make up an imaginary situation with those two.

Dick: Wow!

Shorr: Well, you think about it, Dick.

Martha: Yes, Dick, good luck (Laughing).

Larry: Imagine that you're like the, remember, the woman you once imagined?

Yale: The flying woman? (Reference to a previous image in another session)

Larry: Imagine that you're in that group of eight bicyclists up on top of that (Various people — Oh dear and Oh shit) thing, and, and, and imagine who's with you and what you're doing.

Yale: Hum . . .

Shorr: (Chuckle) While you think of that one, Nancy, ask Martha one.

Nancy: Well, what comes to my mind is a wooden plank in the shape of a Y and you're walking along it — imagine yourself walking along the long part of the Y and you come to where it turns into the V, and what do you see at either end of that V and which way would you go?

Shorr: Well, we'll start with Martha.

(Mumbled talking)

Martha: I saw water. I saw the plank at the end of — of a ship or boat and I just saw water.

Shorr: Are you happy with that answer? Remember what you asked her. (This is directed to Nancy)

Nancy: No.

Shorr: What did you ask her?

Nancy: Ah, I wanted to know what, who was at either end of the V.

Martha: Oh, I thought you said what.

Nancy: Or what, or who.

Martha: Well, I just saw a vast ocean — I don't see anyone at the end of that, I see that vast huge sea.

Shorr: But you say that there's a separate road up . . .

Nancy: Yes and you have to . . .

Shorr: And you want her to see something different on each one?

Nancy: Yes, something different on each one and you have to decide which way you're going to go, because you have to go this way or that way.

Martha: Yeah, I'm not going off that plank. I have to take it off the boat which I'm obviously going to have to do because there's just water there and I'm not going, I'm not going in it that way. So if I have to take that Y and put it someplace else. . . . (Sigh) I'm in the woods with it and I don't know, it doesn't matter which way I go 'cause I don't know what's at the end of either one of those paths. What I'll have to do is try one and if I don't like that one, I'll go back to the beginning and try and try another one, try the other one.

Nancy: Well, if you can see the end of the paths and you see something at the end of one and you know that you have to decide which way to go and you cannot come back, what would you do, or see?

Martha: What would I see at the end . . . I see a house at the end of one . . . I don't know where that other one's going, I just don't know. I don't see where it's going, it's just going into the woods, and I don't know, I, I don't see it.

Shorr: You want to go into it?

Martha: I'm not afraid to go into it.

Shorr: Go. Why not try it?

Martha: Okay — okay, it's like I came out the end of the woods, and the woods are — huh — it's the woods I used to play in — and then there is an open field. I used to love that particular field, like when you come out from all the woods. I like being in the woods but I like coming out too. So there was a sense of openness and freedom.

Shorr: Why don't you go towards the house more?

Martha: The house is very, it's a very nice, it's a warm welcome kind of a feeling I get from the house — and there's very plain people in there — I don't know them, I don't think, but they're good people and, and they're very comfortable and I like that house too, I like the feeling I get from being in it. . . .

Shorr: Does it represent anything to you? Does it have meaning — this place, this childhood place and the house?

Martha: The childhood place was a place where I would go because I couldn't face what was happening in my own home and I'd go off and be alone there and feel all right. It's like the only place that I had a sense of peace because when I was back in the house with my family, it was just hell. So that was a good feeling, you know it was . . . nothing could touch me there.

Shorr: And the house — what did you feel about that?

Martha: And the house was, I don't know where this house came from. I don't recognize that as any house I've ever been in, it's just like a little old one-room house and the thing I, that kinda comes to my mind is, I used to wish that I had been a pioneer when — when it was cut and dried what you had to do, you had to work to survive and there wasn't time to, to worry about that — should your kids take dancing lessons or some insignificant thing — it was, it was a simple cut and dried life. I used to think, God, maybe I should have lived then — life would not be so complicated.

Shorr: So what do these images mean to you? What do you think about them? Does it relate to your life today in any way?

(Pause)

Martha: My life is so complicated right now that I would like to be in a real peaceful spot. Yeah, yeah. Where nobody can touch me, either this quiet, little. . . . Yeah, which is kinda what I do, see I turn to a physical thing. Always when I can't handle something, I always go into some sort of physical activity with great vigor.

Shorr: So it's pretty illustrative of you, this, these two things you saw, huh?

Martha: Probably.

Shorr: I'm going to pull a switch. I want Yale to ask Larry an imaginary situation and Larry will have to answer before yours.

Dick: Sneak.

Yale: Yeah, mine is sort of prejudiced by his question to me.

(Everyone laughs)

Yale: No. no. Larry, you're on the back of a seat of a motorcycle, who's driving it and what's happening?

Larry: Do I have to answer or anything?

(Everyone laughs)

Shorr: There are no policemen. (Larry has had bad experiences with motorcycles)

Larry: Oh, I didn't know. Well, I don't like motorcycles, as you know, and I think that I'm trying to see who's driving it. I get this picture of sort of a playgirl, you know with the long hair and all that, you know – but she's really just fucked in her head, 'cause we're just going like a son-of-a-bitch, you know, so all I can do is figure how to tail out of the god damn thing. (Robert laughs; Nora says, "Fall off gracefully.") Yeah, that's my whole concern. (Group laughs) How to get off and be cool (Everyone laughs) at 80 miles an hour, you know. I had an image of that guy they have at automobile shows where they slide for life, you know, or he slides along and the smoke pouring out but he's, but he does it just right. I was thinking, if I could pull that off?

Roberta: Are you holding onto her?

Larry: No, not any more. I'm . . . ah, no, I'm not holding onto her, huh, uh.

Martha: Who is this girl?

Larry: I don't know. . . . She's almost like a, like a pop art, you know, kind of with the big Hollywood smile. I mean (Robert: "Barbarella.") Raquel Welch. You know what I mean. It was, it got, that got me thinking about it, but she's like just really, just you know, what's her name, there was a movie that was put out about a spy girl, you know (Yale: "Barbarella, is that what you mean?") Is that who it is, yeah, that, that type of thing, you know it just really – Barbarella.

Nancy: But do you do everything with so much finesse, but can you just let reality in and know that you're going to die if you don't get the fuck off that thing, can't you. . . .

(Background talking during all of the previous)

Larry: I think I do everything, I would die with finesse.

Yale: Wait a second, Larry. (Everyone laughing)

Larry: That's very important to me.

Robert: It was important to Byron too – You really think that she's definitely bound for a crackup, huh, there's no two ways about it, there, if you stay on, she's going to crash.

Larry: Good chance, I wouldn't say definitely. I'd say there was a damn good chance.

Martha: You couldn't talk her out of it?

Larry: I don't think she's aware. She's not aware of the perils, you see. She's in for the image and everything and it's just not – it's, I, it just does not cross her mind.

Yale and Arly: Well, were you in the image?

Larry: What image?

Nora: Uh, huh.

Arly: Well, you can't tell her to stop the fucking motorcycle and let you get off?

Nancy: You have no control?

Arly: Do you have to "finesse" it with her?

Larry: No, I . . . (Pause)

Shorr: An awful lot of danger involved.

Nancy: Yeah.

Larry: Oh, I don't think that would change, that's what I said, I don't think that would change my picture of decorum. There are ways to get off a motorcycle, no matter what. (Laughs)

Shorr: The most important thing is . . .

Roberta: In a life or death situation, you'd still hang onto the control thing.

Larry: Well, I feel that emotionally I don't know if in truth you know that's something that may be really true, although everytime I cracked up on a motorcycle I did it really pretty good, I think . . .

Nancy: You were cool and cracked up.

Robert: With aplomb.

Larry: That's right!

Nancy: But would you rather get off, than reach over and just turn something off or grab her arms or feet?

(Miscellaneous talking and laughing)

Larry: Yeah, grab her arms — (Laughs)

Roberta: Grab her boobs.

Arly: She'll hit you with a tit.

Nancy: I mean, it's almost like you have no power to do anything except get off gracefully.

Larry: That's about the way I see it. I don't think I do have much power. I mean to do anything else. I could throttle her or something like that but these would be a . . . (Pause)

Arly: Could you, could you force yourself to say, "Stop this motorcycle, I want to get off," or is that uncouth?

(All speaking at once)

Martha: Stop and let me off.

Nancy: It's not cool.

Robert: I forgot something, I . . .

Yale: I've got a letter to mail, would you pull over to the next mailbox. (Laughs)

Shorr: Well, how does this relate to your life when you think of this image? Is it protective of anything in your life? (Pause)

Larry: I think it fairly well exemplifies how I handle situations of this type, not that I don't have day-to-day life and death situations too often, but situations that are tricky in, in a respect. I think this is about the way I handle them, I try and do it very, very coolly whether I feel it or not.

Shorr: That fact that you include a woman in this without Yale indicating that there's a woman or anybody else that I know of, right, Yale?

Larry: Well, no, no of course not.

(Everyone Laughing)

Shorr: You think that's important that you got the woman on the bike?

Larry: Well, I think — you see I have — I get a pretty positive feeling about the whole situation. I think that it, is (Sigh) at least it's resolved, it's my resolving a conflict with, with women, that kind of woman is the woman that I had for a long time as an idealized image — idealized woman.

Nancy: A problem we didn't know about.

(Everyone laughs)

Larry: Well, I'm a transvestite. (Offered in a humorous fashion) (Laughing) Anyway, it's a Hollywood broad, it's a swinging, you know, hip chick. All that shit and I guess after all this in (Laughingly) my mind, the best way out of it is just to get off the motorcycle —

Roberta: And let her go screaming into the wind?

Larry: Because, because there's no way, there's no way that I'm going to be able to, to, talk with her.

Roberta: Yeah, it's like you can't deal with it, there's just no level that you can communicate, or nothing you know.

Robert: She won't listen to reason. Oh, then I can just win with the big smile and, azzoom, you know, and this is the whole thing and she wants a guy who's going to go along and say, "Faster, faster," you know, but like I've fractured my asshole with this kind of cunt and those kind of motorcycles and that's it.

Shorr: You want no more part of that.

Larry: No more, no more (Background talking) and I want to get out as coolly as possible, you know, without any hassle.

Shorr: But you're not facing that in life today?

Larry: No, it's something that I think I've resolved pretty well.

Yale: What would happen if you got off the motorcycle without cool, you just reach over and turn off the ignition, and, ah.

Larry: Uh, huh, very hard for me to believe that I would do it, it's not impossible, but it's like eating left-handed. I mean, you know, I guess I could do it. I could imagine it — aah, but I think I'd have a lot of . . .

Roberta: Can you scream at her for jeopardizing your life, like, "God damn stupid bitch," you know — I mean can you, you know . . .

Larry: Can, but ah —

Yale: Why is it still . . .

Larry: She couldn't care less, I mean, you know.

Robert: Is that the feeling you . . .

Arly: Yeah, but can you care less?

Nancy: Yeah, but it makes you feel good, to get it out.

Yale: Yeah, that's the point, I think Arly has a point there. Can you, can you turn off the key and get off and to hell with what she thinks about you. I mean it's like you're still getting off, and getting off and, getting off her way.

Larry: No, I'm getting off my way, not her way. This is my way of getting off.

Yale: Well, I don't understand that.

Martha: I don't see anything wrong with the way he got off that, that he walked away from a situation. He just turned his back on it.

Roberta: He wasn't going to walk away. He was going at 80 miles an hour, going to try to go off gracefully, you know, without damaging . . .

(Everyone talking)

Martha: Did you get off safely in your picture? That was the impression I got.

Larry: Oh yeah.

Martha: You got off and left and I . . .

Larry: I got off safely, yeah, I got off.

Robert: The details were a little vague, I think they . . .

Nora: Yah, it was a little vague to me, Larry, because you said you would die for them.

Larry: Well, oh well, I hadn't exactly figured it out then I, I really . . .

Nora: But at least you would keep it cool?

Arly: Yeah, that's what you said.

Larry: Well, I don't expect to die.

Nora: That's different than getting off safely.

Larry: Uh huh, no, I will get off safely, but with finesse.

Shorr: Do you have a reaction to that, Nina? What Larry just said?

Yale: (Laughs)

Larry: Just a motorcycle problem (Group laughter) Harley-Davidson.

Yale: Who's riding in back of your motorcycle? (Laughs)

Larry: Yamaha hangup.

Martha: I think it's great.

(Group laughter)

Nina: I'm so nervous with that fucking thing going, I can't follow anything. I'm just catching words here and there and blanking out. (Laughs)

Shorr: No, now – say something to the damn tape recorder, so it doesn't intimidate you. Why do you let that define you? (Roberta squeals, "more softly")

Nina: (Very quietly) Ah, I don't know.

Larry: Just because everybody's going to play it tomorrow night and laugh, (Everyone laughs) sit around and (Background talking and laughing) listen to it.

Nina: That's what I'm afraid of, I'm afraid of, of being foolish.

Shorr: Well, nobody will hear you but this group – on a replay, how do you like that, except myself. Is that fair?

Nina: Well, I still think that I'll come off foolish.

Shorr: Then you're always coming off foolish in group. I mean, after all, we can tape any session.

Nina: I hope nobody remembers. (Laughs)

(Background talking)

Shorr: (M/L) What's the most difficult thing to say to the tape recorder? Since you're investing it with power.

Nina: Just to talk.

Shorr: (Focus) No, say something to it, so it doesn't define you.

Nina: (Loudly) FUCK OFF!

Shorr: Good, now what did you think of Larry and the motorcycle?

Nina: (Chuckle) I, I thought that what he did was fine. I, you know, I didn't think going 80 miles and hour was any different than going 20 miles an hour. I felt, you know, he had to just get off.

Larry: It calls for a little more agility. (Group laughter)

Nina: I thought – I thought you'd do it anyway, no matter what.

Roberta: We all have great faith in him.

Arly: There is a little pocket parachute.

Nora: I'd like to see it myself (Laughingly) at 80 miles an hour.

Roberta: I'd like to see you take a different type of control of the scene, you know, like confronting her.

Larry: If you were driving the motorcycle, I could and more. There's the difference. Any woman in this group I think I could handle.

Arly: But why, why?

Larry: Because these women in here I have communication with, and I realize that they know me. Yeah, I mean this broad is detached from me.

Arly: Yeah, but you're giving her power, because you said —

Larry: No, I'm not giving her power, man. I used to give her power when I was trying to fuck her, trying to make something out of her. I'm not giving her any power.

Arly: Then why do you have to give up?

Larry: She doesn't have any, I just bail off of the motorcycle.

Arly: But you said you had to do it with a sense of finesse. You wouldn't die.

Larry: But that's for me. I think I would do that, I think I would do that.

Arly: But if Roberta were driving the motorcycle, would you do the same thing?

Larry: I could do the same thing but I wouldn't have to do the same thing. I could reach over to Roberta and say, "Roberta, would you please slow down, we're going too fast."

Arly: If you couldn't say that to some of them or —

Larry: This particular girl, this is my fantasy. Arly is not going to listen to that.

(Everyone laughs)

Arly: Okay, that's different than what I heard you saying. I thought, what I was getting from you is that she wasn't going to listen. It's that you couldn't say, "Stop this motorcycle, you're jeopardizing my life."

Larry: Oh, I could, but it's not going to stop that motorcycle.

Arly: Oh, okay, but I mean, in other words, her presence couldn't stop you from saying what you want to say?

Larry: No, I just, in this particular situation, I'm going to have to do it the best way I can and that's, you know, in order to save my life is what it amounts to, and the only way I could save my life with her, with Roberta, with Nina or anybody or you, you know, it could be done differently but not with this girl.

Dick: You assumed or you stated all along that you're going to die, I mean, that this thing is doomed.

Martha: No

Roberta: No, no he changed it, he changed it.

(Various "no's")

Larry: I'm not going to die, I'm going to live forever. (Underlying conversations) If I stay on, there's a damn good possibility I will die, yes.

Dick: Then, she's going to kill herself, is what she's doing?

Larry: I don't know what she's going to do, I'm not really (Laughingly) concerned.

Dick: You're sure, sure that there's going to be a crackup?

Larry: Yeah, positive.

Robert: I notice that you're disguising your voice, by the way.

(Group laughing)

Larry: What!

(Everyone laughs and various talking)

Yale: Is that why you've got that pebble in your mouth?

Larry: (Mutters) Yeah, a pebble here.

(Group laughing)

Dick: Is there also a way possibly that you won't die, that you could ride it out?

Larry: That's a very slim possibility, I feel. You see, motorcycles has got me in a very bad way. It's a tough subject 'cause I think I've used up my chances on a motorcycle. (Group laughter) I don't have too many "freebies" left. (Group laughter)

Shorr: Dick, why don't you ask Roberta an imaginary situation?

Roberta: (In a quiet voice) I tried to get missed.

Shorr: I know.

Larry: Buried all the rice.

Roberta: I am ready for it.

Shorr: She still has hers.

Dick: O.K., there are three birds flying. Can you imagine that?

Roberta: Three birds flying?

Shorr: Will you say it louder, Dick? I didn't hear you.

Dick: (Loudly) There are three birds flying and you're one of them. Which one are you? And what's it about?

Roberta: All right! Yeah, I saw the three of them and I was in the middle, you know, like a V-type situation. I like them this way. Feels great. (Laughing) I've never flown before — fantastic! Then we get a little closer and we kind of huddle (Laughs) as we fly. What do we think? Who are they?

Dick: Who's in front of you?

Roberta: I was kind of like — in that — those birds were back there, those, those beautiful birds. Aaah, who are they? I immediately thought of the children, you know, Jimmy and Carol — great day, it's beautiful, I didn't see the tornado.

Yale: (Laughs)

Shorr: Dick, you had it with one in front, one in the middle, something like that and one in the back. You mean, you had it in a direct line?

Martha: In a line.

Dick: Yeah, I, I set it up as a line, yeah.

Shorr: Where there's one, two, three right in front of each other?

Dick: I wanted to know which one you were, and you said you were in the middle.

Roberta: Oooooooohhhhhh — I did, didn't I, you see I was seeing it different. That's why. Okay. If I would be in the middle, then it would be different. Then there would be a man in front and — someone else, or you know.

Yale: A spare.

(Laughter)

Roberta: You know more about me than you need to know.

Larry: A spare (Laugh) — a back-up stud.

Roberta: No, I saw it, you know, like children instead, in the back.

Larry: Children in the back?

Roberta: Well, you know if that, that's the direction. If I'm not in front, then the man's in front. Okay. The first impression I had was that I was flying and I had both kids on the side, okay, that's going like flying, okay but the situation he wants is someone in the front, me in the middle and someone in the back, well then I feel like I'd be – well with other people, if I'm in the middle in this particular situation, I'm comfortable, you know, the man's in front and the children in back.

Shorr: You have sort of a family scene there.

Roberta: Yeah – yeah, there's something to that.

Nancy: Are there any conflicts between you wanting to go up front with the fellow? I like the V-shape better myself, because it shows you do or are having some sort of a problem with your children as far as responsibility and guilt and all this sort of thing, but if you are in the other line with a man in front and the children in back, do you have any conflict in trying to get forward or do you feel a pull of any kind?

Roberta: I didn't, no, no, it was kind of like nice and I was wondering why I was there. It feels so good. No, no I love the unity, I love that effect, you know, like I want to gather it in.

Nancy: So, in other words, it's more comfortable. It's more comfortable being in the center of – the man in front and the children behind, than you in the front and the children behind?

Roberta: Oh, no, no, no, they're comparable, see, you know, parallel feeling.

Nancy: But in reality, they are totally opposite. They're not comparable, in reality you're not either. Right?

Roberta: Okay, let me, you know, get a feel on that I – (Pause) – Okay, if there's a tornado and I'm (Laughter) you know, in front with the kids, I tend to get a little nervous. Yeah, I do tend to get a little nervous and I really feel a lot more comfortable, you know, with a man in front, you know, and the kids in back, but will fly the tornado. When there's trouble, you know, where the hell are they? I need the man, and I do feel like, you know, that kind of feels good to be able to rely on him.

Nancy: Yeah, but if there is no tornado – the feeling, the feeling that I'm having is sometime, I might be inflicting a lot of my own problems and my own feelings of remarriage and stuff. Do you feel that if there is no tornado, is there a definite difference in your feeling?

Roberta: A bit incomplete with the kids – you know it feels good and, and it's comfortable, but again, it's like in case of trouble – like I'm all alone.

Nancy: It would be easy to give up your place in the front with the children and let a man take over. There's no problem.

Roberta: Well, you know, I'm going to make sure it's a good strong bird. You know, I know that. I mean, he'd have to be a goose instead. (Group laughter)

Shorr: So what does that mean to your life?

Roberta: Well, I'd, I'd be willing to give up, you know, the leader, sole responsibility for, you know, a nice relationship.

Shorr: Sounds like it's coming off good. Martha, how about asking one of Nancy.

Martha: Aaah, okay. Let's see. Picture a scale of justice. What do you see on either side and how does it relate to you? In other words, which one's heavier and what is it?

Yale: I think we've got justice sitting here right there, very proper as you. (Points to Shorr)

Nancy: Hey, I'm just like the statue (Laughter) now that you mention it. I was getting very regal up there, wasn't I. Aaah, I'm looking down instead of up. That's funny. Okay, I'm really having a problem here with authority, uumm. Now I'm looking at eye level to a statue that is holding a scale in either hand, but it is not the statue of justice that has a blindfold over its eyes and it should, ummmm. It is of a very — human, soft person, that is holding out these two dishes or plates or trays or whatever, with a lot of compassion and understanding and in the right hand, there is — all kinds of real pretty, shiny things — extremely brilliant, radiating, fantastic amounts of energy — and in the left hand — is a pile of rusty keys — and — it's sort of like I'm afraid of both of them in reality.

Martha: Which one were you the most, between them?

Nancy: They weigh totally the same. They weigh equally the same. Aah, the keys are frightening, because I know it's like confinement, imprisonment, aah hardship, slavery, which is from my slavery days. Oh no, I was a slave. It's a comfortable feeling with the keys, although it's, it's something that I know that's over and I don't want to have anything more to do with it. It's sad — lethargic. It's a feeling about it that's sad, but it's over with, and of thing and the sparkly things I really am moving towards, but I'm very afraid of them because I don't know what's there. I don't if that's really, really what belongs to me or not.

Martha: Who is that woman who's holding this stuff so compassionately?

Nancy: Oh, it has to be me, I'm sure. I'm sure. I'm sure that it's probably me.

Nora: Nancy, explain the keys to me a little better.

Nancy: The keys?

Nora: Yea.

Nancy: Well, they're old rusty keys, with round loops on them and —

Nora: Fantastic, but what do they represent, that's what I'm losing.

Nancy: Well, they represent a lot of years, I would say, that were spent imprisoned, just years that I have spent in imprisonment and now that I'm not in prison anymore. They're old and rusty — I feel like I'm looking back on my life and I see it in blocks, like a child's box of toys and you see building blocks in it and like they're numbered or lettered according to the phase of life that I went through and like the life that I have today I feel is just like a bunch of these blocks that are, that are built and this block I was imprisoned in, this situation or this feeling or this ignorance which is, whatever you want to call it. As I grew out of that into another stage of life or another aspect, each block that I passed through is like a prison with a key on it.

Nina: You're in possession of all of these keys, nobody else has them?

Nancy: No, they're there, I have them.

Dick: Can you throw them away?

Nancy: Oh yes, they're thrown away, they are old and rusty already, and I don't feel like I would ever be imprisoned again. Aaah, I don't feel restricted now like I was before, like I had no choice up until lately.

Shorr: What about that other side, can you luxuriate in the other side?

Nancy: Yeah, it seems like it would be.

Shorr: Experience the joy of it.

Nancy: Well this is it. There really hasn't been much joy up until recently and I don't know if I could really accept it or not right now or do you want me to go home and think about it?

(Laughter)

Shorr: Right now.

Nancy: (Laughs) Oh rats, I hate this spur-of-the-moment decision. Aaah.

Shorr: I'll take joy anytime I could get it.

Nancy: What's her last name? – It's, it's strange, I want to go to it and I know damn well I deserve everything that's there, I know it's mine, I earned it by physical labor. In reality, it's not just because I'm me, which is enough.

Shorr: Stop explaining and start experiencing it.

Nancy: Oh, I know, my body starts shaking, as I go towards it, it just starts vibrating so terribly much that the plates start shaking and all the little things start tingling –

Yale: Will you let some of that joy show in your face?

Nancy: You mean it hasn't?

Yale: It wasn't.

Nancy: Well, I'm too worried about the job – I feel out of place, I, totally feel out of place. If I could change those shiny things to earth things, I would feel comfortable.

Shorr: (Focus) (IS) Change them.

Nancy: Aaah that, see that. I'm really fooling myself. I keep thinking I want all the shiny luxury things. I don't, I really don't. I would feel out of place with them and now that they're earth things, like dirt and plants and things like that and flowers – and trees and butterflies.

Shorr: Seems more natural.

Nancy: Yes, yes, then I can really luxuriate in that, I can just fall down and let it cover me up and it feels satiny and smooth and it smells just heavenly – Yeah, that's much better.

Shorr: The gold sounds like it's a false position of some sort.

Nancy: Yeah, I think it was, well I don't think it was, I know it was. You're right – realistically I'm much more comfortable here.

Nora: If they're earth things, do they still weigh the same?

Nancy: Oh yes, I think of them as higher though than the keys, but I don't understand how that is except that they're higher up – aah – the weights are –

Robert: They're not as hard to carry.

Nancy: Yeah, maybe that's it, they're much, they're higher up on the scale. Although I'm sure they weigh physically as much or more but it's not, it's not the burden, the keys are sort of dead and heavy, whereas this is strong but higher.

Shorr: You like that?

Nancy: Oh yeah, yeah, yeah. Now I have to go home and clean my mental closet out and get rid of all those diamonds and satins (Laughs) and jewels. (Group laughter) I want a pair of satin sheets (Laughingly). Okay, I'll go home and play in the grass. That's probably better. You know, really to put a little tag line on it, where I work. You know, it's all man-made structure and all and everytime the gardeners mow the lawn I have a horrible urge. I pick up handfuls of grass and stick them in my pocket and I take it in and put it on my desk, and the smell of cut grass, it's so delicious. Have you ever smelled fresh cut grass?

Shorr: I believe so.

Roberta: Live in California!

Nancy: Oh, it smells so good. I wish they would get that into a perfume of some kind, you know.

Robert: "Eau de Grasse."

(Group laughter)

Yale: "Newly Mown."

Shorr: Robert, ask an imaginary situation of Nora.

Robert: Of Nora?

Shorr: Un huh.

Robert: Hoo − Ummmm − (IS) You're in the, on the observation deck on the top of the Empire State Building and a man is coming towards you −

Nora: I'm standing by one of those telescopes − and I'm looking out at the city that I've never seen before and it's all so different and it's very exciting and I'm urging him to come on to see it with me and to look out and see what I've found, and it's chilly − I don't see myself in a coat but I see him in a topcoat which is unusual here − and it's a good place to be, that would be a nice place to be.

Nina: Are you sharing it with him?

Nora: Yes, I, I'm hurrying him on to see what I see and to share it 'cause it's going to be something new and awfully nice.

Shorr: What do you see?

Nora: Oh, I see these huge tall buildings and, oh, just a skyline I've never seen before − and the busiest harbor I've ever seen. My goodness, except for looking through it, the ships are going in like this, like cars on a freeway. (Laughingly) Of course, they can't do, but it's very busy and it's − seems very different and extremely exciting to me.

Nancy: After you look through the telescope and you turn away, what do you do?

Nora: We get in the elevator to go down and go somewhere else to see something in the city.

Robert: What does he say to you?

Nora: What does he say? (Quietly) "That was marvelous, what shall we do now?" It just seems, it's a very nice image, I really like it. I really like that.

Nancy: Would you feel that as out − between the two of you, which one would take charge and take the lead?

Nora: I can't see a leader, I can see two people just so anxious to go see what there is to see and one is urging this way and one is urging that way and so you go both. There's no leader.

Robert: Spontaneous interaction type.

Nora: Yeah, I love that scene − thanks, Robert, write me another. I love it.

Shorr: Self-explanatory. Yale, how about that imaginary situation you got before.

Yale: Yeah, riding a bicycle on the high-wire. I can only get the troupe up to three people at any one time. (Group laughter) Yeah, well it's like, I had to put it in a situation. At first I was out at one of the ends of the poles, sort of hanging on, and then I was sort of imagining who I would feel comfortable with on the other side. Can I be comfortable riding the bicycle and basically in control of the situation? And I can think of a number of people, like Helen or Nora, who I'd feel comfortable with out at the other end of the pole. Aaah, it's not a real dynamic situation. I don't imagine moving. It's just sort of a balancing act, you know, like who do I feel comfortable with in what situations. I put Harriet (woman friend) out on the end of one of the poles and boy it was just hard work to get her balanced. In fact, it was almost impossible. You know it was like she let go and I sort of poke her with the pole and it was, I guess, physically impossible. If you try to pull her up, why she'd go down a little bit further on the pole. Something of that sort, no one really at the moment. I was just about to say if I started to drive along, funny, well then I imagine seeing another bicycle coming in from the opposite (Laughs) direction.

(Group laughter)

Robert: (Laughing) Who's driving that "son-of-a-bitch?"

(Group laughter and talking)

Yale: I don't know — it's probably a woman.

Nora: Lousy women drivers. (Sarcastically)

Yale: Right, always going the wrong way on a one-way street.

Nina: Would you try to see how much you could do on a bicycle, like handstands or on one hand or two hands or —

Yale: Aaah, I don't think I would have thought of that, I can imagine it now that you asked me, but I don't think that I could have conceived of that myself.

Nancy: It seems like the one coming towards you is obviously not a woman driver as you said. You're really wound up in conflict or combat with women. There's nothing else but the combat?

(Laughs)

Yale: (Laughs) Yes.

Nancy: Yes, there is, or no, there isn't?

Yale: Yeah, I think you're right there. I think of it as meeting someone not necessarily as being combative.

Nancy: Well, if it was a woman driver coming towards you, when you met, what would the result be? What would you do?

Yale: (Laughs) That's your woman (to Larry) driver. I mean you just pedal faster.

Nancy: I want to see you jump out of her way, Yale.

(Group laughter and background talking)

Yale: I don't go for these Hollywood tricks. No, I see us sort of getting off our bicycles and holding the bicycle on one side as a counterbalance and just balancing there, facing each other for awhile, aaah —

Nancy: It would be like a partnership act?

Yale: I, I haven't gotten that far.

Nancy: Oh!

Robert: Are there spectators, Yale?

Yale: Aaah!

Robert: Is there a crowd?

Yale: Sort of phantom crowds. I don't see the crowd, but I feel their presence.

Nina: Is there a net below just in case?

Robert: No.

Yale: I hope so. (Laughs) (Group laughs) I don't see one.

Yale: Me and the woman, though I imagine in some cases, it's easier to — for each of us to go by each other and continue in the directions we were going. It is to turn one of the bicycles around and sort of have a bicycle built for two, in the middle of the high-wire and then go off in the same direction.

Roberta: Do you still see yourself meeting, exchanging, able to work it out and still continue?

Yale: Well, I'm not sure, it's like I got two solutions or two pictures.

Roberta: It's obvious — I don't like that.

Robert: Well, suppose that the person on the bike coming toward you were Harriet?

Yale: ... We don't get that close — I'd back up aways and then she backs up aways — bikes are always ten feet apart.

Shorr: What does it say about you?

Yale: Ah — says I got to go down the path and when I do meet someone, I've got to risk trying to put the bicycles together and do a bicycle built for two. I see the whole thing as being trust. Whom do I trust and how does the trust balance out?

Nancy: And where your responsibility is?

Yale: Yes and no.

Nancy: Well, like when you were on one side and you had Harriet or somebody else on the other and you said it's hard for her to stay on there. If you were the one who was responsible to pick her up and put her back — if you got to give that up —

Yale: Yeah, but if I saw her falling off, I didn't feel "AAAAAAAGH," you know, calamity. I should jump after her, you know, that's something I should get to make an effort at. I guess there is some responsibility in it but I don't, I don't feel that it's a calamity.

Shorr: You're exercising trust more now in this thing?

Yale: Yeah.

Shorr: More than the responsibility?

Yale: Yeah, I certainly see it as something in regards to trust.

Roberta: I don't see you as terribly nervous up there either. I see you able to deal with it.

Shorr: How high up was it, Larry, that imaginary situation you gave to Yale?

Larry: Oh, waaaay up.

    (Group laughing and talking)

Yale: I was high up too. I wouldn't want to fall off that thing. I'm not sure that there's a safety net down below.

Larry: No, no.

Nancy: It wasn't the fear of falling. It was the fear of encounter?

Yale: It was encounter and it would stretch between the Empire State Building. Well one, I think, Nina brought up something which I would like to emphasize. I wish I had been flamboyant up there. I seem to be confident to certainly go by someone else on the high wire, but whether I trust enough to make a bicycle built for two and then go wheeling off with the woman up front, or whether I'd be confident enough to be flamboyant, while I'm doing my own thing by standing on my head on the seat of the bicycle or whatever.

(Group laughter)

Nora: Thank you for explaining your image.

Body Routes to Conflict

One of the most powerful means to group interaction involves imagery in sensing one's body or a body part and then imagining handing that part to different persons in the group. As an example, I might suggest (IS): "Imagine your heart, imagine handing it to Bill." My patients' responses to this imaginary act, the myriad of comments, hesitations, false starts and facial reactions have been too numerous and varied to catalogue; the degrees of difficulty or simplicity they have encountered encompass an immeasurable spectrum.

My experience verifies that people relate the heart to love and feelings of tenderness. Noting the relative ease or difficulty with which the patient performs the task is an indication of his sense of his own love feelings (or lack of them); it also reveals how "safe" or "fearful" he feels about the person to whom he hands his heart.

I remember an experience in group therapy in which I asked Theresa, a detached young woman, to imagine (IS) placing her heart on the ground, next to Gerald's heart. I then asked Gerald, who was also prone to detachment, to (IS) imagine placing his heart next to Theresa's. With most detached persons, the giving and taking of love feelings is extremely difficult, implying, as it does, an inherent commitment.

Both Theresa and Gerald closed their eyes for a long time. Then Theresa slowly put her imagined heart on the floor, Gerald following suit a moment later. Both people then appeared to reflect for a time, saying and doing nothing. (They both told me at later times that they didn't want to "act out" the feelings they had had, but rather to allow themselves to really *feel*.) At last Theresa was about to "join" her heart with Gerald's and spoke of warm feelings for his heart. Gerald, despite prolonged concentration, was unable to join his heart to Theresa's heart. Theresa at this point expressed feelings of betrayal; Gerald became defensive. So it is that powerful feelings of interaction can occur through "body routes." (I must add that in a subsequent session Gerald finally did hand his heart to Theresa, and despite extreme caution was finally able to trust it to her.)

Other body imagery can be elicited by asking each person in the group (IS): "Imagine something inside Ned's guts." As the group goes around with each person describing his or her imagery, Ned's reactions — and the resultant interactions — reveal the interpersonal conflicts that exist and may also provide a vehicle for focusing for change. (IS) "Say something from your head to the head of another person in group." (IS) "From your heart to someone else's heart." (IS) "From your guts to someone else's guts." (IS) "From your vagina to Al's penis." — The interactions which result in the group sessions from such imaginary situations are immensely valuable in the revealing of conflicts and their resolutions.

One patient, Fred, seemed to be so intellectually bound that he could express virtually no emotion. At one point I asked the other members in his group (IS): "Imagine entering Fred's head and share your imagery." One response: "I see a giant computer inside, with thousands of levers and pulleys. On the other side are rows and rows of buttons, and a mechanical lever is pushing them in computer order." This from Clara. And each of the other people reported similar mechanical gadgetry and computer-like hardware in Fred's head. Fred was visibly shaken by their reports, and in time was able to allow himself to express feelings instead of mere description.

One of the most compelling body routes I've used in group therapy involves asking Hank (IS): "Imagine entering Jason's body." That body part through which Hank would imagine entering Jason may reveal conflicts and defenses present in both of them. While Hank is "moving about" inside of Jason, he experiences surprising imagery and many heretofore unsuspected feelings. And what he *avoids* as he travels around in there may be equally as revealing. Jason, listening in his imagination to Hank's inside-the-body travel, may express a whole host of defensive reactions, conflict awareness, and other unanticipated reactions which, at some time, may lead to the possibility of focusing approaches.

Focusing Approaches

The focusing approaches in group therapy are quite similar to those used in individual sessions, the main difference of course being that they occur in front of other people – the group members – in open view. It may happen that the focusing of an individual to be defined in a manner consistent with his true self-image may bring him in direct opposition to another group member or even the group as a whole.

Cathartic expression of feeling towards other group members is of course quite direct and utilizes little imagery; but one of the values of interaction imagery is precisely that it can lead to cathartic expression. Additionally, imagery can be used to make the patient aware of tender, warm feelings; it may involve imagining his parents or other nongroup members.

Interaction Imagery/Cathartic Imagery

Imagery that relates to intimacy can be elicited in the group by having each member (IS) "Imagine holding one particular group member in your arms – Chuck, for example – as you would hold a baby." When the group has gone around, each person reporting his imagery and associated feelings, Chuck will express his reactions to those reports. As a variation, it is possible to imagine the adult's being a baby. The responses to this particular imaginary situation are invariably strong ones and usually involve extensive interaction. A further variation involves (IS): "Imagine pushing so-and-so in a baby carriage." Or (IS) "Imagine pushing *me* in a baby carriage." Transference reactions and the abrupt exposure of conflicting feelings often surface during such an exercise.

To ask each person in the group to imagine holding *himself* in his arms as a baby is useful in eliciting conflict areas that relate to historical self-concepts or self-images which contrast with present ones. People whose early lives were highly traumatic and accompanied by frequent and powerful feelings of terror often cannot allow themselves to "go" with this imagery at all and flatly refuse to attempt it. Others, who find no difficulty with the imagery and find it accompanied by tender, soft feelings, demonstrate by example that such positive emotion is not beyond reach.

It is helpful for certain individuals who were badly neglected as children to (IS) imagine holding their mother or father — as an infant — in their arms. Or, the imaginary roles may be reversed.

Jane, a thirty-eight-year-old woman, found this kind of imagery very difficult to allow herself within the group situation. Her mother had totally neglected her deprived her of love, and competed fiercely with her when Jane was only a child What follows below is an excerpt from an audiotape of a particular session in which Jane experienced the imagery of holding her "infant" mother in her arms. She then reversed the roles and imagined being held by her mother. Although she was very bright and quite accomplished, Jane had introjected severe feelings of inferiority and self-doubt; she had often expressed a fear of retaliation on the part of her strong, controlling mother. The imaginary situation served, in this case, as a focusing experience of the cathartic/imagery type. It resulted in a changed self-concept, verified by her own reports of her feelings and by the judgment of her group in this session and subsequent ones.

Jane: . . . I like both ways, but, I'm imagining holding my mother. Once I said, you know, she was probably a squalling, angry baby and that she was hurt before I got her, which is kind of a weird thing — I mean, if I had her as a baby, I think it'd take all the psychiatrists in the world to find out what was wrong with her — (Long silence) and turning it around the other way, I feel that, you know, like if she poked at me and — she didn't really hold me like a baby and she never held me as if I was responsive — that — she was never responsive to me and never, made me feel like a baby. I feel hopeless. I feel that, you can talk about a lot of things in therapy, but like this happened before I even remembered. Like before I could even — talk about things — how is it ever possible? You know, I must have been so angry and a nothing from the way she treated me that I don't know how I'll ever get over it.

Shorr: Over what?

Jane: The anger I feel about that is so — so unverbal. I think that's what the world is like.

Shorr: (Focus) (IS) Well, what do you want to say to her or scream at her to liberate yourself from her?

Jane: But you see, I guess that's the point. I could. I could think about having myself if I could scream at her.

Ned: You could scream.

Shorr: It's still there.

Ned: You don't have to say anything.

Andy: Sometimes the words aren't necessary.

Shorr: What did you say you were?

Jane: (Tries to talk, but no words come.)

Shorr: Implicit or explicit.

Jane: I wasn't a person. I wasn't anything.

Shorr: So, you do know. (Focus) (IS) O.K., now how about screaming that. (FTS) "I am not . . ."

Jane: I am not a piece of bread. I'm – I'm a person. (Not very loud)

Shorr: Try that again – 'cause there's a lot more pain in it – than that. (Said very softly)

Jane: I'M NOT A – I'M NOT A ROCK, I'M NOT DEAD, I'M A LIVING – BABY THAT NEEDS THINGS. (Sobs) I'M SO MUCH – FROM THE VERY BEGINNING.

Shorr: But you don't need her.

Jane: What?

Shorr: But you don't need her. She's never going to give it to you. She never did. She never will. You can't hold back on all that anger lest she might turn away from you someday. You have to . . .

Jane: (SCREAMS VERY LOUDLY) (Pause) I guess I need to have cried from the very beginning and yelled and screamed.

Shorr: Uh huh.

Jane: I think I feel how my sister did, now. But – my – but she could never give it to me. Like, and – and never would you know. I mean . . .

Shorr: That's why it happened in the first place, because there wasn't anyone else around that could be for you but right now, and since then, there are many that could be there for you. And then you can liberate yourself. Otherwise you stand there waiting forever for her to come through to you and she never will.

Jane: She hates to – she hates . . .

Shorr: And all your anger and your . . .

Jane: She hates. That's all she can probably do – is to hate.

Shorr: Yeah.

Jane: She makes me – I guess maybe I'm afraid that if I get angry too, then that's all I know how to do is to be angry.

Shorr: I don't think so. That's just a way of keeping yourself immobilized.

Jane: (SCREAMS AND CRIES LOUDLY) You know, I feel like as if babies have a right to scream like that.

Andy: You do have the right to scream. Go on. Go on. Go on.

Min: Don't muffle it, Jane. Let it go.

Andy: Don't cover it up.

Jane: (SCREAMS) I – I – I – set it off to go. Like I screamed at three weeks of age.

Shorr: At three weeks?

Jane: (SCREAMS AND SOBS LOUDLY)

Shorr: Kinda like a baby. Not like an adult. You were thirty before you're born.

Jane: (SCREAMS) I'M A BABY, I HAVE THE RIGHT TO BE ANGRY.

Shorr: Sure. Damn right.

Andy: Good.

Jane: (Pause) It doesn't feel like – it doesn't, it doesn't. I mean, you know. What is it now about being angry?

Shorr: What does it do now?

Jane: Oh boy!

Shorr: You have never heard a baby get angry? You never saw a baby angry? Or cry?

Jane: (Pause) Yeah, because I never was.

Andy: You don't have to. You don't have to scream either.

Shorr: (IS) How about feeling like you're hungry, and you want a bottle, and what are you going to do? Go through the feeling of it. Like you're a baby – not 30 years old, remember.

Jane: But . . .

Shorr: You're hungry. Now, come on. Don't intellectualize it. You're allowed. You are *allowed* to feel hungry.

Jane: But . . .

Shorr: (Focus) SCREAM AT HER

Jane: It – you know, like – boy! Did I have it rotten when I was a real baby, you know?

Shorr: I know.

Jane: Yeah, you can do it now, Jane.

Shorr: You better! Now!

Jane: All right. I . . .

Shorr: Selfish!

Ned: Take your glasses off. 'Cause you keep touching your face and don't express yourself.

Jane: They didn't let me do that when I was a real baby, yeah. Boy, that's a good way not to get fed all right.

Andy: Just go on and scream. Now just start screaming.

Jane: (SCREAMS AND CRIES LOUDLY)

Shorr: (IS) Here's a bottle, Jane. Try it. A bottle of good milk. Try it. Take it. It's yours. (Jane is sobbing) Sorry you had to cry for it. (Jane cries) Take it. (Jane sobs) Can you drink it, Jane? Can you let yourself drink it?

Jane: Oh, no, no.

Shorr: Huh?

Jane: I'm afraid I'd throw it up.

Shorr: You're allowed.

Jane: (Sobs) I don't know whether I can drink it.

Shorr: (IS) If I put you in a straitjacket, could you take the – the bottle?

Jane: Not if I'm still angry.

Shorr: (IS) But things are better in a straitjacket. I mean, just break out of it and just drink — and enjoy it.

Jane: Oohh.

Hank: You deserve it. It's yours.

Shorr: That's what you wanted is a straitjacket.

Jane: Yeah.

Shorr: (Focus) (IS) So break out of the straitjacket and just accept that bottle.

Jane: Hooohhh! (GASPING)

Shorr: (IS) Just drink it and enjoy it. Let it be yours.

Jane: Oohh.

Shorr: Relax. (Jane is breathing hard. Shorr hums a lullaby) Let it be.

Jane: Oh!

Shorr: You don't need that straitjacket anymore. Straitjacket says you can't be human. Live by schedules, minutes, seconds. Never cry. Never feel. Never want.

Jane: I don't know where I am. I got a tingle all over. You know I don't know what's happened.

Shorr: Let it be. Just be. It's O.K. You don't have to know anything. Just — just let yourself relax and . . .

Hank: That's true.

Shorr: No one's going to hurt you. No — no schedules to meet. No requirements. No nothing. No straitjackets. (Jane is breathing hard) You're all right. (Pause) What would you like right now, Jane?

Jane: What would I like?

Shorr: Hmmm? (Jane laughs) Huh? What would you like?

Jane: Well, I don't know — I don't know where I am.

Shorr: You're O.K. You're here, and you're comfortable and, you know, among friends. Everybody loves you. (Jane sobs) That's where you are.

Hank: That's right.

Shorr: And what do you like? What would you like to have? (Jane cries) Ask for something. You'll get it.

Jane: (Sobs) I don't care.

Shorr: Come on.

Min: Come on, Jane.

Shorr: Ask for something.

Jane: Oh. (Pause) I'm ashamed.

Shorr: You are? Come on. (Jane cries) You have rights. Ask for whatever you want. Come on.

Jane: (Sobs) I don't know. I — I'm really ashamed to show all this feeling. I really am.

Hank: What do you want?

Shorr: (IS) What do you imagine a baby shows?

Jane: I don't know what a baby shows.

Shorr: O.K., what do you want? You're allowed. You hear me? You're allowed. You hear me? You're allowed.

Jane: I'm a poor baby. (Pause) I feel terrible.

Shorr: No, you're not. It doesn't feel guilty for wanting.

Jane: I don't know where I am.

Shorr: There's no guilt for wanting. It's O.K. just to be and want.

Theresa: What do you want, Jane?

Hank: (Pause) Jane, nothing has disappeared. (Jane sobs) We're right here.

Jane: (Sobbing) I am being so much of a baby, nobody will love me.
(Pause)

Min: A real baby, Jane.

Shorr: It's normal not to be a robot, you know. You deserve everything you want. You're not a robot. You're a human being. Do you feel guilty of being human? Or needing and wanting?

Jane: That makes me feel so good.

Shorr: You're not a robot anymore. That's what she wanted.

Jane: (Sobs) That's exactly what she wanted.

Shorr: You're not that anymore.

Hank; No, that's the real you, and you have a right to have everything you want.

Jane: (Sobs and cries) I don't see why I was a robot. (Cries)

Hank: But you're not.

Shorr: Don't — don't give her that power.

Hank: No.

Shorr: How 'bout — How 'bout smiling.

Hank: You can be real. You . . .
(Several people talk at once and Jane sobs)

Shorr: How 'bout some smiles and, uh, laughter?

Hank: Let it in.

Jane: I WANT TO BE LOVED AND CARED FOR. (Sobs)

Theresa: Don't be ashamed of it.

Jane: I'm ashamed of it. (Sobs)

Theresa: There's nobody to be ashamed of.

Jane: I'm ashamed of it. (Sobs) I am really ashamed to be. I — I sort of tingle all over. I'm afraid I'll go out of control.

Shorr: No, you won't.

Hank and Andy: No. No, you won't. (Jane sobs)

Ned: That's your circulation coming back.

Shorr: Here's the real Jane. (Jane laughs)

Jane: I'm afraid the real Jane would get killed for doing this.

Shorr: Nooo.

Jane: Oh yeah.

Shorr: No.

Jane: (Sobs) I don't know where I am. I — (Cries) I want a friend.

Hank: We all do. I do. Everybody does.

Jane: (Sobbing and crying) I went too far.

Hank: You only did what comes naturally.

Shorr: Don't be afraid to let it in, Jane. Let it happen.

Hank: Yeah.

Shorr: It's true.

Shorr: Laugh, coo, laugh – anything. (Jane laughs)

Hank: Come on. Let it in. It's great. I know it. It shows. I can feel it.

Jane: (She breaks into a beautiful smile)

(Group laughs and talks)

Jane: (Laughing) Goo, like a baby. I won't act like a baby. My mother said I was so serious all the time.

(Group laughs and talks)

Hank: Yeah, I know that's bullshit.

Shorr: Can't always think about what – follow the robot on, you know? You wanted to be a robot. She had you wired to be a robot. You had to think of your next move. How could you be anything but serious?

Jane: Yeah. I wanted that robot dead.

Shorr: Right.

Hank: You have a happiness and a joy really that, when it first came through, that – that was the first time I ever saw you that way. It came through from you.

Shorr: No more crying – (Hank talks at same time) only laughing.

Jane: It might turn into a better world, but I don't know if I really feel that.

Hank: You're in a better one now.

Jane: Yeah, I know.

Shorr: It's called "After laughing." (Group laughter)

Jane: Oh, I don't know if I can believe it. I can try. I can look at it.

Shorr: Come on. (Focus) I don't _____. (FTS) I don't want to hear the robot _____.

Jane: NO, I DON'T WANT TO HEAR THAT ROBOT AGAIN. Ah, no, I – I –

(Group: Very serious and then laughter)

Jane: . . . I HATE THAT ROBOT.

Shorr: Feel free.

Jane: Oh, God! I can't believe it. (Laughs) (Laughs) (Laughs) It might be nice. The world would really be something.

Shorr: Uh, huh.

Jane: Yeah.

Shorr: You don't need all that compulsive behavior anymore.

(Jane sighs, then laughs. Group laughs and talks)

Hank: Oh God! You're too much – that's beautiful.

(Group laughter)

Jane: What is the point. Oh, no. (Laughs)

Shorr: If you don't have to be compulsive, then you're free. Compulsion is a robot. You don't need that.

Jane: I don't know how to be anything else, but, gee, I can try.

Shorr: I think you've done it already.

Min: Yeah.

Hank: You're doing it right now.

Min: . . . Natural. It's there.

Shorr: You don't need the robot anymore.

Jane: WOW! IT'S REAL.

(Group laughter and talk)

Jim: You're real.

Hank: You're real.

Jane: (Laughing) I — I might ask my mother if she's real. I don't know what she'd say. (Laughs)

Shorr: She'd say, "This is a recording."

Jane: " . . . a recording."

Jim: Push the button and . . . (Jane laughs)

Jane: She's the one who isn't real — not me.

Hank: That's right! Right!

Shorr: I think we got it.

Jim: Hey, that's nice. It's kind of a nice circle here. Jesus Christ!

Shorr: My mother, the robot.

Jane: (Laughs) That's for sure.

Hank: That's right.

Andy: I think you act real.

Jane: I'm real. (Laughs)

(Group laughter and talk)

Jane: She wasn't there ever. (Laughs) She wasn't there.

Shorr: That's right. She never was. Call the robot nevermore. (Jane sighs) Now's your chance.

Hank: She was an automated mind – with a bad plug-in

Min: Wired. (Jane laughs)

Shorr: That's right.

Jane: With a bad plug-in! (Laughs)

Shorr: That's right. She was programmed.

(Laughter)

Jane: She was. She really was sick. She got sick a long time ago and she never recovered.

Shorr: That's right.

Jane: She died, and she didn't know it.

Shorr: That's right.

(Group laughter)

Jane: God damn! That's what comes of freedom.

(Laughter)

Shorr: I can feel the coils and springs coming out of your mother now.

(Jane laughs)

Hank: Boing! Tisssh!

Jane: Now that my mother's problem is straightened out . . .

(Laughter)

Hank: They had to put her tog — they had to screw her to put her together.

(Laughter)

Jane: My mother's a robot.

Shorr: That's what I say!

Hank: Be glad you're human.

Jane: To have a real live baby. She had one, but I — but she didn't ever know it.

Shorr: No, she would never know it.

Jane: Oh!

Andy: You ought to teach something like that.

Hank: Yeah, this was something.

Min: (Jane is laughing) Back to your seat.

Hank: It's incredible. Something tonight. I'll tell you that.

Jane: Oh! (Laughs)

Shorr: You finally found out who your mother was.

Jane: Hah! She never had real deep problems — she just — she never was.

Shorr: That's right. She never existed.

Estelle: What's — what kind? — What's wrong.

Ned: No problems.

Andy: She never had any, because she never existed.

Jane: And I've been trying to find out a long time what happened to her.

(Laughs)

(Group laughter)

Hank: Mmmm. This is different, Jane. I'll let you.

Shorr: I'll tell you what really happened. She changed her oil every 5,000 miles.

Andy: She got lubed.

Jane: She squeaks, but she never gets anything. (Laughs)

Shorr: Exactly right.

Hank: And ruins every man.

Jane: Oh, really?

Hank: Really got a man.

Shorr: Terrific. Hey, there! That's great.

Hank: Oh, that's too much, Joe.

Shorr: That's right.

Jane: Oh, that's wonderful.

Shorr: You got a heart — you got a heart and your mother doesn't have one.

Jane: Really.

Shorr: Your mother doesn't have one.

Jane: Really.

Shorr: Your mother doesn't have one.

Jane: She knows. People are all around me.

Shorr: Right, Right.

Jim: That's good.

Shorr: Can't tell your mother without a program card.

Jane: (Laughs) I don't know if I can look at her again.

   (Group laughter)

   (Group laughter and talk)

Jane: How — how can you analyze my mother? How can you — (Laughs) I can't think of anything that can analyze her.

Shorr: I'd need — I'd need a vernier scale.

Jane: (Laughs) Yeah. That's my problem. (Laughs) I took my problems to a computer.

Shorr: My mother, the robot.

Jane: The machine shop.

Shorr: That's right. And in terms of ecology I think we know where to dump her.

   (Group talk and noises)

Shorr: All right.

Jane: GOO! GOO! GOO! GOO! WAH! WAH! WAH!

Hank: Where does . . . ?

Jane: Now you've got me wondering. What did you say, dump her?

Shorr: Hmm?

Hank: Do you know where to dump her?

Jane: Oh dump — oh, yes.

Shorr: You see . . .

Jane: In a field, I guess.

Shorr: Any kind of behavior's all right. That's what you misunderstand. Not prescribed, rigid, programmed behavior.

Jane: Yeah, but why — so I can act?

Shorr: Of course. You can let go.

Jane: I was trying to be a robot all my life. (Laughs) (Group talk) She bore me, so I thought I must be a robot.

Shorr: Right, Right. Get her a pouch.

Jane: Never mind, walk into a robot.

   (Group talk)

Shorr: What's that?

Ned: It's just like the shell just fell off of that . . .

   (Group laughter and talk)

Andy: . . fantastic . . .

Shorr: I'm allowed to be a person. (Group talk) I'm allowed to be a person. I have to be compulsive against just being anything I want to be. That's more real than all the programmed shit in the world.

Jim: It's really nice to have you here, Jane.

   (Group talk and laughter)

Hank: Welcome. Welcome to the world. (Laughter and then quiet)

Shorr: Yea. Terrific!

Hank: Boy! (Laughter) Change yourself.

Shorr: You can't — your mother won't allow you to be a baby. Like with you. How the hell could she allow you to be anything? As you grow older, there's nothing allowable ever. You're wondering whether it's allowable to cry, to — to scream, to laugh, to hold your arms — do anything.

Hank: That's right.

Shorr: It's all there. Let it be.

Hank: That's right. That's right. If a mother can't even let a baby be, for Christ's sake! What — what the hell's going to happen?

Ned: Everything, because that got beyond all her intellectual shit.

(Group talk and laughter)

Shorr: That was certainly totally non-intellectual.

Min: Yeah.

Jane: Heard myself cry like a baby, 'cause it just . . .

Min: It really did.

(Group talk)

Hank: Yeah, it sounded like a baby . . .

Min: Sounded like a baby . . .

Hank: That was a very demanding bottle. That's the truth.

Min: Undoubtedly.

Hank: Yeah.

Min: That was a baby crying.

Shorr: That was like, preverbal. Wasn't even words that could do that.

Jane: Right. (Chuckles) That was — that wasn't me, was it? (Laughter)

(Group laughter)

Shorr: That's right.

Jane: Me.

Hank: Well, it wasn't any robot. I'll tell you that.

Jane: I'm me — a real — a live person — all right. (Group laughter) I feel a lot better.

Min: So do I. (Group laughter)

(Several people talk at once)

Min: . . . Jane be?

Jane: (Laughs) I'm just going to be. I really am.

Min: Great!

Shorr: You really felt a lot. Tremendous!

Hank: You felt right back to your source of it. Incredible!

Jane: Yeah.

Shorr: I don't see anybody ever say, "Gee, I think you're too intellectual, Jane." Anyone . . . (Group chuckles) Yeah. It's 'cause it's real.

Jim: That's the way you started out, too. You said it was before the — before you could talk.

Hank: That's right.

Jim: Didn't you?

Shorr: You knew right where it was.

Hank: You really knew where it was.

Ned: Yeah, 'cause you saw her with some other baby, and you started — I saw you — it really got to you.

Jane: Right. I guess I felt it's real. Like it's really — how could you talk about something that happened. I didn't even know you could feel it.

    (Laughs)

Jim: Sometimes you say some of the greatest things, Jane.

Jane: That's really good. You know, like uh — yeah — I was stopped, because I couldn't talk about. (Laughs) Oh, but I — I really thought that I can't talk about it and express it. How could I, you know, do it?

Shorr: That's — that was the robot.

Jane: It — it must be all around me. I must be helpless about it. But — I — all the time I could have held and expressed the feeling.

Shorr: Right.

Jane: But I didn't know that. (Laughs)

Shorr: See, the robot demanded the intellectual explanation.

Jane: Yeah.

Shorr: But you don't need that.

Ned: That's right.

Shorr: To hell with the explanation. Let it happen.

Jane: I would be angry again like that.

Min: Let the laughter come through, Jane. It's terrific — physically. It's beautiful. It's wonderful.

Jane: Yeah, but that's — but I can be angry too.

Min: Yeah, you can be that too.

Hank: You can do anything you want to do.

Jim: But now you can laugh too. It's just like . . .

    (Group talk)

Ned: You know that your feelings are smarter than your head now.

Jane: Yeah.

    (Group laughter)

Hank: That's right.

Jane: (Laughs) Yeah.

Hank: Smarter, stronger . . .

Jane: Yeah.

Hank: . . . more alive — and the whole thing.

Jane: Yeah.

Estelle: You see what happened when you let out the anger and then the laughter comes out.

Jane: Yeah.

Jim: Your feelings are smarter than your head. That's . . .

    (Group talk)

Min: Write that down, Jane.

Jim: Yeah, I just did. (Laughter)

Shorr: What was that?

Min: Feelings are . . .

Jim: Your feelings are smarter than your head. That's really neat.

Jane: WHEW! (Laughs)

Shorr: That's what you're reacting to.

Hank: No more robot.

Jane: Down with robots. Down . . . (Loudly, but with laughter)

Jim: Going to picket your mother's house tomorrow. "Down with robots!"

Jane: Bumper stickers and do a whole campaign.

Shorr: Very good. Go tell Frankenstein about this.

Hank: Yeah.

Shorr: Don't build robots.

Jane: I could have told him his mistake before he experimented.

    (Group laughter)

Min: You certainly could, Jane.

Hank: I'll never forget when — when the first laughter came through — Wow!

Jane: I really did it, didn't I?

Hank: Uh! Pretty wild. Wow!

Jim: Finally! I got my money's worth tonight.

Hank: Yeah. (Group laughter) You can't say this was boring.

    (Group laughter)

Jane: WHEW! (Sighs)

Task Imagery

Task imagery is an additional tool for focusing, useful in the recognition of conflicts and for the possibility of change. The group as a whole is asked, for example, the task imagery (IS): "Imagine you are a fetus about to birth." Each person closes his eyes and imagines himself going through the process. The reactions, as one would expect, are enormously different. Some persons don't want to leave the warmth of the womb. Here is one man's report:

"I find myself in a womb. It is comfortable, warm and secure. I began to feel an ever mounting pressure pushing me down towards the vagina. I resist. I prop my hands and feet against the lower wall so as not to be pushed out. The pressure mounts ever increasingly and I find myself inexorably being forced out. Great fear overwhelms me as I realize that I didn't have the strength to resist.

"As my head exits, the fear diminishes quite a bit. All of a sudden I plop out. Fear has left me and I feel angry at those handling me so roughly, but I no longer feel afraid. In fact, I am amused at my previous fears.

"I feel that I am always afraid of transitions. I fear the event most before it happens rather than when it does actually come about. I frequently feel joy after having survived through such emotions."

I may "force" the person to make the attempt to birth, supportively urging him on. Other group members may urge him on as well. For some people, this represents the choice they must make in order to establish a new self-concept. Facing their feelings of "rottenness" and now deserving is an important element of this task imagery. Others recreate their own actual birth scene, experiencing pain or pleasure and recounting imaginary dialogues with their mothers and fathers. Feelings forgotten early in life and reminiscent imagery may erupt, clarifying some heretofore hidden self-concept. It serves as a wonderful vehicle of feeling reaction in those who observe them and may, in turn, trigger reminiscent imagery in them.

Another example of task imagery that I have used requires asking the group (IS): "Imagine a lock attached to something, and then imagine a series of keys; choose one to open the lock." The imagery develops as the person finds the right key and proceeds further as he reports what the opened lock has revealed. What has been unlocked may be deep feelings, perhaps the very most secret feelings he possesses. At some point in the sequence of the imagery he may need to redo some aspect of it or be urged on.

Ned, a forty-year-old man, reports his experience with this particular task imagery in group therapy. He is struggling with a "double bind": torn between living his own life or living the other person's life, leaving him in limbo. Here is his own report:

"The situation in group was to imagine a lock. The following is what I first saw and wished to communicate to the group. I instantly saw a large, very old-style lock on a large steel door in a steel wall — all of it colored gun-metal. It was dark, but I could see the wall and door. It's surface was very smooth and cold and covered with moisture, like dew drops. This was all apprehended immediately, and just as quickly I saw in my hand a ring of keys, all of which, save one, were old, rusted and unused. The exception, which I felt without hesitation, would open the lock — was made of gold and had brilliant rubies, emeralds encrusting it. I put it in the lock and immediately the door opened and I beheld a brilliantly colored world. It contained everything our ordinary world has, but the colors were so intense, I was caught breathless and became afraid. I, immediately, felt it the world I could have if I just would reach out and take it. I fearfully ventured out and saw the intense color lessen but remain naturally strong.

"I looked back at the door and saw it still against the rear of the door. I saw that part of this new world that would exist if the door were closed. I knew that if I closed it, that I would be forever in this new delightful world and that I could never even, if I tried, get back to that dark limbo-like tomb.

"At this time, I stopped momentarily and got no response from the group, and the imaginary situation passed to others. While others were talking, I saw a further scene in this sequence which I reported after several minutes.

"Looking back at 'limbo,' the dark side of the door, I saw a woman — she may have been my mother, my wife or as I said at the time, a Brand X female. My mother beckoned me back into limbo and pointed to another world. She seemed to deny my right to be in my world and imply that either I should live in limbo or her world.

"My world was full of intense colors; many things were irridescent and when things, birds, people, etc., moved, they left trails of color behind them for several feet. In my mother's world, the colors were almost of sunset or dawn: reds, yellows, purples, blacks, but not somber. I didn't like it, because of the limited range of color. I knew that given a choice, I would prefer limbo to living in her world and that I could reject her world without worrying about her feelings.

"My wife also beckoned me in a like manner and while my mother had beckoned me, I have not even gone into limbo or her world but had seen it from afar and had rejected it. But when my wife beckoned me, I crossed limbo and went into her world which was colored in all colors of pastel. The contours were soft. No mountains, canyons or places of danger existed in her world.

"She seemed to indicate without words that in order to have her love, not only must I accept her world as valid for her, but that I must live in it wholly, make it my own and renounce my own world. To me, this was merely a soft prison and if I were to accept it, its lack of surprise and excitement would bore me. Again, I would choose 'limbo' to this if forced to. I would prefer to live in my own world.

"I got no group response from this and it passed on again. Later I got pissed off at the group for their lack of response − this provoked some reaction. They seemed to believe my world was exclusive. However, when I visualized a woman in my world, she seemed to be in it but not constrained by it. I did not feel that she had rejected or accepted it or her own vision of life. We simply talked. I didn't withhold my appreciation of her nor she of me. It was very pleasant.

"About this time, Joe asked me to close the door back into limbo. Since I had repeatedly indicated that I felt that if I could, it would be closed forever. I felt that all that it required was an exercise of will to close the door, but when asked to do this, I felt a great reluctance to do it. I felt that the woman in limbo would be intensely hurt or injured and at the same time, I felt if I didn't close it, I'd be back in limbo soon myself. Trying very hard, the most I could do, was to shut it to the point that just its outline appeared. In order to make it easier, I imagined a vision of me as I might be. I saw beautiful scenes and places, all of these to the point of closing the door. When in interaction with the group, they called these scenes lollipops or goodies, to make it easy.

"I then allowed just any scene to come up, and I saw a volcano in violent eruption. But in all these circumstances, the almost invisible outline of the door persisted over them. At this point, however, I realized that even if I ever returned to limbo, I would never close the door which I was in limbo and that sooner or later I'd leave limbo for good and live in my own world.

"I feel the above shows my perpetual double bind about living. If I live in my world, I'll hurt those with whom I live and if I give in to them, I won't be able to live except in some kind of limbo. Living in limbo denies me to them and them to me. I feel it is an expression of anger at not being allowed to be myself which punished the significiant other and also myself."

Here is another report of a man in group to Task Imagery: "Imagine trying to herd a group of horses into a corral a mile away."

"I'm in the country with rolling hills all around. I can see my destination ahead and it really looks far away. I'm a little unsure as how to begin so I mounted one of the horses thinking that the rest would follow. It's not working at all. I'll try to herd them from behind. I'm riding around the back perimeter of the group, hoping to push them as a group forward. This doesn't even begin to work. I'm getting frustrated. I feel like someone has trusted me to complete this job, and I can't even get started. It's an easy job, it seems, but I can't do it. I again ride around the back of them all, trying to move them forward, but nothing. They won't budge. I can see them eating and not even noticing my presence. I'm really frustrated now. It's now like a mental block. There is no fuckin' way those horses are going to move for me.

"What started out to be a seemingly simple request is now totally impossible. I can't even force my mind to see them walking or running forward. They just won't move. I feel terrible. Joe asked me to imagine this and I can't even begin to do it. 'I can't do it, Joe; they won't move.'

Shorr: "Take charge of the situation."

"That very second Joe said 'take charge,' I ran up to the horse with confidence to move mountains, and started to slap them on the ass saying. 'Come on you sons-of-bitches, get going.' I'm running around slapping them in the butt and they are all going. I'm really in charge of the total situation. I can feel the confidence with every slap. 'Come on you sons-of-bitches, let's get going.'

"I can see the group of horses all paying close attention to what I want them to do. I've got them all running together towards the pen a mile away. I remount my horse and ride alongside of them, occasionally slapping one that gets out of the main group.

"Now I can see them all running into the pen and I close the gate behind them feeling good. I put my horse in a separate stable and give him a pat of appreciation as I walk away."

Other examples of task imagery may be utilized. Here are a few additional ones:

1. Imagine descending or ascending 1,000 steps.
2. Imagine you are caught in a blizzard and it appears that you may not be able to survive.
3. Imagine you are invisible and cannot get anyone to recognize you.

There are countless other task imageries that one can utilize as part of a focusing approach. An important part of task imagery is to ask the person to face the part of the imagery that is difficult for him. Often one must ask a person to redo the imagery in a way consistent with an attempt to change his self-image.

Body Focusing

The body focusing technique in group therapy has already been mentioned in the chapter on Imagery and the Focusing Approaches. In the section entitled, "Imagine in What Part of Your Body Your Mother Resides," the question was raised in the course of intensive group interaction. In group therapy this area can be approached by asking the entire group (IS): "In what part of your body does your anger reside?" Each person senses his or her response and, in turn, shares it with the group. Invariably, it provides the opportunity for various persons in the group to deal with unexpressed anger and to find a way of directing it towards others who have defined them falsely.

One man had his anger "buried" in his chest, and after repeated urging "to get it out," found himself imagining the experience of vomiting it out — "in a black stench." While it was done solely in his imagination it nevertheless gripped him with the reality and intensity of an anger buried for a lifetime. It was focused against his father, who had been a crushing force in his life.

It is possible to ask (IS): "In what part of your body does your joy (or revenge, or self-doubt or misery) reside?"

Here is a report by Fred, a thirty-five-year-old man, in which the Finish-the-Sentence approach led to Body Focusing imagery in a group therapy session:

" 'I must not allow myself to be' . . . was the Finish-the-Sentence question that was asked of all the members in the group. When it came my turn, I responded with, 'I must not allow myself to be *judged.*' Then I was asked to expand my statement. I began to get images of something inside of me.

"At that time I felt that there was a whole part of me inside that I had never explored. It came in the form and shape of a pie inside of me and I knew that if I could take a slice of that pie and see exactly what I really am, what my ingredients are, it would be the best thing I could do for myself. Joe then asked me to 'imagine getting inside myself to have a piece of that pie.' I closed my eyes to imagine that. I then announced that I had a knife in my right hand, and became fearful of the find. I felt I would be unable to deal with the unknown, good or bad. Immediately, I thought of my relationship with music. What if I spent most of my thirty-five years in the wrong direction? What if I didn't want to be a musician? The truth would be too painful to see. The group urged me to take a chance. At first, I balked, but suddenly I said, 'O.K.' I don't even recall why it was as easy to say, 'I'll take a piece of pie,' as it was to resist through my fear. But I did agree.

"As I closed my eyes, I remember feeling only a slight self-consciousness. I was having great difficulty getting the knife near my body. I started squirming uncontrollably. My face contorted as the resistance grew stronger. Then I said to myself, 'There is a beautiful part of me in that pie that I should see.' Yet, I still hesitated.

"Somebody made a joke about something. I didn't hear it, but in the background, I did hear the laughter. I felt judged. Maybe the joke was the amount of time I was taking. I was getting colder and more frightened. Time rolled on. As the frustration of the moment mounted, it was like holding your nose and jumping into a swimming pool for an early morning dip. Suddenly I made the incision. I cut from the upper hip bone on my left side down through the base of my pelvic bone. And I sliced again to form a piece of pie. I guess I was crying. I know I was.

"I opened my eyes to examine what I held in my hand. I had good feelings about what had just transpired. Christ! It was exactly what I did not want to see! Pie that was filled with the alphabet, emerged in a black, sticky substance, a filler like one would find in a blueberry pie. The letters of the alphabet all seemed to spell out the word 'judgment' hundreds of times. I put the pie down on the floor and looked away from it disheartened that I found what I knew was there somewhere inside me. It was in the way of something perhaps beautiful.

"Joe asked, could I change pies. I agreed to change fillings, but I felt the crust was good. I wished to leave it alone. I made the filler switch. Its ingredients were woven into space. Letters spelled out self-discovery, creativity, energy, vitality, essence. All floating around in my new pie filling. I felt much better. Really peaceful. Slowing down. The moments were longer. No pressure. No demands. I was floating around in space somewhere, at my own pace. I didn't know who I was. I expressed to the group my desire to savor things. 'I would like to be able to dissect things and follow them through to their essence.' I guess a long time went by.

"I heard Joe ask me if I'd like a drink of clear spring water. His voice sounded barely audible. I felt I was in a trance of some kind.

"I said, 'Why not. Sounds as good as anything.' I bent over and took in a mouthful of water from a brook. Sitting back in my chair and closing my eyes, I swallowed the water very slowly following it down my throat and into my stomach. I drank more. It tasted so good and I was in tune with my experience. Peace.

"Joe suggested that I get up and say something to each member of the group. I remember floating over to Jane and telling her how sad I was for her putting herself in an impossible bind during Christmas holiday.

" 'Liza, you are beautiful!' I said.

"I don't recall what I said to Hank.

" 'Richard, I wish I could really get to know you, because I like your sense of being human.' Richard expressed that he would like that, someday.

" 'Lynne, I wish you really knew me. I don't show too much of myself to you.' She responded with her lovely smile.

"On to Jim. 'You're still a little too heavy for me. I respect your growth, but you're too down and weighty. I can't handle that yet.' I don't remember how Jim responded to that.

"I told Angie that she should slow her movements down. She agreed completely.

" 'Helen, you really show me somebody in this group, but I don't know who it really is, because it sure as hell isn't you. I haven't the foggiest who you really are.' She stared at me like a poor, wounded animal.

" 'Eloise, I respect your contributions to the people in the group. You have fine insight. But I don't know who *you* are. You are very quiet about yourself.'

" 'Yale, whatever I have done to help you get your new job is purely an act of friendship and nothing more. I have no other interests invested. I also feel that at this moment in your life, you are walking a tightrope without a net.'

"I don't remember what I said to Joe, but I remember remaining peaceful.

"I realized I had to start to know Dennis sooner or later, so I shook his hand and slowly drawled, 'Hey!' My eyes got teary.

"I didn't feel nervous throughout the group experience, and the few times I started to feel slightly self-conscious, I quickly nipped the feeling in the bud. I wasn't afraid of anybody or anything. It was a beautiful feeling.

"I can call myself a 'judgaholic.' I have to deal with it from day to day. And I am. Soon it will be easier to deal with. It will be an enemy for awhile. But not forever."

Debra had tried to develop changes in her attitude towards her father, who had rejected her. That relationship had influenced all her relationships with men. Using the Body Focusing approach, she (IS) imagined entering her father's body. Other approaches had been attempted previously with no change in her attitude. This Body Focusing experience was able to make a change in her self-image and her attitude towards men:

"He is sitting rigidly, as usual, and stiffly in the chair in the living room, listening to some dreary and heavy music. I close my eyes and climb up his arm which is warm and hairy and enter through his mouth, because he ate delicious corned beef and lots of dill pickles and it smells good – indeed it is warm and smooth and dark but not a bit scary – I climb up and down, onto his ribs and play like it is a ladder. I come towards the front and pat his heart – it is beating softly and evenly and I touch it – I put my ear next to it. I climb down into his legs and they are crossed so it is annoying. I'd like to uncross them and slide up and down. So I go up again past the delicious smells in his stomach and up into his throat where he is humming softly, and then up into his head – the brain in his head is moaning softly and I am impatient – I see the images of dark, poverty-stricken farms and I put my fingers softly in the brain tissues and will good and happy images to appear – I hear and feel some movement. I climb down towards his legs again and see a ghastly sight. He is having trouble walking and I can see why. The entrance to his penis is blocked and sore, like a lump of clay has hardened and the tissue is irritated all around it. I am enraged and sick and angry and can't wait to dislodge it – tenderly and most carefully I try to loosen it without making too much noise, but it soon comes loose and I am so angry I just pull it out and climb up and out of his mouth very quickly and throw it a mile away. Then just as quickly I climb back up into his mouth and back down into his penis and softly touch it to see if it isn't sore anymore – and I climb down into his legs and I feel his muscles tensing up as if he would like to run, and I climb back into his brain and will another part of it to play great early jazz, and I can hear him laughing and I hear him calling, 'Debra, Debra, where are you? Let's go for a walk. Come on now. I'll carry you on my shoulders and we can walk around the block. Listen to that music – isn't it wonderful? Come on, Debra, it's time for daddy and his little girl to have fun!!!!!!!!!!!' "

Some Concluding Observations

The use of imagery in individual therapy and group therapy is ever increasing. In order to study imagery in a systematic way, one must be concerned with:

1. The use of imagery to make the patient aware of his internal conflicts between historical negative self-concepts and his potentially positive contemporary self-concepts. This involves the use of Dual Imagery, Body Route Imagery, Nonsymbolic Imagery, as well as Symbolic Imagery.

2. The use of imagery to help the person focus for a change in his self-definition against the archaic forces and self-defeating defenses. This involves the use of Cathartic Imagery, Task Imagery, and many Body Focusing Imageries.

3. The use of imagery when combined with dialogue to heighten awareness and focus for change. The use of listening to one's own Imagery and Dialogue audiotape at a later point as a further possibility of awareness and change.

4. The use of imagery in group therapy for the awareness of internal conflicts which involves Dual Imagery, Group Imagery and Body Route Imagery. Additionally, the use of imagery as Cathartic Imagery, Task Imagery and the various Body Focusing Imageries in the focusing approaches for change.

5. The infinite possibilities of creativity on the part of the therapist and his patients to utilize therapy more effectively in order to help resolve their conflicts.

CHAPTER 17

Imagery as a Projective Device

The term "projective method" has been firmly established in psychological parlance. The Rorschach Ink Blot test is so widely known that even the general population is aware of its existence, if not its specific functions. The TAT is not far behind in common recognition. The fact that visual imagery can be a projective device is relatively new.

Projective tests enable the subject to project himself into a planned situation. The Rorschach uses the function of perception, a highly integrated act, as the basis of its operation. The analyses of fantasy in story form are organized by the intellect but take their meaning from the affect or emotional quality. Free drawing and handwriting are also projective. In all these methods, clinical experience with many persons and their responses and styles gives us the core of the diversity of possible interpretation.

In 1974, the Shorr Imagery Test (SIT) was developed from another modality – the waking images that are constantly going on in our minds. Recent models of personality have moved away from energy discharge or drive satisfaction toward a view of human beings as information processing and image-making creatures. Utilizing this capacity, the Shorr Imagery Test "tunes in" to this constant and ubiquitous stream of conscious and unconscious imaging.

Cards or inkblots or pictures of persons or things are not necessary. Originating from a body of knowledge of how individuals respond to certain imaginary situations (when they are asked to close their eyes and to trust their imagery), specific kinds of interpretations are possible based on clinical experience. In all projective devices it is mandatory that the subject be able to bypass his own censorship so that he can reveal himself without being aware, in advance, of what is being revealed.

The use of visual imagery as a modality that can bypass the censorship of the individual came out of the clinical experience of introducing imaginary situations into the fabric of the therapeutic process. In working with thousands of imagery productions of several thousand persons – patients, students, workshop participants, and trainees – certain imaginary situations indicated particular kinds of conflicts, feelings, defenses, styles, and other subjective meanings.

The most difficult part of the development of the Shorr Imagery Test was to devise a reliable quantitative scoring method. On many of the items the subject imagines he *is* what he *sees* in his imaginary projection, and then finishes the following sentences:

"I feel _____"
"The adjective that best describes me is _____"
"I wish _____"
"I must _____"
"I secretely _____"
"I need _____"
"I will _____"
"Never refer to me as _____"

With these sentences it is then possible to get scoring samples that will yield a high interscorer reliability. For those trained in psycho-imagination approaches, a 1% level of confidence of interscorer reliability was achieved.

The SIT uses imaginary situations to reveal a wide range of personality variables including the individual's personal world, relationships between self and others, self image, body image, sexual attitudes, and internal and external forces acting upon the person.

Use of the Test

The SIT will be found useful in the comprehensive study of personality and in the interpretation of personality disorders. The questions given in this manual are essentially for adults. The SIT can be used as a quantitative screening device to detect disturbed persons and can also be used qualitatively for in-depth personality analysis.

The SIT is a projective test of personality. We believe that it is a realiable, valid indicator of specific areas of conflict within the personality, as well as a powerful and accurate method of assessing the personality dynamics and defenses of individuals.

Rationale of the Test

Diagnostic techniques using affective visual imagery and psychodynamic principles for personality exploration so far have received scarce attention by clinicians and practicing psychotherapists. We believe the SIT offers a possible use of imagery for such purposes.

The test is designed to elicit and score the degree of conflict in the visual images projected by the subject. We feel that unconscious conflicts are a major cause of psychological disturbance among individuals and that the presence of such conflicts is graphically revealed by the items of this test. Such presentations in the psychotherapy situation can bring the conflicts to awareness, where they can be dealt with and resolved. The items in the SIT are designed to identify the areas of conflict in the individual and the degree of personality disturbance. Previous work by Shorr (1967, 1972, 1973, 1974,) in developing the concepts of Dual Imagery, Task Imagery, etc., have shown the importance of visual imagery as an indicator of the personality conflicts, the strategies of defense, the self-images, the self-other images, and other ranges of personality functions.

The rationale for our beliefs concerning personality conflict is much more extensively stated in Dr. Shorr's books (1972, 1974).

Item Selection

The SIT is based primarily on clinical experience using Psycho-Imagination Therapy with hundreds of patients. The primary tool is a series of imaginary situations directed to the patient, whose reactions and styles in response become the material for further therapeutic work. A very small portion of another tool, the Finish-the-Sentence technique, has also been included. Fourteen imaginary situations are included, plus one item that includes four Finish-the-Sentence questions.* The items were selected, on the basis of clinical experience, as being those that reflect accurately many phases of the subject's personality and emotional conflicts. While we have developed a "Conflict" score for separate diagnostic and comparative purposes, the most interesting and powerful application of the test is for in-depth personality analysis.

Reliability

For a test to merit clinical application, it must have some degree of reliability.

Interscorer Reliability. The conflict of a subject on the SIT is essentially obtained by subjective processes. The interscorer reliability values reported, therefore, are of some interest. The scores reported have not been corrected for restrictions on the sample.

Two estimates of interscorer reliability have been made thus far. Both the samples were taken before the test manual, with its scoring guide, was completed.

First Study. In the first estimate, seven scorers with various levels of education and histories of exposure to PsychoImagination processes were compared. The scorers are characterized as follows:

> Scorer J. holds a Ph.D. and is a clinical psychologist who has worked with Psycho-Imagination Therapy for nine years. He is the author of the SIT.
> Scorer D. holds a Ph.D. in clinical psychology and has been involved with Psycho-Imagination processes for three years.
> Scorer C is a Ph.D. candidate in clinical psychology and has been involved with Psycho-Imagination processes for six years.

---

*Two of the Finish-the-Sentence completions first appeared in the Miale-Holsopple Sentence Completion Test published in 1954. These are "Worse than being lonely is. . . ." and "No one can repair the damage caused by. . . ." Dr. Shorr developed nearly identical Finish-the-Sentence items independently, and later discovered the Miale-Holsopple Sentence Completion Test.

Scorers P, L and H hold M.A.'s in Marriage, Family and Child Counseling. They have worked with Psycho-Imagination Therapy for about six months.

Scorer G is an undergraduate psychology student. G's involvement with Psycho-Imagination Therapy is limited to seminars and library work for about six months.

Each of the seven scored, independently, the first two items on thirteen protocols not used in the standardization sample. The results are presented in Table 1.

The obtained means range from 4.38 to 6.15, with a mean of means of 5.44. The obtained standard deviations ranged from 1.32 to 1.91 with a mean of 1.62. Average standard errors of measurement for the means and standard deviations were 0.45 and 0.32, respectively.

A test of the difference between means showed six of the 21 pairs to be significantly different at the 0.05 level of confidence. Four of the six were differences between the least experienced and educated scorers and the others. A difference in means of about one point was required to be considered significant.

The reliability coefficients, calculated for a 21-item test by the Spearman-Brown formula, averaged 0.93. All but three of them were above 0.85, and two of the three lower values were pairs with the least experienced and educated scorer. Because of the low N, the confidence limits for reliability of the 21-item test are rather broad.

Second Study. In the second estimate of interscorer reliability, two pairs of scorers, matched for their level of education and degree of experience with Psycho-Imagination Therapy, were compared. Each pair scored, independently, 20 protocols from the standardization sample. The two pairs scored different protocols. The results are given in Table 2.

The first pair of scorers, who were more educated and more experienced in Psycho-Imagination Therapy, correlated well (r = 0.93) and agreed with one another within 0.4 points. The other pair correlated well (r = 0.90), but were biased in their scoring with a mean difference in total score of 14.3 points. This continues the pattern of P low and H high that they set during the first study, and indicates a need for further training. It is expected that the large number of samples of scoring provided in the manual, plus the rules for scoring provided, which were formulated after these studies were done, will reduce the likelihood of bias. Further work is contemplated in this area.

Evidence for Validity

No quantitative measures of the validity of the SIT have yet been made. We hope in the future to show its predictive validity as an indicator of potential resistance or gain in psychotherapy and its concurrent validity as a diagnostic instrument or as a measure of in-depth personality analysis comparable to that available to a therapist in a long-term relationship.* We hope that the concept of internal personality conflict can be shown to be related to the conflict scores on the test. When the data are available, we will report the validity of each inference made from the test, and we will report the degree of confidence we have in each inference. We expect to present explicit evidence for each interpretation. It is appropriate to warn the test user than an inference about a personality characteristic based on a specific item is subject to error. It is reasonable to note such inferences and make use of them in later counseling effort.

Conflict

Each conversation and each list of sentence completions associated with a particular image, or the image taken as a whole, is scored for degree of conflict as indicated on the test form. If the conversation and sentence completions for a particular image seems difficult to score, they may be read together and then be scored separately. However, each image must be scored for conflict on its own merit, avoiding a possible halo effect from previous or overall impressions of the protocol.

The five scoring levels are:

		Score
P1	A positive response	1
C1	A conflict response	2
C2	An increased conflict response	3
C3	A severe conflict response	4
C3*	An extreme conflict response	5

C1   is scored when there is evidence of some conflict in the subject's response to the item.

C2   is scored when there is overt conflict in the responses.

C3   is scored when there is severe conflict in the responses.

C3* is scored when images of blood, mutilation, suicide, or murder occur, or when the subject refuses to answer in a dangerous situation.

Some additional general rules for scoring are as follows: If there is no verbal response in the conversation, score at least a C2. If the response shows great conflict, score C3. If the response is self-destructive, score C3*.

The higher the total score, the more conflicted the individual is considered to be. Lower scores would show the least conflicted individuals. There are 21 places in the test that can be scored in this quantitative manner. Other differentiations

*See Bibliography for special mention of a monograph that deals with this last point.

are based on frequency of response to the images reported for each question.

The minimum possible conflict score on the Shorr Imagery Test is 21. The maximum is 105. The scoring sheet is laid out so the conflict scores can be converted easily to numerical values and the numerical values added to give a total conflict score.

The scoring of conflict is, to a certain extent, subjective. However, reasonable interscorer reliability was obtained with relatively untrained scorers, as shown in the section on Reliability.

Training

A scorer should be able to train himself to score the SIT for conflict by studying the sample answers given in the scoring criteria section.* Scorers in the interscorer reliability study were trained by Dr. Shorr in the course of developing the test.

At this point we feel training beyond the Manual is not needed by a qualified clinician to do quantitative scoring. The Monograph and item interpretation are intended to assist users in evolving qualitative interrogations with the SIT.

Time

Scoring the test takes about 15 to 40 minutes. Users are cautioned against scoring the test during administration. This practice precludes reflection on the responses and reference to the examples given.

Overall Interpretations

We feel that, overall, the SIT can be used to make statements about the subject's mood; potential for action; place on a dependence-independence continuum, on a sadism-masochism continuum, on an aggressive-passive continuum; worries (sex, economics, significant others, hostility, remorse, abstract worries, understanding); conflicts, both internal and external; solution techniques; presses (significant others, job, health, drugs, enemies, environment); definition of self; definition by others; potential for attitude change; body image; frustration tolerance; defenses; awareness; needs; impulses; wishes; and sense of making a difference to others or of allowing others to make a difference to him or her. We hope to be able to publish demonstrations of the validity of these interpretations in the future.

Group Shorr Imagery Test

The regular SIT was put on tape for group administration by C. Smith, T. Kard, L. Squire, and M. Vale in an unpublished study at California State Univer-

---

*Scored sample responses taken from the standardization protocols are given for most items in Appendix A.

sity at San Diego in 1977. The individual testee is asked to write out his responses to the same test items that are ordinarily written by the examiner in the SIT. So long as the testee can adequately hear the tape, no ordinary limit can be put on the size of the group upon which it is administered.

Scoring and Interpretation

The test can be scored reliably for degree of conflict in the personality after studying the sample responses given in the Manual. Instructions are given for determining a quantitative score for the test. The most interesting and powerful application of the test is for in-depth personality analysis. A sample of the theoretical basis for such an analysis is given in the monograph included with the set. It contains a near verbatim blind analysis by the Institute staff of one SIT record.

We must point out, however, that formal validation needed to support interpretations suggested in the Manual cannot be presented at this time. The interpretations suggested are based on Dr. Shorr's clinical experience with the use of these images as therapeutic tools.

Norms

Normative data, based on a sample population of one hundred four (104) state university students, are included in the Manual.*

Research

Interscorer reliability ranged from 0.51 to 0.88, significant at the 0.05 level. There was no significant difference between the means of the four scorers at the 0.05 level. Three of the four persons doing the study had no prior training in Psycho-Imagination theory. They used the guidelines in the Manual for scoring.

Test-retest reliability of the GSIT was 0.56, significant at the 0.01 level. There was no significant difference between the means and standard deviations obtained on either presentation of the GSIT and the means and standard deviations presented in the Manual at the 0.01 level of confidence.

Concurrent validity with the Taylor Manifest Anxiety Scale (MAS) was significant, $r = 0.23$ ($p \leq 0.05$) for the first administration, and $r = .33$ ($p \leq 0.01$) for the second administration.

Sex Differences

No sex differences were found in comparing the results of men and women who took the GSIT.

---

*The group form and normative data were developed originally by Claire Smith, Terri Kard, Lisa Squire, and Melanie Vale, graduate students at California State University, San Diego.

Work in progress includes enlargement of the normative samples to 400 persons. Comparing the SIT population to the GSIT showed no statistical differences, both having nearly identical distributions. Tentative comparisons with the additional normative samples compared with the originally used populations (SIT and GSIT) show no statistical differences and have nearly identical distributions.

The tape for the GSIT runs one hour and four minutes, giving more than sufficient time for administration and imagery production on the part of the testees. Unlike any other tests, only problems of motivation and rare technical difficulties may prevent adequate administration of the test.

Just as a qualitative, in-depth interpretation can be developed from the SIT, similarly such interpretation or diagnostic factors can be equally determined from the GSIT.

Supplementary Shorr Imagery Test

Soon after the SIT was originally developed, many researchers requested an alternate form for possible test-retest purposes. It could also be argued that if the number of unrepeated imaginary situations could be increased to 28 plus 8 Finish-the-Sentence questions, a marked increase in personality information could thus be achieved.

Certain problems arose. There was no adequate substitute for the Three Boxes. No other imaginary situation that Dr. Shorr laboriously worked with through trial and error could duplicate the Three Boxes. As a matter of fact, the Three Doors revealed quite another set of personality information. After quite a lot of trials with various workshop groups, training class persons and patients, it was decided since an alternate form did not seem feasible, a supplementary form could be developed. This encompassed a shorter form of nine imaginary situations plus four Finish-the-Sentence questions. Incorporated into the SSIT were items newly "discovered" since 1974. Among them were asking the testee to imagine himself in an area the shape of a circle. This item has proved to be valuable as an information gatherer of the phenomenological world view of the testee. The Three Doors, previously discussed in Chapter II, was added, plus certain unconscious images, body images, task images and self-image images.

So all in all, the SIT (or GSIT), when given in conjunction with the Supplementary Shorr Imagery Test, can give us 23 imaginary situations plus 8 Finish-the-Sentence questions to work with. The SSIT can be given by itself for personality evaluation at a shorter time (20 minutes to 30 minutes) and for "testing the limits" of what may not have been clearly established in the SIT (or GSIT) administration.

It has exceeded our fondest expectations, appearing to reveal an enormous amount of additional personality information. It has the possibility of being used as a screening device, since it can be given in one-half the time of the SIT administration.

Of course, quantitative scoring to assess degree of conflict can be used, plus the already mentioned clinical interpretation of qualitative nature.

At present, normative data is being gathered upon the general populations. The goal is to collect data from four hundred men and women. It is expected that about fifty Swedish men and women tested by Swedish psychologists will be included as part of the general population. They, of course, have faced the enormous task of translating the SSIT into the Swedish language. The SIT was previously translated by investigators in Umea, Sweden, and found to be extremely informative in conjunction with studies of headache patients.

Shorr Parent Imagery Test

The Shorr Parent Imagery Test (SPIT) is now under construction and promises to be of greater dimension than any of the previous tests. While the previous tests investigated the individual and his or her phenomenological world, the Shorr Parent Imagery Test investigates the child and his or her reactions to both of his parents, and then each of the parents to the child, then the reactions of each of the parents to each other.

For example, from the view of the child of ten years of age, we ask him or her to imagine himself being pushed in a baby stroller by his mother. Then the individual is asked to imagine what he or she feels, sees and does. The same imaginary sequence is then repeated, this time with the individuals father in place of the mother.

The mother separately would then be asked to imagine pushing the child in a stroller and asked to say what she feels, sees and does. The father separately would then imagine pushing the child in a stroller, and would be asked to report his feelings and actions.

If other dimensions are to be investigated, then the mother is asked to imagine pushing her husband in a stroller and to report her feelings and actions. The father, likewise, could be asked to imagine pushing his wife in a stroller and to report his feelings and actions.

The test is primarily constructed for parent-child reactions, so that husband-wife imagined interactions could be left out (or done at a later time), and it then allows us to concentrate on the parents-child reaction primarily.

If a child psychologist were to examine the results of the child's view of himself in relation to each parent, and then the parents' view of the child (and of each other), we have all the ingredients of an interview plus an enormous amount of information that may bypass ordinary observations and censorship.

At present, investigators on our team are determining which age categories of children would be most responsive to these parent-child imaginary situations. Most parents were already found to respond with relative ease to this type of imaginary situation. Normative data on at least 1,000 children, separated by age categories, are being gathered. An equal number of parents, with age not being the central question, are also being gathered. We will publish the test, using 20 items, as soon as our data gathering is complete.

It is our opinion that no comparable test of this kind has ever been constructed previously.

Waking imagery can thus be utilized as a projective device to proved psychodynamic awareness and to reveal degree of conflict.

CHAPTER 18

Summary

A person's imagery, more than any other mental function, indicates how he organizes his world. The central importance of imagery in man has been eloquently stated by Sylvia Ashton Warner, who has taught children of Moiri tribesmen in New Zealand and children in Colorado. She states: "The pictures in (man's) mind are part of his mind as an organ is part of his body, are indispensable to the life of the mind as the heart to the body." (Warner, 1972, p.14)

Only in the last decade has the function of imagination regained respectability among psychological investigators. In addition, the use of visual imagery as a therapeutic agent in individual and group therapy from the Behaviorists, Gestaltists and the Psychosynthesis group has mushroomed and is gaining momentum. But, while the experimental investigation of imagination and imagery has increased enormously in the work of Singer (1965), Segal (1971), Pavio (1971), Richardson (1969), Sheehan (1972), Klinger, et al. (1971), the systematic investigation of imagery in psychotherapy has not been attempted within a large scope of dimensions. The experimentalist engaged in the investigation of imagery, invariably, does not carry a *full* work load of psychotherapy with his patients. Likewise, the psychotherapist engaged in the full time psychotherapeutic experience with patients would be hard put to set up experimental designs. In this book I have been aware of this schism since my own emphasis has been almost exclusively in the practice of psychotherapy. However, whenever and wherever possible, I have attempted to incorporate what the experimentalist has made known to us into the psychotherapeutic experience. From this book one hopes the researcher will gain insights to incorporate into his experimental designs. Both the researcher and the clinician should complement each other's work.

Allow me to point out at least one example of how research and clinical experience can complement each other. Goldberger and Holt (1958) studied fourteen subjects who spent eight hours lying in isolation in a soundproof room under conditions of uniform stimulation. Diffused light let in through halved ping pong balls covering the eyes, were used in combination with a steady input of monotonous white noise through earphones. While the visual imagery of some subjects became quite bizarre in their isolation, they did not necessarily mistake these images, however bizarre, for hallucinatory perceptions. Goldberger and Holt concluded that reality testing remained relatively unimpaired while the sensory functions were involved in the experience of imagery. The subjects' capacity for judging the plausability and implausability of such experiences was also unimpaired.

Patients deeply immersed in their own imagery with powerful reactions and feelings even for prolonged periods in a therapeutic session do not lose their power of reality testing however bizarre and weird the imagery may be. Neurotic patients will emerge with no impairment in their judgment of the plausability or implausability of their imagery. I have observed it with hundreds of patients over thousands of hours in deep imagery involvement. This conclusion then, can be reached from both vantage points of experience, experimental or clinical.

I do not know of any psychotherapeutic procedures that do not depend in one manner or another on the presence of imagery. Is there a psychotherapeutic procedure that does not depend on the patient's ability to recall and to recreate situations and persons, real or imagined, which are a central part of a person's inner world regardless of whether they are verbalized in a therapy session? Sheehan accurately states, "Only through the image can they be actualized and 'animated' and so brought into relationship with each other, with the person of the therapist and with the here-and-now of the patient's actual life circumstances." (Sheehan, 1972, p. 73.)

Perhaps the most important factor about imagery as it is used in psychotherapy is its ability to bypass the usual censorship of the person. Lowenstein (1956) makes the point that the patient through hearing himself vocalize may control his own reactions to his thoughts. In short, he is "editing" and in so doing attempts to control the reactions of the analyst. Because we cannot usually tell in advance what effect or meaning the imagery will have, we may reveal in imagery what we would not ordinarily reveal in verbal conversation. The use of imagery has a prime value in that it can help break resistances usually found in verbal transactions. Indeed, we reach a near ultimate of the elimination of verbal insights and analysis by the exclusive use of symbolic imagery.

Another function of imagery that has special relevance to psychotherapy is the fact that images can be transformed, reexperienced and reshaped in line with a healthier self-concept. Gardner Murphy anticipated the concept of transformation of imagery when he stated: "But images ... are manipulated just as are muscular acts, and they may be rearranged, freshly reconstituted, to give new and better satisfactions." (Murphy, 1947, p. 550.) In this book the development of the concept of transformation of images is demonstrated by use of Task Imagery, Cathartic Imagery and Body Focusing.

The patient's awareness of his internal conflicts should be one of the most important functions of imagery. This complementary opposition within experience results in a bipolarization of imagery. Dual Imagery is an impressive means of demonstrating this phenomenon. Other methods that help define conflicts involve concrete Nonsymbolic Imagery, Symbolic Imagery, Imagery in Dreams as well as Depth Imagery. The implication is that the patient in becoming aware of his internal conflicts can hopefully do something to resolve them.

In this book, I have tried to emphasize that imagery can be comingled with dialogue to develop meanings and awareness during therapeutic sessions. There are others who work exclusively with Symbolic Imagery who would prefer a hypnoidal state that tends to minimize dialogue. My own opinion is that both procedures should be utilized so long as it serves the best interest of the patient. Moreover, the possibility of greater awareness in the patient is increased by listening to audiotapes of his sessions with special reference to his own imagery.

Insofar as group therapy is concerned, the systematic use of imagery is presented covering a wide range of areas. These include Cathartic Imagery; Dual Imagery; the use of the patient's own imagination in interaction with the other members; the Transformation of imagery; Group Imagery; the use of Task Imagery; and Body Focusing.

It is all but impossible to imagine a therapist that had poor knowledge and experience of his own images. Again, Sheehan graphically clarifies this point: "Where his capacity to image is limited, there he fails to comprehend with ease the experience of his patient; in fact he may be tempted to disregard, disbelieve or dismiss those experiences of his patients which his own imaginal disposition does not allow him to share." (Sheehan, 1972, p. 73.) It appears sound to assume that the greater the range of imagery the therapist possesses, the greater his effectiveness.

A practical application of the active use of imagery for the patient when not in a therapy session is for him to receive greater awareness and increased meaning from the stream of images in his waking existence. One patient reported that when he was in a state of anxiety, he asked himself to imagine something different in each hand and then proceeded to speak to each image in turn. From his images, he began to clarify the conflicts beneath his anxiety, developed increased meaning and then set a course of behavior that he felt would resolve the conflict. Certainly, when one can learn to transform negative images into positive images, greater control over the anticipation of events and pessimism may be secured. It is possible for the patient to develop this skill independent of the therapist following a certain therapeutic experience using imagery.

The creative use of imagery in psychotherapy, whether it be by the patient or therapist, is a goal not to be achieved for its own sake. The range of the dimensions inherent in helping a patient make a basic change within himself are so vast that creativity becomes mandatory if we are to meet the formidable problems therapy presents.

BIBLIOGRAPHY

Alexander, Eugene D. In-the-body travel: a growth experience with fantasy, *Psychotherapy,* 1971, *8,* No. 4, 319–324.

Allport, G. W. Pattern and growth in personality. New York: Holt, Rinehart & Winston, 1961.

Assagioli, Roberto. *Psycho-synthesis: a manual of principles and techniques.* New York: Hobbs, Dorman, 1965.

Bach, G. R. *Intensive group therapy.* New York: Ronald Press, 1954.

Bachelard, Gaston. *The psychoanalysis of fire.* Boston: Beacon Press, 1964.

Baldwin, J. M. *Social and ethical interpretations in mental development: a study in social psychology.* New York: Macmillan, 1897.

Barron, Frank. *Creativity and personal freedom.* New York: D. Van Nostrand, 1968.

Bartlett, Francis. Significance of patients' work on the therapeutic process, *Contemporary Psychoanalysis,* 1973, *9,* No. 4, 405–416.

Battegay, R. Individual psychotherapy and group psychotherapy as single treatment methods and in combination, *Acta Psychiatricia Scandinavica,* 1972, *48,* 43–48.

Berdach, Elsie and Backan, Paul. Body position and the free recall of early memories, *Psychotherapy: Theory, Research and Practice,* 1967, *4,* No. 3, 101–102.

Binswanger, L. *Being-in-the-world: selected papers of Ludwig Binswanger.* J. Needleman (Trans.). New York: Basic Books, 1963.

Binswanger, Ludwig. *Sigmund Freud: reminiscences of a friendship.* New York: Grune & Stratton, 1957.

Boss, Medard. *The analysis of dreams.* New York: Philosophical Library, 1958.

Brenman, M., Gill, M., and Knight, R. Spontaneous fluctuations in the depth of hypnosis. In R. K. Knight (Ed.) *Psychoanalytic Psychiatry and Psychology,* Austin Riggs Monograph Series, Vol. 1. New York: International Universities Press, 1954.

Breuer, J. and Freud, S. *Studies in hysteria.* (1895) Standard Edition, 2. London: Hogarth Press, 1953.

Bugental, J. F. T. *Challenge of humanistic psychology.* New York: McGraw-Hill, 1967.

Buhler, C. and Massarik, F. *The course of human life. A study of goals in humanistic perspective.* New York: Springer, 1968.

Burnham, D., Gladston, A., and Gibson, R. *Schizophrenia and the need-fear dilemma.* New York: International Universities Press, 1969.

Butler, J. M. Self-ideal congruence in psychotherapy, *Psychotherapy,* 1968, *5,* 13–17.

Caslant, E. *Method of development of the supernormal faculties.* Paris: Meyer, 1927.

Clynes, Manfred. Sentics: biocybernetics of emotion communication, *Annals of the New York Academy of Sciences,* 1973, *200,* No. 3, 57–131.

Cooley, C. H. *Human nature and the social order.* New York: Scribners', 1902.

Dellas, Marie and Gaier, E. M. Identifications of creativity, *Psychological Bulletin,* 1970, *73,* 55–73.

Demille, R. *Put your mother on the ceiling.* New York: Viking Press, 1973.

Desoille, R. *The directed daydream.* Monograph No. 8. New York: The Psychosynthesis Research Foundation, 1965.

Ellenberger, Henri. *The discovery of the unconscious.* New York: Basic Books, 1970.

Ferenczi, Sandor. *Further contributions to the theory and technique of psychoanalysis.* London: Hogarth Press, 1950.

Ferenczi, Sandor. *Final contributions to the problems and methods of psychoanalysis.* New York: Basic Books, 1955.

Fingarette, H. *The self in transformation.* New York: Basic Books, 1963.

Fisher, C. A. A study of the preliminary stages of the construction of dreams and images, *Journal of the American Psychoanalytic Association,* 1967, *5,* 5–60.

Fisher, Seymour. *Body experience in fantasy and behavior.* New York: Appleton Century Crofts, 1970.

Frankl, Victor. *Man's search for meaning.* Boston: Beacon Press, 1966.

Freud, Anna. *The ego and the mechanisms of defense.* New York: International Universities Press, 1946.

Freud, Sigmund. *The ego and the id.* New York: Norton, 1923.

Freud, Sigmund. *An autobiographical study.* (1925) Standard Edition. 12: 3–70. London: Hogarth Press, 1959.

Freud, Sigmund. *Character and culture.* New York: Collier Books. 1963.

Freud, Sigmund. *On creativity and the unconscious.* New York: Basic Books, 1970.

Freytag, Fredericka F. *Hypnosis and the body image.* New York: Julian Press, 1961.

Frisch, Max. *I'm not stiller.* New York: Vantage Books, 1958.

Fromm, Erich. Remarks on the problem of free association. *Psychiatric Research Reports, 2,* American Psychiatric Association, 1955.

Gary, Romain. *The roots of heaven.* New York: Simon & Schuster, 1958.

Gendlin, E. *Experiencing and the creation of meaning.* New York: The Free Press of Glencoe, 1962.

Goldberger, L. and Holt, R. Experimental interference with reality contact (perceptual isolation): method and group results, *Journal of Nervous and Mental Disease Disorders, 127,* 99–112.

Gordon, C. and Gergen, K. H. *The self in social interaction,* Vol. 1. New York: John Wiley & Sons, Inc., 1968.

Gorman, Warren. *Body image and the image of the brain.* St. Louis: Warren Green, 1969.

Gough, H. G. and Heilbrun, A. B., Jr. *The adjective check list manual.* Palo Alto, Calif.: Consulting Psychologists Press, 1965.

Gough, H. G., Lazzari, R., and Fioravanti, M. Self versus ideal self: a comparison of five adjective check list indices, *Journal of Consulting and Clinical Psychology,* 1978, *46,* No. 5, 1085–1091.

Gruenwald, D. Hypnotic technique without hypnosis in the treatment of dual personality, *The Journal of Nervous and Mental Disease,* 1971, *153,* No. 1, 41–46.

Hammer, Max. The directed daydream technique, *Psychotherapy,* 1967, *4,* No. 4, 173–181.

Hammer, Max. *The theory and practice of psychotherapy with specific disorders.* Springfield, Illinois: Charles C. Thomas, 1972.

Healy, William, Bronner, Augusta, and Bowers, Anna. *The structure and meaning of psychoanalysis.* New York: Alfred A. Knopf, 1930.

Hilgard, E. R. and Tart, C. T. Responsiveness to suggestion following induction of hypnosis, *Journal of Abnormal Psychology,* 1966, *71,* 196–208.

Holt, R. R. Imagery: the return of the ostracised, *American Psychologist,* 1964, *19,* 254–264.

Horney, Karen. *Our inner conflicts.* New York: W. W. Norton, 1945.

Horney, Karen. *Neurosis and human growth.* New York: W. W. Norton, 1950.

Horowitz, E. L. Spatial localization of the self, *Journal of Social Psychology,* 1935, *6,* 379–387.

Horowitz, Mardi. *Image formation and cognition.* New York: Appleton Century Crofts, 1970.

Horowitz, M. and Becker, Stephanie S. The compulsion to repeat trauma: experimental study of intrusive thinking after stress, *Journal of Nervous and Mental Disease,* 1971, *153,* No. 1, 32–40.

James, W. *The principles of psychology.* New York: Holt, 1890.

Jellinek, Augusta. Spontaneous imagery: a new psychotherapeutic approach, *American Journal of Psychotherapy,* 1949, *3,* No. 3, 372–391.

Jones, E. *Papers on psychoanalysis* (4th Edition). London: Bailliere, Tindall and Cox, 1948.

Jung, Carl. *Contributions to analytical psychology.* New York: Harcourt Brace, 1928.

Jung, Carl. *Memories, dreams, reflections.* Arriela Jaffe (Ed.) New York: Pantheon Books, 1961.

Kanzer, M. Image formation during free association, *Psychoanalytic Quarterly,* 1958, *27,* 475–485.

Kinch, J. W. A formalized theory of the self-concept, *American Journal of Sociology,* 1963, *68,* 481–486.

Klein, George. *Perception, motives and personality.* New York: Alfred A. Knopf, 1970.

Klinger, Eric. *Structure and functions of fantasy.* New York: Wiley Interscience, 1971.

Kubie, L. The induced hypnotic reverie in the recovery of regressed amnesic data, *Bulletin of the Meninger Clinic,* 1943, 7.

Laing, R. D. *The divided self.* Chicago: Quadrangle Books, 1962.

Laing, R. D. *The self and others.* Chicago: Quadrangle Books, 1962.

Laing, R. D. Violence and love, *Journal of Existentialism,* 1975, *5,* No. 20, 411–422.

Laing, R. D., Phillipson, H., and Lee, A. R. *Interpersonal perception.* New York: Springer, 1966.

Leary, T. F. *Interpersonal diagnosis of personality.* New York: Ronald Press, 1957.

Leuner, Hanscarl. Guided affective imagery (GAI): a method of intensive psychotherapy, *American Journal of Psychotherapy,* 1969, *23,* No. 1, 4–22.

Lowenstein, R. M. Some remarks on the role of speech in psychoanalytic technique, *International Journal of Psychoanalysis,* 1956, *37,* 460–467.

Maddi, Salvatore. The search for meaning. *Nebraska Symposium on Motivation.* Lincoln, Nebraska: University of Nebraska Press, 1970.

Maslow, A. H. *Toward a psychology of being.* Princeton, New Jersey: Van Nostrand, 1962.

May, Rollo, Angell, E., and Ellenberger, H. F. *Existence: a new dimension of psychiatry and psychology.* New York: Basic Books, 1958.

May, Rollo. On the phenomenological bases of psychotherapy, *Review of Existential Psychology and Psychiatry,* 1964, *4,* No. 1, 22–36.

May, Rollo. Passion for form, *Review of Existential Psychology and Psychiatry,* 1967, *7,* No. 1, 6–12.

McDougall, W. *The energies of men.* London: Methuen, 1932.

Mead, G. H. *Mind, self, and society.* Chicago: University of Chicago Press, 1934.

Miller, Arthur. The role of P.E.N., *Saturday Review,* June 1966, *4.*

Murphy, Gardner. *Personality. A biosocial approach to origins and structure.* New York: Harper, 1947.

Nye, Robert D. *Conflict among humans.* New York: Springer, 1973.

Paivio, Allan. Imagery and synchronic ideation, *Abstract Guide,* XXth International Congress of Psychology, Tokyo, Japan, 1972, 127–128.

Paivio, Allan. *Imagery and verbal processes.* New York: Holt, Rinehart and Winston, 1971.

Peirce, C. S. Questions concerning certain faculties claimed for man, *Journal of Speculative Philosophy,* 1968, *2,* 103–114.

Perls, F., Hefferline, R. F., and Goodman, P. *Gestalt therapy.* New York: Dell, 1951.

Pervin, L. A., and Lilly, R. S. Social desirability and self-ideal self on the semantic differential, *Educational and Psychological Measurement,* 1967, *27,* 845–853.

Raven, B. H. and Rubin, J. Z. *Social psychology: people in groups.* New York: Wiley, 1976.

Reiff and Scheerer. *Memory and hypnotic age regression.* New York: International Universities Press, 1959.

Reyher, J. Free imagery, *Journal of Clinical Psychology,* 1963, *19,* 454–459.

Richardson, Alan. *Mental imagery.* New York: Springer, 1969.

Rosen, E. Self-appraisal and perceived desirability of MMPI personality traits, *Journal of Counseling Psychology,* 1956, *3,* 44–51.

Rossi, Ernest Lawrence. *Dreams and the growth of personality.* New York: Pergamon Press, 1972.

Sadler, William A. *Existence and love. A new approach to existential phenomenology.* New York: Charles Scribner & Sons, 1969.

Schacter, S. and Singer, J. E. Cognitive, social and physiological determinants of emotional states, *Psychological Revue,* 1962, *69,* 379–399.

Schneider, D. J. *Social psychology.* Reading, Mass.: Addison-Wesley, 1976.

Schutz, W. C. *Joy. Expanding human awareness.* New York: Grove Press, 1967.

Secord, P. F., and Backman, C. W. *Social psychology.* New York: McGraw-Hill, 1974.

Segal, Sydney and Glicksman, Michael. Relaxation and the perky effect: the influence of body position on judgement of imagery, *American Journal of Psychology,* 1967, *60,* 257–262.

Segal, Sydney J. (Ed.), *Imagery: current cognitive processes.* New York: Academic Press, 1971.

Seidenberg, R. Who owns the body?, *Existential Psychiatry,* Summer-Fall 1969, 93–105.

Shahn, Ben. Imagination and intention, *Review of Existential Psychiatry,* 1967, *7,* No. 1, 13–17.

Shapiro, David L. The significance of the visual image in psychotherapy, *Psychotherapy: Theory, Research and Practice,* 1970, *7,* No. 4, 209–212.

Sheehan, P. W. Functional similarity of imagining to perceiving, *Perceptual and Motor Skills,* 1966, *23,* 1011–1013.

Sheehan, Peter W. *The function and nature of imagery.* New York: Academic Press, 1972.

Shorr, Joseph E. The existential question and the imaginary situation as therapy, *Existential Psychiatry: The Journal of the American Ontoanalytic Association,* Winter, 1967.

Shorr, Joseph E. *Psycho-imagination therapy: the integration of phenomenology and imagination.* New York: Intercontinental Medical Book Corporation, 1972.

Shorr, Joseph E. In what part of your body does your mother reside? *Psychotherapy: Theory, Research and Practice,* 1973, *10,* No. 2, 31–34.

Shorr, Joseph E. *Shorr imagery test.* Institute for Psycho-Imagination Therapy, Los Angeles, 1974.

Shorr, Joseph E. Task imagery as therapy, *Psychotherapy: Theory,* Research and Practice, Summer 1975, *12,* No. 2.

Shorr, Joseph E. Dual imagery, *Psychotherapy: Theory, Research and Practice,* Fall 1976, *13,* No. 2.

Shorr, Joseph E. *Group Shorr imagery test.* Institute for Psycho-Imagination Therapy, Los Angeles, 1977.

Shorr, Joseph E. *Supplementary Shorr imagery test.* Institute for Psycho-Imagination Therapy, Los Angeles, 1978.

Shorr, Joseph E. Clinical use of categories of therapeutic imagery. In J. S. Singer and K. Pope (Eds.) *The power of human imagination.* New York: Plenum Publishing Co., 1978.

Shorr, Joseph E. Imagery as a projective device, *Imagery Bulletin* of the American Association for the Study of Mental Imagery, Los Angeles, Vol. I, No. 2, July, 1978.

Shorr, Joseph E. *Go see the movie in your head.* New York: Popular Library, 1978.

Shorr, Joseph E. Imagery as a method of self-observation in therapy, *Imagery Bulletin* of the American Association for the Study of Mental Imagery, Los Angeles, Vol. II, No. 2, May, 1979.

Shorr, Joseph E. *Shorr parent imagery test.* Institute for Psycho-Imagination Therapy, Los Angeles (in press).

Shrauger, J. Sidney and Schoeneman, Thomas J. Symbolic interactionist view of self-concept: through the looking glass darkly, *Psychological Bulletin,* 1979, *86,* No. 3, 549–573.

Silberer, H. Report on a method of eliciting and observing certain symbolic hallucinations phenomena. In Rapaport (Ed.) *Organization and pathology of thought.* New York: Columbia University Press, 1951.

Singer, Jerome L. *Daydreaming: an introduction to the experimental study of inner experience.* New York: Random House, 1966.

Singer, Jerome L. Imagery and daydream techniques employed in psychotherapy: some practical and theoretical implications. In Spielberger, C. (Ed.) *Current topics in clinical and community psychology,* Vol. 3. New York: Academic Press, 1971.

Singer, Jerome L. *The child's world of make-believe.* New York: Academic Press, 1973.

Singer, Jerome L. and Pope, K. (Eds.) *The power of human imagination.* New York: Plenum Publishing Co., 1978.

Smith, Barbara Hernstein. The new imagism, *Midway,* 1969, *9,* No. 3, 27–44.

Spiegel, Rose. Specific problems of communication in psychiatric conditions, *American Handbook of Psychiatry*, Vol I. Silvano Ariete (Ed.) New York: Basic Books, 1959.

Stampfl, T. G. and Leavis, D. J. Essentials of implosive therapy: a learning theory based on psychodynamic behavioral therapy, *Journal of Abnormal Psychology*, 1967, *72*, 496–503.

Straus, Erwin W. (Ed.) *Phenomenology, pure and applied.* Pittsburgh: Duquesne University Press, 1964.

Sullivan, Harry S. *The interpersonal theory of psychiatry.* New York: W. W. Norton, 1953.

Szalita, A. B. Regression and perception in psychotic states, *Psychiatry*, 1958, *12,* 53.

Szalita, A. B. Reanalysis, *Contemporary Psychoanalysis*, 1968, *4,* No. 2, 83–102.

Tart, Charles T. (Ed.) *Altered states of consciousness.* New York: John Wiley, 1969.

Tillich, Paul. *The courage to be.* New Haven: Yale University Press, 1952.

Ullman, Montague. Dreams and the therapeutic process, *Psychiatry*, 1958, *21,* No. 2, 123–131.

Van Den Berg, J. An existential explanation of the guided daydream in psychotherapy, *Review of Existential Psychiatry*, 1962, *2,* No. 1, 5–35.

Vernon, J. A. *Inside the black room.* New York: Clarkson N. Potter, Inc., 1963.

Vespe, Raymond. Ontological analysis and synthesis in existential psychotherapy, *Existential Psychiatry,* Summer-Fall 1967, 83–92.

Wann, T. W. *Behaviorism and phenomenology.* Chicago: University of Chicago Press, 1964.

Warner, Sylvia A. *Spearpoint.* New York: Alfred A. Knopf, 1972.

Warren, M. Significance of visual images during the analytic session, *Journal of the American Psychoanalytic Association,* 1961, *9,* 504–518.

Weisman, Avery D. *The existential core of psychoanalysis.* Boston: Little Brown & Co., 1965.

Weisskopf-Joelson, E. Experimental studies of "meaning" through integration, *Annals of the New York Academy of Sciences.* Patterns of integration from biochemical to behavioral process. *193,* 260–272.

Werner, H. and Kaplan, B. *Symbol formation: an organismic developmental approach to language and the expression of thought.* New York: Wiley, 1962.

Wilson, Colin. *New pathways in psychology. Maslow and the post Freudian revolution.* New York: Taplinger Publishing Co., 1972.

Wolf, Alexander and Schwartz, Emanuel K. *Psychoanalysis in groups.* New York: Grune & Stratton, 1962.

Wolpe, J. *The practice of behavior therapy.* New York: Pergamon Press, 1969.

Wylie, R. C. *The self-concept.* (Rev. ed.) Lincoln, Nebraska: University of Nebraska Press, 1974.

Ziller, R. C. *The social self.* New York: Pergamon Press, 1973.

Zubek, John P. (Ed.) *Sensory deprivation: fifteen years of research.* New York: Appleton Century Crofts, 1969.